866 54

D1082955

Lineberger Memorial
Library

Lutheran Theological Southern Seminary   Columbia, S. C.

THE BICENTENNIAL EDITION
OF THE
WORKS OF JOHN WESLEY

Editor-in-Chief FRANK BAKER

*The Directors of the Bicentennial Edition of
the Works of John Wesley
gratefully acknowledge the financial support
in the preparation of this volume of
The R. W. Fair Foundation of Tyler, Texas
in dedication to
Robert J. and Sallie Kidd Fair
and children
Lula Fair Ray, Claude L. Fair, Corrie Fair Arnold, Nobie Fair Ray
Vonie Fair Arthur, Robert Walter Fair, Willie Fair Ray*

866 54

THE WORKS OF
JOHN WESLEY

VOLUME 2

SERMONS
II
34–70

EDITED BY

ALBERT C. OUTLER

ABINGDON PRESS

NASHVILLE

1985

The Works of John Wesley, Volume 2
SERMONS, II, 34–70

Copyright © 1985 by Abingdon Press

All rights reserved.
No part of this book may be reproduced in any manner
whatsoever without written permission of the publisher
except brief quotations embodied in critical articles
or reviews. For information address Abingdon Press,
Nashville, Tennessee.

Library of Congress Cataloging in Publication Data
(Revised for vol. 2. Sermons II, 34-70)

Wesley, John, 1703-1791.
The works of John Wesley.
Includes indexes.
Contents: v. 1. Sermons I, 1-33—v. 2. Sermons II, 34-70 / edited by
Albert C. Outler.
1. Methodist Church—Collected works. 2. Theology—
Collected works—18th century. I. Outler, Albert Cook,
1908-   . II. Title.
BX8217.W5 1985   252'.07   83-22434

ISBN 0-687-46211-8 (v. 2)
ISBN 0-687-46210-X (v. 1)

THE MONOGRAM USED ON THE CASE AND HALF-TITLE IS
ADAPTED BY RICHARD P. HEITZENRATER FROM ONE OF
JOHN WESLEY'S PERSONAL SEALS

MANUFACTURED BY THE PARTHENON PRESS AT
NASHVILLE, TENNESSEE, UNITED STATES OF AMERICA

THE BICENTENNIAL EDITION OF
THE WORKS OF JOHN WESLEY

THIS edition of the works of John Wesley reflects the quickened interest in the heritage of Christian thought that has characterized both ecumenical insurgency and dominant theological perspectives during the last half-century. A fully critical presentation of Wesley's writings had long been a desideratum in order to furnish documentary sources illustrating his contribution to both catholic and evangelical Christianity.

Several scholars, notably Professor Albert C. Outler, Professor Franz Hildebrandt, Dean Merrimon Cuninggim, and Dean Robert E. Cushman, discussed the possibility of such an edition. Under the leadership of Dean Cushman, a Board of Directors was formed in 1960 comprising the deans of four sponsoring theological schools of Methodist-related universities in the United States: Drew, Duke, Emory, and Southern Methodist. They appointed an Editorial Committee to formulate plans, and enlisted an international and interdenominational team of scholars for the Wesley Works Editorial Project.

The works were divided into units of cognate material, with a separate editor (or joint editors) responsible for each unit. Dr. Frank Baker was appointed textual editor for the whole project, with responsibility for supplying each unit editor with a collated critical text for his consideration and use. The text seeks to represent Wesley's thought in its fullest and most deliberate expression, in so far as this can be determined from the available evidence. Substantive variant readings in any British edition published during Wesley's lifetime are shown in appendices to the units, preceded by a summary of the problems faced and the solutions reached in the complex task of securing and presenting Wesley's text. The aim throughout is to enable Wesley to be read with maximum ease and understanding, and with minimal intrusion by the editors.

It was decided that the edition should include all Wesley's original or mainly original prose works, together with one volume devoted to his *Collection of Hymns for the use of the People called*

Methodists, and another to his extensive work as editor and publisher of extracts from the writings of others. An essential feature of the project is a Bibliography outlining the historical settings of over 450 items published by Wesley and his brother Charles, sometimes jointly, sometimes separately. The Bibliography also offers full analytical data for identifying each of the two thousand editions of these 450 items that were published during the lifetime of John Wesley, and notes the location of copies. An index is supplied for each unit, and a General Index for the whole edition.

The Delegates of the Oxford University Press agreed to undertake publication, but announced in June 1982 that because of severe economic problems they would regretfully be compelled to withdraw from the enterprise with the completion in 1983 of Vol. 7, the *Collection of Hymns.* The Abingdon Press offered its services, beginning with the publication of the first volume of the *Sermons* in 1984, the bicentennial year of the formation of American Methodism as an autonomous church. The new title now assumed, however, refers in general to the bicentennial of Wesley's total activities as author, editor, and publisher, from 1733 to 1791, especially as summarized in the first edition of his collected works in thirty-two volumes, 1771–1774.

Dean Robert E. Cushman of Duke University undertook general administration and promotion of the project until 1971, when he was succeeded by Dean Joseph D. Quillian, Jr., of Southern Methodist University, these two universities having furnished the major support and guidance for the enterprise. During the decade 1961–70 literary planning was undertaken by the Editorial Committee, chaired by Dean Quillian. International conferences were convened in 1966 and 1970, bringing together all available unit editors with the committee, who thus completed their task of achieving a common mind upon editorial principles and procedure. Throughout this decade Dr. Eric W. Baker of London, England, serving as a General Editor along with Dean William R. Cannon and Dean Cushman, assisted the Directors in British negotiations, as well as at the conferences. In 1969 the Directors appointed Dr. Frank Baker, early attached to the project as bibliographer, and later as textual editor, as their Editor-in-Chief also. In 1971 they appointed a new Editorial Board to assist him in coordinating the preparation of the various units for publication. Upon Dean Quillian's retirement in 1981 he was succeeded as President of the project by Dean James E. Kirby, Jr., also of Southern Methodist University.

Other sponsoring bodies were successively added to the original four: The United Methodist Board of Higher Education and Ministry, The Commission on Archives and History of The United Methodist Church, and Boston University School of Theology. For the continuing support of the sponsoring institutions the Directors express their profound thanks. They gratefully acknowledge also the encouragement and financial support that have come from the Historical Societies and Commissions on Archives and History of many Annual Conferences, as well as the donations of The World Methodist Council, The British Methodist Church, private individuals, and foundations.

On June 9, 1976, The Wesley Works Editorial Project was incorporated in the State of North Carolina, U.S.A., as a nonprofit corporation. In 1977 by-laws were approved governing the appointment and duties of the Directors, their Officers, and their Executive Committee.

THE BOARD OF DIRECTORS

The Board of Directors

President: James E. Kirby, Dean of Perkins School of Theology, Southern Methodist University, Dallas, Texas

Vice-President: Robert E. Cushman, The Divinity School, Duke University, Durham, North Carolina

Secretary: Donald H. Treese, Associate General Secretary of the Division of the Ordained Ministry, the United Methodist Board of Higher Education and Ministry, Nashville, Tennessee

Treasurer: Thomas A. Langford, The Divinity School, Duke University, Durham, North Carolina

Editor-in-Chief: Frank Baker, The Divinity School, Duke University, Durham, North Carolina

Associate Editor-in-Chief: Richard P. Heitzenrater, Perkins School of Theology, Southern Methodist University, Dallas, Texas

James M. Ault, Bishop of The United Methodist Church, Pittsburgh, Pennsylvania

Dennis M. Campbell, Dean of The Divinity School, Duke University, Durham, North Carolina

William R. Cannon, Bishop of The United Methodist Church, Emory University, Atlanta, Georgia

Rupert E. Davies, Bristol, England

Joe Hale, General Secretary of The World Methodist Council, Lake Junaluska, North Carolina

Gerald O. McCulloh, Nashville, Tennessee

Richard Nesmith, Dean of Boston University School of Theology, Boston, Massachusetts

Thomas W. Ogletree, Dean of The Theological School of Drew University, Madison, New Jersey

William K. Quick, Detroit, Michigan

Kenneth E. Rowe, Drew University, Madison, New Jersey

Jim L. Waits, Dean of Candler School of Theology, Emory University, Atlanta, Georgia

David L. Watson, Board of Discipleship, Nashville, Tennessee

Charles Yrigoyen, Jr., Executive Secretary of The Commission on Archives and History of The United Methodist Church, Drew University, Madison, New Jersey

The Editorial Board

The Editor-in-Chief *(chairman)*; the President and the Associate Editor-in-Chief *(ex officio)*; William R. Cannon, Robert E. Cushman, Rupert E. Davies, Gerald O. McCulloh, Kenneth E. Rowe, and David L. Watson.

CONTENTS

SERMONS ON SEVERAL OCCASIONS (1788), 54–70

ILLUSTRATIONS

SIGNS, SPECIAL USAGES, ABBREVIATIONS

[ ]	Indicate editorial insertions or substitutions in the original text, or (with a query) doubtful readings.
. . .	Indicate a passage omitted by the writer from the original and so noted by Wesley, usually by a dash.
[. . .]	Indicate a passage omitted from the original text to which the present editor is drawing attention. (N.B. The distinguishing editorial brackets are not used in the introductions and footnotes.)
[[ ]]	Entries within double brackets are supplied by the editor from shorthand or cipher, from an abstract or similar document in the third person, or reconstructed from secondary evidence.
a, b, c,	Small superscript letters indicate footnotes supplied by Wesley.
1, 2, 3,	Small superscript figures indicate footnotes supplied by the editor.
Cf.	'Cf.' before a scriptural or other citation indicates that Wesley was quoting with more than minimal inexactness, yet nevertheless displaying the passage as a quotation.
See	'See' before a citation indicates an undoubted allusion, or a quotation which was not displayed as such by Wesley, and which is more than minimally inexact.
π;	π; indicates a quotation which has not yet been traced to its source.

Wesley's publications. Where a work by Wesley was first published separately its title is italicized—except in the Contents, opening titles, and Appendices A and B—even where (as occasionally in the *Sermons*), the eventual title thus italicized is not that under which it was first published; where it first appeared within a different work such as a collected volume, the title is given within quotation marks. References such as *'Bibliog,* No. 3' are to the forthcoming Bibliography in this edition (Vols. 33–34), which has a different numbering system from Richard Green's *Wesley Bibliography,* although cross-references to Green's numbers are given in the new Bibliography.

Abbreviations. The following are used in addition to many common and obvious ones such as B[oo]k, ch[apter], c[irca], col[umn], com[ment], cont[inued], ed[itio]n, espec[ially], intro[duction, ductory], l[ine], MS[S], n[ote], orig[inal], p[age], para[graph] or ¶, P[ar]t, Sect[ion] or §, st[anza/s], ver[se/s], Vol[ume].

AM	Wesley, John, *Arminian Magazine* (1778–97), cont. as *Methodist Magazine* (1798–1821), and *Wesleyan Methodist Magazine* (1822–1913).
ANF	*Ante-Nicene Fathers* (New York, 1978–79).

AV	Authorized Version of the Bible, 1611 ('King James Version').
BCP	*The Book of Common Prayer as Revised and Settled at the Savoy Conference, Anno 1662*, London, William Pickering, 1844 (which adds marginal numbering for the successive liturgical units).
BL	The British Library, London (formerly British Museum).
Boston	Boston, Thomas, *Human Nature in its Fourfold State*, Edinburgh, 1720.
Bibliog	Bibliography of the publications of John and Charles Wesley, in preparation by Frank Baker to form Vols. 33–34 of this edn.
Christian Lib.	Wesley, John, ed., *Christian Library*, 50 vols., Bristol, 1749–55.
Curnock	Curnock, Nehemiah, ed., *The Journal of the Rev. John Wesley, A.M., . . . enlarged from Original Manuscripts*, 8 vols., London, 1909–16.
CWJ	Wesley, Charles, *Journal*, ed., Thomas Jackson, 2 vols., London, 1849.
DNB	*The Dictionary of National Biography*, ed. Sir Leslie Stephen and Sir Sidney Lee, 22 vols., Oxford, Oxford University Press, 1921–23.
General Rules	Wesley, John, *The Nature, Design, and General Rules of the United Societies . . .* , Newcastle, Gooding, 1743 (*Bibliog*, No. 73).
Homilies	*Certain Sermons or Homilies appointed to be read in Churches in the Time of the late Queen Elizabeth* (1623), Oxford, University Press, 1840.
Jackson	Jackson, Thomas, ed., *The Works of the Rev. John Wesley*, 3rd edn., 14 vols., London, Mason, 1829–31.
JWJ	Wesley, John, *Journal*, in preparation by W. Reginald Ward to form Vols. 18–24 of this edn.; cf. Curnock.
Kempis	*De Imitatione Christi*, published by John Wesley as *The Christian's Pattern*, London, Rivington, 1735 (*Bibliog*, No. 4).
LACT	Library of Anglo-Catholic Theology (Oxford, 1841–63).
Law, *Serious Call*	Law, William, *A Serious Call to a Devout and Holy Life* (1729), as reprinted in his *Works*, 9 vols., London, 1762, Vol. IV.
LCC	Library of Christian Classics (Philadelphia, 1953—).
LPT	Library of Protestant Thought (Oxford, 1964—).
Loeb	The Loeb Classical Library, London, Heinemann; Cambridge, Massachusetts, Harvard University Press.
MA	Methodist Archives, The John Rylands University Library of Manchester.
MM	*Methodist Magazine* (London, 1798–1821).
Migne, *PG, PL*	Migne, J. P., ed., *Patrologiae Cursus Completus, Series Graeca* (Paris, 1857–66), and *Series Latina* (Paris, 1878–90).

Moore	Moore, Henry, *Life of the Rev. John Wesley*, 2 vols., London, Kershaw, 1824–25.
NEB	New English Bible.
Notes	Wesley, John, *Explanatory Notes upon the New Testament*, London, Bowyer, 1755 (*Bibliog*, No. 209).
NPNF, I, II	*Nicene and Post-Nicene Fathers of the Christian Church*, First Series (New York, 1886–90), and Second Series (New York, 1890–1900).
OED	*The Oxford English Dictionary upon Historical Principles*, Oxford, Clarendon Press, 1933.
Poet. Wks.	Wesley, John and Charles, *The Poetical Works*, ed. G. Osborn, 13 vols., London, Wesleyan-Methodist Conference Office, 1868–72.
Seymour	[Seymour, A. C. H.], *The Life and Times of Selina, Countess of Huntingdon*, 2 vols., London, Painter, 1840.
SOSO	Wesley, John, *Sermons on Several Occasions*, 1746–60, 1771, 1787–88.
Southey	Southey, Robert, *The Life of Wesley*, ed. C. C. Southey (including *in full*, as does that of 1846, 'Remarks on the Life and Character of John Wesley', by Alexander Knox), 2 vols., London, Longman, etc., 1864.
Sugden	Sugden, E. H., ed., *Wesley's Standard Sermons*, 2 vols., London, Epworth Press, 1921.
Telford	Telford, John, ed., *The Letters of the Rev. John Wesley*, 8 vols., London, Epworth Press, 1931.
TR	*Textus Receptus* (the 'Received Text', which underlies the AV).
Tyerman (*JW*)	Tyerman, Luke, *The Life and Times of the Rev. John Wesley*, 3 vols., London, Hodder and Stoughton, 1870–71.
[Wesley,] *Works*	Wesley, John, *The Works of the Rev. John Wesley*, 32 vols., Bristol, Pine, 1771–74, (*Bibliog*, No. 334).
WHS	*The Proceedings of the Wesley Historical Society* (Burnley and Chester, 1898—).
WMM	*Wesleyan Methodist Magazine* (1822–1913).

THE ORIGINAL, NATURE, PROPERTIES, AND USE OF THE LAW

THE LAW ESTABLISHED THROUGH FAITH, DISCOURSE I & II

AN INTRODUCTORY COMMENT

The most patent danger in Wesley's delicate balancing of faith alone and *holy living was its possible tilt toward moralism ('inherent righteousness'); something of this sort did eventually occur in Methodism after Wesley's death, despite all his earnest efforts to safeguard his gospel against it. But the opposite extreme, antinomianism, was already a clear and present danger among the Methodists; several versions of it were even then being vigorously asserted, as if antinomianism were a valid consequence of 'faith alone'. This controversy had emerged with the Revival itself, in Wesley's disagreements with the Moravians (cf. JWJ, November 1, 1739, April 19-26, 1740). It had been carried forward by the reckless rhetoric of men like William Cudworth, minister of the Grey Eagle Street Church in London, although Wesley had found its substance in the more sophisticated teachings of James Hervey and others.*

In 1741 (September 3) Wesley had debated the issue of faith and good works with Count von Zinzendorf in London. Wesley's Journal *record of this passage at arms, along with his earlier denunciations of Whitefield's 'Calvinism', etc., had drawn fire from the antinomians (and from some Calvinists). In 1745, Cudworth had published a twenty-five page* Dialogue Between a Preacher of God's Righteousness and a Preacher of Inherent Righteousness, *in which he spoke 'for God' and allowed Wesley to speak for 'inherent righteousness'; cf.* Christ Alone Exalted *(1747), in which Cudworth's tract is No. VIII. The urgency of this is evident from the manuscript Minutes of the second Annual Conference in Bristol, August 2, 1745, in Questions 24-26 and their answers:*

Q. 24. *Wherein may we come to the very edge of antinomianism?*
A.   (1). *In exalting the merits and love of Christ.*
       (2). *In rejoicing evermore.*

I

Q. 25. What can we do to stop the progress of antinomianism?
A.   (1). Pray without ceasing that God would speak for himself.
*   (2). Write one or two more dialogues.*
Q. 26. Doth faith supersede (set aside the necessity of) holiness or good works?
A.   In no wise. So far from it that it implies both, as a cause doth its effects.

The proposed 'one or two more dialogues' promptly appeared in the same year: A Dialogue between an Antinomian and his Friend *and* A Second Dialogue between an Antinomian and his Friend. *The first dialogue was a sort of reenactment of the 1741 debate with Zinzendorf, with Zinzendorf's original words now translated from the Latin and with Wesley's original replies revised. The second pamphlet was Wesley's rejoinder to Cudworth's* Dialogue; *it concludes with what was intended to be a recapitulation of the discussion as a whole. Unsurprisingly, though, these dialogues had not concluded the affair, as we see from many* Journal *entries over the ensuing five years (see especially October 30 and December 11, 1749, etc.). It was, therefore, both urgent and appropriate for Wesley to follow his thirteen sermons on the Sermon on the Mount with three additional sermonic essays on the complex, dynamic interdependence of 'Law and Gospel' in his doctrine of salvation. This was the aim and occasion of the following sermons.*

Despite their complex development, the sermon outlines are plain and simple. The 'original' of the Law is man's inborn moral sense—not 'natural' in the deist sense but, rather, as an aspect of the residual imago Dei. *The 'nature' of the Law is* Christological, *as if Torah and Christ are in some sense to be equated. The 'properties' of the Law are threefold, and here Wesley follows the standard Puritan exegesis of Rom. 7:12 as to the Law's holiness and its instrumentality in the delineation of the just and the good. Incidentally, seven of the eight contemporary editions of this sermon here read 'properties', in the plural; only the text of* Works *(1771) has 'property' (but both Jackson and Sugden seem to have preferred the singular). Wesley's brief discussion of the 'uses of the Law' ignores the fact of the extended debate over 'the* third *use of the Law' between the Lutherans and the Calvinists, and obscures the further fact that Wesley has come down squarely on the Puritan side of the argument: the threefold 'use' of the Law is to convict, convert, and* sustain the believer—*in and after justification (see below, No. 34, IV.1 and n.).*

The twin discourses entitled 'The Law Established through Faith' amount to a single essay in two parts. In the first, Wesley turns on his critics and charges them with 'voiding the Law' by (1) 'not preaching it at all', and (2) by preaching 'faith' so as to 'supersede the necessity of holiness'. In the second part, he argues that the Law is and ought to be 'established by faith': (1) by a doctrine in which salvation by faith is understood as the foundation on which the whole enterprise of Christian living must rest; (2) by preaching 'faith alone' so as to promote 'holiness' rather than to supersede or subordinate it; and (3) by the manifestation of holy living in Christian hearts and lives.

What we have here, then, is a further variation on the central theme of the preceding thirteen sermons: the distinctive character of evangelical ethics in which the fides caritate formata is always the consequent of the sola fide, never its alternative. They also have in them (Discourse II, II.1-6) one of Wesley's most interesting and original proposals: that 'faith is in order to love' and, therefore, that 'love will exist after faith'—which may or may not be an amendment of 1 Cor. 13:13; cf. Wesley's Notes on this verse: 'Faith, hope, and love are the sum of perfection on earth; love alone is the sum of perfection in heaven.'

These sermons were 'tracts for the times' and not the distillate of oral preaching. This appears from the fact that we have no record of Wesley's having preached on Rom. 7:12, ever, and there are only two clear references to his use of Rom. 3:31 (June 27 and August 2, 1741). A possible third reference may be in the Journal entry for April 25, 1745: 'I preached at Little Horton and Bradford.' Here I 'could not but observe how God has made void all their labour who "make void the law through faith".' More than likely, though, this is either a comment on a local circumstance or, at most, one of the 'heads' in a sermon with another, unspecified text. For a publishing history of Nos. 34-36 and a list of variant readings in their successive texts, see Appendix, Vol. 4; see also Bibliog, No. 130.

The Original, Nature, Properties, and Use of the Law

Romans 7:12

*Wherefore the law is holy, and the
commandment holy, and just, and good.*

1. Perhaps there are few subjects within the whole compass of
religion so little understood as this. The reader of this Epistle is
usually told, 'By "the law" St. Paul means the Jewish law;' and so,
apprehending himself to have no concern therewith, passes on
10 without farther thought about it. Indeed some are not satisfied
with this account; but observing the Epistle is directed to the
Romans, thence infer that the Apostle in the beginning of this
chapter alludes to the old Roman law. But as they have no more
concern with this than with the ceremonial law of Moses, so they
15 spend not much thought on what they suppose is occasionally
mentioned, barely to illustrate another thing.
2. But a careful observer of the Apostle's discourse will not be
content with those slight explications of it. And the more he
weighs the words, the more convinced he will be that St. Paul, by
20 'the law' mentioned in this chapter, does not mean either the
ancient law of Rome or the ceremonial law of Moses. This will
clearly appear to all who attentively consider the tenor of his
discourse. He begins the chapter, 'Know ye not, brethren (for I
speak to them that know the law)'—to them who have been
25 instructed therein from their youth—'that the law hath dominion
over a man as long as he liveth?'[a] What? The law of Rome only, or
the ceremonial law? No, surely; but the *moral* law. 'For', to give a
plain instance, 'the woman that hath an husband is bound by the
(moral) law to her husband as long as he liveth. But if her husband
30 be dead, she is loosed from the law of her husband.'[b] 'So, then, if
while her husband liveth she be married to another man, she shall

---

[a] [Rom. 7,] ver. 1. [b] Ver. 2.

be called an adulteress: but if her husband be dead she is free from that law, so that she is no adulteress, though she be married to another man.'c From this particular instance the Apostle proceeds to draw that general conclusion: 'Wherefore, my brethren', by a plain parity of reason, 'ye also are become dead to 5 the law', the whole Mosaic institution, 'by the body of Christ' offered for you, and bringing you under a new dispensation: 'that ye should' without any blame 'be married to another, even to him who is raised from the dead', and hath thereby given proof of his authority to make the change, 'that ye should bring forth fruit 10 unto God'.d And this we can do now, whereas before we could not: 'For when we were in the flesh', under the power of the flesh, that is, of corrupt nature (which was necessarily the case till we knew the power of Christ's resurrection)[1], 'the motions of sins which were by the law', which were shown and inflamed by the 15 Mosaic law, not conquered, 'did work in our members', broke out various ways, 'to bring forth fruit unto death.'e 'But now we are delivered from the law', from that whole moral as well as ceremonial economy; 'that being dead whereby we were held'—that entire institution being now as it were dead, and 20 having no more authority over us than the husband when dead hath over his wife—'that we should serve' him who died for us and rose again 'in newness of spirit', in a new spiritual dispensation, 'and not in the oldness of the letter'f—with a bare outward service, according to the letter of the Mosaic institution. 25

3. The Apostle having gone thus far in proving that the Christian had set aside the Jewish dispensation, and that the moral law itself, though it could never pass away, yet stood on a different foundation from what it did before, now stops to propose and answer an objection. 'What shall we say then? Is the 30 law sin?' So some might infer from a misapprehension of those words, 'the motions of sin which were by the law'. 'God forbid!' saith the Apostle, that we should say so. 'Nay', the law is an irreconcilable enemy to sin, searching it out wherever it is. 'I had not known sin but by the law. I had not known lust', evil desire, to 35 be sin, 'except the law had said, Thou shalt not covet.'g After opening this farther in the four following verses, he subjoins this

---

c Ver. 3.   d Ver. 4.   e Ver. 5.
f Ver. 6.   g Ver. 7.

---

[1] See Phil. 3:10.

general conclusion with regard more especially to the moral law, from which the preceding instance was taken: 'Wherefore the law is holy, and the commandment holy, and just, and good.'

4. In order to explain and enforce these deep words, so little
5 regarded because so little understood, I shall endeavour to show, first, the original of this law; secondly, the nature thereof; thirdly, the properties, that it is 'holy, and just, and good'; and fourthly, the uses of it.

I. 1. I shall, first, endeavour to show the original of the moral
10 law, often called 'the law' by way of eminence.[2] Now this is not, as some may possibly have imagined, of so late an institution as the time of Moses. Noah declared it to men long before that time, and Enoch before him.[3] But we may trace its original higher still, even beyond the foundation of the world to that period, unknown
15 indeed to men, but doubtless enrolled in the annals of eternity, when 'the morning stars' first 'sang together',[4] being newly called into existence. It pleased the great Creator to make these his first-born sons intelligent beings, that they might know him that created them. For this end he endued them with understanding,
20 to discern truth from falsehood, good from evil; and as a necessary result of this, with liberty, a capacity of choosing the one and refusing the other. By this they were likewise enabled to offer him a free and willing service: a service rewardable in itself, as well as most acceptable to their gracious Master.
25 2. To employ all the faculties which he had given them, particularly their understanding and liberty, he gave them a law, a complete model of all truth, so far as was intelligible to a finite being, and of all good, so far as angelic minds were capable of embracing it. It was also the design of their beneficent Governor
30 herein to make way for a continual increase of their happiness; seeing every instance of obedience to that law would both add to the perfection of their nature and entitle them to an higher reward, which the righteous Judge would give in its season.

---

[2] 'In its highest degree'; cf. this seventeenth- eighteenth-century usage of 'eminence' in *OED*, 8c.

[3] The notion of the revelation of the moral law to Noah is reflected in the decision of 'the council of Jerusalem' (Acts 15:1-20, echoing Gen. 9:12-17; cf. 2 Pet. 2:5 and Heb. 11:7). Enoch's special place in covenant history may be seen in Wisd. 4:10; Jude 14; in the apocryphal book of Enoch, 106-7; and in Ecclus. 44:16, 'a sign of knowledge [of the Law] to all generations'.

[4] Job 38:7.

3. In like manner, when God in his appointed time had created a new order of intelligent beings, when he had raised man from the dust of the earth, breathed into him the breath of life, and caused him to become a living soul,[5] endued with power to choose good or evil, he gave to this free, intelligent creature the same law 5 as to his first-born children[6]—not wrote indeed upon tables of stone, or any corruptible substance, but engraven on his heart by the finger of God, wrote in the inmost spirit both of men and of angels—to the intent it might never be far off, never hard to be understood; but always at hand, and always shining with clear 10 light, even as the sun in the midst of heaven.

4. Such was the original of the law of God. With regard to man, it was coeval with his nature. But with regard to the elder sons of God, it shone in its full splendour 'or ever the mountains were brought forth, or the earth and the round world were made'.[7] But 15 it was not long before man rebelled against God, and by breaking this glorious law wellnigh effaced it out of his heart; 'the eyes of his understanding' being *darkened*[8] in the same measure as his soul was 'alienated from the life of God'.[9] And yet God did not despise the work of his own hands; but being reconciled to man 20 through the Son of his love, he in some measure re-inscribed the law on the heart of his dark, sinful creature.[10] 'He' again 'showed thee, O man, what is good' (although not as in the beginning), 'even to do justly, and to love mercy, and to walk humbly with thy God.'[11] 25

5. And this he showed not only to our first parents, but likewise to all their posterity, by 'that true light which enlightens every man that cometh into the world'.[12] But notwithstanding this light, all flesh had in process of time 'corrupted their way before him';[13] till he chose out of mankind a peculiar people,[14] to whom he gave a 30 more perfect knowledge of his law. And the heads of this, because

[5] Gen. 2:7.

[6] I.e., the angels, as in Gen. 6:2, 4; Job 38:7; and Ps. 82:6; cf. No. 141, 'The Image of God', for Wesley's early view of God's gift of the Law to Adam.

[7] Cf. Ps. 90:2 (BCP).   [8] Cf. Eph. 1:18.

[9] Eph. 4:18. Cf. also Charles Wesley, 'The Beatitudes', 'Alien from the life of God', in *Hymns and Sacred Poems* (1749), I. 35, 37.

[10] This notion of 're-inscription' is crucial for Wesley's doctrine of the human *in se* as a divine gift (exceeding 'nature') and of 'prevenient grace'.

[11] Cf. Mic. 6:8.

[12] Cf. John 1:9; cf. this illuminist motif with similar ideas in No. 10, 'The Witness of the Spirit, I', I.12 and n.

[13] Cf. Gen. 6:12.   [14] 1 Pet. 2:9.

they were slow of understanding, he wrote on two tables of stone; which he commanded the fathers to teach their children through all succeeding generations.

6. And thus it is that the law of God is now made known to them
5 that know not God. They hear, with the hearing of the ear, the things that were written aforetime for our instruction.[15] But this does not suffice. They cannot by this means comprehend the height and depth and length and breadth thereof.[16] God alone can reveal this by his Spirit. And so he does to all that truly believe, in
10 consequence of that gracious promise made to all the Israel of God: 'Behold, the days come, saith the Lord, that I will make a new covenant with the house of Israel. . . . And this shall be the covenant that I will make. . . . I will put my law in their inward parts, and write it in their hearts; and I will be their God, and they
15 shall be my people.'[h]

II. 1. The nature of that law which was originally given to angels in heaven and man in paradise, and which God has so mercifully promised to write afresh in the hearts of all true believers, was the second thing I proposed to show. In order to
20 which I would first observe that although 'the law' and 'the commandment' are sometimes differently taken (the commandment meaning but a part of the law) yet in the text they are used as equivalent terms, implying one and the same thing. But we cannot understand here, either by one or the other, the ceremonial law.
25 'Tis not the ceremonial law whereof the Apostle says, in the words above recited, 'I had not known sin but by the law:' this is too plain to need a proof. Neither is it the ceremonial law which saith, in the words immediately subjoined, 'Thou shalt not covet.'[17] Therefore the ceremonial law has no place in the present
30 question.

2. Neither can we understand by the law mentioned in the text the Mosaic dispensation. 'Tis true the word is sometimes so understood: as when the Apostle says, speaking to the Galatians, 'The covenant which was confirmed before' (namely with
35 Abraham the father of the faithful), 'the law', i.e. the Mosaic dispensation, 'which was four hundred and thirty years after,

[h] Jer. 31:31, 33.

---

[15] See Rom. 15:4.   [16] See Eph. 3:18.   [17] Rom. 7:7; cf. Exod. 20:17.

cannot disannul.'[i] But it cannot be so understood in the text; for the Apostle never bestows so high commendations as these upon that imperfect and shadowy dispensation. He nowhere affirms the Mosaic to be a *spiritual* law; or that it is 'holy, and just, and good'. Neither is it true that God 'will write that law in the hearts'[18] of them whose 'iniquities he remembers no more'.[19] It remains that 'the law', eminently so termed, is no other than the moral law.

3. Now this law is an incorruptible picture of the high and holy One that inhabiteth eternity.[20] It is he whom in his essence no man hath seen or can see, made visible to men and angels. It is the face of God unveiled; God manifested to his creatures as they are able to bear it; manifested to give and not to destroy life; that they may see God and live. It is the heart of God disclosed to man. Yea, in some sense we may apply to this law what the Apostle says of his Son—it is 'the streaming forth' or outbeaming 'of his glory, the express image of his person'.[21]

4. 'If virtue', said the ancient heathen, 'could assume such a shape as that we could behold her with our eyes, what wonderful love would she excite in us!'[22] If virtue could do this! It is done already. The law of God is all virtues in one, in such a shape as to be beheld with open face by all those whose eyes God hath enlightened. What is the law but divine virtue and wisdom assuming a visible form? What is it but the original ideas of truth and good, which were lodged in the uncreated mind from

---

[i] Chap. 3, ver. 17.

---

[18] Cf. Jer. 31:33.

[19] Cf. Heb. 8:12; 10:17.

[20] See Isa. 57:15. This view of the moral law as a divine hypostasis is a prime factor in Wesley's Christology (i.e., Christ as Torah incarnate), soteriology (i.e., the *justice* of justification), and ethics (i.e., the correlation of the moral law and holy living).

[21] Cf. Heb. 1:3. Wesley's text of 1771 quotes the Greek orig. here. Cf. No. 15, *The Great Assize*, II.1 and n.

[22] Cf. Cicero, *De Officiis (On Moral Obligations)*, I.5: 'You see here . . . the true form of virtue; "and if", as Plato says, "it could be seen with the bodily eye it would awaken a marvellous love of wisdom"—cf. *Phaedrus*, 250d: '[wisdom's] loveliness would be transporting if only there were a visible image of her.' Note the comment in the Elizabethan Homily, 'On Repentance', Pt. III (*Homilies*, p. 486): 'Plato doth in a certain place write that if virtue could be seen with bodily eyes, all men would be wonderfully inflamed and kindled with the love of it.' Cf. Samuel Clarke, *Discourse Concerning the Unchangeable Obligations of Natural Religion and the Truth and Certainty of the Christian Revelation* (1706), p. 89, where in place of wisdom and virtue Clarke prefers the phrase 'universal justice'. See also *A Farther Appeal*, Pt. II, III.22 (11:269 in this edn.).

eternity, now drawn forth and clothed with such a vehicle as to appear even to human understanding?

5. If we survey the law of God in another point of view, it is supreme, unchangeable reason; it is unalterable rectitude; it is
5   the everlasting fitness of all things[23] that are or ever were created. I am sensible what a shortness, and even impropriety, there is in these and all other human expressions, when we endeavour by these faint pictures to shadow out the deep things of God. Nevertheless we have no better, indeed no other way, during this
10 our infant state of existence. As 'we' now 'know' but 'in part', so we are constrained to 'prophesy', i.e. speak of the things of God, 'in part' also.[24] 'We cannot order our speech by reason of darkness'[25] while we are in this house of clay.[26] While I am 'a child' I must 'speak as a child'. But I shall soon 'put away childish
15 things'. For 'when that which is perfect is come, that which is in part shall be done away.'[27]

6. But to return. The law of God (speaking after the manner of men) is a copy of the eternal mind, a transcript of the divine nature; yea, it is the fairest offspring of the everlasting Father, the
20 brightest efflux of his essential wisdom, the visible beauty of the Most High.[28] It is the delight and wonder of cherubim and seraphim and all the company of heaven,[29] and the glory and joy of every wise believer, every well instructed child of God upon earth.

III. 1. Such is the nature of the ever-blessed law of God. I am,
25 in the third place, to show the properties of it. Not all, for that would exceed the wisdom of an angel; but those only which are mentioned in the text. These are three: It is 'holy, just, and good'. And first, 'the law is holy.'

2. In this expression the Apostle does not appear to speak of its
30 effects, but rather of its nature. As St. James, speaking of the same thing under another name, says, 'The wisdom from above' (which

---

[23] Clarke, *Demonstration of the Being and Attributes of God*, Prop. XII. But see No. 17, 'The Circumcision of the Heart', II.3, where Wesley had denounced the notion of 'everlasting fitness'.

[24] See 1 Cor. 13:9.

[25] Job 37:19.

[26] See Job 4:19. Cf. also No. 28, 'Sermon on the Mount, VIII', §21 and n.

[27] 1 Cor. 13:10, 11.

[28] Cf. Col. 1:15-19, for a striking parallel between Wesley's characterizations of the Law and the Christological metaphors in Colossians.

[29] Cf. BCP, Communion, Sanctus.

is no other than this law, written in our heart) 'is first pure,'ʲ
ἀγνή—chaste, spotless, internally and essentially holy.[30] And
consequently, when it is transcribed into the life, as well as the
soul, it is (as the same Apostle terms it), θρησκεία καθαρὰ καὶ
ἀμίαντος, 'pure religion and undefiled';ᵏ or, the pure, clean, 5
unpolluted worship of God.

3. It is indeed in the highest degree pure, chaste, clean, holy.
Otherwise it could not be the immediate offspring, and much less
the express resemblance of God, who is essential holiness. It is
pure from all sin, clean and unspotted from any touch of evil. It is 10
a chaste virgin, incapable of any defilement, of any mixture with
that which is unclean or unholy. It has no fellowship with sin of
any kind; for 'what communion hath light with darkness?'[31] As sin
is in its very nature enmity to God, so his law is enmity to sin.

4. Therefore it is that the Apostle rejects with such abhorrence 15
that blasphemous supposition that the law of God is either sin
itself or the cause of sin. 'God forbid'[32] that we should suppose it
is the cause of sin because it is the discoverer of it; because it
detects the hidden things of darkness,[33] and drags them out into
open day. 'Tis true, by this means (as the Apostle observes, verse 20
13) 'sin appears to be sin.'[34] All its disguises are torn away, and it
appears in its native deformity. 'Tis true likewise that 'sin by the
commandment becomes exceeding sinful.'[35] Being now committed against light and knowledge, being stripped even of the poor
plea of ignorance, it loses its excuse as well as disguise, and 25
becomes far more odious both to God and man. Yea, and it is true
that 'sin worketh death by that which is good,'[36] which in itself is
pure and holy. When it is dragged out to light it rages the more:
when it is restrained it bursts out with greater violence. Thus the
Apostle, speaking in the person of one who was convinced of sin 30
but not yet delivered from it, 'sin taking occasion by the

ʲ *Ibid.* [Jas. 3:17].
ᵏ [Jas.] 1:27.

---

[30] All nine edns. in Wesley's lifetime read 'internally', and this would seem to mean
'inherently', or something like that. Jackson, sensing that 'eternally' would fit Wesley's
argument more consistently (by adding a temporal dimension), changed the reading either
conjecturally or on the basis of a MS *erratum* now lost. Sugden followed Jackson here
without comment; it is a reasonable guess that Wesley had written 'eternally', and that his
printer had misread him, although his writing in 1750 was perfectly legible.

[31] 2 Cor. 6:14.   [32] Rom. 7:7.   [33] 1 Cor. 4:5.
[34] Cf. Rom. 7:13.   [35] Cf. *ibid.*   [36] Cf. *ibid.*

commandment',[37] detecting and endeavouring to restrain it, disdained the restraint, and so much the more 'wrought in me all manner of concupiscence' (verse 8)—all manner of foolish and hurtful desire,[38] which that commandment sought to restrain.

5 Thus 'when the commandment came, sin revived' (verse 9). It fretted and raged the more. But this is no stain on the commandment. Though it is abused it cannot be defiled. This only proves that 'the heart' of man 'is desperately wicked.'[39] But 'the law' of God 'is holy' still.[40]

10 5. And it is, secondly, *just*. It renders to all their due. It prescribes exactly what is right, precisely what ought to be done, said, or thought, both with regard to the Author of our being, with regard to ourselves, and with regard to every creature which he has made. It is adapted in all respects to the nature of things, of

15 the whole universe and every individual. It is suited to all the circumstances of each, and to all their mutual relations, whether such as have existed from the beginning, or such as commenced in any following period. It is exactly agreeable to the fitnesses of things, whether essential or accidental. It clashes with none of

20 these in any degree, nor is ever unconnected with them. If the word be taken in that sense, there is nothing *arbitrary* in the law of God: although still the whole and every part thereof is totally dependent upon his will, so that 'Thy will be done'[41] is the supreme universal law both in earth and heaven.

25 6. 'But is the will of God the cause of his law? Is his will the original of right and wrong? Is a thing therefore right because God wills it? Or does he will it because it is right?'

I fear this celebrated question[42] is more curious than useful.

---

[37] Rom. 7:11.
[38] See 1 Tim. 6:9.
[39] Jer. 17:9.
[40] Rom. 7:12.
[41] Matt. 6:10; 26:42.
[42] 'Celebrated', indeed, at least since Plato, who understood 'God' as the Supreme Agent of the Supreme Good, as in the *Philebus* 230, 'the *cause* of the [cosmic] mixture', or the *Timaeus* 28c-29c, 'the *Maker* and Father of this universe'. In the tradition of Christian Platonism (from Origen to St. Bonaventura—and on to Descartes, Malebranche to John Norris) God's will and 'the good' had been understood as reciprocals. Scotus, Ockham, Calvin were concerned to stress God's freedom from extrinsic norms of any sort and tended to define 'the good' in terms of God's untrammelled will. The deists and 'natural law' moralists (Fiddes, Shaftesbury, Clarke, and even Butler) point to 'the good' as the norm by which even God is bound. The Calvinists (Ames, Perkins, Whitaker, Twisse) argued in retort that God is unbeholden to any norm or power other than his own will. Cf. Heinrich Heppe's extensive collection of quotations to this same effect from the classical

And perhaps in the manner it is usually treated of it does not so well consist with the regard that is due from a creature to the Creator and Governor of all things. 'Tis hardly decent for man to call the supreme God to give an account to him! Nevertheless, with awe and reverence we may speak a little. The Lord pardon us 5 if we speak amiss!

7. It seems, then, that the whole difficulty arises from considering God's will as distinct from God.[43] Otherwise it vanishes away. For none can doubt but God is the cause of the law of God. But the will of God is God himself. It is God considered 10 as willing thus or thus. Consequently, to say that the will of God, or that God himself, is the cause of the law, is one and the same thing.

8. Again: if the law, the immutable rule of right and wrong, depends on the nature and fitnesses of things, and on their 15 essential relations to each other (I do not say their eternal relations; because the eternal relations of things existing in time is little less than a contradiction); if, I say, this depends on the nature and relations of things, then it must depend on God, or the will of God; because those things themselves, with all their 20 relations, are the work of his hands. By his will, 'for his pleasure' alone, they all 'are and were created'.[44]

9. And yet it may be granted (which is probably all that a considerate person would contend for) that in every particular case God wills this or this (suppose that men should honour their 25 parents) because it is right, agreeable to the fitness of things, to the relation wherein they stand.[45]

10. The law then is right and just concerning all things. And it is *good* as well as *just*. This we may easily infer from the fountain whence it flowed. For what was this but the goodness of God? 30 What but goodness alone inclined him to impart that divine copy of himself to the holy angels? To what else can we impute his bestowing upon man the same transcript of his own nature? And what but tender love constrained him afresh to manifest his will to fallen man? Either to Adam or any of his seed, who like him were 35

Reformed dogmaticians in *Reformed Dogmatics* (London, George Allen and Unwin, 1950), ch. V, §§18-39, pp. 81-100.

[43] Cf. Wesley's later pamphlet on this point, *Thoughts upon God's Sovereignty*, 1777 (*Bibliog*, No. 367; Vol. 12 of this edn.).

[44] Cf. Rev. 4:11.

[45] Note this effort to assimilate the good essence of rationalism into an ethical theory, partly to avoid notions of sovereignty which might lend support to the antinomians.

'come short of the glory of God'?[46] Was it not mere love that
moved him to publish his law, after the understandings of men
were darkened?[47] And to send his prophets to declare that law to
the blind, thoughtless children of men? Doubtless his goodness it
5 was which raised up Enoch and Noah to be preachers of
righteousness; which caused Abraham, his friend, and Isaac and
Jacob, to bear witness to his truth. It was his goodness alone
which, when 'darkness' had 'covered the earth, and thick
darkness the people',[48] gave a written law to Moses, and through
10 him to the nation whom he had chosen. It was his love which
explained these living oracles by David and all the prophets that
followed; until, when the fullness of time was come, he sent his
only-begotten Son, 'not to destroy the law, but to fulfil',[49] to
confirm every jot and tittle thereof, till having wrote it in the
15 hearts of all his children, and put all his enemies under his feet,
'he shall deliver up' his mediatorial 'kingdom to the Father', 'that
God may be all in all'.[50]

11. And this law which the goodness of God gave at first, and
has preserved through all ages, is, like the fountain from whence
20 it springs, full of goodness and benignity. It is mild and kind; it is
(as the Psalmist expresses it) 'sweeter than honey and the
honeycomb'.[51] It is winning and amiable. It includes 'whatsoever
things are lovely or of good report. If there be any virtue, if there
be any praise'[52] before God and his holy angels, they are all
25 comprised in this: wherein are hid all the treasures of the divine
wisdom and knowledge and love.

12. And it is *good* in its effects, as well as in its nature. As the
tree is, so are its fruits. The fruits of the law of God written in the
heart are 'righteousness and peace and assurance for ever'.[53] Or
30 rather, the law itself is righteousness, filling the soul with a peace
that passeth all understanding,[54] and causing us to rejoice
evermore in the testimony of a good conscience toward God.[55] It
is not so properly a pledge as an 'earnest of our inheritance',[56]
being a part of the purchased possession. It is God made manifest
35 in our flesh, and bringing with him eternal life; assuring us by
that pure and perfect love that we are 'sealed unto the day of

---

[46] Rom. 3:23.   [47] See Eph. 4:18.   [48] Cf. Isa. 60:2.
[49] Cf. Matt. 5:17.   [50] Cf. 1 Cor. 15:24, 28.
[51] Ps. 19:10.   [52] Cf. Phil. 4:8.
[53] Cf. Isa. 32:17.   [54] See Phil. 4:7.
[55] See 2 Cor. 1:12; 1 Pet. 3:21.   [56] Eph. 1:14.

redemption';[57] that he will 'spare us, as a man spareth his own son that serveth him, in the day when he maketh up his jewels',[58] and that there remaineth for us 'a crown of glory which fadeth not away'.[59]

IV. 1. It remains only to show, in the fourth and last place, the uses of the law.[60] And the first use of it, without question, is to convince the world of sin. This is indeed the peculiar work of the Holy Ghost, who can work it without any means at all, or by whatever means it pleaseth him, however insufficient in themselves, or even improper to produce such an effect. And accordingly, some there are whose hearts have been broken in pieces in a moment, either in sickness or in health, without any visible cause, or any outward means whatever. And others (one in an age) have been awakened to a sense of 'the wrath of God abiding on them'[61] by hearing that 'God was in Christ, reconciling the world unto himself'.[62] But it is the ordinary method of the Spirit of God to convict sinners by the law. It is this which, being set home on the conscience, generally breaketh the rocks in pieces. It is more especially this part of 'the word of God' which 'is' ζῶν [. . .] καὶ ἐνεργής, 'quick and powerful', full of life and energy, 'and sharper than any two-edged sword'.[63] This, in the hand of God and of those whom he hath sent, 'pierces' through all the folds of a deceitful heart, and 'divides asunder even the soul and spirit', yea, as it were, the very 'joints and marrow'.[64] By this is the sinner discovered to himself. All his fig leaves are torn away, and he sees that he is 'wretched, and poor, and miserable, and blind, and naked'.[65] The law flashes conviction on every side. He feels himself a mere sinner. He has nothing to pay. His 'mouth is stopped,' and he stands 'guilty before God'.[66]

---

[57] Eph. 4:30.   [58] Cf. Mal. 3:17.

[59] Cf. 1 Pet. 5:4. Note here, again, the high correlations between the law and the saving work of Christ. Salvation *through* Christ is, therefore, *to* the law (i.e., holy living).

[60] Calvin had long since focused this problem of the uses of the law in *Institutes*, II.vii: '(1) to convict of unrighteousness (§6); (2) the restraint of wickedness (§10); (3) to teach *believers* "the nature of the Lord's will to which they aspire and to confirm them in the understanding of it".' Cf. Heppe, *Reformed Dogmatics*, XIII. 281-300. Lutherans had tended to deemphasize this third use; cf. Heinrich Schmid, *The Doctrinal Theology of the Evangelical Lutheran Church*, pp. 512-20. The Anglicans had transformed it into a basic premise of their ethics of benevolence and virtue (as in Hammond, Butler, *et al.*). Wesley's revised order, (1) to convince, (2) to convert, (3) to sustain, seems to have been his own.

[61] Cf. John 3:36.   [62] 2 Cor. 5:19.   [63] Heb. 4:12.

[64] *Ibid.*   [65] Cf. Rev. 3:17.   [66] Cf. Rom. 3:19.

2. To slay the sinner is then the first use of the law; to destroy the life and strength wherein he trusts, and convince him that he is dead while he liveth; not only under sentence of death, but actually dead unto God, void of all spiritual life, 'dead in
5   trespasses and sins'.[67] The second use of it is to bring him unto life, unto Christ, that he may live. 'Tis true, in performing both these offices it acts the part of a severe schoolmaster. It drives us by force, rather than draws us by love.[68] And yet love is the spring of all. It is the spirit of love which, by this painful means, tears
10   away our confidence in the flesh, which leaves us no broken reed whereon to trust, and so constrains the sinner, stripped of all, to cry out in the bitterness of his soul, or groan in the depth of his heart,

I give up every plea beside
15   'Lord, I am damned—but thou hast died.' [69]

3. The third use of the law is to keep us alive.[70] It is the grand means whereby the blessed Spirit prepares the believer for larger communications of the life of God.

I am afraid this great and important truth is little understood,
20   not only by the world, but even by many whom God hath taken out of the world, who are real children of God by faith. Many of these lay it down as an unquestioned truth that when we come to Christ we have done with the law; and that in *this* sense, 'Christ is the end of the law . . . to everyone that believeth.'[71] 'The end of
25   the law'. So he is, 'for righteousness', for justification, 'to everyone that believeth'. Herein the law is at an end. It justifies none, but only brings them to Christ; who is also, in another respect, 'the end' or scope 'of the law'—the point at which it continually aims. But when it has brought us to him it has yet a
30   farther office, namely, to keep us with him. For it is continually exciting all believers, the more they see of its height and depth and length and breadth,[72] to exhort one another so much the more:

---

[67] Eph. 2:1.
[68] Cf. No. 47, 'Heaviness through Manifold Temptations', III.9.
[69] John and Charles Wesley, *Hymns and Sacred Poems* (1739), p. 94 (*Poet. Wks.*, I.85). See No. 11, *The Witness of the Spirit*, II, III.7 and n.
[70] This greater stress on the third use (*viz.*, the moral influence) of the law is significant; it supports a positive evangelical ethic.
[71] Rom. 10:4.   [72] See Eph. 3:18.

Closer and closer let us cleave
To his beloved embrace;
Expect his fullness to receive,
And grace to answer grace.[73]

4. Allowing then that every believer has done with the law, as it means the Jewish ceremonial law, or the entire Mosaic dispensation (for these Christ 'hath taken out of the way');[74] yea, allowing we have done with the moral law as a means of procuring our justification (for we are 'justified freely by his grace, through the redemption that is in Jesus');[75] yet in another sense we have not done with this law. For it is still of unspeakable use, first, in convincing us of the sin that yet remains both in our hearts and lives, and thereby keeping us close to Christ, that his blood may cleanse us every moment; secondly, in deriving strength from our Head into his living members, whereby he empowers them to do what his law commands; and thirdly, in confirming our hope of whatsoever it commands and we have not yet attained, of receiving grace upon grace,[76] till we are in actual possession of the fullness of his promises.

5. How clearly does this agree with the experience of every true believer! While he cries out: 'O what love have I unto thy law! All the day long is my study in it,'[77] he sees daily in that divine mirror more and more of his own sinfulness. He sees more and more clearly that he is still a sinner in all things; that neither his heart nor his ways are right before God; and that every moment sends him to Christ. This shows him the meaning of what is written: 'Thou shalt make a plate of pure gold, and grave upon it, Holiness to the Lord. And it shall be upon Aaron's forehead' (the type of our great High Priest) 'that Aaron may bear the iniquities of the holy things, which the children of Israel shall hallow in all their holy gifts' (so far are our prayers or holy things from atoning for the rest of our sins); 'and it shall be always upon his forehead, that they may be accepted before the Lord.'[1]

6. To explain this by a single instance. The law says, 'Thou

---

[1] Exod. 28:36, 38.

---

[73] John and Charles Wesley, 'At Parting', *Hymns and Sacred Poems* (1742), p. 160 (*Poet. Wks.*, II.222).

[74] Cf. 2 Thess. 2:7.   [75] Rom. 3:24.

[76] See John 1:16.

[77] Cf. Ps. 119:97 (BCP).

shalt not kill,'[78] and hereby (as our Lord teaches) forbids not only
outward acts but every unkind word or thought.[79] Now the more I
look into this perfect law, the more I feel how far I come short of
it; and the more I feel this, the more I feel my need of his blood to
5 atone for all my sin, and of his Spirit to purify my heart, and make
me 'perfect and entire, lacking nothing'.[80]

7. Therefore I cannot spare the law one moment, no more than
I can spare Christ; seeing I now want it as much to keep me to
Christ as ever I wanted it to bring me to him. Otherwise this 'evil
10 heart of unbelief' would immediately 'depart from the living
God'.[81] Indeed each is continually sending me to the other—the
law to Christ, and Christ to the law. On the one hand, the height
and depth of the law constrain me to fly to the love of God in
Christ; on the other, the love of God in Christ endears the law to
15 me 'above gold or precious stones';[82] seeing I know every part of it
is a gracious promise, which my Lord will fulfil in its season.

8. Who art thou then, O man, that 'judgest the law, and
speakest evil of the law'?[83] That rankest it with sin, Satan, and
death, and sendest them all to hell together? The Apostle James
20 esteemed 'judging' or 'speaking evil of the law' so enormous a
piece of wickedness that he knew not how to aggravate the guilt of
judging our brethren more than by showing it included this. So
now, says he, 'thou art not a doer of the law but a judge!'[84] A judge
of that which God hath ordained to judge thee. So thou hast set
25 up thyself in the judgment seat of Christ, and cast down the rule
whereby he will judge the world! O take knowledge what
advantage Satan hath gained over thee![85] And for the time to come
never think or speak lightly of, much less dress up as a scarecrow,
this blessed instrument of the grace of God. Yea, love and value it
30 for the sake of him from whom it came, and of him to whom it
leads. Let it be thy glory and joy, next to the cross of Christ.
Declare its praise, and make it honourable before all men.

9. And if thou art throughly convinced that it is the offspring of
God, that it is the copy of all his imitable perfections, and that it 'is

---

[78] Exod. 20:13; Deut. 5:17.
[79] See Matt. 5:21-22.
[80] Jas. 1:4.
[81] Cf. Heb. 3:12.
[82] Cf. Ps. 119:127 (BCP).
[83] Cf. Jas. 4:11.
[84] *Ibid.*
[85] See 2 Cor. 2:11.

holy, and just, and good',[86] but especially to them that believe; then instead of casting it away as a polluted thing, see that thou cleave to it more and more. Never let the law of mercy and truth, of love to God and man, of lowliness, meekness, and purity forsake thee. 'Bind it about thy neck: write it on the table of thy 5 heart.'[87] Keep close to the law if thou wilt keep close to Christ; hold it fast; let it not go. Let this continually lead thee to the atoning blood, continually confirm thy hope, till all 'the righteousness of the law is fulfilled in thee',[88] and thou art 'filled with all the fullness of God'.[89]   10

10. And if thy Lord hath already fulfilled his word, if he hath already 'written his law in thy heart',[90] then 'stand fast in the liberty wherewith Christ hath made thee free.'[91] Thou art not only made free from Jewish ceremonies, from the guilt of sin and the fear of hell (these are so far from being the whole, that they are the 15 least and lowest part of Christian liberty), but what is infinitely more, from the power of sin, from serving the devil, from offending God.[92] O stand fast in this liberty, in comparison of which all the rest is not even worthy to be named. Stand fast in loving God with all thy heart and serving him with all thy strength. 20 This is perfect freedom;[93] thus to keep his law and to walk in all his commandments blameless.[94] 'Be not entangled again with the yoke of bondage.'[95] I do not mean of Jewish bondage; nor yet of bondage to the fear of hell: these, I trust, are far from thee. But beware of being entangled again with the yoke of sin, of any 25 inward or outward transgression of the law. Abhor sin far more than death or hell; abhor sin itself far more than the punishment of it. Beware of the bondage of pride, of desire, of anger; of every evil temper or word or work. 'Look unto Jesus',[96] and in order thereto 'look' more and more 'into the perfect law, the law of 30 liberty', and 'continue therein';[97] so shalt thou daily 'grow in grace, and in the knowledge of our Lord Jesus Christ.'[98]

---

[86] Rom. 7:12.   [87] Cf. Prov. 3:3.   [88] Cf. Rom. 8:4.
[89] Eph. 3:19.   [90] Cf. Rom. 2:15.   [91] Cf. Gal. 5:1.
[92] Note this claim to a freedom from the power of sin (*posse non peccare*); cf. intro. to No. 13, *On Sin in Believers*. Cf. also No. 40, *Christian Perfection*, II.2.
[93] Cf. the 'Collect for Peace', BCP, Morning Prayer: 'O God . . . whose service is perfect freedom'.
[94] See Luke 1:6.   [95] Gal. 5:1.
[96] Cf. Heb. 12:2.
[97] Cf. Jas. 1:25.
[98] Cf. 2. Pet. 3:18.

The Law Established through Faith

Discourse I

Romans 3:31

Do we then make void the law through faith?
God forbid! Yea, we establish the law.

1. St. Paul having in the beginning of this Epistle laid down his general proposition, namely, that 'the gospel of Christ is the power of God unto salvation to everyone that believeth'[1]—the powerful means whereby God makes every believer a partaker of
10 present and eternal salvation—goes on to show that there is no other way under heaven whereby men can be saved.[2] He speaks particularly of salvation from the guilt of sin, which he commonly terms justification. And that all men stood in need of this, that none could plead their own innocence, he proves at large by
15 various arguments addressed to the Jews as well as the heathens. Hence he infers (in the nineteenth verse of this chapter) 'that every mouth', whether of Jew or heathen, must 'be stopped' from excusing or justifying himself, 'and all the world become guilty before God. Therefore', saith he, by his own obedience, 'by the
20 works of the law, shall no flesh be justified in his sight.'[a] 'But now the righteousness of God without the law', without our previous obedience thereto, 'is manifested;[b] even the righteousness of God which is by faith of Jesus Christ unto all and upon all that believe; for there is no difference'[c] as to their need of justification, or the
25 manner wherein they attain it. 'For all have sinned, and come short of the glory of God,'[d] the glorious image of God wherein they were created: and all (who attain) 'are justified freely by his grace, through the redemption that is in Jesus Christ;[e] whom

[a] [Rom. 3,] ver. 20. [b] Ver. 21. [c] Ver. 22.
[d] Ver. 23. [e] Ver. 24.

[1] Rom. 1:16. [2] See Acts 4:12.

God hath set forth to be a propitiation through faith in his blood;[f] . . . that he might be just, and yet the justifier of him which believeth in Jesus';[g] that without any impeachment to his justice he might show him mercy for the sake of that propitiation. 'Therefore we conclude' (which was the grand position he had undertaken to establish) 'that a man is justified by faith, without the works of the law.'[h]

2. It was easy to foresee an objection which might be made, and which has in fact been made in all ages; namely, that to say 'we are justified without the works of the law' is to abolish the law. The Apostle, without entering into a formal dispute, simply denies the charge. 'Do we then', says he, 'make void the law through faith? God forbid! Yea, we establish the law.'

3. The strange imagination of some[3] that St. Paul, when he says, 'A man is justified without the works of the law,' means only the *ceremonial* law, is abundantly confuted by these very words. For did St. Paul 'establish' the *ceremonial* law? It is evident he did not. He did 'make void' that law through faith, and openly avowed his doing so. It was the *moral* law only of which he might truly say, we do not make void but 'establish' this 'through faith'.

4. But all men are not herein of his mind. Many there are who will not agree to this. Many in all ages of the church, even among those who bore the name of Christians, have contended that 'the faith once delivered to the saints'[4] was designed to make void the whole law.[5] They would no more spare the moral than the ceremonial law, but were for 'hewing', as it were, 'both in pieces before the Lord':[6] vehemently maintaining, 'If you establish any law, "Christ shall profit you nothing. [. . .] Christ is become of no effect to you; [. . .] ye are fallen from grace."'[7]

---

[f] Ver. 25. [g] Ver. 26. [h] Ver. 28.

---

[3] *Viz.*, the Anabaptists and Quakers, as Wesley understood them.
[4] Jude 3.
[5] This is antinomianism without the label; Wesley thought he had found this tendency in the Gnostics, the Montanists, the 'spiritual Franciscans', and, more lately, in the Moravians. The term itself seems to have been coined in the Lutheran controversies with Johannes Agricola (cf. *Schaff-Herzog Encyclopedia*); Milton appears to have brought the word into English in his *Colasterion* (1645); cf. his *Works* (1738), I. 295. The *OED* also cites Rogers, Burnet, and Waterland as having used it in their references to the lawlessness of the Puritan Commonwealth. Samuel Johnson, in his *Dictionary*, ignores it. See Wesley's *Second Dialogue Between an Antinomian and His Friend* (1745), where he quotes William Cudworth as holding an antinomian view.
[6] Cf. 1 Sam. 15:33. [7] Gal. 5:2, 4.

5. But is the zeal of these men according to knowledge?[8] Have they observed the connection between the law and faith? And that, considering the close connection between them, to destroy one is indeed to destroy both? That to abolish the moral law is, in truth, to abolish faith and the law together, as leaving no proper means either of bringing us to faith or of 'stirring up that gift of God'[9] in our soul?

6. It therefore behoves all who desire either to come to Christ, or to 'walk in him whom they have received',[10] to take heed how they 'make void the law through faith'; to secure us effectually against which let us inquire, first, which are the most usual ways of 'making void the law through faith'; and, secondly, how we may follow the Apostle, and by faith 'establish the law'.

I. 1. Let us, first, inquire which are the most usual ways of 'making void the law through faith'. Now the way for a preacher to make it all void at a stroke is not to preach it at all. This is just the same thing as to blot it out of the oracles of God. More especially when it is done with design; when it is made a rule, 'not to preach the law'—and the very phrase, 'a preacher of the law', is used as a term of reproach, as though it meant little less than 'an enemy to the gospel'.

2. All this proceeds from the deepest ignorance of the nature, properties, and use of the law; and proves that those who act thus either know not Christ, are utter strangers to the living faith, or at least that they are but babes in Christ, and as such 'unskilled in the word of righteousness'.[11]

3. Their grand plea is this, that preaching the gospel (that is, according to their judgment, the speaking of nothing but the sufferings and merits of Christ) answers all the ends of the law. But this we utterly deny. It does not answer the very first end of the law, namely, the convincing men of sin, the awakening those who are still asleep on the brink of hell. There may have been here and there an exempt case. One in a thousand may have been awakened by the gospel. But this is no general rule. The ordinary method of God is to convict sinners by the law, and that only.[12]

---

[8] See Rom. 10:2.   [9] Cf. 2 Tim. 1:6.
[10] Cf. Col. 2:6.   [11] Cf. Heb. 5:13.
[12] See above, No. 34, 'The Original, Nature, Properties, and Use of the Law', IV. 1. See also, Wesley's letter to Ebenezer Blackwell(?), Dec. 20, 1751 ('Of Preaching Christ'), and its distinction between preaching the law to the complacent and unrepentant and the consolations of the gospel to the despairing.

The gospel is not the means which God hath ordained, or which our Lord himself used, for this end. We have no authority in Scripture for applying it thus, nor any ground to think it will prove effectual. Nor have we any more ground to expect this from the nature of the thing. 'They that be whole', as our Lord himself observes, 'need not a physician, but they that be sick.'[13] It is absurd therefore to offer a physician to them that are whole, or that at least imagine themselves so to be. You are first to convince them that they are sick; otherwise they will not thank you for your labour. It is equally absurd to offer Christ to them whose heart is whole, having never yet been broken. It is, in the proper sense, 'casting pearls before swine'. Doubtless 'they will trample them under foot'; and it is no more than you have reason to expect if they also 'turn again and rend you'.[14]

4. 'But although there is no command in Scripture to offer Christ to the careless sinner, yet are there not scriptural precedents for it?' I think not: I know not any. I believe you can't produce one, either from the four evangelists, or the Acts of the Apostles. Neither can you prove this to have been the practice of any of the apostles from any passage in all their writings.

5. 'Nay, does not the Apostle Paul say, in his former Epistle to the Corinthians, "We preach Christ crucified"?'[i] and in his latter, "We preach not ourselves, but Christ Jesus the Lord"?'[j]

We consent to rest the cause on this issue: to tread in his steps, to follow his example. Only preach you just as St. Paul preached, and the dispute is at an end.

For although we are certain he *preached Christ* in as perfect a manner as the very chief of the apostles, yet who *preached the law* more than St. Paul? Therefore he did not think the gospel answered the same end.

6. The very first sermon of St. Paul's which is recorded concludes in these words: 'By him all that believe are justified from all things, from which ye could not be justified by the law of Moses. Beware therefore lest that come upon you which is spoken of in the Prophets: Behold, ye despisers, and wonder and perish; for I work a work in your days, a work which you will in no

---

[i] Chap. 1, ver. 23.
[j] Chap. 4, ver. 5.

---

[13] Cf. Matt. 9:12.

[14] Cf. Matt. 7:6.

wise believe, though a man declare it unto you.'ᵏ Now it is manifest, all this is 'preaching the law', in the sense wherein you understand the term; even although great part of, if not all, his hearers were either 'Jews or religious proselytes'ˡ, and therefore
5 probably many of them, in some degree at least, convinced of sin already. He first reminds them that they could not be justified by the law of Moses, but only by faith in Christ; and then severely threatens them with the judgments of God, which is, in the strongest sense, 'preaching the law'.

10   7. In his next discourse, that to the heathens at Lystra,ᵐ we do not find so much as the name of Christ. The whole purport of it is that they should 'turn from those vain idols unto the living God'. Now confess the truth. Do not you think if you had been there you could have preached much better than he? I should not wonder if
15 you thought too that his *preaching so ill* occasioned his being *so ill treated;* and that his being *stoned* was a just judgment upon him for not *preaching Christ!*¹⁵

    8. To the jailor indeed, when he 'sprang in and came trembling, and fell down before Paul and Silas, [. . .] and said,
20 Sirs, What must I do to be saved?', he immediately 'said, Believe in the Lord Jesus Christ.'ⁿ And in the case of one so deeply convinced of sin, who would not have said the same? But to the men of Athens you find him speaking in a quite different manner, reproving their superstition, ignorance, and idolatry, and strongly
25 moving them to repent, from the consideration of a future judgment, and of the resurrection from the dead.º Likewise 'when Felix sent for Paul', on purpose that he might 'hear him concerning the faith in Christ'; instead of preaching Christ in *your* sense (which would probably have caused the governor either to
30 mock or to contradict and blaspheme) 'he reasoned of righteousness, temperance, and judgment to come', till 'Felix' (hardened as he was) 'trembled'.ᵖ Go thou and tread in his steps. *Preach* Christ to the careless sinner by 'reasoning of righteousness, temperance, and judgment to come'!

ᵏ Acts 13:39-45.
ˡ Ver. 43.
ᵐ Chap. 14, ver. 15, etc.
ⁿ Chap. 16, ver. 29-31.
º Chap. 17, ver. 22-31.
ᵖ Chap. 24, ver. 24-25.

¹⁵ A rare recourse to sarcasm, addressed to William Cudworth and his associates.

9. If you say, 'But he *preached Christ* in a different manner in his epistles,' I answer, [(1),] he did not there preach at all, not in that sense wherein we speak; for 'preaching' in our present question means speaking before a congregation. But waiving this I answer, (2), his epistles are directed, not to unbelievers, such as those we are now speaking of, but to 'the saints of God'[16] in Rome, Corinth, Philippi, and other places. Now unquestionably he would speak more of Christ to these than to those who were without God in the world. And yet, (3), every one of these is full of the law, even the Epistles to the Romans and the Galatians, in both of which he does what you term preaching the law, and that to believers as well as unbelievers.

10. From hence 'tis plain you know not what it is to 'preach Christ', in the sense of the Apostle. For doubtless St. Paul judged himself to be preaching Christ both to Felix, and at Antioch, Lystra, and Athens: from whose example every thinking man must infer that not only the declaring the love of Christ to sinners, but also the declaring that he will come from heaven in flaming fire, is, in the Apostle's sense, 'preaching Christ'. Yea, in the full scriptural meaning of the word. To preach Christ is to preach what he hath revealed, either in the Old or New Testament; so that you are then as really preaching Christ when you are saying, 'The wicked shall be turned into hell, and all the people that forget God,'[17] as when you are saying, 'Behold the Lamb of God, which taketh away the sin of the world!'[18]

11. Consider this well: that to 'preach Christ' is to preach all things that Christ hath spoken: all his promises; all his threatenings and commands; all that is written in his Book. And then you will know how to preach Christ without making void the law.

12. 'But does not the greatest blessing attend those discourses wherein we peculiarly preach the merits and sufferings of Christ?'

Probably, when we preach to a congregation of mourners or of believers, these will be attended with the greatest blessing; because such discourses are peculiarly suited to their state. At least these will usually convey the most comfort. But this is not always the greatest blessing. I may sometimes receive a far greater by a discourse that cuts me to the heart and humbles me to the dust. Neither should I receive that comfort if I were to preach or

---

[16] Cf. Rom. 1:7, etc.   [17] Ps. 9:17 (BCP).   [18] John 1:29.

to hear no discourses but on the sufferings of Christ. These by
constant repetition would lose their force, and grow more and
more flat and dead, till at length they would become a dull round
of words, without any spirit or life or virtue. So that thus to
5 'preach Christ' must, in process of time, make void the gospel as
well as the law.[19]

II. 1. A second way of 'making void the law through faith' is the
teaching that faith supersedes the necessity of holiness. This
divides itself into a thousand smaller paths—and many there are
10 that walk therein. Indeed there are few that wholly escape it; few
who are convinced we 'are saved by faith' but are sooner or later,
more or less, drawn aside into this by-way.

2. All those are drawn into this by-way who, if it be not their
settled judgment that faith in Christ entirely sets aside the
15 necessity of keeping his law, yet suppose either, (1), that holiness
is less necessary now than it was before Christ came; or, (2), that a
less degree of it is necessary; or, (3), that it is less necessary to
believers than to others. Yea, and so are all those who, although
their judgment be right in the general, yet think they may take
20 more liberty in particular cases than they could have done before
they believed. Indeed the using the term *liberty* in such a manner
for 'liberty from obedience or holiness' shows at once that their
judgment is perverted, and that they are guilty of what they
imagined to be far from them; namely, of 'making void the law

---

[19] Cant phrases among the sectarians and antinomians in praise of those who offered
God's easy pardon (for Christ's sake) and in contempt of those who added moral demands
to the gospel, either as precondition or necessary fruit of it, always drew Wesley's ire; cf.
Nos. 46, 'The Wilderness State', III.1; 88, 'On Dress', §21; and 99, *The Reward of
Righteousness*, I.3. See also his letter to his brother Charles, Nov. 4, 1772: 'If we duly join
faith and works in all our preaching, we shall not fail of a blessing. But of all preaching,
what is usually called gospel preaching is the most useless, if not the most mischievous; a
dull, yea or lively, harangue on the sufferings of Christ or salvation by faith without
strongly inculcating holiness. I see more and more that this naturally tends to drive
holiness out of the world;' and to Mary Bishop, Oct. 18, 1778 (1:25, n. 51, in this edn.).
See also 'Thoughts Concerning Gospel Ministers', (*AM*, 1784, VII. 550-53).
   Wesley was joined in this value judgment by Simon Patrick. Cf. Wesley's extract in *AM*
(1778), I. 402-3; John Selden (*Table Talk*, Nos. 1, 5); Jonathan Swift, and Richard Steele
(cf. *Tatler*, No. 66, Sept. 10, 1709); Robert Bolton (*A Discourse About the State of True
Happiness*); and Joseph Glanvill (*An Essay Concerning Preaching*, pp. 26-27). Glanvill has a
list of 'phantastical phrases' used by the 'gospel preachers': 'roll upon Christ, close with
Christ, get into Christ . . . O, this is savoury! This is precious! This is spiritual teaching,
indeed!'

through faith', by supposing faith to supersede holiness.[20]

3. The first plea of those who teach this expressly is that we are now under the covenant of grace, not works;[21] and therefore we are no longer under the necessity of performing the works of the law.

And who ever was under the covenant of works? None but Adam before the fall. He was fully and properly under that covenant, which required perfect, universal obedience, as the one condition of acceptance, and left no place for pardon, upon the very least transgression. But no man else was ever under this, neither Jew nor Gentile, neither before Christ nor since. All his sons were and are under the covenant of grace. The manner of their acceptance is this: the free grace of God, through the merits of Christ, gives pardon to them that believe, that believe with such a faith as, working by love, produces all obedience and holiness.[22]

4. The case is not therefore, as you suppose, that men were *once* more obliged to obey God, or to work the works of his law, than they are *now*. This is a supposition you cannot make good. But we should have been obliged, if we had been under the covenant of works, to have done those works antecedent to our acceptance. Whereas now all good works, though as necessary as ever, are not antecedent to our acceptance, but consequent upon it. Therefore the nature of the covenant of grace gives you no ground, no encouragement at all, to set aside any instance or degree of obedience, any part or measure of holiness.

5. 'But are we not "justified by faith, without the works of the law"?'[23] Undoubtedly we are, without the works either of the ceremonial or the moral law. And would to God all men were convinced of this! It would prevent innumerable evils: antinomianism in particular—for, generally speaking, they are the Pharisees who make the antinomians. Running into an extreme so palpably contrary to Scripture, they occasion others to run into the opposite one. These, seeking to be justified by works, affright those from allowing any place for them.

6. But the truth lies between both.[24] We are, doubtless,

---

[20] Cf. No. 127, 'On the Wedding Garment', §18: 'The imagination that faith *supersedes* holiness is the marrow of antinomianism.'

[21] Cf. No. 6, 'The Righteousness of Faith', §1 and n.

[22] The *fides caritate formata*; note Wesley's clear implication that the *sola fide* produces the impetus to holy living and guidance in it. Cf. No. 2, *The Almost Christian*, II.6 and n.

[23] Rom. 3:28.

[24] See Intro. on Wesley's 'Theological Method and the Problem of Development', espec. pp. 54-66, Vol. 1 of this edn.

'justified by faith'. This is the corner-stone of the whole Christian building. 'We are justified without the works of the law' as any previous condition of justification. But they are an immediate fruit of that faith whereby we are justified. So that if good works
5 do not follow our faith, even all inward and outward holiness, it is plain our faith is nothing worth; we are yet in our sins.[25] Therefore that we are 'justified by faith', even by 'faith without works', is no ground for 'making void the law through faith'; or for imagining that faith is a dispensation from any kind or degree of holiness.
10   7. 'Nay, but does not St. Paul expressly say, "Unto him that worketh not, but believeth on him that justifieth the ungodly, his faith is counted for righteousness"?[26] And does it not follow from hence that faith is to a believer in the room, in the place, of righteousness? But if faith is in the room of righteousness or
15 holiness, what need is there of this too?'

This, it must be acknowledged, comes home to the point, and is indeed the main pillar of antinomianism. And yet it needs not a long or laboured answer.[27] We allow, (1), that God 'justifies the ungodly', him that till that hour is totally ungodly, full of all evil,
20 void of all good; (2), that he justifies 'the ungodly that worketh not', that till that moment worketh no good work—neither can he: for an evil tree cannot bring forth good fruit;[28] (3), that he justifies him 'by faith alone', without any goodness or righteousness preceding; and (4), that 'faith is' then 'counted to him for
25 righteousness', namely, for *preceding righteousness;* i.e. God, through the merits of Christ, accepts him that believes as if he had already fulfilled all righteousness. But what is all this to your point? The Apostle does not say either here or elsewhere that this faith is counted to him for *subsequent righteousness.*[29] He does teach
30 that there is no righteousness *before* faith; but where does he teach that there is none *after* it? He does assert holiness cannot *precede* justification; but not that it need not *follow* it. St. Paul therefore

---

[25] See 1 Cor. 15:17.
[26] Rom. 4:5.
[27] Another summary of Wesley's version of *sola fide;* cf. Nos. 5, 'Justification by Faith', espec. intro.; and 20, *The Lord Our Righteousness,* §4 and n. But note the lessened emphasis on penal satisfaction as compared, say, to Hervey's *Theron and Aspasio,* (Dialogues III-IV; cf. *Eleven Letters,* II. 15-34), and Calvinist evangelicals in general. The crucial point is that *sola fide* and holy living are related here in a definite *progression.* What follows is yet another summary of Wesley's view of the *ordo salutis,* on the point of justification.
[28] See Matt. 7:18.
[29] I.e., the traditional doctrine of double justification.

gives you no colour for 'making void the law' by teaching that faith supersedes the necessity of holiness.

III. 1. There is yet another way of 'making void the law through faith', which is more common than either of the former. And that is, the doing it practically; the making it void in *fact*, 5 though not in *principle*; the *living* as if faith was designed to excuse us from holiness.

How earnestly does the Apostle guard us against this, in those well-known words: 'What then? Shall we sin, because we are not under the law, but under grace? God forbid!'q A caution 10 which it is needful thoroughly[30] to consider, because it is of the last importance.

2. The being 'under the law' may here mean, (1), the being obliged to observe the ceremonial laws; (2), the being obliged to conform to the whole Mosaic institution; (3), the being obliged 15 to keep the whole moral law as the condition of our acceptance with God; and, (4), the being under the wrath and curse of God, under sentence of eternal death; under a sense of guilt and condemnation, full of horror and slavish fear.

3. Now although a believer is 'not without law to God, but 20 under the law to Christ',[31] yet from the moment he believes he is not 'under the law', in any of the preceding senses. On the contrary, he is 'under grace', under a more benign, gracious dispensation. As he is no longer under the ceremonial law, nor under the Mosaic institution; as he is not obliged to keep even the 25 moral law as the condition of his acceptance, so he is delivered from the wrath and the curse of God, from all sense of guilt and condemnation, and from all that horror and fear of death and hell whereby he was 'all his life' before 'subject to bondage'.[32] And he now performs (which while 'under the law' he could not do) a 30 willing and universal obedience. He obeys, not from the motive of slavish fear, but on a nobler principle, namely, the grace of God

q Rom. 6:15.

---

[30] In his early and middle periods, Wesley's typical spelling here was 'throughly'; as the century wore on he came more and more to adopt the 'modern' spelling, as here, even in 1750.

[31] 1 Cor. 9:21. Cf. Cudworth's exegesis of this text: 'It does not mean "we are under the law to Christ" but rather "in a [new] law of love and liberty"' (*A Dialogue Between a Preacher of God's Righteousness and a Preacher of Inherent Righteousness*, p. 9).

[32] Cf. Heb. 2:15.

ruling in his heart, and causing all his works to be wrought in love.

4. What then? Shall this evangelical principle of action be less powerful than the legal? Shall we be less obedient to God from filial love than we were from servile fear?

5 'Tis well if this is not a common case; if this practical antinomianism, this unobserved way of 'making void the law through faith', has not infected thousands of believers.

Has it not infected you? Examine yourself honestly and closely. Do you not do now what you durst not have done when you was

10 'under the law', or (as we commonly call it) 'under conviction'? For instance: you durst not then indulge yourself in food. You took just what was needful, and that of the cheapest kind. Do you not allow yourself more latitude now? Do you not indulge yourself a *little* more than you did? O beware lest you 'sin because you are

15 not under the law, but under grace'!

5. When you was under conviction, you durst not indulge the lust of the eye in any degree. You would not do anything, great or small, merely to gratify your curiosity. You regarded only cleanliness and necessity, or at most very moderate convenience,

20 either in furniture or apparel; superfluity and finery of whatever kind, as well as fashionable elegance, were both a terror and an abomination to you.

Are they so still? Is your conscience as tender now in these things as it was then? Do you still follow the same rule both in

25 furniture and apparel, trampling all finery, all superfluity, everything useless, everything merely ornamental, however fashionable, under foot? Rather, have you not resumed what you had once laid aside, and what you could not then use without wounding your conscience? And have you not learned to say, 'Oh, I am not *so*

30 *scrupulous* now.' I would to God you were! Then you would not sin thus 'because you are not under the law, but under grace'.

6. You was once scrupulous, too, of commending any to their face; and still more of suffering any to commend *you*. It was a stab to your heart; you could not bear it; you sought the honour that

35 cometh of God only. You could not endure such conversation, nor any conversation which was not good to the use of edifying. All idle talk, all trifling discourse, you abhorred; you hated as well as feared it, being deeply sensible of the value of time, of every precious fleeting moment.[33] In like manner you dreaded and

---

[33] Cf. No. 93, 'On Redeeming the Time'.

abhorred idle expense; valuing your money only less than your time, and trembling lest you should be found an unfaithful steward even of the mammon of unrighteousness.[34]

Do you now look upon praise as deadly poison, which you can neither give nor receive but at the peril of your soul?[35] Do you still dread and abhor all conversation which does not tend to the use of edifying, and labour to improve every moment that it may not pass without leaving you better than it found you? Are not you less careful as to the expense both of money and time? Cannot you now lay out either as you could not have done once? Alas! How has that 'which should have been for your health proved to you an occasion of falling'![36] How have you 'sinned, because you was not under the law, but under grace'!

7. God forbid you should any longer continue thus to 'turn the grace of God into lasciviousness'![37] O remember how clear and strong a conviction you once had concerning all these things! And at the same time you was fully satisfied from whom that conviction came. The world told you you was in a delusion; but you knew it was the voice of God. In these things you was not *too scrupulous* then; but you are not now *scrupulous enough.* God kept you longer in that painful school that you might learn those great lessons the more perfectly. And have you forgot them already? O recollect them, before it is too late. Have you suffered so many things in vain? I trust it is not yet in vain. Now use the conviction without the pain. Practise the lesson without the rod. Let not the mercy of God weigh less with you now than his fiery indignation did before. Is love a less powerful motive than fear? If not, let it be an invariable rule, 'I will do nothing now I am *under grace* which I durst not have done when *under the law*'.

8. I cannot conclude this head without exhorting you to examine yourself, likewise, touching sins of omission.[38] Are you as clear of these, now you are 'under grace', as you was when 'under the law'? How diligent was you then in hearing the Word of God! Did you neglect any opportunity? Did you not attend thereon day and night? Would a small hindrance have kept you away? A little

---

[34] Cf. No. 51, *The Good Steward.*

[35] For Wesley's comments on 'the praise of men' (or flattery), cf. No. 14, *The Repentance of Believers*, I.7 and n.

[36] Cf. Ps. 69:23; Acts 27:34.

[37] Cf. Jude 4.

[38] Cf. No. 14, *The Repentance of Believers*, I.14 and n.

business? A visitant? A slight indisposition? A soft bed? A dark or
cold morning? Did not you then fast often? Or use abstinence to
the uttermost of your power? Was not you much in prayer (cold
and heavy as you was) while you was hanging over the mouth of
5 hell? Did you not speak and not spare, even for an unknown God?
Did you not boldly plead his cause? Reprove sinners? And avow
the truth before an adulterous generation? And are you now a
believer in Christ? Have you the 'faith that overcometh the
world'?[39] What! and are less zealous for your Master now than you
10 was when you knew him not? Less diligent in fasting, in prayer, in
hearing his Word, in calling sinners to God? O repent! See and
feel your grievous loss! Remember from whence you are fallen![40]
Bewail your unfaithfulness! Now be zealous and do the first
works; lest, if you continue to 'make void the law through faith',
15 God cut you off, and 'appoint' you your 'portion with the
unbelievers'![41]

---

[39] Cf. 1 John 5:4, 5.
[40] See Rev. 2:5.
[41] Luke 12:46.

The Law Established through Faith

Discourse II

Romans 3:31

Do we then make void the law through faith?
God forbid! Yea, we establish the law.

1. It has been shown in the preceding discourse which are the most usual ways of 'making void the law through faith'. Namely, first, the not preaching it at all, which effectually makes it all void at a stroke, and this under colour of 'preaching Christ' and magnifying the gospel—though it be, in truth, destroying both the one and the other. Secondly, the teaching (whether directly or indirectly) that faith supersedes the necessity of holiness, that this is less necessary now, or a less degree of it necessary, than before Christ came; that it is less necessary to us because we believe than otherwise it would have been; or that Christian liberty is a liberty from any kind or degree of holiness—so perverting those great truths that we are now under the *covenant of grace* and not of *works*; that 'a man is justified by faith, without the works of the law';[1] and that 'to him that worketh not, but believeth, his faith is counted for righteousness'.[2] Or, thirdly, the doing this practically: the making void the law in practice though not in principle; the living or acting as if faith was designed to excuse us from holiness; the allowing ourselves in sin 'because we are not under the law, but under grace'.[3] It remains to inquire how we may follow a better pattern, how we may be able to say with the Apostle, 'Do we then make void the law through faith? God forbid! Yea, we establish the law.'

2. We do not indeed establish the old ceremonial law: we know that is abolished for ever. Much less do we establish the whole Mosaic dispensation—this, we know, our Lord has 'nailed to his

[1] Cf. Rom. 3:28.   [2] Rom. 4:5.
[3] Rom. 6:15.

33

cross'.[4] Nor yet do we so establish the moral law (which, it is to be feared, too many do) as if the fulfilling it, the keeping all the commandments, were the condition of our justification. If it were so, surely 'in his sight should no man living be justified'.[5] But all
5　this being allowed, we still, in the Apostle's sense, 'establish the law', the moral law.

I. 1. We 'establish the law', first, by our doctrine: by endeavouring to preach it in its whole extent, to explain and enforce every part of it in the same manner as our great Teacher
10　did while upon earth. We establish it by following St. Peter's advice, 'If any man speak, let him speak as the oracles of God;'[6] as the holy men of old, moved by the Holy Ghost, spoke and wrote for our instruction; and as the apostles of our blessed Lord, by the direction of the same Spirit. We establish it whenever we speak in
15　his name, by keeping back nothing from them that hear; by declaring to them without any limitation or reserve the whole counsel of God. And in order the more effectually to establish it we use herein great plainness of speech. 'We are not as many that corrupt the word of God', καπηλεύουσι[7] (as artful men their bad
20　wines); we do not cauponize, mix, adulterate, or soften it to make it suit the taste of the hearers. 'But as of sincerity, but as of God, in the sight of God speak we in Christ,' as having no other aim than by 'manifestation of the truth to commend ourselves to every man's conscience in the sight of God'.[8]
25　2. We then, by our doctrine, establish the law when we thus openly declare it to all men, and that in the fullness wherein it is delivered by our blessed Lord and his apostles; when we publish

---

[4] Cf. Col. 2:14.　　　　　[5] Cf. Rom. 3:20.　　　　　[6] 1 Pet. 4:11.

[7] An odd corruption of 2 Cor. 2:17 (καπηλεύοντες), which Wesley has changed from St. Paul's graceful participle to an awkward contract form of the present indicative. Both in classical Greek and koine the literal meaning is 'to trade', 'to peddle', 'to drive a bargain'. Walther Bauer's comment on it is that 'because of the tricks of small tradesmen the word came close to meaning *adulterate*'; cf. Arndt and Gingrich, *Greek-English Lexicon, loc. cit.* But Bengel (*Gnomon)*, whom Wesley follows in his *Notes* on this passage, had made much of the implication of dishonesty, and so also have modern translators (as in the NEB, 'hawking the word of God about'). Wesley's usage of the English verb, 'cauponize' ('adulterate'), is cited by the *OED,* but it does not appear in Johnson's *Dictionary* (which has *cauponate:* 'to sell wine or victuals'); cf. Poole's *Annotations* here: 'The Greek word signifies, "To sell victuals for money" and because such kind of people make no conscience to deceive, cheat, and deal fraudulently with their customers, it is sometimes used to signify "corrupting or deceiving".' Cf. also No. 18, 'The Marks of the New Birth', I.5.

[8] Cf. 2 Cor. 4:2.

it in the height and depth and length and breadth thereof.[9] We then establish the law when we declare every part of it, every commandment contained therein, not only in its full, literal sense, but likewise in its spiritual meaning; not only with regard to the outward actions which it either forbids or enjoins, but also with respect to the inward principle, to the thoughts, desires, and intents of the heart.

3. And indeed this we do the more diligently, not only because it is of the deepest importance—inasmuch as all the fruit, every word and work, must be only evil continually if the tree be evil, if the dispositions and tempers of the heart be not right before God—but likewise because, as important as these things are, they are little considered or understood; so little that we may truly say of the law, too, when taken in its full spiritual meaning, it is 'a mystery which was hid from ages and generations since the world began'.[10] It was utterly hid from the heathen world. They, with all their boasted wisdom, neither 'found out God'[11] nor the law of God, not in the letter, much less in the spirit of it. 'Their foolish hearts were' more and more 'darkened'; while 'professing themselves wise, they became fools'.[12] And it was almost equally hid, as to its spiritual meaning, from the bulk of the Jewish nation. Even these, who were so ready to declare concerning others, 'this people that know not the law is accursed',[13] pronounced their own sentence therein, as being under the same curse, the same dreadful ignorance. Witness our Lord's continual reproof of the wisest among them for their gross misinterpretations of it. Witness the supposition, almost universally received among them, that they needed only to make clean the outside of the cup, that the paying tithe of mint, anise, and cummin,[14] outward exactness, would atone for inward unholiness, for the total neglect both of justice and mercy, of faith and the love of God. Yea, so absolutely was the spiritual meaning of the law hidden from the wisest of them, that one of their most eminent rabbis comments thus on those words of the Psalmist, 'If I incline unto iniquity with my heart, the Lord will not hear me.'[15] 'That is', saith

---

[9] See Eph. 3:18.   [10] Cf. Col. 1:26.
[11] Cf. Job 11:7.
[12] Cf. Rom. 1:21-22.
[13] Cf. John 7:49.
[14] See Matt. 23:23.
[15] Cf. Ps. 66:16 (BCP); Ps. 66:18 (AV).

he, 'if it be only in my heart, if I do not commit outward wickedness, the Lord will not regard it; he will not punish me unless I proceed to the outward act!'[16]

4. But alas! the law of God, as to its inward spiritual meaning, is 5 not hid from the Jews or heathens only, but even from what is called the Christian world; at least, from a vast majority of them. The spiritual sense of the commandments of God is still a mystery to these also. Nor is this observable only in those lands which are overspread with Romish darkness and ignorance. But 10 this is too sure, that the far greater part, even of those who are called 'Reformed Christians', are utter strangers at this day to the law of Christ, in the purity and spirituality of it.

5. Hence it is that to this day 'the scribes and Pharisees'—the men who have the form but not the power of religion, and who are 15 generally wise in their own eyes,[17] and righteous in their own conceits—'hearing these things are offended',[18] are deeply offended when we speak of the religion of the heart,[19] and particularly when we show that without this, were we to 'give all our goods to feed the poor',[20] it would profit us nothing. But 20 offended they must be, for we cannot but speak the truth as it is in Jesus.[21] It is our part, whether they will hear or whether they will forbear,[22] to deliver our own soul.[23] All that is written in the Book of God we are to declare, not as pleasing men, but the Lord.[24] We

---

[16] Cf. Henry, *Exposition*, Ps. 66:18.

Wesley's 'eminent rabbi' was almost certainly David Kimchi, and Kimchi's actual teaching had been quite the opposite of what Henry and Wesley allege. In his *Sepher Tehillim 'im pirush rabbenu David Kimchi (The Book of Psalms with Commentary by our Rabbi David Kimchi* [Berlin, 1767]), the comment (p. 37) is that 'if I incline to an iniquity in my heart to do it, it is as if I had announced that intention with my lips. *The sin lies in the evil thought'* [italics added].

However, Dom Ambrose Janvier's *Rabbi Davidis Kimchi Commentarii in Psalmos . . . ex Hebraeo Latiné Redditi* (1702) has an editorial footnote which, in effect, turns Kimchi's notion upside down. There is a copy of Janvier in the library of Christ Church which was there in Wesley's day. Thus, both Janvier and Henry agree in their distortion of Kimchi's point, and Wesley seems to have followed them without checking out Kimchi's own text.

[17] Isa. 5:21.   [18] Cf. Matt. 15:12.

[19] Cf. No. 25, 'Sermon on the Mount, V', IV.13 and n.

[20] Cf. 1 Cor. 13:3.   [21] See Eph. 4:21.   [22] Ezek. 2:5, 7; 3:11.

[23] See Ezek. 14:14, 20; 33:9. Wesley uses this cliché to connote extreme exasperation and finality; cf. JWJ, May 2, 1740, June 18, 1741, and Aug. 24, 1744; and his letter to the Mayor of Newcastle upon Tyne, July 12, 1743; to John Bennet, Nov. 3, 1749; and to William Law, Jan. 6, 1756. Cf. also Nos. 49, 'The Cure of Evil-speaking', I.6, III.3; 88, 'On Dress', §22; *General Rules*, §7; *Predestination Calmly Considered*, §33; and 'A Short History of the People Called Methodists'.

[24] See 1 Thess. 2:4.

are to declare not only all the promises but all the threatenings, too, which we find therein. At the same time that we proclaim all the blessings and privileges which God had prepared for his children, we are likewise to 'teach all the things whatsoever he hath commanded'.[25] And we know that all these have their use; either for the awakening those that sleep, the instructing the ignorant, the comforting the feeble-minded,[26] or the building up and perfecting of the saints.[27] We know that 'all Scripture given by inspiration of God is profitable' either 'for doctrine' or 'for reproof', either 'for correction' or 'for instruction in righteous- ness;' and 'that the man of God', in the process of the work of God in his soul, has need of every part thereof, that he 'may' at length 'be perfect, throughly furnished unto all good works'.[28]

6. It is our part thus to 'preach Christ' by preaching all things whatsoever he hath revealed. We may indeed, without blame, yea, and with a peculiar blessing from God, declare the love of our Lord Jesus Christ. We may speak in a more especial manner of 'the Lord our righteousness'.[29] We may expatiate upon the grace of 'God in Christ, reconciling the world unto himself'.[30] We may, at proper opportunities, dwell upon his praise, as bearing 'the iniquities of us all', as 'wounded for our transgressions' and 'bruised for our iniquities', that 'by his stripes we might be healed'.[31] But still we should not 'preach Christ'[32] according to his word if we were wholly to confine ourselves to this. We are not ourselves clear before God unless we proclaim him in all his offices. To preach Christ as a workman that needeth not to be ashamed[33] is to preach him not only as our great 'High Priest, taken from among men, and ordained for men, in things pertaining to God';[34] as such, 'reconciling us to God by his blood',[35] and 'ever living to make intercession for us';[36] but likewise as the Prophet of the Lord, 'who of God is made unto us wisdom',[37] who by his word and his Spirit 'is with us always',[38]

---

[25] Cf. John 14:26.
[26] See 1 Thess. 5:14.
[27] See Eph. 4:12.
[28] 2 Tim. 3:16-17.
[29] Jer. 23:6; 33:16. Cf. No. 20 by this title.
[30] 2 Cor. 5:19.
[31] Cf. Isa. 53:5, 6.
[32] Cf. his letter of Dec. 20, 1751 ('Of Preaching Christ').
[33] 2 Tim. 2:15.
[34] Heb. 5:1.
[35] Cf. Rom. 5:9, 10.
[36] Cf. Heb. 7:25.
[37] 1 Cor. 1:30.
[38] Cf. Matt. 28:20.

'guiding us into all truth';[39] yea, and as remaining a King for ever;
as giving laws to all whom he has bought with his blood; as
restoring those to the image of God whom he had first reinstated
in his favour; as reigning in all believing hearts until he has
'subdued all things to himself';[40] until he hath utterly cast out all
sin, and 'brought in everlasting righteousness.'[41]

II. 1. 'We establish the law', secondly, when we so preach faith
in Christ as not to supersede but produce holiness: to produce
all manner of holiness, negative and positive, of the heart and of
the life.

In order to this we continually declare (what should be
frequently and deeply considered by all who would not 'make void
the law through faith') that faith itself, even Christian faith, the
faith of God's elect, the faith of the operation of God, still is only
the handmaid of love.[42] As glorious and honourable as it is, it is
not the end of the commandment. God hath given this honour to
love alone. Love is the end of all the commandments of God.[43]
Love is the end, the sole end, of every dispensation of God, from
the beginning of the world to the consummation of all things. And
it will endure when heaven and earth flee away; for 'love' alone
'never faileth'.[44] Faith will totally fail; it will be swallowed up in
sight, in the everlasting vision of God. But even then love,

> Its nature and its office still the same,
> Lasting its lamp and unconsumed its flame,
> In deathless triumph shall for ever live,
> And endless good diffuse, and endless praise receive.[45]

---

[39] Cf. John 16:13.   [40] Cf. Phil. 3:21.   [41] Cf. Dan. 9:24.

[42] This unconventional subordination of faith, as a means, to love as an end, may be an
echo from St. Ignatius of Antioch, *Epistle to the Ephesians*, 14:1: 'The beginning [of the
Christian life] is faith but the end is love.' It was more explicitly stated by Thomas Collier
in *The Marrow of Christianity* (1647), p. 28: 'The effect of faith is such as that God by it
works up the soul to an internal and external conformity to Christ in some measure, with a
spiritual and eternal conformity in perfection in another world, where *faith shall cease*, and
love and unity be made perfect' [italics added]. The idea, without the language, appears in
John Norris, Discourse III, 'That the Law is not Made Void Through Faith', *Practical
Discourses*, III. 76-102. But the contrary (and more general) view had been stated by John
Goodwin in his *Imputatio Fidei*: 'Now love is but one duty of the Law and therefore cannot
be many, much less all,' etc. Cf. No. 91, 'On Charity', II.6.

[43] See 1 Tim. 1:5.

[44] 1 Cor. 13:8.

[45] Matthew Prior, 'Charity' (ll. 57-58, 35-36, with 'its' substituted for 'thy'). See No. 22,
'Sermon on the Mount, II', III.17, and also *A Collection of Moral and Sacred Poems* (1744), I.
87-89.

2. Very excellent things are spoken of faith, and whosoever is a partaker thereof may well say with the Apostle, 'Thanks be to God for his unspeakable gift.'[46] Yet still it loses all its excellence when brought into a comparison with love. What St. Paul observes concerning the superior glory of the gospel above that of the law may with great propriety be spoken of the superior glory of love above that of faith: 'Even that which was made glorious hath no glory in this respect, by reason of the glory that excelleth. For if that which is done away is glorious, much more doth that which remaineth exceed in glory.'[47] Yea, all the glory of faith before it is done away arises hence, that it ministers to love. It is the great temporary means which God has ordained to promote that eternal end.

3. Let those who magnify faith beyond all proportion, so as to swallow up all things else, and who so totally misapprehend the nature of it as to imagine it stands in the place of love,[48] consider farther that as love will exist after faith, so it did exist long before it. The angels, who from the moment of their creation beheld the face of their Father that is in heaven,[49] had no occasion for faith in its general notion, as it is the evidence of things not seen.[50] Neither had they need of faith in its more particular acceptation, faith in the blood of Jesus; for he took not upon him the nature of angels, but only the seed of Abraham. There was therefore no place before the foundation of the world for faith either in the general or particular sense. But there was for love. Love existed from eternity, in God, the great ocean of love. Love had a place in all the children of God, from the moment of their creation. They received at once from their gracious Creator to exist, and to love.

4. Nor is it certain (as ingeniously and plausibly as many have descanted upon this) that faith, even in the general sense of the word, had any place in paradise. It is highly probable, from that short and uncircumstantial account which we have in Holy Writ, that Adam, before he rebelled against God, walked with him by sight and not by faith.

[46] 2 Cor. 9:15.
[47] 2 Cor. 3:10-11.
[48] Wesley's interpretation of Protestant versions of 'faith *alone*' which exclude hope and love; cf. the tendency in the early debates at Trent to integrate the three of the Pauline virtues, in Hubert Jedin, *A History of the Council of Trent*, Vol. II, chs. V, VII-VIII. Note Wesley's opposite tendency: to subsume 'faith' into 'love'.
[49] See Matt. 18:10.
[50] Heb. 11:1.

> For then his reason's eye was strong and clear,
> And as an eagle can behold the sun,
> Might have beheld his Maker's face as near,
> As th' intellectual angels could have done.[51]

5 He was then able to talk with him face to face, whose face we cannot now see and live; and consequently had no need of that faith whose office it is to supply the want of sight.[52]

5. On the other hand, it is absolutely certain, faith, in its particular sense, had then no place. For in that sense it necessarily 10 presupposes sin, and the wrath of God declared against the sinner; without which there is no need of an atonement for sin in order to the sinner's reconciliation with God. Consequently, as there was no need of an atonement before the fall, so there was no place for faith in that atonement; man being then pure from every 15 stain of sin, holy as God is holy. But love even then filled his heart. It reigned in him without a rival. And it was only when love was lost by sin that faith was added, not for its own sake, nor with any design that it should exist any longer than until it had answered the end for which it was ordained—namely, to restore man to the 20 love from which he was fallen. At the fall therefore was added this evidence of things unseen,[53] which before was utterly needless; this confidence in redeeming love, which could not possibly have any place till the promise was made that the seed of the woman should bruise the serpent's head.[54]

25   6. Faith then was originally designed of God to re-establish the law of love. Therefore, in speaking thus, we are not undervaluing it, or robbing it of its due praise, but on the contrary showing its real worth, exalting it in its just proportion, and giving it that very place which the wisdom of God assigned it from the beginning. It 30 is the grand means of restoring that holy love wherein man was originally created. It follows, that although faith is of no value in

---

[51] Sir John Davies, *Nosce Teipsum*, 'Of Human Knowledge' (1599), st. 3. Orig. (quoted accurately in *A Collection of Moral and Sacred Poems*, I.15):
> And when their reason's eye was sharp and clear,
> And (as an eagle can behold the sun)
> Could have approached th' Eternal Light as near
> As th' intellectual angels could have done.

Davies and Wesley shared the same Platonic ideas of religious intuition. See No. 128, 'The Deceitfulness of the Human Heart', II. 8, where Wesley quotes from another verse of this same poem.

[52] Cf. No. 10, 'The Witness of the Spirit, I', I.12 and n.

[53] See Heb. 11:1.   [54] See Gen. 3:15.

itself (as neither is any other means whatsoever) yet as it leads to that end—the establishing anew the law of love in our hearts—and as in the present state of things it is the only means under heaven for effecting it, it is on that account an unspeakable blessing to man, and of unspeakable value before God.   5

III. 1. And this naturally brings us to observe, thirdly, the most important way of 'establishing the law'; namely, the establishing it in our own hearts and lives. Indeed, without this, what would all the rest avail? We might establish it by our doctrine; we might preach it in its whole extent; might explain and enforce every part   10 of it. We might open it in its most spiritual meaning, and declare the mysteries of the kingdom;[55] we might preach Christ in all his offices, and faith in Christ as opening all the treasures of his love. And yet, all this time, if the law we preached were not established in our hearts we should be of no more account before God than   15 'sounding brass or tinkling cymbals'.[56] All our preaching would be so far from profiting ourselves that it would only increase our damnation.

2. This is therefore the main point to be considered: How may we establish the law in our own hearts so that it may have its full   20 influence on our lives? And this can only be done by faith.

Faith alone it is which effectually answers this end, as we learn from daily experience. For so long as we walk by faith, not by sight,[57] we go swiftly on in the way of holiness. While we steadily look, not at the things which are seen, but at those which are not   25 seen,[58] we are more and more crucified to the world and the world crucified to us.[59] Let but the eye of the soul be constantly fixed, not on the things which are temporal, but on those which are eternal,[60] and our affections are more and more loosened from earth and fixed on things above. So that faith in general is the   30 most direct and effectual means of promoting all righteousness and true holiness; of establishing the holy and spiritual law in the hearts of them that believe.

3. And by faith, taken in its more particular meaning for a confidence in a pardoning God, we establish his law in our own   35

---

[55] Matt. 13:11.

[56] Cf. 1 Cor. 13:1. Later, Wesley will use 'rumbling' in place of 'tinkling'; cf. No. 89, 'The More Excellent Way', §4 and n.

[57] 2 Cor. 5:7.   [58] See 2 Cor. 4:18.

[59] See Gal. 6:14.   [60] See 2 Cor. 4:18.

hearts in a still more effectual manner. For there is no motive which so powerfully inclines us to love God as the sense of the love of God in Christ. Nothing enables us like a piercing conviction of this to give our hearts to him who was given for us.

5 And from this principle of grateful love to God arises love to our brother also. Neither can we avoid loving our neighbour, if we truly believe the love wherewith God hath loved us. Now this love to man, grounded on faith and love to God, 'worketh no ill to our neighbour'.[61] Consequently it is, as the Apostle observes, 'the

10 fulfilling of the' whole negative 'law'.[62] 'For this, Thou shalt not commit adultery, Thou shalt not kill, Thou shalt not steal, Thou shalt not bear false witness, Thou shalt not covet; and if there be any other commandment, it is briefly comprehended in this saying, Thou shalt love thy neighbour as thyself.'[63] Neither is

15 love content with barely working no evil to our neighbour. It continually incites us to do good: as we have time and opportunity, to do good in every possible kind and in every possible degree to all men.[64] It is therefore the fulfilling of the positive, likewise, as well as of the negative law of God.

20 4. Nor does faith fulfil either the negative or positive law as to the external part only; but it works inwardly by love to the purifying of the heart, the cleansing it from all vile affections. 'Everyone that hath this' faith 'in him purifieth himself, even as he is pure'[65]—purifieth himself from every earthly, sensual desire,

25 from all vile and inordinate affections; yea, from the whole of that carnal mind which is enmity against God.[66] At the same time, if it have its perfect work, it fills him with all goodness, righteousness, and truth. It brings all heaven into his soul, and causes him to walk in the light, even as God is in the light.[67]

30 5. Let us thus endeavour to establish the law in ourselves; not sinning 'because we are under grace',[68] but rather using all the power we receive thereby 'to fulfil all righteousness'.[69] Calling to mind what light we received from God while his Spirit was convincing us of sin, let us beware we do not put out that light.

35 What we had then attained let us hold fast. Let nothing induce us

---

[61] Cf. Rom. 13:10.

[62] *Ibid.*

[63] Rom. 13:9.

[64] See Gal. 6:10.

[65] An interesting amendment of 1 John 3:3; note Wesley's conscious substitution of 'faith' in place of 'hope'.

[66] See Rom. 8:7.

[67] See 1 John 1:7.

[68] Cf. Rom. 6:15.

[69] Matt. 3:15.

to build again what we have destroyed; to resume anything, small or great, which we then clearly saw was not for the glory of God or the profit of our own soul; or to neglect anything, small or great, which we could not then neglect without a check from our own conscience. To increase and perfect the light which we had 5 before, let us now add the light of faith. Confirm we the former gift of God by a deeper sense of whatever he had then shown us, by a greater tenderness of conscience, and a more exquisite sensibility of sin. Walking now with joy and not with fear, in a clear, steady sight of things eternal, we shall look on pleasure, 10 wealth, praise—all the things of earth—as on bubbles upon the water;[70] counting nothing important, nothing desirable, nothing worth a deliberate thought, but only what is 'within the veil',[71] where 'Jesus sitteth at the right hand of God'.[72]

6. Can *you* say, 'Thou art merciful to my unrighteousness; my 15 sins thou rememberest no more'?[73] Then for the time to come see that you fly from sin, as from the face of a serpent.[74] For how exceeding sinful does it appear to you now! How heinous above all expression! On the other hand, in how amiable a light do you now see the holy and perfect will of God! Now, therefore, labour 20 that it may be fulfilled, both in you, by you, and upon you. Now watch and pray that you may sin no more, that you may see and shun the least transgression of his law. You see the motes which you could not see before when the sun shines into a dark place. In like manner you see the sins which you could not see before, now 25 the sun of righteousness shines in your heart. Now, then, do all diligence to walk in every respect according to the light you have received. Now be zealous to receive more light daily, more of the knowledge and love of God, more of the Spirit of Christ, more of his life, and of the power of his resurrection. Now use all the 30 knowledge and love and life and power you have already attained. So shall you continually go on from faith to faith. So shall you daily increase in holy love, till faith is swallowed up in sight, and the law of love established to all eternity.

---

[70] Cf. Erasmus, *Proverbs and Adages* (1569): 'Man is but a bubble . . . on the water;' see also Henry King, *Sic Vita* (1657): 'Like to the falling of a star . . . Or bubbles which on water stood/Even such is man . . .;' and Pope, *Essay on Man*, III.19: 'Like bubbles on the sea'. Wesley repeats the metaphor in Nos. 86, *A Call to Backsliders*, II.1; and 126, 'On Worldly Folly', II.5. Cf. also *An Earnest Appeal*, §42 (11:60 in this edn.).

[71] Heb. 6:19.   [72] Cf. Col. 3:1.

[73] Cf. Heb. 8:12.

[74] See Rev. 12:14.

THE NATURE OF ENTHUSIASM

AN INTRODUCTORY COMMENT

With SOSO, *1-36, the barebones of Wesley's doctrine of salvation had been exposed and his understanding of the imperatives of grace expounded. The logical next step was a stocktaking of the impact of the Methodist Revival within the Church of England and a positive delineation of the terms for a fruitful coexistence of the Methodists with the ecclesiastical establishment. Nos. 37-39 are designed, at least in part, to aid this process of what Wesley intended as a sort of mutual accommodation.*

Very early on in the Revival the Methodists had been tagged with the label 'enthusiasts', which was reason enough for them to be deplored, since to eighteenth-century English ears, 'enthusiasm' had long been a near synonym for 'fanaticism'. Sober men recalled the excesses of Cromwell's Commonwealth, the disruptive claims of the Quakers, Ranters, and others, to superior illuminations and sanctity. Lord Shaftesbury, in 1711, had included 'A Letter Concerning Enthusiasm' in Vol. I of his Characteristics of Men, Manners, Opinions, Times, *in which he held up enthusiasms, ancient and modern, to lighthearted contempt. The Methodists, then, were obvious targets for scorn with their claims of assurance and their irregular ways of worship. Their critics varied from moderate and serious men like Josiah Tucker and Joseph Trapp to intemperate pamphleteers such as those listed in Richard Green's* Anti-Methodist Publications; *and, always, the main charge was enthusiasm; cf. Umphrey Lee,* Historical Backgrounds of Early Methodist Enthusiasm, *and Ronald A. Knox,* Enthusiasm, *chs. xvii-xxi. Henry Moore, in his* Life of John Wesley *(1826), I. 464, reports a bitter exchange between Wesley and Joseph Butler (the ablest intellect in the Anglican hierarchy) on August 18, 1739, in which Butler had expressed his horror of what he regarded as Wesley's presumptions: 'Sir, the pretending to extraordinary revelations, and gifts of the Holy Ghost is a horrid thing—a very horrid thing.' Shortly, another bishop, Edmund Gibson of London, the Church's greatest canonist, would be warning his people against Methodist 'enthusiasm' (*A Pastoral Letter to the People of His Diocese . . .

By Way of Caution Against Lukewarmness on the one hand and Enthusiasm on the Other). *In October, the Vicar of Furneaux Pelham, the Revd. Charles Wheatly, an eminent liturgist, would describe the Methodists to his audience in St. Paul's Cathedral as 'rapturous enthusiasts'* (St. John's Test of Knowing Christ . . . A Sermon . . . Designed as a Support to Good Christians Against the Discouragements of some New Enthusiasts). *George Whitefield was a more vulnerable target here than Wesley, but they were blurred together in their critics' minds; and in any case the issue was larger than the individuals involved. Six years and a hundred pamphlets later, the Vicar of Battersea, the Revd. Thomas Church, had published some* Remarks on the Rev. Mr. John Wesley's Last Journal, *in which he anticipated Dr. Johnson's definition of enthusiasm as 'a vain confidence of divine favour' and classified Wesley and his people under this sign (cf. Wesley's* Answer to Mr. Church's Remarks, *also 1745). In 1749 an anonymous blast would come from the Bishop of Exeter, George Lavington,* The Enthusiasm of Methodists and Papists Compared; *this lent official sanction to the rumours about some sort of affinity between the Methodist sectaries and the Roman Catholic heretics and traitors.*

Obviously, what the Methodists and others needed rather badly was a calm and constructive restatement of the issue. 'The Nature of Enthusiasm' is Wesley's contribution to this need in these circumstances. There are only two reports of Wesley's having preached from Acts 26:24 before 1750 (May 30, 1741, and May 1, 1747) and there is nothing quite like Wesley's argument here in his earlier replies to Church, Gibson, and others. He had, however, already formulated his basic definition of enthusiasm, as one may see from the Journal *entry for January 17, 1739: 'I was with two persons who I doubt [i.e., think] are properly* enthusiasts. *For, first, they think to attain the end without the means, which is* enthusiasm, *properly so called. Again, they think themselves inspired by God, and are not. But false, imaginary inspiration is* enthusiasm. . . . *it contradicts the law and the testimony [i.e., the Scriptures].'*

The following sermon is an exercise in irony. Wesley does not propose to rehabilitate the term, nor defend himself. Instead, he chooses to take his critics' own premise that enthusiasm is 'false confidence' and argue from that to a different conclusion: that the really serious case of false confidence is to be seen in the 'almost Christian' who regards himself as something he is not. The 'men of reason' had equated enthusiasm and fanaticism; Wesley suggests that the real equation is with nominal

Christianity. *He goes on to probe more deeply, and includes those charismatics 'who imagine God dictates the very words they speak, pointing out that "God has given us our own reason for a guide, though never excluding the secret assistance of his Spirit".' In this way he seeks to clear himself and his people from a clutter of misunderstandings, to blunt the reckless charges of his detractors, and to provide his readers, then and now, with a useful guide for evaluating their claims as to the inner witness of the Spirit and their own assurance of God's favour. It makes this sermon an interesting digression in the unfolding exposition of the Wesleyan vision of the* ordo salutis *and sets the stage for 'A Caution against Bigotry', for a commendation of 'Catholic Spirit', and a preparation for the climax of the whole progression: the sermon on* Christian Perfection. *The sermon was reprinted as a pamphlet in 1755, 1778, and 1789; for its publishing history and a list of variant readings, see Appendix, Vol. 4 of this edn.*

The Nature of Enthusiasm

Acts 26:24

And Festus said with a loud voice, Paul, thou art beside thyself.

1. And so say all the world, the men who know not God, of all that are of Paul's religion, of everyone who is so a follower of him as he was of Christ. It is true there is a sort of religion—nay, and it is called Christianity too—which may be practised without any such imputation, which is generally allowed to be consistent with common sense. That is, a religion of form, a round of outward duties performed in a decent, regular manner. You may add orthodoxy thereto, a system of right opinions; yea, and some quantity of heathen morality. And yet not many will pronounce that 'much *religion* hath made you mad.'[1] But if you aim at the religion of the heart,[2] if you talk of righteousness and peace and joy in the Holy Ghost,[3] then it will not be long before *your* sentence is passed: 'Thou art beside thyself.'

---

[1] Cf. Acts 26:24.
[2] See below, §10; and No. 25, 'Sermon on the Mount, V', IV. 13 and n.
[3] Rom. 14:17.

2. And it is no compliment which the men of the world pay you herein. They for once mean what they say. They not only affirm but cordially believe that every man is beside himself who says the love of God is shed abroad in his heart by the Holy Ghost given unto him,[4] and that God has enabled him to rejoice in Christ with joy unspeakable and full of glory.[5] If a man is indeed alive to God, and dead to all things here below;[6] if he continually sees him that is invisible,[7] and accordingly walks by faith and not by sight;[8] then they account it a clear case—beyond all dispute 'much *religion* hath made him mad.'

3. It is easy to observe that the determinate thing which the world accounts madness is that utter contempt of all temporal things, and steady pursuit of things eternal; that divine conviction of things not seen;[9] that rejoicing in the favour of God; that happy, holy love of God; and that testimony of his Spirit with our spirit that we are the children of God.[10] That is, in truth, the whole spirit and life and power of the religion of Jesus Christ.

4. They will, however, allow [that] in other respects the man acts and talks like one in his senses. In other things he is a reasonable man: 'tis in these instances only his head is touched. It is therefore acknowledged that the madness under which he labours is of a particular kind. And accordingly they are accustomed to distinguish it by a particular name—*enthusiasm*.[11]

5. A term this which is exceeding frequently used, which is scarce ever out of some men's mouths. And yet it is exceeding rarely understood, even by those who use it most. It may be therefore not unacceptable to serious men, to all who desire to understand what they speak or hear, if I endeavour to explain the meaning of this term, to show what 'enthusiasm' is. It may be an encouragement to those who are unjustly charged therewith; and may possibly be of use to some who are justly charged with it—at

---

[4] See Rom. 5:5.   [5] 1 Pet. 1:8.   [6] See Rom. 6:11.
[7] See Heb. 11:27.   [8] See 2 Cor. 5:7.   [9] See Heb. 11:1.
[10] See Rom. 8:16.

[11] Cf. the long entry on 'Enthusiasm' in Chambers's *Cyclopaedia*, particularly Chambers's denial of the validity of the claims of 'enthusiasts' to superior insight by virtue of 'immediate revelation'. But see also Theophilus Evans, *The History of Modern Enthusiasm from the Reformation on to the Present Times* (1st edn., 1752; 2nd edn., 1757), and his thesis that 'a pretence to extraordinary revelation has always been the criterion of an enthusiastic brain . . .' (Pref., ii). Cf. also Johnson, *Dictionary*: 'A vain belief of private revelation, a vain confidence of divine favour or communication.' He cites Locke: 'Enthusiasm is founded neither on reason nor divine revelation but rises from the conceits of a warmed or overweening brain.'

least to others who might be so were they not cautioned against it.

6. As to the word itself, it is generally allowed to be of Greek extraction. But whence the Greek word ἐνθουσιασμός is derived none has yet been able to show.[12] Some have endeavoured to derive it from ἐν Θεῷ, 'in God', because all enthusiasm has reference to him. But this is quite forced, there being small resemblance between the word derived and those they strive to derive it from. Others would derive it from ἐν θυσίᾳ, 'in sacrifice', because many of the enthusiasts of old were affected in the most violent manner during the time of sacrifice. Perhaps it is a fictitious word, invented from the noise which some of those made who were so affected.

7. It is not improbable that one reason why this uncouth[13] word has been retained in so many languages was because men were no better agreed concerning the meaning than concerning the derivation of it. They therefore adopted the Greek word because they did not understand it: they did not translate it into their own tongues because they knew not how to translate it, it having been always a word of loose, uncertain sense, to which no determinate meaning was affixed.

8. It is not therefore at all surprising that it is so variously taken at this day, different persons understanding it in different senses quite inconsistent with each other. Some take it in a good sense, for a divine impulse or impression superior to all the natural faculties, and suspending for the time, either in whole or in part, both the reason and the outward senses. In this meaning of the word both the prophets of old and the apostles were proper 'enthusiasts'; being at divers times so filled with the Spirit, and so influenced by him who dwelt in their hearts, that the exercise of their own reason, their senses, and all their natural faculties, being suspended, they were wholly actuated by the power of God, and 'spake' only 'as they were moved by the Holy Ghost'.[14]

---

[12] An odd assertion, in view of the numerous instances of ἐνθουσιάζω, and its cognates, in Plato—sixteen of them cited in D. F. Astius, *Lexicon Platonicum* (Leipzig, 1835), p. 717. E.g., in the *Timaeus*, 71E, ἐνθουσιασμός is directly related to ἐν Θεῷ and signifies a sort of 'divine inspiration' antithetical to φρόνησις ('rationality'). See also other instances of this usage (and the idea of divine 'possession') in classical and patristic Greek in Liddell and Scott, *Greek-English Lexicon;* and Lampe, *Patristic Greek Lexicon.*

[13] Johnson, *Dictionary*, defines 'uncouth' as 'odd, strange, unusual', and quotes usages in this sense from Spenser, Shakespeare, and Milton. Cf. Wesley's references to Boehme's 'hard, uncouth words' in 'Thoughts Upon Jacob Behmen', in *AM* (1781), IV. 271.

[14] 2 Pet. 1:21. Earlier, Isaac Watts had spoken positively of enthusiasm as 'an overpowering impression . . . made on the mind by God himself that gives a convincing

9. Others take the word in an indifferent sense, such as is neither morally good nor evil. Thus they speak of the enthusiasm of the poets, of Homer and Virgil in particular. And this a late eminent writer extends so far as to assert, there is no man excellent in his profession, whatsoever it be, who has not in his temper a strong tincture of enthusiasm.[15] By enthusiasm these appear to understand an uncommon vigour of thought, a peculiar fervour of spirit, a vivacity and strength not to be found in common men; elevating the soul to greater and higher things than cool reason could have attained.

10. But neither of these is the sense wherein the word enthusiasm is most usually understood. The generality of men, if no farther agreed, at least agree thus far concerning it, that it is something evil; and this is plainly the sentiment of all those who call the religion of the heart enthusiasm. Accordingly I shall take it in the following pages as an evil—a misfortune, if not a fault.[16]

11. As to the nature of enthusiasm, it is undoubtedly a disorder of the mind, and such a disorder as greatly hinders the exercise of reason. Nay, sometimes it wholly sets it aside: it not only dims but shuts the eyes of the understanding.[17] It may therefore well be accounted a species of madness: of madness rather than of folly, seeing a fool is properly one who draws wrong conclusions from right premises, whereas a madman draws right conclusions, but from wrong premises. And so does an enthusiast. Suppose his

and indubitable evidence of truth and divinity: so were the prophets and apostles inspired' (cited by Johnson, *Dictionary,* under 'inspiration'). Later, John Fletcher will remind Richard Hill that 'the word "enthusiasm" may be used in a good or bad sense. . . . The true enthusiasts . . . are really inspired by the grace and love of God;' cf. Letter V, *Fourth Check to Antinomianism,* in *Works* (1825), II. 16-17.

[15] Anthony Ashley Cooper, Third Earl of Shaftesbury. In his *Characteristics,* I. 3-55, he has a 'Letter Concerning Enthusiasm' (Sept. 7, 1707). Shaftesbury distinguishes between 'enthusiasm' as self-deception and what he calls 'a noble enthusiasm', the inspiration 'allotted to heroes, statesmen, poets, orators, musicians, and even philosophers' (pp. 53-54; cf. II. 393-94; III. 30-37). 'Inspiration is a *real* feeling of Divine Presence and enthusiasm is a *false* one' (p. 53). But Shaftesbury is opposed to anything like persecution of 'enthusiasts' and insists (p. 22) that 'good humour is not only the best security against *enthusiasm,* but the best foundation of *piety* and *true religion.*' Wesley read this in Oxford in 1730. But he also could have found the same point in Dryden's *Juvenal* (pref.): 'Imaging is, in itself, the very height and life of poetry which, by a kind of enthusiasm or extraordinary emotion of the soul, makes it seem to us that we behold those things which the poet [beheld].'

[16] Luther was greatly disturbed by the enthusiasts of his day (Schwärmer, as he called them contemptuously). And in *The Augsburg Confession,* V, those 'who think that the Holy Ghost cometh to men without the external Word' are condemned.

[17] See Eph. 1:18.

premises true, and his conclusions would necessarily follow. But here lies his mistake: his premises are false. He imagines himself to be what he is not. And therefore, setting out wrong, the farther he goes the more he wanders out of the way.

5   12. Every enthusiast then is properly a madman. Yet his is not an ordinary, but a religious madness. By religious I do not mean that it is any part of religion. Quite the reverse: religion is the spirit of a sound mind, and consequently stands in direct opposition to madness of every kind.[18] But I mean it has religion
10 for its object; it is conversant about religion. And so the enthusiast is generally talking of religion, of God or of the things of God; but talking in such a manner that every reasonable Christian may discern the disorder of his mind. Enthusiasm in general may then be described in some such manner as this: a religious madness
15 arising from some falsely imagined influence or inspiration of God; at least from imputing something to God which ought not to be imputed to him, or expecting something from God which ought not to be expected from him.

13.   There are innumerable sorts of enthusiasm. Those which
20 are most common, and for that reason most dangerous, I shall endeavour to reduce under a few general heads, that they may be more easily understood and avoided.

The first sort of enthusiasm which I shall mention is that of those who imagine they have the *grace* which they have not. Thus
25 some imagine, when it is not so, that they have 'redemption' through Christ, 'even the forgiveness of sin'.[19] These are usually such as 'have no root in themselves',[20] no deep repentance or thorough conviction. Therefore 'they receive the word with joy.' And 'because they have no deepness of earth', no deep work in
30 their heart, therefore the seed 'immediately springs up'.[21] There is immediately a superficial change which, together with that light joy, striking in with the pride of their unbroken heart and with their inordinate self-love, easily persuades them they have already 'tasted the good word of God, and the powers of the world
35 to come'.[22]

---

[18] So also Chambers's *Cyclopaedia*, where it is argued that 'God, when he makes the prophet, doth not unmake the man. He leaves his faculties in their natural state to enable him to judge of his inspirations, whether they be of divine original, or no.' Cf. Nos. 4, *Scriptural Christianity*, IV.2 and n. (espec. Locke's definition of 'madmen'); and 11, *The Witness of the Spirit*, II, IV.2 and n.

[19] Cf. Col. 1:14.   [20] Mark 4:17.
[21] Matt. 13:5, 17, 20, etc.   [22] Heb. 6:5.

14. This is properly an instance of the first sort of enthusiasm; it is a kind of madness, arising from the imagination that they have that grace which in truth they have not; so that they only deceive their own souls. Madness it may justly be termed, for the reasonings of these poor men are right, were their premises good; but as those are a mere creature of their own imagination, so all that is built on them falls to the ground. The foundation of all their reveries[23] is this: they imagine themselves to have faith in Christ. If they had this they would be 'kings and priests to God',[24] possessed of 'a kingdom which cannot be moved'.[25] But they have it not. Consequently all their following behaviour is as wide of truth and soberness as that of the ordinary madman who, fancying himself an earthly king, speaks and acts in that character.

15. There are many other enthusiasts of this sort. Such, for instance, is the fiery zealot for religion; or (more probably) for the opinions and modes of worship which he dignifies with that name. This man also strongly imagines himself to be a believer in Jesus, yea, that he is a champion for the faith which was once delivered to the saints.[26] Accordingly all his conduct is formed upon that vain imagination. And allowing his supposition to be just, he would have some tolerable plea for his behaviour; whereas now it is evidently the effect of a distempered brain, as well as of a distempered heart.

16. But the most common of all the enthusiasts of this kind are those who imagine themselves Christians and are not. These abound not only in all parts of our land, but in most parts of the habitable earth. That they are not Christians is clear and undeniable, if we believe the oracles of God. For Christians are holy; these are unholy. Christians love God; these love the world. Christians are humble; these are proud. Christians are gentle; these are passionate. Christians have the mind which was in Christ;[27] these are at the utmost distance from it. Consequently they are no more Christians than they are archangels. Yet they imagine themselves so to be; and they can give several reasons for

---

[23] The *OED* illustrates this use of the word to mean a fanciful idea by a quotation from Samuel Palmer, *Moral Essays* (1710), p. 325: 'The most ridiculous bigot thinks himself in the right, and . . . believes his reveries acceptable to God.' Johnson, *Dictionary*, defines it as 'loose musing; irregular thought', and quotes Locke: 'Revery is when ideas float in our mind, without any reflection or regard of the understanding.'

[24] Rev. 1:6.   [25] Heb. 12:28.

[26] Jude 3.

[27] See Phil. 2:5.

it. For they have been *called so* ever since they can remember.
They were 'christened' many years ago. They embrace the
'Christian opinions' vulgarly termed the Christian or catholic
faith. They use the 'Christian modes of worship', as their fathers
5 did before them. They live what is called a good 'Christian life', as
the rest of their neighbours do. And who shall presume to think or
say that these men are not Christians? Though without one grain
of true faith in Christ, or of real, inward holiness! Without ever
having tasted the love of God, or been 'made partakers of the
10 Holy Ghost'![28]

17. Ah, poor self-deceivers! Christians ye are not. But you are
enthusiasts in an high degree. Physicians, heal yourselves.[29] But
first know your disease: your whole life is enthusiasm, as being all
suitable to the imagination that you have received that grace of
15 God which you have not. In consequence of this grand mistake,
you blunder on day by day, speaking and acting under a character
which does in no wise belong to you. Hence arises that palpable,
glaring inconsistency that runs through your whole behaviour,
which is an awkward mixture of real heathenism and imaginary
20 Christianity. Yet still, as you have so vast a majority on your side,
you will always carry it by mere dint of numbers that you are the
only men in your senses, and all are lunatics who are not as you
are. But this alters not the nature of things. In the sight of God
and his holy angels—yea, and all the children of God upon
25 earth—you are mere madmen, mere enthusiasts all. Are you not?
Are you not 'walking in a vain shadow', a shadow of religion, a
shadow of happiness? Are you not still 'disquieting yourselves in
vain'?[30] With misfortunes as imaginary as your happiness or
religion? Do you not fancy yourselves great or good? Very
30 knowing, and very wise! How long? Perhaps till death brings you
back to your senses—to bewail your folly for ever and ever!

18. A second sort of enthusiasm is that of those who imagine
they have such *gifts* from God as they have not. Thus some have
imagined themselves to be endued with a power of working
35 miracles, of healing the sick by a word or a touch, of restoring
sight to the blind; yea, even of raising the dead, a notorious
instance of which is still fresh in our own history.[31] Others have

---

[28] Heb. 6:4.   [29] See Luke 4:23.   [30] Cf. Ps. 39:7 (BCP).
[31] This was probably the affair of Dr. Thomas Emes, a physician who had served among
the poor in Moorfields and was 'a great stickler for the party [of French Prophets]'; cf. his
entry in *DNB*. He 'died Dec. 22, 1707, and was buried in Bunhill-fields the 25th *ditto*. [Sir

undertaken to prophesy, to foretell things to come, and that with the utmost certainty and exactness. But a little time usually convinces these enthusiasts. When plain facts run counter to their predictions, experience performs what reason could not, and sinks them down into their senses.   5

19. To the same class belong those who in preaching or prayer imagine themselves to be so influenced by the Spirit of God as in fact they are not. I am sensible indeed that without him we can do nothing,[32] more especially in our public ministry; that all our preaching is utterly vain unless it be attended with his power, and   10 all our prayer, unless his Spirit therein help our infirmities. I know if we do not both preach and pray by the Spirit it is all but lost labour, seeing the help that is done upon earth, he doth it himself,[33] who worketh all in all.[34] But this does not affect the case before us. Though there is a real influence of the Spirit of God,   15 there is also an imaginary one; and many there are who mistake the one for the other. Many suppose themselves to be under that influence when they are not, when it is far from them. And many others suppose they are more under that influence than they really are. Of this number, I fear, are all they who imagine that   20 God dictates the very words they speak, and that consequently it is impossible they should speak anything amiss, either as to the matter or manner of it. It is well known how many enthusiasts of this sort also have appeared during the present century; some of whom speak in a far more authoritative manner than either St.   25 Paul or any of the apostles.[35]

20. The same sort of enthusiasm, though in a lower degree, is frequently found in men of a private character. They may likewise imagine themselves to be influenced or directed by the Spirit when they are not. I allow, 'if any man have not the Spirit of   30

Richard Bulkley, John Lacy, *et al.*] began to prophesy that this Dr. Emes would raise from the grave with a new life in glorious body on the 25th of May, 1708. . . . Bunhill-fields was sufficiently crowded on the 25th of May, in expectation of such a miraculous sight, as some thousands of people now living may very well remember. But, notwithstanding all the prophecies in his favour, there was no resurrection nor any the least symptom of it' (Theophilus Evans, *Enthusiasm*, pp. 105-6); but see also 'Historical Chronicle', Jan. 1740, *Gent's Mag.*: 'At Staines, the wife of one Collet, a tanner, having lain dead three days, just before she was to be nailed up in her coffin, opened her eyes and spoke.' See also George Hickes, *The Spirit of Enthusiasm Exorcised* (1709), pp. 508-30. Cf. No. 116, 'What is Man? Ps. 8:4', §12.

[32] See John 15:5.   [33] Ps. 74:13 (BCP).   [34] 1 Cor. 12:6.

[35] For Wesley's distinction between the 'extraordinary gifts' of the Spirit and the 'ordinary fruits' to be expected of all Christians, cf. No. 4, *Scriptural Christianity*, § 4 and n.

Christ, he is none of his;'[36] and that if ever we either think, speak, or act aright, it is through the assistance of that blessed Spirit. But how many impute things to him, or expect things from him, without any rational or scriptural ground! Such are they who
5 imagine they either do or shall receive 'particular directions' from God, not only in points of importance, but in things of no moment, in the most trifling circumstances of life. Whereas in these cases God has given us our own reason for a guide; though never excluding the 'secret assistance' of his Spirit.

10 21. To this kind of enthusiasm they are peculiarly exposed who expected to be directed of God, either in spiritual things or in common life, in what is justly called an *extraordinary* manner. I mean by visions or dreams, by strong impressions or sudden impulses on the mind. I do not deny that God has of old times
15 manifested his will in this manner, or that he can do so now. Nay, I believe he does, in some very rare instances. But how frequently do men mistake herein! How are they misled by pride and a warm imagination to ascribe such impulses or impressions, dreams or visions, to God, as are utterly unworthy of him! Now this is all
20 pure enthusiasm, all as wide of religion as it is of truth and soberness.

22. Perhaps some may ask, 'Ought we not then to inquire what is *the will of God* in all things? And ought not his will to be the rule of our practice? Unquestionably it ought. But how is a sober
25 Christian to make this inquiry? To know what is 'the will of God'? Not by waiting for supernatural dreams. Not by expecting God to reveal it in visions. Not by looking for any 'particular impressions', or sudden impulses on his mind. No; but by consulting the oracles of God. 'To the law and to the testimony.'[37]
30 This is the general method of knowing what is 'the holy and acceptable will of God'.[38]

23. 'But how shall I know what is the will of God in such and such a particular case? The thing proposed is in itself of an indifferent nature, and so left undetermined in Scripture.' I
35 answer, the Scripture itself gives you a general rule, applicable to all particular cases: 'The will of God is our sanctification.'[39] It is his will that we should be inwardly and outwardly holy; that we

---

[36] Rom. 8:9.
[37] Isa. 8:20.
[38] Cf. Rom. 12:1, 2.
[39] Cf. 1 Thess. 4:3.

should *be good and do good* in every kind, and in the highest degree whereof we are capable. Thus far we tread upon firm ground. This is as clear as the shining of the sun. In order therefore to know what is the will of God in a particular case we have only to apply this general rule.

24. Suppose, for instance, it were proposed to a reasonable man to marry, or to enter into a new business. In order to know whether this is the will of God, being assured, 'It is the will of God concerning me that I should be as holy and do as much good as I can,' he has only to inquire, 'In which of these states can I be most holy, and do the most good?'[40] And this is to be determined partly by reason and partly by experience. Experience tells him what advantages he has in his present state, either for being or doing good; and reason is to show what he certainly or probably will have in the state proposed. By comparing these he is to judge which of the two may most conduce to his being and doing good; and as far as he knows this, so far he is certain what is the will of God.

25. Meantime the assistance of his Spirit is supposed during the whole process of the inquiry. Indeed 'tis not easy to say in how many ways that assistance is conveyed. He may bring many circumstances to our remembrance; may place others in a stronger and clearer light; may insensibly open our mind to receive conviction, and fix that conviction upon our heart. And to a concurrence of many circumstances of this kind in favour of what is acceptable in his sight he may superadd such an unutterable peace of mind, and so uncommon a measure of his love, as will leave us no possibility of doubting that *this*, even *this*, is his will concerning us.

26. This is the plain, scriptural, rational way to know what is the will of God in a particular case. But considering how seldom this way is taken, and what a flood of enthusiasm must needs break in on those who endeavour to know the will of God by unscriptural, irrational ways, it were to be wished that the expression itself were far more sparingly used. The using it as some do, on the most trivial occasions, is a plain breach of the third commandment. It is a gross way of taking the name of God in vain, and betrays great irreverence toward him. Would it not be far better then to use

---

[40] This had been Wesley's rationale for refusing to move from Oxford to Epworth, despite his family's pleadings; cf. his letter to his father, Dec. 10, 1734, espec. §§4-6, 16.

other expressions, which are not liable to such objections? For example: instead of saying on any particular occasion, 'I want to know what is the will of God,' would it not be better to say, 'I want to know what will be most for my improvement, and what will
5 make me most useful.' This way of speaking is clear and unexceptionable. It is putting the matter on a plain, scriptural issue, and that without any danger of enthusiasm.

27. A third very common sort of enthusiasm (if it does not coincide with the former) is that of those who think to attain the
10 end without using the means, by the immediate power of God. If indeed those means were providentially withheld they would not fall under this charge. God can, and sometimes does in cases of this nature, exert his own immediate power. But they who expect this when they have those means and will not use them are proper
15 enthusiasts. Such are they who expect to understand the Holy Scriptures without reading them and meditating thereon; yea, without using all such helps as are in their power, and may probably conduce to that end. Such are they who *designedly* speak in the public assembly without any premeditation. I say
20 'designedly', because there may be such circumstances as at some times make it unavoidable. But whoever *despises* that great means of speaking profitably is so far an enthusiast.

28. It may be expected that I should mention what some have accounted a fourth sort of enthusiasm, namely, the imagining
25 those things to be owing to the providence of God which are not owing thereto. But I doubt. I know not what things they are which are not owing to the providence of God; in ordering, or at least in governing, of which this is not either directly or remotely concerned. I expect nothing but sin; and even in the sins of others
30 I see the providence of God to *me*. I do not say, his *general providence,* for this I take to be a sounding word which means just nothing.[41] And if there be a *particular providence* it must extend to all persons and all things. So our Lord understood it, or he could never have said, 'Even the hairs of your head are all numbered.'[42]
35 And, 'Not a sparrow falleth to the ground'[43] without 'the will of your Father which is in heaven.'[44] But if it be so, if God presides

---

[41] See No. 67, 'On Divine Providence', §23 and n.: 'But I have not done with this same general providence yet. By the grace of God I will sift it to the bottom. And I hope to show it is such stark, staring nonsense as every man of sense ought to be utterly ashamed of.'
[42] Luke 12:7.   [43] Cf. Matt. 10:29.
[44] Matt. 18:14.

universis tanquam singulis, et singulis tanquam universis—over the whole universe as over every single person, over every single person as over the whole universe[45]—what is it (except only our own sins) which we are not to ascribe to the providence of God? So that I cannot apprehend there is any room here for the charge of enthusiasm.

29. If it be said the charge lies here: 'When you impute *this* to providence you imagine yourself the peculiar favourite of heaven,' I answer, you have forgot some of the last words I spoke: *Praesidet universis tanquam singulis*—his providence is over all men in the universe as much as over any single person. Don't you see that he who believing this imputes anything which befalls him to providence does not therein make himself any more the favourite of heaven than he supposes every man under heaven to be? Therefore you have no pretence upon this ground to charge him with enthusiasm.

30. Against every sort of this it behoves us to guard with the utmost diligence, considering the dreadful effects it has so often produced, and which indeed naturally result from it. Its immediate offspring is pride; it continually increases this source from whence it flows, and hereby it alienates us more and more from the favour and from the life of God. It dries up the very springs of faith and love, of righteousness and true holiness;[46] seeing all these flow from grace. But 'God resisteth the proud and giveth grace' only 'to the humble.'[47]

31. Together with pride there will naturally arise an unadvisable and unconvincible spirit; so that into whatever error or fault the enthusiast falls there is small hope of his recovery. For reason will have little weight with him (as has been justly and frequently observed) who imagines he is led by an higher guide, by the immediate wisdom of God. And as he grows in pride, so he must grow in unadvisableness, and in stubbornness also. He must be less and less capable of being convinced, less susceptible of persuasion; more and more attached to his own judgment and his own will, till he is altogether fixed and immovable.

---

[45] Cf. Augustine, *Confessions*, III.xi: '*O tu bone omnipotens, qui sic curas unumquemque nostrum tamquam solum cures, et sic omnes, tamquam singulos*' ('O thou Omnipotent Good who carest for every one of us as if thou didst care for him only, and so for all as if they were but one'). See also Nos. 54, 'On Eternity', §20; 67, 'On Divine Providence', §26; and 77, 'Spiritual Worship', I.8. Cf. also, *Some Observations on Liberty*, §57.

[46] Eph. 4:24.   [47] 1 Pet. 5:5.

32. Being thus fortified both against the grace of God and against all advice and help from man, he is wholly left to the guidance of his own heart, and of the king of the children of pride.[48] No marvel then that he is daily more rooted and grounded
5 in contempt of all mankind, in furious anger, in every unkind disposition, in every earthly and devilish temper. Neither can we wonder at the terrible outward effects which have flowed from such dispositions in all ages; even all manner of wickedness, all the works of darkness, committed by those who called themselves
10 Christians while they wrought with greediness such things as were hardly named even among the heathens.

Such is the nature, such the dreadful effects, of that many-headed monster,[49] enthusiasm! From the consideration of which we may now draw some plain inferences with regard in our
15 own practice.

33. And, first, if enthusiasm be a term, though so frequently used yet so rarely understood, take *you* care not to talk of you know not what, not to use the word till you understand it. As in all other points, so likewise in this, learn to think before you speak.
20 First, know the meaning of this hard word; and then use it if need require.

34. But if so few, even among men of education and learning, much more among the common sort of men, understand this dark, ambiguous word, or have any fixed notion of what it means,
25 then, secondly, beware of judging or calling any man an enthusiast upon common report. This is by no means a sufficient ground for giving any name of reproach to any man; least of all is it a sufficient ground for so black a term of reproach as this. The more evil it contains, the more cautious you should be how you
30 apply it to anyone; to bring so heavy an accusation without full proof being neither consistent with justice nor mercy.

35. But if enthusiasm be so great an evil, beware you are not entangled therewith yourself. Watch and pray that you fall not into the temptation.[50] It easily besets those who fear or love God.
35 O beware you do not think of yourself more highly than you ought to think.[51] Do not imagine you have attained that grace of God to

[48] See Job 41:34.
[49] See Horace, *Epistles* I.i. 76, '*Belua multorum es capitum*'; see also JWJ, Oct. 26, 1740, and *A Second Letter to the Author of the Enthusiasm of Methodists and Papists Compar'd* (1751), §10.
[50] See Matt. 26:41.   [51] See Rom. 12:3.

which you have not attained. You may have much joy; you may have a measure of love, and yet not have living faith. Cry unto God that he would not suffer you, blind as you are, to go out of the way; that you may never fancy yourself a believer in Christ till Christ is revealed in you, and till his Spirit witnesses with your spirit that you are a child of God.[52]

36. Beware you are not a fiery, persecuting enthusiast. Do not imagine that God has called you (just contrary to the spirit of him you style your Master) to destroy men's lives, and not to save them.[53] Never dream of forcing men into the ways of God. Think yourself, and let think.[54] Use no constraint in matters of religion. Even those who are farthest out of the way never 'compel to come in' by any other means than reason, truth, and love.[55]

37. Beware you do not run with the common herd of enthusiasts, fancying you are a Christian when you are not. Presume not to assume that venerable name unless you have a clear, scriptural title thereto; unless you have the mind which was in Christ,[56] and walk as he also walked.[57]

38. Beware you do not fall into the second sort of enthusiasm, fancying you have those *gifts* from God which you have not. Trust not in visions or dreams, in sudden impressions or strong impulses of any kind. Remember, it is not by these you are to know what is 'the will of God' on any particular occasion, but by applying the plain Scripture rule, with the help of experience and reason, and the ordinary assistance of the Spirit of God. Do not lightly take the name of God in your mouth: do not talk of 'the will of God' on every trifling occasion. But let your words as well as your actions be all tempered with reverence and godly fear.

39. Beware, lastly, of imagining you shall obtain the end without using the means conducive to it. God *can* give the end without any means at all; but you have no reason to think he *will*. Therefore constantly and carefully use all these means which he has appointed to be the ordinary channels of his grace. Use every

[52] Orig. (1750, 1755), 'and that'; see Rom. 8:16.
[53] See Luke 9:56.
[54] See No. 7, 'The Way to the Kingdom', I.6 and n.
[55] Cf. Luke 14:23. Wesley was consistently opposed to coercion in matters of religion and in favour of religious toleration. Cf., e.g., Nos. 38, 'A Caution against Bigotry', II.5; 39, 'Catholic Spirit'; 74, 'Of the Church', I.19. See also his letter 'To a Roman Catholic Priest' (? May 1735—see 25:428-30 in this edn.), his letter to a Roman Catholic, July 18, 1749, and two letters to the editors of *Freeman's Journal*, Mar. 23 and Mar. 31, 1780.
[56] See Phil. 2:5.
[57] See 1 John 2:6.

means which either reason or Scripture recommends as
conducive (through the free love of God in Christ) either to the
obtaining or increasing any of the gifts of God. Thus expect a
daily growth in that pure and holy religion which the world always
5 did, and always will, call enthusiasm; but which to all who are
saved from real enthusiasm—from merely nominal Christianity—is the wisdom of God and the power of God,[58] the glorious
image of the Most High, righteousness and peace, a fountain of
living water, springing up into everlasting life![59]

[58] See 1 Cor. 1:24.
[59] See John 4:14.

A CAUTION AGAINST BIGOTRY

AN INTRODUCTORY COMMENT

Part of the price of peace in eighteenth-century Britain, after the bitter quarrels of Civil War and Restoration, was a general lessening of partisan zeal and bigotry. The latitudinarians had made a positive virtue of toleration. Others had accepted it grudgingly as the lesser of two evils. The main concern of all, in both church and civil state, was surcease from religious turmoil. It was, therefore, inevitable that the Methodist Revival should revive fears of new religious disruptions; and Wesley's claim to an extraordinary vocation, his blithe disregard for parish boundaries and for the conventions of ministerial courtesy, along with his employment of lay preachers in busy rotation across the three kingdoms, did nothing to allay such fears. In his interview with Joseph Butler[1] the bishop's brusque judgment betrayed a genuine anxiety: 'Well sir, since you ask my advice, I will give it to you very freely. You have no business here; you are not commissioned to preach in this diocese. Therefore, I advise you to go hence.' Wesley's calm defiance in his response summed up his evangelical self-understanding then and thereafter:

My Lord, my business on earth is to do what good I can. Wherever, therefore, I think I can do most good, there must I stay, so long as I think so. At present I think I can do most good here; therefore here I stay. As to my preaching here, a dispensation of the Gospel is committed to me, and woe is me if I preach not the Gospel, wherever I am in the habitable world. Your Lordship knows, being ordained a priest, by the commission I then received I am a priest of the church universal. And being ordained a Fellow of a College, I was not limited to any particular cure, but have an indeterminate commission to preach the word of God in any part of the Church of England. I do not therefore conceive that, in preaching here by this commission, I break any human law. When I am convinced I do, then it will be time to ask, 'Shall I obey God or man?' But if I should be convinced in the meanwhile, that I could advance the glory of God, and the salvation of souls in any other place, more than in Bristol; in that hour, by God's help, I will go hence; which till then I may not do.[2]

He had already made a similar declaration in a letter to an unnamed

---

[1] See above, p. 44.
[2] Moore, *Wesley*, I.465.

critic (March 28, 1739) in reply to a complaint that he was invading other men's parishes:

'A dispensation of the gospel is committed to me, and woe is me if I preach not the gospel.' But where shall I preach it upon the principles you mention? [Answer: Nowhere.]. . . Suffer me now to tell you my principles in this matter. I look upon all the world as my parish; thus far I mean, that in whatever part of it I am, I judge it meet, right, and my bounden duty, to declare unto all that are willing to hear the glad tidings of salvation. This is the work which I know God has called me to. And sure I am that his blessing attends it.[3]

Thus, in much the same way that the Methodists had come by the label 'enthusiasts', they also had come to be regarded as 'bigots' in the current general sense of 'excessive or irrational zealots'; cf. Johnson's definition in his Dictionary, and see also Chambers's Cyclopaedia, for a quaint story about the term's coinage, viz., in a courtly outburst of outraged dignity: 'No, by-God!'. With the Revival now in full flood, and with Wesley as sole head of a tightly organized, highly partisan group of zealous preachers and people, there was an obvious occasion for a carefully considered statement about proper and improper zeal addressed to critics and to Methodists alike—'a caution against bigotry', defined as 'too strong an attachment to, or fondness for, our own party, opinion, church, and religion'.[4]

In this sermon Wesley studiously avoids an apologetic stance. Rather, he will redefine the problem by asking about the proper business of true apostles and answering it by reference to the gospel story of the casting out of devils (taken here as a metaphor for the whole conflict between Christ and the forces of evil and also for the ministry of salvation). Does it really matter who may venture this task and who may be forbidden it—and on what grounds? Would it really be better for evil to go unchallenged, souls to go unsaved, if this were not to be done 'properly'? Given his predictable answers to such questions, Wesley is then able to argue that valid ministry should be measured by fruits rather than forms. Further, he will imply that churchmen might, indeed, be actually grateful for the work of the Methodists and that, in their turn, the Methodists should renounce all bigotry discovered within themselves. In effect, this is a positive, if also indirect, plea for a carefully considered religious pluralism both in theology and praxis.

There is no record of any other instance of Wesley's using Mark

---

[3] *Letters*, 25:615-16 in this edn.

[4] For other uses by Wesley of 'bigotry', cf. *Notes* on 1 John 4:21, and *Hymns and Spiritual Songs* (1753), Preface, for which see *Bibliog*, No. 199; and Vol. 7 of this edn., pp. 736-37.

9:38-39 as a sermon text—from which we may infer that it was written on purpose for this particular time and occasion. But its underlying pragmatism can be seen as essential in Wesley's concepts of theological method and of Christian community-in-diversity. Thus, it was a useful rejoinder to those who took Methodist bigotry as a matter of course and yet also a timely antidote to Methodist 'zeal without knowledge'; for a sequel, see No. 92, 'On Zeal'.

A Caution against Bigotry

Mark 9:38-39

And John answered him, saying, Master, we saw one casting out devils in thy name, and we forbade him, because he followeth not us. And Jesus said, Forbid him not.

1. In the preceding verses we read that after the twelve had been disputing 'which of them should be the greatest', Jesus 'took a little child, and set him in the midst of them, and taking him in his arms said unto them, Whosoever shall receive one of these little children in my name receiveth me; and whosoever receiveth 10 me receiveth not me (only), but him that sent me.'[1] Then 'John answered' (that is, said with reference to what our Lord had spoken just before), 'Master, we saw one casting out devils in thy name, and we forbade him, because he followeth not us.' As if he had said: 'Ought we to have received him? In receiving him, 15 should we have received thee? Ought we not rather to have forbidden him? Did not we do well therein?' 'But Jesus said, Forbid him not.'

2. The same passage is recited by St. Luke, and almost in the same words. But it may be asked: 'What is this to us? Seeing no 20 man now "casts out devils". Has not the power of doing this been withdrawn from the church for twelve or fourteen hundred years? How then are *we* concerned in the case here proposed, or in our Lord's decision of it?'

---

[1] See Mark 9:34, 36-37.

3. Perhaps more nearly than is commonly imagined, the case proposed being no uncommon case. That we may reap our full advantage from it I design to show, first, in what sense men may, and do now, 'cast out devils'; secondly, what we may understand
5 by, 'He followeth not us.' I shall, thirdly, explain our Lord's direction, 'Forbid him not,' and conclude with an inference from the whole.

I. 1. I am, in the first place, to show in what sense men may, and do now, 'cast out devils'.
10 In order to have the clearest view of this we should remember that (according to the scriptural account) as God dwells and works in the children of light, so the devil dwells and works in the children of darkness. As the Holy Spirit possesses the souls of good men, so the evil spirit possesses the souls of the wicked.
15 Hence it is that the Apostle terms him 'the god of this world'[2]—from the uncontrolled power he has over worldly men. Hence our blessed Lord styles him 'the prince of this world'[3]—so absolute is his dominion over it. And hence St. John, 'We know that we are of God,' and all who are not of God, 'the whole world',
20 ἐν τῷ πονηρῷ κεῖται[4]—not, lieth in wickedness, but 'lieth in the wicked one'[5]—lives and moves in him, as they who are not of the world do in God.

2. For the devil is not to be considered only as 'a roaring lion, going about seeking whom he may devour';[6] nor barely as a subtle
25 enemy who cometh unawares upon poor souls and 'leads them captive at his will';[7] but as he who dwelleth in them and walketh in them; who 'ruleth the darkness' or wickedness 'of this world',[8] of worldly men and all their dark designs and actions, by keeping possession of their hearts, setting up his throne there, and
30 bringing every thought into obedience to himself. Thus the 'strong one armed keepeth his house'; and if this 'unclean spirit' sometime 'go out of a man', yet he often returns with 'seven spirits worse than himself; and they enter in and dwell there.'[9] Nor can he be idle in his dwelling. He is continually 'working in' these

[2] 2 Cor. 4:4.
[3] John 12:31, etc.
[4] 1 John 5:19.
[5] Cf. No. 12, 'The Witness of Our Own Spirit', §10 and n.
[6] Orig. (1750), 'and seeking'; cf. 1 Pet. 5:8.
[7] Cf. 2 Tim. 2:26.
[8] Cf. Eph. 6:12.
[9] Cf. Luke 11:21, 24, 26.

'children of disobedience'.[10] He works in them with power, with mighty energy, transforming them into his own likeness, effacing all the remains of the image of God, and preparing them for every evil word and work.

3. It is therefore an unquestionable truth that the god and prince of this world still possesses all who know not God. Only the manner wherein he possesses them now differs from that wherein he did it of old time. Then he frequently tormented their bodies as well as souls, and that openly, without any disguise; now he torments their souls only (unless in some rare cases) and that as covertly as possible. The reason of this difference is plain. It was then his aim to drive mankind into superstition. Therefore he wrought as openly as he could. But 'tis his aim to drive *us* into infidelity. Therefore he works as privately as he can; for the more secret he is, the more he prevails.

4. Yet if we may credit historians there are countries even now where he works as openly as aforetime. 'But why in savage and barbarous countries only? Why not in Italy, France, or England?' For a very plain reason: he knows his men. And he knows what he hath to do with each. To Laplanders[11] he appears barefaced; because he is to fix them in superstition and gross idolatry. But with you he is pursuing a different point. He is to make you idolize yourselves, to make you wiser in your own eyes than God himself, than all the oracles of God. Now in order to this he must not appear in his own shape. That would frustrate his design. No; he uses all his art to make you deny his being, till he has you safe in his own place.

5. He reigns, therefore, although in a different way, yet as absolute in one land as in the other. He has the gay Italian infidel in his teeth as sure as the wild Tartar. But he is fast asleep in the mouth of the lion, who is too wise to wake him out of sleep. So he

---

[10] Cf. Eph. 2:2.

[11] This stereotype of Laplanders as notoriously superstitious was a fixture in English folklore, reinforced by reports such as Giles Fletcher, *Of the Russe Commonwealth . . . with the manners and fashion of the People of that Country* (1591); Sir Jerome Horsey's 'treatise' 'of Russia and other Northeastern Regions'; in the 4th edn. of Samuel Purchas, *Purchas His Pilgrimage* (1626); and by Milton's simile, 'riding through the air . . . to dance with Lapland witches' (*Paradise Lost*, ii. 663-65). The likeliest direct source for Wesley was Thomas Salmon, *Modern History*, I. 654-58; but see also Aubry de la Motraye, *Travels Through Europe*, II. 283 ff.; and John Ray, *Wisdom of God Manifested in the Works of Creation*, Pt. II, p. 402. For other remarks by Wesley on Laplanders, cf. No. 69, 'The Imperfection of Human Knowledge', II.7; and his *Survey*, IV. 109.

only plays with him for the present, and when he pleases swallows him up.

The god of this world holds his English worshippers full as fast as those in Lapland. But it is not his business to affright them, lest
5 they should fly to the God of heaven. The prince of darkness therefore does not appear while he rules over these his willing subjects. The conqueror holds his captives so much the safer because they imagine themselves at liberty. Thus the 'strong one armed keepeth his house, and his goods are in peace':[12] neither
10 the deist nor nominal Christian suspects he is there; so he and they are perfectly at peace with each other.

6. All this while he works with energy in them. He blinds the eyes of their understanding so that the light of the glorious gospel of Christ cannot shine upon them.[13] He chains their souls down to
15 earth and hell with the chains of their own vile affections. He binds them down to the earth by love of the world, love of money, of pleasure, of praise. And by pride, envy, anger, hate, revenge, he causes their souls to draw nigh unto hell; acting the more secure and uncontrolled because they know not that he acts at all.

20 7. But how easily may we know the cause from its effects! These are sometimes gross and palpable. So they were in the most refined of the heathen nations. Go no farther than the admired, the virtuous Romans. And you will find these, when at the height of their learning and glory, 'filled with all
25 unrighteousness, fornication, wickedness, covetousness, maliciousness; full of envy, murder, debate, deceit, malignity; whisperers, backbiters, despiteful, proud, boasters, disobedient to parents, covenant-breakers, without natural affection, implacable, unmerciful'.[14]

30 8. The strongest parts of this description are confirmed by one whom some may think a more unexceptionable witness. I mean their brother heathen, Dion Cassius, who observes that before Caesar's return from Gaul not only gluttony and lewdness of every kind were open and barefaced; not only falsehood,
35 injustice, and unmercifulness abounded in public courts as well as private families; but the most outrageous robberies, rapine, and murders were so frequent in all parts of Rome that few men

---

[12] Cf. Luke 11:21.   [13] See 2 Cor. 4:4.
[14] Cf. Rom. 1:29-31; see also later negative judgments on Roman degeneracy from their ancient virtues in Tacitus, *Annals*, I, III, IV, VI; and his *De origine et situ Germanorum* (A.D. 98); Juvenal, *Satires*, I, II, IV; and Suetonius, *Lives of the Caesars* (121).

went out of doors without making their wills, as not knowing if they should return alive.[15]

9. As gross and palpable are the works of the devil among many (if not all) the modern heathens. The *natural religion* of the Creeks, Cherokees, Chicasaws, and all other Indians bordering on our southern settlements (not of a few single men, but of entire nations) is to torture all their prisoners from morning to night, till at length they roast them to death; and upon the slightest undesigned provocation to come behind and shoot any of their own countrymen. Yea, it is a common thing among them for the son, if he thinks his father lives too long, to knock out his brains; and for a mother, if she is tired of her children, to fasten stones about their necks, and throw three or four of them into the river one after another.[16]

10. It were to be wished that none but heathens had practised such gross, palpable works of the devil. But we dare not say so. Even in cruelty and bloodshed, how little have the Christians come behind them! And not the Spaniards or Portuguese alone, butchering thousands in South America. Not the Dutch only in the East Indies, or the French in North America, following the Spaniards step by step. Our own countrymen, too, have wantoned in blood, and exterminated whole nations: plainly proving thereby what spirit it is that dwells and works in the children of disobedience.[17]

11. These monsters might almost make us overlook the works of the devil that are wrought in our own country. But, alas! We cannot open our eyes even here without seeing them on every side. Is it a small proof of his power that common swearers, drunkards, whoremongers, adulterers, thieves, robbers, sodom-

[15] Cf. Cassius Dio Cocceianus (*c.* A.D. 150-*c.* A.D. 235), *Dio's Roman History*, xl. 44-50 (Loeb, 53:476-83).

[16] Wesley had been frustrated in his intentions to go to the native Americans as a missionary; Oglethorpe and the Georgia Trustees wanted his work restricted to Savannah. His first-hand contacts with the Indians were, therefore, limited. Here, obviously, he is passing on hearsay about them to readers who would have had no way of knowing that later scholars would conclude that his condemnations of the Indians 'were extremely harsh and unrealistic'; cf. J. Ralph Randolph, 'John Wesley and the American Indian: A Study in Disillusionment', *Meth. Hist.*, X.3:11 (Apr. 1972); see also Randolph's fuller study of Wesley on the Indians in his *British Travelers Among the Southern Indians* (Norman, Oklahoma, Univ. of Oklahoma Press, 1973). For further comments by Wesley on the Indians, cf. No. 69, 'The Imperfection of Human Knowledge', II.6; and JWJ, Feb. 18, 1773.

[17] See Eph. 2:2.

ites, murderers, are still found in every part of our land? How triumphant does the prince of this world reign in all these children of disobedience!

12. He less openly but no less effectually works in dissemblers, talebearers, liars, slanderers; in oppressors and extortioners; in the perjured, the seller of his friend, his honour, his conscience, his country. And yet these may talk of religion or conscience still! Of honour, virtue, and public spirit. But they can no more deceive Satan than they can God. He likewise knows those that are his: and a great multitude they are, out of every nation and people,[18] of whom he has full possession at this day.

13. If you consider this you cannot but see in what sense men may now also 'cast out devils'; yea, and every minister of Christ does cast them out, if his Lord's work prosper in his hand.[19] By the power of God attending his Word he brings these sinners to repentance: an entire inward as well as outward change, from all evil to all good. And this is in a sound sense to 'cast out devils', out of the souls wherein they had hitherto dwelt. The strong one can no longer keep his house. A stronger than he is come upon him, and hath cast him out, and taken possession for himself,[20] and made it an habitation of God through his Spirit.[21] Here then the energy of Satan ends, and the Son of God 'destroys the works of the devil'.[22] The understanding of the sinner is now enlightened, and his heart sweetly drawn to God. His desires are refined, his affections purified; and being filled with the Holy Ghost he grows in grace till he is not only holy in heart, but in all manner of conversation.

14. All this is indeed the work of God. It is God alone who can cast out Satan. But he is generally pleased to do this by man, as an instrument in his hand, who is then said to 'cast out devils in his name'—by his power and authority. And he sends whom he will send[23] upon this great work; but usually such as man would never have thought of. For 'his ways are not as our ways, neither his thoughts as our thoughts.'[24] Accordingly he chooses the weak to confound the mighty; the foolish to confound the wise:[25] for this plain reason, that he may secure the glory to himself, that 'no flesh may glory in his sight'.[26]

---

[18] See Rev. 7:9, used here ironically. [19] See Isa. 53:10.
[20] See Luke 11:21-22. [21] See Eph. 2:22. [22] Cf. 1 John 3:8.
[23] See Exod. 4:13; also cf. No. 4, *Scriptural Christianity*, IV.2 and n.
[24] Cf. Isa. 55:8. [25] See 1 Cor. 1:27. [26] Cf. Rom. 3:20.

II. 1. But shall we not *forbid* one who thus 'casteth out devils', if 'he followeth not us'? This it seems was both the judgment and practice of the Apostle, till he referred the case to his Master. 'We forbade him', saith he, 'because he followeth not us,' which he supposed to be a very sufficient reason. What we may understand 5 by this expression, 'He followeth not us,' is the next point to be considered.

The lowest circumstance we can understand thereby is, 'He has no outward connection with us. We do not labour in conjunction with each other. He is not our fellow-helper in the 10 gospel.' And indeed whensoever our Lord is pleased to send many labourers into his harvest, they cannot all act in subordination to, or connection with, each other. Nay, they cannot all have personal acquaintance with, nor be so much as known to, one another. Many there will necessarily be in different 15 parts of the harvest, so far from having any mutual intercourse that they will be as absolute strangers to each other, as if they had lived in different ages. And concerning any of these whom we know not we may doubtless say, 'He followeth not us.'

2. A second meaning of this expression may be, 'He is *not of our* 20 *party.*' It has long been matter of melancholy consideration to all who pray for the peace of Jerusalem[27] that so many several parties are still subsisting among those who are all styled Christians.[28] This has been particularly observable in our own countrymen, who have been continually dividing from each other upon points 25 of no moment, and many times such as religion had no concern in. The most trifling circumstances have given rise to different parties, which have continued for many generations. And each of these would be ready to object to one who was on the other side, 'He followeth not us.' 30

3. That expression may mean, thirdly, 'He differs from us in our *religious opinions.*'[29] There was a time when all Christians were of one mind, as well as of one heart.[30] So great grace was upon them all when they were first filled with the Holy Ghost. But how

[27] Ps. 122:6.

[28] As the Tory son of a Tory family, Wesley had been involved in the turmoils of party strife all his life. When this sermon was written, he had lived under 'the Whig supremacy' for thirty-five disapproving years.

[29] Another sample of Wesley's doctrinal pluralism; cf. No. 7, 'The Way to the Kingdom', I.6 and n.

[30] See Acts 4:32.

short a space did this blessing continue! How soon was that
unanimity lost, and difference of opinion sprang up again, even in
the church of Christ! And that not in nominal but in real
Christians; nay, in the very chief of them, the apostles themselves!
5 Nor does it appear that the difference which then began was ever
entirely removed. We do not find that even those pillars in the
temple of God, so long as they remained upon earth, were ever
brought to think alike, to be of one mind, particularly with regard
to the ceremonial law. 'Tis therefore no way surprising that
10 infinite varieties of opinion should now be found in the Christian
church. A very probable consequence of this is that whenever we
see any 'casting out devils' he will be one that in this sense
'followeth not us'—that is not of our opinion. 'Tis scarce to be
imagined he will be of our mind in all points, even of religion. He
15 may very probably think in a different manner from us even on
several subjects of importance, such as the nature and use of the
moral law, the eternal decrees of God, the sufficiency and efficacy
of his grace, and the perseverance of his children.

4. He may differ from us, fourthly, not only in opinion, but
20 likewise in some points of practice. He may not approve of that
manner of worshipping God which is practised in our
congregation, and may judge that to be more profitable for his
soul which took its rise from Calvin, or Martin Luther.[31] He may
have many objections to that liturgy which we approve of beyond
25 all others, many doubts concerning that form of church
government which we esteem both apostolical and scriptural.
Perhaps he may go farther from us yet: he may, from a principle of
conscience, refrain from several of those which we believe to be
the ordinances of Christ. Or if we both agree that they are
30 ordained of God, there may still remain a difference between us
either as to the manner of administering those ordinances or the
persons to whom they should be administered. Now the
unavoidable consequence of any of these differences will be that
he who thus differs from us must separate himself with regard to

---

[31] A casual reflection of Wesley's unselfconscious Anglicanism; his own tradition is *not*
Calvinist or Lutheran, not even Puritan. In other places he freely passes judgment on
Calvin and on Luther (cf. No. 104, 'On Attending the Church Service', §25; and his letter
to Mrs. Hutton, Aug. 22, 1744: 'I love Calvin a little, Luther more . . .'), but in typical
Anglican fashion regards them both as aliens. For other references to Luther see No. 14,
The Repentance of Believers, I.9 and n.

those points from our society. In this respect therefore 'he followeth not us;' he is 'not (as we phrase it) of our church'.

5. But in a far stronger sense 'he followeth not us' who is not only of a different church, but of such a church as we account to be in many respects antiscriptural and antichristian:[32] a church 5 which we believe to be utterly false and erroneous in her doctrines, as well as very dangerously wrong in her practice, guilty of gross superstition as well as idolatry; a church that has added many articles to the faith which was once delivered to the saints;[33] that has dropped one whole commandment of God,[34] and made 10 void several of the rest by her traditions; and that pretending the highest veneration for, and strictest conformity to, the ancient church, has nevertheless brought in numberless innovations without any warrant either from antiquity or Scripture. Now most certainly 'he followeth not us' who stands at so great a distance 15 from us.

6. And yet there may be a still wider difference than this. He who differs from us in judgment or practice may possibly stand at a greater distance from us in affection than in judgment. And this indeed is a very natural and a very common effect of the other. 20

---

[32] Wesley's fears of 'popery' and detestation of 'the errors of the Church of Rome' were inherited from a long tradition of Anglican anti-Roman polemics. Despite his generally tolerant spirit, best shown in his open *Letter to a Roman Catholic*, 1749 (cf. Michael Hurley, ed., *John Wesley's Letter to a Roman Catholic*, 1968), he followed in the familiar succession of John Jewel, *An Apology or Answer in Defence of the Church of England* (1562); Richard Hooker, *Laws of Ecclesiastical Polity* (1594-97); William Chillingworth, *The Religion of Protestants* (1637); Edward Stillingfleet, *Origines Sacrae* (1662); and John Tillotson, *Works*. In 1753, he published a slight pamphlet of his own, *The Advantage of the Members of the Church of England over those of the Church of Rome* (*Bibliog*, No. 205; Vol. 13 of this edn.). Then in 1756 he published *A Roman Catechism with a Reply Thereto* (*Bibliog*, No. 218; Vol. 13 of this edn.), an unacknowledged abridgement of Bishop John Williams, *A Catechism Truly Representing the Doctrines and Practices of the Church of Rome* (1st edn., 1686; 3rd edn., 1713). In 1779, he returned to the attack once more with *Popery Calmly Considered* (*Bibliog*, No. 401; Vol. 13 of this edn.). Even so, he had always considered the piety and devotion of Roman Catholics like De Renty, Lopez, Fénelon, *et al.*, authentic; thus, he always insisted that truly 'catholic spirit' must also include the Romans.

[33] See Jude 3.

[34] *The Catechism of the Council of Trent for Parish Priests* (1566) takes the whole of Exod. 20:2-6 as 'The First Commandment' and makes 20:17 into 'The Ninth' and 'Tenth Commandments' (distinguishing between two kinds of covetousness). The Douai Bible (1582, 1609) has the following note on Exod. 20:4-5: 'All such images . . . are forbidden by this [first] commandment as are made to be adored and served. . . . But otherwise, images, pictures, or representations even in the house of God, even in the very sanctuary, so far from being forbidden, are expressly authorized by the Word of God.' *The Childes Catechism* (Paris, 1678) had followed this line of division. Thus, anti-Romans could claim that the Romans had dropped 'the second commandment'; the Romans could claim that their official documents had been misunderstood.

The differences which begin in points of opinion seldom terminate there. They generally spread into the affections, and then separate chief friends. Nor are any animosities so deep and irreconcilable as those that spring from disagreement in religion.
5 For this cause the bitterest enemies of a man are those of his own household.[35] For this the father rises against his own children, and the children against the father;[36] and perhaps persecute each other even to the death, thinking all the time they are doing God service. It is therefore nothing more than we may expect if those
10 who differ from us either in religious opinions or practice soon contract a sharpness, yea, bitterness toward us; if they are more and more prejudiced against us, till they conceive as ill an opinion of our persons as of our principles. An almost necessary consequence of this will be, they will speak in the same manner as
15 they think of us. They will set themselves in opposition to us, and, as far as they are able hinder our work, seeing it does not appear to them to be the work of God, but either of man or of the devil. He that thinks, speaks, and acts in such a manner as this, in the highest sense 'followeth not us'.
20 7. I do not indeed conceive that the person of whom the Apostle speaks in the text (although we have no particular account of him either in the context or in any other part of Holy Writ) went so far as this. We have no ground to suppose that there was any material difference between him and the apostles; much less that
25 he had any prejudice either against them or their Master. It seems we may gather thus much from our Lord's own words which immediately follow the text, 'There is no man which shall do a miracle in my name that can lightly speak evil of me.'[37] But I purposely put the case in the strongest light, adding all the
30 circumstances which can well be conceived; that being forewarned of the temptation in its full strength we may in no case yield to it and fight against God.[38]

III. 1. Suppose then a man have no intercourse with us, suppose he be not of our party, suppose he separate from our
35 Church, yea, and widely differ from us both in judgment, practice, and affection; yet if we see even this man 'casting out

---

[35] See Matt. 10:36.
[36] See Matt. 10:21, etc.   [37] Mark 9:39.
[38] An echo here of Gamaliel's warning (Acts 5:39) against religious persecution as 'fighting against God'.

devils' Jesus saith, 'Forbid him not.' This important direction of
our Lord, I am, in the third place, to explain.

2. If we see this man casting out devils—but 'tis well if in such a
case we would believe even what we saw with our eyes, if we did
not give the lie to our own senses. He must be little acquainted 5
with human nature who does not immediately perceive how
extremely unready we should be to believe that any man does cast
out devils who 'followeth not us' in all or most of the senses above
recited. I had almost said, in any of them; seeing we may easily
learn even from what passes in our own breasts how unwilling 10
men are to allow anything good in those who do not in all things
agree with themselves.

3. 'But what is a sufficient, reasonable proof that a man does (in
the sense above) cast out devils?' The answer is easy. Is there full
proof, first, that a person before us was a gross, open sinner? 15
Secondly, that he is not so now; that he has broke off his sins, and
lives a Christian life? And thirdly, that his change was wrought by
his hearing this man preach? If these three points be plain and
undeniable, then you have sufficient, reasonable proof, such as
you cannot resist without wilful sin, that this man casts out devils. 20

4. Then 'forbid him not.' Beware how you attempt to hinder
him, either by your authority or arguments or persuasions. Do not
in any wise strive to prevent his using all the power which God has
given him. If you have *authority* with him, do not use that authority
to stop the work of God. Do not furnish him with *reasons* why he 25
ought not any more to speak in the name of Jesus. Satan will not
fail to supply him with these if you do not second him therein.
Persuade him not to depart from the work. If he should give place
to the devil[39] and you, many souls might perish in their iniquity,[40]
but their blood would God require at *your* hands.[41] 30

5. 'But what if he be only a *layman* who casts out devils? Ought
I not to forbid him then?'

Is the fact allowed? Is there reasonable proof that this man has
or does 'cast out devils'? If there is, forbid him not; no, not at the
peril of your soul. Shall not God work by whom he will work? 'No 35
man can do these works unless God is with him'[42]—unless God
hath sent him for this very thing. But if God hath sent him, will
you call him back? Will you forbid him to go?

[39] Eph. 4:27.
[41] See 2 Sam. 4:11.

[40] See 2 Pet. 2:12.
[42] Cf. John 3:2.

6. 'But I do not know that he is sent of God.' 'Now herein is a marvellous thing' (may any of the seals of his mission say, any whom he hath brought from Satan to God) 'that ye know not whence this man is, and behold he hath opened mine eyes! If this man were not of God, he could do nothing.'[43] If you doubt the fact, send for the parents of the man; send for his brethren, friends, acquaintance. But if you cannot doubt this, if you must needs acknowledge that 'a notable miracle hath been wrought', then with what conscience, with what face can you charge him whom God hath sent 'not to speak any more in his name'?[44]

7. I allow that it is *highly expedient,* whoever preaches in his name should have an outward as well as an inward call; but that it is *absolutely necessary* I deny.

'Nay, is not the Scripture express? "No man taketh this honour unto himself, but he that is called of God, as was Aaron." '[a]

Numberless times has this text been quoted on the occasion, as containing the very strength of the cause.[45] But surely never was so unhappy a quotation. For, first, Aaron was not called to preach at all. He was called to 'offer gifts and sacrifice for sin'.[46] That was his peculiar employment. Secondly, these men do not offer sacrifice at all, but only preach, which Aaron did not. Therefore it is not possible to find one text in all the Bible which is more wide of the point than this.

8. 'But what was the practice of the apostolic age?' You may easily see in the Acts of the Apostles. In the eighth chapter we read: 'There was a great persecution against the church which was at Jerusalem; and they were all scattered abroad throughout the regions of Judea and Samaria, except the apostles.'[b] 'Therefore they that were scattered abroad went everywhere preaching the word.'[c] Now, were all these outwardly called to preach? No man in his senses can think so. Here then is an undeniable proof what was the practice of the apostolic age.

[a] Heb. 5:4.
[b] [Acts 8], Ver. 1.
[c] Ver. 4.

---

[43] Cf. John 9:30, 33.
[44] Cf. Acts 4:16-17.
[45] Cf. Wesley's own sermon on this text, written at Cork in 1789 (No. 121, 'Prophets and Priests').
[46] Cf. Heb. 5:1.

Here you see not one but a multitude of 'lay preachers', men that were only sent of God.[47]

9. Indeed so far is the practice of the apostolic age from inclining us to think it was *unlawful* for a man to preach before he was ordained, that we have reason to think it was then accounted necessary. Certainly the practice and the direction of the Apostle Paul was to *prove* a man before he was ordained at all. 'Let these' (the deacons), says he, 'first be proved; then let them use the office of a deacon.'[d] Proved? How? By setting them to construe a sentence of Greek? And asking them a few commonplace questions?[48] O amazing proof of a minister of Christ! Nay; but by making a clear, open trial (as is still done by most of the Protestant Churches in Europe) not only whether their lives be holy and unblameable, but whether they have such gifts as are absolutely and indispensably necessary in order to edify the church of Christ.

10. 'But what if a man has these? And has brought sinners to repentance? And yet the bishop will not ordain him?' Then the bishop does 'forbid him to cast out devils'. But I dare not forbid him. I have published my reasons to all the world.[49] Yet 'tis still insisted I ought to do it. You who insist upon it, answer those reasons. I know not that any have done this yet, or even made a feint of doing it. Only some have spoken of them as very weak and trifling. And this was prudent enough. For 'tis far easier to despise—at least, seem to despise—an argument than to answer it. Yet till this is done I must say, when I have reasonable proof that any man does cast out devils, whatever others do I dare not forbid him, lest I be found even to fight against God.[50]

11. And whosoever thou art that fearest God, 'forbid him not,' either directly or indirectly. There are many ways of doing this. You indirectly forbid him if you either wholly deny, or despise and make little account of the work which God has wrought by his hands.[51] You indirectly forbid him when you discourage him in

---

[d] 1 Tim. 3:10.

---

[47] Is Wesley here recalling the case of his own grandfather, John Wesley, of Whitchurch? See Adam Clarke, *Memoirs of the Wesley Family* (1823), p. 353.

[48] A reference to the sometimes inadequate canonical examinations for Holy Orders; cf. Norman Sykes, *Church and State in England in the XVIIIth Century* (Cambridge, England, Univ. Press, 1934), pp. 106-10.

[49] See *A Farther Appeal*, Pt. III (1745), III.8-17 (11:294-303 in this edn.).

[50] See Acts 5:39.   [51] See Mark 6:2.

his work by drawing him into disputes concerning it, by raising objections against it, or frighting him with consequences which very possibly will never be. You forbid him when you show any unkindness toward him either in language or behaviour; and
5 much more when you speak of him to others either in an unkind or a contemptuous manner, when you endeavour to represent him to any either in an odious or a despicable light. You are forbidding him all the time you are speaking evil of him or making no account of his labours. O forbid him not in any of these ways;
10 nor by forbidding others to hear him, by discouraging sinners from hearing that word which is able to save their souls.

12. Yea, if you would observe our Lord's direction in its full meaning and extent, then remember his word, 'He that is not for us is against us, and he that gathereth not with me, scattereth.'[52]
15 He that gathereth not men into the kingdom of God assuredly scatters them from it. For there can be no neuter in this war: everyone is either on God's side or on Satan's. Are you on God's side? Then you will not only not forbid any man that 'casts out devils', but you will labour to the uttermost of your power to
20 forward him in the work. You will readily acknowledge the work of God, and confess the greatness of it. You will remove all difficulties and objections, as far as may be, out of his way. You will strengthen his hands by speaking honourably of him before all men, and avowing the things which you have seen and heard.
25 You will encourage others to attend upon his word, to hear him whom God hath sent. And you will omit no actual proof of tender love which God gives you an opportunity of showing him.

IV. 1. If we willingly fail in any of these points, if we either directly or indirectly forbid him 'because he followeth not us',
30 then we are 'bigots'. This is the inference I draw from what has been said. But the term 'bigotry', I fear, as frequently as it is used, is almost as little understood as 'enthusiasm'. It is too strong an attachment to, or fondness for, our own party, opinion, Church, and religion. Therefore he is a bigot who is so fond of any of
35 these, so strongly attached to them, as to forbid any who casts out devils, because he differs from himself in any or all these particulars.

2. Do *you* beware of this. Take care, first, that you do not

---

[52] Cf. Luke 11:23.

convict yourself of bigotry by your unreadiness to believe that any man does cast out devils who differs from you. And if you are clear thus far, if you acknowledge the fact, then examine yourself, secondly: 'Am I not convicted of bigotry in this, in forbidding him directly or indirectly? Do I not directly forbid him on this ground, 5 because he is not of my *party?* Because he does not fall in with my *opinions?* Or because he does not worship God according to that scheme of religion which I have received from my fathers?'

3. Examine yourself: 'Do I not indirectly, at least, forbid him on any of these grounds? Am I not sorry that God should thus own 10 and bless a man that holds such erroneous opinions? Do I not discourage him because he is not of my Church? By disputing with him concerning it, by raising objections, and by perplexing his mind with distant consequences? Do I show no anger, contempt, or unkindness of any sort, either in my words or 15 actions? Do I not mention behind his back his (real or supposed) faults? His defects or infirmities? Do not I hinder sinners from hearing his word?' If you do any of these things you are a bigot to this day.

4. 'Search me, O Lord, and prove me. Try out my reins and my 20 heart.'[53] 'Look well if there be any way of *bigotry* in me, and lead me in the way everlasting.'[54] In order to examine ourselves throughly let the case be proposed in the strongest manner. What if I were to see a Papist, an Arian, a Socinian casting out devils? If I did, I could not forbid even him without convicting myself of 25 bigotry. Yea, if it could be supposed that I should see a Jew, a deist, or a Turk doing the same, were I to forbid him either directly or indirectly I should be no better than a bigot still.

5. O stand clear of this. But be not content with not forbidding any that casts out devils. 'Tis well to go thus far; but do not stop 30 here. If you will avoid all bigotry, go on. In every instance of this kind, whatever the instrument be, acknowledge the finger of God. And not only acknowledge but rejoice in his work, and praise his name with thanksgiving. Encourage whomsoever God is pleased to employ, to give himself wholly up thereto. Speak well 35 of him wheresoever you are; defend his character and his mission. Enlarge as far as you can his sphere of action. Show him all kindness in word and deed. And cease not to cry to God in his behalf, that he may save both himself and them that hear him.[55]

---

[53] Cf. Ps. 26:2. [54] Cf. Ps. 139:24 (BCP). [55] See 1 Tim. 4:16.

6. I need add but one caution. Think not the bigotry of another is any excuse for your own. 'Tis not impossible that one who casts out devils himself may yet forbid you so to do. You may observe this is the very case mentioned in the text. The apostles forbade
5 another to do what they did themselves. But beware of retorting.[56] It is not your part to return evil for evil.[57] Another's not observing the direction of our Lord is no reason why you should neglect it. Nay, but let him have all the bigotry to himself. If he forbids *you*, do not you forbid *him*. Rather labour and watch and pray the
10 more, to confirm your love toward him. If he speaks all manner of evil of *you*,[58] speak all manner of good (that is true) of *him*. Imitate herein that glorious saying of a great man (O that he had always breathed the same spirit!) 'Let Luther call me an hundred devils; I will still reverence him as a messenger of God.'[59]

---

[56] Cf. No. 42, 'Satan's Devices', §5, proem and n.

[57] Cf. 1 Thess. 5:15.

[58] See Matt. 5:11.

[59] Cf. Calvin's letter to Bullinger (in *Opera*, XI. 586:774): '*Saepe dicere solitus sum: etiam si me diabolum vocaret, me tamen hoc illi honoris habiturum, ut insignem Dei servum agnoscam* . . .'. In a MS letter from Charles Wesley to George Whitefield, Sept. 1, 1740, this same quotation is paraphrased differently: 'I would adopt that noble saying of Calvin, "*Etsi Lutherus centum diabolos nuncuperavit, ego illum nihilominus agnoscam et diligam ut ministrum et angelum Dei*"' (MA). This obvious discrepancy here between two similar texts suggests an intermediary source for the Wesleys; but none has yet been located. Calvin's letter to Bullinger had not been published in English in 1750; this translation here may have been Wesley's own.

CATHOLIC SPIRIT

AN INTRODUCTORY COMMENT

There was a nondogmatic strain in Anglicanism that had discouraged the formulation of creeds, confessions, and systematic treatises. Wesley had inherited this tradition from his mother. He was opinionated and partisan, like his father, with a stubborn loyalty to what he understood to be the essential core of Christian truth. But he never supposed that this core ever had been or ever could be captured in a single form of words. This mistrust of rigid statements may have had some connection with his ingrained impulse to revise almost any sentence that might be set before him, including his own—and also his careless way with quotations. He agreed with the Cambridge Platonists before him that most of the cruel controversies in religion that had spilled so much blood and ink were quarrels about 'opinions'—i.e., subsidiary doctrines affecting the fullness and variety of religious language, not its primary object. He also agreed with William of St. Thierry that love is the surest way to truth and the highest goal of thought. He had a clear enough view for himself of the Christian essentials (cf. No. 7, 'The Way to the Kingdom', I.6 and n.) but never ever tried to formulate them in an unrevisable statement. He had ventured his most elaborate summary of them in an open Letter to a Roman Catholic (1749); his least elaborate ('love of God and love of neighbour') is repeated endlessly throughout the sermons; e.g., No. 120, 'The Unity of the Divine Being', §16: 'True religion is right tempers towards God and man. It is, in two words, gratitude and benevolence: gratitude to our Creator and supreme Benefactor, and benevolence to our fellow creatures. In other words, it is the loving God with all our heart, and our neighbour as ourselves.' In every case, his concern is to narrow the field of irreducible disagreement between professing, practising Christians and to transfer their concerns from argument about faith in Christ to faith itself and to its consequences.

'Catholic Spirit' is the most formal articulation of this nondogmatic method in theology. In it we find yet another statement of 'essentials'—and it goes with his method that Wesley believes he could presuppose a consensus here. Then we come to Wesley's effort to redeem

controversy in general by the spirit of Christian love and forbearance. Given clarity as to the essentials and liberty as to 'opinions', he is glad for Methodists 'to think and let think'. Here, then, is a charter for a distinctive sort of doctrinal pluralism—one that stands at an equal distance from dogmatism on the one extreme and indifferentism on the other.

The mood and method of 'Catholic Spirit' run widely through the entire Wesleyan corpus and must have been heard in his oral preaching as well. But as for the use of this particular text, 2 Kgs. 10:15, there are only three other recorded instances (November 23, 1740; September 8, 1749; and November 3, 1749). This sermon was republished separately in 1755 (and again in 1770), with an appended hymn by Charles Wesley (seven six-line stanzas) on 'Catholic Love':

> Weary of all this wordy strife,
> These notions, forms, and modes, and names,
> To Thee, the Way, the Truth, the Life,
> Whose love my simple heart inflames,
> Divinely taught, at last I fly,
> With thee and thine to live and die.

In some ears such language, and the attitude behind it, would inevitably sound soft-headed. Its deeper concern, however, may represent Wesley's most important contribution to the cause of Christian unity and to the requisite spirit in which that cause may best be served.

For a stemma illustrating this sermon's publishing history and a list of variant readings, see Appendix, Vol. 4; see also Bibliog, No. 211.

Catholic Spirit

2 Kings 10:15

And when he was departed thence, he lighted on Jehonadab the son of Rechab coming to meet him. And he saluted him and said, Is thine heart right, as my heart is with thy heart? And Jehonadab answered, It is. If it be, give me thine hand.

1. It is allowed even by those who do not pay this great debt that love is due to all mankind, the royal law, 'Thou shalt love thy neighbour as thyself,'[1] carrying its own evidence to all that hear it. And that, not according to the miserable construction put upon it by the zealots of old times, 'Thou shalt love thy neighbour', thy relation, acquaintance, friend, 'and hate thine enemy.' Not so. 'I say unto you', said our Lord, 'Love your enemies, bless them that curse you, do good to them that hate you, and pray for them that despitefully use you and persecute you; that ye may be the children'—may appear so to all mankind—'of your Father which is in heaven, who maketh his sun to rise on the evil and on the good, and sendeth rain on the just and on the unjust.'[2]

2. But it is sure, there is a peculiar love which we owe to those that love God. So David: 'All my delight is upon the saints that are in the earth, and upon such as excel in virtue.'[3] And so a greater than he: 'A new commandment I give unto you, that ye love one another: as I have loved you, that ye also love one another. By this shall all men know that ye are my disciples, if ye have love one to another.'[a] This is that love on which the Apostle John so frequently and strongly insists. 'This', said he, 'is the message that ye heard from the beginning, that we should love one another.'[b] 'Hereby perceive we the love of God, because he laid down his life for us. And we ought', if love should call us thereto, 'to lay down our lives for the brethren.'[c] And again, 'Beloved, let

---

[a] John 13:34-35. [b] 1 John 3:11. [c] Ver. 16.

[1] Jas. 2:8; cf. Lev. 19:18; Matt. 19:19, etc.
[2] Cf. Matt. 5:43-45. [3] Ps. 16:3 (BCP).

us love one another; for love is of God. He that loveth not,
knoweth not God; for God is love.'[d] 'Not that we loved God, but
that he loved us, and sent his Son to be the propitiation for our
sins. Beloved, if God so loved us, we ought also to love one
5 another.'[e]

3. All men approve of this. But do all men practise it? Daily
experience shows the contrary. Where are even the Christians
who 'love one another, as he hath given us commandment'?[4] How
many hindrances lie in the way! The two grand, general
10 hindrances are, first, that they can't all think alike; and in
consequence of this, secondly, they can't all walk alike; but in
several smaller points their practice must differ in proportion to
the difference of their sentiments.

4. But although a difference in opinions or modes of worship
15 may prevent an entire external union, yet need it prevent our
union in affection? Though we can't think alike, may we not love
alike? May we not be of one heart, though we are not of one
opinion? Without all doubt we may. Herein all the children of
God may unite, notwithstanding these smaller differences. These
20 remaining as they are, they may forward one another in love and
in good works.

5. Surely in this respect the example of Jehu himself, as mixed a
character as he was of, is well worthy both the attention and
imitation of every serious Christian. 'And when he was departed
25 thence, he lighted on Jehonadab the son of Rechab coming to
meet him. And he saluted him and said, Is thine heart right, as my
heart is with thy heart? And Jehonadab answered, It is. If it be,
give me thine hand.'

The text naturally divides itself into two parts. First a question
30 proposed by Jehu to Jehonadab, 'Is thine heart right, as my heart
is with thy heart?' Secondly, an offer made on Jehonadab's
answering, 'It is.'—'If it be, give me thine hand.'

I. 1. And, first, let us consider the question proposed by Jehu
to Jehonadab, 'Is thine heart right, as my heart is with thy heart?'
35 The very first thing we may observe in these words is that here
is no inquiry concerning Jehonadab's opinions. And yet 'tis
certain he held some which were very uncommon, indeed quite

---

[d] Chap. 4, ver. 7-8.   [e] Ver. 10-11.

---

[4] Cf. 1 John 3:23.

peculiar to himself; and some which had a close influence upon practice, on which likewise he laid so great a stress as to entail them upon his children's children, to their latest posterity. This is evident from the account given by Jeremiah, many years after his death. 'I took Jaazaniah and his brethren, and all his sons, and the whole house of the Rechabites; . . . and set before them pots full of wine, and cups, and said unto them, Drink ye wine. But they said, We will drink no wine; for Jonadab (or Jehonadab) the son of Rechab our father' (it would be less ambiguous if the words were placed thus: Jehonadab 'our father the son of Rechab', out of love and reverence to whom he probably desired his descendants might be called by his name) 'commanded us, saying, Ye shall drink no wine, neither ye nor your sons for ever. Neither shall ye build house, nor sow seed, nor plant vineyard, nor have any; but all your days ye shall dwell in tents. . . . And we have obeyed, and done according to all that Jonadab our father commanded us.'[f]

2. And yet Jehu (although it seems to have been his manner, both in things secular and religious, to 'drive furiously')[5] does not concern himself at all with any of these things, but lets Jehonadab abound in his own sense.[6] And neither of them appears to have given the other the least disturbance touching the opinions which he maintained.

3. 'Tis very possible that many good men now also may entertain peculiar opinions; and some of them may be as singular herein as even Jehonadab was. And 'tis certain, so long as 'we know' but 'in part',[7] that all men will not see all things alike. It is an unavoidable consequence of the present weakness and shortness of human understanding that several men will be of several minds, in religion as well as in common life. So it has been from the beginning of the world, and so it will be 'till the restitution of all things'.[8]

4. Nay farther: although every man necessarily believes that every particular opinion which he holds is true (for to believe any

---

[f] Jer. 35:3-10 [Note the similarity between Wesley's suggested word order and that adopted for the NEB].

---

[5] Cf. 2 Kgs. 9:20.

[6] A proverbial expression derived from the late Latin *abundare in suo sensu:* 'to follow one's own opinion'. (See *OED* for a citation from Taverner's *Proverbs*, 1552, along with later examples, including Edmund Burke, 1775.)

[7] 1 Cor. 13:12.   [8] Cf. Acts 3:21.

opinion is not true is the same thing as not to hold it) yet can no man be assured that all his own opinions taken together are true. Nay, every thinking man is assured they are not, seeing *humanum est errare et nescire*[9]—to be ignorant of many things, and to mistake
5 in some, is the necessary condition of humanity. This therefore, he is sensible, is his own case. He knows in the general that he himself is mistaken; although in what particulars he mistakes he does not, perhaps cannot, know.

5. I say, perhaps he cannot know. For who can tell how far
10 invincible ignorance[10] may extend? Or (what comes to the same thing) invincible prejudice; which is often so fixed in tender minds that it is afterwards impossible to tear up what has taken so deep a root. And who can say, unless he knew every circumstance attending it, how far any mistake is culpable? Seeing all guilt must
15 suppose some concurrence of the will—of which he only can judge who searcheth the heart.

6. Every wise man therefore will allow others the same liberty of thinking which he desires they should allow him; and will no more insist on their embracing his opinions than he would have
20 them to insist on his embracing theirs. He bears with those who differ from him, and only asks him with whom he desires to unite

[9] The first part of this sentence is a familiar classical proverb; cf. Sophocles, *Antigone* ('To err from the right path is common to mankind'); Cicero, *Philippics*, XXI.ii.5; Seneca, *Naturales Quaestiones* (*Natural Questions*), iv.2; Plutarch, *Against Colotes* ('To err in opinion, though it be not part of wisdom, is at least human'); Augustine, Sermon 164:14. Cf. also, Jerome, *Epistles*, 57:12 (Migne, *PL*, XXII.579): '*Scio quod nescio . . .*'); and George Buchanan, *Geflugelte Wörte* (Berlin, 1961), 567-68.

Pope's *Essay on Criticism*, l. 525, popularized this in the first half of 'To err is human, to forgive divine.' Wesley seems to have regarded '*et nescire*', 'to be ignorant', as also an integral part of 'the maxim received in all ages', quoting his amplified version no fewer than four times in the *Sermons:* cf. Nos. 51, *The Good Steward*, II.9; 57, 'On the Fall of Man', II.2; 62, 'The End of Christ's Coming', III.3. See also his *Short Address to the Inhabitants of Ireland*, §15.

[10] 'Invincible' because rooted in one's social influences and prejudices; cf. Francis Bacon's so-called 'idols' of one's 'tribe', 'cave', 'market-place', or 'theatre' as in No. 31, 'Sermon on the Mount, XI', II.5 and n. Cf. St. Thomas, *Summa Theologica* I-II ('Human Acts'), Q. 76, 2nd art. ('Whether Ignorance is a Sin?'): '[Ignorance] is not imputed as a sin to man if he fails to know what he is unable to know. Consequently, such ignorance is called *invincible* because it cannot be overcome by study . . .; wherefore it is evident that no invincible ignorance is a sin. . . .' But 'even inculpable ignorance' 'excludes from salvation' those who do not 'know' 'that there is a God who will reward those who seek him'; cf. Canon George D. Smith, ed., *The Teaching of the Catholic Church*, I.17. What might have surprised Wesley, though, is that 'the Church teaches no less clearly that actual membership of the [Roman] Catholic Church is not necessary for the salvation of those in invincible ignorance of her true nature' (*ibid.*, II.709). Cf. No. 55, *On the Trinity*, §18.

in love that single question. 'Is thine heart right, as my heart is with thy heart?'

7. We may, secondly, observe that here is no inquiry made concerning Jehonadab's mode of worship, although 'tis highly probable there was in this respect also a very wide difference 5 between them. For we may well believe Jehonadab, as well as all his posterity, worshipped God at Jerusalem, whereas Jehu did not; he had more regard to state policy than religion. And therefore although he slew the worshippers of Baal, and 'destroyed Baal out of Israel', yet 'from the' convenient 'sin of 10 Jeroboam', the worship of 'the golden calves, he departed not'.ᵍ

8. But even among men of an upright heart, men who desire 'to have a conscience void of offence',[11] it must needs be that as long as there are various opinions there will be various ways of worshipping God; seeing a variety of opinion necessarily implies a 15 variety of practice. And as in all ages men have differed in nothing more than in their opinions concerning the Supreme Being, so in nothing have they more differed from each other than in the manner of worshipping him. Had this been only in the heathen world it would not have been at all surprising, for we know these 20 'by their wisdom knew not God';[12] nor therefore could they know how to worship him. But is it not strange that even in the Christian world, although they all agree in the general, 'God is a Spirit, and they that worship him must worship him in spirit and in truth,'[13] yet the particular modes of worshipping God are 25 almost as various as among the heathens?

9. And how shall we choose among so much variety? No man can choose for or prescribe to another. But everyone must follow the dictates of his own conscience in simplicity and godly sincerity.[14] He must be fully persuaded in his own mind,[15] and 30 then act according to the best light he has. Nor has any creature power to constrain another to walk by his own rule. God has given no right to any of the children of men thus to lord it over the conscience of his brethren. But every man must judge for himself, as every man must give an account of himself to God.[16] 35

ᵍ 2 Kgs. 10:28-29.

---

[11] Acts 24:16.
[13] John 4:24.
[15] See Rom. 14:5.
[16] See Rom. 14:12.

[12] Cf. 1 Cor. 1:21.
[14] See 2 Cor. 1:12.

10. Although therefore every follower of Christ is obliged by the very nature of the Christian institution to be a member of some particular congregation or other, some church, as it is usually termed (which implies a particular manner of worship-
5 ping God; for 'two cannot walk together unless they be agreed');[17] yet none can be obliged by any power on earth but that of his own conscience to prefer this or that congregation to another, this or that particular manner of worship. I know it is commonly supposed that the place of our birth fixes the church to which we
10 ought to belong; that one, for instance, who is born in England ought to be a member of that which is styled 'the Church of England', and consequently to worship God in the particular manner which is prescribed by that church. I was once a zealous maintainer of this, but I find many reasons to abate of this zeal. I
15 fear it is attended with such difficulties as no reasonable man can get over. Not the least of which is that if this rule had took place, there could have been no Reformation from popery, seeing it entirely destroys the right of private judgment on which that whole Reformation stands.[18]
20 11. I dare not therefore presume to impose my mode of worship on any other. I believe it is truly primitive and apostolical. But my belief is no rule for another. I ask not therefore of him with whom I would unite in love, 'Are you of my Church? Of my congregation? Do you receive the same form of church
25 government and allow the same church officers with me? Do you

---

[17] Cf. Amos 3:3.
[18] Cf. Nos. 105, 'On Conscience'; 12, 'The Witness of Our Own Spirit', §6; 18, 'The Marks of the New Birth', II.2; and 129, 'Heavenly Treasure in Earthen Vessels', I.1. Cf. also Benjamin Ibbot, *A Course of Sermons, preached for the lecture founded by the Honourable Robert Boyle, Esq., at the Church of St. Mary-le-Bow, in the Years 1713 and 1714, Wherein The True Notion of the Exercise of Private Judgment . . . in Matters of Religion is Stated and the Objections Against it Answered;* Vicesimus Knox, *Essays Moral and Literary* (Dublin, 1786), V.21; and *The Old Whig,* No. 4, I.32-33: 'The reformation owes its being to men, who had the honesty and courage to oppose their own private judgments to the established opinions of the whole Christian world; to think for themselves, though threatened with all the terrors of civil punishment in the present life, and damnation in a future state, for such dreadful impiety and insolence; and to protest against those errors in opinion and superstitions in practice, which the church had sanctified and the state established.'
   Compare this with Kant's later definition of 'enlightenment': 'Man's release from . . . his inability to make use of his own understanding ['private judgment'] without direction from another', in *What is Enlightenment?* (1784), §1. See also Wesley's refutation (JWJ, Mar. 25, 1743) of Richard Challoner's denial of the right of 'private judgment', in *The Grounds of the Old Religion* (1742), and his repeated insistence 'on the right of private judgment' in JWJ, May 30, 1746, and in *An Earnest Appeal,* §§61-62 (11:70-71, in this edn.).

join in the same form of prayer wherein I worship God?' I inquire
not, 'Do you receive the Supper of the Lord in the same posture
and manner that I do?' Nor whether, in the administration of
baptism, you agree with me in admitting sureties for the baptized,
in the manner of administering it, or the age of those to whom it
should be administered. Nay, I ask not of you (as clear as I am in
my own mind) whether you allow baptism and the Lord's Supper
at all. Let all these things stand by: we will talk of them, if need be,
at a more convenient season.[19] My only question at present is this,
'Is thine heart right, as my heart is with thy heart?'

12. But what is properly implied in the question? I do not mean
what did Jehu imply therein, but what should a follower of Christ
understand thereby when he proposes it to any of his brethren?

The first thing implied is this: Is thy heart right with God? Dost
thou believe his being, and his perfections? His eternity,
immensity, wisdom, power; his justice, mercy, and truth? Dost
thou believe that he now 'upholdeth all things by the word of his
power'?[20] And that he governs even the most minute, even the
most noxious, to his own glory, and the good of them that love
him? Hast thou a divine evidence, a supernatural conviction, of
the things of God? Dost thou 'walk by faith, not by sight'?[21]
'Looking not at temporal things, but things eternal'?[22]

13. Dost thou believe in the Lord Jesus Christ, 'God over all,
blessed for ever'?[23] Is he 'revealed in' thy soul?[24] Dost thou 'know
Jesus Christ and him crucified'?[25] Does he 'dwell in thee, and
thou in him'?[26] Is he 'formed in thy heart by faith'?[27] Having
absolutely disclaimed all thy own works, thy own righteousness,
hast thou 'submitted thyself unto the righteousness of God',[28]
'which is by faith in Christ Jesus'?[29] Art thou 'found in him, not
having thy own righteousness, but the righteousness which is by
faith'?[30] And art thou, through him, 'fighting the good fight of
faith, and laying hold of eternal life'?[31]

[19] See Acts 24:25.
[20] Cf. Heb. 1:3.
[21] 2 Cor. 5:7.
[22] Cf. 2 Cor. 4:18.
[23] Cf. Rom. 9:5.
[24] Cf. Gal. 1:16.
[25] 1 Cor. 2:2.
[26] Cf. John 6:56; 1 John 4:13, 15.
[27] Cf. Gal. 4:19; Eph. 3:17.
[28] Cf. Rom. 10:3.
[29] Rom. 3:22.
[30] Cf. Phil. 3:9.
[31] Cf. 1 Tim. 6:12.

14. Is thy faith ἐνεργουμένη δἰ ἀγάπης—filled with the energy of love?[32] Dost thou love God? I do not say 'above all things', for it is both an unscriptural and an ambiguous expression, but 'with all thy heart, and with all thy mind, and with all thy soul, and with all thy strength'?[33] Dost thou seek all thy happiness in him alone? And dost thou find what thou seekest? Does thy soul continually 'magnify the Lord, and thy spirit rejoice in God thy Saviour'?[34] Having learned 'in everything to give thanks',[35] dost thou find it is 'a joyful and a pleasant thing to be thankful'?[36] Is God the centre of thy soul? The sum of all thy desires? Art thou accordingly 'laying up' thy 'treasure in heaven',[37] and 'counting all things else dung and dross'?[38] Hath the love of God cast the love of the world out of thy soul? Then thou art 'crucified to the world'.[39] 'Thou art dead' to all below, 'and thy life is hid with Christ in God.'[40]

15. Art thou employed in doing 'not thy own will, but the will of him that sent thee'?[41] Of him that sent thee down to sojourn here a while, to spend a few days in a strange land, till having finished the work he hath given thee to do thou return to thy Father's house? Is it thy meat and drink 'to do the will of thy Father which is in heaven'?[42] Is 'thine eye single'[43] in all things? Always fixed on him? Always 'looking unto Jesus'?[44] Dost thou point at him in whatsoever thou dost? In all thy labour, thy business, thy conversation? Aiming only at the glory of God in all? 'Whatsoever' thou dost, either 'in word or deed, doing it all in the name of the Lord Jesus, giving thanks unto God, even the Father, through him'?[45]

16. Does the love of God constrain thee to 'serve' him 'with fear'?[46] To 'rejoice unto him with reverence'?[47] Art thou more afraid of displeasing God than either of death or hell? Is nothing so terrible to thee as the thought of 'offending the eyes of his glory'?[48] Upon this ground dost thou 'hate all evil ways',[49] every transgression of his holy and perfect law? And herein 'exercise'

---

[32] Cf. Gal. 5:6, orig., πίστις δἰ ἀγάπης ἐνεργουμένη ('faith active in love'); Wesley's reversal has the effect of a different nuance ('the energy *of* love'). See above, No. 2, *The Almost Christian*, II.6 and n.

[33] Cf. Mark 12:30; Luke 10:27. [34] Cf. Luke 1:46-47. [35] 1 Thess. 5:18.
[36] Cf. Ps. 147:1 (BCP). [37] Cf. Matt. 6:20. [38] Cf. Phil. 3:8.
[39] Cf. Gal. 6:14. [40] Cf. Col. 3:3. [41] Cf. John 6:38.
[42] Cf. Matt. 7:21, etc. [43] Matt. 6:22. [44] Heb. 12:2.
[45] Cf. Col. 3:17. [46] Cf. Ps. 2:11. [47] *Ibid.* (BCP).
[48] Cf. Isa. 3:8. [49] Ps. 119:104 (BCP).

thyself 'to have a conscience void of offence toward God and toward man'?[50]

17. Is thy heart right toward thy neighbour? Dost thou 'love as thyself'[51] all mankind without exception? 'If you love those only that love you, what thank have you?'[52] Do you 'love your enemies'?[53] Is your soul full of goodwill, of tender affection toward them? Do you love even the enemies of God? The unthankful and unholy? Do your bowels yearn over them? Could you 'wish yourself (temporally) accursed'[54] for their sake? And do you show this by 'blessing them that curse you, and praying for those that despitefully use you and persecute you'?[55]

18. Do you show your love by your works? While you have time, as you have opportunity, do you in fact 'do good to all men'[56]—neighbours or strangers, friends or enemies, good or bad? Do you do them all the good you can? Endeavouring to supply all their wants, assisting them both in body and soul to the uttermost of your power? If thou art thus minded, may every Christian say—yea, if thou art but sincerely desirous of it, and following on till thou attain—then 'thy heart is right, as my heart is with thy heart.'

II. 1. 'If it be, give me thine hand.' I do not mean, 'Be of my opinion.' You need not. I do not expect nor desire it. Neither do I mean, 'I will be of your opinion.' I cannot. It does not depend on my choice. I can no more think than I can see or hear as I will. Keep you your opinion, I mine; and that as steadily as ever. You need not even endeavour to come over to me, or bring me over to you. I do not desire you to dispute those points, or to hear or speak one word concerning them. Let all opinions alone on one side and the other. Only 'give me thine hand.'

2. I do not mean, 'Embrace my modes of worship,' or, 'I will embrace yours.' This also is a thing which does not depend either on your choice or mine. We must both act as each is fully persuaded in his own mind.[57] Hold you fast that which you believe

---

[50] Cf. Acts 24:16.
[51] Lev. 19:18, etc.
[52] Cf. Luke 6:32.
[53] Matt. 5:44.
[54] Cf. Rom. 9:3.
[55] Cf. Matt. 5:44.
[56] Cf. Gal. 6:10.
[57] See Rom. 14:5.

is most acceptable to God, and I will do the same. I believe the
episcopal form of church government to be scriptural and
apostolical. If you think the presbyterian or independent is better,
think so still, and act accordingly. I believe infants ought to be
5 baptized, and that this may be done either by dipping or
sprinkling.[58] If you are otherwise persuaded, be so still, and follow
your own persuasion. It appears to me that forms of prayer are of
excellent use, particularly in the great congregation.[59] If you judge
extemporary prayer to be of more use, act suitably to your own
10 judgment. My sentiment is that I ought not to forbid water
wherein persons may be baptized, and that I ought to eat bread
and drink wine as a memorial of my dying Master. However, if
you are not convinced of this, act according to the light you have. I
have no desire to dispute with you one moment upon any of the
15 preceding heads. Let all these smaller points stand aside. Let
them never come into sight. 'If thine heart is as my heart', if thou
lovest God and all mankind, I ask no more: 'Give me thine hand.'

3. I mean, first, love me. And that not only as thou lovest all
mankind; not only as thou lovest thine enemies or the enemies of
20 God, those that hate thee, that 'despitefully use thee and
persecute thee';[60] not only as a stranger, as one of whom thou
knowest neither good nor evil. I am not satisfied with this. No; 'If
thine heart be right, as mine with thy heart', then love me with a
very tender affection, as a friend that is closer than a brother; as a
25 brother in Christ, a fellow-citizen of the new Jerusalem, a
fellow-soldier engaged in the same warfare, under the same
Captain of our salvation.[61] Love me as a companion in the
kingdom and patience of Jesus,[62] and a joint-heir of his glory.[63]

4. Love me (but in an higher degree than thou dost the bulk of
30 mankind) with the love that is 'long-suffering and kind';[64] that is
patient if I am ignorant or out of the way, bearing and not
increasing my burden; and is tender, soft, and compassionate
still; that 'envieth not' if at any time it please God to prosper me in
his work even more than thee. Love me with the love that 'is not
35 provoked' either at my follies or infirmities, or even at my acting

---

[58] Note Wesley's casual self-identification as Anglican, here as elsewhere.
[59] As distinguished from the religious society or informal worship group.
[60] Cf. Matt. 5:44.   [61] See Heb. 2:10.
[62] See Rev. 1:9.
[63] See Rom. 8:17.
[64] Cf. 1 Cor. 13:4.

(if it should sometimes so appear to thee) not according to the will of God. Love me so as to 'think no evil' of me, to put away all jealousy and evil surmising. Love me with the love that 'covereth all things', that never reveals either my faults or infirmities; that 'believeth all things', is always willing to think the best, to put the fairest construction on all my words and actions; that 'hopeth all things',[65] either that the thing related was never done, or not done with such circumstances as are related, or, at least, that it was done with a good intention, or in sudden stress of temptation. And hope to the end that whatever is amiss will, by the grace of God, be corrected, and whatever is wanting supplied, through the riches of his mercy in Christ Jesus.

5. I mean, secondly, commend me to God in all thy prayers; wrestle with him in my behalf, that he would speedily correct what he sees amiss and supply what is wanting in me. In thy nearest access to the throne of grace beg of him who is then very present with thee that my heart may be more as thy heart, more right both toward God and toward man; that I may have a fuller conviction of things not seen,[66] and a stronger view of the love of God in Christ Jesus; may more steadily walk by faith, not by sight,[67] and more earnestly grasp eternal life. Pray that the love of God and of all mankind may be more largely poured into my heart; that I may be more fervent and active in doing the will of my Father which is in heaven,[68] more zealous of good works,[69] and more careful to abstain from all appearance of evil.

6. I mean, thirdly, provoke me to love and to good works.[70] Second thy prayer as thou hast opportunity by speaking to me in love whatsoever thou believest to be for my soul's health. Quicken me in the work which God has given me to do, and instruct me how to do it more perfectly. Yea, 'smite me friendly and reprove me'[71] whereinsoever I appear to thee to be doing rather my own will than the will of him that sent me.[72] O speak and spare not, whatever thou believest may conduce either to the amending my faults, the strengthening my weakness, the building me up in love, or the making me more fit in any kind for the Master's use.

7. I mean, lastly, love me not in word only, but in deed and in

[65] Cf. 1 Cor. 13:4-7.
[66] See Heb. 11:1.
[67] 2 Cor. 5:7.
[68] Matt. 12:50.
[69] Titus 2:14.
[70] See Heb. 10:24.
[71] Ps. 141:5 (BCP).
[72] See John 6:38.

truth.[73] So far as in conscience thou canst (retaining still thy own opinions and thy own manner of worshipping God), join with me in the work of God, and let us go on hand in hand. And thus far, it is certain, thou mayst go. Speak honourably, wherever thou art, of
5 the work of God, by whomsoever he works, and kindly of his messengers. And if it be in thy power, not only sympathize with them when they are in any difficulty or distress, but give them a cheerful and effectual assistance, that they may glorify God on thy behalf.

10 8. Two things should be observed with regard to what has been spoken under this last head. The one, that whatsoever love, whatsoever offices of love, whatsoever spiritual or temporal assistance, I claim from him whose heart is right, as my heart is with his, the same I am ready, by the grace of God, according to
15 my measure, to give him. The other, that I have not made this claim in behalf of myself only, but of all whose heart is right toward God and man, that we may all love one another as Christ hath loved us.[74]

III. 1. One inference we may make from what has been said.
20 We may learn from hence what is a 'catholic spirit'.

There is scarce any expression which has been more grossly misunderstood and more dangerously misapplied than this. But it will be easy for any who calmly consider the preceding observations to correct any such misapprehensions of it, and to
25 prevent any such misapplication.

For from hence we may learn, first, that a catholic spirit is not *speculative latitudinarianism*.[75] It is not an indifference to all opinions. This is the spawn of hell, not the offspring of heaven. This unsettledness of thought, this being 'driven to and fro, and

---

[73] See 1 John 3:18.

[74] See John 13:34.

[75] A tradition of toleration of theoretical differences that had arisen as an alternative to a tragic century of divisive controversy and conflict. Its theory had been laid down by the Cambridge Platonists (Whichcote, More, Cudworth); its ecclesiological implications had been set out, in different ways, by Hoadly and Tillotson; some of its unintended practical effects had been made evident in the Bangorian controversy; cf. Sykes, *From Sheldon to Secker: Aspects of English Church History, 1660–1768* (Cambridge, England, Univ. Press, 1959), pp. 146-52, for a brief review of this movement. What is significant is that Wesley could have rejected latitudinarianism with such vehemence in the course of espousing yet another form of 'comprehension'. It means that he felt closer to Richard Baxter, *The True Catholick and Catholick Church Described* (1660), in *Works* (1854), IV.729-58.

tossed about with very wind of doctrine',[76] is a great curse, not a blessing; an irreconcilable enemy, not a friend, to true catholicism. A man of a truly catholic spirit has not now his religion to seek. He is fixed as the sun in his judgment concerning the main branches of Christian doctrine. 'Tis true he is always 5 ready to hear and weigh whatsoever can be offered against his principles. But as this does not show any wavering in his own mind, so neither does it occasion any. He does not halt between two opinions,[77] nor vainly endeavour to blend them into one. Observe this, you who know not what spirit ye are of, who call 10 yourselves men of a catholic spirit only because you are of a muddy understanding; because your mind is all in a mist; because you have no settled, consistent principles, but are for jumbling all opinions together. Be convinced that you have quite missed your way: you know not where you are. You think you are got into the 15 very spirit of Christ, when in truth you are nearer the spirit of antichrist. Go first and learn the first elements of the gospel of Christ, and then shall you learn to be of a truly catholic spirit.

2. From what has been said we may learn, secondly, that a catholic spirit is not any kind of *practical latitudinarianism.* It is not 20 indifference as to public worship or as to the outward manner of performing it. This likewise would not be a blessing but a curse. Far from being an help thereto it would, so long as it remained, be an unspeakable hindrance to the worshipping of God in spirit and in truth.[78] But the man of a truly catholic spirit, having weighed all 25 things in the balance of the sanctuary,[79] has no doubt, no scruple at all concerning that particular mode of worship wherein he joins. He is clearly convinced that *this* manner of worshipping God is both scriptural and rational. He knows none in the world which is more scriptural, none which is more rational. Therefore 30 without rambling hither and thither he cleaves close thereto, and praises God for the opportunity of so doing.

3. Hence we may, thirdly, learn that a catholic spirit is not indifference to all congregations. This is another sort of latitudinarianism, no less absurd and unscriptural than the 35 former. But it is far from a man of a truly catholic spirit. He is

---

[76] Cf. Eph. 4:14: an ironic reference to Elijah's challenge to the Israelites but not in the 'catholic spirit' here advocated.
[77] See 1 Kgs. 18:21.
[78] See John 4:23-24.
[79] Cf. No. 10, 'The Witness of the Spirit, I', II.8 and n.

fixed in his congregation as well as his principles. He is united to one, not only in spirit, but by all the outward ties of Christian fellowship. There he partakes of all the ordinances of God. There he receives the Supper of the Lord. There he pours out his soul in
5 public prayer, and joins in public praise and thanksgiving. There he rejoices to hear the word of reconciliation,[80] the gospel of the grace of God. With these his nearest, his best beloved brethren, on solemn occasions he seeks God by fasting. These particularly he watches over in love, as they do over his soul, admonishing,
10 exhorting, comforting, reproving, and every way building up each other in the faith. These he regards as his own household, and therefore according to the ability God has given him naturally cares for them, and provides that they may have all the things that are needful for life and godliness.
15   4. But while he is steadily fixed in his religious principles, in what he believes to be the truth as it is in Jesus; while he firmly adheres to that worship of God which he judges to be most acceptable in his sight; and while he is united by the tenderest and closest ties to one particular congregation; his heart is enlarged
20 toward all mankind, those he knows and those he does not; he embraces with strong and cordial affection neighbours and strangers, friends and enemies. This is catholic or universal love. And he that has this is of a catholic spirit. For love alone gives the title to this character—catholic love is a catholic spirit.
25   5. If then we take this word in the strictest sense, a man of a catholic spirit is one who in the manner above mentioned 'gives his hand' to all whose 'hearts are right with his heart'. One who knows how to value and praise God for all the advantages he enjoys: with regard to the knowledge of the things of God, the
30 true, scriptural manner of worshipping him; and above all his union with a congregation fearing God and working righteousness.[81] One who, retaining these blessings with the strictest care, keeping them as the apple of his eye, at the same time loves as friends, as brethren in the Lord, as members of Christ and
35 children of God, as joint partakers now of the present kingdom of God, and fellow-heirs of his eternal Kingdom, all of whatever opinion or worship or congregation who believe in the Lord Jesus Christ; who love God and man; who, rejoicing to please and

[80] 2 Cor. 5:19.
[81] See Acts 10:35.

fearing to offend God, are careful to abstain from evil and zealous of good works.[82] He is the man of a truly catholic spirit who bears all these continually upon his heart, who having an unspeakable tenderness for their persons, and longing for their welfare, does not cease to commend them to God in prayer, as well as to plead 5 their cause before men; who speaks comfortably to them,[83] and labours by all his words to strengthen their hands in God. He assists them to the uttermost of his power in all things, spiritual and temporal. He is ready 'to spend and be spent for them';[84] yea, 'to lay down his life for'[85] their sake. 10

6. Thou, O man of God, think on these things. If thou art already in this way, go on. If thou hast heretofore mistook the path, bless God who hath brought thee back. And now run the race which is set before thee,[86] in the royal way of universal love. Take heed lest thou be either wavering in thy judgment or 15 straitened in thy bowels.[87] But keep an even pace, rooted in the faith once delivered to the saints[88] and grounded in love,[89] in true, catholic love, till thou art swallowed up in love for ever and ever.[90]

---

[82] Titus 2:14.
[83] See 2 Chron. 32:6.
[84] Cf. 2 Cor. 12:15.
[85] Cf. John 13:37.
[86] See Heb. 12:1.
[87] See 2 Cor. 6:12.
[88] Jude 3.
[89] See Eph. 3:17.
[90] The three edns. of 'Catholic Spirit' as a separate sermon append the poem 'Catholic Love', by Charles Wesley (*Poet. Wks.*, VI.71-72).

Chriſtian Perfection:

A

SERMON,

Preached by

JOHN WESLEY, M. A.
Fellow of *Lincoln-College, Oxford.*

LONDON:

Printed by W. STRAHAN, and ſold by THO-
MAS HARRIS, at the *Looking Glaſs* and *Bible,* on *London-Bridge,* and at the *Foundery,*
near *Upper Moorfields.* MDCCXLI.

[Price Sixpence.]

CHRISTIAN PERFECTION

AN INTRODUCTORY COMMENT

If, for Wesley, salvation was the total restoration of the deformed image of God in us, and if its fullness was the recovery of our negative power not to sin and our positive power to love God supremely, this denotes that furthest reach of grace and its triumphs in this life that Wesley chose to call 'Christian Perfection'. Just as justification and regeneration are thresholds for the Christian life in earnest ('what God does for *us'), so also sanctification is 'what God does* in *us', to mature and fulfil the human potential according to his primal design. Few Christians had ever denied some such prospect,* in statu gloriae; *few, in the West at least, had ever envisioned it as a realistic possibility* in this life. *Those few were obscure exceptions like Robert Gell and Thomas Drayton—or William Law in a very different sense. Thus, Wesley's encouragement to his people to 'go on to perfection' and to* 'expect *to be made perfect in love in this life' aroused lively fears that this would foster more of the self-righteous perfection*ism *already made objectionable by earlier pietists.*

Obviously, this fear was in the background of an unofficial hearing granted Wesley by Bishop Edmund Gibson at Whitehall in the latter end of the year 1740 (cf. Wesley's version of the hearing in his Plain Account of Christian Perfection as believed and taught by the Rev. Mr. John Wesley, from the year 1725 to the year 1765, *§12; note its omission from the Journal—and other discrepancies between the historical data in the* Plain Account . . . *and other sources). The bishop felt entitled to a direct account of Wesley's teaching, since the Methodist movement was headquartered in his diocese, even if not within his jurisdiction. Wesley's response was candid: 'I told him, without any disguise or reserve ['what I meant by perfection']. When I ceased speaking, he said, "Mr. Wesley, if this be all you mean, publish it to all the world. If anyone then can confute what you say, he may have free leave." I answered, "My Lord, I will," and accordingly wrote and published the sermon on* Christian Perfection.' *The sermon's title page indicates that it had been 'preached by John Wesley, M.A., Fellow of Lincoln College, Oxford' in 1741 (or earlier). There is, however, no* *other record of the place or occasion of its being preached and no other record of Wesley's use of Phil. 3:12, except as the motto of* The Character of a Methodist, *which Wesley dates (in* A Plain Account . . . ,§*10) as in 1739; the extant first edition is dated 1742. This 1741 sermon is the one that Wesley chooses to place here, out of sequence but with a clear logic, as the crown of* SOSO, *III (1750).*

Wesley's doctrinal position on this point had, of course, been staked out long before, in 'The Circumcision of the Heart' (1733), in which he had described the goal of Christian living as 'the being so "renewed in the image of our mind" as to be "perfect as our Father in heaven is perfect" '. Thereafter, he stoutly maintained that he had never wavered from that first baseline nor ever had encountered serious difficulty in harmonizing 'Christian perfection' with his later emphases on 'faith alone' and 'assurance'. In A Plain Account . . . *he recalls that 'the first tract I ever wrote expressly on [perfection]' was* The Character of a Methodist; *in it, the label 'Methodist' is used provocatively as the idealized equivalent of 'perfect Christian'; the paradigm for both is taken from Clement of Alexandria's description of the perfect Christian in his* Stromateis, *VII.*

In 1741 (as Wesley continues, in A Plain Account . . . , §*13), he and his brother published 'a second volume of hymns', in the preface of which John came as close as he ever would to an unnuanced claim for sinless perfection—'freedom from* all *self-will and even "wandering thoughts" '. It was so close in fact that soon afterwards he felt obliged to qualify such a claim. Even so, the critical reaction was less against his particular formulations than the bare idea itself—*'there is no perfection on earth!' *Wesley found this all the more disconcerting since he was confident that he and his brother 'were clear on justification by faith, and careful to ascribe the* whole *of salvation to the mere grace of God' (§11).*

Protestants, convinced of the simul justus et peccator—*and used to translating* perfectio *as some sort of perfected perfection—were bound to see in the Wesleyan doctrine, despite all its formal disclaimers, a bald advertisement of spiritual pride and, implicitly, works-righteousness. Even the Methodists, working from their own unexamined Latin traditions of forensic righteousness, tended to interpret 'perfection' in terms of a spiritual elitism—and so misunderstood Wesley and the early Eastern traditions of* τελειότης *as a never ending aspiration for all of love's fullness (perfecting perfection). Thus, 'Christian Perfection' came to be the most distinctive and also the most widely misunderstood of all Wesley's doctrines. He continued to teach it, however, in season and out, as the farthest horizon of his vision of Christian existence, an idea with radical implications for personal ethics and for social transformation as well. First and last, it is his doctrine of grace carried to its climax—'grace abounding'. It is, also, a doctrine of 'double justification' by God's pardoning and reconciling grace; the 'relative change' in No. 43,* The Scripture Way of Salvation, *I.4, and also the 'real change' (ibid.) which involves the believer in an actual and lively participation in God's own loving business in creation.*

The text here is based on the first edition of 1741, collated against the six other editions issued during Wesley's lifetime. For a stemma illustrating its publishing history and a list of variant readings, see Appendix, Vol. 4; see also Bibliog, *No. 53.*

Christian Perfection

Philippians 3:12

Not as though I had already attained,
either were already perfect.

1. There is scarce any expression in Holy Writ which has given   5
more offence than this. The word 'perfect' is what many cannot
bear. The very sound of it is an abomination to them. And
whosoever 'preaches perfection' (as the phrase is),[1] i.e. asserts
that it is attainable in this life, runs great hazard of being
accounted by them worse than a heathen man or a publican.   10
2. And hence some have advised, wholly to lay aside the use of
those expressions, 'because they have given so great offence'. But
are they not found in the oracles of God? If so, by what authority
can any messenger of God lay them aside, even though all men

---

[1] E.g., Robert Gell in his *Essay Towards the Amendment of the Last English Translation of the Bible* (1659), where his Sermon 20 is entitled, 'Some Saints Without Sin for a Season'. On p. 797, Gell cites Dr. Thomas Drayton and Mr. William Parker as having 'preached perfection' and as having defended it in *A Revindication of the Possibility of a Total Mortification of Sin in this Life; and of the Saints' Perfect Obedience to the Law of God, to be the Orthodox Protestant Doctrine* (1658). On pp. 797–804 Gell sets out a catena of Scripture texts that *'prove* a possibility of ἀναμαρτησία—the having of no sin . . . according to the will of God'. This leads to his triumphant conclusion, based on 2 Tim. 3:16-17, 'That the man of God may be *perfect,* throughly furnished to every good work . . .'.

should be offended?² We have not so learned Christ;³ neither may
we thus give place to the devil.⁴ Whatsoever God hath spoken,
that will we speak, whether men will hear or whether they will
forbear:⁵ knowing that then alone can any minister of Christ be
5 'pure from the blood of all men', when he hath 'not shunned to
declare unto them all the counsel of God'.⁶

3. We may not therefore lay these expressions aside, seeing
they are the words of God, and not of man.⁷ But we may and ought
to explain the meaning of them, that those who are sincere of
10 heart may not err to the right hand or to the left from the mark of
the prize of their high calling.⁸ And this is the more needful to be
done because in the verse already repeated the Apostle speaks of
himself as not perfect: 'Not', saith he, 'as though I were already
perfect.'⁹ And yet immediately after, in the fifteenth verse, he
15 speaks of himself, yea and many others, as perfect. 'Let us', saith
he, 'as many as be perfect, be thus minded.'

4. In order therefore to remove the difficulty arising from this
seeming contradiction, as well as to give light to them who are
pressing forward to the mark, and that those who are lame be not
20 turned out of the way,¹⁰ I shall endeavour to show,

First, in what sense Christians are *not,* and

Secondly, in what sense they *are,* perfect.

I. 1. In the first place I shall endeavour to show in what sense
Christians are *not perfect.* And both from experience and
25 Scripture it appears, first, that they are not perfect in knowledge:
they are not *so* perfect in this life as to be free from ignorance.
They know, it may be, in common with other men, many things
relating to the present world; and they know, with regard to the
world to come, the general truths which God hath revealed. They
30 know likewise (what 'the natural man receiveth not', for these
things 'are spiritually discerned')¹¹ 'what manner of love it is
wherewith the Father hath loved them, that they should be called
the sons of God'.¹² They know 'the mighty working of his Spirit'¹³
in their hearts, and the wisdom of his providence directing all

---

² See Matt. 26:33.   ³ See Eph. 4:20.
⁴ See Eph. 4:27.   ⁵ See Ezek. 2:5, 7; 3:11.
⁶ Acts 20:26-27.   ⁷ See 1 Thess. 2:13.
⁸ See Phil. 3:14.   ⁹ Phil. 3:12.
¹⁰ See Heb. 12:13.
¹¹ Cf. 1 Cor. 2:14; cf. No. 10, 'The Witness of the Spirit, I', I.12 and n.
¹² Cf. 1 John 3:1.   ¹³ Cf. Eph. 1:19.

their paths, and causing all things to work together for their good.[14] Yea, they know in every circumstance of life what the Lord requireth of them, and how 'to keep a conscience void of offence both toward God and toward man'.[15]

2. But innumerable are the things which they know not. 'Touching the Almighty himself', 'they cannot search him out to perfection.'[16] 'Lo, these are but a part of his ways; but the thunder of his power who can understand?'[17] They cannot understand, I will not say, how 'there are three that bear record in heaven, the Father, the Son, and the Holy Spirit, and these three are one;'[18] or how the eternal Son of God 'took upon himself the form of a servant';[19] but not any one attribute, not any one circumstance of the divine nature. Neither is it for them 'to know the times and seasons'[20] when God will work his great works upon the earth; no, not even those which he hath in part revealed, by his servants the prophets, since the world began. Much less do they know when God, having 'accomplished the number of his elect, will hasten his kingdom';[21] when 'the heavens shall pass away with a great noise, and the elements shall melt with fervent heat.'[22]

3. They know not the reasons even of many of his present dispensations with the sons of men; but are constrained to rest here, though 'clouds and darkness are round about him, righteousness and judgment are the habitation of his seat.'[23] Yea, often with regard to his dealings with themselves doth their Lord say unto them, 'What I do, thou knowest not now; but thou shalt know hereafter.'[24] And how little do they know of what is ever before them, of even the visible works of his hands! How 'he spreadeth the north over the empty place, and hangeth the earth upon nothing.'[25] How he unites all the parts of this vast machine by a secret chain which cannot be broken. So great is the ignorance, so very little the knowledge of even the best of men.[26]

4. No one then is so perfect in this life as to be free from ignorance. Nor, secondly, from mistake, which indeed is almost an unavoidable consequence of it; seeing those who 'know but in

---

[14] See Rom. 8:28.
[15] Cf. Acts 24:16.
[16] Cf. Job 37:23.
[17] Cf. Job 26:14.
[18] Cf. 1 John 5:7; see below, No. 55, *On the Trinity*.
[19] Cf. Phil. 2:7.
[20] Cf. Acts 1:7.
[21] Cf. Mark 13:20.
[22] 2 Pet. 3:10.
[23] Ps. 97:2 (BCP).
[24] John 13:7.
[25] Cf. Job 26:7.
[26] See below, No. 69, 'The Imperfection of Human Knowledge'.

part'[27] are ever liable to err touching the things which they know not. 'Tis true the children of God do not mistake as to the things essential to salvation. They do not 'put darkness for light, or light for darkness',[28] neither 'seek death in the error of their life'.[29] For they are 'taught of God',[30] and the way which he teaches them, the way of holiness, is so plain that 'the wayfaring man, though a fool, need not err therein.'[31] But in things unessential to salvation they do err, and that frequently. The best and wisest of men are frequently mistaken even with regard to facts; believing those things not to have been which really were, or those to have been done which were not. Or suppose they are not mistaken as to the fact itself, they may be with regard to its circumstances; believing them, or many of them, to have been quite different from what in truth they were. And hence cannot but arise many farther mistakes. Hence they may believe either past or present actions which were or are evil to be good; and such as were or are good to be evil. Hence also they may judge not according to truth with regard to the characters of men; and that not only by supposing good men to be better, or wicked men to be worse, than they are, but by believing them to have been or to be good men who were or are very wicked; or perhaps those to have been or to be wicked men who were or are holy and unreprovable.

5. Nay, with regard to the Holy Scriptures themselves, as careful as they are to avoid it, the best of men are liable to mistake, and do mistake day by day; especially with respect to those parts thereof which less immediately relate to practice. Hence even the children of God are not agreed as to the interpretation of many places in Holy Writ; nor is their difference of opinion any proof that they are not the children of God on either side. But it is a proof that we are no more to expect any living man to be *infallible* than to be *omniscient*.

6. If it be objected to what has been observed under this and the preceding head that St. John speaking to his brethren in the faith says, 'Ye have an unction from the Holy One, and know all things,'[a] the answer is plain—'Ye know all things that are needful

---

[a] 1 John 2:20.

---

[27] Cf. 1 Cor. 13:9, 12.
[28] Cf. Isa. 5:20.
[29] Wisd. 1:12. Cf. No. 6, 'The Righteousness of Faith', §2 and n.
[30] John 6:45; 1 Thess. 4:9.   [31] Cf. Isa. 35:8.

for your soul's health.' That the Apostle never designed to extend this farther, that he could not speak it in an absolute sense, is clear first from hence: that otherwise he would describe the disciple as 'above his Master';[32] seeing Christ himself, as man, knew not all things. 'Of that hour', saith he, 'knoweth no man, no, not the Son, but the Father only.'[33] It is clear, secondly, from the Apostle's own words that follow: 'These things have I written unto you concerning them that deceive you,'[34] as well as from his frequently repeated caution, 'Let no man deceive you,'[35] which had been altogether needless had not those very persons who had that unction from the Holy One[36] been liable not to ignorance only but to mistake also.

7. Even Christians therefore are not *so* perfect as to be free either from ignorance or error. We may, thirdly, add: nor from infirmities. Only let us take care to understand this word aright. Let us not give that soft title to known sins, as the manner of some is. So, one man tells us, 'Every man has his infirmity, and mine is drunkenness.' Another has the infirmity of uncleanness; another of taking God's holy name in vain; and yet another has the infirmity of calling his brother, 'Thou fool ,'[37] or returning 'railing for railing'.[38] It is plain that all you who thus speak, if ye repent not, shall with your infirmities go quick into hell.[39] But I mean hereby not only those which are properly termed 'bodily infirmities', but all those inward or outward imperfections which are not of a moral nature. Such are weakness or slowness of understanding, dullness or confusedness of apprehension, incoherency of thought, irregular quickness or heaviness of imagination. Such (to mention no more of this kind) is the want of a ready or of a retentive memory. Such in another kind are those which are commonly in some measure consequent upon these: namely slowness of speech, impropriety of language, ungraceful-ness of pronunciation—to which one might add a thousand nameless defects either in conversation or behaviour. These are the infirmities which are found in the best of men in a larger or smaller proportion. And from these none can hope to be perfectly freed till the spirit returns to God that gave it.[40]

---

[32] Matt. 10:24.   [33] Cf. Matt. 24:36.
[34] Cf. 1 John 2:26.   [35] Eph. 5:6; 1 John 3:7.
[36] 1 John 2:20.   [37] Matt. 5:22.
[38] 1 Pet. 3:9.   [39] See Ps. 55:15 (AV).
[40] See Eccles. 12:7.

8. Nor can we expect till then to be wholly free from temptation. Such perfection belongeth not to this life. It is true, there are those who, being given up to work all uncleanness with greediness,[41] scarce perceive the temptations which they resist
5 not, and so seem to be without temptation. There are also many whom the wise enemy of souls, seeing [them] to be fast asleep in the dead form of godliness, will not tempt to gross sin, lest they should awake before they drop into everlasting burnings.[42] I know there are also children of God who, being now 'justified freely',
10 having found 'redemption in the blood of Christ',[43] for the present feel no temptation. God hath said to their enemies, 'Touch not mine anointed, and do my children no harm.'[44] And for this season, it may be for weeks or months, he causeth them to 'ride on high places';[45] he beareth them as on eagles' wings,[46] above all the
15 fiery darts of the wicked one.[47] But this state will not last always, as we may learn from that single consideration that the Son of God himself, in the days of his flesh, was tempted even to the end of his life. Therefore so let his servant expect to be; for 'it is enough that he be as his Master.'[48]

20   9. Christian perfection therefore does not imply (as some men seem to have imagined) an exemption either from ignorance or mistake, or infirmities or temptations. Indeed, it is only another term for holiness. They are two names for the same thing. Thus everyone that is perfect is holy, and everyone that is holy is, in the
25 Scripture sense, perfect. Yet we may, lastly, observe that neither in this respect is there any absolute perfection on earth. There is no 'perfection of degrees',[49] as it is termed; none which does not admit of a continual increase. So that how much soever any man hath attained, or in how high a degree soever he is perfect, he hath

---

[41] Eph. 4:19.   [42] Isa. 33:14.   [43] Cf. Rom. 3:24.
[44] Cf. 1 Chron. 16:22; Ps. 105:15.   [45] Cf. Deut. 32:13.
[46] See Exod. 19:4.   [47] Eph. 6:16.   [48] Matt. 10:25.
[49] For the notion that in the ladder of perfections there is an unsurpassable top rung, cf. Thomas Drayton, *The Proviso, or Condition of the Promises* (1657), where he distinguishes between the 'manifold perfection' attributed by the Papists to their 'saints', the perfection of *parts* (some partial perfection in this respect or that) and 'the *perfection of degrees*, when holiness in a full degree is attained by us . . .' (p. 37). 'This is threefold: the first is of love to God above all and to our neighbour as ourselves. . . . The second is . . . when the saints are wholly dead with [Christ] to sin. The third is *perfectio patriae* . . . with Christ after his ascension and glorification . . .' (p. 38). Wesley opts for a perfection of love, to God and neighbour, and quietly ignores the other two. But note that, on p. 46, Drayton affirms that 'the work which God hath given us to do must be perfected and finished *in this life*'. Cf. also No. 83, 'On Patience', §10; and Wesley's letter to William Dodd, Mar. 12, 1756.

still need to 'grow in grace',[50] and daily to advance in the knowledge and love of God his Saviour.

II. 1. In what sense then are Christians perfect? This is what I shall endeavour, in the second place, to show. But it should be premised that there are several stages in Christian life as well as in natural: some of the children of God being but new-born babes, others having attained to more maturity. And accordingly St. John, in his first Epistle,[b] applies himself severally to those he terms little children, those he styles young men, and those whom he entitles fathers.[51] 'I write unto you, little children', saith the Apostle, 'because your sins are forgiven you;' because thus far ye have attained, being 'justified freely',[52] you 'have peace with God, through Jesus Christ'.[53] 'I write unto you, young men, because ye have overcome the wicked one;' or (as he afterwards adds) 'because ye are strong, and the word of God abideth in you.' Ye have quenched the fiery darts of the wicked one,[54] the doubts and fears wherewith he disturbed your first peace, and the witness of God that your sins are forgiven now 'abideth in your heart'.[55] 'I write unto you, fathers, because ye have known him that is from the beginning.' Ye have known both the Father and the Son and the Spirit of Christ in your inmost soul. Ye are 'perfect men, being grown up to the measure of the stature of the fullness of Christ'.[56]

2. It is of these chiefly I speak in the latter part of this discourse; for these only are properly Christians.[57] But even babes in Christ[58] are in such a sense perfect, or 'born of God'[59] (an expression taken also in divers senses) as, first, not to commit sin.[60] If any doubt of this privilege of the sons of God, the question is not to be decided by abstract reasonings, which may be drawn out into an endless length, and leave the point just as it was before. Neither is it to be determined by the experience of this or that particular person. Many may suppose they do not commit sin when they do, but this

---

[b] Chap. 2, ver. 12, etc.

---

[50] 2 Pet. 3:18.
[51] Cf. No. 13, *On Sin in Believers*, III.2 and n.
[52] Rom. 3:24.
[53] Rom. 5:1.
[54] Eph. 6:16.
[55] Cf. 1 John 2:14, 27.
[56] Cf. Eph. 4:13.
[57] Taken literally, this would mean that none but the perfect are 'proper Christians'. In 1750 and thereafter, Wesley altered this to read, 'these only are perfect Christians.'
[58] 1 Cor. 3:1.
[59] 1 John 3:9; 4:7.
[60] See No. 19, 'The Great Privilege of those that are Born of God'.

proves nothing either way. 'To the law and to the testimony'[61] we appeal. 'Let God be true, and every man a liar.'[62] By his Word will we abide, and that alone. Hereby we ought to be judged.

3. Now the Word of God plainly declares that even those who are justified, who are born again in the lowest sense, do not 'continue in sin'; that they cannot 'live any longer therein';[c] that they are 'planted together in the likeness of the death of Christ';[d] that their 'old man is crucified with him, the body of sin being destroyed, so that thenceforth they do not serve sin'; that 'being dead with Christ, they are freed from sin';[e] that they are 'dead unto sin', and 'alive unto God';[f] that 'sin hath not[63] dominion over them', who are 'not under the law, but under grace'; but that these, 'being made free from sin, are become the servants of righteousness'.[g]

4. The very least which can be implied in these words is that the persons spoken of therein, namely all real Christians or believers in Christ, are made free from outward sin.[64] And the same freedom which St. Paul here expresses in such variety of phrases St. Peter expresses in that one: 'He that hath suffered in the flesh hath ceased from sin; that he no longer should live . . . to the desires of men, but to the will of God.'[h] For this 'ceasing from sin', if it be interpreted in the lowest sense, as regarding only the outward behaviour, must denote the ceasing from the outward act, from any outward transgression of the law.

5. But most express are the well-known words of St. John in the third chapter of his first Epistle (verse eight, etc.): 'He that committeth sin is of the devil; for the devil sinneth from the beginning. For this purpose the Son of God was manifested, that he might destroy the works of the devil. Whosoever is born of God doth not commit sin; for his seed remaineth in him, and he cannot sin, because he is born of God.'[65] And those in the fifth, verse eighteen: 'We know that whosoever is born of God sinneth

---

[c] Rom. 6:1,2.
[e] Ver. 6,7.
[g] Ver. 14, [15,]18.

[d] Ver. 5.
[f] Ver. 11.
[h] 1 Pet. 4:1-2.

[61] Isa. 8:20.
[62] Rom. 3:4.
[63] Altered from 1750 onwards to 'no more'.
[64] For this crucial distinction between *outward* sin and all other, cf. No. 13, *On Sin in Believers*, intro., III.1-9, and n.
[65] 1 John 3:8-9.

not. But he that is begotten of God keepeth himself, and that wicked one toucheth him not.'

6. Indeed it is said this means only, he sinneth not *wilfully;* or he doth not commit sin *habitually;* or, *not as other men do;* or, *not as he did before.* But by whom is this said? By St. John? No.[66] There is no such word in the text, nor in the whole chapter, nor in all this Epistle, nor in any part of his writings whatsoever. Why, then, the best way to answer a bold[67] assertion is simply to deny it. And if any man can prove it from the Word of God, let him bring forth his strong reasons.

7. And a sort of reason there is which has been frequently brought to support these strange assertions, drawn from the examples recorded in the Word of God: 'What!', say they, 'did not Abraham himself commit sin, prevaricating and denying his wife? Did not Moses commit sin when he provoked God "at the waters of strife"?[68] Nay, to produce one for all, did not even David, "the man after God's own heart",[69] commit sin in the matter of Uriah the Hittite, even murder and adultery?' It is most sure he did. All this is true. But what is it you would infer from hence? It may be granted, first, that David, in the general course of his life, was one of the holiest men among the Jews. And, secondly, that the holiest men among the Jews *did sometimes commit sin.* But if you would hence infer that *all Christians do, and must commit sin, as long as they live,* this consequence we utterly deny. It will never follow from those premises.

8. Those who argue thus seem never to have considered that declaration of our Lord: 'Verily I say unto you, among them that are born of women there hath not risen a greater than John the Baptist. Notwithstanding, he that is least in the kingdom of heaven is greater than he.'[i] I fear indeed there are some who have imagined 'the kingdom of heaven' here to mean the kingdom of

---

[i] Matt. 11:11.

---

[66] A flat negative to comments like those of James Hervey and William Cudworth (see No. 18, 'The Marks of the New Birth', I.5 and n.). But notice Wesley's qualifications of the absolute in Nos. 14, *The Repentance of Believers,* I.20, II.3-4; 18, 'The Marks of the New Birth', I.4-5; 19, 'The Great Privilege of those that are Born of God', II.2; 13, *On Sin in Believers,* IV.1-3. The irony here is that Wesley is moved to denounce qualifications of the doctrine when made by others and then come up with some of his own as if oblivious to the discrepancies involved in any such argument.

[67] I.e., 'impudent'; note Johnson's definition of 'bold' as 'impudent'.

[68] Ps. 106:32. [69] Acts 13:22.

glory. As if the Son of God had just discovered to us that the least glorified saint in heaven is greater than any man upon earth! To mention this is sufficiently to refute it. There can therefore no doubt be made but 'the kingdom of heaven' here (as in the

5 following verse, where it is said to be 'taken by force')[70] or, 'the kingdom of God', as St. Luke expresses it, is that kingdom of God on earth whereunto all true believers in Christ, all real Christians, belong. In these words then our Lord declares two things. First, that before his coming in the flesh among all the children of men,

10 there had not been one greater than John the Baptist; whence it evidently follows that neither Abraham, David, nor any Jew was greater than John. Our Lord, secondly, declares that he which is least in the kingdom of God (in that kingdom which he came to set up on earth, and which 'the violent' now began 'to take by

15 force') is greater than he. The plain consequence is, the least of these who have now Christ for their King is greater than Abraham or David or any Jew ever was. None of them was ever greater than John. But the least of these is greater than he.[71] Not 'a greater prophet' (as some have interpreted the word), for this is palpably

20 false in fact, but greater in the grace of God and the knowledge of our Lord Jesus Christ. Therefore we cannot measure the privileges of real Christians by those formerly given to the Jews. 'Their ministration' (or dispensation) we allow 'was glorious'; but ours 'exceeds in glory'.[72] So that whosoever would bring down the

25 Christian dispensation to the Jewish standard, whosoever gleans up the examples of weakness recorded in the law and the prophets, and thence infers that they who have 'put on Christ'[73] are endued with no greater strength, doth 'greatly err, neither knowing the Scriptures nor the power of God'.[74]

30   9. 'But are there not assertions in Scripture which prove the same thing, if it cannot be inferred from those examples? Does not the Scripture say expressly, 'Even a just man sinneth seven

---

[70] Cf. Matt. 11:12.

[71] The previous three sentences are found only in the first separate edition of 1741 (p. 20) and the second of 1743 (p. 11). The passage was omitted from the first collected edition of 1750 (and henceforth), apparently because of a simple error of the compositor's eye slipping from one occurrence of 'is greater than he' to another five lines lower. It seems highly unlikely that Wesley himself deliberately omitted this logical extension of his argument.

[72] Cf. 2 Cor. 3:8-9.

[73] Gal. 3:27.

[74] Cf. Matt. 22:29.

times a day"?' I answer, No. The Scripture says no such thing. There is no such text in all the Bible. That which seems to be intended is the sixteenth verse of the twenty-fourth chapter of the Proverbs, the words of which are these: 'A just man falleth seven times, and riseth up again.'[75] But this is quite another thing. For, first, the words 'a day' are not in the text. So that if a just man falls seven times in his life it is as much as is affirmed here. Secondly, here is no mention of 'falling into sin' at all: what is here mentioned is 'falling into temporal affliction'. This plainly appears from the verse before, the words of which are these: 'Lay not wait, O wicked man, against the dwelling of the righteous; spoil not his resting place.' It follows, 'For a just man falleth seven times, and riseth up again: but the wicked shall fall into mischief.' As if he had said, 'God will deliver him out of his trouble. But when thou fallest, there shall be none to deliver thee.'

10. But, however, in other places, continue the objectors, Solomon does assert plainly, 'There is no man that sinneth not;'[j] yea, 'there is not a just man upon earth that doth good, and sinneth not.'[k] I answer: Without doubt, thus it was in the days of Solomon. Yea, thus it was from Adam to Moses, from Moses to Solomon, and from Solomon to Christ. There was *then* no man that sinned not. Even from the day that sin entered into the world there was not a just man upon earth that did good and sinned not, *until* the Son of God was manifested 'to take away our sins'.[76] It is unquestionably true that 'the heir, as long as he is a child, differeth nothing from a servant.'[77] And that 'even so' they (all the holy men of old who were under the Jewish dispensation) 'were', during that infant state of the church, 'in bondage under the elements of the world. But when the fullness of the time was

[j] 1 Kgs. 8:46; 2 Chron. 6:36.
[k] Eccles. 7:20.

---

[75] Cf. the Elizabethan 'Homily or an Information for Them That Take Offence at Certain Places in the Holy Scriptures', Pt. II, *Homilies*, p. 335. See also No. 9, 'The Spirit of Bondage and of Adoption', I.7 and n.

[76] 1 John 3:5. It was from this way of expressing the effect of Christ's atonement that Cudworth developed his notion of guiltless perfection (i.e., 'from the guilt of *all* our sins, past and future'); cf. his *Dialogue*, p. 11. See also James Relly's *Union: Or a Treatise of the Consanguinity and Affinity Between Christ and His Church* (1759), p. 112, where the thesis is that those 'in Christ' are, on the ground of the 'consanguinity' with him, rendered 'sinless'. Wesley recoiled from this as antinomian; cf. his two *Dialogues Between an Antinomian and His Friend.* Cf. also No. 43, *The Scripture Way of Salvation*, III.11.

[77] Gal. 4:1.

come, God sent forth his Son, made under the law, to redeem
them that were under the law, that they might receive the
adoption of sons;'[78] that they might receive that 'grace which is
now made manifest by the appearing of our Saviour, Jesus Christ,
5 who hath abolished death, and brought life and immortality to
light through the gospel.'[1] Now therefore they 'are no more
servants, but sons'.[79] So that, whatsoever was the case of those
under the law, we may safely affirm with St. John that since the
gospel was given, 'He that is born of God sinneth not.'[80]

10 11. It is of great importance to observe, and that more carefully
than is commonly done, the wide difference there is between the
Jewish and the Christian dispensation, and that ground of it
which the same Apostle assigns in the seventh chapter of his
Gospel, verse thirty-eight, etc. After he had there related those
15 words of our blessed Lord, 'He that believeth on me, as the
Scripture hath said, out of his belly shall flow rivers of living
water,' he immediately subjoins, 'This spake he of the Spirit,' οὖ
ἔμελλον λαμβάνειν οἱ πιστεύοντες εἰς αὐτόν,[81] 'which they
who should believe on him were afterwards to receive. For the
20 Holy Ghost was not yet given, because that Jesus was not yet
glorified.'[82] Now the Apostle cannot mean here (as some have
taught) that the miracle-working power of the Holy Ghost was
not yet given. For this was given: our Lord had given it to all his
apostles when he first sent them forth to preach the gospel. He
25 then gave them 'power over unclean spirits to cast them out',
power to 'heal the sick', yea, to 'raise the dead'.[83] But the Holy
Ghost was not yet given in his sanctifying graces, as he was after
Jesus was glorified. It was then when 'he ascended up on high,
and led captivity captive', that he 'received those gifts for men,
30 yea, even for the rebellious, that the Lord God might dwell
among them.'[84] And 'when the day of Pentecost was fully come',[85]
then first it was that they who 'waited for the promise of the
Father'[86] were made more than conquerors over sin by the Holy
Ghost given unto them.

---

[1] 2 Tim. 1:10.

---

[78] Cf. Gal. 4:3-5.   [79] Cf. Gal. 4:7.   [80] 1 John 5:18.
[81] Thus *TR*; modern editors read πιστεύσαντες.
[82] Cf. John 7:38-39.   [83] Matt. 10:1, 8.
[84] Cf. Ps. 68:18.   [85] Acts 2:1.
[86] Cf. Acts 1:4.

12. That this great salvation from sin was not given till Jesus was glorified St. Peter also plainly testifies, where speaking of his 'brethren in the flesh'[87] as now 'receiving the end of their faith, the salvation of their souls', he adds: 'Of which salvation the prophets have inquired and searched diligently, who prophesied of the grace (i.e. the gracious dispensation) that should come unto you; searching what, or what manner of time, the Spirit of Christ which was in them did signify, when it testified beforehand the sufferings of Christ and the glory (the glorious salvation) that should follow. Unto whom it was revealed that not unto themselves, but unto us they did minister the things which are now reported unto you by them that have preached the gospel unto you with the Holy Ghost sent down from heaven' (viz., at the day of Pentecost, and so unto all generations, into the hearts of all true believers). On this ground, even 'the grace which was brought unto them by the revelation of Jesus Christ', the Apostle might well build that strong exhortation, 'Wherefore, girding up the loins of your mind, . . . as he which hath called you is holy, so be ye holy in all manner of conversation.'[m]

13. Those who have duly considered these things must allow that the privileges of Christians are in no wise to be measured by what the Old Testament records concerning those who were under the Jewish dispensation, seeing the fullness of times is now come, the Holy Ghost is now given, the great salvation of God is brought unto men by the revelation of Jesus Christ. The kingdom of heaven is now set up on earth; concerning which the Spirit of God declared of old (so far is David from being the pattern or standard of Christian perfection), 'He that is feeble among them at that day, shall be as David; and the house of David shall be as God, as the angel of the Lord before them.'[n]

14. If therefore you would prove that the Apostle's words, 'He that is born of God sinneth not,' are not to be understood according to their plain, natural, obvious meaning, it is from the New Testament you are to bring your proofs; else you will fight as one that beateth the air.[88] And the first of these which is usually brought is taken from the examples recorded in the New

[m] 1 Pet. 1:9,10, etc.
[n] Zech. 12:8.

---

[87] Cf. 1 Pet. 4:2, 6.   [88] See 1 Cor. 9:26.

Testament. 'The Apostles themselves (it is said) committed sin;
nay the greatest of them, Peter and Paul: St. Paul by his sharp
contention with Barnabas,[89] and St. Peter by his dissimulation at
Antioch.'[90] Well; suppose both Peter and Paul did then commit
5 sin. What is it you would infer from hence? That *all the other
apostles* committed sin sometimes? There is no shadow of proof in
this. Or would you thence infer that *all the other Christians* of the
apostolic age committed sin? Worse and worse. This is such an
inference as one would imagine a man in his senses could never
10 have thought of. Or will you argue thus?—'If two of the apostles
did once commit sin, then *all other Christians, in all ages,* do, and
will commit sin as long as they live.' Alas, my brother! a child of
common understanding would be ashamed of such reasoning as
this. Least of all can you with any colour of argument infer that
15 any man *must* commit sin at all. No; God forbid we should thus
speak. No necessity of sinning was laid upon *them.* The grace of
God was surely sufficient for them. And it *is* sufficient for *us* at
this day. With the temptation which fell on *them* that *was* a way to
escape, as there *is* to every soul of man in every temptation; so that
20 whosoever is tempted to any sin *need* not yield; for no man is
tempted above that he is able to bear.[91]

15. 'But St. Paul besought the Lord thrice, and yet he could not
escape from his temptation.' Let us consider his own words
literally translated: 'There was given to me a thorn, to the flesh,[92]
25 an angel or messenger of Satan, to buffet me. Touching this I
besought the Lord thrice, that it (or he)[93] might depart from me.
And he said unto me, My grace is sufficient for thee: for my
strength is made perfect in weakness. Most gladly therefore will I
rather glory in these my weaknesses, that the strength of Christ
30 may rest upon me. Therefore I take pleasure in weaknesses . . . ;
for when I am weak, then am I strong.'[94]

16. As this Scripture is one of the strongholds of the patrons of
sin, it may be proper to weigh it thoroughly. Let it be observed

---

[89] Acts 15:39. See also No. 19, 'The Great Privilege of those that are Born of God',
II.3-8.

[90] Cf. Gal. 2:11-14.   [91] See 1 Cor. 10:13.

[92] All edns. except that of 1787 retain this literal translation of the dative τῇ, as it stands
in the Greek of 2 Cor. 12:7; in 1787 this was changed to 'in the flesh'.

[93] This parenthetical phrase—there are no parentheses here in Wesley's text—is added
to the text of 1750 and subsequent edns., suggesting that Wesley had thought of 'Satan' as
a likely referent in the 'thorn' metaphor.

[94] Cf. *Notes* on 2 Cor. 12:7-10.

then, first, it does by no means appear that this thorn, whatsoever it was, occasioned St. Paul to commit sin, much less laid him under any necessity of doing so. Therefore from hence it can never be proved that any Christian *must* commit sin. Secondly, the ancient Fathers inform us it was bodily pain: 'a violent headache', saith Tertullian,° to which both Chrysostom and St. Jerome agree. St. Cyprian expresses it a little more generally, in those terms, 'many and grievous torments of the flesh and of the body'.ᵖ Thirdly, to this exactly agree the Apostle's own words, 'A thorn to the flesh to smite, beat, or buffet me. . . . My strength is made perfect in weakness'⁹⁵—which same word occurs no less than four times in these two verses only.⁹⁶ But, fourthly, whatsoever it was, it could not be either inward or outward sin. It could no more be inward stirrings than outward expressions of pride, anger, or lust. This is manifest beyond all possible exception from the words that immediately follow: 'Most gladly will I glory in these my weaknesses, that the strength of Christ rested upon me.' What! Did he glory in pride, in anger, in lust? Was it through these 'weaknesses' that the strength of Christ rested upon him? He goes on: 'Therefore I take pleasure in weaknesses; for when I am weak, then am I strong;'⁹⁷ i.e. when I am weak *in body*, then am I strong *in spirit*. But will any man dare to say, When I am weak by pride or lust, then am I strong in spirit? I call you all to record this day, who find the strength of Christ resting upon you, can *you* glory in anger, or pride, or lust? Can *you* take pleasure in *these* infirmities? Do *these* weaknesses make you strong? Would you not leap into hell, were it possible, to escape them? Even by yourselves, then, judge whether the Apostle could

---

° *De Pudic* [*itia*, §13 ('Of Purity'); cf. *Ancient Christian Writers* (ed., J. Quasten *et. al.*), 28:88. What Tertullian actually said is '. . . *per dolorem, ut aiunt, auriculae vel capitis*' ('as they say, an earache or a headache'). Notice Tertullian's distinction between Paul's 'thorn' and the fate of blasphemers and incestuous persons who are 'deservedly delivered over completely into the possession of Satan himself and not just an angel of his'. Chrysostom understood 'the thorn' as a metaphor for all of Paul's various indignities suffered at the hands of 'public executions' (cf. *Letters to Olympias*, 2, in *NPNF*, I, IX.295). For Cyprian, see *Treatise* IX.9, in *A Library of Fathers* (1839), III.222-23].

ᵖ '*Carnis et corporis multa ac gravia tormenta*', *De Mortalitate* [*Of Mortality*. Wesley was using Dean Fell's famous Oxford edn. of 1682; cf. 1690 edn., p. 161; see also, Migne, *PL*, IV:613].

---

⁹⁵ Cf. 2 Cor. 12:7, 9.
⁹⁶ I.e., ἀσθενεία, which, with its cognates, appears four times in ver. 9-10.
⁹⁷ Cf. 2 Cor. 12:9-10.

glory and take pleasure in them! Let it be, lastly, observed, that this thorn was given to St. Paul 'above fourteen years'[98] before he wrote this Epistle, which itself was wrote several years before he finished his course. So that he had after this a long course to run,
5 many battles to fight, many victories to gain, and great increase to receive in all the gifts of God and the knowledge of Jesus Christ. Therefore from any spiritual weakness (if such it had been) which he *at that time* felt, we could by no means infer that he was never made strong, that Paul the aged, the father in Christ, still
10 laboured under the same weaknesses; that he was in no higher state till the day of his death. From all which it appears that this instance of St. Paul is quite foreign to the question, and does in no wise clash with the assertion of St. John, 'He that is born of God sinneth not.'

15 17. 'But does not St. James directly contradict this? His words are, "In many things we offend all."[q] And is not *offending* the same as *committing sin?*' In this place I allow it is. I allow *the persons here spoken of* did commit sin; yea, that they *all* committed *many* sins. But who are 'the persons here spoken of'? Why, those 'many
20 masters' or 'teachers'[99] whom God had not sent (probably the same 'vain men' who taught that 'faith without works'[100] which is so sharply reproved in the preceding chapter); not the Apostle himself, nor any real Christian. That in the word 'we' (used by a figure of speech common in all other as well as the inspired
25 writings) the Apostle could not possibly include himself or any other true believer appears evidently, first, from the use of the same word in the ninth verse: 'Therewith (saith he) bless *we* God and therewith curse *we* men. Out of the same mouth proceedeth blessing and cursing.'[101] True; but not out of the mouth of the
30 Apostle, nor of anyone who is in Christ a new creature.[102] Secondly, from the verse immediately preceding the text, and manifestly connected with it: 'My brethren, be not many masters (or teachers), knowing that *we* shall receive the greater condemnation: for in many things *we* offend all.'[103] 'We'! Who?

[q] Chap. 3, ver. 2.

---

[98] 2 Cor. 12:2.
[100] Cf. Jas. 2:20.
[101] Jas. 3:9-10.
[102] See 2 Cor. 5:17.
[103] Jas. 3:1-2.

[99] Cf. Jas. 3:1.

Not the apostles, not true believers; but they who know they should 'receive the greater condemnation'[104] because of those many offences. But this could not be spoke of the Apostle himself, or of any who trod in his steps, seeing 'there is no condemnation for them who walk not after the flesh, but after the Spirit.'[105] Nay, thirdly, the very verse itself proves that 'we offend all'[106] cannot be spoken either of all men, or of all Christians; for in it there immediately follows the mention of a man who 'offends not', as the 'we' first mentioned did; from whom therefore he is professedly contradistinguished, and pronounced 'a perfect man'.[107]

18. So clearly does St. James explain himself and fix the meaning of his own words. Yet, lest anyone should still remain in doubt, St. John, writing many years after St. James, puts the matter entirely out of dispute by the express declarations above recited. But here a fresh difficulty may arise. How shall we reconcile St. John with himself? In one place he declares, 'Whosoever is born of God doth not commit sin.'[108] And again, 'We know that he which is born of God sinneth not.'[109] And yet in another he saith, 'If we say that we have no sin, we deceive ourselves, and the truth is not in us.'[110] And again, 'If we say that we have not sinned we make him a liar, and his word is not in us.'[111]

19. As great a difficulty as this may at first appear, it vanishes away if we observe, first, that the tenth verse fixes the sense of the eighth: 'If we say we have no sin' in the former being explained by, 'If we say we have not sinned' in the latter verse.[112] Secondly, that the point under present consideration is not whether we *have or have not sinned heretofore*,[113] and neither of these verses asserts that we *do sin, or commit sin* now. Thirdly, that the ninth verse explains both the eighth and tenth: 'If we confess our sins, he is faithful and just to forgive us our sins, and to cleanse us from all unrighteousness.'[114] As if he had said, 'I have before affirmed, "The blood of Jesus Christ cleanseth us from all sin." But let no man say, I need it not; I have no sin to be cleansed from. If we say

---

104 Jas. 3:1.
106 Jas. 3:1.
108 1 John 3:9.
110 1 John 1:8.
112 1 John 1:8, 10.
114 1 John 1:9.

105 Cf. Rom. 8:1.
107 Jas. 3:2.
109 Cf. 1 John 5:18.
111 1 John 1:10.
113 See 2 Cor. 13:2.

"that we have no sin", "that we have not sinned", we deceive
ourselves, and make God a liar. But if we confess our sins, he is
faithful and just, not only to forgive our sins, but also to cleanse us
from all unrighteousness, that we may go and sin no more.'[115]

5   20. St. John therefore is well consistent with himself, as well as
with the other holy writers; as will yet more evidently appear if we
place all his assertions touching this matter in one view. He
declares, first, 'The blood of Jesus Christ cleanseth us from all
sin.' Secondly, 'No man can say I have not sinned, I have no sin to
10 be cleansed from.' Thirdly, 'But God is ready both to forgive our
past sins and to save us from them for the time to come.' Fourthly,
'These things I write unto you', saith the Apostle, 'that ye may not
sin: but if any man should sin', or 'have sinned' (as the word might
be rendered)[116] he need not continue in sin, seeing 'we have an
15 advocate with the Father, Jesus Christ the righteous.'[117] Thus far
all is clear. But lest any doubt should remain in a point of so vast
importance the Apostle resumes this subject in the third chapter,
and largely explains his own meaning. 'Little children', saith
he, 'let no man deceive you (as though I had given any
20 encouragement to those that continue in sin); 'he that doth
righteousness is righteous, even as he is righteous. He that
committeth sin is of the devil; for the devil sinneth from the
beginning. For this purpose the Son of God was manifested, that
he might destroy the works of the devil. Whosoever is born of
25 God doth not commit sin; for his seed remaineth in him, and he
cannot sin, because he is born of God. In this the children of God
are manifest, and the children of the devil.'[r] Here the point, which
till then might possibly have admitted of some doubt in weak
minds, is purposely settled by the last of the inspired writers, and
30 decided in the clearest manner. In conformity therefore both to
the doctrine of St. John, and to the whole tenor of the New
Testament, we fix this conclusion: 'A Christian is so far perfect as
not to commit sin.'

[r] [1 John 3,] ver. 7-10.

---

[115] Cf. John 5:14.
[116] A softening, in 1750, of the arbitrary dictum in the first two edns. which read, 'as the
word should rather be rendered'; cf. Wesley's *Notes* on 1 John 1:10: 'Yet still we are to
retain, even to our lives' end, a deep sense of our past sins. . . . "If we say we have not
sinned, we make [God] a liar," who saith, "All have sinned." '
[117] Cf. 1 John 2:1.

21. This is the glorious privilege of every Christian; yea, though he be but 'a babe in Christ'.[118] But it is only of those who 'are strong in the Lord',[119] and 'have overcome the wicked one', or rather of those who 'have known him that is from the beginning',[120] that it can be affirmed they are in such a sense 5 perfect as, secondly, to be freed from evil thoughts and evil tempers. First, from evil or sinful thoughts. But here let it be observed that thoughts concerning evil are not always evil thoughts; that a thought concerning sin and a sinful thought are widely different. A man, for instance, may think of a murder 10 which another has committed, and yet this is no evil or sinful thought. So our blessed Lord himself doubtless thought of or understood the thing spoken by the devil when he said, 'All this will I give thee if thou wilt fall down and worship me.'[121] Yet had he no evil or sinful thought, nor indeed was capable of having any. 15 And even hence it follows that neither have real Christians; for 'everyone that is perfect is as his master.'[s] Therefore, if he was free from evil or sinful thoughts, so are they likewise.

22. And indeed, whence should evil thoughts proceed in the servant who is 'as his master'? 'Out of the heart of man (if at all) 20 proceed evil thoughts.'[t] If therefore his heart be no longer evil, then evil thoughts can no longer proceed out of it. If the tree were corrupt, so would be the fruit. But the tree is good. The fruit therefore is good also.[u] Our Lord himself bearing witness: 'Every good tree bringeth forth good fruit. A good tree cannot bring 25 forth evil fruit, as a corrupt tree cannot bring forth good fruit.'[v]

23. The same happy privilege of real Christians St. Paul asserts from his own experience: 'The weapons of our warfare', saith he, 'are not carnal, but mighty through God to the pulling down of strongholds; casting down imaginations' (or 'reasonings' rather, 30 for so the word λογισμούς signifies: all the reasonings of pride and unbelief against the declarations, promises, or gifts of God) 'and every high thing that exalteth itself against the knowledge of

---

[s] [Cf.] Luke 6:40 [not τέλειος but κατηρτισμένος (i.e., 'expert' or 'fully equipped'); cf. below, II.24; see also Wesley's own translation in *Notes*, 'every (disciple) that is perfected shall be as his master'].

[t] Mark 7:21.　　　　　　　　　　　　　　　　　　[u] Matt. 12:33.

[v] Matt. 7:17-18.

---

[118] Cf. 1 Cor. 3:1.　　　　　　　　　　　　　　[119] Cf. Eph. 6:10.
[120] 1 John 2:13, 14.　　　　　　　　　　　　　　[121] Cf. Matt. 4:9.

God; and bringing into captivity every thought to the obedience of Christ.'[w]

24. And as Christians indeed are freed from evil thoughts, so are they, secondly, from evil tempers. This is evident from the above-mentioned declaration of our Lord himself: 'The disciple is not above his master; but everyone that is perfect shall be as his master.' He had been delivering just before some of the sublimest doctrines of Christianity, and some of the most grievous to flesh and blood: 'I say unto you, love your enemies, do good to them which hate you: and unto him that smiteth thee on the one cheek, offer also the other.'[122] Now these he well knew the world would not receive, and therefore immediately adds, 'Can the blind lead the blind? Will they not both fall into the ditch?'[123] As if he had said, 'Do not confer with flesh and blood[124] touching these things, with men void of spiritual discernment, the eyes of whose understanding God hath not opened,[125] lest they and you perish together.'[126] In the next verse he removes the two grand objections with which these wise fools[127] meet us at every turn: 'these things are too grievous to be borne,'[128] or, 'they are too high to be attained,'[129] saying, 'The disciple is not above his master.' Therefore if I have suffered be content to tread in my steps. And doubt ye not then but I will fulfil my word: 'For everyone that is perfect shall be as his master.' But his Master was free from all sinful tempers. So therefore is his disciple, even every real Christian.

25. Every one of these can say with St. Paul, 'I am crucified with Christ: nevertheless I live; yet not I, but Christ liveth in me'[130]—words that manifestly describe a deliverance from inward as well as from outward sin. This is expressed both negatively, 'I live not'—my evil nature, the body of sin, is destroyed—and positively, 'Christ liveth in me'—and therefore all that is holy, and just, and good. Indeed both these, 'Christ liveth in me,' and 'I live not,' are inseparably connected; for 'what communion hath light with darkness' or 'Christ with Belial?'[131]

---

[w] 2 Cor. 10:[4,] 5, etc.

---

[122] Luke 6:27, 29.
[124] See Gal. 1:16.
[126] See Job 34:15.
[128] Cf. Matt. 23:4.
[130] Gal. 2:20.

[123] Luke 6:39.
[125] See Eph. 1:18; 4:18.
[127] See Rom. 1:22.
[129] Cf. Ps. 139:6 (AV).
[131] 2 Cor. 6:14-15.

26. He therefore who liveth in true believers hath 'purified their hearts by faith'[132], insomuch that 'everyone that hath Christ in him, the hope of glory'[133], 'purifieth himself even as he is pure'[x]. He is purified from pride; for Christ was lowly of heart. He is pure from self-will or desire; for Christ desired only to do the will 5 of his Father, and to finish his work. And he is pure from anger, in the common sense of the word; for Christ was meek and gentle, patient and long-suffering. I say, 'in the common sense of the word'; for all anger is not evil. We read of our Lord himself that he once 'looked round with anger'.[y] But with what kind of anger? 10 The next word shows, συλλυπούμενος, being *at the same time* 'grieved for the hardness of their hearts'. So then he was *angry at the sin,* and in the same moment *grieved for the sinners;* angry or displeased *at the offence,* but sorry *for the offenders.* With anger, yea, hatred, he looked upon *the thing;* with grief and love upon the 15 *persons.* Go thou that art perfect, and do likewise.[134] 'Be thus angry, and *thou* sinnest not:'[135] feeling a displacency[136] at every offence against God, but only love and tender compassion to the offender.

27. Thus doth Jesus 'save his people from their sins':[137] and not 20 only from outward sins, but also from the sins of their hearts; from evil thoughts and from evil tempers. 'True', say some, 'we shall thus be saved from our sins, but not till death; not in this world.' But how are we to reconcile this with the express words of St. John? 'Herein is our love made perfect, that we may have 25 boldness in the day of judgment: because as he is, so are we *in this world.*'[z] The Apostle here beyond all contradiction speaks of himself and other living Christians, of whom (as though he had foreseen this very evasion, and set himself to overturn it from the

[x] 1 John 3:3.
[y] Mark 3:5.
[z] 1 John 4:17.

---

[132] Cf. Acts 15:9.
[133] Cf. Col. 1:27.
[134] See Luke 10:37.
[135] Cf. Eph. 4:26.
[136] 'Displacency' was a familiar eighteenth-century antonym to 'complacency' and is defined in Johnson's *Dictionary* as 'disgust'. But Johnson derives it from 'the Latin, *displicentia*', which throws light on the fact that the first four edns. of Wesley's text read 'displicency' here. This was altered in 1771 and 1787 to 'displacency', and is cited thus as an example in *OED.*
[137] Cf. Matt. 1:21.

foundation) he flatly affirms that not only at or after death but 'in this world' they are as their Master.

28. Exactly agreeable to this are his words in the first chapter of this Epistle: 'God is light, and in him is no darkness at all. If we
5 walk in the light, as he is in the light, we have fellowship one with another, and the blood of Jesus Christ his Son cleanseth us from all sin.' And again, 'If we confess our sins, he is faithful and just to forgive us our sins, and to cleanse us from all unrighteousness.'ªª Now it is evident the Apostle here ·also speaks of a deliverance
10 wrought 'in this world'. For he saith not, 'the blood of Christ will cleanse' (at the hour of death, or in the day of judgment) but it 'cleanseth (at the time present) us (living Christians) from all sin.' And it is equally evident that if *any sin* remain we are not cleansed from *all sin:* if *any* unrighteousness remain in the soul it is not
15 cleansed from *all* unrighteousness. Neither let any sinner against his own soul say that this relates to justification only, or the cleansing us from the guilt of sin. First, because this is confounding together what the Apostle clearly distinguishes, who mentions first, 'to forgive us our sins', and then 'to cleanse us
20 from all unrighteousness'.¹³⁸ Secondly, because this is asserting justification by works in the strongest sense possible. It is making all inward as well as outward holiness necessarily previous to justification. For if the cleansing here spoken of is no other than the cleansing us from the guilt of sin, then we are not cleansed
25 from guilt; i.e. are not justified, unless on condition of 'walking in the light, as he is in the light'.¹³⁹ It remains, then, that Christians are saved in this world from all sin, from all unrighteousness; that they are now in such a sense perfect as not to commit sin, and to be freed from evil thoughts and evil tempers.¹⁴⁰

30 29. Thus hath the Lord fulfilled the things he spake by his holy prophets, which have been since the world began:¹⁴¹ by Moses in particular, saying, 'I will circumcise thine heart, and the heart of thy seed, to love the Lord thy God with all thy heart, and with all thy soul;'ᵇᵇ by David, crying out, 'Create in me a clean

---

ªª Ver. [5,] 6, etc.
ᵇᵇ Deut. 30:6.

---

¹³⁸ 1 John 1:9.
¹³⁹ Cf. 1 John 1:7.
¹⁴⁰ See below, No. 41, *Wandering Thoughts*, II.2.
¹⁴¹ See Luke 1:70.

heart, and renew a right spirit within me;'[142] and most remarkably by Ezekiel, in those words: 'Then will I sprinke clean water upon you, and ye shall be clean; from all *your* filthiness, and from *all* your idols will I cleanse you. A new heart also will I give you, and a new spirit will I put within you, and cause you to walk in my 5 statutes, and ye shall keep my judgments, and do them. . . . Ye shall be my people, and I will be your God. I will also save you from all your uncleannesses. . . . Thus saith the Lord your God, In the day that I shall have cleansed you from all your iniquities . . . the heathen shall know that I the Lord build the ruined 10 places; . . . I the Lord have spoken it, . . . and I will do it.'[cc]

30. 'Having therefore these promises, dearly beloved', both in the law and in the prophets, and having the prophetic word confirmed unto us in the gospel by our blessed Lord and his apostles, 'let us cleanse ourselves from all filthiness of flesh and 15 spirit, perfecting holiness in the fear of God.'[143] 'Let us fear lest' so many promises 'being made us of entering into his rest' (which he that hath entered into 'is ceased from his own works') 'any of us should come short of it.'[144] 'This one thing let us do: forgetting those things which are behind, and reaching forth unto those 20 things which are before, let us press toward the mark for the prize of the high calling of God in Christ Jesus;'[145] crying unto him day and night till we also are 'delivered from the bondage of corruption into the glorious liberty of the sons of God.'[146]

[cc] Ezek. 36:25, etc.

---

[142] Ps. 51:10 (AV).

[143] 2 Cor. 7:1.

[144] Cf. Heb. 4:1, 10.

[145] Cf. Phil. 3:13-14.

[146] Cf. Rom. 8:21. This last division was a conscious rejection of the idea behind the slogan, *simul justus et peccator.* Cf. No. 46, 'The Wilderness State', II.6-8. Thus Wesley comes yet again, in II.21-28, to the verge of a doctrine of sinless perfection. Cf. also No. 13, *On Sin in Believers,* V.2 and n.

THE
PROMISE
OF
SANCTIFICATION

Ezekiel 36:25, etc.

By the Reverend Mr. Charles Wesley.

1. God of all power, and truth, and grace,
    Which shall from age to age endure;
    Whose word, when heaven and earth shall pass,
10   Remains, and stands for ever sure.

2. Calmly to thee my soul looks up,
    And waits thy promises to prove;
    The object of my stedfast hope,
    The seal of thine eternal love.

15 3. That I thy mercy may proclaim,
    That all mankind thy truth may see,
    Hallow thy great and glorious name,
    And perfect holiness in me.

4. Chose from the world if now I stand,
20   Adorned in righteousness divine,
    If brought unto the promised land
    I justly call the Saviour mine;

5. Perform the work thou hast begun,
    My inmost soul to thee convert:
25   Love me, for ever love thine own,
    And sprinkle with thy blood my heart.

6. Thy sanctifying Spirit pour
    To quench my thirst, and wash me clean;
    Now, Father, let the gracious shower
30   Descend, and make me pure from sin.

7. Purge me from every sinful blot;
    My idols all be cast aside:
    Cleanse me from every evil thought,
    From all the filth of self and pride.

35 8. Give me a new, a perfect heart,
    From doubt, and fear, and sorrow free;
    The mind which was in Christ impart,
    And let my spirit cleave to thee.

9. O take this heart of stone away,
40   (Thy rule it doth not, cannot own)
    In me no longer let it stay:
    O take away this heart of stone.

10. The hatred of my carnal mind
    Out of my flesh at once remove;
  Give me a tender heart, resigned,
    And pure, and filled with faith and love.

11. Within me thy good Spirit place,   5
    Spirit of health, and love and power;
  Plant in me thy victorious grace,
    And sin shall never enter more.

12. Cause me to walk in Christ my way,
    And I thy statutes shall fulfil;   10
  In every point thy law obey.
    And perfectly perform thy will.

13. Hast thou not said, who canst not lie,
    That I thy law shall keep and do?
  Lord, I believe, though men deny: 15
    They all are false; but thou art true.

14. O that I now, from sin released,
    Thy word might to the utmost prove!
  Enter into the promised rest,
    The Canaan of thy perfect love!   20

15. There let me ever, ever dwell;
    By thou my God, and I will be
  Thy servant: O set to thy seal;
    Give me eternal life in thee.

16. From all remaining filth within   25
    Let me in Thee salvation have:
  From actual, and from inbred sin
    My ransomed soul persist to save.

17. Wash out my old orig'nal stain:
    Tell me no more, It cannot be,   30
  Demons or men! The Lamb was slain,
    His blood was all poured out for me.

18. Sprinkle it, Jesus, on my heart!
    One drop of thy all-cleansing blood
  Shall make my sinfulness depart,   35
    And fill me with the life of God.

19. Father, supply my every need:
    Sustain the life thyself hast given;
  Call for the corn, the living bread,
    The manna that comes down from heaven.   40

20. The gracious fruits of rightcousness,
    Thy blessings' unexhausted store,
  In me abundantly increase;
    Nor let me ever hunger more.

21. Let me no more in deep complaint
    'My leanness, O my leanness!' cry,
    Alone consumed with pining want
    Of all my Father's children I!

22. The painful thirst, the fond desire
    Thy joyous presence shall remove,
    While my full soul doth still require
    Thy whole eternity of love.

23. Holy, and true, and righteous Lord,
    I wait to prove thy perfect will:
    Be mindful of thy gracious word,
    And stamp me with thy Spirit's seal.

24. Thy faithful mercies let me find
    In which thou causest me to trust;
    Give me the meek and lowly mind,
    And lay my spirit in the dust.

25. Show me how foul my heart hath been,
    When all renewed by grace I am;
    When thou hast emptied me of sin,
    Show me the fullness of my shame.

26. Open my faith's interior eye,
    Display thy glory from above;
    And all I am shall sink and die,
    Lost in astonishment and love.

27. Confound, o'erpower me with thy grace!
    I would be by myself abhorred,
    (All might, all majesty, all praise,
    All glory be to Christ my Lord!)

28. Now let me gain perfection's height!
    Now let me into nothing fall!
    Be less than nothing in thy sight,
    And feel that Christ is all in all![147]

---

[147] This poem was incorporated in the 1st edn. of 1741, omitted from the 2nd edn. of 1743 (which was compressed into 24 pages) and from the first two edns. of the collected *Sermons*, which may possibly have derived from the 1743 edn. It was restored by Wesley to his *Works* (1771), and also to the last edn. of *SOSO* (1787). It had already been reprinted in *Hymns and Sacred Poems* (1742), pp. 261–64.

WANDERING THOUGHTS

AN INTRODUCTORY COMMENT

In the conclusion of Christian Perfection *(II.28), Wesley had boldly stated 'that Christians are saved in this world from all sin', that 'they are now in such a sense perfect as not to commit sin and to be freed from evil thoughts and evil tempers.' Taken literally, this flew in the face of obvious experience and of Wesley's own previous qualifications. And, of course, it was taken literally, thus provoking easy misinterpretations which could not then be easily refuted. Wesley was more willing to qualify such overstatements than to acknowledge them as such, or to seem to contradict himself. Thus, at least as early as March 1757, he had begun to explain that 'wandering thoughts', properly understood, were not to be included in that class of sins that are properly so called. He did this again on November 30, 1760 (in Spitalfields) and January 1, 1761 (at the West Street Chapel). Professor Frank Baker has reviewed the complicated bibliographic evidence and finds no support for Sugden's conjecture of a published version of* Wandering Thoughts *as early as 1761; that comes a year later, printed in Bristol by Elizabeth Farley. It was also reprinted, line for line, in York in 1763. Also in 1763, a second edition of the separate sermon was printed (also in Bristol) by William Pine, who was printing an undated second edition of* SOSO, III, *with* Wandering Thoughts *quietly inserted after* Christian Perfection, *as an obvious addendum, and before 'Satan's Devices' (the original sequel to* Christian Perfection *in 1750). For further details of this publishing history, along with a list of variant readings in the twelve extant editions from Wesley's lifetime, see Appendix, Vol. 4.*

What this means, however, is that the prime function of Wandering Thoughts *was to deny what Wesley had never really intended to affirm, and to do this with a new sermon that was, in effect, an extended annotation of II.28 of* Christian Perfection. *It also means that* Wandering Thoughts *was probably contained in that edition of 'the four volumes of sermons' stipulated in the Model Deed of 1763 as a doctrinal standard for Methodist trustees and preachers. In any case the idea was clearly in Wesley's mind. The question of the sermon as 'a standard' is far less important, however, than its link with* On Sin in Believers *and* The Repentance of Believers *as a trio of needed qualifiers of* Christian Perfection—*of both the general idea and of the sermon of 1741.*

Wandering Thoughts

2 Corinthians 10:4

Bringing into captivity every thought to the obedience of Christ.

5   1. But will God so 'bring every thought into captivity to the obedience of Christ' that no wandering thought will find a place in the mind, even while we remain in the body? So some have vehemently maintained; yea, have affirmed that none are perfected in love unless they are so far perfected in understanding
10   that all wandering thoughts are done away; unless not only every affection and temper be holy, and just, and good,[1] but every individual thought which arises in the mind be wise and regular.
      2. This is a question of no small importance. For how many of those who fear God, yea, and love him, perhaps with all their
15   heart, have been greatly distressed on this account! How many, by not understanding it right, have not only been distressed, but greatly hurt in their souls! Cast into unprofitable, yea, mischievous reasonings, such as slackened their motion towards God, and weakened them in running the race set before them.[2]
20   Nay, many, through misapprehensions of this very thing, have cast away the precious gift of God. They have been induced first to doubt of, and then to deny, the work God had wrought in their souls; and hereby have grieved the Spirit of God,[3] till he withdrew and left them in utter darkness.
25   3. How is it, then, that amidst the abundance of books which have been lately published almost on all subjects, we should have

---

[1] See Rom. 7:12.
[2] See Heb. 12:1.   [3] See Eph. 4:30.

none upon 'wandering thoughts'?[4] At least none that will at all satisfy a calm and serious mind? In order to do this in some degree I purpose to inquire,

    I.   What are the several sorts of wandering thoughts?
    II.   What are the general occasions of them?
    III. Which of them are sinful, and which not?
    IV. Which of them we may expect and pray to be delivered from?

I. 1. I purpose to inquire, first, What are the several sorts of wandering thoughts? The particular sorts are innumerable; but in general they are of two sorts—thoughts that wander from God, and thoughts that wander from the particular point we have in hand.

2. With regard to the former, all our thoughts are naturally of this kind. For they are continually wandering from God: we think nothing about him. God is not in all our thoughts: we are one and all, as the Apostle observes, 'without God in the world'.[5] We think of what we love; but we do not love God; therefore we think not of him. Or if we are now and then constrained to think of him for a time, yet as we have no pleasure therein, nay, rather, as these thoughts are not only insipid, but distasteful and irksome to us, we drive them out as soon as we can, and return to what we love to think of. So that the world and the things of the world— what we shall eat, what we shall drink, what we shall put on,[6] what we shall see, what we shall hear, what we shall gain, how we shall please our senses or our imagination—takes up all our time, and engrosses all our thoughts. So long therefore as we love the world, that is, so long as we are in our natural state, all our thoughts from morning to evening, and from evening to morning, are no other than wandering thoughts.

3. But many times we are not only 'without God in the world', but also 'fighting against him',[7] as there is in every man by nature 'a carnal mind which is enmity against God'.[8] No wonder, therefore, that men abound with *unbelieving* thoughts, either saying in their hearts, There is no God,[9] or questioning, if not

---

[4] This sense of 'wandering thoughts' as meaning 'random' or 'undirected by reason' is cited by *OED* from as early as the fifteenth century.
[5] Eph. 2:12.   [6] See Matt. 6:25.
[7] Cf. Acts 5:39.   [8] Cf. Rom. 8:7.
[9] Ps. 14:1.

denying, his power or wisdom, his mercy, or justice, or holiness.
No wonder that they so often doubt of his providence, at least of
its extending to all events; or that, even though they allow it, they
still entertain *murmuring* or *repining* thoughts. Nearly related to
5 these, and frequently connected with them, are *proud* and *vain*
imaginations.[10] Again: sometimes they are taken up with *angry,
malicious,* or *revengeful* thoughts; at other times with airy scenes of
pleasure, whether of sense or imagination; whereby the earthy
sensual mind becomes more *earthy* and *sensual* still. Now by all
10 these they make flat war with God; these are wandering thoughts
of the highest kind.

4. Widely different from these are the other sort of wandering
thoughts, in which the heart does not wander from God, but the
understanding wanders from the particular point it had then in
15 view. For instance: I sit down to consider those words in the verse
preceding the text, 'The weapons of our warfare are not carnal,
but mighty through God.'[11] I think, 'This ought to be the case with
all that are called Christians. But how far is it otherwise! Look
round into almost every part of what is termed the Christian
20 world! What manner of weapons are these using? In what kind of
warfare are they engaged,

> While men, like fiends, each other tear
> In all the hellish rage of war?[12]

See how *these* Christians love one another.[13] Wherein are they
25 preferable to Turks and pagans? What abomination can be found
among Mahometans or heathens which is not found among
Christians also?' And thus my mind runs off, before I am aware,
from one circumstance to another. Now all these are in some
sense wandering thoughts; for although they do not wander from
30 God, much less fight against him, yet they do wander from the
particular point I had in view.

II. Such is the nature, such are the sorts (to speak rather
usefully than philosophically) of wandering thoughts. But what

[10] A conflation of Luke 1:51 and Rom. 1:21.   [11] 2 Cor. 10:4.
[12] A couplet from Charles Wesley's 'For Peace', in *Hymns of Intercession for All Mankind* (1758), p. 4 (*Poet Wks.*, VI.112). In 1758 Britain was in the midst of what came to be called 'The Seven Years' War' (1756–63); cf. Basil Williams, *The Whig Supremacy, 1714–1760*, pp. 330-50. It was a sort of world war involving most of Europe, together with India and Canada.
[13] Cf. No. 22, 'Sermon on the Mount, II', III.8 and n.

are the general occasions of them? This we are in the second place to consider.

1. And it is easy to observe that the occasion of the former sort of thoughts which oppose or wander from God are, in general, sinful tempers. For instance: why 'is not God in all the thoughts',[14] in any of the thoughts, of a natural man? For a plain reason: be he rich or poor, learned or unlearned, he is an atheist (though not vulgarly so called)—he neither knows nor loves God. Why are his thoughts continually wandering after the world? Because he is an idolater. He does not indeed worship an image, or bow down to the stock of a tree; yet is he sunk into equally damnable idolatry: he loves, that is, worships the world. He seeks happiness in the things that are seen, in the pleasures that perish in the using. Why is it that his thoughts are perpetually wandering from the very end of his being, the knowledge of God in Christ? Because he is an unbeliever; because he has no faith, or at least no more than a devil.[15] So all these wandering thoughts easily and naturally spring from that evil root of unbelief.

2. The case is the same in other instances: pride, anger, revenge, vanity, lust, covetousness—every one of them occasion[s] thoughts suitable to their own nature. And so does every sinful temper of which the human kind is capable. The particulars it is hardly possible, nor is it needful, to enumerate. It suffices to observe that as many evil tempers[16] as find a place in any soul, so many ways that soul will depart from God, by the worst kind of wandering thoughts.

3. The occasions of the latter kind of wandering thoughts are exceeding various. Multitudes of them are occasioned by the natural union between the soul and body. How immediately and how deeply is the understanding affected by a diseased body! Let but the blood move irregularly in the brain, and all regular thinking is at an end. Raging madness ensues, and then farewell to all evenness of thought. Yea, let only the spirits be hurried or agitated to a certain degree, and a temporary madness, a delirium, prevents all settled thought. And is not the same irregularity of thought in a measure occasioned by every nervous disorder?[17] So

[14] Cf. Ps. 10:4.
[15] See Jas. 2:19.
[16] Cf. No. 40, *Christian Perfection*, II.28.
[17] Note the presupposed psychophysical parallelism here; see below, III.4 and n.

does 'the corruptible body press down the soul, and cause it to muse about many things'.[18]

4. But does it only cause this in the time of sickness or preternatural disorder? Nay, but more or less at all times, even in a state of perfect health. Let a man be ever so healthy, he will be more or less delirious every four and twenty hours. For does he not sleep? And while he sleeps is he not liable to dream? And who then is master of his own thoughts, or able to preserve the order and consistency of them? Who can then keep them fixed to any one point, or prevent their wandering from pole to pole?[19]

5. But suppose we are awake, are we always so awake that we can steadily govern our thoughts? Are we not unavoidably exposed to contrary extremes by the very nature of this machine, the body? Sometimes we are too heavy, too dull and languid, to pursue any chain of thought. Sometimes, on the other hand, we are too lively. The imagination, without leave, starts to and fro, and carries us away, hither and thither, whether we will or no; and all this from the merely natural motion of the spirits, or vibration of the nerves.[20]

6. Farther: how many wanderings of thought may arise from those various associations of our ideas[21] which are made entirely

[18] Cf. Wisd. 9:15; see also IV.4, below. Note how casually Wesley resorts to an apocryphal text; the line between canonical and apocryphal Scripture is by no means absolute. Actually, the Wisdom of Solomon is his favourite apocryphal writing, and he quotes 9:15 at least eight other times in his sermons over sixty years, from 1730 (No. 141, 'The Image of God', II.1) to 1790 (No. 129, 'Heavenly Treasure in Earthen Vessels', II.1, 3); there are also frequent references in his letters. For an Anglican bishop's views on the Christian use of 'Wisdom literature', cf. John Wilkins, *Sermons* (2nd edn., 1680), and his *Ecclesiastes* (1679).

[19] Cf. Nos. 93, 'On Redeeming the Time', *passim.;* and 24, 'Human Life a Dream', §4 and n. Wesley, like Law before him, regarded sleep as a begrudged necessity; cf. also, below, III.7.

[20] An echo of David Hartley's *Observations on Man* (1749), with its doctrine of 'association' and 'vibrations'. Hartley expanded Locke's theories of the association of ideas far past Locke's original horizon, and added an explanation of human behaviour on his hypothesis of impalpable nervous vibrations ('vibratiuncles'). Samuel Taylor Coleridge, in his *Religious Musings*, spoke of 'Hartley, of mortal kind the wisest . . .'. Wesley's summary of the doctrine, in his 'A Thought on Necessity' (*AM*, 1780, III.485-92), concluded that it was necessitarian. See also his earlier (1774) summary of Hartley's theory in *Thoughts upon Necessity*, I.4: 'all our thoughts depend upon the vibrations of the fibres of the brain; and, of consequence, . . . unavoidably follow those vibrations;' cf. also IV.2-3.

[21] A central notion in the reigning psychology of Wesley's time, rooted in Locke and John Gay (1699–1745), *Dissertation Concerning the Fundamental Principles of Virtue and Morality* (1731), but given a radically new twist by David Hume, *A Treatise of Human Nature* (1738–40)—which Wesley may never have read. His knowledge of associationist

without our knowledge and independently on our choice! How these connections are formed we cannot tell; but they are formed in a thousand different manners. Nor is it in the power of the wisest or holiest of men to break those associations, or to prevent what is the necessary consequence of them, and matter of daily 5 observation. Let the fire but touch one end of the train,[22] and it immediately runs on to the other.

7. Once more: let us fix our attention as studiously as we are able on any subject, yet let either pleasure or pain arise, especially if it be intense, and it will demand our immediate attention, and 10 attach our thought to itself. It will interrupt the steadiest contemplation, and divert the mind from its favourite subject.

8. These occasions of wandering thoughts lie within, are wrought into our very nature. But they will likewise naturally and necessarily arise from the various impulse[s] of outward objects. 15 Whatever strikes upon the organ of sense, the eye or ear, will raise a perception in the mind. And accordingly, whatever we see or hear will break in upon our former train of thought. Every man, therefore, that does anything in our sight, or speaks anything in our hearing, occasions our mind to wander more or less from the 20 point it was thinking of before.

9. And there is no question but those evil spirits who are continually 'seeking whom they may devour'[23] make use of all the foregoing occasions to hurry and distract our minds. Sometimes by one, sometimes by another of these means, they will harass and 25 perplex us, and, so far as God permits, interrupt our thoughts, particularly when they are engaged on the best subjects. Nor is this at all strange: they well understand the very springs of thought, and know on which of the bodily organs the imagination, the understanding, and every other faculty of the mind, more 30 immediately depends. And hereby they know how, by affecting those organs, to affect the operations dependent on them. Add to this that they can inject a thousand thoughts without any of the preceding means; it being as natural for spirit to act upon spirit as for matter to act upon matter. These things being considered, we 35

---

theory came mainly from Hartley's more recent *Observations*, where the attempt had been made to explain the emergence and development of all knowledge and value judgments from 'the association of ideas'. It was, in effect, a determinist view, though Hartley had hoped to avoid any such conclusion. Cf. Frederick Copleston, *A History of Philosophy*, Vol. V (see index for 'association of ideas').

[22] I.e., a fuse, as of gunpowder.   [23] Cf. 1 Pet. 5:8.

cannot wonder[24] that our thought so often wanders from any point which we have in view.

III. 1. What kind of wandering thoughts are sinful, and what not, is the third thing to be inquired into. And, first, all those
5 thoughts which wander from God, which leave him no room in our minds, are undoubtedly sinful. For all these imply practical atheism,[25] and by these we are without God in the world. And so much more are all those which are contrary to God, which imply opposition or enmity to him. Such are all murmuring,
10 discontented thoughts, which say, in effect, 'We will not have thee to rule over us;' all unbelieving thoughts, whether with regard to his being, his attributes, or his providence. I mean his particular providence over all things as well as all persons in the universe: that without which 'not a sparrow falls to the ground', by which
15 'the hairs of our head are all numbered'.[26] For as to a general providence (vulgarly so called) contradistinguished from a particular, it is only a decent, well-sounding word, which means just nothing.[27]

2. Again: all thoughts which spring from sinful tempers are
20 undoubtedly sinful. Such, for instance are those that spring from a revengeful temper, from pride, or lust, or vanity. 'An evil tree cannot bring forth good fruit;'[28] therefore if the tree be evil, so must the fruit be also.[29]

3. And so must those be which either produce or feed any sinful
25 temper; those which either give rise to pride or vanity, to anger or love of the world, or confirm and increase these or any other unholy temper, passion, or affection. For not only whatever flows from evil is evil, but also whatever leads to it; whatever tends to alienate the soul from God, and to make or keep it 'earthly,
30 sensual, and devilish'.[30]

---

[24] All edns. before 1787 read 'admire', in its root meaning *(admiror)* of 'be surprised'. *OED* notes that this usage was, however, already obsolescent in the late eighteenth century.

[25] Cf. No. 23, 'Sermon on the Mount, III', I.11 and n.

[26] Cf. Matt. 10:29-30.

[27] For more on Wesley's rejection of this distinction, see below, No. 67, 'On Divine Providence', §23 and n.

[28] Cf. Matt. 7:17, 18.

[29] See Matt. 12:33.

[30] Cf. Jas. 3:15. It should be noted that while only the first edition uses 'earthy' instead of the AV's 'earthly' (the latter supported also by Wesley's *Notes*), yet in the echo of the same text in I.3 all editions use 'earthy'.

4. Hence even those thoughts which are occasioned by weakness or disease, by the natural mechanism of the body, or by the laws of vital union, however innocent they may be in themselves, do nevertheless become sinful when they either produce or cherish and increase in us any sinful temper—sup- 5 pose the desire of the flesh, the desire of the eye, or the pride of life.[31] In like manner the wandering thoughts which are occasioned by the words or actions of other men, if they cause or feed any wrong disposition, then commence[32] sinful. And the same we may observe of those which are suggested or injected by 10 the devil. When they minister to any earthly or devilish temper (which they do whenever we give place to them, and thereby make them our own) then they are equally sinful with the tempers to which they minister.

5. But abstracting from[33] these cases, wandering thoughts in 15 the latter sense of the word—that is, thoughts wherein our understanding wanders from the point it has in view—are no more sinful than the motion of the blood in our veins, or of the spirits in our brain. If they arise from an infirm constitution or from some accidental weakness or distemper they are as innocent 20 as it is to have a weak constitution or a distempered body. And surely no one doubts but a bad state of nerves, a fever of any kind, and either a transient or a lasting delirium, may consist with perfect innocence. And if they should arise in a soul which is united to a healthful body, either from the natural union between 25 the body and soul,[34] or from any of ten thousand changes which may occur in those organs of the body that minister to

[31] See 1 John 2:16; see No. 7, 'The Way to the Kingdom', II.2 and n.

[32] Cf No. 25, 'Sermon on the Mount, V', III.3, where Wesley uses 'commence' in this same sense of graduation, of entering into a new state or phase.

[33] I.e., 'leaving out of account', a familiar eighteenth-century usage.

[34] Note Wesley's effort here to concede as much as possible to the 'associations' and their body-mind monism. He himself was, of course, a thoroughgoing body-mind dualist, as may be seen in Nos. 3, 'Awake, Thou That Sleepest', I.9; 51, *The Good Steward*, I.4; 82, 'On Temptation', I.1-2; 86, *A Call to Backsliders*, II.2; 99, *The Reward of Righteousness*, II.1-6; 116, 'What is Man? Ps. 8:4', §12; 129, 'Heavenly Treasure in Earthen Vessels', II.1; 140, 'The Promise of Understanding', I.2. See also the *Survey*, V.67, 254; and *Notes* on Mark 4:26.

In this Wesley was following an ancient dualist tradition back to Descartes and Plato but reasserted in his time by men like Malebranche, *Treatise Concerning the Search After Truth*, tr. by T. Taylor (1694); James Keill, *Essays on Several Parts of the Animal Economy* (1717), p. vii.; Samuel Pike, *Philosophia Sacra: Or, the Principles of Natural Philosophy Extracted From Divine Revelation* (1753), p. 7; Robert Bolton, *On the Employment of Time* (1750), pp. 8 ff.; all of whom Wesley had read with some attention.

thought—in any of these cases they are as perfectly innocent as the causes from which they spring. And so they are when they spring from the casual, involuntary associations of our ideas.

6. If our thoughts wander from the point we had in view by
5 means of other men variously affecting our senses, they are equally innocent still: for it is no more a sin to understand what I see and hear, and in many cases cannot help seeing, hearing, and understanding, than it is to have eyes and ears. 'But if the devil injects wandering thoughts, are not those thoughts evil?' They are
10 troublesome, and in that sense evil; but they are not sinful.[35] I do not know that he spoke to our Lord with an audible voice; perhaps he spoke to his heart only when he said, 'All these things will I give thee, if thou wilt fall down and worship me.'[36] But whether he spoke inwardly or outwardly, our Lord doubtless understood
15 what he said. He had therefore a thought correspondent to those words. But was it a sinful thought? We know it was not. 'In him was no sin,'[37] either in action, or word, or thought. Nor is there any sin in a thousand thoughts of the same kind which Satan may inject into any of our Lord's followers.

20   7. It follows that none of these wandering thoughts (whatever unwary persons have affirmed, thereby grieving whom the Lord had not grieved) are inconsistent with perfect love. Indeed if they were, then not only sharp pain, but sleep itself would be inconsistent with it. Sharp pain; for whenever this supervenes,
25 whatever we were before thinking of, it will interrupt our thinking, and of course draw our thoughts into another channel. Yea, and sleep itself, as it is a state of insensibility and stupidity; and such as is generally mixed with thoughts wandering over the earth, loose, wild, and incoherent.[38] Yet certainly these are
30 consistent with perfect love: so then are all wandering thoughts of this kind.

IV. 1. From what has been observed it is easy to give a clear answer to the last question—what kind of wandering thoughts we may expect and pray to be delivered from.
35   From the former sort of wandering thoughts, those wherein the heart wanders from God; from all that are contrary to his will,

---

[35] Cf. No. 13, *On Sin in Believers*, intro., III.1-9, and n.
[36] Matt. 4:9.
[37] 1 John 3:5.
[38] Cf., above, II.4 and n.

or that leave us without God in the world, everyone that is perfected in love is unquestionably delivered.[39] This deliverance therefore we may expect; this we may, we ought to pray for. Wandering thoughts of this kind imply unbelief, if not enmity against God. But both of these he will destroy, will bring utterly to 5 an end. And, indeed, from all sinful wandering thoughts we shall be absolutely delivered. All that are perfected in love are delivered from these; else they were not saved from sin. Men and devils will tempt them all manner of ways; but they cannot prevail over them. 10

2. With regard to the latter sort of wandering thoughts the case is widely different. Till the cause is removed we cannot in reason expect the effect should cease. But the causes or occasions of these will remain as long as we remain in the body. So long therefore we have all reason to believe the effects will remain also. 15

3. To be more particular. Suppose a soul, however holy, to dwell in a distempered body; suppose the brain be so throughly disordered as that raging madness follows; will not all the thoughts be wild and unconnected, as long as that disorder continues? Suppose a fever occasions that temporary madness 20 which we term a delirium, can there be any just connection of thought till that delirium is removed? Yea, suppose what is called a nervous disorder to rise to so high a degree as occasions at least a partial madness, will there not be a thousand wandering thoughts? And must not these irregular thoughts continue as long 25 as the disorder which occasions them?

4. Will not the case be the same with regard to those thoughts that necessarily arise from violent pain? They will more or less continue while that pain continues, by the inviolable order of nature. This order likewise will obtain where the thoughts are 30 disturbed, broken, or interrupted, by any defect of the apprehension, judgment, or imagination, flowing from the natural constitution of the body. And how many interruptions may spring from the unaccountable and involuntary associations of our ideas! Now all these are directly or indirectly caused by the 35 corruptible body pressing down the mind.[40] Nor therefore can we expect them to be removed till 'this corruptible shall put on incorruption.'[41]

---

[39] No. 40, *Christian Perfection*, II.28, more amplified than qualified—and reasserted.
[40] See Wisd. 9:15. See above, II.3 and n.   [41] 1 Cor. 15:54.

5. And then only, when we lie down in the dust, shall we be delivered from those wandering thoughts which are occasioned by what we see and hear among those by whom we are now surrounded. To avoid these we must go out of the world.[42] For as
5 long as we remain therein, as long as there are men and women round about us, and we have eyes to see and ears to hear,[43] the things which we daily see and hear will certainly affect our mind, and will more or less break in upon and interrupt our preceding thoughts.

10 6. And as long as evil spirits roam to and fro in a miserable, disordered world, so long they will assault (whether they can prevail or no) every inhabitant of flesh and blood. They will trouble even those whom they cannot destroy: they will attack, if they cannot conquer. And from these attacks of our restless,
15 unwearied enemies, we must not look for an entire deliverance till we are lodged 'where the wicked cease from troubling, and where the weary are at rest'.[44]

7. To sum up the whole: to expect deliverance from those wandering thoughts which are occasioned by evil spirits is to
20 expect that the devil should die or fall asleep; or at least should no more go about as a roaring lion.[45] To expect deliverance from those which are occasioned by other men is to expect either that men should cease from the earth, or that *we* should be absolutely secluded from them, and have no intercourse with them; or that
25 having eyes we should not see, neither hear with our ears, but be as senseless as stocks or stones. And to pray for deliverance from those which are occasioned by the body is in effect to pray that we may leave the body. Otherwise it is praying for impossibilities and absurdities; praying that God would reconcile contradictions by
30 continuing our union with a corruptible body without the natural, necessary consequences of that union. It is as if we should pray to be angels and men, mortal and immortal, at the same time. Nay, but when that which is immortal is come, mortality is done away.[46]

8. Rather let us pray, both with the spirit and with the
35 understanding, that 'all' these 'things may work together for our good';[47] that we may suffer all infirmities of our nature, all the

---

[42] See 1 Cor. 5:10.   [43] Deut. 29:4.
[44] Cf. Job 3:17.
[45] 1 Pet. 5:8.
[46] See 1 Cor. 13:10; 15:53, 54.
[47] Cf. Rom. 8:28.

interruptions of men, all the assaults and suggestions of evil spirits, and in all be 'more than conquerors'.[48] Let us pray that we may be delivered from all sin; that both root and branch may be destroyed; that we may be 'cleansed from all pollution of flesh and spirit',[49] from every evil temper and word and work; that we may 'love the Lord our God with all our heart, with all our mind, with all our soul, and with all our strength';[50] that all 'the fruit of the Spirit' may be found in us—not only 'love, joy, peace'; but also 'long-suffering, gentleness, goodness; fidelity, meekness, temperance.'[51] Pray that all 'these things may flourish and abound',[52] may increase in you more and more, till an abundant 'entrance be ministered unto you into the everlasting kingdom of our Lord Jesus Christ'![53]

[48] Rom. 8:37.
[49] Cf. 2 Cor. 7:1.
[50] Cf. Mark 12:30.
[51] Cf. Gal. 5:22-23; see also *Notes*.
[52] Cf. 2 Pet. 1:8.
[53] 2 Pet. 1:11.

SATAN'S DEVICES

The variety and vehemence of the attacks upon his doctrines, and against Christian perfection in particular, never ceased to baffle Wesley. These attacks seemed to him to proceed from a lack of serious interest in the distinctive vision of holy living that he was trying to put into words. Nor could he help being further dismayed by the distortions of that vision that were being spread abroad by some of his own self-professed disciples. There is an illuminating discussion of these problems of misinterpretation on this very point in the Minutes *for June 17, 1747. Clearly, then, the sermon* Christian Perfection *required yet another sequel which would acknowledge the abuses of the doctrines and also take his critics to task for ignoring the crucial distinction between valid* use *and illicit* abuse. *Most of all, Wesley wanted to reduce such dismal janglings by making still further clarifications.*

He had found his clue, of course, in the conviction that the world in general was ruled by Satan and his minions. Cf. No. 12, 'The Witness of Our Own Spirit', § 10 and n. This satanocratic perspective had been shared by the generality of Puritan theologians, but it had been given a special turn by William Spurstowe, better known for his membership in the anti-Laudian group that styled itself 'Smectymnuus'. One of the discourses in Spurstowe's Spiritual Chymist: Or, Six Decades of Divine Meditations *(1666) is entitled 'Σατάνα Νοήματα: Or, the Wiles of Satan'—and this was one of the volumes owned and read by the Holy Club. Spurstowe, of course, had no concern whatever with any notion of Christian perfection; his interest was in pointing out Satan's alertness in distorting Christian truth in the minds of believers and his effectiveness in annulling the benefits of mere orthodoxy.*

Thus, 'Satan's Devices' is Wesley's elaboration of this suggestion on the point of sanctification in particular; it is also a warning to his people against Satan's insinuations in general. He had already preached on 2 Cor. 2:11 four times before 1750 (October 31, 1739;

December 29, 1740; January 18, 1741 [twice]). He would return to it again (May 1, 1774; February 6, 1785; February 9, 1785) with no indication, however, as to which specific 'device' he may have had in view on any of these occasions. In the first edition (1750) the sermon has its text without a title; that appears for the first time in Works *(1771), III. 232-51.*

Satan's Devices

2 Corinthians 2:11

We are not ignorant of his devices.

1. The devices whereby the subtle 'god of this world'[1] labours to destroy the children of God, or at least to torment whom he 5 cannot destroy, to perplex and hinder them in running the race which is set before them,[2] are numberless as the stars of heaven or the sand upon the sea-shore.[3] But it is of one of them only that I now propose to speak (although exerted in various ways), whereby he endeavours to divide the gospel against itself, and by one part 10 of it to overthrow the other.

2. The inward kingdom of heaven, which is set up in the heart of all that 'repent and believe the gospel',[4] is no other than 'righteousness and peace and joy in the Holy Ghost'.[5] Every babe in Christ knows we are made partakers of these the very hour that 15 we believe in Jesus. But these are only the first-fruits of his Spirit;[6] the harvest is not yet. Although these blessings are inconceivably great, yet we trust to see greater than these. We trust to 'love the Lord our God' not only as we do now, with a weak though sincere affection, but 'with all our heart, with all our 20 mind, with all our soul, and with all our strength'.[7] We look for power to 'rejoice evermore', to 'pray without ceasing', and 'in everything to give thanks'; knowing 'this is the will of God concerning' us 'in Christ Jesus'.[8]

---

[1] 2 Cor. 4:4.　　　　[2] See Heb. 12:1.　　　　[3] See Gen. 22:17.
[4] Mark 1:15.　　　　[5] Rom. 14:17.　　　　[6] See Rom. 8:23.
[7] Cf. Mark 12:30.　　　　　　　[8] Cf. 1 Thess. 5:16-18.

3. We expect to be 'made perfect in love', in that love which 'casts out' all painful 'fear',[9] and all desire but that of glorifying him we love, and of loving and serving him more and more. We look for such an increase in the experimental knowledge and love
5 of God our Saviour as will enable us always to 'walk in the light, as he is in the light'.[10] We believe the whole 'mind' will be in us 'which was also in Christ Jesus';[11] that we shall love every man so as to be ready 'to lay down our life for his sake',[12] so as by this love to be freed from anger and pride, and from every unkind
10 affection. We expect to be 'cleansed' from all our idols, 'from all filthiness', whether 'of flesh or spirit';[13] to be 'saved from all our uncleannesses',[14] inward or outward; to be 'purified as he is pure'.[15]

4. We trust in his promise who cannot lie,[16] that the time will
15 surely come when in every word and work we shall 'do his' blessed 'will on earth, as it is done in heaven';[17] when all our conversation shall be 'seasoned with salt',[18] all meet to 'minister grace to the hearers';[19] when 'whether we eat or drink, or whatever we do', it shall be done 'to the glory of God';[20] when all
20 our words and deeds shall be 'in the name of the Lord Jesus, giving thanks unto God, even the Father, through him'.[21]

5. Now this is the grand device of Satan: to destroy the first work of God in the soul, or at least to hinder its increase by our expectation of that greater work. It is therefore my present design,
25 first, to point out the several ways whereby he endeavours this; and, secondly, to observe how we may retort[22] these fiery darts of the wicked one[23]—how we may rise the higher by what he intends for an occasion of our falling.

I. 1. I am, first, to point out the several ways whereby Satan
30 endeavours to destroy the first work of God in the soul, or at least to hinder its increase by our expectation of that greater work.

---

[9] 1 John 4:18.　　　　　　　　　　　　　　　　　　[10] 1 John 1:7.
[11] Cf. Phil. 2:5.　　　　　　　　　　　　　　　　　　[12] Cf. John 13:37.
[13] 2 Cor. 7:1.　　　　　　　　　　　　　　　　　　　[14] Cf. Ezek. 36:29.
[15] Cf. 1 John 3:3.　　　　　　　　　　　　　　　　　[16] See Titus 1:2.
[17] Cf. Matt. 6:10.　　　　　　　　　　　　　　　　　[18] Col. 4:6.
[19] Eph. 4:29.
[20] Cf. 1 Cor. 10:31.　　　　　　　　　　　　　　　　[21] Cf. Col. 3:17.
[22] A then common usage based on its root meaning of *retorqueo*, 'to twist or hurl back'. Cf. Wesley's letter to Mrs. Pendarves, Aug. 12, 1731; and Nos. 38, 'A Caution against Bigotry', IV.6; and 75, 'On Schism', II.15.
[23] Eph. 6:16.

And, (1), he endeavours to damp our joy in the Lord[24] by the consideration of our own vileness, sinfulness, unworthiness; added to this, that there *must* be a far greater change than is yet, or we cannot see the Lord. If we knew we *must* remain as we are, even to the day of our death, we might possibly draw a kind of comfort, poor as it was, from that necessity. But as we know, we need not remain in this state, as we are assured, there is a greater change to come—and that unless sin be all done away in this life we cannot see God in glory[25]—that subtle adversary often damps the joy we should otherwise feel in what we have already attained, by a perverse representation of what we have not attained, and the absolute necessity of attaining it. So that we cannot rejoice in what we have, because there is more which we have not. We cannot rightly taste the goodness of God, who hath done so great things for us, because there are so much greater things which as yet he hath not done. Likewise the deeper conviction God works in us of our present unholiness, and the more vehement desire we feel in our heart of the entire holiness he hath promised, the more are we tempted to think lightly of the present gifts of God, and to undervalue what we have already received because of what we have not received.

2. If he can prevail thus far, if he can damp our joy, he will soon attack our peace also. He will suggest, 'Are you fit to see God? He is of purer eyes than to behold iniquity.[26] How then can you flatter yourself so as to imagine he beholds *you* with approbation? God is holy; you are unholy. What communion hath light with darkness?[27] How is it possible that *you*, unclean as you are, should be in a state of acceptance with God? You see indeed the mark, the prize of your high calling.[28] But do you not see it is afar off? How can you presume then to think that all your sins are already blotted out? How can this be until you are brought nearer to God, until you bear more resemblance to him?' Thus will he endeavour, not only to shake your peace, but even to overturn the very foundation of it; to bring you back by insensible degrees to the point from whence you set out first: even to seek for

---

[24] Cf. Wesley's account of the aftermath of his Aldersgate experience (JWJ, May 24, 1738): May 26 ('My soul continued in peace, but yet in heaviness, because of manifold temptations'); and May 28 ('I waked in peace, but not in joy').

[25] The echo of a doctrine of sinless perfection? Cf. No. 13, *On Sin in Believers*, V.2 and n.

[26] See Hab. 1:13.　　　　　　　　　　　　　　　　　[27] 2 Cor. 6:14.

[28] See Phil. 3:14.

justification by works, or by your own righteousness; to make something in *you* the ground of your acceptance, or at least necessarily previous to it.

3. Or if we hold fast—'other foundation can no man lay than that which is laid, even Jesus Christ;'[29] and I am 'justified freely by God's grace, through the redemption which is in Jesus'[30]—yet he will not cease to urge, 'But "the tree is known by its fruits."[31] And have you the fruits of justification? Is "that mind in you which was in Christ Jesus"?[32] Are you "dead unto sin and alive unto"[33] righteousness? Are you made conformable to the death of Christ, and do you know the power of his resurrection?' And then, comparing the small fruits we feel in our souls with the fullness of the promises, we shall be ready to conclude: 'Surely God hath not said that my sins are forgiven me! Surely I have not received the remission of my sins; for what lot have I among them that are sanctified?'[34]

4. More especially in the time of sickness and pain he will press this with all his might: 'Is it not the word of him that cannot lie, "Without holiness no man shall see the Lord"?[35] But you are not holy. You know it well; you know holiness is the full image of God. And how far is this above, out of your sight? You cannot attain unto it.[36] Therefore all your labour has been in vain. All these things you have suffered in vain. You have spent your strength for nought.[37] You are yet in your sins and must therefore perish at the last.' And thus, if your eye be not steadily fixed on him who hath borne all your sins, he will bring you again under that 'fear of death' whereby you was so long 'subject unto bondage';[38] and by this means impair, if not wholly destroy, your peace as well as joy in the Lord.

5. But his masterpiece of subtlety is still behind. Not content to strike at your peace and joy, he will carry his attempts farther yet: he will level his assault against your righteousness also. He will

---

[29] Cf. 1 Cor. 3:11.   [30] Cf. Rom. 3:24.   [31] Cf. Matt. 12:33.
[32] Cf. Phil. 2:5.   [33] Cf. Rom. 6:11.
[34] For a sample of a quite similar barrage of negative suggestions, cf. No. 2, *The Almost Christian*, II.7, 9. If it is one of 'Satan's devices' to raise doubts in believers' minds as to the reality of their present salvation, what is to be made of Wesley's habit of disparaging the faith of most conventional Christians?
[35] Cf. Heb. 12:14.   [36] See Ps. 139:6 (AV).
[37] See Isa. 49:4; note this instance of Wesley's allowing Satan to 'cite Scripture for his purpose', as in Shakespeare's *Merchant of Venice*, I. iii.99.
[38] Heb. 2:15.

endeavour to shake, yea, if it be possible, to destroy the holiness you have already received by your very expectation of receiving more, of attaining all the image of God.

6. The manner wherein he attempts this may partly appear from what has been already observed. For, first, by striking at our joy in the Lord he strikes likewise at our holiness: seeing joy in the Holy Ghost[39] is a precious means of promoting every holy temper; a choice instrument of God whereby he carries on much of his work in a believing soul. And it is a considerable help not only to inward but also to outward holiness. It strengthens our hands to go on in the work of faith and in the labour of love;[40] manfully to 'fight the good fight of faith,' and to 'lay hold on eternal life.'[41] It is peculiarly designed of God to be a balance both against inward and outward sufferings; to 'lift up the hands that hang down' and confirm 'the feeble knees'.[42] Consequently, whatever damps our joy in the Lord proportionably obstructs our holiness. And therefore so far as Satan shakes our joy he hinders our holiness also.

7. The same effect will ensue if he can by any means either destroy or shake our peace. For the peace of God is another precious means of advancing the image of God in us. There is scarce a greater help to holiness than this: a continual tranquility of spirit, the evenness of a mind stayed upon God, a calm repose in the blood of Jesus. And without this it is scarce possible to grow in grace, and in the vital knowledge of our Lord Jesus Christ.[43] For all fear (unless the tender, filial fear) freezes and benumbs the soul. It binds up all the springs of spiritual life, and stops all motion of the heart toward God. And doubt, as it were, bemires the soul, so that it sticks fast in the deep clay. Therefore in the same proportion as either of these prevail, our growth in holiness is hindered.

8. At the same time that our wise adversary endeavours to make our conviction of the necessity of perfect love an occasion of shaking our peace by doubts and fears, he endeavours to weaken, if not destroy, our faith. Indeed these are inseparably connected, so that they must stand or fall together. So long as faith subsists

[39] Rom. 14:17.
[40] 1 Thess. 1:3.
[41] 1 Tim. 6:12.
[42] Heb. 12:12.
[43] See 2 Pet. 3:18.

we remain in peace; our heart stands fast while it believes in the Lord. But if we let go our faith, our filial confidence in a loving, pardoning God, our peace is at an end, the very foundation on which it stood being overthrown. And this is the only foundation of holiness as well as of peace. Consequently whatever strikes at this strikes at the very root of all holiness. For without this faith, without an abiding sense that Christ loved me and gave himself for me,[44] without a continuing conviction that God for Christ's sake is merciful to me a sinner,[45] it is impossible that I should love God. 'We love him because he first loved us;'[46] and in proportion to the strength and clearness of our conviction that he hath loved us and accepted us in his Son. And unless we love God it is not possible that we should love our neighbour as ourselves; nor, consequently, that we should have any right affections either toward God or toward man. It evidently follows that whatever weakens our faith must in the same degree obstruct our holiness. And this is not only the most effectual but also the most compendious way of destroying all holiness; seeing it does not affect any one Christian temper, any single grace or fruit of the Spirit, but, so far as it succeeds, tears up the very root of the whole work of God.

9. No marvel, therefore, that the ruler of the darkness of this world[47] should here put forth all his strength. And so we find by experience. For it is far easier to conceive than it is to express the unspeakable violence wherewith this temptation is frequently urged on them who hunger and thirst after righteousness.[48] When they see in a strong and clear light, on the one hand the desperate wickedness of their own hearts, on the other hand the unspotted holiness to which they are called in Christ Jesus; on the one hand the depth of their own corruption, of their total alienation from God; on the other the height of the glory of God, that image of the Holy One wherein they are to be renewed; there is many times no spirit left in them; they could almost cry out, 'With God this is impossible.'[49] They are ready to give up both faith and hope, to

---

[44] Gal. 2:20.

[45] Cf. No. 3, *'Awake, Thou That Sleepest,'* III.6 and n.; see also the climactic passage in the account of Wesley's heartwarming experience of May 24, 1738 (JWJ, §14): 'an assurance was given me that [Christ] had taken away *my* sins, even *mine*, and saved *me* from the law of sin and death.'

[46] 1 John 4:19.

[47] Eph. 6:12.

[48] Matt. 5:6.

[49] See Matt. 19:26, etc.

cast away that very confidence whereby they are to overcome all things, and do all things, through Christ strengthening them;[50] whereby, 'after' they 'have done the will of God', they are to 'receive the promise'.[51]

10. And if they 'hold fast the beginning of their confidence steadfast unto the end',[52] they shall undoubtedly receive the promise of God, reaching through both time and eternity. But here is another snare laid for our feet. While we earnestly pant for that part of the promise which is to be accomplished here, for 'the glorious liberty of the children of God',[53] we may be led unawares from the consideration of the glory which shall hereafter be revealed. Our eye may be insensibly turned aside from that 'crown which the righteous Judge' hath promised to 'give at that day to all that love his appearing';[54] and we may be drawn away from the view of that incorruptible inheritance which is reserved in heaven for us.[55] But this also would be a loss to our souls, and an obstruction to our holiness. For to walk in the continual sight of our goal is a needful help in our running the race that is set before us.[56] This it was, the having 'respect unto the recompense of reward', which of old time encouraged Moses rather 'to suffer affliction with the people of God than to enjoy the pleasures of sin for a season; esteeming the reproach of Christ greater riches than the treasures of Egypt'.[57] Nay, it is expressly said of a greater than him, that 'for the joy that was set before him, he endured the cross, and despised the shame,' till he 'sat down at the right hand of the throne of God'.[58] Whence we may easily infer how much more needful for us is the view of that joy set before us, that we may endure whatever cross the wisdom of God lays upon us, and press on through holiness to glory.

11. But while we are reaching to this, as well as to that glorious liberty which is preparatory to it, we may be in danger of falling into another snare of the devil, whereby he labours to entangle the children of God. We may take too much 'thought for tomorrow',[59]

---

[50] See Phil. 4:13.
[51] Heb. 10:36.
[52] Cf. Heb. 3:14.
[53] Rom. 8:21.
[54] Cf. 2 Tim. 4:8.
[55] See 1 Pet. 1:4.
[56] See Heb. 12:1.
[57] Heb. 11:25-26.
[58] Cf. Heb. 12:2. Although Wesley did use the phrase 'greater than he' (see above, *Christian Perfection*, II.8, and n.71), yet he was not uncomfortable with 'greater than him', used at the beginning of this sentence. His frequent use of colloquialisms has often been obscured by later editors.
[59] Cf. Matt. 6:34.

so as to neglect the improvement of today. We may so expect 'perfect love' as not to use that which is already 'shed abroad in our hearts'.[60] There have not been wanting instances of those who have greatly suffered hereby. They were so taken up with what 5 they were to receive hereafter as utterly to neglect what they had already received. In expectation of having five talents more, they buried their one talent in the earth.[61] At least they did not improve it as they might have done to the glory of God and the good of their own souls.

10 12. Thus does the subtle adversary of God and man endeavour to make void the counsel of God by dividing the gospel against itself, and making one part of it overthrow the other—while the first work of God in the soul is destroyed by the expectation of his perfect work. We have seen several of the ways wherein he 15 attempts this by cutting off, as it were, the springs of holiness; but this he likewise does more directly by making that blessed hope an occasion of unholy tempers.

13. Thus, whenever our heart is eagerly athirst for all the great and precious promises, when we pant after the fullness of God, as 20 the hart after the water brook,[62] when our soul breaketh out in fervent desire, 'Why are his chariot wheels so long a-coming?'[63] he will not neglect the opportunity of tempting us to murmur against God. He will use all his wisdom and all his strength if haply, in an unguarded hour, we may be influenced to repine at 25 our Lord for thus delaying his coming. At least he will labour to excite some degree of fretfulness or impatience; and perhaps of envy at those whom we believe to have already attained the prize of our high calling.[64] He well knows that by giving way to any of these tempers we are pulling down the very thing we would build 30 up. By *thus* following after perfect holiness we become more unholy than before.[65] Yea, there is great danger that our last state should be worse than the first;[66] like them of whom the Apostle speaks in those dreadful words, 'It had been better they had never known the way of righteousness, than after they had known it to 35 turn back from the holy commandment delivered to them.'[67]

14. And from hence he hopes to reap another advantage, even

---

[60] Rom. 5:5.   [61] See Matt. 25:14-30.   [62] See Ps. 42:1.
[63] Cf. Judg. 5:28.   [64] See Phil. 3:14.
[65] Note this qualification of I.1, above; Wesley never uses the term 'perfectionism', but he does regard both the idea and the attitude as a deterrent to true holiness.
[66] See. Matt. 12:45.   [67] Cf. 2 Pet. 2:21.

to bring up an evil report of the good way. He is sensible how few are able to distinguish (and too many are not willing so to do) between the accidental abuse and the natural tendency of a doctrine. These, therefore, will he continually blend together with regard to the doctrine of Christian perfection, in order to prejudice the minds of unwary men against the glorious promises of God. And how frequently, how generally—I had almost said, how universally—has he prevailed herein! For who is there that observes any of these accidental ill effects of this doctrine, and does not immediately conclude, 'This is its natural tendency'? And does not readily cry out, 'See, these are the fruits (meaning the natural, necessary fruits) of such doctrine!' Not so. They are fruits which may accidentally spring from the abuse of a great and precious truth. But the abuse of this, or any other scriptural doctrine, does by no means destroy its use.[68] Neither can the unfaithfulness of man, perverting his right way, 'make the promise of God of none effect'.[69] No; let God be true and every man a liar.[70] The word of the Lord, it shall stand. 'Faithful is he that hath promised;'[71] 'he also will do it.'[72] Let not us then be 'removed from the hope of the gospel'.[73] Rather let us observe—which was the second thing proposed—how we may retort these fiery darts of the wicked one;[74] how we may rise the higher by what he intends for an occasion of our falling.

II. 1. And, first, does Satan endeavour to damp your joy in the Lord by the consideration of your sinfulness, added to this, that without entire, universal 'holiness no man can see the Lord'?[75] You may cast back this dart upon his own head while, through the grace of God, the more you feel of your own vileness the more you rejoice in confident hope that all this shall be done away. While you hold fast this hope, every evil temper you feel, though you hate it with a perfect hatred, may be a means, not of lessening your humble joy, but rather of increasing it. 'This and this', may you say, 'shall likewise perish from the presence of the Lord. Like as the wax melteth at the fire, so shall this melt away before his face.'[76] By this means the greater that change is which remains to

---

[68] Cf. No. 20, *The Lord Our Righteousness*, II.20 and n.   [69] Gal. 3:17.
[70] Rom. 3:4.   [71] Cf. Heb. 10:23.
[72] Cf. 1 Thess. 5:24.   [73] Col. 1:23.
[74] See Eph. 6:16; for 'retort' see above, §5, proem and n.
[75] Cf. Heb. 12:14.   [76] See Ps. 68:2 (BCP).

be wrought in your soul, the more may you triumph in the Lord
and rejoice in the God of your salvation[77]—who hath done so
great things for you already,[78] and will do so much greater things
than these.

5   2. Secondly, the more vehemently he assaults your peace with
that suggestion: 'God is holy; you are unholy. You are immensely
distant from that holiness without which you cannot see God.'[79]
How then can you be in the favour of God? How can you fancy
you are justified?'—take the more earnest heed to hold fast that,
10 'not by works of righteousness which I have done'[80] I am 'found in
him'.[81] I am 'accepted in the Beloved',[82] 'not having my own
righteousness' (as the cause either in whole or in part of our
justification before God), 'but that which is by faith in Christ, the
righteousness which is of God by faith'.[83] O bind this about your
15 neck; write it upon the table of thy heart;[84] wear it as a bracelet
upon thy arm,[85] as frontlets between thine eyes:[86] I am 'justified
freely by his grace, through the redemption that is in Jesus
Christ'.[87] Value and esteem more and more that precious truth,
'By grace we are saved through faith.'[88] Admire more and more
20 the free grace of God in so loving the world as to give 'his only
Son, that whosoever believeth on him might not perish but have
everlasting life'.[89] So shall the sense of the sinfulness you feel on
the one hand, and of the holiness you expect on the other, both
contribute to establish your peace, and to make it flow as a river.[90]
25 So shall that peace flow on with an even stream, in spite of all
those mountains of ungodliness, which shall become a plain in
the day when the Lord cometh to take full possession of your
heart.[91] Neither will sickness or pain, or the approach of death,
occasion any doubt or fear. You know a day, an hour, a moment
30 with God is as a thousand years.[92] He cannot be straitened for
time wherein to work whatever remains to be done in your soul.
And God's time is always the best time.[93] Therefore be thou
'careful for nothing'. Only 'make thy request known unto him,'

---

[77] See Hab. 3:18.   [78] See Luke 1:49.   [79] See Heb. 12:14.
[80] Cf. Titus 3:5.   [81] Phil. 3:9.   [82] Eph. 1:6.
[83] Cf. Phil. 3:9.   [84] See. Prov. 3:3.   [85] See Ezek. 16:11.
[86] See Exod. 13:16; Deut. 6:8; 11:18.   [87] Cf. Rom. 3:24.
[88] Cf. Eph. 2:8.   [89] Cf. John 3:16.   [90] See Isa. 48:18.
[91] An echo of Isa. 40:3-4, and of Luke 3:5-6.   [92] See Ps. 90:4.
[93] Wesley may have found this slogan in John Spencer, ΚΑΙΝΑ ΚΑΙ ΠΑΛΑΙΑ:
Things New and Old (1658), pp. 5, 140 (note the para. captions); he might also have known
Bishop John Wilkins, *Discourse Concerning the Beauty of Providence* (6th edn., 1680), in *Sermons,*

and that, not with doubt or fear, but 'thanksgiving';[94] as being previously assured, he cannot withhold from thee any manner of thing that is good.

3. Thirdly, the more you are tempted to give up your shield, to cast away your faith, your confidence in his love, so much the more take heed that you hold fast that whereunto you have attained.[95] So much the more labour to 'stir up the gift of God which is in you.'[96] Never let that slip: I have 'an advocate with the Father, Jesus Christ the righteous';[97] and 'the life I now live, I live by faith in the Son of God, who loved me and gave himself for me.'[98] Be this thy glory and crown of rejoicing. And see that no one take thy crown. Hold that fast: 'I know that my Redeemer liveth, and shall stand at the latter day upon the earth.'[99] And I now 'have redemption in his blood, even the forgiveness of sins'.[100] Thus, being filled with all peace and joy in believing,[101] press on in the peace and joy of faith to the renewal of thy whole soul in the image of him that created thee.[102] Meanwhile, cry continually to God that thou mayst see that prize of thy high calling, not as Satan represents it, in a horrid[103] dreadful shape, but in its genuine native beauty; not as something that *must* be, or thou wilt go to hell, but as what *may* be, to lead thee to heaven. Look upon it as the most *desirable* gift which is in all the stores of the rich mercies of God. Beholding it in this true point of light, thou wilt hunger after it more and more: thy whole soul will be athirst for God, and for this glorious conformity to his likeness. And having received a good hope of this, and strong consolation through grace, thou wilt no more be weary or faint in thy mind, but wilt follow on till thou attainest.

4. In the same power of faith press on to glory. Indeed this is the same prospect still. God hath joined from the beginning pardon, holiness, heaven. And why should man put them asunder? O

p. 164: 'God's time is the best, and he never fails his own season.' It is unlikely that Wesley would have known J. S. Bach's since famous cantata No. 106 (*c.* 1708–17), with its magnificent first chorus, *'Gottes Zeit ist die allerbeste Zeit'* ('God's time is always the best time'); what is plain is that the idea was in the air and believed by fervent Christians generally. And the idea turns up elsewhere in John Wesley in his letter to Ann Bolton, July 18, 1773 (cf. also No. 18, 'The Marks of the New Birth', I.7 and n.), and in Charles's hymns, as in *Hymns and Sacred Poems* (1742), p. 107 (*Poet. Wks.*, II.163).

[94] Cf. Phil. 4:6. [95] See 1 Tim. 4:6. [96] Cf. 2 Tim. 1:6.
[97] 1 John 2:1. [98] Gal. 2:20. [99] Job. 19:25.
[100] Cf. Col. 1:14. [101] Rom. 15:13; see also Pref., §10.
[102] See Col. 3:10.
[103] Used adverbially to qualify 'dreadful'.

beware of this. Let not one link of the golden chain be broken.[104] God for Christ's sake hath forgiven me. He is now renewing me in his own image.[105] Shortly he will make me meet for himself, and take me to stand before his face. I, whom he hath justified
5 through the blood of his Son,[106] being thoroughly sanctified by his Spirit, shall quickly ascend to the 'New Jerusalem, the city of the living God'. Yet a little while and I shall 'come to the general assembly and church of the first-born, and to God the judge of all, and to Jesus the Mediator of the new covenant'.[107] How soon
10 will these shadows flee away, and the day of eternity dawn upon me! How soon shall I drink of 'the river of the water of life, going out of the throne of God and of the Lamb! There all his servants shall praise him, and shall see his face, and his name shall be upon their foreheads. And no night shall be there; and they have no
15 need of a candle or the light of the sun. For the Lord God enlighteneth them, and they shall reign for ever and ever.'[108]

5. And if you thus 'taste of the good word, and of the powers of the world to come',[109] you will not murmur against God, because you are not yet 'meet for the inheritance of the saints in light'.[110]
20 Instead of repining at your not being wholly delivered, you will praise God for thus far delivering you. You will magnify God for what he hath done, and take it as an earnest of what he will do. You will not fret against him because you are not yet renewed, but bless him because you shall be; and because 'now is your
25 salvation' from all sin 'nearer than when you' first 'believed'.[111] Instead of uselessly tormenting yourself because the time is not fully come you will calmly and quietly wait for it, knowing that it 'will come and will not tarry'.[112] You may therefore the more cheerfully endure as yet the burden of sin that still remains in you,
30 because it will not always remain. Yet a little while and it shall be clean gone. Only 'tarry thou the Lord's leisure: be strong, and he shall comfort thy heart; and put thou thy trust in the Lord.'[113]

6. And if you see any who appear (so far as man can judge, but God alone searcheth the hearts) to be already partakers of their
35 hope, already 'made perfect in love';[114] far from envying the grace

---

[104] The golden chain linking heaven and earth, *Iliad*, viii. 19; this metaphor had become familiar in English literature, as in Milton, *Paradise Lost*, ii. 1004, 1051. Cf. No. 56, 'God's Approbation of His Works', I.14 and n.
[105] See Col. 3:10.   [106] See Rom. 5:9.   [107] Heb. 12:22-24.
[108] Cf. Rev. 22:1-5.   [109] Heb. 6:5.   [110] Cf. Col. 1:12.
[111] Cf. Rom. 13:11.   [112] Heb. 10:37.
[113] Ps. 27:16 (BCP; cf. AV, ver. 14).   [114] 1 John 4:18.

of God in them, let it rejoice and comfort your heart. Glorify God for their sake. 'If one member is honoured', shall not 'all the members rejoice with it'?[115] Instead of jealousy or evil surmising concerning them, praise God for the consolation. Rejoice in having a fresh proof of the faithfulness of God in fulfilling all his promises. And stir yourself up the more to 'apprehend that for which you also are apprehended of Christ Jesus'.[116]

7. In order to this, redeem the time.[117] Improve the present moment. Buy up every opportunity of growing in grace, or of doing good. Let not the thought of receiving more grace tomorrow make you negligent of today. You have one talent now. If you expect five more, so much the rather improve that you have. And the more you expect to receive hereafter, the more labour for God now. Sufficient for the day is the grace thereof.[118] God is now pouring his benefits upon you. Now approve yourself a faithful steward of the present grace of God. Whatever may be tomorrow, give all diligence today to 'add to your faith courage, temperance, patience, brotherly kindness, and the fear of God,' till you attain that pure and perfect love. Let 'these things be' now 'in you and abound'. Be not now slothful or unfruitful. So shall an entrance be ministered 'into the everlasting kingdom of our Lord Jesus Christ'.[119]

[8]. Lastly, if in time past you have abused this blessed hope of being holy as he is holy, yet do not therefore cast it away. Let the abuse cease, the use remain.[120] Use it now to the more abundant glory of God and profit of your own soul. In steadfast faith, in calm tranquility of spirit, in full assurance of hope, rejoicing evermore for what God hath done, 'press' ye 'on unto perfection.'[121] Daily growing in the knowledge of our Lord Jesus Christ,[122] and going on from strength to strength, in resignation, in patience, in humble thankfulness for what ye have attained and for what ye shall, run the race set before you, 'looking unto Jesus',[123] till through perfect love ye enter into his glory.

---

[115] Cf. 1 Cor. 12:26.
[116] Cf. Phil. 3:12.
[117] See Eph. 5:16.
[118] A play on Matt. 6:34 ('Sufficient unto the day is the *evil* thereof'); cf. No. 85, 'On Working Out Our Own Salvation', III.4: 'No man sins because he has not grace, but because he does not use the grace which he hath.'
[119] 2 Pet. 1:5-8, 11.
[120] Cf. No. 20, *The Lord Our Righteousness*, II.20 and n.
[121] Cf. Heb. 6:1.   [122] See 2 Pet. 3:18.   [123] Cf. Heb. 12:1-2.

The Scripture-Way *of* SALVATION:

A

SERMON

On EPHES. ii. 8.

By JOHN WESLEY.

LONDON,

Printed; and Sold at the FOUNDERY.
MDCCLXV.

THE SCRIPTURE WAY OF SALVATION

AN INTRODUCTORY COMMENT

In 1750 Wesley had concluded the third volume of his Sermons on Several Occasions: In Three Volumes *with the sermon on 'Satan's Devices'. Ten years later, he decided to publish yet another, fourth, volume and to open it with his sermon on* Original Sin. *During that decade, however, he had become embroiled in an unpleasant controversy with a Scottish dissenter, Robert Sandeman, and his disciples, on the relative merits of 'a faith of* adherence' *(Sandeman's notion of faith as an act of will) and 'a faith of* assurance' *(Wesley's 'heart religion'). In 1757 Sandeman had expounded his views in two volumes,* Letters on Theron and Aspasio, Addressed to the Author *(James Hervey), under the pen name 'Palaemon'. His advocacy of salvation by assent had seemed dangerous to Wesley; already it had encouraged Thomas Maxfield and George Bell in their rush into antinomianism. Wesley's reaction was, therefore, as vehement as anything he ever published:* A Sufficient Answer to the Letters to the Author of Theron and Aspasio *(1757; reprinted in* Works, *1773, Vol. XX). He followed this up in 1762 with three pamphlets in the same vein:* Thoughts on the Imputed Righteousness of Christ; A Blow at the Root: or Christ Stabbed in the House of His Friends; *and* Cautions and Directions given to the Greatest Professors in the Methodist Societies. *In 1763 he continued with* Farther Thoughts Upon Christian Perfection.

The controversy, of course, had a history. Nathaniel Culverwell had explored it a century before in 'The White Stone', a chapter in A Discourse on the Light of Nature *(1st edn., 1652; 3rd. edn., 1661):*

Assurance is the top and triumph of faith. Faith—that's our victory 'by which we overcome the world'. But assurance—that's our triumph by which 'we are more than conquerors'. 'Tis flos fidei, *the very lustre and eminency of faith. Faith—that's the root; assurance the top-branch, the flourishing of faith. Justifying faith—that does not only dwell in the understanding, in* nudo assensus; *but requires an act of the will, to which must embrace a promise. Indeed, it calls for an act resulting from the whole soul, which must receive Christ offered unto it. But now, assurance consists only in the mind, and so there you have the difference between the Faith of Adherence and the Faith of Assurance. . . . When I say that every believer may be assured of his salvation, I don't say that every believer* is *assured of it. . . . A man may be a true child of God and certainly saved, though he have not assurance . . . ; he may be in a safe though in a sad condition. 'Tis required to the* bene esse, *not to the* esse *of a believer* (p. 103).

Wesley could never have agreed, after 1738, that assurance 'consists only in the mind'; when he published his extract from Culverwell in the Christian Library *(1752), Vol. XVII, he omitted the passage just quoted.*

He would also have known of William Allen's threefold distinction in The Glass of Justification *(1658): 'Faith, as it justifies, hath three acts: credence, adherence, confidence' (p. 43); this is very close to his own idea. And he also knew the famous summary of the question in Arthur Bedford's* The Doctrine of Assurance *(1738), Appendix, p. 36:*

> *To put this controversy into as clear a light as I can, I shall only add that there is a 'faith of adherence' and a 'faith of assurance'. The 'faith of adherence' is a saving faith, wrought in the heart of a sinner by the Spirit and Word of God, whereby he is convinced of his sin and misery and of his disability in himself and all other creatures, to recover him out of his lost condition—[he] not only assenteth to the truth of the promise of the Gospel, but receives and rests on the death and righteousness of Christ Jesus, therein held for pardon of sin and for the accepting and accounting of his person as righteous in the sight of God. And thus he* hopes, *though he hath no certainty. The 'faith of assurance' is that whereby a man absolutely knows all this to be true in his own particular case. So that the faith of adherence is general but the faith of assurance is particular. Now this 'faith of adherence' alone is sufficient to bring a man to heaven, because the promises are given in general to every one who believes. And, therefore, to limit salvation to a particular degree of faith is to destroy all those promises on which thousands of Christians have hitherto depended for their eternal comfort. From which 'uncharitableness, false doctrine and heresy, Good Lord, deliver us!'*

Given, however, the still unsettled state of mind among the Methodists in 1765, Wesley decided to sum up the matter yet once more: to correlate the faith that saves with the faith that sanctifies. This was the task he set himself in The Scripture Way of Salvation. *In it, he gathered up the best residues of earlier sermons—*Salvation by Faith, *'Justification by Faith', and 'The Circumcision of the Heart'. Here he could reemphasize the point that in the Christian life all is of grace—'preventing', 'justifying', 'accompanying', and 'sanctifying'. He could have made Henry Smith's point yet again, that 'good works are* the *way to come to heaven, though they be not the* cause *why we shall come to heaven.'[1] The result is the most successful summary of the Wesleyan vision of the* ordo salutis *in the entire sermon corpus.*

When, therefore, he was reordering and republishing his Sermons

---

[1] See *Sermons*, ed. by Thomas Fuller (1675), p. 562.

in 1771, he could see the logic of adding The Scripture Way of Salvation *to the sequence of* Christian Perfection, Wandering Thoughts, *and 'Satan's Devices'. Later, in 1787, he would revert to the order of 1760 and, in effect, discard* The Scripture Way of Salvation. *Clearly, whatever the gain here in terms of the legal function of* SOSO, *its effect was an obvious loss in terms of doctrinal substance.*

Of all the written sermons, this one had the most extensive history of oral preaching behind it: forty instances of his using Eph. 2:8 before 1765, nine in 1738, including the first written sermon on it (No. 1, Salvation by Faith). *The text continued to be a favourite: twenty recorded instances in the quarter century following 1765. The* Scripture Way of Salvation *went through five further editions in Wesley's lifetime. For its publishing history and a list of variant readings, see Appendix, Vol. 4; see also* Bibliog, No. 265.

The Scripture Way of Salvation

Ephesians 2:8

Ye are saved through faith.

1. Nothing can be more intricate, complex, and hard to be understood, than religion as it has been often described. And this 5 is not only true concerning the religion of the heathens, even many of the wisest of them, but concerning the religion of those also who were in some sense Christians; yea, and men of great name in the Christian world, men 'who seemed to be pillars'[1] thereof. Yet how easy to be understood, how plain and simple a 10 thing, is the genuine religion of Jesus Christ! Provided only that

---

[1] Gal. 2:9, οἵ δοκοῦντες στύλοι εἶναι. . . . Later, in No. 82, 'On Temptation', §2, Wesley will argue for a different translation: 'by a careful consideration of every text in the New Testament wherein this word [δόκειν] occurs, I am fully convinced that it nowhere lessens, but everywhere strengthens, the sense of the word to which it is annexed. Accordingly, ὁ δόκει ἔχειν does not mean "what he *seems* to have" but on the contrary, "who he *assuredly* hath".' Cf. his translation to this same effect in the *Notes;* and see also Nos. 85, 'On Working Out Our Own Salvation', III.7; 90, 'An Israelite Indeed', I.5; 128, 'The Deceitfulness of the Human Heart', III.3. He nowhere notices the irony of Paul's use of δοκοῦντες in Gal. 2:9.

we take it in its native form, just as it is described in the oracles of God. It is exactly suited by the wise Creator and Governor of the world to the weak understanding and narrow capacity of man in his present state. How observable is this both with regard to the
5 end it proposes and the means to attain that end! The end is, in one word, salvation: the means to attain it, faith.

2. It is easily discerned that these two little words—I mean faith and salvation—include the substance of all the Bible, the marrow, as it were, of the whole Scripture. So much the more should we
10 take all possible care to avoid all mistake concerning them, and to form a true and accurate judgment concerning both the one and the other.

Let us then seriously inquire,
I. What is salvation?
15 II. What is that faith whereby we are saved? And
III. How we are saved by it.

I. 1. And first let us inquire, What is *salvation?* The salvation which is here spoken of is not what is frequently understood by that word, the going to heaven, eternal happiness. It is not the
20 soul's going to paradise, termed by our Lord 'Abraham's bosom'.[2] It is not a blessing which lies on the other side death, or (as we usually speak) in the other world. The very words of the text itself put this beyond all question. 'Ye *are* saved.' It is not something at a distance: it is a present thing, a blessing which, through the free
25 mercy of God, ye are now in possession of. Nay, the words may be rendered, and that with equal propriety, 'Ye *have been* saved.' So that the salvation which is here spoken of might be extended to the entire work of God, from the first dawning of grace in the soul till it is consummated in glory.
30 2. If we take this in its utmost extent it will include all that is wrought in the soul by what is frequently termed 'natural conscience', but more properly, 'preventing grace';[3] all the

---

[2] Luke 16:22. Cf. the Talmudic tractate *Kiddushin*, 72*b*, and the comment of Kaufmann Kohler in *The Jewish Encyclopedia*, 'Abraham's Bosom'. Bengel, *Gnomon, loc. cit.*, comments that 'the Jews used to call the state of the righteous dead "the bosom of Abraham" and "the Garden of Eden".' See No. 115, 'Dives and Lazarus', I.3 and n.

[3] A special gracious activity of the Holy Spirit in the heart and will, always in anticipation *(praeveniens)* of any human initiative or act of choice. 'Pre-venting' grace (distantly kin to what the Calvinists called 'common grace', save that it is uniquely the work of the Holy Spirit) 'goes before' conscious awareness of one's condition, to 'turn', to 'draw', to stir up 'the desires after God . . . all the convictions which the Holy Spirit . . . works in every child of man.' Thus, it displaces 'natural conscience' (the notion of which presupposes

'drawings' of 'the Father',[4] the desires after God, which, if we yield to them, increase more and more; all that 'light' wherewith the Son of God 'enlighteneth everyone that cometh into the world',[5] *showing* every man 'to do justly, to love mercy, and to walk humbly with his God';[6] all the *convictions* which his Spirit from time to time works in every child of man. Although it is true the generality of men stifle them as soon as possible, and after a while forget, or at least deny, that ever they had them at all.

3. But we are at present concerned only with that salvation which the Apostle is directly speaking of. And this consists of two general parts, justification and sanctification.

Justification is another word for pardon.[7] It is the forgiveness of all our sins, and (what is necessarily implied therein) our acceptance with God. The price whereby this hath been procured for us (commonly termed the 'meritorious cause' of our justification)[8] is the blood and righteousness of Christ, or (to

human autonomy and free will); it signifies the divine initiative in all human 're-actions' that aspire to faith. Thus, 'preventing' (prevenient) grace is the theological principle that assigns an absolute priority to the indwelling Spirit and yet allows for actual and valid human involvement, since the actions of the Holy Spirit are 'resistible', as the decrees of the Father are not (cf. the canons of the Second Council of Orange, A.D. 529).

Wesley's teaching here reaches back to Jerome, at least (cf. *Epistles*, 31, 33, 34, 62), and thence through the Middle Ages to Martin Bucer, Johann Gropper, and *The King's Book (A Necessary Doctrine and Erudition for Any Christian Man*, 'The Article of Free Will') to Fénelon (*Christian Counsel*, ch. XXI). But it assumes an even more crucial role in Wesley's thought, especially in his stress upon the Holy Spirit as its agent and on its transformation of 'natural conscience' (e.g., the analogue between its role in Wesley's ethics to the role of 'conscience' in Joseph Butler's *Fifteen Sermons*, II and III). It was in this sense that John Fletcher could rightly 'deny that Mr. Wesley is an Arminian', since 'Arminius held that man hath a will to turn to God *before* grace prevents him' (*Works*, 1825, I.229), whereas, for Wesley, it is the Spirit's prevenient motion by which 'we ever are moved and inspired to *any* good thing'. The early Wesley tended to ground 'preventing grace' in baptism; the mature Wesley linked it more closely to repentance; the late Wesley correlates it with the order of salvation as a whole; cf. No. 85, 'On Working Out Our Own Salvation', I.21 ('God *breathes* into us every good desire, and brings every good desire to good effect'), and III.3-4, Wesley's most compact and complete statement of the doctrine and its import. But see also *Notes* on Rom. 2:14, together with the comment in *Predestination Calmly Considered* (1752), §45; and yet another comment in *Some Remarks on Mr. Hill's Review* (1772), 12:xvi. Cf. Charles Rogers's Duke University dissertation, *The Doctrine of Prevenient Grace in John Wesley*. For other references to will and liberty, cf. No. 60, 'The General Deliverance', I.4 and n.

[4] Cf. John 6:44; and below, No. 47, 'Heaviness through Manifold Temptations', III.9 and n.

[5] Cf. John 1:9.   [6] Cf. Mic. 6:8.

[7] See No. 5, 'Justification by Faith', II.5 and n.

[8] An echo of the bitter controversy about the 'causes' of justification between the Roman Catholics, the Calvinists, and the Anglicans; cf. Nos. 5, 'Justification by Faith', II.5; and 20, *The Lord Our Righteousness*, intro.; see also C. F. Allison, *The Rise of Moralism*, ch. 1.

express it a little more clearly) all that Christ hath done and suffered for us till 'he poured out his soul for the transgressors.'⁹ The immediate effects of justification are, the peace of God, a 'peace that passeth all understanding',¹⁰ and a 'rejoicing in *hope* of
5 the glory of God',¹¹ 'with *joy* unspeakable and full of glory'.¹²

4. And at the same time that we are justified, yea, in that very moment, *sanctification* begins. In that instant we are 'born again', 'born from above',¹³ 'born of the Spirit'.¹⁴ There is a *real* as well as a *relative* change.¹⁵ We are inwardly renewed by the power of God.
10 We feel the 'love of God shed abroad in our heart by the Holy Ghost which is given unto us',¹⁶ producing love to all mankind, and more especially to the children of God; expelling the love of the world, the love of pleasure, of ease, of honour, of money; together with pride, anger, self-will, and every other evil
15 temper—in a word, changing the 'earthly, sensual, devilish'¹⁷ mind into 'the mind which was in Christ Jesus'.¹⁸

5. How naturally do those who experience such a change imagine that all sin is gone! That it is utterly rooted out of their heart, and has no more any place therein! How easily do they
20 draw that inference, 'I *feel* no sin; therefore I *have* none.' It does not *stir;* therefore it does not *exist:* it has no *motion;* therefore it has no *being.*

Session VI of Trent (ch. VII) had listed five distinguishable 'causes' of justification and had specified ' "the meritorious cause" as the atoning Passion and death of Jesus Christ who "merited our justification . . . unto God the Father" '. The Calvinists had countered this by insisting on the atonement as the *formal* cause of the justification *of the elect* (as in Davenant, Downham, and others). This had focused the issue: the idea of 'formal cause' entailed a doctrine of predestination on the one hand and irresistible grace on the other; the notion of 'meritorious cause' did not. Wesley had tried to hold to the good intentions of both views but finally was forced to come down on the side of 'meritorious cause' (as in No. 20, *The Lord Our Righteousness*). No other single point (which embraces the correlative issue of 'good works after faith') so excited the Calvinist polemic against him from 1765, both until and after his death.

⁹ Cf. Isa. 53:12.
¹⁰ Cf. Phil. 4:7.
¹¹ Cf. Rom. 5:2.   ¹² 1 Pet. 1:8.
¹³ John 3:3, 7. Cf. No. 3, *'Awake, Thou That Sleepest'*, I.2 and n.
¹⁴ John 3:6, 8.
¹⁵ Cf. No. 19, 'The Great Privilege of those that are Born of God', I.1 and n. The 'relative change' denotes the new relationship between God and his pardoned child; the 'real change' is in the actual heart and will of the justified one, which is the equivalent of regeneration, 'the new birth'—which in turn is the beginning of a new lifelong process of sanctification or holy living; cf. Nos. 18, 'The Marks of the New Birth'; and 45, 'The New Birth'.
¹⁶ Cf. Rom. 5:5. Cf. No. 3, *'Awake, Thou That Sleepest'*, II.10 and n.
¹⁷ Jas. 3:15.   ¹⁸ Cf. Phil. 2:5.

6. But it is seldom long before they are undeceived, finding sin was only suspended, not destroyed. Temptations return and sin revives, showing it was but stunned before, not dead. They now feel two principles in themselves, plainly contrary to each other: 'the flesh lusting against the spirit'[19], nature opposing the grace of God. They cannot deny that although they still feel power to believe in Christ and to love God, and although his 'Spirit' still 'witnesses with' their 'spirits that' they 'are the children of God';[20] yet they feel in themselves, sometimes pride or self-will, sometimes anger or unbelief. They find one or more of these frequently *stirring* in their heart, though not *conquering;* yea, perhaps 'thrusting sore at them, that they' may 'fall; but the Lord is' their 'help'.[21]

7. How exactly did Macarius, fourteen hundred years ago, describe the present experience of the children of God! 'The unskilful (or unexperienced), when grace operates, presently imagine they have no more sin. Whereas they that have discretion cannot deny that even we who have the grace of God may be molested again. . . . For we have often had instances of some among the brethren who have experienced such grace as to affirm that they had no sin in them. And yet after all, when they thought themselves entirely freed from it, the corruption that lurked within was stirred up anew, and they were wellnigh burnt up.'[22]

---

[19] Cf. Gal. 5:17. [20] Cf. Rom. 8:16.

[21] Cf. Ps. 118:13 (BCP). See Nos. 13, *On Sin in Believers;* 14, *The Repentance of Believers;* and 41, *Wandering Thoughts.*

[22] There was a fourth-century Egyptian hermit with this name who was renowned for his miracles and spiritual counsel. He was, however, probably not the author of the homilies and other pieces attributed to him in, Migne, *PG*, XXXIV; neither Palladius nor Rufinus makes any mention of them. Cf. Werner Jaeger, *Two Rediscovered Works of Ancient Christian Literature: Gregory of Nyssa and Macarius* (Leiden, E. J. Brill, 1954). Still, Wesley knew and loved the 'Macarian homilies'; he extracted and published twenty-two of them in Vol. I of the *Christian Lib.* (1749); for the passage cited here, cf. Homily IX, pp. 95-97. But cf. Migne, *PG*, XXXIV.623-34, and the Eng. tr. (which Wesley knew), 'By a Presbyter of the Church of England', *The Spiritual Homilies of Macarius the Egyptian* (1721), Homily XVII, 'Concerning the Spiritual Unction and Glory of Christians. And that without Christ it is Impossible to be Saved, or to be made Partaker of Eternal Life', p. 267: 'But the unsteady and unskilful, whenever grace operates, tho' but in part, imagine presently they have no more sin. Whereas they that have discretion and are prudent, never have the confidence to deny that we who even have the grace of God, are molested with obscene and filthy thoughts. For we have often had instances of some among the brethren, that have experienced such a degree of joy and grace, as to affirm that for five or six years running, concupiscence had withered quite away; and yet after all, when they thought themselves freed entirely from it, the corruption that lurked within, was stirred up anew, and they were even burnt up.' See also No. 112, *On Laying the Foundation of the New Chapel*, II.3.

8. From the time of our being 'born again' the gradual work of sanctification takes place. We are enabled 'by the Spirit' to 'mortify the deeds of the body',[23] of our evil nature. And as we are more and more dead to sin, we are more and more alive to God.
5 We go on from grace to grace, while we are careful to 'abstain from all appearance of evil',[24] and are 'zealous of good works',[25] 'as we have opportunity doing good to all men';[26] while we walk in all his ordinances blameless,[27] therein worshipping him in spirit and in truth;[28] while we take up our cross and deny ourselves every
10 pleasure that does not lead us to God.

9. It is thus that we wait for entire sanctification, for a full salvation from all our sins, from pride, self-will, anger, unbelief, or, as the Apostle expresses it, 'Go on to perfection.'[29] But what is perfection? The word has various senses: here it means perfect
15 love. It is love excluding sin; love filling the heart, taking up the whole capacity of the soul. It is love 'rejoicing evermore, praying without ceasing, in everything giving thanks'.[30]

II. But what is that 'faith through which we are saved'?[31] This is the second point to be considered.
20 1. Faith in general is defined by the Apostle, ἔλεγχος πραγμάτων οὐ βλεπομένων—'an evidence', a divine 'evidence and conviction' (the word means both), 'of things not seen'[32]—not visible, not perceivable either by sight or by any other of the external senses. It implies both a supernatural *evidence* of God and
25 of the things of God, a kind of spiritual *light* exhibited to the soul, and a supernatural *sight* or perception thereof. Accordingly the Scripture speaks sometimes of God's giving light, sometimes a power of discerning it. So St. Paul: 'God, who commanded light to shine out of darkness, hath shined in our hearts, to give us the
30 light of the knowledge of the glory of God in the face of Jesus

---

[23] Cf. Rom. 8:13.
[24] 1 Thess. 5:22.
[25] Titus 2:14.
[26] Cf. Gal. 6:10.
[27] Cf. Luke 1:6.
[28] See John 4:23, 24.
[29] Heb. 6:1.
[30] Cf. 1 Thess. 5:16-18.
[31] Cf. Eph. 2:8.
[32] Cf. Heb. 11:1; this, obviously, is a quotation from memory, since even *TR* here reads πραγμάτων ἔλεγχος. See No. 3, *'Awake, Thou That Sleepest'*, I.1 and n.; also, *An Earnest Appeal*, §§6-7 (11:46-47 in this edn.).

Christ.'[33] And elsewhere the same Apostle speaks 'of the eyes of' our 'understanding being opened'.[34] By this twofold operation of the Holy Spirit—having the eyes of our soul both *opened* and *enlightened*—we see the things which the natural 'eye hath not seen, neither the ear heard'.[35] We have a prospect of the invisible things of God. We see the *spiritual world*, which is all round about us, and yet no more discerned by our natural faculties than if it had no being; and we see the *eternal world*, piercing through the veil which hangs between time and eternity. Clouds and darkness then rest upon it no more,[36] but we already see the glory which shall be revealed.[37]

2. Taking the word in a more particular sense, faith is a divine evidence and conviction, not only that 'God was in Christ, reconciling the world unto himself',[38] but also that Christ 'loved *me*, and gave himself for *me*'.[39] It is by this faith (whether we term it the *essence*, or rather a *property* thereof) that we 'receive Christ';[40] that we receive him in all his offices, as our Prophet, Priest, and King.[41] It is by this that he 'is made of God unto us wisdom, and righteousness, and sanctification, and redemption'.[42]

3. 'But is this the "faith of assurance" or "faith of adherence"?' The Scripture mentions no such distinction. The Apostle says: 'There is one faith, and one hope of our calling,' one Christian, saving faith, as 'there is one Lord' in whom we believe, and 'one God and Father of us all.'[43] And it is certain this faith necessarily implies an *assurance* (which is here only another word for *evidence*, it being hard to tell the difference between them) that 'Christ loved *me*, and gave himself for *me*.' For 'he that believeth' with the true, living faith, 'hath the witness in himself.'[44] 'The Spirit witnesseth with his spirit that he is a child of God.'[45] 'Because he

[33] Cf. 2 Cor. 4:6.
[34] Eph. 1:18.
[35] Cf. 1 Cor. 2:9.
[36] An echo of Addison's *Cato;* cf. No. 117, 'On the Discoveries of Faith', §8 and n.
[37] Rom. 8:18. Yet another instance of the theory that our knowledge 'of God and the things of God' is a sort of *sight*, a direct intuition of 'the eternal world'. See No. 10, 'The Witness of the Spirit, I', I.12 and n.
[38] 2 Cor. 5:19.
[39] Gal. 2:20.
[40] Cf. Col. 2:6.
[41] For this Reformed concept of 'offices' and its import for Wesley's Christology, see Deschner, *Wesley's Christology,* chs. III–VI.
[42] Cf. 1 Cor. 1:30.   [43] Cf. Eph. 4:4-6.
[44] 1 John 5:10.   [45] Rom. 8:16.

is a son, God hath sent forth the Spirit of his Son into his heart, crying, Abba, Father;'⁴⁶ giving him an assurance that he is so, and a childlike confidence in him. But let it be observed that, in the very nature of the thing, the assurance goes before the
5 confidence. For a man cannot have a childlike confidence in God till he knows he is a child of God. Therefore confidence, trust, reliance, adherence, or whatever else it be called, is not the first, as some have supposed, but the second branch or act of faith.

4. It is by this faith we 'are saved', justified and sanctified,
10 taking that word in its highest sense. But how are we justified and sanctified by faith? This is our third head of inquiry. And this being the main point in question, and a point of no ordinary importance, it will not be improper to give it a more distinct and particular consideration.

15   III. 1. And first, how are we justified by faith? In what sense is this to be understood? I answer, faith is the condition, and the only condition, of justification. It is the condition: none is justified but he that believes; without faith no man is justified. And it is the only condition: this alone is sufficient for justification. Everyone
20 that believes is justified, whatever else he has or has not. In other words: no man is justified till he believes; every man when he believes is justified.

2. 'But does not God command us to *repent* also? Yea, and to "bring forth fruits meet for repentance"?⁴⁷ To "cease", for
25 instance, "from doing evil", and "learn to do well"?⁴⁸ And is not both the one and the other of the utmost necessity? Insomuch that if we willingly neglect either we cannot reasonably expect to be justified at all? But if this be so, how can it be said that faith is the only condition of justification?'

30   God does undoubtedly command us both to repent and to bring forth fruits meet for repentance; which if we willingly neglect we cannot reasonably expect to be justified at all. Therefore both repentance and fruits meet for repentance are in some sense necessary to justification.⁴⁹ But they are not necessary

---

⁴⁶ Cf. Gal. 4:6.
⁴⁷ Matt. 3:8.   ⁴⁸ Cf. Isa. 1:16-17.
⁴⁹ Elsewhere, Wesley stresses repentance as the normal preparatory state for the reception of justifying faith and, in that sense, 'necessary'; cf. No. 14, *The Repentance of Believers*, II.6 and n. See also Law's insistence in *A Practical Treatise upon Christian Perfection* (1726), in *Works* (1762), III. 84-86, that 'Repentance and sorrow for sin are [strictly] necessary to salvation.'

in the *same sense* with faith, nor in the *same degree*. Not in the *same degree;* for those fruits are only necessary *conditionally*, if there be time and opportunity for them. Otherwise a man may be justified without them, as was the 'thief' upon the cross (if we may call him so; for a late writer has discovered that he was no thief, but a very honest and respectable person!)[50] But he cannot be justified without faith: this is impossible. Likewise let a man have ever so much repentance, or ever so many of the fruits meet for repentance, yet all this does not at all avail: he is not justified till he believes. But the moment he believes, with or without those fruits, yea, with more or less repentance, he is justified. Not in the *same sense:* for repentance and its fruits are only *remotely* necessary, necessary in order to faith; whereas faith is *immediately* and *directly* necessary to justification. It remains that faith is the only condition which is *immediately* and *proximately* necessary to justification.

3. 'But do you believe we are sanctified by faith? We know you believe that we are justified by faith; but do not you believe, and accordingly teach, that we are sanctified by our works?'

So it has been roundly and vehemently affirmed for these five and twenty years.[51] But I have constantly declared just the contrary, and that in all manner of ways. I have continually testified in private and in public that we are sanctified, as well as justified, by faith. And indeed the one of these great truths does exceedingly illustrate the other. Exactly as we are justified by faith, so are we sanctified by faith. Faith is the condition, and the only condition of sanctification, exactly as it is of justification. It is the condition: none is sanctified but he that believes; without faith no man is sanctified. And it is the only condition: this alone is sufficient for sanctification. Everyone that believes is sanctified,

---

[50] See Matt. 27:38 and Mark 15:27. The 'late writer' was not Bengel, Burkitt, Heylyn, Henry, or Poole—and Wesley makes nothing of the idea that one of the λῃσταί was 'very honest and respectable'. This interpretation goes back, of course, to Josephus's account of the Zealots in his *Jewish War*, II. Josephus's first English translator, William Whiston (1737), may have been Wesley's 'late writer'; cf. his *Six Dissertations* (1734), No. I. See also Karl Rengstorf's article on λῃστής in Gerhard Kittel, ed., *Theological Dictionary of the New Testament*, IV.262: 'When Jesus was crucified and was thus punished as a political rebel against Rome, two others condemned as λῃσταί suffered with him. The title on the cross marked him as one of them.' Cf. also Haim Cohn, *The Trial and Death of Jesus* (New York, Harper and Row, 1967), p. 208.

[51] I.e., approximately from 1739, with Wesley's insistence in his preface to *Hymns and Sacred Poems* on good works following upon faith (see *Bibliog*, No. 13; and Vol. 12 of this edn.).

whatever else he has or has not. In other words: no man is sanctified till he believes; every man when he believes is sanctified.[52]

4. 'But is there not a repentance consequent upon, as well as a
5 repentance previous to, justification? And is it not incumbent on all that are justified to be "zealous of good works"?[53] Yea, are not these so necessary that if a man willingly neglect them he cannot reasonably expect that he shall ever be sanctified in the full sense, that is, "perfected in love"?[54] Nay, can he "grow" at all "in grace,
10 in the" loving "knowledge of our Lord Jesus Christ"?[55] Yea, can he retain the grace which God has already given him? Can he continue in the faith which he has received, or in the favour of God? Do not you yourself allow all this, and continually assert it? But if this be so, how can it be said that faith is the only condition
15 of sanctification?'

5. I do allow all this, and continually maintain it as the truth of God. I allow there is a repentance consequent upon, as well as a repentance previous to, justification.[56] It is incumbent on all that are justified to be zealous of good works. And these are so
20 necessary that if a man willingly neglect them, he cannot reasonably expect that he shall ever be sanctified. He cannot 'grow in grace', in the image of God, the mind which was in Christ Jesus;[57] nay, he cannot retain the grace he has received, he cannot continue in faith, or in the favour of God.

25 What is the inference we must draw herefrom? Why, that both repentance, rightly understood, and the practice of all good works, works of piety, as well as works of mercy (now properly so called, since they spring from faith) are in some sense necessary to sanctification.

30 6. I say 'repentance rightly understood'; for this must not be confounded with the former repentance. The repentance consequent upon justification is widely different from that which is antecedent to it. This implies no guilt, no sense of condemnation, no consciousness of the wrath of God. It does not

---

[52] Cf. Wesley's repetition of this emphasis on the close correlation between justification and sanctification in No. 107, 'On God's Vineyard', I.5-6.

[53] Titus 2:14.   [54] Cf. 1 John 2:5; 4:12, 18.   [55] 2 Pet. 3:18.

[56] See Nos. 14, *The Repentance of Believers*, proem, §2, and n.; 13. *On Sin in Believers;* and 8, 'The First-fruits of the Spirit', for other versions of this notion of 'repentance consequent upon justification'. The idea goes back to the *poenitentia secunda* of Tertullian (at least) and is a correlate of the doctrine of double justification.

[57] See Phil. 2:5.

suppose any doubt of the favour of God, or any 'fear that hath torment'.[58] It is properly a conviction wrought by the Holy Ghost of the 'sin' which still 'remains'[59] in our heart, of the φρόνημα σαρκός,[60] 'the carnal mind',[61] which 'does still *remain*', as our Church speaks, 'even in them that are regenerate'[62]—although it 5 does no longer *reign*,[63] it has not now dominion over them. It is a conviction of our proneness to evil, of an heart 'bent to backsliding',[64] of the still continuing tendency of the 'flesh' to 'lust against the Spirit'.[65] Sometimes, unless we continually watch and pray, it lusteth to pride, sometimes to anger, sometimes to love of 10 the world, love of ease, love of honour, or love of pleasure more than of God. It is a conviction of the tendency of our heart to self-will, to atheism, or idolatry; and above all to unbelief, whereby in a thousand ways, and under a thousand pretences, we are ever 'departing' more or less 'from the living God'.[66] 15

7. With this conviction of the sin *remaining* in our hearts there is joined a clear conviction of the sin remaining in our lives, still *cleaving* to all our words and actions. In the best of these we now discern a mixture of evil, either in the spirit, the matter, or the manner of them; something that could not endure the righteous 20 judgment of God, were he 'extreme to mark what is done amiss'.[67] Where we least suspected it we find a taint of pride of self-will, of unbelief or idolatry; so that we are now more ashamed of our best duties than formerly of our worst sins. And hence we cannot but feel that these are so far from having anything meritorious in 25 them, yea, so far from being able to stand in sight of the divine justice, that for those also we should be guilty before God were it not for the blood of the covenant.[68]

---

[58] Cf. 1 John 4:18.
[59] Cf. John 9:41.
[60] Cf. No. 13, *On Sin in Believers*, intro., I.3, III.1-9, and IV.1.
[61] Rom. 8:7.
[62] Cf. Art. IX, 'Of Original or Birth Sin'.
[63] Cf. No. 13, *On Sin in Believers*, intro., I.6, and n. This distinction between 'voluntary' and 'involuntary' sins is crucial. Voluntary sins ('sins properly so called') generate guilt and alienation; their 'reign' must be broken by God's pardoning mercy. The φρόνημα σαρκός remains, but has lost its dominion in the believer's heart; it does not, therefore, annul his assurance that God will pardon subsequent sins on the basis of 'consequent repentance'.
[64] Hos. 11:7.
[65] Cf. Gal. 5:17.
[66] Heb. 3:12.
[67] Ps. 130:3 (BCP).
[68] Exod. 24:8; Heb. 10:29.

8. Experience shows that together with this conviction of sin *remaining* in our hearts and *cleaving* to all our words and actions, as well as the guilt which on account thereof we should incur were we not continually sprinkled with the atoning blood, one thing
5 more is implied in this repentance, namely, a conviction of our helplessness, of our utter inability to think one good thought, or to form one good desire; and much more to speak one word aright, or to perform one good action but through his free, almighty grace, first preventing us, and then accompanying us every
10 moment.[69]

9. 'But what good works are those, the practice of which you affirm to be necessary to sanctification?' First, all works of piety,[70] such as public prayer, family prayer, and praying in our closet; receiving the Supper of the Lord; searching the Scriptures by
15 hearing, reading, meditating; and using such a measure of fasting or abstinence as our bodily health allows.

10. Secondly, all works of mercy, whether they relate to the bodies or souls of men; such as feeding the hungry, clothing the naked, entertaining the stranger, visiting those that are in prison,
20 or sick, or variously afflicted; such as the endeavouring to instruct the ignorant, to awaken the stupid sinner, to quicken the lukewarm, to confirm the wavering, to comfort the feeblemind-ed,[71] to succour the tempted,[72] or contribute in any manner to the saving of souls from death. This is the repentance, and these the
25 fruits meet for repentance, which are necessary to full sanctification. This is the way wherein God hath appointed his children to wait for complete salvation.

11. Hence may appear the extreme mischievousness of that seemingly innocent opinion that 'there is no sin in a believer; that
30 all sin is destroyed, root and branch, the moment a man is justified.'[73] By totally preventing that repentance[74] it quite blocks up the way to sanctification. There is no place for repentance in him who believes there is no sin either in his life or heart. Consequently there is no place for his being 'perfected in love',[75]
35 to which that repentance is indispensably necessary.

---

[69] Cf. above, I.2 and n.   [70] Cf. No. 14, *The Repentance of Believers*, I.13 and n.
[71] 1 Thess. 5:14.   [72] See Heb. 2:18.
[73] I.e., the view of men like Philip Molther (and, thereafter, of William Cudworth and James Relly); cf. No. 40, *Christian Perfection*, II.10 and n. And, since it denied the necessity of a 'second repentance', Wesley regarded it as a premise for antinomianism.
[74] I.e., 'second repentance'; cf. No. 14, *The Repentance of Believers*, proem, §§1-3, *et seq.*
[75] Cf. 1 John 4:18.

12. Hence it may likewise appear that there is no possible danger in *thus* expecting full salvation. For suppose we were mistaken, suppose no such blessing ever was or can be attained, yet we lose nothing. Nay, that very expectation quickens us in using all the talents which God has given us; yea, in improving them all, so that when our Lord cometh he will 'receive his own with increase'.[76]

13. But to return. Though it be allowed that both this repentance and its fruits are necessary to full salvation, yet they are not necessary either in the *same sense* with faith or in the *same degree*. Not in the same degree; for these fruits are only necessary *conditionally*, if there be time and opportunity for them. Otherwise a man may be sanctified without them. But he cannot be sanctified without faith. Likewise let a man have ever so much of this repentance, or ever so many good works, yet all this does not at all avail: he is not sanctified till he believes. But the moment he believes, with or without those fruits, yea, with more or less of this repentance, he is sanctified. Not in the *same sense;* for this repentance and these fruits are only *remotely* necessary, necessary in order to the continuance of his faith, as well as the increase of it; whereas faith is *immediately* and *directly* necessary to sanctification. It remains that faith is the only condition which is *immediately* and *proximately* necessary to sanctification.[77]

14. 'But what is that faith whereby we are sanctified, saved from sin and perfected in love?' It is a divine evidence and conviction, first, that God hath promised it in the Holy Scripture. Till we are thoroughly satisfied of this there is no moving one step farther. And one would imagine there needed not one word more to satisfy a reasonable man of this than the ancient promise, 'Then will I circumcise thy heart, and the heart of thy seed, to love the Lord your God with all your heart, and with all your soul.'[78] How clearly does this express the being perfected in love! How strongly imply the being saved from all sin! For as long as love takes up the whole heart, what room is there for sin therein?

15. It is a divine evidence and conviction, secondly, that what

[76] Cf. Matt. 25:27.

[77] The parallel here between faith and repentance in relation to both justification and sanctification is important for Wesley's solution to his problem of 'the remains of sin'; it is his alternative to the Lutheran *simul justus et peccator*. Faith is the only and equally necessary condition in both cases.

[78] Deut. 30:6. An echo of No. 17, 'The Circumcision of the Heart'.

God hath promised he is *able* to perform. Admitting therefore that 'with men it is impossible' to bring a clean thing out of an unclean, to purify the heart from all sin, and to fill it with all holiness, yet this creates no difficulty in the case, seeing 'with
5 God all things are possible.'[79] And surely no one ever imagined it was possible to any power less than that of the Almighty! But if God speaks, it shall be done. God saith, 'Let there be light: and there is light.'[80]

16. It is, thirdly, a divine evidence and conviction that he is able
10 and willing to do it *now*. And why not? Is not a moment to him the same as a thousand years?[81] He cannot want more time to accomplish whatever is his will. And he cannot want or stay for any more *worthiness* of *fitness* in the persons he is pleased to honour. We may therefore boldly say, at any point of time, 'Now is
15 the day of salvation.'[82] '*Today* if ye will hear his voice, harden not your hearts.'[83] 'Behold! all things are now ready! Come unto the marriage!'[84]

17. To this confidence, that God is both able and willing to sanctify us *now*, there needs to be added one thing more, a divine
20 evidence and conviction that *he doth it*. In that hour it is done. God says to the inmost soul, 'According to thy faith be it unto thee!'[85] Then the soul is pure from every spot of sin; 'it is clean from all unrighteousness.'[86] The believer then experiences the deep meaning of those solemn words, 'If we walk in the light, as he is in
25 the light, we have fellowship one with another, and the blood of Jesus Christ his Son cleanseth us from all sin.'[87]

18. 'But does God work this great work in the soul *gradually* or *instantaneously?*' Perhaps it may be gradually wrought in some. I mean in this sense—they do not advert to the particular moment
30 wherein sin ceases to be. But it is infinitely desirable, were it the will of God, that it should be done instantaneously; that the Lord should destroy sin 'by the breath of his mouth'[88] in a moment, in the twinkling of an eye.[89] And so he generally does, a plain fact of

[79] Cf. Matt. 19:26, etc.
[80] Cf. Gen. 1:3.
[81] See 2 Pet. 3:8; Ps. 90:4.
[82] 2 Cor. 6:2.
[83] Heb. 4:7.
[84] Matt. 22:4.
[85] Cf. Matt. 9:29.
[86] Cf. 1 John 1:9.
[87] 1 John 1:7.
[88] Job 15:30; Ps. 33:6.
[89] 1 Cor. 15:52.

which there is evidence enough to satisfy any unprejudiced person. *Thou* therefore look for it every moment. Look for it in the way above described; in all those 'good works' whereunto thou art 'created anew in Christ Jesus'.[90] There is then no danger. You can be no worse, if you are no better for that expectation. For were 5 you to be disappointed of your hope, still you lose nothing. But you shall not be disappointed of your hope: it will come, and will not tarry.[91] Look for it then every day, every hour, every moment. Why not this hour, this moment? Certainly you may look for it *now*, if you believe it is by faith. And by this token may you surely 10 know whether you seek it by faith or by works. If by works, you want something to be done *first, before* you are sanctified. You think, 'I must first *be* or *do* thus or thus.' Then you are seeking it by works unto this day. If you seek it by faith, you may expect it *as you are:* and if as you are, then expect it *now.* It is of importance to 15 observe that there is an inseparable connection between these three points—expect it *by faith,* expect it *as you are,* and expect it *now!* To deny one of them is to deny them all: to allow one is to allow them all. Do *you* believe we are sanctified by faith? Be true then to your principle, and look for this blessing just as you are, 20 neither better, nor worse; as a poor sinner that has still nothing to pay, nothing to plead but 'Christ died.'[92] And if you look for it as you are, then expect it *now.* Stay for nothing. Why should you? Christ is ready. And he is all you want. He is waiting for you. He is at the door![93] Let your inmost soul cry out, 25

> Come in, come in, thou heavenly Guest!
> Nor hence again remove:
> But sup with me, and let the feast
> Be everlasting love.[94]

---

[90] Eph. 2:10.
[91] See Heb. 10:37.
[92] Rom. 5:6, 8, etc.
[93] See Rev. 3:20.
[94] Cf. Wesley, *Hymns on God's Everlasting Love* (II), London, Strahan, 1742 (*Bibliog*, No. 47), Hymn 8, p. 25 (*Poet. Wks.*, III.66); the orig. has been slightly retouched.

ORIGINAL SIN

AN INTRODUCTORY COMMENT

One of the prime targets in orthodox Christianity for the deists and other apostles of enlightenment was the doctrine of original sin and total depravity. It was a cherished conviction of theirs that men, once freed from their superstitious errors, would recover their innate moral virtue: viz., the power to will the good and to do it (cf. Carl Becker, The Heavenly City of the Eighteenth-Century Philosophers, *and Peter* Gay, The Enlightenment*). The early Wesley was never more than lightly touched by these attacks, save for a passing flirtation with the newly fashionable cult of 'the noble savage'. His view of mankind's primal ruin is delineated in his very early sermon on Gen. 1:27,* [1] *and this is presupposed elsewhere in his comments on anthropology.*

But when a new optimism about man's innate virtue, with a corresponding denial of the Pauline and Augustinian notions of 'the Fall' and 'original sin', began to be urged by professed Christians, Wesley was quick to sense a radical challenge and to react on behalf of his people. To him, Article IX, 'Of Original or Birth Sin', had always seemed unexceptionable: '. . . Man is very far gone from original righteousness and is of his own nature *inclined to evil. . . . And this infection of nature doth remain . . . whereby the lust of the flesh, called in Greek,* φρόνημα σαρκός, *is not subject to the Law of God.'*

The issue had come into focus for him in 1740, when Dr. John Taylor, an eminent Dissenting minister in Norwich and a Hebrew scholar of growing fame, published an influential treatise, The Scripture Doctrine of Original Sin: Proposed to Free and Candid Examination *(cf. Alexander Gordon's comment on it in the* DNB: *'The effect of [this book] in combating the [orthodox] view of human nature was widespread and lasting. Its influence in Scotland is signalised by* Robert Burns, Epistle to John Goudie; *in New England, according to* Jonathan Edwards, *"no one book did so much towards rooting out the underlying ideas of the Westminster Confession".'). It had been quickly answered by two other Dissenting ministers,* Samuel Hebden, *in an*

---

[1] No. 141, 'The Image of God'.

appendix to Man's Original Righteousness *(1741), and in* The
Doctrine of Original Sin . . . Vindicated *(1741), and by Dr. David
Jennings,* A Vindication of the Scripture Doctrine of Original Sin
*(1740). Wesley joined the fray in 1757 with the longest treatise that he
ever wrote (in four disjointed parts),* The Doctrine of Original Sin:
According to Scripture, Reason, and Experience *(pp. 522).*[2] *Its
first part is most nearly Wesley's own answer to Taylor; in the others he
borrows heavily from Jennings, Hebden, Isaac Watts, Thomas Boston,
and others.*

*Meanwhile, he had been preaching on Gen. 6:5 (once in 1751; again
in 1754 and 1757; and six times in 1758). Even so, he realized that
oral preaching would not suffice in the circumstances and that his full
length volume was more than most of his people would read.
Accordingly, in 1759, he reformulated his own summary of Part I of*
The Doctrine of Original Sin *in sermon form and published it
separately in 1759. In 1760 he placed it at the head of the added fourth
volume of SOSO. In 1766 he asked his preachers in Conference, 'Have
the sermons on* Wandering Thoughts, In-being Sin *[i.e., this
present sermon; cf. Samuel Johnson's definition of 'inbeing'],* The
Lord Our Righteousness, *and* The Scripture Way of Salvation,
*been carefully dispersed?' and, to a negative answer, directed them to 'do
it now'.*[3] *In his mind, therefore, and in the logic of his soteriology, this
sermon was a major doctrinal statement in which he sought to compound
the Latin tradition of total depravity with the Eastern Orthodox view of
sin as disease (III.3) and of salvation as* θεραπεία ψυχῆς.[4] *Thus, it
still stands as a sufficient answer to all simple-minded references to
Wesley as a Pelagian.*

*For other references to 'original', 'inbred', 'inbeing' sin, cf. Nos. 5,
'Justification by Faith', I.5-9; 6, 'The Righteousness of Faith', II.6; 7,
'The Way to the Kingdom', II.1-7; 14,* The Repentance of
Believers, *I.20; 21, 'Sermon on the Mount, I', I.13; 47, 'Heaviness
through Manifold Temptations', III.9; and* Notes on Rom. 7:9. *For a
stemma illustrating the transmission of the text through the thirteen
extant editions issued in Wesley's lifetime, together with a list of variant
readings, see Appendix, Vol. 4; see also* Bibliog, No. 236.

---

[2] See *Bibliog*, No. 222; and Vol. 12 of this edn.

[3] *Minutes*, 1766, *Q*. [27].

[4] Cf. the origins of this idea of ϑεραπεία, in Robert E. Cushman, *Therapeia: Plato's
Conception of Philosophy* (Chapel Hill, N.C., Univ. of North Carolina Press, 1958), chs. II,
VI, X-XI.

Original Sin

Genesis 6:5

And God saw that the wickedness of man was great in the earth, and that every imagination of the thoughts of his heart was only evil continually.

1. How widely different is this from the fair pictures of human nature which men have drawn in all ages! The writings of many of the ancients abound with gay descriptions of the dignity of man; whom some of them paint as having all virtue and happiness in his
10 composition, or at least entirely in his power, without being beholden to any other being; yea, as self-sufficient, able to live on his own stock, and little inferior to God himself.[1]

2. Nor have heathens alone, men who were guided in their researches by little more than the dim light of reason, but many
15 likewise of them that bear the name of Christ, and to whom are entrusted the oracles of God,[2] spoke as magnificently concerning the nature of man, as if it were all innocence and perfection. Accounts of this kind have particularly abounded in the present century; and perhaps in no part of the world more than in our own
20 country. Here not a few persons of strong understanding, as well as extensive learning, have employed their utmost abilities to show what they termed 'the fair side of human nature'. And it must be acknowledged that if their accounts of him be just, man is still but 'a little lower than the angels', or (as the words may be
25 more literally rendered), 'a little less than God'.[3]

3. Is it any wonder that these accounts are very readily received

---

[1] Virgil and Ovid could have been read in this way (cf. *The Doctrine of Original Sin*, Pt. I, II.9); and so also Plato and Aristotle. Plato's vision of the nobility and transcendence of the human spirit had become a Renaissance commonplace, as one may see in Thomas More's *Utopia* (1551), or in James Harrington's *Common-Wealth of Oceana* (1656). Cf. No. 128, 'The Deceitfulness of the Human Heart', §§1-2.

[2] Cf. No. 5, 'Justification by Faith', §2 and n.

[3] Ps. 8:5; Heb. 2:7, 9. Only in Ps. 8:5 is the Hebrew *elohim* (אלהים) translated 'angels' in the AV; elsewhere it is translated 'God' (and in the Geneva Bible even Ps. 8:5 reads 'God'). As noted above, the innate virtue of man had been celebrated by the deists generally and by Shaftesbury, Bolingbroke, and Pope in particular. Bolingbroke, *Works*

by the generality of men? For who is not easily persuaded to think favourably of himself? Accordingly writers of this kind are almost universally read, admired, applauded. And innumerable are the converts they have made, not only in the gay but the learned world. So that it is now quite unfashionable to talk otherwise, to say anything to the disparagement of human nature; which is generally allowed, notwithstanding a few infirmities, to be very innocent and wise and virtuous.

4. But in the meantime, what must we do with our Bibles? For they will never agree with this. These accounts, however pleasing to flesh and blood, are utterly irreconcilable with the scriptural. The Scripture avers that 'by one man's disobedience all men were constituted sinners';[4] that 'in Adam all died',[5] spiritually died, lost the life and the image of God; that fallen, sinful Adam then 'begat a son in his own likeness';[6] nor was it possible he should beget him in any other, for 'who can bring a clean thing out of an unclean?'[7] That consequently *we*, as well as other men, 'were by nature'[8] 'dead in trespasses and sins',[9] 'without hope, without God in the world',[10] and therefore 'children of wrath';[11] that every man may say, 'I was shapen in wickedness, and in sin did my mother conceive me;'[12] that 'there is no difference, in that all have sinned, and come short of the glory of God,'[13] of that glorious image of God wherein man was originally created. And hence, when 'the Lord looked down from heaven upon the children of men, he saw they were all gone out of the way, they were altogether become abominable, there was none righteous, no not one', none that truly 'sought after God'.[14] Just agreeable, this, to what is declared by the Holy Ghost in the words above recited: 'God saw', when he looked down from heaven before, 'that the wickedness of man was great in the earth'; so great that 'every imagination of the thoughts of his heart was only evil continually'.[15]

(1777), V. 351, had appealed to those who sought enlightenment: 'Let us be convinced, however, in opposition to atheists and divines, that the general state of mankind in the present scheme of providence is a state not only tolerable but happy.' The same point had been made in Pope's *Essay on Man* (as in III.232):

> Man, like his Maker, saw that all was right;
> To virtue, in the paths of pleasure, trod,
> And owned a Father when he owned a God.

See also James Burgh, *The Dignity of Human Nature* (1754), a volume read by Wesley.
[4] Cf. Rom. 5:19 *(Notes)*.   [5] 1 Cor. 15:22.   [6] Gen. 5:3.   [7] Job 14:4.
[8] Eph. 2:3.   [9] Eph. 2:1.   [10] Eph. 2:12.   [11] Eph. 2:3; 6:4.
[12] Cf. Ps. 51:5 (BCP).   [13] Rom. 3:22-23.   [14] Cf. Ps. 14:3-4 (BCP).   [15] Gen. 6:5.

This is God's account of man: from which I shall take occasion, first, to show what men were before the flood; secondly, to inquire whether they are not the same now; and, thirdly, to add some inferences.

5 I. 1. I am, first, by opening the words of the text, to show what men were before the flood. And we may fully depend on the account here given. For God saw it, and he cannot be deceived. He 'saw that the wickedness of man was great'. Not of this or that man; not of a few men only; not barely of the greater part, but of *man in* 10 *general*, of men universally. The word includes the whole human race, every partaker of human nature. And it is not easy for us to compute their numbers, to tell how many thousands and millions they were. The earth then retained much of its primeval beauty and original fruitfulness. The face of the globe was not rent and torn as 15 it is now; and spring and summer went hand in hand. 'Tis therefore probable it afforded sustenance for far more inhabitants than it is now capable of sustaining. And these must be immensely multiplied while men begat sons and daughters for seven or eight hundred years together.[16] Yet among all this inconceivable number 20 *only* Noah 'found favour with God'.[17] He alone (perhaps including part of his household) was an exception from the universal wickedness, which by the just judgment of God in a short time after brought on universal destruction. All the rest were partakers in the same guilt, as they were in the same punishment.

25 2. 'God saw all the imaginations of the thoughts of his heart'—of his soul, his inward man, the spirit within him, the

---

[16] There had been a lively debate about the perfections of the antediluvian earth and the causes of the Flood; cf. Chambers's *Cyclopaedia* ('Deluge'), for a summary of popular wisdom on this point. Thomas Burnet, in his *Sacred Theory of the Earth*, had speculated that the hitherto smooth earth's outer crust had cracked and had opened up the pent-up floods beneath. This theory had then been attacked by Erasmus Warren and John Keill, but William Whiston sought to advance the debate with his own *New Theory of the Earth* (read by Newton in manuscript and praised by Locke). Whiston's theory had included the hypothesis of the earth's collision with a huge comet.

For Wesley's review of Burnet's theory, cf. JWJ, Jan. 17, 1770: 'He is doubtless one of our first-rate writers, both as to sense and style; his language is remarkably clear, unaffected, nervous, and elegant. And as to his theory, none can deny that it is ingenious, and consistent with itself. And it is highly probable (1) that the earth arose out of the chaos in some such manner as he describes; (2) that the antediluvian earth was without high or abrupt mountains, and without sea, being one uniform crust, enclosing the great abyss; (3) that the flood was caused by the breaking of this crust, and its sinking into the abyss of waters; and (4) that the present state of the earth, both internal and external, shows it to be the ruins of the former earth.'

[17] Cf. Gen. 6:8; Luke 1:30.

principle of all his inward and outward motions. He 'saw all the imaginations'. It is not possible to find a word of a more extensive signification. It includes whatever is formed, made, fabricated within; all that is or passes in the soul: every inclination, affection, passion, appetite; every temper, design, thought. It must of consequence include every word and action, as naturally flowing from the fountains, and being either good or evil according to the fountain from which they severally flow.

3. Now God 'saw that all' this, the whole thereof, 'was evil', contrary to moral rectitude; contrary to the nature of God, which necessarily includes all good; contrary to the divine will, the eternal standard of good and evil; contrary to the pure, holy image of God, wherein man was originally created, and wherein he stood when God, surveying the works of his hands, saw them all to be 'very good';[18] contrary to justice, mercy, and truth, and to the essential relations which each man bore to his Creator and his fellow creatures.

4. But was there not good mingled with the evil? Was there not light intermixed with the darkness? No, none at all: 'God saw that the whole imagination of the heart' of man 'was *only* evil.' It cannot indeed be denied but many of them, perhaps all, had good motions put into their hearts. For the spirit of God did then also 'strive with man',[19] if haply he might repent; more especially during that gracious reprieve, the hundred and twenty years while the ark was preparing. But still 'in his flesh dwelt no good thing:'[20] all his nature was purely evil. It was wholly consistent with itself, and unmixed with anything of any opposite nature.

5. However, it may still be matter of inquiry, 'Was there no intermission of this evil? Were there no lucid intervals, wherein something good might be found in the heart of man?' We are not here to consider what the grace of God might occasionally work in his soul.[21] And abstracting[22] from this, we have no reason to

---

[18] Gen. 1:31.   [19] Gen. 6:3.   [20] Cf. Rom. 7:18.

[21] I.e., prevenient grace, from which Wesley could infer that God's saving grace might find 'occasions' for action outside the scope of his ordinary dispensations (cf. No. 43, *The Scripture Way of Salvation*, I.2 and n.); for a comment on this doctrine of 'occasional' grace, cf. Michael Hurley, 'Salvation Today and Wesley Today' in *The Place of Wesley in the Christian Tradition*, Kenneth E. Rowe, ed., pp. 94–116. See also No. 91, 'On Charity', I.2 and n.

[22] I.e., 'disregarding'; cf. *OED*. Later edns. of the *Sermons* (1768 and thereafter) misread this as 'abstracted from'; see also below, No. 47, 'Heaviness through Manifold Temptations', III.1.

believe there was any intermission of that evil. For God, who 'saw the whole imagination of the thoughts of his heart to be *only* evil', saw likewise that it was always the same, that it 'was only evil *continually*'—every year, every day, every hour, every moment. 5 He never deviated into good.

II. Such is the authentic account of the whole race of mankind, which he who knoweth what is in man, who searcheth the heart and trieth the reins,[23] hath left upon record for our instruction. Such were all men before God brought the flood upon the earth. 10 We are, secondly, to inquire whether they are the same now.

1. And this is certain, the Scripture gives us no reason to think any otherwise of them. On the contrary, all the above-cited passages of Scripture refer to those who lived after the flood. It was above a thousand years after that God declared by David 15 concerning the children of men, 'They are all gone out of the way' of truth and holiness; 'there is none righteous, no, not one.'[24] And to this bear all the prophets witness in their several generations. So Isaiah concerning God's peculiar people (and certainly the heathens were in *no better* condition): 'The whole head is sick, and 20 the whole heart faint. From the sole of the foot even unto the head there is no soundness, but wounds and bruises and putrifying sores.'[25] The same account is given by all the apostles, yea, by the whole tenor of the oracles of God. From all these we learn concerning man in his natural state,[26] unassisted by the grace of 25 God, that 'all the imaginations of the thoughts of his heart' are still 'evil, only evil', and that 'continually'.

2. And this account of the present state of man is confirmed by daily experience. It is true the natural man discerns it not. And this is not to be wondered at. So long as a man born blind 30 continues so, he is scarce sensible of his want. Much less, could we suppose a place where all were born without sight, would they be sensible of the want of it. In like manner, so long as men remain in their natural blindness of understanding they are not sensible of their spiritual wants, and of this in particular.[27] But as 35 soon as God opens the eyes of their understanding they see the

[23] See Rev. 2:23; cf. also, Jer. 17:10.
[24] Cf. Ps. 14:4 (BCP).
[25] Isa. 1:5-6.
[26] Cf. No. 9, 'The Spirit of Bondage and of Adoption', §5 and n.
[27] Cf. No. 10, 'The Witness of the Spirit, I', I.12 and n.

state they were in before; they are then deeply convinced that 'every man living', themselves especially, are by nature 'altogether vanity';[28] that is, folly and ignorance, sin and wickedness.[29]

3. We see, when God opens our eyes, that we were before ἄθεοι ἐν [τῷ] κόσμῳ—'without God', or rather, 'atheists in the world'.[30] We had by nature no knowledge of God, no acquaintance with him. It is true, as soon as we came to the use of reason we learned 'the invisible things of God, even his eternal power and godhead', from 'the things that are made'.[31] From the things that are seen we inferred the existence of an eternal, powerful being that is not seen. But still, although we acknowledged his being, we had no acquaintance with him. As we know there is an emperor of China, whom yet we do not know, so we knew there was a King of all the earth; but yet we knew him not. Indeed we could not, by any of our natural faculties. By none of these could we attain the knowledge of God. We could no more perceive him by our natural understanding than we could see him with our eyes. For 'no one knoweth the Father but the Son, and he to whom the Son willeth to reveal him. And no one knoweth the Son but the Father, and he to whom the Father revealeth him.'[32]

4. We read of an ancient king who, being desirous to know what was the *natural language* of men, in order to bring the matter to a certain issue made the following experiment: he ordered two infants, as soon as they were born, to be conveyed to a place prepared for them, where they were brought up without any instruction at all, and without ever hearing an human voice. And what was the event? Why, that when they were at length brought out of their confinement, they spake no language at all, they uttered inarticulate sounds, like those of other animals.[33] Were

---

[28] Ps. 39:6 (BCP).

[29] Cf. Thomas Hobbes's famous epigram: 'No arts; no letters; no society; and which is worst of all, continual fear and danger of violent death; and the life of man, solitary, poor, nasty, brutish, and short' (*Leviathan*, Pt. I, ch. xiii).

[30] Eph. 2:12. Cf. also Nos. 79, 'On Dissipation', §7; 130, 'On Living without God', §1. Cf. also Wesley's *Notes*, and the Geneva Bible, where the marginal note is to 'atheists'.

[31] Cf. Rom. 1:20.

[32] Cf. Matt. 11:27.

[33] Cf. Herodotus, *History*, ii.2 (Loeb, 117:275-76); note how blithely Wesley has altered the story's original point to his own purposes. The ancient king was Psammetichus of Egypt, and the reported experiment was much as Wesley has it. But, 'when the shepherd [caretaker] . . . opened the door . . . both the children ran to him stretching out their hands and calling, "Bekos". . . . On command he brought the children into the king's

two infants in like manner to be brought up from the womb
without being instructed in any religion, there is little room to
doubt but (unless the grace of God interposed) the event would
be just the same. They would have no religion at all: they would
5　know no more of God than the beasts of the field, than the 'wild
ass's colt'.[34] Such is *natural religion*, abstracted from traditional,
and from the influences of God's spirit!

5. And having no knowledge, we can have no love of God: we
cannot love him we know not. Most men *talk* indeed of loving
10　God, and perhaps imagine that they do. At least few will
acknowledge they do not love him. But the fact is too plain to be
denied. No man loves God by nature, no more than he does a
stone, or the earth he treads upon. What we love, we delight in:
but no man has naturally any delight in God. In our natural state
15　we cannot conceive how anyone should delight in him. We take
no pleasure in him at all; he is utterly tasteless to us. To love God!
It is far above, out of our sight. We cannot naturally attain unto
it.[35]

6. We have by nature not only no love, but no fear of God. It is
20　allowed, indeed, that most men have, sooner or later, a kind of
senseless, irrational fear, properly called 'superstition'; though
the blundering Epicureans gave it the name of 'religion'.[36] Yet
even this is not natural, but acquired; chiefly by conversation or
from example. By nature 'God is not in all our thoughts.'[37] We
25　leave him to manage his own affairs, to sit quietly, as we imagine,
in heaven, and leave us on earth to manage ours. So that we have
no more of the fear of God before our eyes[38] than of the love of
God in our hearts.[39]

7. Thus are all men 'atheists in the world'.[40] But atheism itself

presence. Psammetichus heard them himself and inquired to what language this word
"Bekos" might belong. He was told it was a Phrygian word signifying "bread" [or food].
Reasoning from this fact, the Egyptians confessed that the Phrygians were older [in their
culture] than they.'

[34] Job 11:12. But see below, No. 106, 'On Faith, Heb. 11:6', I.4, for the story of Hai Ebn
Yokton, and for a very different inference as to our natural knowledge of God.

[35] See Ps. 139:5.

[36] Cf. Lucretius, *De Rerum Natura (On the Nature of Things)*, I.101, '*Tantum religio potuit
suadere malorum*' ('So potent was religion in persuading men to evil deeds').

[37] Cf. Ps. 10:4.　　　　　　　　　　　　　　　　　　　[38] See Rom. 3:18.

[39] See Rom. 5:5. Again, cf. the later Wesley's assertion (in No. 85, 'On Working Out
Our Own Salvation', III.4) that 'there is no man that is in a state of mere nature, . . . no
man, unless he has quenched the Spirit, that is wholly void of the grace of God.'

[40] Eph. 2:12; see above, II.3.

does not screen us from *idolatry*. In his natural state every man born into the world is a rank idolater.[41] Perhaps indeed we may not be such in the vulgar sense of the word. We do not, like the idolatrous heathens, worship molten or graven images. We do not bow down to the stock of a tree, to the work of our own hands. We do not pray to the angels or saints in heaven, any more than to the saints that are upon earth. But what then? We 'have set up our idols in our heart';[42] and to these we bow down, and worship them. We worship ourselves when we pay that honour to ourselves which is due to God only. Therefore all pride is idolatry; it is ascribing to ourselves what is due to God alone. And although pride was not made for man, yet where is the man that is born without it? But hereby we rob God of his unalienable right, and idolatrously usurp his glory.

8. But pride is not the only sort of idolatry which we are all by nature guilty of. Satan has stamped his own image on our heart in *self-will* also. 'I will', said he, before he was cast out of heaven, 'I will sit upon the sides of the north.'[43] I will do my own will and pleasure, independently on that of my Creator. The same does every man born into the world say, and that in a thousand instances. Nay, and avow it, too, without ever blushing upon the account, without either fear or shame. Ask the man, 'Why did you do this?' He answers, 'Because I had a mind to it.' What is this but, 'Because it was my will;' that is, in effect, because the devil and I are agreed; because Satan and I govern our actions by one and the same principle. The will of God meantime is not in his thoughts, is not considered in the least degree; although it be the supreme rule of every intelligent creature, whether in heaven or earth, resulting from the essential, unalterable relation which all creatures bear to their Creator.

9. So far we bear the image of the devil, and tread in his steps. But at the next step we leave Satan behind, we run into an idolatry whereof he is not guilty: I mean *love of the world,* which is now as natural to every man as to love his own will. What is more natural to us than to seek happiness in the creature instead of the

---

[41] Cf. Thomas Manton, *Works* (1681), IV.41: "Every man is naturally an idolater, and he makes the creature his God;' also, Stephen Charnock, *Works* (1684), I.4: 'that secret atheism which is in the heart of every man by nature'. Cf. also No. 23, 'Sermon on the Mount, III', I.11 and n.

[42] Cf. Ezek. 14:3, 4, 7.

[43] Cf. Isa. 14:13.

Creator? To seek that satisfaction in the works of his hands which can be found in God only? What more natural than the desire of the flesh?[44] That is, of the pleasure of sense in every kind? Men indeed talk magnificently of despising these low pleasures,
5 particularly men of learning and education. They affect to sit loose[45] to the gratification of those appetites wherein they stand on a level with the beasts that perish. But it is mere affectation; for every man is conscious to himself that in this respect he is by nature a very beast. Sensual appetites, even those of the lowest
10 kind, have, more or less, the dominion over him. They lead him captive, they drag him to and fro, in spite of his boasted reason. The man, with all his good breeding and other accomplishments, has no pre-eminence over the goat. Nay, it is much to be doubted whether the beast has not the pre-eminence over him! Certainly
15 he has, if we may hearken to one of their modern oracles, who very decently tells us:

> Once in a season, beasts too taste of love:
> Only the beast of reason is its slave,
> And in that folly drudges all the year.[46]

20 A considerable difference indeed, it must be allowed, there is between man and man, arising (beside that wrought by preventing grace) from difference of constitution and of education. But notwithstanding this, who that is not utterly ignorant of himself can here cast the first stone at another?[47] Who
25 can abide the test of our blessed Lord's comment on the seventh

---

[44] See 1 John 2:16; see below, II.10, 11; cf. also No. 7, 'The Way to the Kingdom', II.2 and n.

[45] A colloquialism in Wesley's time, as may be seen in Addison, *The Spectator*, No. 119 (July 17, 1711), and earlier in Francis Atterbury, *Sermons* (Pref., p. xi.). Cf. Nos. 88, 'On Dress', §12; and 108, 'On Riches', II.12. Charles Wesley used it in *Hymns and Sacred Poems* (1749), II. 286 (*Poet. Wks.*, V. 429): 'Sit loose to all below.'

[46] Cf. Thomas Otway, *The Orphan; or the Unhappy Marriage*, Act V, sc. 1:

> Once in a season they [deer] taste of love:
> Only the beast of reason is its slave,
> And in that folly drudges all the year.

Wesley had read Otway's *Orphan* while at Oxford (it was even performed in Charleston in 1736 during his time in nearby Georgia). This is all the more remarkable in view of his denunciations of the English theatre (following after William Law and Jeremy Collier, *et al.*). Clearly, this did not deter him from reading widely in English drama, from Shakespeare to Douglas Home, or from putting his recollections to his own uses. Cf. No. 89, 'The More Excellent Way', V.4 and n.

[47] See John 8:7.

commandment: 'He that looketh upon a woman to lust after her hath committed adultery with her already in his heart'?[48] So that one knows not which to wonder at most, the ignorance or the insolence of those men who speak with such disdain of them that are overcome by desires which every man has felt in his own breast! The desire of every pleasure of sense, innocent or not, being natural to every child of man.

10. And so is 'the desire of the eye',[49] the desire of the pleasures of the imagination.[50] These arise either from great, or beautiful, or uncommon objects—if the two former do not coincide with the latter; for perhaps it would appear upon a diligent inquiry that neither *grand* nor *beautiful* objects please any longer than they are *new;* that when the novelty of them is over, the greatest part, at least, of the pleasure they give is over; and in the same proportion as they become familiar they become flat and insipid. But let us experience this ever so often, the same desire will remain still. The inbred thirst continues fixed in the soul. Nay, the more it is indulged, the more it increases, and incites us to follow after another and yet another object; although we leave every one with an abortive hope and a deluded expectation. Yea,

> The hoary fool, who many days
> Has struggled with continued sorrow,
> Renews his hope, and fondly lays
> The desperate bet upon tomorrow!
>
> Tomorrow comes! 'Tis noon! 'Tis night!
> This day like all the former flies:
> Yet on he goes, to seek delight
> Tomorrow, till tonight he dies![51]

---

[48] Cf. Matt. 5:28.

[49] 1 John 2:16, see above, II.9 and n.

[50] Addison wrote at least nine essays in *The Spectator* on 'The Pleasures of the Imagination' (Nos. 411-14, 416-18, 420, 421). Bishop Berkeley also used the phrase in an issue of *The Guardian*, No. 49 (May 7, 1713). Thomas Hobbes, *Leviathan*, 'Of the Passions', Pt. I, ch. vi, speaks of 'the pleasures of the mind'. See also Cicero, *De Senectute,* xiv. 50.

The phrase was a favourite of Wesley's, as in Nos. 68, 'The Wisdom of God's Counsels', §16; 73, 'Of Hell', I.1; 81, 'In What Sense we are to Leave the World', §11; 84, *The Important Question*, I.3; 90, 'An Israelite Indeed', I.1; and *Notes* on 1 John 2:16. Cf. also Nos. 78, 'Spiritual Idolatry', I.12 (where he says history gratifies the imagination and pleases us by touching our passions); 107, 'On God's Vineyard', V. 3; 108, 'On Riches', II.3; and 125, 'On a Single Eye', II.1.

[51] Cf. Matthew Prior, 'To the Honourable Charles Montague', st. 4, 5, orig., 'blindly lays' and 'on he runs'. Wesley printed this in *AM* (1779), II.153, as 'The Pursuit of Happiness'—without credit to Prior.

11. A third symptom of this fatal disease, the love of the world, which is so deeply rooted in our nature, is 'the pride of life',[52] the desire of praise, of 'the honor that cometh of men'.[53] This the greatest admirers of human nature allow to be strictly natural—as natural as the sight or hearing, or any other of the external senses. And are they ashamed of it, even men of letters, men of refined and improved understanding? So far from it that they glory therein; they applaud themselves for their love of applause! Yea, eminent Christians, so called, make no difficulty of adopting the saying of the old, vain heathen, *Animi dissoluti est et nequam negligere quid de se homines sentiant:*[54] 'Not to regard what men think of us is the mark of a wicked and abandoned mind.' So that to go calm and unmoved 'through honour and dishonour, through evil report and good report'[55], is with them a sign of one that is indeed 'not fit to live; away with such a fellow from the earth.'[56] But would one imagine that these men had ever heard of Jesus Christ or his apostles? Or that they knew who it was that said, 'How can ye believe, who receive honour one of another, and seek not that honour which cometh of God only?'[57] But if this be really so; if it be impossible to believe, and consequently to please God, so long as we 'receive (or *seek*) honour one of another, and seek not the honour which cometh of God only'; then in what a condition are all mankind! The Christians as well as the heathens! Since they all seek 'honour one of another'! Since it is as natural for them so to do, themselves being the judges, as it is to see the light which strikes upon their eye, or to hear the sound which enters their ear; yea, since they account it the sign of a virtuous mind to seek the praise of men, and of a vicious one to be content with 'the honour which cometh of God only'!

III. 1. I proceed to draw a few inferences from what has been said. And, first, from hence we may learn one grand, fundamental difference between Christianity, considered as a system of doctrines, and the most refined heathenism. Many of the ancient

---

[52] 1 John 2:16; see above, II.9 and n.

[53] Cf. John 5:41, 44.

[54] A paraphrase of Cicero, *De Officiis (On Moral Obligations)*, I.xxviii.99: '*Nam neglegere, quid de se quisque sentiat, non solum arrogantis est, sed etiam omnino dissoluti*' ('For to disregard what others think of you is not only arrogant but actually unprincipled'). Thus, Wesley makes Cicero's point but in his own Latin.

[55] 2 Cor. 6:8 *(Notes)*.   [56] Cf. Acts 22:22.

[57] Cf. John 5:44.

heathens have largely described the vices of particular men. They have spoken much against their covetousness or cruelty, their luxury or prodigality. Some have dared to say that 'no man is born without vices of one kind or another.'[58] But still, as none of them were apprised of the fall of man, so none of them knew his total corruption. They knew not that all men were empty of all good, and filled with all manner of evil. They were wholly ignorant of the entire depravation of the whole human nature, of every man born into the world, in every faculty of his soul, not so much by those particular vices which reign in particular persons as by the general flood of atheism and idolatry, of pride, self-will, and love of the world. This, therefore, is the first, grand, distinguishing point between heathenism and Christianity. The one acknowledges that many men are infected with many vices, and even born with a proneness to them; but supposes withal that in some the natural good much overbalances the evil. The other declares that all men are 'conceived in sin', and 'shapen in wickedness';[59] that hence there is in every man a 'carnal mind which is enmity against God, which is not, cannot be, subject to his law',[60] and which so infects the whole soul that 'there dwelleth in him, in his flesh', in his natural state, 'no good thing;'[61] but 'all the imagination of the thoughts of his heart is evil', *only* evil', and that 'continually.'

2. Hence we may, secondly, learn that all who deny this—call it 'original sin' or by any other title—are but heathens still in the fundamental point which differences heathenism from Christianity. They may indeed allow that men have many vices; that some are born with us; and that consequently we are not born altogether so wise or so virtuous as we should be; there being few that will roundly affirm we are born with as much propensity to good as to evil, and that every man is by nature as virtuous and wise as Adam was at his creation. But here is the shibboleth:[62] Is man by nature filled with all manner of evil? Is he void of all good?

---

[58] Horace, *Satires*, I.iii. 68, '*vitiis nemo sine nascitur*'. Cf. *The Doctrine of Original Sin* (1757), p. 217 (II.vi. 1, Vol. 12 in this edn.), where the same passage is quoted, along with supporting testimony from Horace and Seneca.
[59] Cf. Ps. 51:5 (BCP).   [60] Cf. Rom. 8:7.
[61] Cf. Rom. 7:18.
[62] Cf. Judg. 12:4-6, and also *OED* for examples of this term (meaning 'a catchword'). Wesley had denied that good works was a Methodist shibboleth in his *Second Letter to Dr. Free* (1758); he would also warn his own people against making perfection a shibboleth of their own; see *Farther Thoughts on Christian Perfection* (1763), *Q.–A.* 34, included in *A Plain Account of Christian Perfection*.

Is he wholly fallen? Is his soul totally corrupted? Or, to come back
to the text, is 'every imagination of the thoughts of his heart evil
continually'? Allow this, and you are so far a Christian. Deny it,
and you are but an heathen still.

5   3. We may learn from hence, in the third place, what is the
proper nature of religion, of the religion of Jesus Christ. It is
θεραπεία ψυχῆς,[63] God's method of healing a soul which is *thus
diseased.* Hereby the great Physician of souls applies medicine to
heal *this sickness;* to restore human nature, totally corrupted in all
10   its faculties. God heals all our atheism by the knowledge of
himself, and of Jesus Christ whom he hath sent; by giving us faith,
a divine evidence and conviction of God and of the things of
God—in particular of this important truth: Christ loved *me,* and
gave himself for *me.*[64] By repentance and lowliness of heart the
15   deadly disease of pride is healed; that of self-will by resignation, a
meek and thankful submission to the will of God. And for the love
of the world in all its branches the love of God is the sovereign
remedy. Now this is properly religion, 'faith thus working by
love',[65] working the genuine, meek humility, entire deadness to
20   the world, with a loving, thankful acquiescence in and conformity
to the whole will and Word of God.

    4. Indeed if man were not thus fallen there would be no need of
all this. There would be no occasion for this work in the heart, this
'renewal in the spirit of our mind'.[66] The 'superfluity of godliness'
25   would then be a more proper expression than the 'superfluity of
naughtiness'.[67] For an outside religion without any godliness at all
would suffice to all rational intents and purposes. It does
accordingly suffice, in the judgment of those who deny this
corruption of our nature. They make very little more of religion
30   than the famous Mr. Hobbes did of reason. According to him,
reason is only 'a well-ordered train of words':[68] according to them,
religion is only a well-ordered train of words and actions. And

[63] Cf. Plato, *Laches,* 185*e; Gorgias,* 513*d; Republic,* 585*d;* see also Cushman, *Therapeia,*
pp. 295-301, for an extended comment on this therapeutic concept of salvation, which
Wesley preferred above all juridical and forensic metaphors. E.g., in the 'Preface' to *The
Doctrine of Original Sin,* §4, he had said: '. . . nor can the Christian philosophy . . . be more
properly defined than in Plato's word: It is θεραπεία Ψυχῆς, "the only true method of
healing a distempered soul".'
[64] Gal. 2:20.   [65] Cf. Gal. 5:6.
[66] Cf. Eph. 4:23.   [67] Jas. 1:21.
[68] Thomas Hobbes (1588–1679), author of *Leviathan* (1651); see Wesley's other
references to him in No. 70, 'The Case of Reason Impartially Considered', §1, II.4. The
quotation is not from Hobbes directly but from John Norris, *Reflections Upon the Conduct of*

they speak consistently with themselves; for if the inside be not 'full of wickedness', if this be clean already, what remains but to 'cleanse the outside of the cup'?[69] Outward reformation, if their supposition be just, is indeed the one thing needful.

5. But ye have not so learned the oracles of God. Ye know that he who seeth what is in man gives a far different account both of nature and grace, of our fall and our recovery. Ye know that the great end of religion is to renew our hearts in the image of God, to repair that total loss of righteousness and true holiness which we sustained by the sin of our first parent.[70] Ye know that all religion which does not answer this end, all that stops short of this, the renewal of our soul in the image of God, after the likeness of him that created it, is no other than a poor farce and a mere mockery of God, to the destruction of our own soul. O beware of all those teachers of lies who would palm this upon you for Christianity! Regard them not, though they should come unto you with 'all the deceivableness of unrighteousness',[71] with all smoothness of language, all decency, yea, beauty and elegance of expression, all professions of earnest goodwill to you, and reverence for the Holy Scriptures. Keep to the plain, old 'faith, once delivered to the saints'[72], and delivered by the Spirit of God to your hearts. Know your disease! Know your cure! Ye were born in sin; therefore 'ye must be born again'[73], 'born of God'.[74] By nature ye are wholly corrupted; by grace ye shall be wholly renewed. 'In Adam ye all died;' in the second Adam, 'in Christ, ye all are made alive.'[75] You 'that were dead in sins hath he quickened'.[76] He hath already given you a principle of life, even 'faith in him who loved *you*, and gave himself for *you*'![77] Now 'go on'[78] 'from faith to faith'[79], until your whole sickness be healed, and all that 'mind be in you which was also in Christ Jesus'![80]

Human Life, p. 44: 'Thus Mr. Hobbes makes reason to be nothing but *"Sequela Nominum"*, a well-ordered train of words.' (Wesley published an extract of Norris's *Reflections* in 1734; see *Bibliog.* No. 3.) Hobbes's own text is in *Leviathan*, I.iv.12: 'The general use of speech is to transfer our mental discourse into verbal, or the train of our thoughts into a train of words;' see also IV.xlvi-xlvii. 370, 379, 383.

[69] Cf. Luke 11:39.

[70] The recovery of the defaced image of God is the axial theme of Wesley's soteriology; cf. Nos. 12, 'The Witness of Our Own Spirit', §16; 45, 'The New Birth', III.1; 85, 'On Working Out Our Own Salvation', §2; 129, 'Heavenly Treasure in Earthen Vessels', I.2; see also Nos. 1, *Salvation by Faith*, §1 and n.; and 5, 'Justification by Faith', I.4 and n.

[71] 2 Thess. 2:10.   [72] Jude 3.   [73] John 3:7.
[74] 1 John 3:9; cf. John 3:8.   [75] Cf. 1 Cor. 15:22.   [76] Cf. Eph. 2:5.
[77] Cf. Gal. 2:20.   [78] Heb. 6:1.   [79] Rom. 1:17.   [80] Phil. 2:5.

THE NEW BIRTH

AN INTRODUCTORY COMMENT

In conventional Anglican soteriology the basic remedy for original sin had always lain in the church and the sacrament of baptism (as it had been in the ancient church, where ἄφεσιν ἁμαρτιῶν, *'remission of sins', is regularly included in the third article of the creeds in connection with belief in the Holy Spirit and the church). The young Wesley had grown up with this tradition and had reproduced it in his publication of 'A Treatise on Baptism' (1758), without any acknowledgement that he had abridged his father's discourse,* The Pious Communicant Rightly Prepared; . . . to which is added, A Short Discourse of Baptism *(1700). Even the mature Wesley had remarked, as if it were a general commonplace, 'that these privileges [of being "born again"] by the free mercy of God, are ordinarily annexed to baptism'.[1] But as tensions in the Revival mounted, between the claims of nominal Christians to baptismal regeneration and the claims of the evangelicals to 'conversion', the whole problem of regeneration in relation both to justification and sanctification became more and more urgent. And now that Wesley had restated his doctrine of original sin, there was an obvious logic in following it with an updated version of his doctrine of 'new birth', with a special reference, in the new situation, to some of his revisions of the conventional notions of baptismal regeneration.*

This written sermon, then, is a sort of distillate of more than sixty oral sermons on John 3:7, reaching back to the 1740s (once in 1740) and continued with increasing frequency in the 1750s (five times in 1755; eleven in 1756; six in 1757; fourteen in 1758; thirteen in 1759). We may see here a rough measure of the importance of the point about 'conversion' as perceived by Wesley and his people. 'The New Birth' is Wesley's conscious effort to provide them with a formal statement of the issue, even though, as an essay, it is clearly incomplete in both its form and argument. Similar comments may be found in Wesley's Notes on Matt. 18:4 *and John 3:7; see also Nos. 1,* Salvation by Faith, *II.7; 19, 'The Great Privilege of those that are Born of God', §1-2; 57, 'On the Fall of Man', II.9-10; and 83, 'On Patience', §9.*

---

[1] See No. 18, 'The Marks of the New Birth', §1.

In addition to its first appearance in SOSO, *IV (1760), and again in* Works *(1771), IV, this sermon was printed separately at least five times during Wesley's lifetime. For its publishing history, together with a list of variant readings, see the Appendix, Vol. 4; see also* Bibliog, *No. 131.i.*

The New Birth

John 3:7

Ye must be born again.

1. If any doctrines within the whole compass of Christianity may be properly termed fundamental they are doubtless these 5 two—the doctrine of justification, and that of the new birth: the former relating to that great work which God does *for us*, in forgiving our sins; the latter to the great work which God does *in us*, in renewing our fallen nature.[1] In order of time neither of these is before the other. In the moment we are justified by the grace of 10 God through the redemption that is in Jesus we are also 'born of the Spirit'[2]; but in order of thinking, as it is termed, justification precedes the new birth. We first conceive his wrath to be turned away, and then his Spirit to work in our hearts.

2. How great importance, then, must it be of to every child of 15 man throughly to understand these fundamental doctrines! From a full conviction of this, many excellent men have wrote very largely concerning justification, explaining every point relating thereto, and opening the Scriptures which treat upon it. Many likewise have wrote on the new birth—and some of them largely 20 enough—but yet not so clearly as might have been desired, nor so deeply and accurately; having either given a dark, abstruse account of it, or a slight and superficial one. Therefore a full and at the same time a clear account of the new birth seems to be wanting still. Such as may enable us to give a satisfactory answer 25 to these three questions: First, why must we be born again? What

[1] Cf. No. 5, 'Justification by Faith', II.1 and n.
[2] John 3:6, 8.

is the foundation of this doctrine of the new birth? Secondly, how
must we be born again? What is the nature of the new birth? And
thirdly, wherefore must we be born again? To what end is it
necessary? These questions, by the assistance of God, I shall
5 briefly and plainly answer, and then subjoin a few inferences
which will naturally follow.

I. 1. And, first, why must we be born again? What is the
foundation of this doctrine? The foundation of it lies near as deep
as the creation of the world, in the scriptural account whereof we
10 read, 'And God', the three-one God,[3] 'said, Let us make man in
our image, after our likeness. So God created man in his own
image, in the image of God created he him.'[a] Not barely in his
natural image, a picture of his own immortality, a spiritual being
endued with understanding, freedom of will, and various
15 affections; nor merely in his *political image*, the governor of this
lower world, having 'dominion over the fishes of the sea, and over
the fowl of the air, and over the cattle, and over all the earth';[4] but
chiefly in his *moral image*,[5] which, according to the ·Apostle, is
'righteousness and true holiness'.[b] In this image of God was man
20 made. 'God is love:'[6] accordingly man at his creation was full of
love, which was the sole principle of all his tempers, thoughts,
words, and actions.[7] God is full of justice, mercy, and truth: so
was man as he came from the hands of his Creator. God is
spotless purity: and so man was in the beginning pure from every
25 sinful blot. Otherwise God could not have pronounced *him* as
well as all the other works of his hands, 'very good'.[c] This he could
not have been had he not been pure from sin, and filled with
righteousness and true holiness. For there is no medium. If we
suppose an intelligent creature not to love God, not to be

[a] Gen. 1:26-27.
[b] Eph. 4:24.
[c] Gen. 1:31. [Cf. No. 141, 'The Image of God'.]

[3] Cf. No. 55, *On the Trinity*, §17 and n.
[4] Cf. Gen. 1:26.
[5] These phrases, 'political image' (i.e., social) and 'moral image', are borrowings
from Isaac Watts, *Ruin and Recovery of Mankind* (1740); cf. Wesley's long quotation from
Watts in *The Doctrine of Original Sin* (1757), pp. 310-11. See also No. 1, *Salvation by Faith*,
§1 and n.
[6] 1 John 4:8, 16.
[7] This passage reappears, in altered form, in J. Wakelin, *Christ and Nicodemus* (1760), a
rare instance of any attention paid to Wesley's sermons outside his own Methodist
constituency.

righteous and holy, we necessarily suppose him not to be good at all; much less to be 'very good'.

2. But although man was made in the image of God, yet he was not made immutable. This would have been inconsistent with that state of trial in which God was pleased to place him. He was therefore created able to stand, and yet liable to fall. And this God himself apprised him of, and gave him a solemn warning against it. Nevertheless 'man did not abide in honour.'[8] He fell from his high estate. He 'ate of the tree whereof the Lord had commanded him, Thou shalt not eat thereof.'[9] By this wilful act of disobedience to his Creator, this flat rebellion against his sovereign, he openly declared that he would no longer have God to rule over him; that he would be governed by his own will, and not the will of him that created him, and that he would not seek his happiness in God, but in the world, in the works of his hands. Now God had told him before, 'In the day that thou eatest' of that fruit 'thou shalt surely die.'[10] And the word of the Lord cannot be broken. Accordingly in that day he did die: he died to God, the most dreadful of all deaths. He lost the life of God: he was separated from him in union with whom his spiritual life consisted. The body dies when it is separated from the soul, the soul when it is separated from God. But this separation from God Adam sustained in the day, the hour, he ate of the forbidden fruit. And of this he gave immediate proof; presently showing by his behaviour that the love of God was extinguished in his soul, which was now 'alienated from the life of God'.[11] Instead of this he was now under the power of servile fear, so that he fled from the presence of the Lord.[12] Yea, so little did he retain even of the knowledge of him who filleth heaven and earth that he endeavoured to 'hide himself from the Lord God, among the trees of the garden'.[d] So had he lost both the knowledge and the love of God, without which the image of God would not subsist. Of this therefore he was deprived at the same time, and became unholy as well as unhappy.[13] In the room of this he had sunk into

[d] Gen. 3:8.

---

[8] Cf. Ps. 49:12 (BCP). [9] Cf. Gen. 3:11, 17.
[10] Gen. 2:17.
[11] Eph. 4:18.
[12] Jonah 1:10.
[13] Cf. below, III.3; also No. 5, 'Justification by Faith', I.4 and n.

pride and self-will, the very image of the devil, and into sensual appetites and desires, the image of the beasts that perish.

3. If it be said, 'Nay, but that threatening, "In the day that thou eatest thereof thou shalt surely die," refers to temporal death, and
5 that alone, to the death of the body only;' the answer is plain: to affirm this is flatly and palpably to make God a liar—to aver that the God of truth positively affirmed a thing contrary to truth. For it is evident Adam did not *die* in this sense 'in the day that he ate thereof'. He lived, in the sense opposite to this death, above nine
10 hundred years after; so that this cannot possibly be understood of the death of the body without impeaching the veracity of God. It must therefore be understood of spiritual death, the loss of the life and image of God.

4. And 'in Adam all died,'[14] all humankind, all the children of
15 men who were then in Adam's loins. The natural consequence of this is that everyone descended from him comes into the world spiritually dead, dead to God, wholly 'dead in sin';[15] entirely void of the life of God, void of the image of God, of all that 'righteousness and holiness'[16] wherein Adam was created. In-
20 stead of this every man born into the world now bears the image of the devil, in pride and self-will; the image of the beast, in sensual appetites and desires. This then is the foundation of the new birth—the entire corruption of our nature.[17] Hence it is that being 'born in sin'[18] we 'must be born again'.[19] Hence everyone
25 that is born of a woman must be born of the Spirit of God.

II. 1. But how must a man be born again? What is the nature of the new birth?[20] This is the second question. And a question it is of the highest moment that can be conceived. We ought not, therefore, in so weighty a concern, to be content with a slight
30 inquiry, but to examine it with all possible care, and to ponder it in our hearts, till we fully understand this important point, and clearly see how we are to be born again.

---

[14] Cf. 1 Cor. 15:22.   [15] Cf. Eph. 2:5; Col. 2:13.
[16] Eph. 4:24.
[17] A recapitulation of the effects of the Fall, as in No. 44, *Original Sin*, I.3, II.9; see also Nos. 57, 'On the Fall of Man'; 60, 'The General Deliverance', I.6-II.2; 69, 'The Imperfection of Human Knowledge', §3; 76, 'On Perfection', I.1-2; 95, 'On the Education of Children', §5; 129, 'Heavenly Treasure in Earthen Vessels', §2; 130, 'On Living without God', §15; and 141, 'The Image of God', II.
[18] Cf. John 9:34.   [19] John 3:7.
[20] See No. 19, 'The Great Privilege of those that are Born of God', I.1-2 and n.

2. Not that we are to expect any minute, philosophical account of the *manner how* this is done. Our Lord sufficiently guards us against any such expectation by the words immediately following the text: wherein he reminds Nicodemus of as indisputable a fact as any in the whole compass of nature—which, notwithstanding, 5 the wisest man under the sun is not able fully to explain. 'The wind bloweth where it listeth', not by thy power or wisdom, 'and thou hearest the sound thereof.' Thou art absolutely assured, beyond all doubt, that it doth blow. 'But thou canst not tell whence it cometh, neither whither it goeth.' The precise manner 10 how it begins and ends, rises and falls, no man can tell. 'So is everyone that is born of the Spirit.'[21] Thou mayst be as absolutely assured of the fact as of the blowing of the wind; but the precise manner how it is done, how the Holy Spirit works this in the soul, neither thou nor the wisest of the children of men is able to 15 explain.

3. However, it suffices for every rational and Christian purpose that without descending into curious, critical inquiries, we can give a plain scriptural account of the nature of the new birth. This will satisfy every reasonable man who desires only the salvation of 20 his soul. The expression, 'being born again', was not first used by our Lord in his conversation with Nicodemus. It was well known before that time, and was in common use among the Jews when our Saviour appeared among them. When an adult heathen was convinced that the Jewish religion was of God, and desired to join 25 therein, it was the custom to baptize him first, before he was admitted to circumcision. And when he was baptized he was said to be 'born again': by which they meant that he who was before a child of the devil was now adopted into the family of God, and accounted one of his children.[22] This expression therefore which 30 Nicodemus, being 'a teacher in Israel',[23] ought to have understood well, our Lord uses in conversing with him; only in a stronger sense than he was accustomed to. And this might be the reason of his asking, 'How can these things be?'[24] They cannot be literally. 'A man' cannot 'enter a second time into his mother's 35 womb and be born'.[25] But they may, spiritually. A man may be

[21] John 3:8.
[22] See an extensive documentation of this in *The Jewish Encyclopedia* ('Birth, New' and 'Baptism').
[23] John 3:10 (Geneva Bible).
[24] John 3:9.   [25] Cf. John 3:4.

'born from above',[26] 'born of God',[27] 'born of the Spirit'[28]—in a manner which bears a very near analogy to the natural birth.

4. Before a child is born into the world he has eyes, but sees not; he has ears, but does not hear. He has a very imperfect use of any other sense. He has no knowledge of any of the things of the world, nor any natural understanding. To that manner of existence which he then has we do not even give the name of life. It is then only when a man is born that we say, he begins to live. For as soon as he is born he begins to see the light and the various objects with which he is encompassed. His ears are then opened, and he hears the sounds which successively strike upon them. At the same time all the other organs of sense begin to be exercised upon their proper objects. He likewise breathes and lives in a manner wholly different from what he did before. How exactly does the parallel hold in all these instances![29] While a man is in a mere natural state, before he is born of God, he has, in a spiritual sense, eyes and sees not; a thick impenetrable veil lies upon them. He has ears, but hears not; he is utterly deaf to what he is most of all concerned to hear. His other spiritual senses are all locked up; he is in the same condition as if he had them not. Hence he has no knowledge of God, no intercourse with him; he is not at all acquainted with him. He has no true knowledge of the things of God, either of spiritual or eternal things. Therefore, though he is a living man, he is a dead Christian. But as soon as he is born of God there is a total change in all these particulars. The 'eyes of his understanding are opened'[30] (such is the language of the great Apostle). And he who of old 'commanded light to shine out of darkness shining on his heart', he sees 'the light of the glory of God', his glorious love, 'in the face of Jesus Christ'.[31] His ears being opened, he is now capable of hearing the inward voice of God, saying, 'Be of good cheer, thy sins are forgiven thee:'[32] 'Go and sin no more.'[33] This is the purport of what God speaks to his heart; although perhaps not in these very words. He is now ready to hear whatsoever 'he that teacheth man knowledge'[34] is pleased

[26] John 3:3. Cf. No. 3, *'Awake, Thou That Sleepest,'* I.2 and n.
[27] 1 John 3:9, etc.   [28] John 3:6, 8.
[29] This point, basic to Wesley's intuitionist epistemology, will be made again, with a remarkable anecdote, in No. 130, 'On Living without God'; see also No. 10, 'The Witness of the Spirit', I', I.12 and n.
[30] Eph. 1:18.   [31] Cf. 2 Cor. 4:6.
[32] Cf. Matt. 9:2.   [33] John 8:11.
[34] Ps. 94:10.

from time to time to reveal to him. He 'feels in his heart' (to use the language of our Church) 'the mighty working of the Spirit of God'.[35] Not in a gross, carnal sense, as the men of the world stupidly and wilfully misunderstand the expression, though they have been told again and again, we mean thereby neither more 5 nor less than this: he feels, is inwardly sensible of, the graces which the Spirit of God works in his heart. He feels, he is conscious of, a 'peace which passeth all understanding'.[36] He many times feels such a joy in God as is 'unspeakable and full of glory'.[37] He feels 'the love of God shed abroad in his heart by the 10 Holy Ghost which is given unto him'.[38] And all his spiritual senses are then 'exercised to discern' spiritual 'good and evil'.[39] By the use of these he is daily increasing in the knowledge of God, of Jesus Christ whom he hath sent, and of all the things pertaining to his inward kingdom. And now he may properly be said *to live:* God 15 having quickened him by his Spirit,[40] he is alive to God through Jesus Christ.[41] He lives a life which the world knoweth not of, a 'life' which 'is hid with Christ in God'.[42] God is continually breathing, as it were, upon his soul, and his soul is breathing unto God. Grace is descending into his heart, and prayer and praise 20 ascending to heaven. And by this intercourse between God and man, this fellowship with the Father and the Son,[43] as by a kind of spiritual respiration, the life of God in the soul is sustained: and the child of God grows up, till he comes to 'the full measure of the stature of Christ'.[44]   25

5. From hence it manifestly appears what is the nature of the new birth. It is that great change which God works in the soul when he brings it into life:[45] when he raises it from the death of sin

---

[35] The echoes here are from the Elizabethan Homily XVII for 'Rogation Week', III; and also XVI, for 'Whitsunday', I. From the former, cf. *Homilies*, p. 434: 'God give us grace, good people, to know these things and to feel them in our hearts. . . . Let us therefore meekly call upon . . . the Holy Ghost . . . that he would assist us . . . that in him we may be able to hear the goodness of God declared unto us for our salvation.' From the latter, cf. *ibid.*, p. 409: '. . . the more it is hid from our understanding, the more it ought to move all men to wonder at the *secret and mighty working of God's Holy Spirit* which is within us. For it is the Holy Ghost . . . that doth quicken the minds of men, stirring up good and godly motions in their hearts [i.e., prevenient grace].' See also No. 130, 'On Living without God', §8; and *A Farther Appeal*, Pt. I, V.24-26 (11:166-70 in this edn.).

[36] Phil. 4:7.   [37] 1 Pet. 1:8.
[38] Cf. Rom. 5:5.   [39] Heb. 5:14.
[40] See 1 Pet. 3:18.   [41] Rom. 6:11.
[42] Col. 3:3.   [43] See 1 John 1:3.
[44] Cf. Eph. 4:13.
[45] Cf. No. 19, 'The Great Privilege of those that are Born of God', I.1 and n.

to the life of righteousness. It is the change wrought in the whole
soul by the almighty Spirit of God when it is 'created anew in
Christ Jesus',[46] when it is 'renewed after the image of God',[47] 'in
righteousness and true holiness',[48] when the love of the world
5 is changed into the love of God, pride into humility, passion
into meekness; hatred, envy, malice, into a sincere, tender,
disinterested love for all mankind. In a word, it is that change
whereby the 'earthly, sensual, devilish' mind[49] is turned into 'the
mind which was in Christ'.[50] This is the nature of the new birth.
10 'So is everyone that is born of the Spirit.'[51]

III. 1. It is not difficult for any who has considered these things
to see the necessity of the new birth, and to answer the third
question: Wherefore, to what ends, is it necessary that we should
be born again? It is very easily discerned that this is necessary,
15 first, in order to holiness. For what is holiness, according to the
oracles of God? Not a bare external religion, a round of outward
duties, how many soever they be, and how exactly soever
performed. No; gospel holiness is no less than the image of God
stamped upon the heart.[52] It is no other than the whole mind
20 which was in Christ Jesus. It consists of all heavenly affections
and tempers mingled together in one. It implies such a continual,
thankful love to him who hath not withheld from us his Son, his
only Son,[53] as makes it natural, and in a manner necessary to us, to
love every child of man; as fills us with 'bowels of mercies,
25 kindness, gentleness, long-suffering'.[54] It is such a love of God as
teaches us to be blameless in all manner of conversation; as
enables us to present our souls and bodies, all we are and all we
have, all our thoughts, words, and actions, a continual sacrifice to
God, acceptable through Christ Jesus.[55] Now this holiness can
30 have no existence till we are renewed in the image of our mind. It
cannot commence in the soul till that change be wrought, till by

---

[46] Cf. Eph. 2:10.   [47] Cf. Col. 3:10.   [48] Eph. 4:24.
[49] Jas. 3:15.   [50] Cf. Phil. 2:5.   [51] John 3:8.
[52] Cf. Wesley's letter to his father, Dec. 10, 1734, §§4, 6 (25:398-99 in this edn.): 'That
course of life tends most to the glory of God wherein we can most promote holiness in
ourselves and others. . . . By holiness I mean, not fasting, or bodily austerity, or any other
external means of improvement, but that inward temper to which all these are subservient,
a renewal of soul in the image of God.'
[53] See Gen. 22:12, 16.
[54] Cf. Col. 3:12. For this concept of holiness as *love* (of God *and* of 'every child of man'),
cf. No. 7, 'The Way to the Kingdom', I.10 and n.
[55] See 1 Pet. 2:5.

the power of the highest overshadowing us[56] we are brought 'from darkness to light, from the power of Satan unto God';[57] that is, till we are born again; which therefore is absolutely necessary in order to holiness.

2. But 'without holiness no man shall see the Lord,'[58] shall see the face of God in glory. Of consequence the new birth is absolutely necessary in order to eternal salvation. Men may indeed flatter themselves (so desperately wicked and so deceitful is the heart of man!)[59] that they may live in their sins till they come to the last gasp, and yet afterward live with God. And thousands do really believe that they have found a 'broad way which leadeth' not 'to destruction'.[60] What danger, say they, can a woman be in, that is so *harmless* and so *virtuous?* What fear is there that so *honest* a man, one of so strict *morality*, should miss of heaven? Especially if over and above all this they constantly attend on church and sacrament. One of these will ask with all assurance, 'What, shall not I do as well as my neighbours?' Yes, as well as your unholy neighbours; as well as your neighbours that die in their sins. For you will all drop into the pit together, into the nethermost hell. You will all lie together in the lake of fire, 'the lake of fire burning with brimstone'.[61] Then at length you will see (but God grant you may see it before!) the necessity of holiness in order to glory—and consequently of the new birth, since none can be holy except he be born again.

3. For the same reason, except he be born again none can be happy even in this world. For it is not possible in the nature of things that a man should be happy who is not holy.[62] Even the poor ungodly poet could tell us,

> *Nemo malus felix*—[63]

no wicked man is happy. The reason is plain: all unholy tempers are uneasy tempers. Not only malice, hatred, envy, jealousy, revenge, create a present hell in the breast, but even the softer passions, if not kept within due bounds, give a thousand times more pain than pleasure. Even 'hope', when 'deferred' (and how

---

[56] See Luke 1:35.   [57] Acts 26:18.   [58] Cf. Heb. 12:14.
[59] See Jer. 17:9.   [60] Cf. Matt. 7:13.   [61] Rev. 19:20.
[62] See above, I.2 and n.

[63] Juvenal, *Satires*, iv. 8-9: *Nemo malus felix, minime corruptor et idem incestus* ('no bad man can be happy: least of all an incestuous seducer'). This dictum of Juvenal's (here levied against Crispinus) is repeated in No. 84, *The Important Question*, III.7.

often must this be the case!) 'maketh the heart sick.'[64] And every desire which is not according to the will of God is liable to 'pierce us through with many sorrows'.[65] And all those general sources of sin, pride, self-will, and idolatry, are, in the same proportion as 5 they prevail, general sources of misery. Therefore as long as these reign in any soul happiness has no place there. But they must reign till the bent of our nature is changed, that is, till we are born again. Consequently the new birth is absolutely necessary in order to happiness in this world, as well as in the world to come.

10 IV. I proposed in the last place to subjoin a few inferences which naturally follow from the preceding observations.

1. And, first, it follows that baptism is not the new birth: they are not one and the same thing. Many indeed seem to imagine they are just the same; at least, they speak as if they thought so. 15 But I do not know that this opinion is publicly avowed by any denomination of Christians whatever. Certainly it is not by any within these kingdoms, whether of the Established Church, or dissenting from it. The judgment of the latter is clearly declared in their *Larger Catechism: 'Q.* What are the parts of a sacrament? *A.* 20 The parts of a sacrament are two: the one, an outward and sensible sign [. . .]; the other, an inward and spiritual grace thereby signified: [. . .] *Q.* What is baptism? *A.* Baptism is a sacrament [. . .] wherein Christ hath ordained the washing with water [. . .] to be a sign and seal of [. . .] regeneration by his 25 Spirit.'[e] Here it is manifest [that] baptism, the sign, is spoken of as distinct from regeneration, the thing signified.

In the Church Catechism likewise the judgment of our Church is declared with the utmost clearness. 'What meanest thou by this word, "sacrament"? I mean an outward and visible sign of an 30 inward and spiritual grace. [. . .] What is the outward part or form in baptism? Water, wherein the person is baptized, "In the name of the Father, Son, and Holy Ghost". What is the inward part or thing signified? A death unto sin, and a new birth unto

---

[e] *Qq.* 163, 165. [Published by the Westminster Assembly in 1647; the ellipses are here added to indicate Wesley's abridgements of the original. Cf. his earlier abridgement of the Westminster *Shorter Catechism* (also in 1647) in the *Christian Lib.*, Vol. XXXI; see also the passage on 'The Sacraments' in the BCP Catechism.]

---

[64] Prov. 13:12.
[65] Cf. 1 Tim. 6:10.

righteousness.'[66] Nothing therefore is plainer than that, according to the Church of England, baptism is not the new birth. But indeed the reason of the thing is so clear and evident as not to need any other authority. For what can be more plain than that the one is an external, the other an internal work? That the one 5 is a visible, the other an invisible thing, and therefore wholly different from each other: the one being an act of man, purifying the body, the other a change wrought by God in the soul. So that the former is just as distinguishable from the latter as the soul from the body, or water from the Holy Ghost.   10

2. From the preceding reflections we may, secondly, observe that as the new birth is not the same thing with baptism, so it does not always accompany baptism; they do not constantly go together. A man may possibly be 'born of water',[67] and yet not be 'born of the Spirit'.[68] There may sometimes be the outward 15 sign where there is not the inward grace. I do not now speak with regard to infants: it is certain, our Church supposes that all who are baptized in their infancy are at the same time born again. And it is allowed that the whole office for the baptism of infants proceeds upon this supposition. Nor is it an objection of any 20 weight against this that we cannot comprehend how this work can be wrought in infants: for neither can we comprehend *how* it is wrought in a person of riper years. But whatever be the case with infants, it is sure all of riper years who are baptized are not at the same time born again. 'The tree is known by its fruits.'[69] And 25 hereby it appears too plain to be denied that divers of those who were children of the devil before they were baptized continue the same after baptism: 'For the works of' their 'father they do';[70] they

---

[66] An abridgement of the section on Baptism in the BCP Catechism. Henry Hammond, *Practical Catechism*, VI.ii.348-57, had made no sharp distinction between the external and internal 'works' in baptism, nor had any of the other representative spokesmen of the Church of England; see, for examples, More and Cross, *Anglicanism*, pp. 423-29, and espec. Jeremy Taylor, *The Great Exemplar; . . . the History of the Life and Death of the Ever-Blessed Jesus Christ* (1649), I.ix, in *Works* (1844), I.129: 'In baptism we are born again. . . . The second birth spoken of in Scripture *is* baptism.' See also Wesley's own 'Treatise on Baptism': 'This regeneration which our Church in so many places ascribes to baptism is more than barely being admitted into the Church. . . . By . . . the water of baptism we are regenerated or born again; whence it is also called by the Apostle, "the washing of regeneration" [Titus 3:5] . . . .' The fact is that Wesley had changed his views on this point; his evangelical concern was to separate 'the new birth' from all 'external acts' in order to support his newer emphasis on 'conversion'. See also *Works* (1771), XIX.275-97.

[67] John 3:5.   [68] John 3:6, 8.
[69] Matt. 12:33.   [70] Cf. John 8:41, 44.

continue servants of sin, without any pretence either to inward or outward holiness.

3. A third inference which we may draw from what has been observed is that the new birth is not the same with sanctification. 5 This is indeed taken for granted by many; particularly by an eminent writer in his late treatise on 'the nature and grounds of Christian regeneration'.[71] To waive several other weighty objections which might be made to that tract, this is a palpable one: it all along speaks of regeneration as a progressive work 10 carried on in the soul by slow degrees from the time of our first turning to God.[72] This is undeniably true of sanctification; but of regeneration, the new birth, it is not true. This is a part of sanctification, not the whole; it is the gate of it, the entrance into it. When we are born again, then our sanctification, our in- 15 ward and outward holiness, begins. And thenceforward we are gradually to 'grow up in him who is our head'.[73] This expression of the Apostle admirably illustrates the difference between one and the other, and farther points out the exact analogy there is between natural and spiritual things. A child is born of a woman 20 in a moment, or at least in a very short time. Afterward he gradually and slowly grows till he attains the stature of a man. In like manner a child is born of God in a short time, if not in a moment. But it is by slow degrees that he afterward grows up to the measure of the full stature of Christ.[74] The same relation 25 therefore which there is between our natural birth and our growth there is also between our new birth and our sanctification.

---

[71] Law, *The Grounds and Reasons of Christian Regeneration or the New Birth* (1739), *Works* (1762), V.155-66. Wesley had reacted sharply against this little book shortly after its publication, as in JWJ, Oct. 23, 1739: 'I read over Mr. Law's book on the new birth: philosophical, speculative, precarious; Behmenish, void, and vain! "O what a fall is there!"' See also CWJ, Oct. 19, 1739. There are, however, echoes of Law's treatise in Wesley's sermon. For instance, Law is much concerned with 'the nature, manner, and necessity of our redemption through Christ's blood, and a life received from him . . .' (§16), and holds it 'proper to inquire when and how this great work is done in the soul' (§29). More, regeneration is defined as consisting 'solely in the *restoration* of the birth of the Son of God in the human soul' *(ibid.)*. The crucial disagreement came over Law's conflation of regeneration and sanctification, where he speaks of 'regeneration . . . as a certain *process*, a *gradual release* from our captivity and disorder, consisting of several *stages* and *degrees*, both of life and death, which the soul must go through before it can have thoroughly put off the old Man' (§49). Even here, Wesley argued for *sanctification* as process, 'a gradual release from our captivity and disorder'. What he denied was that it *had* to go through life *and death* before 'perfection in love' might be attained.
[72] See No. 107, 'On God's Vineyard', I.7.
[73] Cf. Eph. 4:15.   [74] See Eph. 4:13.

4. One point more we may learn from the preceding observations. But it is a point of so great importance as may excuse the considering it the more carefully, and prosecuting it at some length. What must one who loves the souls of men, and is grieved that any of them should perish, say to one whom he sees 5 living in sabbath-breaking, drunkenness, or any other wilful sin? What can he say, if the foregoing observations are true, but 'you must be born again.' 'No', says a zealous man, 'that cannot be. How can you talk so uncharitably to the man? Has he not been baptized already? He cannot be born again now.' Can he not be 10 born again? Do you affirm this? Then he cannot be saved. Though he be as old as Nicodemus was, yet, 'except he be born again, he cannot see the kingdom of God.'[75] Therefore in saying, 'he cannot be born again,' you in effect deliver him over to damnation. And where lies the uncharitableness now? On my 15 side, or on yours? I say, 'He may be born again, and so become an heir of salvation.' You say, 'He cannot be born again.' And if so, he must inevitably perish. So you utterly block up his way to salvation, and send him to hell out of mere charity!

But perhaps the sinner himself, to whom in real charity we say, 20 'You must be born again,' has been taught to say, 'I defy your new doctrine; I need not be born again. I was born again when I was baptized. What! Would you have me deny my baptism?' I answer, first, there is nothing under heaven which can excuse a lie. Otherwise I should say to an open sinner, 'If you have been 25 baptized, do not own it.' For how highly does this aggravate your guilt! How will it increase your damnation! Was you devoted to God at eight days old, and have you been all these years devoting yourself to the devil? Was you, even before you had the use of reason, consecrated to God the Father, the Son, and the Holy 30 Ghost? And have you, ever since you had the use of it, been flying in the face of God, and consecrating yourself to Satan? Does the abomination of desolation,[76] the love of the world, pride, anger, lust, foolish desire, and a whole train of vile affections, stand where it ought not? Have you set up all these accursed things in 35 that soul which was once a 'temple of the Holy Ghost'?[77] Set apart for 'an habitation of God through the Spirit'?[78] Yea, solemnly

[75] Cf. John 3:3.
[76] Matt. 24:15.
[77] 1 Cor. 6:19.
[78] Eph. 2:22.

given up to him? And do you glory in this, that you once belonged to God? O, be ashamed! Blush! Hide yourself in the earth! Never boast more of what ought to fill you with confusion, to make you ashamed before God and man! I answer, secondly, you have
5 already denied your baptism; and that in the most effectual manner. You have denied it a thousand and a thousand times; and you do so still day by day. For in your baptism you renounced the devil and all his works.[79] Whenever therefore you give place to him again, whenever you do any of the works of the devil, then you
10 deny your baptism. Therefore you deny it by every wilful sin; by every act of uncleanness, drunkenness, or revenge; by every obscene or profane word; by every oath that comes out of your mouth. Every time you profane the day of the Lord you thereby deny your baptism; yea, every time you do anything to another
15 which you would not he should do to you.[80] I answer, thirdly, be you baptized or unbaptized, you must be born again. Otherwise it is not possible you should be inwardly holy: and without inward as well as outward holiness you cannot be happy even in this world; much less in the world to come. Do you say, 'Nay, but I do no
20 harm to any man; I am honest and just in all my dealings; I do not curse, or take the Lord's name in vain; I do not profane the Lord's day; I am no drunkard, I do not slander my neighbour, nor live in any wilful sin'? If this be so, it were much to be wished that all men went as far as you do. But you must go farther yet, or you cannot
25 be saved. Still you must be born again. Do you add, 'I do go farther yet; for I not only do no harm, but do all the good I can.' I doubt that fact; I fear you have had a thousand opportunities of doing good which you have suffered to pass by unimproved, and for which therefore you are accountable to God. But if you had
30 improved them all, if you really had done all the good you possibly could to all men, yet this does not at all alter the case. Still you must be born again. Without this nothing will do any good to your poor, sinful, polluted soul. 'Nay, but I constantly attend all the ordinances of God: I keep to my church and sacrament.' It is well
35 you do. But all this will not keep you from hell, except you be born again. Go to church twice a day, go to the Lord's table every week,

---

[79] Cf. in the BCP rite 'For the Ministration of Holy Baptism', the question addressed to 'Godfathers and Godmothers' (in the case of infants) or to an adult baptized directly: 'Dost thou, therefore, in the name of this child, renounce the devil and all his works, the vain pomp and glory of the world . . . ?'
[80] See Matt. 7:12.

say ever so many prayers in private; hear ever so many sermons, good sermons, excellent sermons, the best that ever were preached; read ever so many good books—still you must be born again. None of these things will stand in the place of the new birth. No, nor anything under heaven. Let this, therefore, if you 5 have not already experienced this inward work of God, be your continual prayer, 'Lord, add this to all thy blessings: let me be "born again". Deny whatever thou pleasest, but deny not this: let me be "born from above". Take away whatsoever seemeth thee good, reputation, fortune, friends, health. Only give me this: to be 10 "born of the Spirit"! To be received among the children of God. Let me be born, "not of corruptible seed, but incorruptible, by the Word of God, which liveth and abideth for ever".[81] And then let me daily "grow in grace, and in the knowledge of our Lord and Saviour Jesus Christ"!'[82] 15

[81] 1 Pet. 1:23.
[82] 2 Pet. 3:18.

THE WILDERNESS STATE
HEAVINESS THROUGH MANIFOLD TEMPTATIONS

AN INTRODUCTORY COMMENT

Like that of true love, the course of true faith *never did run smooth (cf. Thomas Goodwin,* A Child of Light Walking in Darkness *(1636); abridged by Wesley in the* Christian Library *(1751), Vol. XI; and Hugh Binning,* Fellowship With God, *especially Sermon XIV). There is, therefore, a natural progress in following a sermon on conversion with two further comments on the peaks and valleys in a Christian pilgrim's progress. That is the point to this particular pair of sermons, Nos. 46, 'The Wilderness State', and 47, 'Heaviness through Manifold Temptations'. By 1760 Wesley knew, from long experience, how regularly any stress on the* necessity *of assurance would raise the levels of religious anxiety amongst his hearers and disciples. Even earlier, he had pondered Thomas à Kempis's generalization* (Imitation, *II. ix. 7): 'I never found anyone so religious and devout that he had not sometimes a withdrawing of grace or felt not some decrease of zeal.' He also remembered how quickly the euphoria of his own Aldersgate experience had passed (cf. JWJ, May 26, 1738, 'My soul continued in peace, but yet in heaviness because of manifold temptations,' and May 28, 'I waked in peace, but not in joy').*

Thus, wary though he was of allegorizing, he found himself turning to the Old Testament story of the sojourn of the Children of Israel in the wilderness of Sinai as a metaphor for the anxieties and depressions that follow upon 'the new birth'. This allegory was already a familiar one among the Puritans. There was, e.g., Samuel Mather's Figures or Types of the Old Testament *(Dublin, 1683); Mather had understood 'wilderness' to mean 'the wilderness of this world' through which 'Christ directs and conducts his people in their travels . . . to the true Canaan' (p. 170; cf. p. 192). Thus it was clear to him that just 'as the Ark of God had led [the Israelites] through the Wilderness, so we are to follow the guidance of Christ through the world' (p. 510). Mather had also cited (pp. 200-201) a quite different interpretation in Jeremiah Burroughs (whom Wesley also knew) in* The Excellency of

Holy Courage in Evil Times *(1661), where 'the wilderness state' is understood as 'an unregenerate condition' before conversion (cf. chs. 25-26 and Burroughs's comments on Heb. 11:27). In Robert Gell's Remaines, I.16, the reference had been transferred from the wilderness of Sinai to Jesus' experience of 'forty days and nights' in the wilderness of Judea. Wesley had followed Gell in this, at least once, in Bristol (cf. JWJ, March 28, 1740): 'From these words, "Then was Jesus led by the Spirit into the wilderness to be tempted of the devil," I took occasion to describe that wilderness state, that state of doubts and fears and strong temptations which so many go through, though in different degrees, after they have received remission of sins.'*

From none of these sources, however, could one have anticipated Wesley's uncommonly sharp distinction, now in 1760, between 'the wilderness state' as 'darkness' (i.e., an actual 'loss of faith' and 'a total loss of joy'; in effect, a relapse from faith into unfaith that simply reverses the positive processes of salvation) and 'heaviness' (religious depression) which is more or less normal, and thus not a valid ground for prolonged anxiety or despair. But this is the distinction which is expounded, along with its psychological implications, in the two sermons here (and also, presumably, in his thirty-five oral sermons on John 16:22). It had been summarized in the manuscript Minutes of 1744 (Q. and A. 10) and then commented on in Wesley's Notes: 'This [John 16:22] gives us no manner of authority to assert that all believers must come into a state of darkness. They never need lose either their peace or their love, or the witness that they are the children of God. They can never lose these, but either through sin, or ignorance, or vehement temptation, or bodily disorders.' This same idea will be repeated in letters to Mrs. Marston, August 11, 1770, and to Rebecca Yeoman, February 5, 1772 (who is urged to read 'The Wilderness State' in 'the fourth volume, and examine yourself thereby'). Charles Wesley, however, had understood 'the wilderness state' rather as Gell had done: 'that [condition] into which the believer is generally led by the Spirit to be tempted as soon as he is baptized by the Holy Ghost' (CWJ, August 26, 1739).

It would be interesting to know how John Wesley understood his own episodes of acute religious anxiety. By 1780 he could 'not remember to have felt lowness of spirits for one quarter of an hour since I was born' (see No. 77, 'Spiritual Worship', III.2). Actually, though, he has been through many such episodes both early and late (as in his letter to 'Varanese', February 6, 1736; or, in JWJ, January 4, 1739; or, again, in a letter to Elizabeth Hardy, May 1758: 'I felt the wrath of God abiding on me. I was afraid of dropping into hell;' and another to Mrs.

Ryan, November 4, 1758). The most remarkable of these is mirrored in an outburst to his brother Charles, June 26, 1766: 'In one of [[my]] last [letters] [[I]] was saying, [[I]] do not feel the wrath of God abiding on [[me]]. . . . [[I do not love God. I never did]]. . . . [[I have no]] direct witness. . . . [[I]] have no more fear than love. Or if [[I have any fear, it is not that of falling]] into hell, but of falling into nothing.' (The words within double brackets are transcribed from shorthand.) Was this a case of 'heaviness' or 'darkness', or what?

'Heaviness through Manifold Temptations' is the linked sequel to 'The Wilderness State', designed to help believers avoid any further slide from depression into 'darkness' or sinful despair. Thus, it seeks to lay out 'the wide and essential difference between "darkness" and "heaviness"'. He had already done this in sixteen oral sermons on 1 Pet. 1:6 between 1754 and 1757, which suggests that the problem of religious anxiety had become more widespread and urgent in and after the upswing in 'professors of perfection' in 1755. At any rate, this particular pair of sermons seems to have been written expressly for SOSO, IV (1760). They were reprinted in Works (1771), IV, and again in SOSO, IV (1787), but were not otherwise printed separately.

The Wilderness State

John 16:22

Ye now have sorrow; but I will see you again, and your heart shall rejoice, and your joy no man taketh from you.

1. After God had wrought a great deliverance for Israel by 5 bringing them out of the house of bondage,[1] they did not immediately enter into the land which he had promised to their fathers, but 'wandered out of the way in the wilderness',[2] and were variously tempted and distressed. In like manner after God has delivered them that fear him from the bondage of sin and 10 Satan; after they are 'justified freely by his grace, through the redemption that is in Jesus',[3] yet not many of them immediately enter into 'the rest' which 'remaineth for the people of God'.[4] The greater part of them wander more or less out of the good way into which he hath brought them. They come as it were into a 'waste 15 and howling desert',[5] where they are variously tempted and tormented. And this some, in allusion to the case of the Israelites, have termed 'a wilderness state'.

2. Certain it is that the condition wherein these are has a right to the tenderest compassion. They labour under an evil and sore 20 disease, though one that is not commonly understood. And for this very reason it is the more difficult for them to find a remedy. Being in darkness themselves, they cannot be supposed to understand the nature of their own disorder; and few of their brethren—nay, perhaps of their teachers—know either what 25 their sickness is, or how to heal it. So much the more need there is to inquire, first, what is the nature of this disease; secondly, what is the cause; and thirdly, what is the cure of it.

I. 1. And, first, what is the nature of this disease into which so many fall after they have believed? Wherein does it properly 30

---

[1] Exod. 13:3.
[2] Cf. Ps. 107:40 (BCP).
[3] Rom. 3:24.
[4] Cf. Heb. 4:9.
[5] Cf. Deut. 32:10.

consist? And what are the genuine symptoms of it? It properly consists in the loss of that faith which God once wrought in their heart. They that are 'in the wilderness' have not now that divine 'evidence', that satisfactory 'conviction of things not seen',[6] which
5 they once enjoyed. They have not now that inward demonstration of the Spirit which before enabled each of them to say, 'The life I live, I live by faith in the Son of God, who loved *me* and gave himself for *me*.'[7] The light of heaven does not now 'shine in their hearts',[8] neither do they 'see him that is invisible';[9] but darkness is
10 again on the face of their souls, and blindness on the eyes of their understanding. The Spirit no longer 'witnesses with their spirits that they are the children of God';[10] neither does he continue as the Spirit of adoption, 'crying in their hearts, Abba, Father'.[11] They have not now a sure trust in his love, and a liberty of
15 approaching him with holy boldness. 'Though he slay me, yet will I trust in him'[12] is no more the language of their heart. But they are shorn of their strength, and become weak and feeble-minded, even as other men.[13]

2. Hence, secondly, proceeds the loss of love, which cannot but
20 rise or fall at the same time, and in the same proportion, with true, living faith. Accordingly they that are deprived of their faith are deprived of the love of God also. They cannot now say, 'Lord, thou knowest all things; thou knowest that I love thee.'[14] They are not now happy in God, as everyone is that truly loves him. They
25 do not delight in him as in time past, and 'smell the odour of his ointments'.[15] Once all their 'desire was unto him, and to the remembrance of his name'.[16] But now even their desires are cold and dead, if not utterly extinguished. And as their love of God is 'waxed cold',[17] so is also their love of their neighbour. They have
30 not now that zeal for the souls of men, that longing after their welfare, that fervent, restless, active desire of their being reconciled to God. They do not feel those 'bowels of mercies'[18] for the sheep that are lost, that tender 'compassion for the ignorant, and them that are out of the way'.[19] Once they were

---

[6] Cf. Heb. 11:1. See No. 3, *'Awake, Thou That Sleepest'*, I.11 and n.
[7] Cf. Gal. 2:20.   [8] Cf. 2 Cor. 4:6.
[9] Cf. Heb. 11:27.   [10] Cf. Rom. 8:16.
[11] Cf. Gal. 4:6.   [12] Job 13:15.
[13] Cf. the story of Samson in Judg. 16:7, 11, 19.
[14] John 21:17.   [15] Cf. John 12:3.
[16] Cf. Isa. 26:8.   [17] Cf. Matt. 24:12.
[18] Col. 3:12.   [19] Cf. Heb. 5:2.

'gentle toward all men', meekly 'instructing' such as 'opposed' the truth,[20] and 'if any was overtaken in a fault, restoring such an one in the spirit of meekness'.[21] But after a suspense perhaps of many days, anger begins to regain its power. Yea, peevishness and impatience thrust sore at them, that they may fall.[22] And it is well if they are not sometimes driven even to 'render evil for evil and railing for railing'.[23]

3. In consequence of the loss of faith and love follows, thirdly, loss of joy in the Holy Ghost. For if the loving consciousness of pardon be no more, the joy resulting therefrom cannot remain. If the Spirit does not witness with our spirit that we are the children of God, the joy that flowed from that inward witness must also be at an end. And in like manner they who once 'rejoiced with joy unspeakable in hope of the glory'[24] of God, now they are deprived of that 'hope full of immortality',[25] are deprived of the joy it occasioned; as also of that which resulted from a consciousness of 'the love of God' then 'shed abroad in their hearts'.[26] For the cause being removed, so is the effect: the fountain being dammed up, those living waters spring no more to refresh the thirsty soul.

4. With loss of faith and love and joy there is also joined, fourthly, the loss of that peace which once passed all understanding. That sweet tranquillity of mind, that composure of spirit, is gone. Painful doubt returns: doubt whether we ever did, and perhaps whether we ever shall, believe. We begin to doubt whether we ever did find in our hearts the real testimony of the Spirit. Whether we did not rather deceive our own souls, and mistake the voice of nature for the voice of God. Nay, and perhaps whether we shall ever hear his voice and find favour in his sight. And these doubts are again joined with servile fear, with that 'fear' which 'hath torment'.[27] We fear the wrath of God, even as before we believed; we fear lest we should be cast out of his presence; and thence sink again into that fear of death from which we were before wholly delivered.

5. But even this is not all. For loss of peace is accompanied with loss of power. We know everyone who has peace with God through Jesus Christ has power over all sin. But whenever he

---

[20] 2 Tim. 2:24-25.
[21] Cf. Gal. 6:1.
[22] Ps. 118:13.
[23] Cf. 1 Pet. 3:9.
[24] Cf. 1 Pet. 1:8.
[25] Wisd. 3:4.
[26] Cf. Rom. 5:5.
[27] 1 John 4:18.

loses the peace of God he loses also the power over sin. While that peace remained, power also remained, even over the besetting sin, whether it were the sin of his nature, his constitution, the sin of his education, or that of his profession; yea, and over those evil
5 tempers and desires which till then he could not conquer. 'Sin' had then 'no more dominion over him';[28] but he hath now no more dominion over sin. He may struggle indeed, but he cannot overcome; the crown is fallen from his head. His enemies again prevail over him, and more or less bring him into bondage. The
10 glory is departed from him,[29] even the kingdom of God which was in his heart. He is dispossessed of righteousness, as well as of peace and joy in the Holy Ghost.[30]

II. 1. Such is the nature of what many have termed, and not improperly, 'the wilderness state'. But the nature of it may be
15 more fully understood by inquiring, secondly, What are the causes of it? These indeed are various. But I dare not rank among these the bare, arbitrary, sovereign will of God. He rejoiceth 'in the prosperity of his servants'.[31] He delighteth not to 'afflict or grieve the children of men'.[32] His invariable 'will is our
20 sanctification',[33] attended with 'peace and joy in the Holy Ghost'.[34] These are his own free gifts; and we are assured 'the gifts of God are' on his part 'without repentance.'[35] He never repenteth of what he hath given, or desires to withdraw them from us. Therefore he never *deserts* us, as some speak: it is we only
25 that *desert* him.[36]

2. [(I).] The most usual cause of inward darkness is *sin* of one kind or another. This it is which generally occasions what is often a complication of sin and misery. And, first, sin of *commission*. This may frequently be observed to darken the soul in a moment;
30 especially if it be a known, a wilful, or presumptuous sin. If, for instance, a person who is now walking in the clear light of God's countenance should be any way prevailed on to commit a single act of drunkenness or uncleanness, it would be no wonder if in

---

[28] Cf. Rom. 6:14.
[29] See Ezek. 10:18.
[30] See Rom. 14:17.
[31] Cf. Ps. 35:27.
[32] Cf. Lam. 3:33.
[33] Cf. 1 Thess. 4:3.
[34] Rom. 14:17.
[35] Rom. 11:29.
[36] The reference here is twofold: to the mystical theories (as in St. John of the Cross) of God's withdrawal from the believer in 'the dark night of the soul', and to Lutheran explanations of religious depressions *(Anfechtungen)* in terms of the concept of the *Deus absconditus* (God's withdrawals of himself).

that very hour he fell into utter darkness. It is true, there have been some very rare cases wherein God has prevented this by an extraordinary display of his pardoning mercy, almost in the very instant. But in general such an abuse of the goodness of God, so gross an insult on his love, occasions an immediate estrangement 5 from God, and a 'darkness that may be felt'.[37]

3. But it may be hoped this case is not very frequent; that there are not many who so despise the riches of his goodness as, while they walk in his light, so grossly and presumptuously to rebel against him. That light is much more frequently lost by giving way 10 to sins of *omission*.[38] This indeed does not immediately quench the Spirit,[39] but gradually and slowly. The former may be compared to pouring water upon a fire; the latter to withdrawing the fuel from it. And many times will that loving Spirit reprove our neglect before he departs from us. Many are the inward checks, the secret 15 notices, he gives before his influences are withdrawn. So that only a train of omissions wilfully persisted in can bring us into utter darkness.

4. Perhaps no sin of omission more frequently occasions this than the neglect of private prayer; the want whereof cannot be 20 supplied by any other ordinance whatever. Nothing can be more plain than that the life of God in the soul does not continue, much less increase, unless we use all opportunities of communing with God, and pouring out our hearts before him. If therefore we are negligent of this, if we suffer business, company, or any avocation 25 whatever, to prevent these secret exercises of the soul (or which comes to the same thing, to make us hurry them over in a slight and careless manner) that life will surely decay. And if we long or frequently intermit them, it will gradually die away.

5. Another sin of omission which frequently brings the soul of a 30 believer into darkness is the neglect of what was so strongly enjoined even under the Jewish dispensation: 'Thou shalt in any wise rebuke thy neighbour, and not suffer sin upon him:'[40] 'Thou shalt not hate thy brother in thy heart.'[41] Now if we do 'hate our brother in our heart', if we do not 'rebuke' him when we see him 35 in a fault, but 'suffer sin upon him', this will soon bring leanness into our own soul; seeing hereby we are 'partakers of his sin'.[42] By

---

[37] Cf. Exod. 10:21.
[38] Cf. No. 14, *The Repentance of Believers*, I.14 and n.
[39] See 1 Thess. 5:19.
[41] *Ibid.*

[40] Lev. 19:17.
[42] Cf. Rev. 18:4.

neglecting to reprove our neighbour we make his sin our own. We become accountable for it to God: we saw his danger, and gave him no warning. So 'if he perish in his iniquity'[43] God may justly 'require his blood at our hands'.[44] No wonder then if by thus
5 grieving the Spirit we lose the light of his countenance.[45]

6. A third cause of our losing this is the giving way to some kind of *inward sin*.[46] For example: we know 'everyone that is proud in heart is an abomination to the Lord;'[47] and that although this pride of heart should not appear in the outward conversation.
10 Now how easily may a soul filled with peace and joy fall into this snare of the devil! How natural is it for him to imagine that he has more grace, more wisdom or strength, than he really has! 'To think more highly of himself than he ought to think!'[48] How natural to glory in something he has received as if he had not
15 received it![49] But seeing God continually 'resisteth the proud, and giveth grace' only 'to the humble',[50] this must certainly obscure, if not wholly destroy, the light which before shone on his heart.

7. The same effect may be produced by giving place to anger, whatever the provocation or occasion be; yea, though it were
20 coloured over with the name of *zeal* for the truth, or for the glory of God. Indeed all zeal which is any other than the flame of love is 'earthly, animal, devilish'.[51] It is the flame of wrath. It is flat, sinful anger, neither better nor worse. And nothing is a greater enemy to the mild, gentle love of God than this. They never did, they never
25 can, subsist together in one breast. In the same proportion as this prevails, love and joy in the Holy Ghost decrease. This is particularly observable in the case of *offence*, I mean, anger at any of our brethren, at any of those who are united with us either by civil or religious ties. If we give way to the spirit of offence but one
30 hour we lose the sweet influences of the Holy Spirit; so that instead of amending them we destroy ourselves, and become an easy prey to any enemy that assaults us.

8. But suppose we are aware of this snare of the devil, we may be attacked from another quarter. When fierceness and anger are
35 asleep, and love alone is waking, we may be no less endangered by

---

[43] Cf. Josh. 22:20.   [44] Cf. 2 Sam. 4:11; Ezek. 3:18; 33:8.
[45] Cf. No. 65, 'The Duty of Reproving our Neighbour'.
[46] Cf. No. 13, *On Sin in Believers*, intro., III.1-9, and n.
[47] Prov. 16:5.   [48] Cf. Rom. 12:3.
[49] See 1 Cor. 4:7.   [50] 1 Pet. 5:5.
[51] Jas. 3:15 *(Notes)*. See No. 92, 'On Zeal', for this point enlarged.

desire, which equally tends to darken the soul. This is the sure effect of any 'foolish desire',[52] any vain or inordinate affection. If we 'set our affection on things of the earth',[53] on any person or thing under the sun, if we desire anything but God and what tends to God, if we seek happiness in any creature, the jealous God will   5
surely contend with us; for he can admit of no rival. And 'if' we 'will' not 'hear' his warning 'voice',[54] and return to him with our whole soul; if we continue to grieve him with our idols, and running after other gods, we shall soon be cold, barren, and dry, and 'the god of this world' will 'blind' and darken 'our hearts'.[55]   10

9. But this he frequently does, even when we do not give way to any positive sin. It is enough, it gives him sufficient advantage, if we do not 'stir up the gift of God which is in us';[56] if we do not 'agonize' continually 'to enter in at the strait gate';[57] if we do not earnestly 'strive for the mastery',[58] and 'take the kingdom of   15
heaven by violence'.[59] There needs no more than not to fight, and we are sure to be conquered. Let us only be careless or 'faint in our mind',[60] let us be easy and indolent, and our natural darkness will soon return, and overspread our soul. It is enough, therefore, if we give way to *spiritual sloth:* this will effectually darken the soul.   20
It will as surely destroy the light of God, if not so swiftly, as murder or adultery.

10. But it is well to be observed that the cause of our darkness (whatsoever it be, whether omission or commission, whether inward or outward sin) is not always nigh at hand. Sometimes the   25
sin which occasioned the present distress may lie at a considerable distance. It might be committed days or weeks or months before. And that God now withdraws his light and peace on account of what was done so long ago is not (as one might at first imagine) an instance of his severity, but rather a proof of his   30
long-suffering and tender mercy. He waited all this time if haply we would see, acknowledge, and correct what was amiss. And in default of this he at length shows his displeasure, if thus, at last,[61] he may bring us to repentance.

---

[52] Cf. 1 Tim. 6:9 *(Notes).*   [53] Cf. Col. 3:2.
[54] Cf. Ps. 95:7; Heb. 3:7, 15.   [55] Cf. 2 Cor. 4:4.
[56] Cf. 2 Tim. 1:6.
[57] Luke 13:24 *(Notes).*
[58] Cf. 2 Tim. 2:5.
[59] Cf. Matt. 11:12 *(Notes).*
[60] Cf. Heb. 12:3.
[61] Orig., 'least', altered in 1771 and 1787.

(II). 1. Another general cause of this darkness is *ignorance;* which is likewise of various kinds. If men know not the Scriptures, if they imagine there are passages either in the Old or New Testament which assert that all believers without exception *must*
5 sometimes be in darkness, this ignorance will naturally bring upon them the darkness which they expect. And how common a case has this been among us! How few are there that do not expect it! And no wonder, seeing they are taught to expect it; seeing their guides lead them into this way. Not only the mystic writers of the
10 Romish Church, but many of the most spiritual and experimental in our own (very few of the last century excepted), lay it down with all assurance as a plain, unquestionable Scripture doctrine, and cite many texts to prove it.

2. Ignorance also of the work of God in the soul frequently
15 occasions this darkness. Men imagine (because so they have been taught, particularly by writers of the Romish communion, whose plausible assertions too many Protestants have received without due examination) that they are not always to walk in 'luminous faith'; that this is only a 'lower dispensation'; that as they rise
20 higher they are to leave those 'sensible comforts', and to live by 'naked faith' (*naked* indeed, if it be stripped both of love and peace and joy in the Holy Ghost!); that a state of light and joy is good, but a state of 'darkness' and 'dryness' is better, that it is by these alone we can be 'purified' from pride, love of the world, and
25 inordinate self-love; and that therefore we ought neither to expect nor desire to 'walk in the light' always.[62] Hence it is (though other reasons may concur) that the main body of pious men in the Romish Church generally walk in a dark uncomfortable way, and if ever they receive, soon lose the light of God.[63]

30 (III). 1. A third general cause of this darkness is *temptation.* When the candle of the Lord first shines on our head, temptation frequently flees away, and totally disappears. All is calm within:

---

[62] Cf. St. John of the Cross, *Ascent of Mount Carmel,* II.ii, in *Complete Works* (1933), I.68 ff.; see also *The Dark Night of the Soul,* I.ix-x, *ibid.,* I.373-80.

[63] Cf. Jean Orcibal, 'The Theological Originality of John Wesley and Continental Spirituality' (see above, Vol. 1, pp. 36, 75). Besides his conventional, lifelong anti-Roman prejudices, Wesley was predisposed to take the gloom of the Jansenists and even of M. de Renty as normative. Thus he ignored the lilting 'folk-spirituality' of the Ursulines, the Oratorians, the Salesians (and eighteenth-century Catholicism generally), so lovingly recounted by Henri Bremond in a classic study, *A Literary History of Religious Thought in France* (French text, 1916; Eng. tr., London, SPCK, 1928, 1930), 2 vols.

perhaps without, too, while God makes our enemies to be at peace with us. It is then very natural to suppose that we shall not see war any more. And there are instances wherein this calm has continued, not only for weeks, but for months or years. But commonly it is otherwise: in a short time 'the winds blow, the 5 rains descend, and the floods arise'[64] anew. They who 'know not either the Son or the Father',[65] and consequently hate his children, when God slackens the bridle which is in their teeth, will show that hatred in various instances. As of old 'he that was born after the flesh persecuted him that was born after the Spirit, 10 even so it is now;'[66] the same cause still producing the same effect. The evil which yet remains in the heart will then also move afresh; anger and many other 'roots of bitterness'[67] will endeavour to spring up. At the same time Satan will not be wanting to cast in his fiery darts;[68] and the soul will have to 'wrestle', not only with the 15 world, not only 'with flesh and blood, but with principalities and powers, with the rulers of the darkness of this world, with wicked spirits in high places'.[69] Now when so various assaults are made at once, and perhaps with the utmost violence, it is not strange if it should occasion not only heaviness, but even darkness in a weak 20 believer. More especially if he was not watching, if these assaults are made in an hour when he looked not for them; if he expected nothing less, but had fondly told himself,

The day of evil would return no more.[70]

2. The force of those temptations which arise from within will 25 be exceedingly heightened if we before thought too highly of ourselves, as if we had been cleansed from all sin. And how naturally do we imagine this during the warmth of our first love! How ready are we to believe that God has 'fulfilled' in us the whole 'work of faith with power'![71] That because we *feel* no sin, 30 we *have* none in us, but the soul is all love! And well may a sharp attack from an enemy whom we supposed to be not only

---

[64] Cf. Matt. 7:25, 27.   [65] Cf. John 8:19.
[66] Gal. 4:29.   [67] Cf. Heb. 12:15.
[68] See Eph. 6:16.   [69] Cf. Eph. 6:12.
[70] Cf. *Letters*, 26:389 (line 8) in this edn., where these exact words occur in a somewhat despairing letter of Oct. 7, 1749, though without quotation marks. This letter, however, is known only through copies of 1828 and 1831, when the elusive quotation was apparently not recognized as such.
[71] Cf. 2 Thess. 1:11.

conquered but slain, throw us into much heaviness of soul, yea, sometimes into utter darkness; particularly when we *reason* with this enemy, instead of instantly calling upon God, and casting ourselves upon him by simple faith who *alone* 'knoweth how to
5 deliver' his [own] 'out of temptation'.[72]

III. These are the usual causes of this second darkness. Inquire we, thirdly, what is the cure of it?
1. To suppose that this is one and the same in all cases is a great and fatal mistake; and yet extremely common even among many
10 who pass for experienced Christians; yea, perhaps take upon them to be 'teachers in Israel',[73] to be the guides of other souls. Accordingly they know and use but one medicine, whatever be the cause of the distemper. They begin immediately to apply the promises, to 'preach the gospel', as they call it. To give comfort is
15 the single point at which they aim, in order to which they say many soft and tender things concerning the love of God to poor, helpless sinners, and the efficacy of the blood of Christ. Now this is 'quackery' indeed, and that of the worse sort, as it tends, if not to kill men's bodies, yet without the peculiar mercy of God to
20 'destroy both' their 'bodies and souls in hell'.[74] It is hard to speak of these 'daubers with untempered mortar',[75] these promise-mongers, as they deserve. They well deserve the title which has been ignorantly given to others: they are 'spiritual mounte-banks'.[76] They do, in effect, make 'the blood of the covenant an
25 unholy thing'.[77] They vilely prostitute the promises of God by thus applying them to all without distinction. Whereas indeed the cure of spiritual, as of bodily diseases, must be as various as are the causes of them. The first thing, therefore, is to find out the cause, and this will naturally point out the cure.
30 2. For instance: is it sin which occasions darkness? What sin? Is it outward sin of any kind? Does your conscience accuse you of committing any sin whereby you grieve the Holy Spirit of God?[78]

---

[72] Cf. 2 Pet. 2:9.   [73] Cf. John 3:10 *(Notes)*.
[74] Cf. Matt. 10:28. Cf. Samuel Johnson's understanding of 'quackery' in the particular sense of medical malpractice.
[75] Cf. Ezek. 13:10, 11, 14, 15; 22:28.
[76] An ironic reference to Bishop George Lavington's application of this label to the Methodists, in *The Enthusiasm of Methodists and Papists Compared*, Pt. II, p. 147: 'Their mountebank's infallible prescription must be swallowed . . .—though they die for it.' See also No. 35, 'The Law Established through Faith, I', I.12 and n.
[77] Heb. 10:29.   [78] Cf. Eph. 4:30.

Is it on this account that he is departed from you, and that joy and peace are departed with him? And how can you expect they should return till you put away the accursed thing?[79] 'Let the wicked forsake his way;'[80] 'cleanse your hands, ye sinners;'[81] 'put away the evil of your doings.'[82] So shall your 'light break out of obscurity':[83] 'the Lord will return and abundantly pardon.'[84]

3. If upon the closest search you can find no sin of commission which causes the cloud upon your soul, inquire next if there be not some sin of omission which separates between God and you. Do you 'not suffer sin upon your brother'?[85] Do you reprove them that sin in your sight? Do you walk in all the ordinances of God? In public, family, private prayer? If not, if you habitually neglect any one of these known duties, how can you expect that the light of his countenance should continue to shine upon you? Make haste to 'strengthen the things that remain';[86] then your soul shall live. 'Today, if ye will hear his voice',[87] by his grace supply what is lacking. When you 'hear a voice behind you, saying, This is the way; walk thou in it,'[88] 'harden not your heart.'[89] Be no more 'disobedient to the heavenly calling'.[90] Till the sin, whether of omission or commission, be removed, all comfort is false and deceitful. It is only skinning the wound over, which still festers and rankles beneath. Look for no peace within till you are at peace with God; which cannot be without 'fruits meet for repentance'.[91]

4. But perhaps you are not conscious of even any *sin of omission* which impairs your peace and joy in the Holy Ghost.[92] Is there not then some *inward sin*, which as a 'root of bitterness springs up' in your heart to 'trouble you'?[93] Is not your dryness and barrenness of soul occasioned by your heart's 'departing from the living God'?[94] Has not 'the foot of pride come against' you?[95] Have you

---

[79] See Josh. 7:13.   [80] Isa. 55:7.   [81] Jas. 4:8.
[82] Isa. 1:16.   [83] Cf. Isa. 58:10.   [84] Cf. Isa. 55:7.
[85] Cf. Lev. 19:17.   [86] Rev. 3:2.   [87] Ps. 95:7; Heb. 3:7, 15; 4:7.
[88] Cf. Isa. 30:21.   [89] Cf. Ps. 95:8; Heb. 3:8, 15; 4:7.   [90] Cf. Acts 26:19.
[91] Matt. 3:8.   [92] Rom. 14:17.
[93] Cf. Heb. 12:15. The following paragraph closely resembles both the forms and substance of the Puritan schemes of self-examination; cf. Robert Bolton, *Works* (3rd edn., 1614), II.27: 'a fruitless and dangerous speculation of a man's own worthiness—rather fasten it upon your corruptions and infirmities, upon your many deficiencies in religious duties and executions of your calling, wants and weaknesses in prayer and inward devotion, dullness and uncheerfulness in religious exercises.' See also Joseph Alleine, 'Letter IX' in *Christian Letters*, published by Wesley in 1767 (see *Bibliog*, No. 301; and Vol. 16 of this edn.); see also 'Letter XVI' and 'Letter XXI'.
[94] Heb. 3:12.   [95] Cf. Ps. 36:11.

not 'thought' of yourself 'more highly than you ought to think'?[96] Have you not in any respect 'sacrificed to your own net, and burnt incense to your own drag'?[97] Have you not ascribed your success in any undertaking to your own courage, or strength, or wisdom?

5 Have you not boasted of something 'you have received, as though you had not received it'?[98] Have you not gloried 'in anything save the cross of our Lord Jesus Christ'?[99] Have you not sought after or desired the praise of men? Have you not taken pleasure in it? If so, you see the way you are to take. If you have fallen by pride,

10 'humble yourself under the mighty hand of God, and he will exalt you in due time.'[100] Have you not forced him to depart from you by giving place to anger? Have you not 'fretted yourself because of the ungodly' or 'been envious against the evil-doers'?[101] Have you not been offended at any of your brethren? Looking at their (real

15 or imagined) sin, so as to sin yourself against the great law of love by estranging your heart from them? Then look unto the Lord, that you may renew your strength, that all this sharpness and coldness may be done away, that love and peace and joy may return together, and you may be invariably 'kind to each other,

20 and tender-hearted; forgiving one another, even as God for Christ's sake hath forgiven you'.[102] Have not you given way to any foolish desire? To any kind or degree of inordinate affection? How then can the love of God have place in your heart, till you put away your idols? 'Be not deceived; God is not mocked:'[103] he will

25 not dwell in a divided heart. As long therefore as you cherish Delilah in your bosom he has no place there. It is vain to hope for a recovery of his light till you pluck out the right eye and cast it from you.[104] O let there be no longer delay. Cry to him that he may enable you so to do! Bewail your own impotence and help-

30 lessness; and the Lord being your helper, enter in at the strait gate:[105] take the kingdom of heaven by violence![106] Cast out every idol from his sanctuary, and the glory of the Lord shall soon appear.[107]

5. Perhaps it is this very thing, the want of striving, *spiritual*
35 *sloth*, which keeps your soul in darkness. You dwell at ease in the land: there is no war in your coasts, and so you are quiet and

---

[96] Cf. Rom. 12:3.   [97] Cf. Hab. 1:16.   [98] See 1 Cor. 4:7.
[99] Cf. Gal. 6:14.   [100] Cf. 1 Pet. 5:6.   [101] Cf. Ps. 37:1 (BCP).
[102] Cf. Eph. 4:32.   [103] Gal. 6:7.
[104] See Matt. 5:29.   [105] Matt. 7:13.
[106] See Matt. 11:12.   [107] See Lev. 9:6.

unconcerned. You go on in the same even track of outward duties, and are content there to abide. And do you wonder meantime that your soul is dead? O stir yourself up before the Lord! Arise, and shake yourself from the dust: wrestle with God for the mighty blessing.[108] Pour out your soul unto God in prayer, and continue therein with all perseverance.[109] Watch! Awake out of sleep, and keep awake! Otherwise there is nothing to be expected but that you will be alienated more and more from the light and life of God.

6. If upon the fullest and most impartial examination of yourself you cannot discern that you at present give way either to spiritual sloth or any other inward or outward sin,[110] then call to mind the time that is past. Consider your former tempers, words, and actions. Have these been right before the Lord? 'Commune with him in your chamber, and be still,'[111] and desire of him to try the ground of your heart, and bring to your remembrance whatever has at any time offended the eyes of his glory.[112] If the guilt of any unrepented sin remain on our soul it cannot be but you will remain in darkness, till, having been 'renewed by repentance',[113] you are again washed by faith in the 'fountain opened for sin and uncleanness'.[114]

7. Entirely different will be the manner of the cure if the cause of the disease be not sin, but *ignorance*. It may be ignorance of the meaning of Scripture; perhaps occasioned by ignorant commentators—ignorant at least in this respect, however knowing or learned they may be in other particulars. And in this case that ignorance must be removed before we can remove the darkness arising from it. We must show the true meaning of those texts which have been misunderstood. My design does not permit me to consider all the passages of Scripture which have been pressed into this service. I shall just mention two or three which are frequently brought to prove that all believers must, sooner or later, 'walk in darkness'.[115]

8. One of these is Isaiah 50:10: 'Who is among you that feareth the Lord, and obeyeth the voice of his servant, that walketh in

---

[108] See Gen. 32:25-26.
[109] See Eph. 6:18.
[110] See No. 8, 'The First-fruits of the Spirit', III.4 and n.
[111] Cf. Ps. 4:4 (BCP).
[112] Isa. 3:8.
[113] Cf. Heb. 6:6. Another instance of 'a second repentance'; see intro. to Nos. 13 and 14 *(On Sin in Believers* and *The Repentance of Believers).*
[114] Zech. 13:1.
[115] Isa. 59:9; John 8:12.

darkness and hath no light? Let him trust in the name of the Lord, and stay upon his God.' But how does it appear either from the text or context that the person here spoken of ever had light? One who is 'convinced of sin'[116] 'feareth the Lord and obeyeth the voice of his servant'. And him we should advise, though he was still dark of soul, and had never seen the light of God's countenance, yet to 'trust in the name of the Lord, and stay upon his God.' This text therefore proves nothing less than that a believer in Christ 'must sometimes "walk in darkness"'.[117]

9. Another text which has been supposed to speak the same doctrine is Hosea 2:14: 'I will allure her, and bring her into the wilderness, and speak comfortably unto her.' Hence it has been inferred that God will bring every believer 'into the wilderness', into a state of deadness and darkness. But it is certain the text speaks no such thing. For it does not appear that it speaks of particular believers at all. It manifestly refers to the Jewish nation; and perhaps to that only. But if it be applicable to particular persons, the plain meaning of it is this: I will draw him by love; I will next convince him of sin, and then comfort him by my pardoning mercy.

10. A third Scripture from whence the same inference has been drawn is that above-recited: 'Ye now have sorrow; but I will see you again, and your heart shall rejoice, and your joy no man taketh from you.' This has been supposed to imply that God would after a time withdraw himself from all believers; and that they could not, till after they had thus sorrowed, have the joy which no man could take from them. But the whole context shows that our Lord is here speaking personally to the apostles, and no others; and that he is speaking concerning those particular events—his own death and resurrection. 'A little while', says he, 'and ye shall not see me;' namely, while I am in the grave. 'And again a little while, and ye shall see me,'[118] when I am risen from

---

[116] Cf. John 8:46.

[117] The intent of 'nothing less than' is to *negate* the predicate of the sentence and is common eighteenth-century usage; in modern ears it can be taken in the opposite sense. Wesley is here going against the interpretations of both Henry, *Exposition,* and Poole, *Annotations,* who understand Isa. 50:10 in terms of what Wesley will call 'heaviness' in the following sermon rather than 'darkness'. Poole makes a distinction between *sin* and *misery* and supposes the prophet to be referring to misery that may pass. Similarly, Henry comments that 'they walk in darkness when . . . their joy in God is interrupted, the testimony of the Spirit is interrupted, and the light of God's countenance eclipsed.'

[118] John 16:16-17.

the dead. 'Ye will weep and lament, and the world will rejoice: but your sorrow shall be turned into joy. . . . Ye now have sorrow,' because I am about to be taken from your head; 'but I will see you again,' after my resurrection, 'and your heart shall rejoice. And your joy', which I will then give you, 'no man taketh from you.'[119] All this we know was literally fulfilled in the particular case of the apostles. But no inference can be drawn from hence with regard to God's dealings with believers in general.

11. A fourth text (to mention no more) which has been frequently cited in proof of the same doctrine is 1 Peter 4:12: 'Beloved, think it not strange concerning the fiery trial which is to try you.' But this is full as foreign to the point as the preceding. The text, literally rendered, runs thus: 'Beloved, wonder not at the burning which is among you, which is for your trial.' Now however this may be accommodated to inward trials, in a secondary sense, yet primarily it doubtless refers to martyrdom and the sufferings connected with it.[120] Neither therefore is this text anything at all to the purpose for which it is cited. And we may challenge all men to bring one text, either from the Old or New Testament, which is any more to the purpose than this.

12. 'But is not darkness much more profitable for the soul than light? Is not the work of God in the heart most swiftly and effectually carried on during a state of inward suffering? Is not a believer more swiftly and throughly purified by sorrow than by joy? By anguish and pain and distress and spiritual martyrdoms than by continual peace?' So the *mystics* teach; so it is written in their books—but not in *the oracles of God*.[121] The Scripture nowhere says that the absence of God best perfects his work in the heart! Rather his presence, and a clear communion with the Father and the Son. A strong consciousness of this will do more in an hour than his absence in an age. Joy in the Holy Ghost will far more effectually purify the soul than the want of that joy; and

[119] John 16:20, 22.

[120] An echo of Henry's *Exposition*, to this same effect; also an indirect refutation of Moravian interpretations of 1 Pet. 4:12.

[121] See No. 5, 'Justification by Faith', §2 and n. Cf. Law's highest mystical flight in *The Spirit of Prayer*, Pt. II (1750) (*Works*, VII. 129-30): 'This "coldness" [i.e., darkness] is the divine offspring. . . . It brings a divine effect, or more fruitful progress in the divine life. . . . Fervour is good and ought to be loved; but tribulation, distress, and coldness in their season are better, because they give means and power of exercising a higher faith, a purer love, and more perfect resignation to God—which are the best state of the soul. . . . Light and darkness equally assist the pious soul; . . . in the darkness he lays hold on God, and so [both light and darkness] do him the same good.'

the peace of God is the best means of refining the soul from the
dross of earthly affections. Away then with the idle conceit that
the kingdom of God is divided against itself; that the peace of
God and joy in the Holy Ghost are obstructive of righteousness;
5 and that 'we are saved', not 'by faith',[122] but by unbelief; not by
hope, but by despair!

13. So long as men dream thus they may well 'walk in
darkness'. Nor can the effect cease till the cause is removed. But
yet we must not imagine it will immediately cease, even when the
10 cause is no more. When either ignorance or sin has caused
darkness, one or the other may be removed, and yet the light
which was obstructed thereby may not immediately return. As
it is the free gift of God, he may restore it sooner or later, as it
pleases him. In the case of sin we cannot reasonably expect that it
15 should immediately return. The sin began before the punishment, which may therefore justly remain after the sin is at an end.
And even in the natural course of things, though a wound cannot
be healed while the dart is sticking in the flesh, yet neither is it
healed as soon as that is drawn out, but soreness and pain may
20 remain long after.

14. Lastly, if darkness be occasioned by manifold, heavy, and
unexpected temptations, the best way for removing and preventing this is—teach believers always to expect temptation;
seeing they dwell in an evil world, among wicked, subtle,
25 malicious spirits, and have an heart capable of all evil.[123] Convince
them that the whole work of sanctification is not (as they
imagined) wrought at once; that when they first believe they are
but as new-born babes,[124] who are gradually to grow up, and may
expect many storms before they come to the full stature of Christ.
30 Above all let them be instructed, when the storm is upon them,
not to reason with the devil, but to pray; to pour out their souls
before God, and show him of their trouble. And these are the
persons unto whom chiefly we are to apply the great and precious
promises—not to the ignorant, till the ignorance is removed;
35 much less to the impenitent sinner. To these we may largely and
affectionately declare the loving-kindness of God our Saviour,

---

[122] Cf. Eph. 2:8.

[123] An unusually explicit avowal of the 'remains of sin'; see intro. to No. 13, *On Sin in
Believers*, III.1-9 and n. But notice the distinctions here between 'involuntary sins' (as in
On Sin in Believers) and 'heaviness' (as in the following sermon).

[124] 1 Pet. 2:2.

and expatiate upon his tender mercies, which have been ever of old. Here we may dwell upon the faithfulness of God, whose 'word is tried to the uttermost',[125] and upon the virtue of that blood which was shed for us, to 'cleanse us from all sin'.[126] And God will then bear witness to his word, and bring their souls out 5 of trouble. He will say, 'Arise, shine; for thy light is come, and the glory of the Lord is risen upon thee.'[127] Yea, and that light, if thou walk humbly and closely with God, will 'shine more and more unto the perfect day'.[128]

---

[125] Ps. 119:140 (BCP).
[126] Cf. 1 John 1:7.
[127] Isa. 60:1.
[128] Cf. Prov. 4:18.

Heaviness through Manifold Temptations

1 Peter 1:6

*Now for a season, if need be, ye are in
heaviness through manifold temptations.*

5 1. In the preceding discourse I have particularly spoken of that
darkness of mind into which those are often observed to fall who
once walked in the light of God's countenance. Nearly related
to this is the *heaviness* of soul which is still more common,
even among believers; indeed almost all the children of God
10 experience this in an higher or lower degree. And so great is the
resemblance between one and the other that they are frequently
confounded together; and we are apt to say indifferently, 'Such an
one is in *darkness*, or such an one is in *heaviness*,' as if they were
equivalent terms, one of which implied no more than the other.[1]
15 But they are far, very far from it. Darkness is one thing; heaviness is another. There is a difference, yea a wide, an essential difference, between the former and the latter. And such
a difference it is as all the children of God are deeply concerned
to understand; otherwise nothing will be more easy than for them
20 to slide out of heaviness into darkness.[2] In order to prevent this I
will endeavour to show,

   I. What manner of persons those were to whom the Apostle
   says, 'Ye are in heaviness.'
   II. What kind of 'heaviness' they were in.
25 III. What were the causes, and
   IV. What were the ends of it.
   I shall conclude with some inferences.

---

[1] Matthew Poole had not confounded the two notions; his point was that 'darkness' has
two different meanings that ought to be distinguished by context: 'Walking in darkness is
[sometimes] put for living in wickedness (John 1:6); [the other sense] is being in misery,
which also frequently cometh under the name of "darkness": that liveth in a most
disconsolate and calamitous condition, together with great despondency or dejection of
spirit' *(Annotations* on Isa. 50:10). But this is an episode from which the steadfast believer
can hope to be delivered, 'especially in the free grace, mercy, and faithfulness of the
Lord. . . '.
[2] Cf. Wesley's letter to Mary Bishop, Sept. 13, 1774: 'The difference between

I. 1. I am in the first place to show what manner of persons those were to whom the Apostle says, 'Ye are in heaviness.' And, first, it is beyond all dispute that they were believers at the time the Apostle thus addressed them. For so he expressly says, verse five: Ye 'who are kept through the power of God by *faith* unto 5 salvation'. Again, verse seven, he mentions 'the trial of their *faith*, much more precious than that of gold which perisheth'. And yet again, verse nine, he speaks of their 'receiving the end of their *faith*, the salvation of their souls'. At the same time, therefore, that they were 'in heaviness', they were possessed of living faith. Their 10 heaviness did not destroy their faith; they still 'endured, [as] seeing him that is invisible'.[3]

2. Neither did their heaviness destroy their peace, the peace that passeth all understanding,[4] which is inseparable from true, living faith. This we may easily gather from the second verse, 15 wherein the Apostle prays, not that 'grace and peace' may be given them, but only that it may 'be multiplied unto them'; that the blessing which they already enjoyed might be more abundantly bestowed upon them.

3. The persons to whom the Apostle here speaks were also full 20 of a living hope. For thus he speaks, verse three: 'Blessed be the God and Father of our Lord Jesus Christ, who according to his abundant mercy hath begotten us again'—me and you, all of us who are 'sanctified by the Spirit', and enjoy the 'sprinkling of the blood of Jesus Christ'—'unto a living hope, unto an inheritance', 25 that is, unto a living hope of an inheritance, 'incorruptible, undefiled, and that fadeth not away.'[5] So that notwithstanding their heaviness they still retained an hope full of immortality.

4. And they still 'rejoiced in hope of the glory of God'.[6] They were filled with joy in the Holy Ghost. So, verse eight, the Apostle 30 having just mentioned the final 'revelation of Jesus Christ'[7]

---

heaviness and darkness of soul (the wilderness state) should never be forgotten. Darkness . . . seldom comes on us but by our own fault. . . . Heaviness . . . may be occasioned by a thousand circumstances, such as frequently neither our wisdom can foresee nor our power prevent.' Cf. below, V.1.

[3] Heb. 11:27.   [4] See Phil. 4:7.
[5] Cf. 1 Pet. 1:2-4.   [6] Cf. Rom. 5:2.
[7] The AV of 1 Pet. 1:7 reads, 'the appearing of Jesus Christ'. Wesley changes this in his translation in the *Notes* (as also in the tr. of James Moffatt and the RSV). But in the text of *SOSO* (1787) the term, 'revelation', has been altered to 'redemption', which must have been a printer's error since no Greek scholar would have derived the English 'redemption' from the original ἀποκαλύψει.

(namely, when he cometh to judge the world), immediately adds, 'In whom, though now ye see him not (not with your bodily eyes), yet believing, ye rejoice with joy unspeakable and full of glory.' Their heaviness therefore was not only consistent with living hope, but also with 'joy unspeakable'. At the same time they were thus heavy they nevertheless rejoiced with 'joy full of glory'.

5. In the midst of their heaviness they likewise still enjoyed the love of God which had been shed abroad in their hearts.[8] 'Whom', says the Apostle, 'having not seen, ye love.'[9] Though ye have not yet seen him face to face, yet knowing him by faith ye have obeyed his word, 'My son, give me thy heart.'[10] He is your God, and your love, the desire of your eyes, and your 'exceeding great reward'.[11] Ye have sought and found happiness in him; ye 'delight in the Lord, and he hath given you your heart's desire'.[12]

6. Once more. Though they were heavy, yet were they holy. They retained the same power over sin. They were still 'kept' from this 'by the power of God'. They were 'obedient children, not fashioned according to their former desires', but 'as he that had called them is holy', so were they 'holy in all manner of conversation. . . . Knowing they were redeemed by the precious blood of Christ, a Lamb without spot and without blemish', they had, through the 'faith and hope which they had in God', 'purified their souls by the Spirit'.[13] So that upon the whole their heaviness well consisted with faith, with hope, with love of God and man; with the peace of God, with joy in the Holy Ghost, with inward and outward holiness. It did no way impair, much less destroy, any part of the work of God in their hearts. It did not at all interfere with that 'sanctification of the Spirit' which is the root of all true 'obedience'; neither with the happiness which must needs result from 'grace and peace'[14] reigning in the heart.

II. 1. Hence we may easily learn what kind of heaviness they were in—the second thing which I shall endeavour to show. The word in the original is λυπηθέντες, 'made sorry', 'grieved', from λύπη, 'grief' or 'sorrow'. This is the constant, literal meaning of the word: and this being observed, there is no ambiguity in the expression, nor any difficulty in understanding it. The persons

---

[8] See Rom. 5:5.　　　　　　　　　　　　　　　[9] 1 Pet. 1:8.
[10] Cf. Prov. 23:26.　　　　　　　　　　　　　　[11] Gen. 15:1.
[12] Cf. Ps. 37:4 (BCP).　　　　　　　[13] Cf. 1 Pet. 1:14-15, 19, 21-22.
[14] 1 Pet. 1:2.

spoken of here were *grieved:* the heaviness they were in was neither more nor less than *sorrow* or *grief*—a passion which every child of man is well acquainted with.

2. It is probable our translators rendered it 'heaviness' (though a less common word) to denote two things: first, the degree; and next, the continuance of it. It does indeed seem that it is not a slight or inconsiderable degree of grief which is here spoken of, but such as makes a strong impression upon and sinks deep into the soul. Neither does this appear to be a transient sorrow, such as passes away in an hour; but rather such as having taken fast hold of the heart is not presently shaken off, but continues for some time, as a settled temper, rather than a passion—even in them that have living faith in Christ, and the genuine love of God in their hearts.

3. Even in these this heaviness may sometimes be so deep as to overshadow the whole soul, to give a colour, as it were, to all the affections, such as will appear in the whole behaviour. It may likewise have an influence over the body; particularly in those that are either of a naturally weak constitution, or weakened by some accidental disorder, especially of the nervous kind. In many cases we find 'the corruptible body presses down the soul.'[15] In this the soul rather presses down the body, and weakens it more and more. Nay, I will not say that deep and lasting sorrow of heart may not sometimes weaken a strong constitution, and lay the foundation of such bodily disorders as are not easily removed. And yet all this may consist with a measure of that 'faith which' still 'worketh by love'.[16]

4. This may well be termed a 'fiery trial':[17] and though it is not the same with that the Apostle speaks of in the fourth chapter, yet many of the expressions there used concerning outward sufferings may be accommodated to this inward affliction. They cannot indeed with any propriety be applied to them that are *in darkness:* these do not, cannot, *rejoice;* neither is it true that 'the Spirit of glory and of God resteth upon'[18] them. But he frequently doth on those that are 'in heaviness', so that though 'sorrowful, yet' are they 'always rejoicing'.[19]

---

[15] Cf. Wisd. 9:15. Cf. also No. 41, *Wandering Thoughts*, II.3 and n.
[16] Gal. 5:6. Cf. below, IV.5; and No. 2, *The Almost Christian*, II.6 and n.
[17] 1 Pet. 4:12.
[18] 1 Pet. 4:14.
[19] 2 Cor. 6:10.

III. 1. But to proceed to the third point. What are the causes of such sorrow or heaviness in a true believer? The Apostle tells us clearly: 'Ye are in heaviness', says he, 'through manifold temptations'—ποικίλοις, 'manifold'; not only many in number, 5 but of many kinds. They may be varied and diversified a thousand ways by the change or addition of numberless circumstances. And this very diversity and variety makes it more difficult to guard against them. Among these we may rank all bodily disorders; particularly acute diseases, and violent pain of every kind, 10 whether affecting the whole body or the smallest part of it. It is true, some who have enjoyed uninterrupted health, and have felt none of these, may make light of them, and wonder that sickness or pain of body should bring heaviness upon the mind. And perhaps one in a thousand is of so peculiar a constitution as not 15 to feel pain like other men. So hath it pleased God to show his almighty power by producing some of these prodigies of nature who have seemed not to regard pain at all, though of the severest kind; if that contempt of pain was not owing partly to the force of education, partly to a preternatural cause—to the power either of 20 good or evil spirits who raised those men above the state of mere nature. But abstracting from[20] these particular cases, it is in general a just observation, that

> . . . pain is perfect misery, and extreme
> Quite overturns all patience.[21]

25 And even where this is prevented by the grace of God, where men do 'possess their souls in patience',[22] it may nevertheless occasion much inward heaviness, the soul sympathizing with the body.

2. All diseases of long continuance, though less painful, are apt to produce the same effect. When God 'appoints over us 30 consumption' or 'the chilling and burning ague', if it be not speedily removed it will not only 'consume the eyes', but 'cause sorrow of heart'[23]. This is eminently the case with regard to all

---

[20] Cf. the earlier usage of this phrase as meaning 'disregarding' in No. 44, *Original Sin*, I.5 and n.

[21] Cf. Milton, *Paradise Lost*, vi. 462-64:

> But pain is perfect misery, the worst
> Of evil, and, excessive, overturns
> All patience.

[22] Cf. Luke 21:19.

[23] Cf. Lev. 26:16.

those which are termed 'nervous disorders'. And faith does not overturn the course of nature: natural causes still produce natural effects. Faith no more hinders the 'sinking of the spirits' (as it is called) in an hysteric illness, than the rising of the pulse in a fever.[24]   5

3. Again, when 'calamity cometh as a whirlwind,'[25] and poverty 'as an armed man',[26] is this a little temptation? Is it strange if it occasion sorrow and heaviness? Although this also may appear but a small thing to those who stand at a distance, or who look and 'pass by on the other side',[27] yet it is otherwise to them who feel it.   10 'Having food and raiment' (indeed the latter word, σκεπάσμα- τα, implies lodging as well as apparel) we may, if the love of God is in our hearts, 'be therewith content'.[28] But what shall they do who have none of these? Who as it were 'embrace the rock for a shelter'?[29] Who have only the earth to lie upon, and only the sky to   15 cover them? Who have not a dry, or warm, much less a clean abode for themselves and their little ones? No, nor clothing to keep themselves, or those they love next themselves, from pinching cold, either by day or night? I laugh at the stupid heathen, crying out,   20

> Nil habet infelix paupertas durius in se
> Quam quod ridiculos homines facit! [30]

Has poverty nothing worse in it than this, that it 'makes men liable to be laughed at'? 'Tis a sign this idle poet talked by rote of the things which he knew not. Is not want of food something worse   25 than this? God pronounced it as a curse upon man that he should earn it by 'the sweat of his brow'.[31] But how many are there in this

---

[24] Cf. Chambers's *Cyclopaedia*, on 'Hysteric Affections'; he has no entry for 'nervous disorders'. Johnson, *Dictionary*, defines 'nervous' in the medical terms as, 'Having weak or diseased nerves', and quotes Cheyne: 'Poor, weak, nervous creatures'. Cf. also Wesley's 'Thoughts on Nervous Disorders; particularly that which is usually termed Lowness of Spirits', in *AM* (1786), IX.52-54, 94-97; as well as his entry No. 162, 'Nervous Disorders', in *Primitive Physick* (15th edn., 1772), pp. 105-6.
[25] Cf. Prov. 1:26-27.   [26] Prov. 24:34.   [27] Cf. Luke 10:31, 32.
[28] Cf. 1 Tim. 6:8. Cf. Wesley's comment in his *Notes*: 'That is, raiment and a house to cover us'. This is an overblown inference from any of the noun and verb forms of σκεπάζω, the participial forms of which can be stretched to connote 'shelter' or even 'protection', but not 'lodging'; see Liddell and Scott, *Greek-English Lexicon*.
[29] Job 24:8.
[30] Cf. Juvenal, *Satires*, iii. 152-53: 'Poverty brings no unhappiness worse than this: it exposes men to ridicule' (cf. Loeb 91:42).
[31] Cf. Gen. 3:19.

Christian country that toil and labour, and sweat, and have it not
at last, but struggle with weariness and hunger together? Is it not
worse for one after an hard day's labour to come back to a poor,
cold, dirty, uncomfortable lodging, and to find there not even the
5 food which is needful to repair his wasted strength? You that live
at ease in the earth, that want nothing but eyes to see, ears to hear,
and hearts to understand how well God has dealt with you—is it
not worse to seek bread day by day, and find none? Perhaps to find
the comfort also of five or six children, crying for what he has not
10 to give. Were it not that he is restrained by an unseen hand, would
he not soon 'curse God and die'?[32] O want of bread! Want of
bread![33] Who can tell what this means unless he hath felt it
himself? I am astonished it occasions no more than heaviness
even in them that believe![34]

15 4. Perhaps next to this we may place the death of those who
were near and dear unto us; of a tender parent, and one not much
declined into the vale of years;[35] of a beloved child just rising into
life, and clasping about our heart; of a friend that was as our own
soul[36]—next the grace of God the last, best gift of heaven. And a
20 thousand circumstances may enhance the distress: perhaps the
child, the friend, died in our embrace! Perhaps was snatched
away when we looked not for it! Flourishing, cut down like a
flower! In all these cases we not only may, but ought to be
affected: it is the design of God that we should. He would not
25 have us stocks and stones. He would have our affections
regulated, not extinguished. Therefore

. . . nature unreproved may drop a tear:[37]

There may be sorrow without sin.

5. A still deeper sorrow we may feel for those who are dead
30 while they live, on account of the unkindness, ingratitude,
apostasy of those who were united to us in the closest ties. Who
can express what a lover of souls may feel for a friend, a brother
dead to God? For an husband, a wife, a parent, a child, rushing

---

[32] Job 2:9.   [33] Amos 4:6.
[34] Another example (rare in his time) of Wesley's conscious identification with 'Christ's
poor'. See No. 31, 'Sermon on the Mount, XI', I.6 and n.
[35] Cf. Shakespeare, *Othello*, III. iii. 264-65: 'I am declin'd into a vale of years.'
[36] See 1 Sam. 18:1, 3; 20:17; cf. No. 73, 'Of Hell', I.2.
[37] Cf. Samuel Wesley, Jun., 'The Parish Priest', ll. 5-6, *Poems on Several Occasions*
(1736), p. 65.

into sin as an horse into the battle,[38] and in spite of all arguments and persuasions hasting to work out his own damnation? And this anguish of spirit may be heightened to an inconceivable degree by the consideration that he who is now posting to destruction once ran well in the way of life. Whatever he was in time past serves 5 now to no other purpose than to make our reflections on what he is more piercing and afflictive.

6. In all these circumstances we may be assured our great adversary will not be wanting to improve his opportunity. He who is always 'walking about seeking whom he may devour'[39] will then 10 especially use all his power, all his skill, if haply he may gain any advantage over the soul that is already cast down. He will not be sparing of his fiery darts,[40] such as are most likely to find an entrance, and to fix most deeply in the heart, by their suitableness to the temptation that assaults it. He will labour to inject 15 unbelieving, or blasphemous, or repining thoughts. He will suggest that God does not regard, does not govern the earth; or at least that he does not govern it aright, not by the rules of justice and mercy. He will endeavour to stir up the heart against God, to renew our natural enmity against him. And if we attempt to fight 20 him with his own weapons, if we begin to *reason* with him, more and more heaviness will undoubtedly ensue, if not utter darkness.

7. It has been frequently supposed that there is another cause (if not of darkness, at least) of heaviness, namely, God's withdrawing himself from the soul because it is his sovereign will. 25 Certainly he will do this if we grieve his Holy Spirit, either by outward or inward sin; either by doing evil or neglecting to do good; by giving way either to pride or anger, to spiritual sloth, to foolish desire or inordinate affection.[41] But that he ever withdraws himself because he *will*, merely because it is his good pleasure, I 30 absolutely deny:[42] there is no text in all the Bible which gives any colour for such a supposition. Nay, it is a supposition contrary not only to many particular texts, but to the whole tenor of Scripture. It is repugnant to the very nature of God; it is utterly beneath his majesty and wisdom (as an eminent writer strongly expresses it) 35

---

[38] See Jer. 8:6.
[39] Cf. 1 Pet. 5:8.
[40] Eph. 6:16.
[41] Col. 3:5.
[42] Note this flat rejection of what Wesley understood of the Lutheran doctrine of 'the hiddenness of God' (*Deus absconditus*).

'to play at *bo-peep* with his creatures'.[43] It is inconsistent both with his justice and mercy, and with the sound experience of all his children.

8. One more cause of heaviness is mentioned by many of those who are termed mystic authors. And the notion has crept in, I know not how, even among plain people who have no acquaintance with them. I cannot better explain this than in the words of a late writer, who relates this as her own experience: 'I continued so happy in my Beloved, that although I should have been forced to live a vagabond in a desert, I should have found no difficulty in it. This state had not lasted long when in effect I found myself led into a desert. . . . I found myself in a forlorn condition, altogether poor, wretched, and miserable. . . . The proper source of this grief is the knowledge of ourselves, by which we find that there is an extreme unlikeness between God and us. We see ourselves most opposite to him, and that our inmost soul is entirely corrupted, depraved and full of all kind of evil and malignity, of the world and the flesh and all sorts of abominations.'[44] From hence it has been inferred that the knowledge of ourselves, without which we should perish everlastingly, *must*, even after we have attained justifying faith, occasion the deepest heaviness.

9. But upon this I would observe, (1). In the preceding paragraph this writer says, 'Hearing I had not a true faith in Christ, I offered myself up to God, and immediately felt his love.' It may be so; and yet it does not appear that this was justification. 'Tis more probable it was no more than what are usually termed the 'drawings of the Father'.[45] And if so, the heaviness and darkness which followed was no other than conviction of sin, which in the nature of things must precede that faith whereby we are justified. (2). Suppose she was justified almost the same moment she was convinced of wanting faith, there was then no time for that gradually increasing self-knowledge which uses to precede justification. In this case therefore it came after, and was probably the more severe the less it was expected. (3). It is allowed

[43] I.e., to play a tantalizing game; cf. *OED* for a variety of instances of the phrase, espec. in Daniel Defoe's denunciation of 'men . . . that . . . do nothing but play at bo-peep with God Almighty', in *Enquiry Into the Occasional Conformity of Dissenters* (1697).

[44] π;

[45] Cf. *OED*, 'draw', II.26-28; and letter to Charles Wesley, Apr. 4, 1748: 'So loving a people have I scarce ever seen, nor so strong and general drawings from above' (26:302 in this edn., l. 33).

there will be a far deeper, a far clearer and fuller knowledge of our inbred sin, of our total corruption by nature, after justification, than ever there was before it.[46] But this need not occasion darkness of soul. I will not say that it *must* bring us into heaviness. Were it so the Apostle would not have used that expression, 'if need be';[47] for there would be an absolute, indispensable need of it, for all that would know themselves; that is, in effect, for all that would know the perfect love of God, and be thereby 'made meet to be partakers of the inheritance of the saints in light'.[48] But this is by no means the case. On the contrary, God may increase the knowledge of ourselves to any degree, and increase in the same proportion the knowledge of himself and the experience of his love.[49] And in this case there would be no desert, no misery, no forlorn condition;[50] but love and peace and joy, gradually springing up into everlasting life.[51]

IV. 1. For what ends, then (which was the fourth thing to be considered), does God permit heaviness to befall so many of his children? The Apostle gives us a plain and direct answer to this important question: 'That the trial of their faith, which is much more precious than gold that perisheth though it be tried by fire, may be found unto praise and honour and glory, at the revelation of Jesus Christ.'[a] There may be an allusion to this in that well-known passage of the fourth chapter (although it primarily relates to quite another thing, as has been already observed): 'Think it not strange concerning the fiery trial which is to try you', 'but rejoice that ye are partakers of the sufferings of Christ; that when his glory shall be revealed ye may likewise rejoice with exceeding great joy.'[b]

2. Hence we learn that the first and great end of God's permitting the temptations which bring heaviness on his children is the trial of their faith, which is tried by these, even as gold by the

[a] [1 Pet. 1:] ver. 7.
[b] Ver. 12, etc.

---

[46] Another explicit reference to the 'remains of sin' after justification; see No. 13, *On Sin in Believers*, intro., I.6, and III.8. Note here the phrase 'inbred sin' as synonymous with 'in-being' and 'original' sin in No. 44, *Original Sin*, intro.

[47] 1 Pet. 1:6.   [48] Col. 1:12.

[49] A proportionality between repentance after justification (our self-knowledge) and faith (our knowledge of God and of his grace).

[50] See III.8, above.   [51] John 4:14.

fire. Now we know gold tried in the fire is purified thereby, is separated from its dross. And so is faith in the fire of temptation; the more it is tried, the more it is purified. Yea, and not only purified, but also strengthened, confirmed, increased abundant-
5 ly, by so many more proofs of the wisdom and power, the love and faithfulness of God. This then—to increase our faith—is one gracious end of God's permitting those manifold temptations.

3. They serve to try, to purify, to confirm and increase that living hope also, whereunto 'the God and Father of our Lord
10 Jesus Christ hath begotten us again of his abundant mercy'.[52] Indeed our hope cannot but increase in the same proportion with our faith. On this foundation it stands: believing in his name, living by faith in the Son of God, we hope for, we have a confident expectation of, the glory which shall be revealed.[53] And
15 consequently, whatever strengthens our faith increases our hope also. At the same time it increases our joy in the Lord, which cannot but attend an hope full of immortality.[54] In this view the Apostle exhorts believers in the other chapter, 'Rejoice that ye are partakers of the sufferings of Christ.' On this very account,
20 'Happy are you; for the Spirit of glory and of God resteth upon you.'[55] And hereby ye are enabled, even in the midst of sufferings, to 'rejoice with joy unspeakable and full of glory'.[56]

4. They rejoice the more because the trials which increase their faith and hope increase their love also; both their gratitude to God
25 for all his mercies, and their goodwill to all mankind. Accordingly the more deeply sensible they are of the loving-kindness of God their Saviour, the more is their heart inflamed with love to him who 'first loved us'.[57] The clearer and stronger evidence they have of the glory that shall be revealed, the more do they love him who
30 hath purchased it for them, and 'given them the earnest' thereof 'in their hearts'.[58] And this, the increase of their love, is another end of the temptations permitted to come upon them.

5. Yet another is their advance in holiness, holiness of heart and holiness of conversation; the latter naturally resulting from the
35 former; for a good tree will bring forth good fruit.[59] And all inward holiness is the immediate fruit of the faith that worketh by love.[60]

---

[52] Cf. 1 Pet. 1:3.
[54] Wisd. 3:4.
[56] 1 Pet. 1:8.
[58] 2 Cor. 1:22.
[53] Rom. 8:18.
[55] Cf. 1 Pet. 4:13-14.
[57] 1 John 4:19.
[59] See Matt. 7:17.
[60] See Gal. 5:6. Cf. above, II.3; and No. 2, *The Almost Christian*, II.6 and n.

By this the blessed Spirit purifies the heart from pride, self-will, passion; from love of the world, from foolish and hurtful desires,[61] from vile and vain affections. Beside that, sanctified afflictions have (through the grace of God) an immediate and direct tendency to holiness. Through the operation of his Spirit they 5 humble more and more, and abase the soul before God. They calm and meeken[62] our turbulent spirit, tame the fierceness of our nature, soften our obstinacy and self-will, crucify us to the world, and bring us to expect all our strength from, and to seek all our happiness in, God.   10

6. And all these terminate in that great end, that our faith, hope, love, and holiness, 'may be found' (if it doth not yet appear) 'unto praise' from God himself, 'and honour' from men and angels, 'and glory'[63] assigned by the great Judge to all that have endured to the end. And this will be assigned in that awful day to every man 15 'according to his works',[64] according to the work which God had wrought in his heart, and the outward works which he has wrought for God; and likewise according to what he had suffered; so that all these trials are unspeakable gain. So many ways do these 'light afflictions, which are but for a moment, work out for 20 us a far more exceeding and eternal weight of glory'![65]

7. Add to this the advantage which others may receive by seeing our behaviour under affliction. We find by experience, example frequently makes a deeper impression upon us than precept. And what examples have a stronger influence, not only on those who 25 are partakers of like precious faith, but even on them who have not known God, than that of a soul calm and serene in the midst of storms, sorrowful, yet always rejoicing;[66] meekly accepting whatever is the will of God, however grievous it may be to nature; saying, in sickness and pain, 'The cup which my Father hath 30 given me, shall I not drink it?'[67] In loss or want, 'The Lord gave; the Lord hath taken away; blessed be the name of the Lord!'[68]

V. 1. I am to conclude with some inferences. And, first, how wide is the difference between *darkness* of soul and *heaviness!*

---

[61] 1 Tim. 6:9.
[62] A rare usage; cf. *OED* and also Charles Wesley's hymn on Matt. 5:5, 1.1: 'Meeken my soul, Thou heavenly Lamb', in *Short Hymns on Select Passages of Holy Scripture*, 1762 *(Poet. Wks.*, X. 162).
[63] 1 Pet. 1:7.   [64] Matt. 16:27.
[65] Cf. 2 Cor. 4:17.   [66] 2 Cor. 6:10.
[67] John 18:11.   [68] Job 1:21.

Which nevertheless are so generally confounded with each other, even by experienced Christians! Darkness, or the wilderness state, implies a total loss of joy in the Holy Ghost; heaviness does not; in the midst of this we may 'rejoice with joy unspeakable'.[69]

5 They that are in darkness have lost the peace of God; they that are in heaviness have not. So far from it that at the very time 'peace' as well as 'grace' may 'be multiplied unto' them.[70] In the former the love of God is waxed cold, if it be not utterly extinguished; in the latter it retains its full force, or rather increases daily. In these

10 faith itself, if not totally lost, is however grievously decayed. Their evidence and conviction of things not seen,[71] particularly of the pardoning love of God, is not so clear or strong as in time past; and their trust in him is proportionably weakened. Those, though they see him not, yet have a clear, unshaken confidence in God,

15 and an abiding evidence of that love whereby all their sins are blotted out.[72] So that as long as we can distinguish faith from unbelief, hope from despair, peace from war, the love of God from the love of the world, we may infallibly distinguish *heaviness* from *darkness*.[73]

20 2. We may learn from hence, secondly, that there may be need of *heaviness*, but there can be no need of *darkness*. There may be need of our being in 'heaviness for a season', in order to the ends above recited; at least in this sense, as it is a natural result of those 'manifold temptations' which are needful to try and increase our

25 faith, to confirm and enlarge our hope, to purify our heart from all unholy tempers, and to perfect us in love. And by consequence they are needful in order to brighten our crown, and add to our eternal weight of glory.[74] But we cannot say that darkness is needful in order to any of these ends. It is no way conducive to

30 them: the loss of faith, hope, love, is surely neither conducive to holiness nor to the increase of that reward in heaven which will be in proportion to our holiness on earth.

3. From the Apostle's manner of speaking we may gather, thirdly, that even heaviness is not *always* needful. 'Now, for a

35 season, if need be'; so it is not needful for *all persons;* nor for any person at *all times.* God is able, he has both power and wisdom,

---

[69] 1 Pet. 1:8.　　　　　　　　　　　　　　　　　[70] Cf. 2 Pet. 1:2.
[71] See Heb. 11:1.
[72] See Acts 3:19.
[73] Cf. above, I.1 and n.
[74] 2 Cor. 4:17.

to work when he pleases the same work of grace, in any soul, by other means. And in some instances he does so: he causes those whom it pleaseth him to go on from strength to strength, even till they 'perfect holiness in his fear',[75] with scarce any heaviness at all; as having an absolute power over the heart of man, and 5 moving all the springs of it at his pleasure. But these cases are rare: God generally sees good to try 'acceptable men in the furnace of affliction';[76] so that manifold temptations and heaviness, more or less, are usually the portion of his dearest children. 10

4. We ought therefore, lastly, to watch and pray,[77] and use our utmost endeavours to avoid falling into darkness. But we need not be solicitous how to avoid, so much as how to improve by heaviness. Our great care should be so to behave ourselves under it, so to wait upon the Lord therein, that it may fully answer all the 15 design of his love in permitting it to come upon us; that it may be a means of increasing our faith, of confirming our hope, of perfecting us in all holiness. Whenever it comes, let us have an eye to these gracious ends for which it is permitted, and use all diligence that we may not 'make void the counsel of'[78] God 20 'against ourselves'.[79] Let us earnestly 'work together with him',[80] by the grace which he is continually giving us, in 'purifying ourselves from all pollution both of flesh and spirit',[81] and daily 'growing in the grace of our Lord Jesus Christ',[82] till we are received into his everlasting kingdom! 25

---

[75] Cf. 2 Cor. 7:1.
[76] Cf. Ecclus. 2:5.
[77] Matt. 26:41.
[78] Jer. 19:7.
[79] Cf. Luke 7:30.
[80] Cf. 2 Cor. 6:1.
[81] Cf. 2 Cor. 7:1 (*Notes*).
[82] Cf. 2 Pet. 3:18.

SELF-DENIAL

AN INTRODUCTORY COMMENT

The concluding trio of sermons in SOSO, *IV, suggest that Wesley had finally rounded out his exposition of the 'order of salvation' with his paired essays on the difference between spiritual 'darkness' and 'heaviness'. It was, therefore, time to turn to other, separate problems that continued to arise in any programme of Christian living. This sequence would have seemed natural enough, since Wesley's concept of theology as a* scientia practica *had always meant to him that evangelical doctrine entailed a series of ethical imperatives which issued, in turn, from clear conceptions of sound doctrine.*

It may be somewhat startling to read that, until this sermon, 'no writer in the English tongue [had] described the nature of self-denial in plain and intelligible terms,' when one considers the popularity of this topic in Puritan preaching and such familiar classics as Richard Baxter's Treatise of Self-Denyall *(1660, 1675); William Penn,* No Cross, No Crown . . . *(1669, 1682); Jeremy Taylor,* The Rule and Exercises of Holy Living *(1650), and* The Rule and Exercises of Holy Dying *(1651),* Works, *I. 399-515, 516-604; Thomas Manton,* A Treatise of Self-Denial . . . *in* Works *(1689), IV.17 ff.; and William Law,* Christian Perfection, *and* A Serious Call to a Devout and Holy Life *(1729), in* Works, *Vols. III and IV. And it goes without saying that a reader is free to judge how far Wesley may be compared with such predecessors.*

What he may have had more directly in mind was the fact that the tradition on self-denial had rested on a general consensus, at least in an approval of the ideal. The conventional form of the problem had always come from the discrepancies between profession and practice. In his own lifetime, however, Wesley had seen even the ideal decried, both by the spreading fashions of self-advertised ostentation in eighteenth-century culture and by a rising tide of antinomian rejection of self-denial, on principle. *As far back as 1741 he had been shocked by Count von Zinzendorf's scornful dismissal of self-abnegation as a Christian virtue (cf. JWJ, September 3, 1741: 'We believers do as we please and nothing more; we laugh at all talk of "mortification"'). He had gone on to retort* to this in kind, in his own General Rules *of 1743, by instructing the Methodists to 'trample under foot that enthusiastic doctrine of devils that "we are not to do good unless our heart be free to it."' But the tendency of the new piety to turn 'Christian liberty' into self-indulgence had persisted; there was evident need for yet another distillation of the ancient Christian wisdom on 'cross-bearing' and self-surrender to the will of God; hence, this present sermon.*

The idea, as Wesley defines it here, had been a childhood commonplace in his family; it had been a major premise in Susanna's theory of Christian nurture.[1] A sermon on this topic appears as No. 25 in Wesley's own list of his early sermons.[2] He had preached on Luke 9:23 in Savannah, and very shortly after his return to England (February 21, 1738) he had used the same text for a sermon in one of the oldest churches in the City of London, Great St. Helen's (in Bishopsgate). In the Journal for August 16, 1744, he had printed a letter about self-denial from his friend, the Revd. Henry Piers (Vicar of Bexley), and a few months later (February 17, 1745), he had inserted another letter into the Journal on the same theme, from his 'book steward', William Briggs.

Since then, however, his use of Luke 9:23 had been sparse (only twice, both in 1755). One may suppose, therefore, that our text here had been written expressly for inclusion in the fourth volume of his SOSO; it should be noticed how much more clearly this sermon reflects the problem as it had to be perceived in the 1750s than it would have appeared in 1738. It was, of course, reprinted in the successive editions of SOSO, but never separately.

---

[1] See Nos. 95, 'On the Education of Children', and 96, 'On Obedience to Parents'.
[2] See Heitzenrater, 'John Wesley's Early Sermons', p. 117.

Self-denial

Luke 9:23

And he said to them all, If any man will come after me, let him deny himself, and take up his cross daily, and follow me.

5   1. It has been frequently imagined that the direction here given related chiefly, if not wholly, to the apostles; at least to the Christians of the first ages, or those in a state of persecution. But this is a grievous mistake; for although our blessed Lord is here directing his discourse more immediately to his apostles and
10 those other disciples who attended him in the days of his flesh, yet in them he speaks to us, and to all mankind, without any exception or limitation. The very reason of the thing puts it beyond dispute that the duty which is here enjoined is not peculiar to them, or to the Christians of the early ages. It no more regards any particular
15 order of men, or particular time, than any particular country. No; it is of the most universal nature, respecting all times and all persons. Yea, and all things—not meats and drinks only, and things pertaining to the senses. The meaning is, 'If any man', of whatever rank, station, circumstances, in any nation, in any age of
20 the world, 'will' effectually 'come after me, let him deny himself in all things; let him take up his cross' of whatever kind, yea, and that 'daily, and follow me.'
     2. The 'denying' ourselves and the 'taking up our cross', in the full extent of the expression, is not a thing of small concern. It is
25 not expedient only, as are some of the circumstantials of religion; but it is absolutely, indispensably necessary, either to our becoming or continuing his disciples. It is absolutely necessary, in the very nature of the thing, to our 'coming after him' and 'following him',
·   insomuch that as far as we do not practise it we are not his dis-
30 ciples. If we do not continually 'deny ourselves', we do not learn of him, but of other masters. If we do not 'take up our cross daily', we do not 'come after him', but after the world, or the prince

[1] Col. 2:18.

of the world, or our own 'fleshly mind'.[1] If we are not walking in the way of the cross, we are not following him; we are not treading in his steps, but going back from, or at least wide of, him.

3. It is for this reason that so many ministers of Christ in almost every age and nation, particularly since the Reformation of the Church from the innovations and corruptions gradually crept into it, have wrote and spoke so largely on this important duty, both in their public discourses and private exhortations. This induced them to disperse abroad many tracts upon the subject; and some in our own nation. They knew both from the oracles of God and from the testimony of their own experience how impossible it was not to deny our Master, unless we will deny ourselves; and how vainly we attempt to follow him that was crucified, unless we take up our cross daily.

4. But may not this very consideration make it reasonable to inquire, 'If so much has been said and wrote on the subject already, what need is there to say or write any more?' I answer, there are no inconsiderable numbers, even of people fearing God, who have not had the opportunity either of hearing what has been spoke, or reading what has been wrote upon it. And perhaps if they had read much of what has been written they would not have been much profited. Many who have wrote (some of them large volumes) do by no means appear to have understood the subject. Either they had imperfect views of the very nature of it (and then they could never explain it to others) or they were unacquainted with the due extent of it; they did not see how *exceeding broad* this command is; or they were not sensible of the absolute, the indispensable necessity of it. Others speak of it in so dark, so perplexed, so intricate, so mystical a manner, as if they designed rather to conceal it from the vulgar than to explain it to common readers.[2] Others speak admirably well, with great clearness and strength, on the necessity of self-denial; but then they deal in generals only, without coming to particular instances, and so are of little use to the bulk of mankind, to men of ordinary capacity and education. And if some of them do descend to particulars, it is to those particulars only which do not affect the generality of men, since they seldom, if ever, occur in common life: such as the enduring imprisonment or tortures; the giving up,

---

[2] It may be William Law that he has in mind here, or even Madame Guyon; but it is true that he found such classics as St. John of the Cross's *Ascent of Mt. Carmel* somewhat 'dark, perplexed, and intricate'.

in a literal sense, their houses or lands, their husbands or wives,
children, or life itself—to none of which we are called, nor are
likely to be, unless God should permit times of public persecution
to return. In the meantime, I know of no writer in the English
5 tongue[3] who has described the nature of self-denial in plain and
intelligible terms such as lie level with common understandings,
and applied it to those little particulars which daily occur in common life. A discourse of this kind is wanted still. And it is wanted
the more because in every stage of the spiritual life, although
10 there is a variety of particular hindrances of our attaining grace or
growing therein, yet are all resolvable into these general ones—
either we do not deny ourselves, or we do not take up our cross.

In order to supply this defect in some degree, I shall endeavour
to show, first, what it is for a man to deny himself, and what to take
15 up his cross; and secondly, that if a man be not fully Christ's
disciple, it is always owing to the want of this.

I. 1. I shall, first, endeavour to show what it is for a man to 'deny
himself and take up his cross daily'. This is a point which is of all
others most necessary to be considered and throughly under-
20 stood, even on this account, that it is of all others most opposed,
by numerous and powerful enemies. All our nature must certainly rise up against this, even in its own defence. The world,
consequently, the men who take nature, not grace, for their guide,
abhor the very sound of it. And the great enemy of our souls, well
25 knowing its importance, cannot but move every stone against it.
But this is not all: even those who have in some measure shaken
off the yoke of the devil, who have experienced, especially of late
years, a real work of grace in their hearts, yet are no friends to this
grand doctrine of Christianity, though it is so peculiarly insisted
30 on by their Master. Some of them are as deeply and totally
ignorant concerning it as if there was not one word about it in the
Bible. Others are farther off still, having unawares imbibed strong
prejudices against it. These they have received partly from
outside Christians—men of a fair speech and behaviour who
35 want nothing of godliness but the power, nothing of religion but
the spirit—and partly from those who did once, if they do not
now, 'taste of the powers of the world to come'.[4] But are there any

---

[3] Note the assumption here that Wesley's readers would not have been interested in
cross-checking on so confident a generality.
[4] Cf. Heb. 6:5.

of these who do not both practise self-denial themselves and recommend it to others? You are little acquainted with mankind if you doubt of this. There are whole bodies of men who only do not declare war against it. To go no farther than London, look upon the whole body of predestinarians who by the free mercy of God 5 have lately been called out of the darkness of nature into the light of faith.[5] Are they patterns of self-denial? How few of them even profess to practise it at all! How few of them recommend it themselves, or are pleased with them that do! Rather do they not continually represent it in the most odious colours, as if it were 10 seeking *salvation by works,* or 'seeking to establish our own righteousness'?[6] And how readily do antinomians of all kinds, from the smooth Moravian[7] to the boisterous foul-mouthed Ranter,[8] join the cry with their silly unmeaning cant of 'legality', and 'preaching the law'! Therefore you are in constant danger of 15 being wheedled, hectored, or ridiculed out of this important gospel doctrine either by false teachers or false brethren (more or less beguiled from the simplicity of the gospel) if you are not deeply grounded therein. Let fervent prayer then go before, accompany, and follow what you are now about to read, that it 20 may be written in your heart by the finger of God, so as never to be erased.

2. But what is self-denial? Wherein are we to deny ourselves? And whence does the necessity of this arise? I answer, the will of God is the supreme, unalterable rule for every intelligent 25 creature; equally binding every angel in heaven and every man upon earth. Nor can it be otherwise: this is the natural, necessary result of the relation between creatures and their Creator. But if the will of God be our one rule of action in everything, great and

---

[5] See Col. 1:12-13.

[6] Cf. Rom. 10:3; a caricature that ignores the commonplace that men like Thomas Manton, Lewis Bayley, George Whitefield (indeed, most Calvinists) taught both predestination *and* self-denial. Wesley may have had a special group in mind—e.g., John Cennick, William Cudworth, James Relly, and their disciples.

[7] A sarcastic reference to the elegant Count von Zinzendorf?

[8] If this is a reference to George Fox (cf. the 'foul-mouthed . . . George Fox' in No. 68, 'The Wisdom of God's Counsels', §9), Wesley has confused his seventeenth-century church history. The Ranters proper (men like Laurence Clarkson, Abiezer Coope, Thomas Tany) were indeed famous for their indifference to customary morality and their cultic swearing, but they were condemned and disowned by the Quakers and even by the Muggletonians ('The Seekers'). Cf. Robert Barclay, *The Anarchy of the Ranters, and Other Libertines* . . . (1676); abridged in Barbour and Roberts, *Early Quaker Writings,* pp. 215 ff. Ironically, the 'Primitive Methodists' of the early nineteenth century were also called 'Ranters', because of their boisterous preaching services and class meetings.

small, it follows by undeniable consequence that we are not to do our own will in anything. Here therefore we see at once the nature, with the ground and reason, of self-denial. We see the nature of self-denial: it is the denying or refusing to follow our 5 own will, from a conviction that the will of God is the only rule of action to us. And we see the reason thereof, because we are creatures; because 'it is he that hath made us and not we ourselves.'[9]

3. This reason for self-denial must hold even with regard to the 10 angels of God in heaven; and with regard to man, innocent and holy, as he came out of the hands of his Creator. But a farther reason for it arises from the condition wherein all men are since the Fall. We are all now 'shapen in wickedness, and in sin did our mother conceive us'.[10] Our nature is altogether corrupt, in every 15 power and faculty. And our will, depraved equally with the rest, is wholly bent to indulge our natural corruption. On the other hand, it is the will of God that we resist and counteract that corruption, not at some times, or in some things only, but at all times, and in all things. Here therefore is a farther ground for constant and 20 universal self-denial.

4. To illustrate this a little farther. The will of God is a path leading straight to God. The will of man which once ran parallel with it is now another path, not only different from it, but in our present state directly contrary to it. It leads from God; if therefore 25 we walk in the one, we must necessarily quit the other. We cannot walk in both. Indeed a man of 'faint heart and feeble hands' may 'go in two ways',[11] one after the other; but he cannot walk in two ways at the same time. He cannot at one and the same time follow his own will and follow the will of God; he must choose the one or 30 the other—denying God's will to follow his own, or denying himself to follow the will of God.

5. Now it is undoubtedly pleasing for the time to follow our own will, by indulging, in any instance that offers, the corruption of our nature. But by following it in anything we so far strengthen 35 the perverseness of our will; and by indulging it we continually increase the corruption of our nature. So by the food which is agreeable to the palate we often increase a bodily disease. It gratifies the taste; but it inflames the disorder. It brings pleasure; but it also brings death.

---

[9] Ps. 100:3 (AV).   [10] Cf. Ps. 51:5 (BCP).   [11] Cf. Ecclus. 2:12.

6. On the whole, then, to deny ourselves is to deny our own will where it does not fall in with the will of God, and that however pleasing it may be. It is to deny ourselves any pleasure which does not spring from, and lead to, God; that is, in effect, to refuse going out of our way, though into a pleasant, flowery path; to refuse what we know to be deadly poison, though agreeable to the taste.

7. And everyone that would follow Christ, that would be his real disciple, must not only 'deny himself', but 'take up his cross' also. A cross is anything contrary to our will, anything displeasing to our nature.[12] So that taking up our cross goes a little farther than denying ourselves; it rises a little higher, and is a more difficult task to flesh and blood, it being more easy to forego pleasure than to endure pain.

8. Now in 'running the race which is set before us'[13] according to the will of God, there is often a cross lying in the way; that is, something which is not only not joyous, but grievous, something which is contrary to our will, which is displeasing to our nature. What then is to be done? The choice is plain: either we must 'take up our cross', or we must turn aside from the way of God, 'from the holy commandment delivered to us'[14]—if we do not stop altogether, or turn back to everlasting perdition.

9. In order to the healing of that corruption, that evil disease which every man brings with him into the world, it is often needful to pluck out as it were a right eye, to cut off a right hand; so painful is either the thing itself which must be done, or the only means of doing it; the parting suppose with a foolish desire,[15] with an inordinate affection;[16] or a separation from the object of it, without which it can never be extinguished. In the former kind, the tearing away such a desire or affection when it is deeply rooted in the soul is often like the piercing of a sword, yea, like 'the dividing asunder of the soul and spirit, the joints and marrow'.[17]

---

[12] A notable and rare instance of allegorical interpretation; see also No. 99, *The Reward of Righteousness*, §4. Wesley's standard rule, of course, was that all Scripture is to be interpreted literally unless this leads into an absurdity; cf. No. 21, 'Sermon on the Mount, I', §6 and n.

[13] Cf. Heb. 12:1. [14] Cf. 2 Pet. 2:21.

[15] 1 Tim. 6:9 (*Notes*). [16] Col. 3:5.

[17] Cf. Heb. 4:12. There is a personal note of remembered anguish here, for Wesley had experienced two profoundly disturbing misadventures in love—the successive loss of the only two women he had ever really loved romantically. The first was the Sophy Hopkey affair in Georgia, to which there are some clues in the printed *Journal*, more in Wesley's diary, but the fullest in his several MS journals of his experiences in Georgia, which will appear in print for the first time in the appendix to Vol. 18 of this edn., containing the

The Lord then sits upon the soul 'as a refiner's fire',[18] to burn up all the dross thereof. And this is a cross indeed; it is essentially painful; it must be so in the very nature of the thing. The soul cannot be thus torn asunder, it cannot pass through the fire,
5 without pain.

10. In the latter kind, the means to heal a sin-sick soul,[19] to cure a foolish desire, an inordinate affection, are often painful, not in the nature of the thing, but from the nature of the disease. So when our Lord said to the rich young man, 'Go sell that thou hast
10 and give it to the poor' (as well knowing this was the only means of healing his covetousness), the very thought of it gave him so much pain that 'he went away sorrowful';[20] choosing rather to part with his hope of heaven than his possessions on earth. This was a burden he could not consent to lift, a cross he would not take up.
15 And in the one kind or the other every follower of Christ will surely have need to 'take up his cross daily'.

11. The 'taking up' differs a little from 'bearing his cross'. We are then properly said to 'bear our cross' when we endure what is laid upon us without our choice, with meekness and resignation.
20 Whereas we do not properly 'take up our cross' but when we voluntarily suffer what it is in our power to avoid; when we willingly embrace the will of God, though contrary to our own; when we choose what is painful because it is the will of our wise and gracious Creator.
25 12. And thus it behoves every disciple of Christ to 'take up' as well as to 'bear *his* cross'. Indeed in one sense it is not *his* alone: it

Journals and diaries for Georgia. The scars of this disappointment may be seen as late as Dec. 23, 1782 (in a letter to an unnamed friend), and in his letters to Samuel Bradburn, Feb. 14, 1786, and to Thomas Roberts, Feb. 12, 1789. Even more deeply disturbing, and more recent, had been his espousal to Grace Murray and his loss of her to John Bennet (through the meddling offices of his brother and George Whitefield); cf. JWJ, July 20–Oct. 15, 1749; also Wesley's MS account of her from her birth to her marriage to Bennet (BL Add. MSS. 7119), published in J. A. Leger, *John Wesley's Last Love* (London, J. M. Dent and Sons, Ltd., 1910); see also, Curnock, III. 417-22. There are not many more pathetic letters in the Wesley corpus than the one to Thomas Bigg, Oct. 7, 1749, expressing his anguish over 'the fatal, irrecoverable stroke [that] was struck on Thursday last', when he and Grace Murray 'were torn asunder by a whirlwind' (see 26:388-89 in this edn.).

[18] Cf. Mal. 3:2, 3.

[19] 'Sin-sick soul' had been a part of poetic diction for over a century, and was becoming almost a religious cliché, even in prose, found in Brooke's *Fool of Quality*, Cowper's *Olney Hymns*, and in the Wesleys' *Hymns and Sacred Poems* (1739), p. 92: 'Pity and heal my sin-sick soul.' (Cf. *OED*.)

[20] Matt. 19:21-22.

is common to him and many others, seeing 'there is no temptation befalls any man', εἰ μὴ ἀνθρώπινος, 'but such as is common to men',[21] such as is incident and adapted to their common nature and situation in the present world. But in another sense, as it is considered with all its circumstances, it is *his*; peculiar to himself. It is prepared of God for him; it is given by God to him, as a token of his love. And if he receives it as such, and (after using such means to remove the pressure as Christian wisdom directs) lies as clay in the potter's hand,[22] it is disposed and ordered by God for his good, both with regard to the quality of it and in respect to its quantity and degree, its duration, and every other circumstance.

13. In all this we may easily conceive our blessed Lord to act as the physician of our souls, not merely 'for his own pleasure, but for our profit, that we may be partakers of his holiness'.[23] If in searching our wounds he puts us to pain, it is only in order to heal them. He cuts away what is putrified or unsound in order to preserve the sound part. And if we freely choose the loss of a limb, rather than the whole body should perish, how much more should we choose, figuratively, to cut off a right hand, rather than the whole soul should be cast into hell![24]

14. We see plainly, then, both the nature and ground of 'taking up our cross'. It does not imply the 'disciplining ourselves' (as some speak), the literally tearing our own flesh: the wearing haircloth, or iron girdles, or anything else that would impair our bodily health (although we know not what allowance God may make for those who act thus through involuntary ignorance), but the embracing the will of God, though contrary to our own; the choosing wholesome, though bitter, medicines; the freely accepting temporary pain, of whatever kind, and in whatever degree, when it is either essentially or accidentally necessary to eternal pleasure.

II. 1. I am, secondly, to show that it is always owing to the want either of self-denial or taking up his cross that any man does not throughly 'follow him', is not fully a 'disciple' of Christ.

It is true this may be partly owing, in some cases, to the want of the means of grace; of hearing the true word of God spoken with power; of the sacraments; or of Christian fellowship. But where

---

[21] Cf. 1 Cor. 10:13.
[22] See Jer. 18:6.
[23] Cf. Heb. 12:10.
[24] See Matt. 5:30.

none of these is wanting, the great hindrance of our receiving or growing in the grace of God[25] is always the want of denying ourselves or taking up our cross.

2. A few instances will make this plain. A man hears the word
5 which is able to save his soul. He is well pleased with what he hears, acknowledges the truth, and is a little affected by it. Yet he remains 'dead in trespasses and sins',[26] senseless and unawakened. Why is this? Because he will not part with his bosom sin,[27] though he now knows it is an abomination to the Lord. He came
10 to hear, full of lust and unholy desires; and he will not part with them. Therefore no deep impression is made upon him, but his foolish heart is still hardened; that is, he is still senseless and unawakened, because he will not 'deny himself'.

3. Suppose he begins to awake out of sleep, and his eyes are a
15 little opened, why are they so quickly closed again? Why does he again sink into the sleep of death? Because he again yields to his bosom sin; he drinks again of the pleasing poison. Therefore it is impossible that any lasting impression should be made upon his heart; that is, he relapses into his fatal insensibility because he will
20 not 'deny himself'.

4. But this is not the case with all. We have many instances of those who when once awakened sleep no more. The impressions once received do not wear away; they are not only deep, but lasting. And yet many of these have not found what they seek; they
25 mourn, and yet are not comforted. Now why is this? It is because they do not 'bring forth fruits meet for repentance';[28] because they do not, according to the grace they have received, 'cease from evil and do good'.[29] They do not cease from the easily besetting sin,[30] the sin of their constitution, of their education, or of their
30 profession. Or they omit doing the good they may, and know they ought to do, because of some disagreeable circumstance attending it; that is, they do not attain faith, because they will not 'deny themselves', or 'take up their cross'.

5. 'But this man did receive "the heavenly gift".[31] He did "taste

---

[25] See 2 Pet. 3:18.
[26] Eph. 2:1.
[27] See below, No. 62, 'The End of Christ's Coming', §1, for Wesley's quotation of George Herbert's use of this phrase in verse. Cf. also Nos. 13, *On Sin in Believers*, V.1; and 14, *The Repentance of Believers*, I.3. For Wesley's frequent usage of such phrases as 'bosom sin', 'darling sin', 'darling lust', etc.; cf. No. 25, 'Sermon on the Mount, V', III.2 and n.
[28] Matt. 3:8.   [29] Cf. Isa. 1:16, 17.
[30] See Heb. 12:1; and also *Notes*.   [31] Heb. 6:4.

of the powers of the world to come".[32] He saw "the light of the glory of God in the face of Jesus Christ".[33] The "peace which passeth all understanding" did "rule his heart and mind";[34] and the love of God was shed abroad[35] therein by the Holy Ghost which was given unto him. Yet he is now weak as another man. He again relishes the things of earth, and has more taste for the things which are seen than for those which are not seen.[36] The eye of his understanding[37] is closed again, so that he cannot "see him that is invisible".[38] His love is waxed cold, and the peace of God no longer rules in his heart.' And no marvel: for he has again given place to the devil, and grieved the Holy Spirit of God.[39] He has turned again unto folly, to some pleasing sin, if not in outward act, yet in heart. He has given place to pride, or anger, or desire; to self-will, or stubbornness. Or he did not stir up the gift of God which was in him;[40] he gave way to spiritual sloth, and would not be at the pains of 'praying always, and watching thereunto with all perseverance';[41] that is, he made shipwreck of the faith[42] for want of self-denial and 'taking up his cross daily'.

6. But perhaps he has not made shipwreck of the faith: he has still a measure of the Spirit of adoption, which continues to witness with his spirit that he is a child of God.[43] However, he is not 'going on to perfection';[44] he is not, as once, hungering and thirsting after righteousness,[45] panting after the whole image and full enjoyment of God, as the hart after the water-brook.[46] Rather he is weary and faint in his mind, and as it were hovering between life and death. And why is he thus, but because he hath forgotten the word of God, 'By works is faith made perfect'?[47] He does not use all diligence in working the works of God. He does not 'continue instant in prayer',[48] private as well as public; in communicating, hearing, meditation, fasting, and religious conference. If he does not wholly neglect some of these means, at least he does not use them all, with his might. Or he is not zealous of works of charity,[49] as well as works of piety. He is not merciful after his power, with the full ability which God giveth. He does

---

[32] Cf. Heb. 6:5.
[33] 2 Cor. 4:6.
[34] Cf. Phil. 4:7.
[35] See Rom. 5:5.
[36] Cf. 2 Cor. 4:18.
[37] See Eph. 1:18.
[38] Cf. Heb. 11:27.
[39] See Eph. 4:30.
[40] See 2 Tim. 1:6.
[41] Eph. 6:18.
[42] 1 Tim. 1:19.
[43] Rom. 8:15-16.
[44] Cf. Heb. 6:1.
[45] See Matt. 5:6.
[46] See Ps. 42:1.
[47] Cf. Jas. 2:22.
[48] Rom. 12:12.
[49] See Titus 2:14.

not fervently serve the Lord by doing good to men, in every kind and in every degree he can, to their souls as well as their bodies. And why does he not continue in prayer? Because in times of dryness it is pain and grief unto him. He does not continue in
5 hearing at all opportunities, because sleep is sweet; or it is cold, or dark, or rainy. But why does he not continue in works of mercy?[50] Because he cannot feed the hungry, or clothe the naked, unless he retrench the expense of his own apparel, or use cheaper and less pleasing food. Beside which the visiting the sick or those that
10 are in prison is attended with many disagreeable circumstances. And so are most works of spiritual mercy—reproof, in particular. He *would* reprove his neighbour; but sometimes shame, sometimes fear, comes between. For he may expose himself not only to ridicule but to heavier inconveniences too. Upon these
15 and the like considerations he omits one or more, if not all, works of mercy and piety. Therefore his faith is not made perfect, neither can he grow in grace; namely, because he will not 'deny himself, and take up his daily cross'.

7. It manifestly follows that it is always owing to the want either
20 of self-denial or taking up his cross that a man does not throughly follow his Lord, that he is not fully a disciple of Christ. It is owing to this that he who is dead in sin does not awake, though the trumpet be blown;[51] that he who begins to awake out of sleep yet has no deep or lasting conviction; that he who is deeply and
25 lastingly convinced of sin does not attain remission of sins; that some who have received this heavenly gift retain it not, but make shipwreck of the faith; and that others, if they do not draw back to perdition, yet are weary and faint in their mind, and do not reach the mark of the prize of the high calling of God in Christ Jesus.[52]

30 III. 1. How easily may we learn hence that they know neither the Scripture nor the power of God who directly or indirectly, in public or in private, oppose the doctrine of self-denial and the daily cross! How totally ignorant are these men of an hundred particular texts, as well as of the general tenor of the whole oracles
35 of God! And how entirely unacquainted must they be with true,

---

[50] For this pairing of *piety* (here 'prayer') and *mercy*, cf. No. 14, *The Repentance of Believers*, I.13 and n. 65.

[51] See Amos 3:16; this is both the text and theme of No. 143, 'Public Diversions Denounced'.

[52] See Phil. 3:14.

genuine, Christian experience! Of the manner wherein the Holy Spirit ever did, and does at this day, work in the souls of men! They may talk indeed very loudly and confidently (a natural fruit of ignorance), as though they were the only men who understood either the Word of God, or the experience of his children. But their words are, in every sense, 'vain words':[53] they are weighed in the balance and found wanting.[54]

2. We may learn from hence, secondly, the real cause why not only many particular persons, but even bodies of men, who were once burning and shining lights,[55] have now lost both their light and heat. If they did not hate and oppose, they at least lightly esteemed this precious gospel doctrine. If they did not boldly say, *Abnegationem omnem proculcamus, internecioni damus* ('We trample all self-denial under foot, we devote it to destruction'),[56] yet they neither valued it according to its high importance, nor took any pains in practising it. *Hanc mystici docent,* said that great, bad man—'The mystic writers teach self-denial.'[57] No; the inspired writers. And God teaches it to every soul who is willing to hear his voice.

3. We may learn from hence, thirdly, that it is not enough for a minister of the gospel not to oppose the doctrine of self-denial, to say nothing concerning it. Nay, he cannot satisfy his duty by saying a little in favour of it. If he would indeed be pure from the blood of all men he must speak of it frequently and largely; he must inculcate the necessity of it in the clearest and strongest manner; he must press it with his might on all persons, at all times, and in all places; laying 'line upon line, line upon line, precept upon precept, precept upon precept'.[58] So shall he have a conscience void of offence;[59] so shall he save his own soul and those that hear him.[60]

---

[53] Exod. 5:9.   [54] Dan. 5:27.   [55] See John 5:35.

[56] An echo of the debate, in Latin, between Wesley and Count von Zinzendorf in Gray's Inn Walks, Sept. 3, 1741, reported in Wesley's version in the *Journal.* There, Zinzendorf is quoted as saying, '*Abnegationem omnem respuimus, conculcamus*' (lit. 'we spew out all abnegations [self-denials], we tread them under foot'). *Proculcamus* is a synonym for *conculcamus,* and this tends to confirm the impression that Wesley reconstructed his reports from memory, then and here. The addition of *internecioni damus* is out of order; *ad internecionem do* is a fragment from an earlier passage in the debate. For other references to Zinzendorf, see No. 13, *On Sin in Believers,* I.5 and n.

[57] Apparently yet another snatch from the dispute with Zinzendorf, along with a rare instance of ungracious invective ('that great, *bad* man'!). It is yet another indication that Wesley's rift with the Moravians was still rankling, and a measure of how deep it still went.

[58] Cf. Isa. 28:10, 13.   [59] Acts 24:16.   [60] See 1 Tim. 4:16.

4. Lastly, see that you apply this, every one of you, to your own soul. Meditate upon it when you are in secret; ponder it in your heart. Take care not only to understand it throughly, but to remember it to your life's end. Cry unto the Strong for strength,[61]
5 that you may no sooner understand than enter upon the practice of it. Delay not the time, but practise it immediately, from this very hour. Practise it universally, on every one of the thousand occasions which will occur in all circumstances of life. Practise it daily, without intermission, from the hour you first set your hand
10 to the plough; and perseveringly enduring therein to the end, till your spirit returns to God.

---

[61] A favourite phrase derived from Job 9:19; cf. Nos. 72, 'Of Evil Angels', III.4; 78, 'Spiritual Idolatry', II.4; 80, 'On Friendship with the World', §19; 93, 'On Redeeming the Time', III.2; 98, 'On Visiting the Sick', II.1. See also JWJ, May 26, 1752; and his letters to Mrs. Bennis, Dec. 16, 1772, and to William Minethorp, Nov. 29, 1776.

THE CURE OF EVIL-SPEAKING

AN INTRODUCTORY COMMENT

If, as we saw in 'Self-denial', pietists are all too easily tempted to a sort of religious narcissism, so also they find it hard to resist their strong temptations to high-minded censoriousness. Wesley saw the dangers here and roundly asserts (more hopefully, perhaps, than realistically) that 'a distinguishing mark of a Methodist [is that] he censures no man behind his back.' The magnitude of this problem within the closeknit fellowship of Methodist class meetings, etc., is reflected in a formal compact that was drawn up by the brothers Wesley, in John's own handwriting, and eleven of their colleagues, including Edward and Charles Perronet, on January 29, 1752:

It is agreed by us whose names are underwritten:
1. That we will not listen, or willingly inquire after any ill concerning each other.
2. That if we do hear any ill of each other, we will not be forward to believe it.
3. That as soon as possible we will communicate what we hear, by speaking or writing to the person concerned.
4. That till we have done this we will not write or speak a syllable of it to any other person whatsoever.
5. That neither will we mention it after we have done this to any other person.
6. That we will not make any exception to any of these rules, unless we think ourselves absolutely obliged in conscience so to do.[1]

This concern is confirmed by the fact that Wesley preached against 'evil-speaking' at least nine times in that year, then twice in 1753, and once again in 1758. The effectiveness of these various efforts, and of this written sermon summing up the issue, may be gauged from the fact that we hear no more of it until an oral sermon in 1786, and another written sermon—on how to reprove a neighbour to his face—in 1787 [2] (No. 65, 'The Duty of Reproving our Neighbour').

In light of Wesley's definition of evil-speaking ('neither more nor less than speaking evil of an absent person') it is worth noting that he does not use the terms 'gossip', on the one hand, or 'candour', on the other. This reminds us that, in the eighteenth century, neither term meant to

---

[1] See *Letters,* 26:490 in this edn.
[2] No. 65, 'The Duty of Reproving our Neighbour'.

Wesley what they later came to mean, by cynical extension in the case of 'gossip' and by inference in the case of 'candour' (cf. OED and Johnson's Dictionary).

This 'tract for the times' has no other publishing history than its place as a sort of addendum in SOSO, IV.

The Cure of Evil-speaking

Matthew 18:15-17

If thy brother shall sin against thee, go and tell him his fault between thee and him alone: if he will hear thee, thou hast gained thy brother.

But if he will not hear, take with thee one or two more, that by the mouth of two or three witnesses every word may be established.

And if he will not hear them, tell it to the church: but if he will not hear the church, let him be to thee as an heathen man and a publican.

10   1. 'Speak evil of no man,'[1] says the great Apostle—as plain a command as 'Thou shalt do no murder.'[2] But who even among Christians regards this command? Yea, how few are there that so much as understand it? What is 'evil-speaking'? It is not (as some suppose) the same with lying or slandering. All a man says may be
15 as true as the Bible; and yet the saying of it is evil-speaking. For evil-speaking is neither more nor less than speaking evil of an absent person; relating something evil which was really done or said by one that is not present when it is related.[3] Suppose, having seen a man drunk, or heard him curse or swear, I tell this when he
20 is absent, it is evil-speaking. In our language this is also by an extremely proper name termed 'backbiting'.[4] Nor is there any

---

[1] Titus 3:2.   [2] Matt. 19:18.

[3] The original μηδένα βλασφημεῖν is a prohibition against seditious language (cf. βλασφημέω in Liddell and Scott, *Greek-English Lexicon*, as well as Bauer's commentary in Arndt and Gingrich, *Greek-English Lexicon*), but without reference to the presence or absence of the person blasphemed. This point is ignored in the standard commentaries; it is not even made in the *Notes* on this text. But see No. 14, *The Repentance of Believers*, I.11 and n.

[4] Cf. both Johnson's *Dictionary* and *OED*; they agree with Wesley's stress on malice toward *absent* persons.

material difference between this and what we usually style 'talebearing'. If the tale be delivered in a soft and quiet manner (perhaps with expressions of goodwill to the person, and of hope that things may not be quite so bad) then we call it 'whispering'.[5] But in whatever manner it be done the thing is the same—the same in substance if not in circumstance. Still it is evil-speaking; still this command, 'Speak evil of no man,' is trampled under foot if we relate to another the fault of a third person when he is not present to answer for himself.

2. And how extremely common is this sin among all orders and degrees of men! How do high and low, rich and poor, wise and foolish, learned and unlearned, run into it continually! Persons who differ from each other in all things else, nevertheless agree in this. How few are there that can testify before God, 'I am clear in this matter: I have always set a watch before my mouth, and kept the door of my lips!'[6] What conversation do you hear of any considerable length whereof evil-speaking is not one ingredient? And that even among persons who in the general have the fear of God before their eyes,[7] and do really desire to have a conscience void of offence toward God and toward man.[8]

3. And the very commonness of this sin makes it difficult to be avoided. As we are encompassed with it on every side, so if we are not deeply sensible of the danger, and continually guarding against it, we are liable to be carried away by the torrent. In this instance almost the whole of mankind is, as it were, in a conspiracy against us. And their example steals upon us we know not how, so that we insensibly slide into the imitation of it. Besides, it is recommended from within as well as from without. There is scarce any wrong temper in the mind of man which may not be occasionally gratified by it, and consequently incline us to it. It gratifies our *pride* to relate those faults of others whereof we think ourselves not to be guilty. *Anger*, resentment, and all unkind tempers are indulged by speaking against those with whom we are displeased. And in many cases, by reciting the sins of their neighbours, men indulge their own 'foolish and hurtful desires'.[9]

4. Evil-speaking is the more difficult to be avoided because it frequently attacks us in disguise. We speak thus out of a noble,

---

[5] Cf. Shakespeare, *King John*, IV. ii. 188-89: 'When they talk of him, they shake their heads / And whisper one another in the ear.'
[6] Cf. Ps. 141:3.
[7] Rom. 3:18.
[8] See Acts 24:16.
[9] 1 Tim. 6:9 (*Notes*).

generous ('tis well if we do not say, 'holy') 'indignation' against
these vile creatures! We commit sin from mere hatred of sin! We
serve the devil out of pure zeal for God! It is merely in order to
punish the wicked that we run into this wickedness. So do 'the
5 passions' (as one speaks) 'all justify themselves',[10] and palm sin
upon us under the veil of holiness!

5. But is there no way to avoid the snare? Unquestionably there
is. Our blessed Lord has marked out a plain way for his followers
in the words above recited. None who warily and steadily walks in
10 this path will ever fall into evil-speaking. This rule is either an
infallible preventive or a certain cure of it. In the preceding verses
our Lord had said, 'Woe to the world because of offences!'[11]
Unspeakable misery will arise in the world from this baleful
fountain. ('Offences' are all things whereby anyone is turned out
15 of, or hindered in, the ways of God.) 'For it must be that offences
come.'[12] Such is the nature of things; such the weakness, folly,
and wickedness of mankind. 'But woe to that man', miserable is
that man, 'by whom the offence cometh. Wherefore if thy hand,
thy foot, thine eye cause thee to offend'—if the most dear
20 enjoyment, the most beloved and useful person, turn thee out of
or hinder thee in the way— 'pluck it out, cut them off, and cast
them from thee.'[13] But how can we avoid giving offence to some,
and being offended at others? Especially suppose they are quite in
the wrong, and we see it with our own eyes? Our Lord here
25 teaches us how: he lays down a sure method of avoiding offences
and evil-speaking together. 'If thy brother shall sin against thee,
go and tell him of his fault, between thee and him alone: if he will
hear thee, thou hast gained thy brother. But if he will not hear
thee, take with thee one or two more, that by the mouth of two or
30 three witnesses every word may be established. And if he will not
hear them, tell it to the church: but if he will not hear the church,
let him be to thee as an heathen man and a publican.'

I. 1. First, 'if thy brother shall sin against thee, go and tell him
of his fault, between thee and him alone.' The most literal way of

---

[10] Cf. Francis Hutcheson, 'Concerning Moral Good and Evil', in *An Inquiry Into the Original of Our Ideas of Beauty and Virtue* (1726), Treatise II, Sec. II, viii. 152. Cf. also No. 92, 'On Zeal', §2. For other references to Hutcheson, cf. No. 12, 'The Witness of Our Own Spirit', §5 and n. See also Thomas Browne, *Religio Medici* (1642), I.19: ' . . . as reason is a rebel unto faith, so passion unto reason;' and Pope's *Essay on Man*, ii. 42: 'What reason weaves by passion is undone.'

[11] Matt. 18:7.   [12] *Ibid.*   [13] Cf. Matt. 18:7-9.

following this first rule, where it is practicable, is the best. Therefore, if thou seest with thine own eyes a brother, a fellow-Christian, commit undeniable sin, or hearest it with thine own ears, so that it is impossible for thee to doubt the fact, then thy part is plain: take the very first opportunity of going to him; 5 and if thou canst have access, 'tell him of his fault between thee and him alone.' Indeed great care is to be taken that this is done in a right *spirit,* and in a right *manner.* The success of a reproof greatly depends on the spirit wherein it is given.[14] Be not therefore wanting in earnest prayer to God that it may be given in a lowly 10 spirit; with a deep, piercing conviction that it is God alone who maketh thee to differ, and that if any good be done by what is now spoken, God doth it himself. Pray that he would guard thy heart, enlighten thy mind, and direct thy tongue to such words as he may please to bless. See that thou speak in a meek as well as a lowly 15 spirit; 'for the wrath of man worketh not the righteousness of God.'[15] If he 'be overtaken in a fault', he can no otherwise be 'restored' than 'in the spirit of meekness'.[16] If he 'opposes' the truth, yet he cannot be 'brought to the knowledge' thereof but by 'gentleness'.[17] Still speak in a spirit of tender love, 'which many 20 waters cannot quench'.[18] If love is not conquered, it conquers all things. Who can tell the force of love?

> Love can bow down the stubborn neck,
>   The stone to flesh convert;
> Soften and melt and pierce and break   25
>   An adamantine heart.[19]

Confirm then your love toward him, and you will thereby 'heap coals of fire upon his head'.[20]

    2. But see that the *manner* also wherein you speak be according to the gospel of Christ. Avoid everything in look, gesture, word, 30 and tone of voice that savours of *pride* or self-sufficiency. Studiously avoid everything magisterial or dogmatical; everything that looks like arrogance or assuming. Beware of the most distant approach to disdain, overbearing, or *contempt.* With equal care

---

[14] Cf. No. 65, 'The Duty of Reproving our Neighbour'.
[15] Jas. 1:20.   [16] Cf. Gal. 6:1.
[17] Cf. 2 Tim. 2:25.   [18] S. of S. 8:7.
[19] Charles Wesley, 'Against Hope, Believing in Hope', in John and Charles Wesley, *Hymns and Sacred Poems* (1740), p. 157 (*Poet. Wks.* I. 329).
[20] Cf. Prov. 25:22; Rom. 12:20.

avoid all appearance of *anger*, and though you use great plainness
of speech, yet let there be no reproach, no railing accusation, no
token of any warmth but that of love. Above all, let there be no
shadow of *hate* or ill will, no bitterness or sourness of expression;
5 but use the air and language of sweetness, as well as gentleness,
that all may appear to flow from love in the heart. And yet this
sweetness need not hinder your speaking in the most serious and
solemn manner, as far as may be in the very words of the oracles
of God (for there are none like them), and as under the eye of him
10 who is coming to judge the quick and [the] dead.[21]
    3. If you have not an opportunity of speaking to him in person,
or cannot have access, you may do it by a messenger, by a
common friend in whose prudence as well as uprightness you can
throughly confide. Such a person, speaking in your name, and in
15 the spirit and manner above described, may answer the same end,
and in a good degree supply your lack of service. Only beware you
do not feign want of opportunity in order to shun the cross;
neither take it for granted that you cannot have access without
ever making the trial. Whenever you can speak in your own
20 person it is far better. But you should rather do it by another than
not at all: this way is better than none.
    4. But what if you can neither speak yourself, nor find such a
messenger as you can confide in? If this is really the case, it then
only remains to write. And there may be some circumstances
25 which make this the most advisable way of speaking. One of these
circumstances is when the person with whom we have to do is of
so warm and impetuous a temper as does not easily bear reproof,
especially from an equal or inferior. But it may be so introduced
and softened in writing as to make it far more tolerable. Besides,
30 many will read the very same words which they could not bear to
hear. It does not give so violent a shock to their pride, nor
so sensibly touch their honour. And suppose it makes little
impression at first, they will perhaps give it a second reading, and
upon farther consideration lay to heart what before they
35 disregarded. If you add your name, this is nearly the same thing as
going to him and speaking in person. And this should always be
done, unless it be rendered improper by some very particular
reason.

[21] 2 Tim. 4:1; 1 Pet. 4:5. See also 'The Apostles' Creed' and 'The Creed Commonly
Called Nicene' (BCP).

5. It should be well observed, not only that this is a step which our Lord absolutely commands us to take, but that he commands us to take this step first, before we attempt any other. No alternative is allowed, no choice of anything else; this is the way; walk thou in it.[22] It is true he enjoins us, if need require, to take 5 two other steps. But they are to be taken successively *after* this step, and neither of them *before* it. Much less are we to take any other step either before or beside this. To do anything else, or not to do this, is therefore equally inexcusable.

6. Do not think to excuse yourself for taking an entirely 10 different step by saying, 'Why, I did not speak to anyone till I was so *burdened* that I could not refrain.' You was burdened! It was no wonder you should, unless your conscience was seared;[23] for you was under the guilt of sin, of disobeying a plain commandment of God. You ought immediately to have gone and 'told your brother 15 of his fault between you and him alone'. If you did not, how should you be other than burdened (unless your heart was utterly hardened) while you was trampling the command of God under foot, and 'hating your brother in your heart'?[24] And what a way have you found to *unburden* yourself? God reproves you for a sin 20 of omission, for not telling your brother of his fault; and you comfort yourself under his reproof by a sin of commission, by telling your brother's fault to another person! Ease bought by sin is a dear purchase: I trust in God you will have no ease, but will be burdened so much the more till you 'go to your brother and tell 25 him', and no one else.

7. I know but of one exception to this rule. There may be a peculiar case wherein it is necessary to accuse the guilty, though absent, in order to preserve the innocent. For instance: you are acquainted with the design which a man has against the property 30 or life of his neighbour. Now the case may be so circumstanced that there is no other way of hindering that design from taking effect but the making it known without delay to him against whom it is laid. In this case therefore this rule is set aside, as is that of the Apostle, 'Speak evil of no man,'[25] and it is lawful, yea, it is our 35 bounden duty to speak evil of an absent person, in order to prevent his doing evil to others and himself at the same time. But

[22] See Isa. 30:21.
[23] See 1 Tim. 4:2. Cf. No. 12, 'The Witness of Our Own Spirit', §19 and n.
[24] Cf. Zech. 7:10.
[25] Titus 3:2.

remember meanwhile that all evil-speaking is in its own nature deadly poison. Therefore if you are sometimes constrained to use it as a medicine, yet use it with fear and trembling, seeing it is so dangerous a medicine that nothing but absolute necessity can
5 excuse your using it at all. Accordingly use it as seldom as possible; never but when there is such a necessity. And even then use as little of it as is possible; only so much as is necessary for the end proposed. At all other times, 'go and tell him of his fault, between thee and him alone.'

10   II. 1. But what 'if he will not hear'? If he repay evil for good? If he be enraged rather than convinced? What if he hear to no purpose, and go on still in the evil of his way? We must expect this will frequently be the case; the mildest and tenderest reproof will have no effect, but the blessing we wished for another will return
15 into our own bosom.[26] And what are we to do then? Our Lord has given us a clear and full direction. Then 'take with thee one or two more:' this is the second step. Take one or two whom you know to be of a loving spirit, lovers of God and of their neighbour. See likewise that they be of a lowly spirit, and 'clothed with humility'.[27]
20 Let them also be such as are meek and gentle, patient and longsuffering; not apt to 'return evil for evil, or railing for railing, but contrariwise blessing'.[28] Let them be men of understanding, such as are endued with wisdom from above; and men unbiased, free from partiality, free from prejudice of any kind. Care should
25 likewise be taken that both the persons and their characters be well known to him. And let those that are acceptable to him be chosen preferable to any others.

    2. Love will dictate the manner wherein they should proceed, according to the nature of the case. Nor can any one particular
30 manner be prescribed for all cases. But perhaps in general one might advise, before they enter upon the thing itself, let them mildly and affectionately declare that they have no anger or prejudice toward him, and that it is merely from a principle of goodwill that they now come, or at all concern themselves with his
35 affairs. To make this the more apparent, they might then calmly attend to your repetition of your former conversation with him, and to what he said in his own defence, before they attempted to

---

[26] See Ps. 35:13.
[27] 1 Pet. 5:5.
[28] Cf. 1 Pet. 3:9.

determine anything. After this they would be better able to judge in what manner to proceed, 'that by the mouth of two or three witnesses, every word might be established'; that whatever you have said may have its full force by the additional weight of their authority.   5

3. In order to this, may they not, (1). Briefly repeat what you spoke, and what he answered? (2). Enlarge upon, open, and confirm the reasons which you had given? (3). Give weight to your reproof, showing how just, how kind, and how seasonable it was? And, lastly, enforce the advices and persuasions which you had   10
annexed to it? And these may likewise hereafter, if need should require, bear witness of what was spoken.

4. With regard to this, as well as the preceding rule, we may observe that our Lord gives us no choice, leaves us no alternative, but expressly commands us to do this, and nothing else in the   15
place of it. He likewise directs us when to do this. Neither sooner, nor later: namely, *after* we have taken the first, and *before* we have taken the third step. It is then only that we are authorized to relate the evil another has done to those whom we desire to bear a part with us in this great instance of brotherly love. But let us have a   20
care how we relate it to any other person till both these steps have been taken. If we neglect to take these, or if we take any others, what wonder if we are burdened still! For we are sinners against God and against our neighbour. And how fairly soever we may colour it, yet if we have any conscience our sin will find us out,   25
and bring a burden upon our soul.

III. 1. That we may be throughly instructed in this weighty affair our Lord has given us a still farther direction. 'If he will not hear them'—then and not till then—'tell it to the church.' This is the third step. All the question is how this word, 'the church', is   30
here to be understood. But the very nature of the thing will determine this beyond all reasonable doubt. You cannot tell it to the national church, the whole body of men termed 'the Church of England'.[29] Neither would it answer any Christian end if you could: this therefore is not the meaning of the word. Neither can   35
you tell it to that whole body of people in England with whom you have a more immediate connexion. Nor indeed would this answer

---

[29] Note this unselfconscious assumption that 'church', in its broader denotation, is the Church of England. For Wesley's understanding of himself as Anglican, see Vol. 1, Intro., p. 88.

any good end: the word therefore is not to be understood thus. It would not answer any valuable end to tell the faults of every particular member to 'the church' (if you would so term it), the congregation or *society*[30] united together in London. It remains that you tell it to the elder or elders of the church, to those who are overseers of that flock of Christ to which you both belong, who watch over yours and his soul 'as they that must give account'.[31] And this should be done, if it conveniently can, in the presence of the person concerned, and, though plainly, yet with all the tenderness and love which the nature of the thing will admit. It properly belongs to their office to determine concerning the behaviour of those under their care, and to 'rebuke', according to the demerit of the offence, 'with all authority'.[32] When therefore you have done this, you have done all which the Word of God or the law of love requireth of you. You are not now partaker of his sin, but if he perish his blood is on his own head.[33]

2. Here also let it be observed that this, and no other, is the third step which we are to take; and that we are to take it in its order, after the other two; not before the second, much less the first, unless in some very particular circumstance. Indeed in one case the second step may coincide with this: they may be, in a manner, one and the same. The elder or elders of the church may be so connected with the offending brother that they may set aside the necessity, and supply the place of the 'one or two' witnesses. So that it may suffice to tell it to them after you have told it to your brother, 'between you and him alone'.

3. When you have done this you have delivered your own soul.[34] 'If he will not hear the church', if he persist in his sin, 'let him be to thee as an heathen man and a publican.' You are under no obligation to think of him any more—only when you commend him to God in prayer. You need not speak of him any more, but leave him to his own Master. Indeed you still owe to him, as to all other heathens, earnest, tender goodwill. You owe him courtesy, and as occasion offers all the offices of humanity. But have no friendship, no familiarity with him; no other intercourse than with an open heathen.

---

[30] I.e., the United Society of Methodists, here understood as an *ecclesiola*, most of whose members were registered on one or another parish roll in the Church of England.
[31] Heb. 13:17.   [32] Titus 2:15.   [33] See Ezek. 33:4-6.
[34] See Ezek. 14:14, 20; 33:9. Cf. above, No. 36, 'The Law Established through Faith, II', I.5 and n.

4. But if this be the rule by which Christians walk, which is the land where the Christians live?[35] A few you may possibly find scattered up and down who make a conscience of observing it. But how very few! How thinly scattered upon the face of the earth! And where is there any body of men that universally walk thereby? Can we find them in Europe? Or, to go no farther, in Great Britain or Ireland? I fear not: I fear we may search these kingdoms throughout, and yet search in vain. Alas for the Christian world! Alas for Protestants, for Reformed Christians! 'O who will rise up with me against the wicked? Who will take God's part against the evil-speakers?'[36] 'Art thou the man?'[37] By the grace of God wilt thou be one who art not carried away by the torrent? Art thou fully determined, God being thy helper, from this very hour to set a watch, a continual 'watch before thy mouth, and keep the door of thy lips'?[38] From this hour wilt thou walk by this rule, 'speaking evil of no man'?[39] If thou seest thy brother do evil, wilt thou 'tell him of his fault between thee and him alone'? Afterwards 'take one or two witnesses', and then only 'tell it to the church'? If this be the full purpose of thy heart, then learn one lesson well: *Hear evil of no man.* If there were no hearers, there would be no speakers of evil. And is not (according to the vulgar proverb) the receiver as bad as the thief? If then any begin to speak evil in thy hearing, check him immediately. Refuse to hear the voice of the charmer, charm he never so sweetly:[40] let him use ever so soft a manner, so mild an accent, ever so many professions of goodwill for him whom he is stabbing in the dark, whom he smiteth under the fifth rib.[41] Resolutely refuse to hear, though the whisperer complain of being 'burdened' till he speak. Burdened! thou fool, dost thou 'travail with' thy cursed *secret*, 'as a woman travaileth with child'?[42] Go then and be delivered of thy burden, in the way the Lord hath ordained. First, 'go and tell thy brother of his fault, between thee and him alone.' Next, 'take with thee one or two' common friends, and tell him in their presence. If neither of these steps take effect, then 'tell it to the church.' But at the peril of thy soul tell it to no one else, either before or after, unless in that one exempt case, when it is absolutely needful to preserve

---

[35] See No. 4, *Scriptural Christianity*, IV.1 and n.
[36] Cf. Ps. 94:16 (BCP).   [37] 1 Kgs. 13:14.
[38] Cf. Ps. 141:3.   [39] Cf. Titus 3:2.
[40] See Ps. 58:5 (BCP).   [41] See 2 Sam. 2:23; 3:27.
[42] Cf. Isa. 13:8; Rev. 12:2, etc.

the innocent. Why shouldst thou burden another as well as thyself by making him partaker of thy sin?

5. O that all you who bear the reproach of Christ,[43] who are in derision called 'Methodists', would set an example to the
5 Christian world, so called, at least in this one instance! Put ye away evil-speaking, talebearing, whispering: let none of them proceed out of your mouth. See that you 'speak evil of no man;'[44] of the absent nothing but good. If ye must be distinguished, whether ye will or no, let this be the distinguishing mark of a
10 Methodist: 'He censures no man behind his back: by this fruit ye may know him.'[45] What a blessed effect of this self-denial should we quickly feel in our hearts! How would our 'peace flow as a river',[46] when we thus 'followed peace with all men'![47] How would the love of God abound in our own souls while we thus confirmed
15 our love to our brethren! And what an effect would it have on all that were united together in the name of the Lord Jesus! How would brotherly love continually increase when this grand hindrance of it was removed! All the members of Christ's mystical body would then *naturally care for* each other: 'If one
20 member suffered, all would suffer with it; if one was honoured, all would rejoice with it;'[48] and everyone would love his brother 'with a pure heart fervently'.[49] Nor is this all: but what an effect might this have even on the wild unthinking world! How soon would they descry in us what they could not find among all the
25 thousands of their brethren, and cry (as Julian the Apostate to his heathen courtiers), 'See how these Christians love one another!'[50] By this chiefly would God convince the world, and prepare them also for his kingdom, as we may easily learn from those remarkable words in our Lord's last, solemn prayer: 'I pray for
30 them who will believe in me, that they all may be one, as thou, Father, art in me, and I in thee; that the world may believe that thou hast sent me!'[51] The Lord hasten the time! The Lord enable *us* thus to love one another, not only 'in word and in tongue, but in deed and in truth',[52] even as Christ hath loved us.

---

[43] Heb. 11:26.
[44] Titus 3:2.
[45] Cf. Matt. 7:16, 20.
[46] Cf. Isa. 48:18.
[47] Cf. Heb. 12:14.
[48] Cf. 1 Cor. 12:26.
[49] 1 Pet. 1:22.
[50] See No. 22, 'Sermon on the Mount, II', III.18 and n.
[51] Cf. John 17:20-21.
[52] Cf. 1 John 3:18.

THE USE OF MONEY

AN INTRODUCTORY COMMENT

This sermon completes the series mentioned in the Model Deed of 1763 as 'the first four volumes of sermons'. It is easily the clearest of Wesley's summaries of his economic views. The negative premises of those views had already been laid out in No. 28, 'Sermon on the Mount, VIII', with its lively critique there of covetousness and of surplus accumulation. Moreover, there are at least twenty-seven oral sermons on Luke 16:9 recorded between 1741 and 1758 (including seven in 1750, six in 1752), and this reflects a constant concern and a perplexing problem. Later, as the Methodists prospered, he would return to the theme again and again, with stern warnings against 'the dangers of riches' and with almost pathetic complaints that his warnings were going unheeded. Here, however, we have the live nucleus of an economic view in its entirety, greatly oversimplified but with a prophet's confidence. None of the elements in his statement is original; this particular combination of them, however, is genuinely so. But there was the rub: on his most original point (the radical rejection of surplus accumulation) his own people preferred the way of the world as stubbornly as any others.

That world, in Wesley's day, was largely the creation of an alliance between the new plutocrats of London, Bristol, etc., and the great Whig landed gentry. In ways distortedly described by its anti-bourgeois critics (Max Weber, Werner Sombart, Ernst Troeltsch, R. H. Tawney), this new capitalism had expropriated the so-called 'Calvinist work ethic' and had exploited it to advantages that no good Calvinist would ever have approved. As a result there was a steady accumulation of venture capital in Britain and, correspondingly, a shocking contrast between the Georgian splendours of the newly rich and the grinding misery of the perennial poor (not least, those lately uprooted from ancestral villages and now huddled in and around the cities and pitheads). These masses were Wesley's self-chosen constituency: 'Christ's poor'.

By both birth and breeding Wesley had a deep aversion to ostentation and to arbitrary power conferred by rank or wealth. Conversely, he was deeply committed to a work ethic that saw sloth as sin (even the idleness of excess sleep) and that condemned self-indulgence as a faithless stewardship of God's bounties in creation. Labour, for him, was no mere remedium peccati *(remedy for sin), as it had been for Luther and many medieval moralists, no grim necessity laid on man for that first sin (as Gen. 3:17-20 had often been interpreted). Nor did he see money as anything evil in itself. Thrift, industry, honesty, sobriety, generosity were all Christian virtues; their warrants rested in the twin love of God and neighbour, and thus they were included in the agenda of holy living.*

In this sense, Wesley shared a broad tradition of economic discipline and philanthropy long understood as essential in the Christian ethic. Its first premise was the flat rejection of the arrogant notion 'that men may use their possessions as they list'; this, so ran both medieval and Reformation ethics, was tantamount to atheism.[1] The basic ideas of gaining, saving, and sharing the wealth ran back at least to William Perkins.[2] Wesley had so heartily approved the views of Richard Lucas's Enquiry After Happiness *that he published an abridgement of it in the* Christian Library, *Vol. XL (1754), where on pp. 210-15 there is a rough approximation of some of the ideas in 'The Use of Money' (but note the differences as well). Four of Archbishop Tillotson's sermons had dealt with 'covetousness' in a tone that recurs in Wesley.[3] One may also hear echoes from Giovanni Cardinal Bona's* Guide to Eternity *(1709), especially from the chapter on 'Liberality' (pp. 161-65). Then, too, there had been Jeremy Collier's strictures on acquisitiveness and economic exploitation in* God Not the Origin of Evil . . . *(1726), pp. 28 ff., and also John Chappelow's quaint commendations of thrift and generosity in* The Right Way to be Rich . . . *(2nd edn., 1717).*

For all this, however, Wesley's formula, as summarized here and expounded even more urgently after 1776 in an unavailing counterattack against the huge success of Adam Smith's Wealth of Nations, *has a different final focus than one can find in any of its sources. Work is extolled as honourable, a productive mode of Christian 'asceticism in the world'. Wesley declines to condemn money or trade or technology. He encourages all reasonable provisions for life's 'necessaries and conveniences' for one's self and family—this, indeed, is a Christian's duty. The difference comes in his insistence on 'giving all*

---

[1] Cf. John Strype's analysis of Robert Crowley's comment to this effect in *Information and Peticion against the Oppressours of the Pore Commons of this Realme* (1548) in Strype's *Historical Memorials* . . . (1694) II, Pt. 1, pp. 217-26; Wesley may not have known Crowley, but he knew Strype, and the general idea was already a Christian commonplace.

[2] See Perkins, *Works* (1612), I.769; II.150.

[3] See Tillotson, *Works*, I. 253-74.

you can': an exhortation with so radical an implication that the ordinary conventions of generosity and philanthropy are brought into question. It is as if Wesley regarded surplus accumulation as sinful in itself or as at the least an irresistible temptation to sin. The break here with the economic wisdom of the day (including that of the Quakers) is drastic and deliberate; he challenged his own people, and others, to a more stringent form of self-denial than most of them were prepared for. None of this deterred Wesley, even though he was increasingly dismayed by his inability to persuade the Methodists on this point, as we can see from Nos. 28, 'Sermon on the Mount, VIII'; 87, 'The Danger of Riches'; 108, 'On Riches'; and 131, 'The Danger of Increasing Riches'; see also Nos. 30, 'Sermon on the Mount, X', §26; 61, 'The Mystery of Iniquity', §12; 63, 'The General Spread of the Gospel', §20; 68, 'The Wisdom of God's Counsels', §§8, 16; 80, 'On Friendship with the World', §3; 89, 'The More Excellent Way', VI.4; 90, 'An Israelite Indeed', I.1; 94, 'On Family Religion', III.16, 17; 115, 'Dives and Lazarus', II.1; 122, 'Causes of the Inefficacy of Christianity', §12; and 126, 'On Worldly Folly', I.4.

Wesley's self-chosen title for this sermon is as it stands here and in all its successive editions. On at least two occasions, however, he refers to it under the title of 'The Mammon of Unrighteousness' (as in his open letter to 'The St. James Chronicle', October 29, 1764; and in No. 122, 'Causes of the Inefficacy of Christianity', §8, July 2, 1789). For other comments on Wesley's economic views, cf. Nos. 51, The Good Steward; *and 125, 'On a Single Eye'.*

On no other single point, save only faith alone and holy living, is Wesley more insistent, consistent—and out of step with the bourgeois spirit of his age. It is, therefore, interesting to note that in E. P. Thompson's Marxist condemnations of Wesley's economic and social views as hopelessly reactionary, there is no mention of Wesley's principled rejection of surplus accumulation; cf. The Making of the English Working Class *(New York, Pantheon Books, 1964), pp. 38-44, 353, 362-63 ('Wesley appears to have dispensed with the best and selected unhesitatingly the worst elements of Puritanism'), 380-81, etc. But see also Bernard Semmel,* The Methodist Revolution *(New York, Basic Books, 1973), pp. 71 ff.*

The Use of Money

Luke 16:9

I say unto you, Make unto yourselves friends of the mammon of unrighteousness, that when ye fail, they may receive you into the everlasting habitations.

1. Our Lord, having finished the beautiful parable of the Prodigal Son, which he had particularly addressed to those who murmured at his receiving publicans and sinners, adds another relation of a different kind, addressed rather to the children of
10 God. 'He said unto his disciples'—not so much to the scribes and Pharisees to whom he had been speaking before—'There was a certain rich man, who had a steward, and he was accused to him of wasting his goods. And calling him he said, Give an account of thy stewardship, for thou canst be no longer steward.'ᵃ After
15 reciting the method which the bad steward used to provide against the day of necessity, our Saviour adds, 'His lord commended the unjust steward'—namely in this respect, that he used timely precaution—and subjoins this weighty reflection, 'The children of this world are wiser in their generation than the
20 children of light.'ᵇ Those who seek no other portion than 'this world are wiser' (not absolutely; for they are one and all the veriest fools, the most egregious madmen under heaven, but) 'in their generation', in their own way; they are more consistent with themselves, they are truer to their acknowledged principles, they
25 more steadily pursue their end, 'than the children of light', than they who see 'the light of the glory of God in the face of Jesus Christ'.¹ Then follow the words above recited: 'And I'—the only-begotten Son of God, the Creator, Lord and Possessor of heaven and earth, and all that is therein; the Judge of all, to whom
30 ye are to 'give an account of your stewardship' when ye 'can be no longer stewards'²—'I say unto you' (learn in this respect even of

---

ᵃ [Luke 16:] ver. 1-2 [cf. Wesley's *Notes*].   ᵇ Ver. 8.

---

¹ Cf. 2 Cor. 4:6.   ² Cf. Luke 16:2.

the unjust steward), 'make yourselves friends', by wise, timely precaution, 'of the mammon of unrighteousness.' 'Mammon' means riches or money.[3] It is termed 'the mammon of unrighteousness' because of the unrighteous manner wherein it is frequently procured, and wherein even that which was honestly 5 procured is generally employed. 'Make yourselves friends' of this by doing all possible good, particularly to the children of God; 'that when ye fail', when ye return to dust, when ye have no more place under the sun, those of them who are gone before 'may receive you', may welcome you 'into the everlasting habitations'. 10

2. An excellent branch of Christian wisdom is here inculcated by our Lord on all his followers, namely, the right use of money—a subject largely spoken of, after their manner, by men of the world, but not sufficiently considered by those whom God hath chosen out of the world.[4] These generally do not consider as 15 the importance of the subject requires the use of this excellent talent. Neither do they understand how to employ it to the greatest advantage; the introduction of which into the world is one admirable instance of the wise and gracious providence of God. It has indeed been the manner of poets, orators, and 20 philosophers, in almost all ages and nations, to rail at this as the grand corrupter of the world, the bane of virtue, the pest of human society. Hence nothing so commonly heard as:

Ferrum, ferroque nocentius aurum—[5]

'And gold, more mischievous than keenest steel'. Hence the 25 lamentable complaint,

Effodiuntur opes, irritamenta malorum.[6]

Nay, one celebrated writer gravely exhorts his countrymen, in order to banish all vice at once, to 'throw all their money into the sea': 30

. . . in mare proximum[. . .]
Summi materiem mali![7]

---

[3] Cf. No. 29, 'Sermon on the Mount, IX', §4 and n.   [4] See John 15:19.

[5] Ovid, *Metamorphoses*, I. i. 141; note that Ovid does not use the superlative form and that *ferrum* typically means 'iron'.

[6] *Ibid.*, I. i. 140. In the appendix to Vol. XXXII of his *Works* Wesley supplies a translation: 'Wealth is dug up, incentive to all ill.'

[7] Horace, *Odes*, III. xxiv. 47, 49 ('into the *nearest* sea . . . '); cf. Loeb, 33:253-57, for the passage as a whole. See also No. 87, 'The Danger of Riches', I.4.

But is not all this mere empty rant? Is there any solid reason therein? By no means. For let the world be as corrupt as it will, is gold or silver to blame? 'The love of money', we know, 'is the root of all evil;'[8] but not the thing itself. The fault does not lie in the
5 money, but in them that use it. It may be used ill; and what may not? But it may likewise be used well; it is full as applicable to the best as to the worst uses. It is of unspeakable service to all civilized nations in all the common affairs of life. It is a most compendious instrument of transacting all manner of business, and (if we use it
10 according to Christian wisdom) of doing all manner of good. It is true, were man in a state of innocence, or were all men 'filled with the Holy Ghost', so that, like the infant church at Jerusalem, 'no man counted anything he had his own', but 'distribution was made to everyone as he had need,'[9] the use of it would be
15 superseded; as we cannot conceive there is anything of the kind among the inhabitants of heaven. But in the present state of mankind it is an excellent gift of God, answering the noblest ends. In the hands of his children it is food for the hungry, drink for the thirsty, raiment for the naked. It gives to the traveller and the
20 stranger where to lay his head. By it we may supply the place of an husband to the widow, and of a father to the fatherless; we may be a defence for the oppressed, a means of health to the sick, of ease to them that are in pain. It may be as eyes to the blind, as feet to the lame;[10] yea, a lifter up from the gates of death.[11]
25 　　3. It is therefore of the highest concern that all who fear God know how to employ this valuable talent; that they be instructed how it may answer these glorious ends, and in the highest degree. And perhaps all the instructions which are necessary for this may be reduced to three plain rules, by the exact observance whereof
30 we may approve ourselves faithful stewards of 'the mammon of unrighteousness'.

　　I. 1. The first of these is (he that heareth let him understand!)[12] *Gain all you can.*[13] Here we may speak like the children of the world.[14] We meet them on their own ground. And it is our

---

[8] 1 Tim. 6:10.　　　　　　　　　　　　　　　[9] Cf. Acts 4:31-35.
[10] See Job 29:15.
[11] See Ps. 9:13.
[12] See Matt. 13:43; 15:10, etc.
[13] But cf. Aristotle's strictures against 'sordid gain', as in *Nicomachean Ethics*, IV.i.1121*b*-1122*a*.
[14] See Luke 16:8.

bounden duty to do this. We ought to gain all we can gain without buying gold too dear, without paying more for it than it is worth. But this it is certain we ought not to do: we ought not to gain money at the expense of life; nor (which is in effect the same thing) at the expense of our health. Therefore no gain whatsoever 5 should induce us to enter into, or to continue in, any employ which is of such a kind, or is attended with so hard or so long labour, as to impair our constitution. Neither should we begin or continue in any business which necessarily deprives us of proper seasons for food and sleep in such a proportion as our nature 10 requires. Indeed there is a great difference here. Some employments are absolutely and totally unhealthy—as those which imply the dealing much with arsenic or other equally hurtful minerals, or the breathing an air tainted with steams of melting lead, which must at length destroy the firmest 15 constitution. Others may not be absolutely unhealthy, but only to persons of a weak constitution. Such are those which require many hours to be spent in writing, especially if a person write sitting, and lean upon his stomach, or remain long in an uneasy posture. But whatever it is which reason or experience shows to 20 be destructive of health or strength, that we may not submit to; seeing 'the life is more' valuable 'than meat, and the body than raiment.'[15] And if we are already engaged in such an employ, we should exchange it as soon as possible for some which, if it lessen our gain, will however not lessen our health. 25

2. We are, secondly, to gain all we can without hurting our mind any more than our body. For neither may we hurt this. We must preserve, at all events, the spirit of an healthful mind. Therefore we may not engage or continue in any sinful trade, any that is contrary to the law of God, or of our country. Such are all 30 that necessarily imply our robbing or defrauding the king of his lawful customs.[16] For it is at least as sinful to defraud the king of his right as to rob our fellow subjects. And the king has full as much right to his customs as we have to our houses and apparel. Other businesses there are, which however innocent *in themselves*, 35 cannot be followed with innocence *now* (at least, not in England): such, for instance, as will not afford a competent maintenance

---

[15] Luke 12:23.
[16] Cf. Wesley's prohibition in his *General Rules* against 'buying or selling uncustomed goods' [i.e., smuggling, etc.]. This was a serious problem in Hanoverian England, especially in Cornwall, and Wesley would have none of it.

without cheating or lying, or conformity to some custom which is not consistent with a good conscience. These likewise are sacredly to be avoided, whatever gain they may be attended with provided we follow the custom of the trade; for to gain money we
5 must not lose our souls. There are yet others which many pursue with perfect innocence without hurting either their body or mind. And yet perhaps *you* cannot: either they may entangle you in that company which would destroy your soul—and by repeated experiments it may appear that you cannot separate the one from
10 the other—or there may be an idiosyncrasy, a peculiarity in your constitution of soul (as there is in the bodily constitution of many) by reason whereof that employment is deadly to *you* which another may safely follow. So I am convinced, from many experiments, I could not study to any degree of perfection either
15 mathematics, arithmetic, or algebra, without being a deist, if not an atheist.[17] And yet others may study them all their lives without sustaining any inconvenience. None therefore can here determine for another, but every man must judge for himself, and abstain from whatever he in particular finds to be hurtful to his
20 soul.

3. We are, thirdly, to gain all we can without hurting our neighbour. But this we may not, cannot do, if we love our neighbour as ourselves. We cannot, if we love everyone as ourselves, hurt anyone *in his substance*. We cannot devour the
25 increase of his lands, and perhaps the lands and houses themselves, by gaming, by overgrown bills (whether on account of physic, or law, or anything else), or by requiring or taking such

---

[17] Cf. the comment in Harald Höffding, *A History of Modern Philosophy*, I.260, that 'mathematics did not then [early seventeenth century] form part of the ordinary educational curriculum in England; indeed, it was looked upon as devilry.' See also Wesley's letter to Dr. John Robertson, Sept. 24, 1753: '[Ramsay's *Principles of Religion*] gave me a stronger conviction than ever I had before of the fallaciousness and unsatisfactoriness of the mathematical method of reasoning on religious subjects. . . .' Whitehead, *Life of John Wesley*, II. 464-65, had a different explanation: '[Wesley] never entered far into the more abstruse or higher branches of mathematics, finding they would fascinate his mind, absorb all his attention, and divert him from more important objects.'

For other comments on mathematics and the rationalist method in theology, cf. H.R. McAdoo, *The Spirit of Anglicanism* (New York, Charles Scribner's Sons, 1965), pp. 127-28. Ernst Cassirer believed that the Cambridge Platonists, with their mystical notions of nature (nature as the mirror of the wisdom of God), 'broke with the strongest and most fruitful scientific force of the seventeenth century, *exact mathematics*'; see *The Platonic Renaissance in England* (Austin, Tex., Univ. of Texas Press, 1953), p. 133; cf. chs. 3 and 4. This notion of plastic nature, not wholly reducible to quantification, comes over into Wesley's view of 'natural theology'. It was the basis of his aversion to exact mathematics.

interest as even the laws of our country forbid. Hereby all *pawnbroking* is excluded, seeing whatever good we might do thereby all unprejudiced men see with grief to be abundantly overbalanced by the evil. And if it were otherwise, yet we are not allowed to 'do evil that good may come'.[18] We cannot, consistent 5 with brotherly love, sell our goods below the market price.[19] We cannot study to ruin our neighbour's trade in order to advance our own. Much less can we entice away or receive any of his servants or workmen whom he has need of. None can gain by swallowing up his neighbour's substance, without gaining the 10 damnation of hell.

4. Neither may we gain by hurting our neighbour *in his body*. Therefore we may not sell anything which tends to impair health. Such is, eminently, all that liquid fire commonly called 'drams' or 'spirituous liquor'. It is true, these may have a place in medicine; 15 they may be of use in some bodily disorders (although there would rarely be occasion for them were it not for the unskillfulness of the practitioner). Therefore such as prepare and sell them *only for this end* may keep their conscience clear. But who are they? Who prepare and sell them *only for this end?* Do you 20 know ten such distillers in England? Then excuse these. But all who sell them in the common way, to any that will buy, are poisoners-general. They murder his Majesty's subjects by wholesale, neither does their eye pity or spare.[20] They drive them to hell like sheep. And what is their gain? Is it not the blood of 25 these men? Who then would envy their large estates and sumptuous palaces? A curse is in the midst of them: the curse of God cleaves to the stones, the timber, the furniture of them. The curse of God is in their gardens, their walks, their groves; a fire that burns to the nethermost hell. Blood, blood is there—the 30 foundation, the floor, the walls, the roof are stained with blood![21]

---

[18] Rom. 3:8.

[19] Contrast this with the monastic rule that goods produced by monks should 'sell at a little cheaper rate than men of the world would sell . . . '; 'The Rule of St. Benedict', c. 57, in Owen Chadwick, ed., *Western Asceticism* (LCC, Vol. 12, Philadelphia, Pa., Westminster Press, 1958), p. 527.

[20] See Deut. 13:8; Ezek. 5:11.

[21] This rhetoric sounds more realistic against the background of the appalling social miseries of alcoholism that we know from Hogarth's *Beer Alley* and *Gin Row* and that Wesley knew at first hand and all too intimately. Cf. Rudé, *Hanoverian London, 1714–1808*, p. 20: ' . . . a Bow Street tavern proudly boasted: "Here you may get drunk for a penny, dead drunk for twopence, and get straw for nothing."' Cf. also p. 91, and see Dorothy George, *London Life in the Eighteenth Century*, espec. pp. 27-30, 272, 296-99.

And canst thou hope, O thou man of blood,[22] though thou art 'clothed in scarlet and fine linen, and farest sumptuously every day',[23] canst thou hope to deliver down thy 'fields of blood'[24] to the third generation? Not so; for there is a God in heaven.[25]
5 Therefore thy name shall soon be rooted out. Like as those whom thou hast destroyed, body and soul, 'thy memorial shall perish with thee.'[26]

5. And are not they partakers of the same guilt, though in a lower degree, whether surgeons, apothecaries, or physicians, who
10 play with the lives or health of men to enlarge their own gain?[27] Who purposely lengthen the pain or disease which they are able to remove speedily? Who protract the cure of their patient's body in order to plunder his substance? Can any man be clear before God who does not shorten every disorder *as much as he can,* and remove
15 all sickness and pain *as soon as he can.* He cannot. For nothing can be more clear than that he does not 'love his neighbour as himself';[28] than that he does not 'do unto others as he would they should do unto himself'.[29]

6. This is dear-bought gain. And so is whatever is procured by
20 hurting our neighbour *in his soul:* by ministering, suppose either directly or indirectly, to his unchastity or intemperance, which certainly none can do who has any fear of God, or any real desire of pleasing him. It nearly concerns all those to consider this who have anything to do with taverns, victualling-houses, opera-
25 houses, playhouses, or any other places of public, fashionable diversion. If these profit the souls of men, you are clear; your employment is good, and your gain innocent. But if they are either sinful in themselves, or natural inlets to sin[30] of various kinds, then it is to be feared you have a sad account to make. O
30 beware lest God say in that day, 'These have perished in their iniquity, but their blood do I require at thy hands!'[31]

7. These cautions and restrictions being observed, it is the bounden duty of all who are engaged in worldly business to

---

[22] Ecclus. 34:21.   [23] Cf. Luke 16:19.
[24] Cf. Matt. 27:8; Acts 1:19.   [25] See Dan. 2:28.
[26] Cf. Ps. 9:6.
[27] Cf. Wesley's complaint against self-serving physicians in his letter to 'John Smith', Mar. 25, 1747, §11 (*Letters,* 26:235-36 in this edn.).
[28] Mark 12:33.
[29] Cf. Matt. 7:12.
[30] Cf. No. 96, 'On Obedience to Parents', I.11.
[31] Cf. Ezek. 3:18.

observe that first and great rule of Christian wisdom with respect to money, 'Gain all you can.'[32] Gain all you can by honest industry: use all possible diligence in your calling. Lose no time.[33] If you understand yourself and your relation to God and man, you know you have none to spare. If you understand your particular 5 calling as you ought, you will have no time that hangs upon your hands. Every business will afford some employment sufficient for every day and every hour. That wherein *you* are placed, if you follow it in earnest, will leave you no leisure for silly, unprofitable diversions. You have always something better to do, something 10 that will profit you, more or less. And 'whatsoever thy hand findeth to do, do it with thy might.'[34] Do it *as soon* as possible. No delay! No putting off from day to day, or from hour to hour. Never leave anything till tomorrow which you can do today. And do it *as well* as possible. Do not sleep or yawn over it. Put your whole 15 strength to the work. Spare no pains. Let nothing be done by halves, or in a slight and careless manner. Let nothing in your business be left undone if it can be done by labour or patience.

8. Gain *all* you can, by common sense, by using in your business all the understanding which God has given you. It is 20 amazing to observe how few do this; how men run on in the same dull track with their forefathers. But whatever they do who know not God, this is no rule for *you*. It is a shame for a Christian not to improve upon *them* in whatever he takes in hand. *You* should be continually learning from the experience of others or from your 25 own experience, reading, and reflection, to do everything you have to do better today than you did yesterday. And see that you practise whatever you learn, that you may make the best of all that is in your hands.[35]

II. 1. Having gained all you can, by honest wisdom and 30 unwearied diligence, the second rule of Christian prudence is, *Save all you can.* Do not throw the precious talent into the sea:

---

[32] Cf. above, I.1 and n.

[33] Cf. No. 93, 'On Redeeming the Time'; also Nos. 4, *Scriptural Christianity*, IV.9; 84, *The Important Question*, III.7. See also JWJ, Aug. 1743, and Aug. 1787; and his letters to John Mason, Feb. 17, 1776; and to Ann Bolton, Aug. 8, 1773, and May 13, 1774.

[34] Eccles. 9:10.

[35] Contrast the emphasis here on the correlation between economic efficiency and 'progress' with the Weber-Tawney thesis about the 'Calvinist work ethic'; there the emphasis is on a correlation between 'election' and affluence. There has been an important difference between these two ideas in the subsequent history of capitalism.

leave that folly to heathen philosophers. Do not throw it away in idle expenses, which is just the same as throwing it into the sea. Expend no part of it merely to gratify the desire of the flesh, the desire of the eye, or the pride of life.[36]

5 2. Do not waste any part of so precious a talent merely in gratifying the desires of the flesh; in procuring the pleasures of sense of whatever kind; particularly, in enlarging the pleasure of tasting.[37] I do not mean, avoid gluttony and drunkenness only: an honest heathen would condemn these. But there is a regular, reputable kind of sensuality, an elegant epicurism,[38] which does not immediately disorder the stomach, nor (sensibly, at least) impair the understanding. And yet (to mention no other effects of it now) it cannot be maintained without considerable expense. Cut off all this expense. Despise delicacy and variety, and be content with what plain nature requires.

3. Do not waste any part of so precious a talent merely in gratifying the desire of the eye by superfluous or expensive apparel, or by needless ornaments.[39] Waste no part of it in curiously adorning your houses in superfluous or expensive furniture; in costly pictures, painting, gilding, books; in elegant (rather than useful) gardens. Let your neighbours, who know nothing better, do this: 'Let the dead bury their dead.' But 'What is that to thee?' says our Lord: 'Follow thou me.'[40] Are you willing? Then you are able so to do.

25 4. Lay out nothing to gratify the pride of life, to gain the admiration or praise of men. This motive of expense is frequently interwoven with one or both of the former. Men are expensive in diet, or apparel, or furniture, not barely to please their appetite, or to gratify their eye, their imagination, but their vanity too. 'So long as thou dost well unto thyself, men will speak good of thee.'[41] So

---

[36] 1 John 2:16. Cf. No. 7, 'The Way to the Kingdom', II.2 and n.

[37] A favourite target; see Nos. 68, 'The Wisdom of God's Counsels', §16; 84, *The Important Question*, I.2; 87, 'The Danger of Riches', I.13; 95, 'On the Education of Children', §19 (where the phrase is repeated as a quotation); 111, *National Sins and Miseries*, II.5; and 131, 'The Danger of Increasing Riches', II.10. See also *A Farther Appeal*, Pt. II, II.18 (11:230 in this edn.), where again it appears as a quotation. A probable source here is William Law: 'Some people have no other care than how to give their palate some fresh pleasure and enlarge the happiness of tasting,' *Christian Perfection (Works*, III.38). In his *Serious Call (Works*, IV.115), Law uses the phrase, 'the pleasures of gluttony'.

[38] Cf. No. 9, 'The Spirit of Bondage and of Adoption', I.2 and n.

[39] Cf. No. 88, 'On Dress', §14.

[40] Matt. 8:22; John 21:22.

[41] Ps. 49:18 (BCP).

long as thou art 'clothed in purple and fine linen, and farest sumptuously every day',[42] no doubt many will applaud thy elegance of taste, thy generosity and hospitality. But do not buy their applause so dear. Rather be content with the honour that cometh from God.

5. Who would expend anything in gratifying these desires if he considered that to gratify them is to increase them? Nothing can be more certain than this: daily experience shows, the more they are indulged, they increase the more. Whenever therefore you expend anything to please your taste or other senses, you pay so much for sensuality. When you lay out money to please your eye, you give so much for an increase of curiosity, for a stronger attachment to these pleasures, which perish in the using. While you are purchasing anything which men use to applaud, you are purchasing more vanity. Had you not then enough of vanity, sensuality, curiosity before? Was there need of any addition? And would you pay for it, too? What manner of wisdom is this? Would not the literally throwing your money into the sea be a less mischievous folly?

6. And why should you throw away money upon your children, any more than upon yourself, in delicate food, in gay or costly apparel, in superfluities of any kind? Why should you purchase for them more pride or lust, more vanity, or foolish and hurtful desires?[43] They do not want any more; they have enough already; nature has made ample provision for them. Why should you be at farther expense to increase their temptations and snares, and to 'pierce them through with more sorrows'?[44]

7. Do not *leave it* to them, to throw away. If you have good reason to believe that they would waste what is now in your possession in gratifying and thereby increasing the desire of the flesh, the desire of the eye, or the pride of life (at the peril of theirs and your own soul), do not set these traps in their way. Do not offer your sons or your daughters unto Belial[45] any more than unto Moloch.[46] Have pity upon them, and remove out of their way what

[42] Cf. Luke 16:19.
[43] 1 Tim. 6:9.
[44] Cf. 1 Tim. 6:10.
[45] A demonic figure in the Apocalyptic literature, sometimes identified with Satan himself. Cf. Book of Jubilees 1:20; 15:32; and the Sybilline Oracles 3:63; 2:166. But see also, Milton, *Paradise Lost*, i.490.
[46] A Semitic god (cf. 2 Kgs. 2:16 and 23:10) whose worship included child sacrifice. He also appears in Milton, *Paradise Lost*, i.392.

you may easily foresee would increase their sins, and consequently plunge them deeper into everlasting perdition. How amazing then is the infatuation of those parents who think they can never leave their children enough? What! cannot you leave
5 them enough of arrows, firebrands, and death? Not enough of foolish and hurtful desires? Not enough of pride, lust, ambition, vanity? Not enough of everlasting burnings![47] Poor wretch! Thou fearest where no fear is. Surely both thou and they, when ye are lifting up your eyes in hell, will have enough both of the 'worm
10 that never dieth', and of 'the fire that never shall be quenched'.[48]

8. 'What then would you do if you was in my case? If you had a considerable fortune to leave?' Whether I *would* do it or no, I know what I *ought* to do: this will admit of no reasonable question. If I had one child, elder or younger, who knew the value of money,
15 one who I believed would put it to the true use, I should think it my absolute, indispensable duty to leave that child the bulk of my fortune; and to the rest just so much as would enable them to live in the manner they had been accustomed to do. 'But what if all your children were equally ignorant of the true use of money?' I
20 ought then (hard saying! Who can hear it?)[49] to give each what would keep him above want, and to bestow all the rest in such a manner as I judged would be most for the glory of God.

III. 1. But let not any man imagine that he has done anything barely by going thus far, by *gaining and saving all he can*, if he were
25 to stop here. All this is nothing if a man go not forward, if he does not point all this at a farther end. Nor indeed can a man properly be said to *save* anything if he only *lays it up*.[50] You may as well throw your money into the sea as bury it in the earth. And you may as well bury it in the earth as in your chest, or in the Bank of
30 England.[51] Not to use, is effectually to throw it away. If therefore

---

[47] Isa. 33:14.
[48] Cf. Mark 9:43-46, 48.
[49] John 6:60.
[50] See above, 'An Introductory Comment' to this sermon.
[51] Founded as a joint venture of the government and London financiers in 1694, the Bank of England had become a familiar symbol of capitalism—of the virtues (and to Wesley, the vice) of surplus accumulation. During the Gordon Riots of June 1780, it would become a target of the rioters and would be defended by no less a 'radical' than John Wilkes himself; cf. Rudé, *Hanoverian London, 1714–1808*, pp. 178-81. For Wesley's indirect role in this affair, see his 'Letter to the Printer of the *Public Advertiser*', Jan. 12, 1780, and his comments on Lord George Gordon in JWJ, Nov. 5, 1780 (cf. Curnock's note, VI. 299-300); Dec. 16, 1780; and Jan. 29, 1781; cf. also *AM* (1781), IV.295.

you would indeed 'make yourselves friends of the mammon of unrighteousness', add the third rule to the two preceding. Having first gained all you can, and secondly saved all you can, then give all you can.

2. In order to see the ground and reason of this, consider: when the possessor of heaven and earth brought you into being and placed you in this world, he placed you here not as a proprietor, but a steward.[52] As such he entrusted you for a season with goods of various kinds. But the sole property of these still rests in him, nor can ever be alienated from him. As you yourself are not your own, but his, such is likewise all that you enjoy. Such is your soul, and your body—not your own, but God's. And so is your substance in particular. And he has told you in the most clear and express terms how you are to employ it for him, in such a manner that it may be all an holy sacrifice, acceptable through Christ Jesus.[53] And this light, easy service he has promised to reward with an eternal weight of glory.[54]

3. The directions which God has given us touching the use of our worldly substance may be comprised in the following particulars. If you desire to be a faithful and a wise steward, out of that portion of your Lord's goods which he has for the present lodged in your hands, but with the right of resuming whenever it pleases him, first, provide things needful for yourself—food to eat, raiment to put on, whatever nature moderately requires for preserving the body in health and strength. Secondly, provide these for your wife, your children, your servants, or any others who pertain to your household.[55] If when this is done there be an overplus left, then 'do good to them that are of the household of faith.'[56] If there be an overplus still, 'as you have opportunity, do good unto all men.'[57] In so doing, you *give all you can*; nay, in a sound sense, all you have. For all that is laid out in this manner is really given to God. You 'render unto God the things that are God's',[58] not only by what you give to the poor, but also by that

---

[52] Cf. No. 51, *The Good Steward.*
[53] See 1 Pet. 2:5.   [54] 2 Cor. 4:17.
[55] Cf. No 94, 'On Family Religion', II.3: 'Your servants are secondary children.' See also, Law, *Christian Perfection* (*Works*, III.223); and J. H. Plumb, *The First Four Georges* (London, B. T. Batsford, Ltd., 1956), p. 31, for a comment that this was the typical conception of relationships in English middle-class households in the first half of the eighteenth century.
[56] Gal. 6:10.   [57] *Ibid.*
[58] Cf. Matt. 22:21, etc.

which you expend in providing things needful for yourself and your household.[59]

4. If then a doubt should at any time arise in your mind concerning what you are going to expend, either on yourself or any part of your family, you have an easy way to remove it. Calmly and seriously inquire: (1). In expending this, am I acting according to my character? Am I acting herein, not as a proprietor, but as a steward of my Lord's goods? (2). Am I doing this in obedience to his Word? In what Scripture does he require me so to do? (3). Can I offer up this action, this expense, as a sacrifice to God through Jesus Christ? (4). Have I reason to believe that for this very work I shall have a reward at the resurrection of the just? You will seldom need anything more to remove any doubt which arises on this head; but by this fourfold consideration you will receive clear light as to the way wherein you should go.

5. If any doubt still remain, you may farther examine yourself by prayer according to those heads of inquiry. Try whether you can say to the Searcher of hearts, your conscience not condemning you: 'Lord, thou seest I am going to expend this sum on that food, apparel, furniture. And thou knowest I act herein with a single eye as a steward of thy goods, expending this portion of them thus in pursuance of the design thou hadst in entrusting me with them. Thou knowest I do this in obedience to thy Word, as thou commandest, and because thou commandest it. Let this, I beseech thee, be an holy sacrifice, acceptable through Jesus Christ! And give me a witness in myself that for this labour of love I shall have a recompense when thou rewardest every man according to his works.'[60] Now if your conscience bear you witness in the Holy Ghost that this prayer is well-pleasing to God, then have you no reason to doubt but that expense is right and good, and such as will never make you ashamed.

6. You see then what it is to 'make [to] yourselves friends of the mammon of unrighteousness', and by what means you may procure 'that when ye fail they may receive you into the everlasting habitations'. You see the nature and extent of truly Christian prudence so far as it relates to the use of that great talent—money. *Gain all you can,* without hurting either yourself

---

[59] Cf. No. 87, 'The Danger of Riches', II.8, for this same para., slightly rephrased.
[60] See Matt. 16:27.

or your neighbour, in soul or body, by applying hereto with unintermitted diligence, and with all the understanding which God has given you. *Save all you can,* by cutting off every expense which serves only to indulge foolish desire, to gratify either the desire of the flesh, the desire of the eye, or the pride of life. Waste 5 nothing, living or dying, on sin or folly, whether for yourself or your children. And then, *Give all you can,* or in other words give all you have to God. Do not stint yourself, like a Jew rather than a Christian, to this or that proportion. 'Render unto God', not a tenth, not a third, not half, but 'all that is God's,'[61] be it more or 10 less, by employing all on yourself, your household, the household of faith, and all mankind, in such a manner that you may give a good account of your stewardship when ye can be no longer stewards;[62] in such a manner as the oracles of God direct, both by general and particular precepts; in such a manner that whatever 15 ye do may be 'a sacrifice of a sweet-smelling savour to God',[63] and that every act may be rewarded in that day when the Lord cometh with all his saints.[64]

7. Brethren, can we be either wise or faithful stewards[65] unless we thus manage our Lord's goods? We cannot, as not only the 20 oracles of God, but our own conscience beareth witness. Then why should we delay? Why should we confer any longer with flesh and blood, or men of the world? Our kingdom, our wisdom 'is not of this world'.[66] Heathen custom is nothing to us. We follow no men any farther than they are followers of Christ. Hear ye him. 25 Yea, today, while it is called today, hear and obey his voice.[67] At this hour and from this hour, do his will; fulfil his word in this and in all things. I entreat you, in the name of the Lord Jesus, act up to the dignity of your calling. No more sloth! Whatsoever your hand findeth to do, do it with your might.[68] No more waste! Cut off 30 every expense which fashion, caprice, or flesh and blood demand. No more covetousness! But employ whatever God has entrusted you with in doing good, all possible good, in every possible kind and degree, to the household of faith, to all men. This is no small

[61] Cf. Matt. 22:21.
[62] See Luke 16:2.
[63] Cf. Eph. 5:2.
[64] See 1 Thess. 3:13.
[65] See Luke 12:42.
[66] John 18:36.
[67] See Heb. 3:15.
[68] See Eccles. 9:10.

part of 'the wisdom of the just'.[69] Give all ye have, as well as all ye are, a spiritual sacrifice to him who withheld not from you his Son, his only Son; so 'laying up in store for yourselves a good foundation against the time to come, that ye may attain eternal life'.[70]

---

[69] Luke 1:17.
[70] Cf. 1 Tim. 6:19.

THE GOOD STEWARD

AN INTRODUCTORY COMMENT

In its substance and theme this sermon follows as a sequel to 'The Use of Money', but its form is different and so also is its style. It is one of the very few of Wesley's sermons to the nobility, the fruit of a brief period of closer cooperation between Wesley and the Countess of Huntingdon and her circle of high-born friends in the closing years of the 1760s—an alliance shortly to be disrupted by the controversies stirred up by that provocative Minute of 1770. 'The Use of Money' is clearly to 'plain people' (ad populum). The Good Steward *is an 'inaugural sermon' marking Wesley's somewhat unlikely appointment as 'Chaplain to the Countess Dowager of Buchan'. The Countess had been born Lady Agnes Stewart of Goodtrees (near Edinburgh), and now was the widow of David Erskine, tenth Earl of Buchan. After the latter's triumphant death, December 1, 1767, his son and heir (also a convert to Methodism) 'appointed Mr. Venn, Mr. Fletcher, and Mr. Berridge as his [personal chaplains]'; see the vivid account in Seymour,* Countess of Huntingdon, *II. 14-19. His mother (the Dowager), 'a woman of strong natural understanding and of a highly cultivated mind', seems to have been persuaded by Lady Huntingdon to appoint Mr. Wesley as her own chaplain (ibid., I. 427; see also* WHS, *X. 91-92). This was promptly acknowledged in a mildly stilted letter of Wesley's to Lady Huntingdon on January 4, 1768: 'I am obliged to your Ladyship, and to Lady Buchan, for such a mark of your regard as I did not at all expect. I purpose to return her Ladyship thanks by this post.' On the following May 15, in Edinburgh, he preached to a 'sufficiently crowded house, even with the rich and honourable', and one may suppose that his topic for that occasion had been* The Good Steward *(a concio ad aulam, dated for publication as of May 14). He had already spoken on this same theme in No. 28,* 'Sermon on the Mount, VIII', §§26-27. *He and the well-read in his audience would have recognized the echoes here from* William Law's *classic description of* the stewardship of life itself *in his* Serious Call. *The special obligations of Christian stewardship amongst 'the rich and honourable' had already been analyzed in quite genteel fashion by John Chappelow,* The Right Way to be Rich. *What*

Wesley adds is a vivid description of 'The Last Judgment', echoing his earlier sermon, No. 15, The Great Assize.

Wesley's style here is noticeably more formal than in the generality of his sermons, his learning slightly more in evidence. Even more notable, however, are his brief excursions into speculation (e.g., the controverted question about 'the sleep of death', etc.). The basic message is, of course, familiar from Wesley's earliest interest in holy living: all of life is from God, and our use of all its gifts and bounties are to be received gratefully and administered faithfully as 'good stewards', *and always* ad interim.

What Wesley's chaplaincy to the Dowager Countess amounted to is not altogether clear. He adverts to it in the title of his open Letter to the Rev. Dr. Rutherforth *(March 24, 1768) and, again, on the title page of his memorial sermon on the death of George Whitefield, November 18, 1770 (see No. 53).*

Does his subsequent silence suggest that the appointment lapsed after the 'Calvinist-Arminian' disputes of the 1770s heated up? We do not know. What is certain is that, while it lasted, the patronage of the Erskine family would have aided Wesley's work in Scotland. The sermon itself was first published in Newcastle in 1768 and then inserted into Vol. IV of Wesley's Works *(1771). For the publishing history of its nine extant editions during Wesley's lifetime, and a list of its variant readings, see Appendix, Vol. 4, and* Bibliog, *No. 311.*

The Good Steward

Luke 16:2

Give an account of thy stewardship; for thou canst be no longer steward.

5   1. The relation which man bears to God, the creature to his Creator, is exhibited to us in the oracles of God under various representations. Considered as a sinner, a fallen creature, he is there represented as a *debtor* to his Creator. He is also frequently represented as a *servant,* which indeed is essential to him as a
10 creature, insomuch that this appellation is given to the Son of

God when in his state of humiliation: he 'took upon him the form of a servant, being made in the likeness of men'.[1]

2. But no character more exactly agrees with the present state of man than that of a *steward*.[2] Our blessed Lord frequently represents him as such; and there is a peculiar propriety in the representation. It is only in one particular respect, namely, as he is a sinner, that he is styled a 'debtor'; and when he is styled a 'servant' the appellation is general and indeterminate. But a 'steward' is a servant of a particular kind; such a one as man is in all respects. This appellation is exactly expressive of his situation in the present world, specifying what kind of servant he is to God, and what kind of service his divine master expects from him.

It may be of use, then, to consider this point throughly, and to make our full improvement of it. In order to this let us, first, inquire in what respects we are now God's 'stewards'. Let us, secondly, observe that when he requires our souls of us we 'can be no longer stewards'. It will then only remain, as we may in the third place observe, to 'give an account of our stewardship'.

I. 1. And, first, we are to inquire in what respects we are now God's stewards. We are now indebted to him for all we have; but although a debtor is obliged to return what he has received, yet until the time of payment comes he is at liberty to use it as he pleases. It is not so with a steward: he is not at liberty to use what is lodged in his hands as *he* pleases, but as his master pleases. He has no right to dispose of anything which is in his hands but according to the will of his lord. For he is not the proprietor of any of these things, but barely entrusted with them by another: and entrusted on this express condition, that he shall dispose of all as his master orders. Now this is exactly the case of every man with relation to God. We are not at liberty to use what he has lodged in our hands as *we* please, but as he pleases, who alone is the Possessor of heaven and earth,[3] and the Lord of every creature. We have no right to dispose of anything we have but according to

---

[1] Cf. Phil. 2:7.

[2] Cf. Wesley's *Notes* (Luke 16:1); and also Poole, *Annotations*: 'We are but stewards of the good things God lends us, and must give an account to our Master of them.' Henry, *Exposition*, on the same passage, quotes from Rabbi Kimchi: 'This world is a house; heaven the roof; the stars the lights; the earth . . . a table spread . . .; man is the steward . . .; if he behave himself well, he shall find favour in the eyes of the Lord; if not, he shall be turned out of his stewardship.'

[3] Gen. 14:19, 22.

his will, seeing we are not proprietors of any of these things. They are all, as our Lord speaks, ἀλλότρια[4], 'belonging to another person'; nor is anything properly 'our own' in the land of our pilgrimage.[5] We shall not receive τὰ ἴδια,[6] 'our own things', till

5 we come to our own country. Eternal things only are our own: with all these temporal things we are barely entrusted by another —the Disposer and Lord of all. And he entrusts us with them on this express condition, that we use them only as our Master's goods, and according to the particular directions which he has

10 given us in his Word.

2. On this condition he hath entrusted us with our souls, our bodies, our goods, and whatever other talents we have received: but in order to impress this weighty truth on our hearts it will be needful to come to particulars.

15 And first, God has entrusted us with our *soul*, an immortal spirit made in the image of God,[7] together with all the powers and faculties thereof—understanding, imagination, memory; will, and a train of affections either included in it or closely dependent upon it; love and hatred, joy and sorrow, respecting present good

20 and evil; desire and aversion, hope and fear, respecting that which is to come. All these St. Paul seems to include in two words when he says, 'The peace of God shall keep your *hearts* and *minds*.'[8] Perhaps, indeed the latter word, νοήματα, might rather be rendered 'thoughts',[9] provided we take that word in its most

25 extensive sense, for every perception of the mind, whether active or passive.

3. Now of all these it is certain we are only stewards. God has entrusted us with these powers and faculties, not that we may employ them according to our own will, but according to the

30 express orders which he has given us; although it is true that in doing his will we most effectually secure our own happiness, seeing it is herein only that we can be happy either in time or in eternity. Thus we are to use our understanding, our imagination, our memory, wholly to the glory of him that gave them. Thus our

35 will is to be wholly given up to him, and all our affections to be

---

[4] Luke 16:12.   [5] See Exod. 6:4.
[6] Cf. Acts 4:32; but see also Bauer in Arndt and Gingrich, *Greek-English Lexicon*.
[7] Gen. 1:27; 9:6, etc.
[8] Phil. 4:7.
[9] Cf. Bengel, *Gnomon, loc. cit.*: 'The heart is the seat of one's thoughts.' But see Bauer in Arndt and Gingrich, *Greek-English Lexicon* on νόημα.

regulated as he directs. We are to love and hate, to rejoice and grieve, to desire and shun, to hope and fear, according to the rule which he prescribes whose we are, and whom we are to serve in all things.[10] Even our thoughts are not our own in this sense: they are not at our own disposal, but for every deliberate motion of our 5 mind we are accountable to our great Master.

4. God has, secondly, entrusted us with our *bodies* (those exquisitely wrought machines, so 'fearfully and wonderfully made'),[11] with all the powers and members thereof. He has entrusted us with the organs of *sense*, of sight, hearing, and the 10 rest: but none of these are given us as our own, to be employed according to our own will. None of these are *lent* us in such a sense as to leave us at liberty to use them as we please for a season. No; we have received them on these very terms, that as long as they abide with us we should employ them all in that very manner, 15 and no other, which he appoints.

5. It is on the same terms that he has imparted to us that most excellent talent of *speech*. 'Thou hast given me a tongue', says the ancient writer, 'that I may praise thee therewith.'[12] For this purpose was it given to all the children of men, to be employed in 20 glorifying God. Nothing therefore is more ungrateful, or more absurd, than to think or say, 'our tongues are our own.' That cannot be, unless we have created ourselves, and so are independent on the Most High. Nay, but 'it is he that hath made us, and not we ourselves.'[13] The manifest consequence is that he is still 25 *Lord over us*, in this as in all other respects. It follows that there is not a word of our tongue for which we are not accountable to him.

6. To him we are equally accountable for the use of our *hands* and *feet*, and all the *members* of our body. These are so many talents which are committed to our trust,[14] until the time 30 appointed by the Father.[15] Until then we have the use of all these;

---

[10] See Acts 27:23.

[11] Ps. 139:14. For Wesley's frequent descriptions of the body as a machine, cf. Nos. 56, 'God's Approbation of His Works', I.7; 57, 'On the Fall of Man', II.1, 5; 69, 'The Imperfection of Human Knowledge', I.13; 71, 'Of Good Angels', I.7; 72, 'Of Evil Angels', II.8; 82, 'On Temptation', I.2; 116, 'What is Man? Ps. 8:4', §§1-4; 141, 'The Image of God', II.1. See also his *Thoughts Upon Necessity*, III.9; and his *Survey*, I.27-29, 164; II.275-76; IV.89; V.254. For another comment on his body/soul dualism, see No. 41, *Wandering Thoughts*, III.5 and n.

[12] Augustine, *Confessions*, V.i: '*Accipe sacrificium confessionum mearum de manu linguae meae, quam formasti et excitasti, ut confiteatur nomini tuo.*'

[13] Cf. Ps. 100:3.   [14] See 1 Tim. 1:11.   [15] See Gal. 4:2.

but as stewards, not as proprietors: to the end we should 'render them, not as instruments of unrighteousness unto sin, but as instruments of righteousness unto God'.[16]

7. God has entrusted us, thirdly, with a portion of *worldly goods*,
5 with food to eat, raiment to put on, and a place where to lay our head, with not only the necessaries but the conveniences of life. Above all, he has committed to our charge that precious talent which contains all the rest, *money*. Indeed, it is unspeakably precious if we are 'wise and faithful stewards'[17] of it; if we employ
10 every part of it for such purposes as our blessed Lord has commanded us to do.

8. God has entrusted us, fourthly, with several talents which do not properly come under any of these heads: such is bodily *strength;* such are *health*, a pleasing *person*, an agreeable *address;*
15 such are *learning* and *knowledge* in their various degrees, with all the other advantages of *education*. Such is the *influence* which we have over others, whether by their *love* and *esteem* of us, or by *power*—power to do them good or hurt, to help or hinder them in the circumstances of life. Add to these that invaluable talent of
20 *time*, with which God entrusts us from moment to moment. Add, lastly, that on which all the rest depend, and without which they would all be curses, not blessings: namely, the *grace* of God, the power of his Holy Spirit, which alone worketh in us[18] all that is acceptable in his sight.[19]

25 II. 1. In so many respects are the children of men stewards of the Lord, 'the possessor of heaven and earth'.[20] So large a portion of his goods of various kinds hath he committed to their charge. But it is not for ever, nor indeed for any considerable time. We have this trust reposed in us only during the short, uncertain
30 space that we sojourn here below; only so long as we remain on earth, as this fleeting breath is in our nostrils. The hour is swiftly approaching, it is just at hand, when we 'can be no longer stewards'.[21] The moment the body 'returns to the dust as it was, and the spirit to God that gave it',[22] we bear that character no
35 more; the time of our stewardship is at an end. Part of those goods

---

[16] Cf. Rom. 6:13.
[18] See Eph. 3:20.
[20] Gen. 14:19, 22.
[21] Cf. Luke 16:2.
[22] Cf. Eccles. 12:7.

[17] Cf. Luke 12:42.
[19] See Ps. 19:14; 1 Tim. 2:3.

wherewith we were before entrusted are now come to an end; at least they are so with regard to *us*; nor are we longer entrusted with them—and that part which remains can no longer be employed or improved as it was before.

2. Part of what we were entrusted with before is at an end, at least with regard to us. What have we to do after this life with food, and raiment, and houses, and earthly possessions? The food of the dead is the dust of the earth: they are clothed only with worms and rottenness. They dwell in 'the house prepared for all flesh':[23] their lands know them no more. All their worldly goods are delivered into other hands, and they have 'no more portion under the sun'.[24]

3. The case is the same with regard to the *body*. The moment the spirit returns to God we are no longer stewards of this machine, which is then sown in corruption and dishonour.[25] All the parts and members of which it was composed lie mouldering in the clay. The hands have no longer power to move; the feet have forgot their office; the flesh, the sinews, the bones are all hasting to be dissolved into common dust.

4. Here end also the talents of a *mixed* nature: our *strength*, our *health*, our *beauty;* our *eloquence* and *address;* our faculty of pleasing, of persuading or convincing others. Here end likewise all the *honours* we once enjoyed, all the *power* which was lodged in our hands, all the *influence* which we once had over others, either by the love or the esteem which they bore us. 'Our love, our hatred, our desire is perished:'[26] none regard how we were once affected toward them. They look upon the dead as neither able to help nor hurt them; so that 'a living dog is better than a dead lion.'[27]

5. Perhaps a doubt may remain concerning some of the other talents wherewith we are now entrusted, whether they will cease to exist when the body returns to dust, or only cease to be improvable. Indeed there is no doubt but the kind of *speech* which we now use, by means of these bodily organs, will then be entirely at an end, when those organs are destroyed. It is certain the tongue will no more occasion any vibrations in the air; neither will

[23] Cf. Job 30:23, 'the house appointed for all living'.
[24] Cf. Eccles. 9:6.
[25] See 1 Cor. 15:42-43. Cf. No. 129, 'Heavenly Treasure in Earthen Vessels', I.1.
[26] Cf. Eccles. 9:6.
[27] Eccles. 9:4.

the ear convey these tremulous motions to the common sensory.[28] Even the *sonus exilis*,[29] the low, shrill voice which the poet supposes to belong to a separate spirit, we cannot allow to have a real being; it is a mere flight of imagination. Indeed it cannot be
5 questioned but separate spirits have some way to communicate their sentiments to each other; but what inhabitant of flesh and blood can explain that way? What we term 'speech' they cannot have. So that we can no longer be stewards of this talent when we are numbered with the dead.
10   6. It may likewise admit of a doubt whether our *senses* will exist when the organs of sense are destroyed. Is it not probable that those of the lower kind will cease—the feeling, the smell, the taste—as they have a more immediate reference to the body, and are chiefly, if not wholly, intended for the preservation of it? But
15 will not some kind of *sight* remain, although the eye be closed in death? And will there not be something in the soul equivalent to the present sense of *hearing*? Nay, is it not probable that these will not only exist in the separate state, but exist in a far greater degree, in a more eminent manner than now. When the soul,
20 disentangled from its clay, is no longer

> A dying sparkle in a cloudy place;

when it no longer

> Looks through the windows of the eye and ear,[30]

---

[28] Cf. Chambers's *Cyclopaedia*, 'Sensory': '*Sensorium commune*, the seat of the common sense; or that part or place where the sensible soul is supposed more immediately to preside [over the body/soul interconnections]. . . . Descartes will have it in the conarion or pineal gland.' But see also, John Norris, *Reason and Religion* (1689), II.ii.188. The classical source of the notion is in Aristotle, *De Memoria*, 450*a*, which speaks of 'the primary faculty of perception'. Cf. also No. 124, 'Human Life a Dream', §7.

[29] Cf. Sugden's note, II.468-69; but none of his citations there comes close to the phrase, *sonus exilis*. Could it be Wesley's own Latin translation of Homer's ὤχετο τετριγυῖα (*Iliad*, xxiii. 99-101)? *Vox exilis* is cited in Lewis and Short, *A Latin Dictionary*, as from Quintilian (XI.iii.15), but not *sonus exilis;* and Quintilian was not a 'poet'.

[30] Wesley's adaptation of Sir John Davies's *Nosce Teipsum* ('Of Human Knowledge'), Pt. I, st. 17:

> How can we hope, that through the eye and ear,
> This dying sparkle, in this cloudy place,
> Can recollect these beams of knowledge clear
> Which were infused in the first minds by grace?

St. 15 has the phrase 'windows of the mind' which Wesley conflated with l.1, above. See also *A Collection of Moral and Sacred Poems* (1744), I.17.

but rather is all eye, all ear, all sense, in a manner we cannot yet conceive. And have we not a clear proof of the possibility of this, of seeing without the use of the eye, and hearing without the use of the ear? Yea, and an earnest of it continually? For does not the soul see, in the clearest manner, when the eye is of no use, namely 5 in dreams?[31] Does she not then enjoy the faculty of hearing without any help from the ear? But however this be, certain it is that neither will our *senses*, any more than our *speech*, be entrusted to us in the manner they are now, when the body lies in the silent grave. 10

7. How far the *knowledge* or *learning* which we have gained by *education* will then remain, we cannot tell. Solomon indeed says, 'There is no work, nor device, nor knowledge, nor wisdom, in the grave whither thou goest.'[32] But it is evident, these words cannot be understood in an absolute sense; for it is so far from being true 15 that there is *no knowledge* after we have quitted the body that the doubt lies on the other side, whether there be any such thing as real knowledge till then? Whether it be not a plain, sober truth, not a mere poetical fiction, that

> . . . all these shadows which for things we take, 20
> Are but the empty dreams which in death's sleep we make[33]—

only excepting those things which God himself has been pleased to reveal to man? I will speak for one. After having sought for truth with some diligence for half a century I am at this day hardly sure of anything but what I learn from the Bible. Nay, I positively 25 affirm I know nothing else so certainly that I would dare to stake my salvation upon it.

So much, however, we may learn from Solomon's words, that 'there is no' *such* 'knowledge or wisdom in the grave' as will be of any use to an unhappy spirit; there is 'no device' there whereby he 30 can now improve those talents with which he was once entrusted. For *time* is no more: the time of our trial for everlasting happiness or misery is past. *Our day*, the day of man, is over; 'the day of salvation'[34] is ended. Nothing now remains but the day of the Lord, ushering in wide, unchangeable eternity.[35] 35

8. But still our souls, being incorruptible and immortal, of a

---

[31] Cf. No. 124, 'Human Life a Dream', §4 and n.   [32] Eccles. 9:10.
[33] Cf. Abraham Cowley, *Pindarique Odes*, 'Life', II.22-23. See also, *A Collection of Moral and Sacred Poems* (1744), I.43.
[34] 2 Cor. 6:2; cf. Isa. 49:8.   [35] Cf. No. 54, 'On Eternity', §§1, 5-7.

290   *Sermon 51*   II.8-10

nature 'little lower than the angels'[36] (even if we are to understand that phrase of our original nature, which may well admit of a doubt), when our bodies are mouldered into earth, will remain with all their faculties. Our *memory*, our *understanding*, will be so
5 far from being destroyed, yea, or impaired by the dissolution of the body, that on the contrary we have reason to believe they will be inconceivably strengthened. Have we not the clearest reason to believe that they will then be wholly freed from those defects which now naturally result from the union of the soul with the
10 corruptible body? It is highly probable that from the time these are disunited our memory will let nothing slip; yea, that it will faithfully exhibit everything to our view which was ever committed to it. It is true that the invisible world is in Scripture termed 'the land of forgetfulness';[37] or, as it is still more strongly
15 expressed in the old translation, 'the land where all things are forgotten'.[38] They are forgotten; but by whom? Not by the inhabitants of that land, but by the inhabitants of the earth. It is with regard to them that the unseen world is 'the land of forgetfulness'. All things therein are too frequently forgotten by
20 these; but not by disembodied spirits. From the time they have put off the earthly tabernacle[39] we can hardly think they forget anything.

9. In like manner the *understanding* will doubtless be freed from the defects that are now inseparable from it. For many ages it has
25 been an unquestioned maxim, *humanum est errare et nescire*[40]— 'ignorance and mistake are inseparable from human nature.' But the whole of this assertion is only true with regard to living men, and holds no longer than while 'the corruptible body presses down the soul'.[41] Ignorance indeed belongs to every finite
30 understanding (seeing there is none beside God that knoweth all things), but not mistake. When the body is laid aside, this also is laid aside for ever.

10. What then can we say to an ingenious man who has lately made a discovery that disembodied spirits have not only no senses
35 (not even sight or hearing), but no memory or understanding, no thought or perception, not so much as a consciousness of their

---

[36] Ps. 8:5; Heb. 2:7, 9.   [37] Ps. 88:12 (AV).
[38] *Ibid.* (BCP). Cf. No. 54, 'On Eternity', §20 and n.
[39] See 2 Cor. 5:1; 2 Pet. 1:13, 14.
[40] See above, No. 39, 'Catholic Spirit', I.4 and n.
[41] Wisd. 9:15. Cf. No. 41, *Wandering Thoughts*, II.3 and n.

own existence! That they are in a dead sleep from death to the resurrection![42] *Consanguineus lethi sopor*[43] indeed! Such a sleep we may well call 'a near kinsman of death', if it be not the same thing. What can we say but that ingenious men have strange dreams; and these they sometimes mistake for realities.[44]   5

11. But to return. As the soul will retain its understanding and memory, notwithstanding the dissolution of the body, so undoubtedly the *will*, including all the *affections*, will remain in its full vigour. If our love or anger, our hope or desire, perish, it is only with regard to those whom we leave behind. To them it 10 matters not whether they were the objects of our love or hate, of our desire or aversion. But in separate spirits themselves we have no reason to believe that any of these are extinguished. It is more probable that they work with far greater force than while the soul was clogged with flesh and blood.   15

12. But although all these, although both our knowledge and senses, our memory and understanding, together with our will, our love, hate, and all our affections, remain after the body is dropped off, yet in this respect they are as though they were not; we are no longer stewards of them. The things continue, but our 20

---

[42] This theory runs back to the Anabaptists, at least; cf. G. H. Williams, *The Radical Reformation*, pp. 20-24, 104-6, 580-92. It had been denounced by Calvin in one of his earliest essays. *Psychopannychia; Or, a Refutation of the Error that the Soul Sleeps in the Interval Between Death and the Judgment* (written in 1534; published in 1542). Cf. 'First Part of the Sermon, against the Fear of Death', *Homilies*, pp. 81-85. The same idea is analysed rather differently in John Donne's famous sermon, 'Death's Duel' (Sermon 15 in his *XXVI Sermons* [1660]).

The 'ingenious man' cited here, however, was Edmund Law (archdeacon of Carlisle; later bishop), who had advocated 'mortalism' in a D. D. exercise at Cambridge (1754), published as an 'Appendix' to the 3rd edn. of *The Theory of Religion* (1755). This 'Appendix' had been roundly criticized (e.g., by John Steffe [1758]) but had then been defended by Francis Blackburne, *A Short Historical View Concerning An Intermediate State* . . . (1765), and by Joseph Priestley, *Disquisitions Relating to Matter and Spirit* . . . (1777), Sec. XIII, p. 155, and Sec. XVII, espec. p. 232. It is noteworthy that Wesley would have been so knowledgeable and yet also so casual in his references here and elsewhere to such a controversy; see No. 115, 'Dives and Lazarus', I.3 and n.

[43] Cf. Virgil, *Aeneid*, vi. 278 (borrowed from Homer, *Iliad*, xiv. 231). See also, Wesley's *Survey*, V. 254, where the same phrase appears in a different form, '*consanguineus somni*'. The English quotation which follows is, of course, Wesley's translation of the Latin.

[44] Locke discusses this in his *Essay Concerning Human Understanding* (1690), II.i.17, and espec. II.xix.4. Cf. also No. 57, 'On the Fall of Man', II.2, where Wesley says: 'the soul cannot dispense with [the body's] service, imperfect as it is. For an embodied spirit cannot form one thought but by the mediation of its bodily organs. For thinking is not, as many suppose, an act of a pure spirit, but the act of a spirit connected with a body, and playing upon a set of material keys.' Cf. also his letter to Mrs. Bennis, Oct. 28, 1771; No. 132, 'On Faith, Heb. 11:1', §8; and his *Survey*, I.178.

stewardship does not; we no more act in that capacity. Even the *grace* which was formerly entrusted with us, in order to enable us to be faithful and wise stewards, is now no longer entrusted for that purpose. The days of our stewardship are ended.

5   III. 1. It now remains that, being 'no longer stewards', we 'give an account of our stewardship'. Some have imagined, this is to be done immediately after death, as soon as we enter into the world of spirits. Nay, the Church of Rome does absolutely assert this; yea, makes it an article of faith.[45] And thus much we may allow:
10   the moment a soul drops the body, and stands naked before God, it cannot but know what its portion will be to all eternity. It will have full in its view either everlasting joy or everlasting torment, as it is no longer possible to be deceived in the judgment which we pass upon ourselves. But the Scripture gives us no reason to
15   believe that God will then sit in judgment upon us. There is no passage in all the oracles of God which affirms any such thing. That which has been frequently alleged for this purpose seems rather to prove the contrary; namely, 'It is appointed for men once to die, and after this, the judgment.'[a] For in all reason, the word
20   'once' is here to be applied to judgment as well as death. So that the fair inference to be drawn from this very text is, not that there are two judgments, a particular and a general, but that we are to be judged, as well as to die, once only; not once immediately after death, and again after the general resurrection, but then only

[a] Heb. 9:27.

---

[45] This refers to the so-called 'Doctrine of Particular Judgment', which is not, strictly speaking, 'an article of faith' in the Roman Catholic Church. It affirms, as Wesley says, 'that there are two judgments, a particular and a general'. The first divides the dead into three groups: (1) those free from all sin who are received forthwith into heaven *(mox in coelum recipi)*; (2) those in a state of grace who need further purification; (3) those dying in mortal sin and impenitent who go forthwith to hell *(mox in infernum descendere)*, to be punished in proportion to their sin *(poenis tamen disparibus puniendas)*. See the decree of the Second Council of Lyons (1274) and the *'de sorte defunctorum'* in the 'Union Decree' of Eugenius IV, 1439 (Heinrich Denzinger, *Enchiridion Symbolorum* [24th edn.], 1304–6). Wesley and his Protestant colleagues had collapsed groups (2) and (3) and supposed that 'Purgatory' held out the promise of salvation to souls dying in mortal sin and unrepentant; see Wesley's *Roman Catechism* (abridged from Bishop John Williams), *Qq.* 20-24, where Bellarmine and Trent are misread as if they taught a purgatorial hope for souls dying in mortal sin. But see George Bull, *Some Important Points of Primitive Christianity* (1713), Vol. I, Sermon II, pp. 25-49: 'The soul of every man presently after death hath its proper place and state allotted by God, of happiness or misery, according as the man hath been good or bad in his past life.' Cf. Wesley's teachings on the intermediate state in No. 115, 'Dives and Lazarus', I.3 and n.

'when the Son of Man shall come in his glory, and all his holy angels with him'.[46] The imagination therefore of one judgment at death, and another at the end of the world, can have no place with those who make the written Word of God the whole and sole standard of their faith.

2. The time then when we are to give this account is when the 'great white throne comes down from heaven, and he that sitteth thereon, from whose face the heavens and the earth flee away, and there is found no place for them'.[47] It is then 'the dead, small, and great,' will 'stand before God; and the books' will be 'opened'[48]—the book of Scripture, to them who were entrusted therewith, the book of conscience to all mankind. The 'book of remembrance'[49] likewise (to use another scriptural expression), which had been writing from the foundation of the world,[50] will then be laid open to the view of all the children of men. Before all these, even the whole human race, before the devil and his angels,[51] before an innumerable company of holy angels,[52] and before God the Judge of all;[53] thou wilt appear without any shelter or covering, without any possibility of disguise, to give a particular account of the manner wherein thou hast employed all thy Lord's goods.

3. The Judge of all will then inquire: 'How didst thou employ thy *soul?* I entrusted thee with an immortal spirit, endowed with various powers and faculties, with understanding, imagination, memory, will, affections. I gave thee withal full and express directions how all these were to be employed. Didst thou employ thy *understanding,* as far as it was capable, according to those directions, namely, in the knowledge of thyself and me? My nature, my attributes? My works, whether of creation, of providence, or of grace? In acquainting thyself with my Word? In using every means to increase thy knowledge thereof? In meditating thereon day and night?[54] Didst thou employ thy *memory* according to my will? In treasuring up whatever knowledge thou hadst acquired which might conduce to my glory, to thy own salvation, or the advantage of others? Didst thou store

---

[46] Cf. Matt. 25:31.
[47] Cf. Rev. 20:11.
[48] Cf. Rev. 20:12.
[49] Mal. 3:16.
[50] Matt. 13:35, etc. 'writing' is the erratum in Wesley's *Works* (1771) for 'written' (Mal. 3:16) present in all the other printed edns.
[51] Matt. 25:41.
[52] Heb. 12:22.
[53] Gen. 18:25; Heb. 12:23.
[54] See Josh. 1:8.

up therein, not things of no value, but whatever experience thou hadst learned from my Word; and whatever experience thou hadst gained of my wisdom, truth, power, and mercy? Was thy *imagination* employed, not in painting vain images, much
5 less such as nourished foolish and hurtful desires,[55] but in representing to thee whatever would profit thy soul, and awaken thy pursuit of wisdom and holiness? Didst thou follow my directions with regard to thy *will?* Was it wholly given up to me? Was it swallowed up in mine, so as never to oppose, but always
10 run parallel with it? Were thy *affections* placed and regulated in such a manner as I appointed in my Word? Didst thou give me thy heart? Didst thou not love the world, neither the things of the world?[56] Was I the object of thy love? Was all thy desire unto me, and unto the remembrance of my name? Was I the joy of thy
15 heart, the delight of thy soul, the chief among ten thousand?[57] Didst thou sorrow for nothing but what grieved my spirit? Didst thou fear and hate nothing but sin? Did the whole stream of thy affections flow back to the ocean from whence they came? Were thy *thoughts* employed according to my will? Not in ranging to the
20 ends of the earth, not on folly, or sin; but on "whatsoever things were pure, whatsoever things were holy",[58] on whatsoever was conducive to my "glory", and to "peace and goodwill among men"?'[59]

4. Thy Lord will then inquire, 'How didst thou employ the *body*
25 wherewith I entrusted thee? I gave thee a *tongue* to praise me therewith. Didst thou use it to the end for which it was given? Didst thou employ it, not in evil-speaking or idle-speaking, not in uncharitable or unprofitable conversation; but in such as was good, as was necessary or useful, either to thyself or others? Such
30 as always tended, directly or indirectly, to "minister grace to the hearers"?[60] I gave thee, together with thy other senses, those grand avenues of knowledge, *sight,* and *hearing.* Were these employed to those excellent purposes for which they were bestowed upon thee? In bringing thee in more and more
35 instruction in righteousness[61] and true holiness? I gave thee hands and feet and various *members* wherewith to perform the works which were prepared for thee. Were they employed, not in doing "the will of the flesh",[62] of thy evil nature, or "the will of the

---

[55] 1 Tim. 6:9.   [56] See 1 John 2:15.   [57] S. of S. 5:10.
[58] Cf. Phil. 4:8.   [59] Cf. Luke 2:14.   [60] Eph. 4:29.
[61] 2 Tim. 3:16.   [62] Cf. John 1:13.

mind",[63] the things to which thy reason or fancy led thee, but "the will of him that sent"[64] thee into the world, merely to work out thy own salvation?[65] Didst thou present all thy members, not to sin, as instruments of unrighteousness, but to me alone, through the Son of my love, "as instruments of righteousness"?'[66]

5. The Lord of all will next inquire, 'How didst thou employ the *worldly goods* which I lodged in thy hands? Didst thou use thy food, not so as to seek or place thy happiness therein, but so as to preserve thy body in health, in strength and vigour, a fit instrument for the soul? Didst thou use apparel, not to nourish pride or vanity, much less to tempt others to sin, but conveniently and decently to defend thyself from the injuries of the weather? Didst thou prepare and use thy house and all other conveniences with a single eye to my glory? In every point seeking not thy own honour, but mine; studying to please, not thyself, but me? Once more: in what manner didst thou employ that comprehensive talent, *money?* Not in gratifying the desire of the flesh, the desire of the eye, or the pride of life?[67] Not squandering it away in vain expenses, the same as throwing it into the sea? Not hoarding it up to leave behind thee, the same as burying it in the earth? But first supplying thy own reasonable wants, together with those of thy family; then restoring the remainder to me, through the poor, whom I had appointed to receive it; looking upon thyself as only one of that number of poor whose wants were to be supplied out of that part of my substance which I had placed in thy hands for this purpose; leaving thee the right of being supplied first, and the blessedness of giving rather than receiving?[68] Wast thou accordingly a general benefactor to mankind? Feeding the hungry, clothing the naked, comforting the sick, assisting the stranger, relieving the afflicted according to their various necessities?[69] Wast thou eyes to the blind, and feet to the lame?[70] A father to the fatherless, and an husband to the widow?[71] And didst thou labour to improve all outward works of mercy, as means of saving souls from death?'[72]

---

[63] Cf. *ibid.*   [64] John 6:38.   [65] See Phil. 2:12.
[66] Rom. 6:13.   [67] 1 John 2:16.
[68] See Acts 20:35. A crucial clarification of the rule in No. 50, 'The Use of Money', III.1-2: '*Give* all you can.' Our stewardship of wealth is *to* God, '*through the poor*, whom [God has] appointed to receive it'. Charity is an expression of benevolence but, more, it is a specification of the Christian's accountability to God.
[69] See Matt. 25:35-36.   [70] See Job 29:15.
[71] See Ps. 68:5.   [72] See Jas. 5:20.

6. Thy Lord will farther inquire: 'Hast thou been a wise and faithful steward with regard to the talents of a mixed nature which I lent thee? Didst thou employ thy health and strength, not in folly or sin, not in the pleasures which perished in the using, "not in
5 making provision for the flesh, to fulfil the desires thereof",[73] but in a vigorous pursuit of that better part which none could take away from thee?[74] Didst thou employ whatever was pleasing in thy person or address, whatever advantages thou hadst by education, whatever share of learning, whatever knowledge of things or men
10 was committed thee, for the promoting of virtue in the world, for the enlargement of my kingdom? Didst thou employ whatever share of power thou hadst, whatever influence over others, by the love or esteem of thee which they had conceived, for the increase of their wisdom and holiness? Didst thou employ that inestimable
15 talent of time with wariness and circumspection, as duly weighing the value of every moment, and knowing that all were numbered in eternity? Above all, wast thou a good steward of my grace, preventing, accompanying, and following thee? Didst thou duly observe and carefully improve all the influences of my Spirit?
20 Every good desire? Every measure of light? All his sharp or gentle reproofs? How didst thou profit by "the spirit of bondage and fear" which was previous to "the Spirit of adoption"?[75] And when thou wast made a partaker of this Spirit, "crying in thy heart, Abba, Father",[76] didst thou stand fast in the glorious liberty
25 wherewith I made thee free? Didst thou from thenceforth present thy soul and body, all thy thoughts, thy words, and actions, in one flame of love, as an holy sacrifice, glorifying me with thy body and thy spirit?[77] Then "well done, good and faithful servant! [. . .] Enter thou into the joy of thy Lord!" '[78] And what will remain,
30 either to the faithful or unfaithful steward? Nothing but the execution of that sentence which has been passed by the righteous Judge; fixing thee in a state which admits of no change, through everlasting ages. It remains only that thou be rewarded to all eternity according to thy works.

35   IV. 1. From these plain considerations we may learn, first, how important is this short, uncertain day of life! How precious, above all utterance, above all conception, is every portion of it!

---

[73] Rom. 13:14.   [74] See Luke 10:42.
[75] Rom. 8:15.   [76] *Ibid.*
[77] See 1 Cor. 6:20.   [78] Matt. 25:21, 23.

The least of these a serious care demands;
For though they are little, they are golden sands![79]

How deeply does it concern every child of man to let none of
these run to waste; but to improve them all to the noblest
purposes as long as the breath of God is in his nostrils!   5
    2. We learn from hence, secondly, that there is no employment
of our time, no action or conversation, that is purely *indifferent*. All
is good or bad, because all our time, as everything we have, is *not
our own*. All these are, as our Lord speaks, τὰ ἀλλότρια,[80] the
property of another—of God, our Creator. Now these either are   10
or are not employed according to his will. If they are so employed,
all is good; if they are not, all is evil. Again: it is his will that we
should continually grow in grace and in the living knowledge of
our Lord Jesus Christ.[81] Consequently every thought, word, and
work whereby this knowledge is increased, whereby we grow in   15
grace, is good; and every one whereby this knowledge is not
increased is truly and properly evil.
    3. We learn from hence, thirdly, that there are no works of
supererogation,[82] that we can never do more than our duty; seeing
all we have is not our own, but God's, all we can do is due to him. 20
We have not received this or that, or many things only, but
everything from him: therefore everything is his due. He that
gives us all must needs have a right to all. So that if we pay him
anything less than all we cannot be 'faithful stewards'. And
considering 'every man shall receive his own reward, according to 25
his own labour,'[83] we cannot be 'wise stewards' unless we labour
to the uttermost of our power; not leaving anything undone which
we possibly can do, but putting forth all our strength.
    4. Brethren, 'Who is an understanding man and endued with
knowledge among you?'[84] Let him show the wisdom from above   30

---

[79] Cf. John Gambold, 'Upon Listening to the Vibrations of a Clock', ll.5-6, in his *Works*
(1789), p. 266. Wesley had published this in his *Moral and Sacred Poems* (1744), III.195.
See also Wesley's letter to Samuel Furly, Nov. 10, 1756. Though Wesley and Gambold
had long since parted company, Wesley is still prepared to quote his quondam friend.
[80] Luke 16:12; cf. above, I.1.
[81] See 2 Pet. 3:18.
[82] Cf. Art. XIV, which rejects all such 'voluntary works besides, over and above, God's
commandments'. These may not be claimed 'without arrogance and impiety'. In the
Roman perspective, they are virtuous acts surpassing what is required by moral *duty* or
legal obligation. They are thus compared to other works, 'not as good works to evil ones but
as better works to good ones' (cf. *The New Catholic Encyclopedia*). And even Wesley allows
for this distinction in his doctrine of *facere quod in se est*.
[83] 1 Cor. 3:8.   [84] Cf. Jas. 3:13.

by walking suitably to his character. If he so account of himself as a steward of the manifold gifts of God, let him see that all his thoughts, and words, and works be agreeable to the post God has assigned him. It is no small thing to lay out for God all which you have received from God. It requires all your wisdom, all your resolution, all your patience and constancy; far more than ever you had by nature, but not more than you may have by grace. For his grace is sufficient for you,[85] and 'all things', you know, 'are possible to him that believeth.'[86] By faith, then, 'put on the Lord Jesus Christ;'[87] 'put on the whole armour of God,'[88] and you shall be enabled to glorify him in all your words and works, yea, to bring every thought into captivity to the obedience of Christ.[89]

Edinburgh
May 14, 1768

---

[85] See 2 Cor. 12:9.
[86] Mark 9:23.
[87] Rom. 13:14.
[88] Eph. 6:11.
[89] See 2 Cor. 10:5.

A
SERMON

Preached before the

SOCIETY

FOR

REFORMATION of Manners.

ON

SUNDAY, *January* 30, 1763.

AT THE

CHAPPEL in Weſt-Street, Seven-Dials.

By JOHN WESLEY, M.A.

Late Fellow of LINCOLN COLLEGE, OXFORD.

LONDON:

Printed, and ſold by *William Flexney*, near *Gray's-Inn-gate*, *Holbourn* ; by *Geo. Keith*, in *Grace-church-ſtreet*; by *John Danſon* the *Corner* of *Gutter-lane, Cheapſide* ; by *M. Engle-field*, at the *Bible* in *Weſt-ſtreet, Seven Dials* ; and at the *Foundery, Upper Moor-fields*.

THE REFORMATION OF MANNERS

AN INTRODUCTORY COMMENT

One of the prime concerns of the religious societies introduced into Restoration England by Dr. Anthony Horneck and others had been 'the reformation of manners'—the reinforcement of police control of public vice, drunkenness, prostitution, etc., with assistance from concerned citizens, together with active aid programmes in relief of the ill, the destitute, and the unemployed (cf. Josiah Woodward, An Account of the Societies for the Reformation of Manners, in London, Westminster, and other parts of the Kingdom . . . against prophaneness and debauchery, for the effecting a National Reformation . . . [1699]). *This project was underwritten by a network of neighbourhood 'societies', first organized in 1677 and then reorganized in 1691. The programmes of their annual meetings regularly included special sermons by eminent ministers; cf. the one hundred and twenty-eight sermons by William Wake, Isaac Watts, John Tillotson, Samuel Chandler, Joseph Burroughs, and others, listed in* Early Nonconformity, 1566–1800: A Catalogue of Books in Dr. Williams' Library, London *(Boston, Mass., G. K. Hall and Co., 1968). And, on February 13, 1698, the sermon had been preached (in the morning at St. James's, Westminster, and in the afternoon in St. Bride's, London) by the rector of Epworth parish, Lincolnshire, the Revd. Samuel Wesley, Sen. It was later published in* The Methodist Magazine *(1814), pp. 648-65, 727-36, and should be compared with this present sermon, sixty-eight years later, for their notable similarity.*

This movement of social reform seems to have ceased functioning by 1730 but was then revived in 1757 under the leadership of one 'W. Welsh' (see JWJ, February 2, 1766), and in 1763 John Wesley was invited to preach the 'Annual Sermon'. This took place on January 30, not at one of the fashionable city churches, but in Wesley's own 'Chapel in West Street, Seven Dials', for a society whose one hundred and sixty members numbered seventy Dissenters and only twenty 'regular' Anglicans.

This is another of Wesley's sermons ad aulam ('formal'), in a 'plain' but 'polite' style—and, it might be noted, on the same text as his father

*had used before him. In its substance it is one of the least evangelical of
any of Wesley's sermons after 1738; its definition of 'the church' in §2
sounds more 'congregational' than 'connexional'; its conclusions are
moralistic and hortatory. Its descriptions of public vice and crime in
mid-century London are confirmed, in part at least, by contemporary
observers (e.g., Boswell, Hogarth,* et al.*) and by* George Rudé,
Hanoverian London, 1714–1808, *ch. 5, and* Dorothy George,
London Life in the Eighteenth Century.

*It was printed as a fairly expensive pamphlet ('sixpence') in 1763,
and was then inserted into the* Works *(1771), Vol. IV; its third edition
in Wesley's lifetime is dated 1778. For its publishing history and
variant readings, see Appendix, Vol. 4 in this edn.; and* Bibliog, No.
254.

The Reformation of Manners

Psalm 94:16

Who will rise up with me against the wicked?[1]

1. In all ages men who neither feared God nor regarded man[2]
have combined together and formed confederacies to carry on the   5
works of darkness.[3] And herein they have shown themselves wise
in their generation;[4] for by this means they more effectually
promoted the kingdom of their father the devil[5] than otherwise
they could have done. On the other hand, men who did fear God
and desire the happiness of their fellow-creatures have in every   10
age found it needful to join together in order to oppose the works
of darkness, to spread the knowledge of God their Saviour, and to
promote his kingdom upon earth. Indeed he himself has
instructed them so to do. From the time that men were upon the
earth he hath taught them to join together in his service, and has   15
united them in one body by one spirit.[6] And for this very end he

---

[1] BCP, Psalter.   [2] See Luke 18:2.   [3] Rom. 13:12; Eph. 5:11.
[4] See Luke 16:18, which is also the text for No. 147, 'Wiser than the Children of Light'
(one of the early MS sermons).
[5] See John 8:44.
[6] See Eph. 4:4.

has joined them together, 'that he might destroy the works of the devil',[7] first in them that are already united, and by them in all that are round about them. ·

2. This is the original design of the church of Christ. It is a body
5 of men compacted together in order, first, to save each his own soul, then to assist each other in working out their salvation, and afterwards, as far as in them lies, to save all men from present and future misery, to overturn the kingdom of Satan, and set up the kingdom of Christ.[8] And this ought to be the continued care and
10 endeavour of every member of his church. Otherwise he is not worthy to be called a member thereof, as he is not a living member of Christ.

3. Accordingly this ought to be the constant care and endeavour of all those who are united together in these kingdoms,
15 and are commonly called 'the Church of England'. They are united together for this very end, to oppose the devil and all his works, and to wage war against the world and the flesh, his constant and faithful allies. But do they in fact answer the end of their union? Are all who style themselves 'members of the Church
20 of England' heartily engaged in opposing the works of the devil and fighting against the world and the flesh? Alas, we cannot say this. So far from it that a great part—I fear, the greater part of them—are themselves 'the world', the people that know not God to any saving purpose; are indulging day by day instead of
25 'mortifying the flesh, with its affections and desires';[9] and doing themselves those works of the devil[10] which they are peculiarly engaged to destroy.

4. There is therefore still need, even in this 'Christian country' (as we *courteously* style Great Britain)[11] yea, in this 'Christian
30 church' (if we may give that title to the bulk of our nation) of some to 'rise up against the wicked', and join together 'against the evil-doers'.[12] Nay, there was never more need than there is at this

---

[7] 1 John 3:8.
[8] Cf. this definition of 'the church' with those in No. 74, 'Of the Church'; also No. 92, 'On Zeal', II.5; *Popery Calmly Considered*, I.6; *A Collection of Forms of Prayer (Bibliog, No. 1; Vol. 8 of this edn.)*; his letter to Gilbert Joyce, May 22, 1750; his *Notes* on Matt. 16:18, and on Eph. 3:10 (where the church is defined as 'the theatre of divine wisdom').
[9] Cf. Rom. 8:13; Gal. 5:24 *(Notes)*.
[10] 1 John 3:8.
[11] Cf. this sarcastic touch with the suggestion in No. 65, 'The Duty of Reproving our Neighbour', §8, that 'a little well-placed raillery will pierce deeper than solid argument, [especially] when we have to do with those who are strangers to religion.'
[12] Ps. 94:16 (BCP).

day for 'them that fear the Lord' to 'speak often together'[13] on this very head—how they may 'lift up a standard against'[14] the iniquity which overflows the land. There is abundant cause for all the servants of God to join together against the works of the devil with united hearts and counsels and endeavours, to make a stand for 5 God, and to repress, as much as in them lies, these 'floods of ungodliness'.[15]

5. For this end a few persons in London, towards the close of the last century, united together, and after a while were termed 'The Society for Reformation of Manners'.[16] And incredible good 10 was done by them for near forty years. But then, most of the original members being gone to their reward, those who succeeded them grew faint in their mind, and departed from the work; so that a few years ago the Society ceased, nor did any of the kind remain in the kingdom. 15

6. It is a society of the same nature which has been lately formed. I purpose to show, first, the *nature* of their design, and the *steps* they have hitherto taken; (2), the *excellency* of it, with the various *objections* which have been raised against it; (3), *what manner of men* they ought to be who engage in such a design; and 20 (4), with what *spirit* and in what *manner* they should proceed in the prosecution of it. I shall conclude with an *application* both to them and to all that fear God.

I. 1. I am, first, to show the *nature* of their design, and the *steps* they have hitherto taken. 25

It was on a Lord's Day in August 1757 that in a small company who were met for prayer and religious conversation mention was made of the gross and open profanation of that sacred day, by

---

[13] Cf. Mal. 3:16.
[14] Cf. Isa. 59:19.
[15] Cf. Pss. 18:3 (BCP), and 18:4 (AV); see also 2 Sam. 22:5.
[16] Not one but many; cf. Josiah Woodward, *Account of the . . . Societies . . . .* Queen Mary's Letter of Approval is dated July 9, 1691; King William's Charge to the Societies was dated Feb. 24, 1697. The original society was composed of 'Members of Parliament, Justices of the Peace, and considerable citizens of London' (p. 10). There was 'a second society of tradesmen and others' (p. 11), and 'a third society of constables . . .' (pp. 11-12). 'A fourth . . . is of supporters of the magistrates' (pp. 12-13). 'There are eight other related and mixed bodies of housekeepers and officers in the several quarters of London, Westminster, and Southwark.' (pp. 14-15). 'Nine and thirty religious societies in London, Westminster, and other parts of the nation' (p. 15). Cf. Robert South's comment about the religious societies in *Sermons Preached Upon Several Occasions* (1st edn., 1737; Philadelphia, Sorin and Ball, 1844), II.105: 'Their leverage of influence is the sense of shame that decent people have in the face of the disapproval of polite society.'

persons buying and selling, keeping open shop, tippling in alehouses, and standing or sitting in the streets, roads, or fields, vending their wares as on common days; especially in Moorfields,[17] which was then full of them every Sunday, from one
5 end to the other. It was considered what method could be taken to redress these grievances. And it was agreed that six of them should in the morning wait upon Sir John Fielding[18] for instruction. They did so. He approved of the design, and directed them how to carry it into execution.
10   2. They first delivered petitions to the right honourable the Lord Mayor and the Court of Aldermen, to the Justices sitting at Hicks's Hall,[19] and those in Westminster Hall.[20] And they received from all these honourable benches much encouragement to proceed.
15   3. It was next judged proper to signify their design to many persons of eminent rank, and to the body of the clergy, as well as the ministers of other denominations, belonging to the several churches and meetings in and about the cities of London and Westminster. And they had the satisfaction to meet with a hearty
20 consent and universal approbation from them.
   4. They then printed and dispersed, at their own expense, several thousand books of instruction to constables and other

---

[17] A large open moor north of the walled city, split by the new 'City Road' which led out from the Moorgate (opened in 1415). It was divided into 'Moorfields', 'Middle Moorfields' (later 'Finsbury Pavement'), and 'Upper Moorfields'. In Upper Moorfields there were the Royal Artillery grounds, Bunhill Fields, the Quaker Burying Ground, and, after 1739, Wesley's London headquarters (in the Foundery). It was a favourite resort for the London poor and 'middling sort', and thus a happy hunting ground for mountebanks and petty criminals. It was also the site of many of the great outdoor preaching services held by the Wesleys and Whitefield.

[18] The blind half-brother and successor to Henry Fielding (author of *Tom Jones*) as the chief magistrate at the Bow Street Courts. A man of 'turbulent disposition', he was zealous in his war on crime and criminals and interested in various philanthropic causes. William Cole said of him, in *The Cambridge Chronicle*, June 7, 1766, that 'though stark blind and of no great reputation for strict integrity, he was generally esteemed as a very useful member of society.'

[19] Sir Baptist Hickes, first Viscount of Campden and first 'shopkeeper' ennobled by James I, 'had built at his own cost a sessions-house for the Middlesex magistrates in St. John's Street, Clerkenwell. It was known as Hick's Hall and was in use as a low court from 1612 to 1788' (see *DNB*), and served the boroughs of Holborn, St. Pancras, and Moorfields.

[20] A part of the Palace of Westminster, built by William Rufus and altered by Richard II. It has been used for many purposes and is now incorporated into the New Palace (or Houses of Parliament). In Wesley's time it was in use as 'a low court' (e.g., Common Pleas and the King's Bench) and also as a sort of shopping centre.

parish officers, explaining and enforcing their several duties. And to prevent as far as possible the necessity of proceeding to an actual execution of the laws, they likewise printed and dispersed in all parts of the town dissuasives from sabbath-breaking, extracts from Acts of Parliament against it, and notices to the 5 offenders.

5. The way being paved by these precautions, it was in the beginning of the year 1758 that, after notices delivered again and again, which were as often set at naught, actual informations were made to magistrates against persons profaning the Lord's day. By 10 this means they first cleared the streets and fields of those notorious offenders who, without any regard either to God or the king, were selling their wares from morning to night. They proceeded to a more difficult attempt, the preventing *tippling*[21] on the Lord's day, spending the time in alehouses which ought to be 15 spent in the more immediate worship of God. Herein they were exposed to abundance of reproach, to insult and abuse of every kind; having not only the tipplers and those who entertained them, the alehouse keepers, to contend with, but rich and honourable men, partly the landlords of those alehouse keepers, 20 partly those who furnished them with drink, and in general all who gained by their sins. Some of these were not only men of substance but men in authority; nay, in more instances than one they were the very persons before whom the delinquents were brought. And the treatment they gave those who laid the 25 informations naturally encouraged 'the beasts of the people'[22] to follow their example, and to use them as fellows not fit to live upon the earth. Hence they made no scruple, not only to treat them with the basest language, not only to throw at them mud or stones or whatever came to hand, but many times to beat them 30 without mercy, and to drag them over the stones, or through the

---

[21] Cf. Johnson, *Dictionary:* 'To waste life over the cup.' See also, Shakespeare, *Anthony and Cleopatra*, I.iv.16, 18-20:

> Let us grant it is not amiss to . . . sit
> And keep the turn of tippling with a slave,
> To reel the streets at noon.

[22] I.e., the London mob; from Ps. 68:30 (BCP). Cf. also, No. 107, 'On God's Vineyard', IV.2; JWJ, June 5, 1765; *Free Thoughts on Public Affairs (Bibliog. No. 325; Vol. 15 of this edn.); Thoughts Upon Liberty*, §23 (*Bibliog.* No. 337; Vol. 15 of this edn.). For Wesley's frequent references to 'the great vulgar', cf. No. 31, 'Sermon on the Mount, XI', I.6 and n.

kennels.[23] And that they did not murder them was not for want of will; but the bridle was in their teeth.

6. Having therefore received help from God, they went on to restrain *bakers* likewise from spending so great a part of the Lord's
5 day in exercising the work of their calling.[24] But many of these were more noble than the victuallers. They were so far from resenting this, or looking upon it as an affront, that several who had been hurried down the stream of custom[25] to act contrary to their own conscience, sincerely thanked them for their labour,
10 and acknowledged it as a real kindness.[26]

7. In clearing the streets, fields, and alehouses of sabbath-breakers, they fell upon another sort of offenders as mischievous to society as any, namely, *gamesters* of various kinds. Some of these were of the lowest and vilest class, commonly called 'gamblers',[27]
15 who make a trade of seizing on young and unexperienced men, and tricking them out of all their money. And after they have beggared them, they frequently teach them the same mystery of iniquity.[28] Several nests of these they have rooted out, and constrained not a few of them honestly to earn their bread by the
20 sweat of their brow and the labour of their hands.

8. Increasing in number and strength, they extended their views, and began not only to repress *profane swearing*, but to remove out of our streets another public nuisance and scandal of the Christian name—*common prostitutes*. Many of these were
25 stopped in their mid-career of audacious wickedness. And in order to go to the root of the disease, many of the *houses* that

---

[23] I.e., 'gutters'. Cf. Johnson's definition ('the water-course of a street') and his example from Arbuthnot ('He came in so dirty as if he had been dragged through the kennel'). Cf. also JWJ, June 16, 1763.

[24] The first two edns. added here the footnote: 'They did not mean by this the restraining them from baking provision for the poor.' This was omitted from the edn. in Wesley's *Works* (1771), IV.90.

[25] Cf. No. 25, 'Sermon on the Mount, V', IV.2 and n.

[26] Alexander Mather, later Wesley's trusted assistant, tells how in 1753 he was employed by William Marriott, master baker in the Moorfields area, but served notice that he would leave because of an uneasy conscience about the universal practice of 'the baking of pans' on Sundays. Marriott and a neighbouring baker canvassed all the master bakers in the area to secure a general agreement to give up the practice, but to no avail. He then told his own customers that he himself would bake no more on Sundays. And yet his business flourished the more, and he became one of the mainstays of Wesley's Foundery society. See *AM* (1780), III.96-98.

[27] The noun 'gambler' was a slang word of recent coinage, thus defined in Johnson's *Dictionary*: '*Gambler* (a cant word, I suppose, for *game* or *gamester*), a knave whose practice it is to invite the unwary to game and cheat them.'

[28] See 2 Thess. 2:7.

entertained them have been detected, prosecuted according to
law, and totally suppressed. And some of the poor, desolate
women themselves, though fallen to

> The lowest line of human infamy,[29]

have acknowledged the gracious providence of God, and broke 5
off their sins by lasting repentance. Several of these have been
placed out, and several received into the Magdalen Hospital.[30]
　9. If a little digression may be allowed, who can sufficiently
admire the wisdom of divine providence in the disposal of the
times and seasons so as to suit one occurrence to another? For 10
instance. Just at a time when many of these poor creatures, being
stopped in their course of sin, found a desire of leading a better
life, as it were in answer to that sad question, 'But if I quit the way
I now am in, what can I do to live? For I am not mistress of any
trade; and I have no friends that will receive me:' I say, just at this 15
time, God has prepared the Magdalen Hospital. Here those who
have no trade, nor any friends to receive them, are received with
all tenderness. Here they may live, and that with comfort, being
provided with all things that are needful 'for life and godliness'.[31]
　10. But to return. The number of persons brought to justice 20
From August 1757 to August 1762, is 　　　　　9,596
From thence to the present time,
　　For unlawful gaming, and profane swearing, 　　40
　　For sabbath-breaking, 　　　　　　　　　　　400
　　Lewd women, and keepers of ill houses, 　　　550 25
　　For offering to sale obscene prints, 　　　　___?_
　　　　　In all, 　　　　　　　　　　　　　10,588
　11. In the admission of members into the society no regard is
had to any particular sect or party. Whoever is found upon inquiry
to be a good man is readily admitted. And none who has selfish or 30
pecuniary views will long continue therein; not only because he

---

[29] Apparently, a conflation of a line from Prior's 'Henry and Emma' (line 498) and one
from Samuel Wesley, Jun., 'The Prisons Opened' (*Poems*, 1736, p. 180), l. 110. Prior: 'O
line extreme of human infamy'; Wesley: 'O lowest depth of human misery'. But see also
John Van Brugh, 'the lowest ebb of human infamy' (*The Provoked Wife* [1697], Act III). Cf.
also No. 115, 'Dives and Lazarus', I.2, where Wesley uses the same line as here, applied
there to beggars.
[30] A home for reformed ex-prostitutes, founded in 1758 by Jonas Hanway and Robert
Dingley. Its first location was in Goodman's Fields. Dr. William Dodd preached the
inaugural sermon and acted as its chaplain.
[31] Cf. 2 Pet. 1:3.

can gain nothing thereby, but because he would quickly be a loser, inasmuch as he must commence subscriber as soon as he is a member. Indeed the vulgar cry is 'These are all *Whitfelites.*'[32] But it is a great mistake. About twenty of the constantly sub-
5 scribing members are all that are in connexion with Mr. Whitefield. About fifty are in connexion with Mr. Wesley. About twenty, who are of the established Church, have no connexion with either; and about seventy are Dissenters, who make in all an hundred and sixty. There are indeed many more who assist in the
10 work by occasional subscriptions.

II. 1. These are the *steps* which have been hitherto taken in prosecution of this design. I am, in the second place, to show the *excellency* thereof, notwithstanding the *objections* which have been raised against it. Now this may appear from several considera-
15 tions. And, first, from hence—that the making an open stand against all the ungodliness and unrighteousness which over-spread our land as a flood is one of the noblest ways of confessing Christ in the face of his enemies. It is giving glory to God, and showing mankind that even in these dregs of time,[33]

20

There are, who faith prefer,
Though few, and piety to God.[34]

And what more excellent than to render to God the honour due unto his name?[35] To declare by a stronger proof than words, even by suffering, and running all hazards, 'Verily there is a reward for
25 the righteous; doubtless there is a God that judgeth the earth.'[36]

2. How excellent is the design to prevent in any degree the dishonour done to his glorious name, the contempt which is poured on his authority, and the scandal brought upon our holy religion by the gross, flagrant wickedness of those who are still
30 called by the name of Christ! To stem in any degree the torrent of

---

[32] A clue to the popular pronunciation of 'Whitefield'.

[33] 'Dregs of time'. A variation of Dryden's familiar phrase, 'dregs of life' (in *Aureng-Zebe*, IV.1)? But see also Samuel Wesley, Sen., who cites only 'the father of old' as saying, 'To what dregs of time are we reserved.' Wesley uses it again in No. 102, 'Of Former Times', §2. Cf. also Law, *Serious Call* (*Works*, IV.25); and *Christian Prefection* (*Works*, III.117).

[34] Cf. Milton, *Paradise Lost*, vi.143-44:

All are not of thy train; there be, who faith
Prefer, and piety to God, . . .

See also No. 79, 'On Dissipation', §15; and *An Earnest Appeal*, §52 (11:64 in this edn.).
[35] Pss. 29:2; 96:8 (BCP).   [36] Ps. 58:10 (BCP).

vice, to repress the floods of ungodliness, to remove in any measure those occasions of blaspheming the worthy name whereby we are called,[37] is one of the noblest designs it can possibly enter into the heart of man[38] to conceive.

3. And as this design thus evidently tends to bring 'glory to God 5 in the highest', so it no less manifestly conduces to the establishing 'peace upon earth'.[39] For as all sin directly tends both to destroy our peace with God by setting him at open defiance, to banish peace from our own breasts, and to set every man's sword against his neighbour; so whatever prevents or removes sin does 10 in the same degree promote peace, both peace in our own soul, peace with God, and peace with one another. Such are the genuine fruits of this design, even in the present world. But why should we confine our views to the narrow bounds of time and space? Rather pass over these into eternity. And what fruit of it 15 shall we find there? Let the Apostle speak: 'Brethren, if one of you err from the truth, and one convert him' (not to this or that opinion, but to God!) 'let him know that he who converteth a sinner from the error of his way shall save a soul from death, and hide a multitude of sins.'[a] 20

4. Nor is it to individuals only, whether those who betray others into sin or those that are liable to be betrayed and destroyed by them, that the benefit of this design redounds, but to the whole community whereof we are members. For is it not a sure observation, 'rightousness exalteth a nation'? And is it not as sure 25 on the other hand that 'sin is a reproach to *any* people'?[40] Yea, and bringeth down the curse of God upon them? So far therefore as righteousness in any branch is promoted, so far is the national interest advanced. So far as sin, especially open sin, is restrained, the curse and reproach are removed from us. Whoever therefore 30 they are that labour herein, they are general benefactors. They are the truest friends of their king and country. And in the same proportion as their design takes place, there can be no doubt but God will give national prosperity, in accomplishment of his faithful word, 'Them that honour me, I will honour.'[41] 35

[a] Jas. 5:19-20.

---

[37] See Jas. 2:7.   [38] See 1 Cor. 2:9.
[39] Luke 2:14.
[40] Prov. 14:34.
[41] 1 Sam. 2:30.

5. But it is objected, 'However excellent a design this is, it does not concern *you*. For are there not persons to whom the repressing these offences and punishing the offenders properly belong? Are there not constables and other parish officers, who
5 are bound by oath to this very thing?' There are. Constables and church wardens in particular are engaged by solemn oaths to give due information against profaners of the Lord's day, and all other scandalous sinners. But if they leave it undone, if notwithstanding their oaths they trouble not themselves about the matter, it
10 concerns all that fear God, that love mankind, and that wish well to their king and country, to pursue this design with the very same vigour as if there were no such officers existing. It being just the same thing, if they are of no use, as if they had no being.

6. 'But this is only a pretence; their real design is to get money
15 by giving informations.' So it has frequently and roundly been affirmed, but without the least shadow of truth. The contrary may be proved by a thousand instances: no member of the Society takes any part of the money which is by the law allotted to the informer. They never did from the beginning, nor does any of
20 them ever receive anything to suppress or withdraw their information. This is another mistake, if not wilful slander, for which there is not the least foundation.

7. 'But the design is impracticable. Vice is risen to such an head that it is impossible to suppress it; especially by such means. For
25 what can an handful of poor people do in opposition to all the world?' 'With men this is impossible, but not with God.'[42] And they trust, not in themselves, but him. Be then the patrons of vice ever so strong, to him they are no more than grasshoppers.[43] And all means are alike to him. It is the same thing with God 'to deliver
30 by many or by few'.[44] The small number therefore of those who are on the Lord's side is nothing, neither the great number of those that are against him. Still he doth whatever pleaseth him. And 'there is no counsel or strength against the Lord.'[45]

8. 'But if the end you aim at be really to reform sinners, you
35 choose the wrong means. It is the Word of God must effect this, and not human laws. And it is the work of ministers, not of magistrates. Therefore the applying to these can only produce an outward reformation. It makes no change in the heart.'

[42] Cf. Matt. 19:26.
[44] Cf. 1 Sam. 14:6.
[43] See Jer. 46:23.
[45] Cf. Prov. 21:30.

It is true the Word of God is the chief ordinary means whereby he changes both the hearts and lives of sinners; and he does this chiefly by the ministers of the gospel. But it is likewise true that the magistrate is 'the minister of God'; and that he is designed of God 'to be a terror to evil-doers',[46] by executing human laws upon them. If this does not change the heart, yet to prevent outward sin is one valuable point gained. There is so much the less dishonour done to God, less scandal brought on our holy religion, less curse and reproach upon our nation, less temptation laid in the way of others. Yea, and less wrath heaped up by the sinners themselves against the day of wrath.[47]

9. 'Nay, rather more; for it makes many of them hypocrites, pretending to be what they are not. Others, by exposing them to shame, and putting them to expense, are made impudent and desperate in wickedness; so that in reality none of them are any better, if they are not worse than they were before.'

This is a mistake all over. For (1), where are these hypocrites? We know none who have pretended to be what they were not. (2). The exposing obstinate offenders to shame, and putting them to expense, does not make them desperate in offending, but afraid to offend. (3). Some of them, far from being worse, are substantially better, the whole tenor of their lives being changed. Yea, (4), some are inwardly changed, even 'from darkness to light, and from the power of Satan unto God'.[48]

10. 'But many are not convinced that buying or selling on the Lord's day is a sin.'

If they are not convinced, they ought to be: it is high time they should. The case is as plain as plain can be. For if an open, wilful breach both of the law of God and the law of the land is not sin, pray what is? And if such a breach both of divine and human laws is not to be punished because a man is not convinced it is a sin, there is an end of all execution of justice, and all men may live as they list.

11. 'But *mild* methods ought to be tried first.' They ought. And so they are. A mild admonition is given to every offender before the law is put in execution against him; nor is any man prosecuted till he has express notice that this will be the case unless he will prevent that prosecution by removing the cause of it. In every case the mildest method is used which the nature of the case will bear;

---

[46] Cf. Rom. 13:3, 4.　　　　[47] See Rom. 2:5.　　　　[48] Acts 26:18.

nor are severer means ever applied but when they are absolutely necessary to the end.

12. 'Well, but after all this stir about reformation, what real good has been done?' Unspeakable good; and abundantly more than anyone could have expected in so short a time, considering the small number of the instruments, and the difficulties they had to encounter. Much evil has been already prevented, and much has been removed. Many sinners have been outwardly reformed; some have been inwardly changed. The honour of him whose name we bear, so openly affronted, has been openly defended. And it is not easy to determine how many and how great blessings even this little stand, made for God and his cause against his daring enemies, may already have derived upon our whole nation. On the whole, then, after all the objections that can be made, reasonable men may still conclude, a more excellent design could scarce ever enter into the heart of man.

III. 1. But *what manner of men* ought they to be who engage in such a design? Some may imagine any that are willing to assist therein ought readily to be admitted; and that the greater the number of members, the greater will be their influence. But this is by no means true; matter of fact undeniably proves the contrary. While the former Society for Reformation of Manners consisted of chosen members only, though neither many, rich, nor powerful, they broke through all opposition, and were eminently successful in every branch of their undertaking. But when a number of men, less carefully chosen, were received into that Society, they grew less and less useful till, by insensible degrees, they dwindled into nothing.

2. The *number* therefore of the members is no more to be attended to than the riches or eminence. This is a work of God. It is undertaken in the name of God, and for his sake. It follows that men who neither love nor fear God have no part or lot in this matter.[49] 'Why takest thou my covenant in thy mouth,' may God say to any of these, 'whereas thou' thyself 'hatest to be reformed, and have cast my words behind thee?'[50] Whoever therefore lives in any known sin is not fit to engage in reforming sinners. More especially if he is guilty in any instance, or in the least degree, of

---

[49] Acts 8:21.
[50] Cf. Ps. 50:16-17 (BCP).

profaning the name of God, of buying, selling, or doing any unnecessary work on the Lord's day, or offending in any other of those instances which this society is peculiarly designed to reform. No; let none who stands himself in need of this reformation presume to meddle with such an undertaking. First 5 let him 'pull the beam out of his own eye'.[51] Let him be himself *unblameable* in all things.

3. Not that this will suffice. Everyone engaging herein should be more than a harmless man.[52] He should be a man of *faith;* having at least such a degree of that 'evidence of things not seen'[53] 10 as to 'aim not at the things that are seen, which are temporal, but at those that are not seen, which are eternal';[54] such a faith as produces a steady *fear of God*, with a lasting resolution by his grace to abstain from all that he has forbidden, and to do all that he has commanded. He will more especially need that particular branch 15 of faith, 'confidence in God'.[55] It is this faith which 'removes mountains',[56] which 'quenches the violence of fire',[57] which breaks through all opposition, and enables 'one' to stand against and 'chase a thousand',[58] knowing in whom his strength lies, and even when he has 'the sentence of death in himself, trusting in 20 him who raiseth the dead'.[59]

4. He that has faith and confidence in God will of consequence be a man of *courage*. And such it is highly needful every man should be who engages in this undertaking. For many things will occur in the prosecution thereof which are terrible to nature; 25 indeed so terrible that all who 'confer with flesh and blood'[60] will be afraid to encounter them. Here therefore true courage has its proper place, and is necessary in the highest degree. And this, faith only can supply. A believer can say,

> I fear no denial; 30
> No danger I fear:
> Nor start from the trial;
> For Jesus is near.[61]

---

[51] Cf. Matt. 7:5.
[52] Cf. No. 119, 'Walking by Sight and Walking by Faith', §18, where Wesley speaks of 'hellish harmlessness'; see also No. 32, 'Sermon on the Mount, XII', II.2 and n.
[53] Heb. 11:1. [54] Cf. 2 Cor. 4:18.
[55] Cf. 2 Thess. 3:4. [56] Cf. Matt. 17:20; 1 Cor. 13:2.
[57] Cf. Heb. 11:34. [58] Deut. 32:30; Josh. 23:10.
[59] Cf. 2 Cor. 1:9. [60] Cf. Gal. 1:16.
[61] John and Charles Wesley, *Hymns and Sacred Poems* (1742), p. 137 (*Poet. Wks.*, II. 197). Orig., 'While Jesus is near'.

5. To courage, *patience* is nearly allied; the one regarding future, the other present evils. And whoever joins in carrying on a design of this nature will have great occasion for this. For notwithstanding all his unblameableness, he will find himself just
5 in Ishmael's situation, 'his hand against every man, and every man's hand against him'.[62] And no wonder. If it be true that 'all who will live godly shall suffer persecution,'[63] how eminently must this be fulfilled in them who, not content to live godly themselves, compel the ungodly to do so too, or at least to refrain from
10 notorious ungodliness! Is not this declaring war against all the world? Setting all the children of the devil[64] at defiance? And will not Satan himself, 'the prince of this world',[65] 'the ruler of the darkness'[66] thereof, exert all his subtlety and all his force in support of his tottering kingdom? Who can expect the 'roaring
15 lion'[67] will tamely submit to have the prey plucked out of his teeth? 'Ye have,' therefore, 'need of patience, that when ye have done the will of God ye may receive the promise.'[68]

6. And ye have need of *steadiness*, that ye may 'hold fast this profession of your faith without wavering'.[69] This also should be
20 found in all that unite in this society; which is not a task for a 'double-minded man', for one that 'is unstable in his ways'.[70] He that is as a reed shaken with the wind[71] is not fit for this warfare, which demands a firm purpose of soul, a constant, determined resolution. One that is wanting in this may 'set his hand to the
25 plough'; but how soon will he 'look back'?[72] He may indeed 'endure for a time; but when persecution or tribulation', public or private troubles, 'arise because of the work, immediately he is offended'.[73]

7. Indeed it is hard for any to persevere in so unpleasing a work
30 unless *love* overpowers both pain and fear. And therefore it is highly expedient that all engaged therein have 'the love of God shed abroad in their hearts';[74] that they should all be able to declare, 'we love him, because he first loved us.'[75] The presence of him whom their soul loveth[76] will then make their labour light.

---

[62] Gen. 16:12.
[63] Cf. 2 Tim. 3:12.
[64] 1 John 3:10.
[65] John 12:31; 14:30; 16:11.
[66] Cf. Eph. 6:12.
[67] 1 Pet. 5:8.
[68] Cf. Heb. 10:36.
[69] Cf. Heb. 10:23.
[70] Jas. 1:8.
[71] Matt. 11:7.
[72] Cf. Luke 9:62.
[73] Cf. Mark 4:17.
[74] Cf. Rom. 5:5.
[75] 1 John 4:19.
[76] See S. of S. 3:1, etc.

They can then say, not from the wildness of an heated imagination, but with the utmost truth and soberness,

> With thee conversing, I forget
> All time, and toil, and care;
> Labour is rest, and pain is sweet,
> While thou, my God, art here.[77]

5

8. What adds a still greater sweetness even to labour and pain is the Christian *love of our neighbour*. When they 'love their neighbour', that is, every soul of man, 'as themselves',[78] as their own souls; when 'the love of Christ constrains'[79] them to love one 10 another, 'even as he loved us';[80] when as he 'tasted death for every man',[81] so they are 'ready to lay down their life for their brethren'[82] (including in that number *every man*, every soul for which Christ died), what prospect of danger will then be able to fright them from their labour of love! What suffering will they not be ready 15 to undergo to save one soul from everlasting burnings![83] What continuance of labour, disappointment, pain, will vanquish their fixed resolution! Will they not be

> 'Gainst all repulses steeled, nor ever tired
> With toilsome day, or ill-succeeding night?[84]

20

So love both 'hopeth and endureth all things'. So 'charity never faileth.'[85]

9. Love is necessary for all the members of such a society on another account likewise; even because it 'is not puffed up';[86] it

---

[77] John and Charles Wesley, 'On a Journey', *Hymns and Sacred Poems* (1740), p. 127 (*Poet. Wks.*, I.304). Orig., 'If thou, . . .'. Cf. Milton, *Paradise Lost*, iv.639-40:

> With thee conversing, I forget all time,
> All seasons and their change; all please alike.

See also Nos. 82, 'On Temptation', III.4; 84, *The Important Question*, III.6; Wesley's letter to Hester Ann Roe, Oct. 6, 1776; and JWJ, Mar. 3, 1753, where he quotes the last two lines of this verse.

[78] Cf. Lev. 19:18, etc.

[79] Cf. 2 Cor. 5:14.

[80] Cf. Eph. 5:2.

[81] Cf. Heb. 2:9.

[82] Cf. 1 John 3:16. Notice the definition here of 'brethren' as *every man . . .* and compare it with the similar definition of 'neighbour', cf. No. 7, 'The Way to the Kingdom', I.8 and n.

[83] Isa. 33:14.

[84] Samuel Wesley, Jun., 'The Battle of the Sexes', xxi. 3-4 (*Poems*, 1736, p. 31); cf. Wesley, *A Collection of Moral and Sacred Poems* (1744), III.27.

[85] Cf. 1 Cor. 13:7-8.

[86] 1 Cor. 13:4.

produces not only courage and patience, but *humility*. And Oh! how needful is this for all who are so employed! What can be of more importance than that they should be little, and mean, and base, and vile in their own eyes? For otherwise, should they think
5 themselves anything, should they impute anything to themselves, should they admit anything of a pharisaic spirit, 'trusting in themselves that they were righteous, and despising others',[87] nothing could more directly tend to overthrow the whole design. For then they would not only have all the world, but also God
10 himself to contend with; seeing he 'resisteth the proud, and giveth grace' only 'to the humble'.[88] Deeply conscious therefore should every member of this society be of his own foolishness, weakness, helplessness; continually hanging with his whole soul upon him who alone hath wisdom and strength, with an unspeakable
15 conviction that 'the help which is done upon earth, God doth it himself;'[89] and that it is he *alone* 'who worketh in us, both to will and to do of his good pleasure'.[90]

10. One point more whoever engages in this design should have deeply impressed on his heart, namely, that 'the wrath of
20 man worketh not the righteousness of God.'[91] Let him therefore 'learn of' him 'who was meek' as well as lowly.[92] And let him abide in meekness as well as humility: 'with all lowliness and meekness', let him 'walk worthy of the vocation wherewith he is called'.[93] Let them be 'gentle toward all men',[94] good or bad, for his own sake,
25 for their sake, for Christ's sake. Are any 'ignorant and out of the way'? Let him 'have compassion' upon them.[95] Do they even *oppose* the word and the work of God; yea, set themselves in battle array against it? So much the more hath he need 'in meekness to instruct those who' thus 'oppose themselves', if haply they may
30 'awake out of the snare of the devil', and no more be 'taken captive at his will'.[96]

IV. 1. From the qualifications of those who are proper to engage in such an undertaking as this I proceed to show, fourthly, with what *spirit* and in what *manner* it ought to be pursued. First,
35 with what spirit. Now this first regards the *motive* which is to be

[87] Cf. Luke 18:9.
[89] Cf. Ps. 121:2; Eccles. 3:14.
[91] Jas. 1:20.
[93] Cf. Eph. 4:1, 2.
[95] Heb. 5:2.

[88] 1 Pet. 5:5.
[90] Cf. Phil. 2:13.
[92] Cf. Matt. 11:29.
[94] 2 Tim. 2:24.
[96] Cf. 2 Tim. 2:25-26.

preserved in every step that is taken. For 'if' at any time 'the light which is in thee be darkness, how great is that darkness!' But 'if thine eye be single, thy whole body shall be full of light.'[97] This is therefore continually to be remembered, and carried into every word and action. Nothing is to be spoke or done, either great or 5 small, with a view to any temporal advantage; nothing with a view to the favour or esteem, the love or the praise of men. But the intention, the eye of the mind,[98] is always to be fixed on the glory of God and good of man.

2. But the spirit with which everything is to be done regards the 10 *temper*, as well as the motive. And this is no other than that which has been described above. For the same courage, patience, steadiness, which qualify a man for the work, are to be exercised therein. 'Above all' let him 'take the shield of faith'; this will quench a thousand fiery darts.'[99] Let him exert all the faith which 15 God has given him, in every trying hour. And 'let all his doings be done in love;'[100] never let this be wrested from him. Neither must many waters quench this love, nor the floods of ingratitude drown it.[101] 'Let' likewise that lowly 'mind be in him which was also in Christ Jesus'.[102] Yea, and let him 'be clothed with humility',[103] 20 filling his heart, and adorning his whole behaviour. At the same time let him 'put on bowels of mercies, gentleness, long-suffering';[104] avoiding the least appearance of malice, bitterness, anger, or resentment; knowing it is our calling, not to be 'overcome of evil, but to overcome evil with good'.[105] In order to preserve this 25 humble, gentle love, it is needful to do all things with *recollection* of spirit, *watching* against all *hurry* or dissipation of thought, as well as against pride, wrath, or surliness. But this can be no otherwise preserved than by 'continuing instant in prayer',[106] both before and after he comes into the field, and during the whole action; 30 and by doing all in the *spirit of sacrifice*, offering all to God, through the Son of his love.

3. As to the outward *manner* of acting, a general rule is, let it be expressive of these inward tempers. But to be more particular. (1). Let every man beware not to 'do evil that good may come'.[107] 35

[97] Cf. Matt. 6:22-23.
[98] For Wesley's other uses of this metaphor, see No. 12, 'The Witness of Our Own Spirit', §11 and n.
[99] See Eph. 6:16.   [100] Cf. 1 Cor. 16:14 *(Notes)*.   [101] See S. of S. 8:7.
[102] Cf. Phil. 2:5.   [103] 1 Pet. 5:5.   [104] Cf. Col. 3:12.
[105] Cf. Rom. 12:21.   [106] Rom. 12:12.   [107] Rom. 3:8.

Therefore, 'putting away all lying', let 'every man speak the truth to his neighbour'.[108] Use no *fraud* or *guile*, either in order to detect or to punish any man, but 'by simplicity and godly sincerity'[109] 'commend yourself to men's consciences in the sight of God.'[110] It
5 is probable that by your adhering to these rules fewer offenders will be convicted. But so much the more will the blessing of God accompany the whole undertaking.

4. But let innocence be joined with *prudence*, properly so called. Not that offspring of hell which 'the world' *calls* prudence, which
10 is mere craft, cunning dissimulation; but with that 'wisdom from above'[111] which our Lord peculiarly recommends to all who would promote his kingdom upon earth. 'Be ye therefore wise as serpents', while ye are 'harmless as doves'.[112] This wisdom will instruct you how to suit your words and whole behaviour to the
15 persons with whom you have to do, to the time, place, and all other circumstances. It will teach you to cut off occasion of offence, even from those who seek occasion, and to do things of the most offensive nature in the least offensive manner that is possible.

20 5. Your *manner of speaking*, particularly to offenders, should be at all times deeply *serious* (lest it appear like insulting or triumphing over them), rather inclining to *sad;* showing that you pity them for what they do, and sympathize with them in what they suffer. Let your *air* and *tone* of voice, as well as words, be
25 *dispassionate, calm, mild;* yea, where it would not appear like dissimulation, even *kind* and *friendly*. In some cases, where it will probably be received as it is meant, you may *profess* the *goodwill* you bear them; but at the same time (that it may not be thought to proceed from fear, or any wrong inclination) professing your
30 *intrepidity* and inflexible *resolution* to oppose and punish vice to the uttermost.

V. 1. It remains only to make some application of what has been said, partly to you who are already engaged in this work, partly to all that fear God, and more especially to them that love as well as
35 fear him.

---

[108] Cf. Eph. 4:25.   [109] Cf. 2 Cor. 1:12.
[110] Cf. 2 Cor. 4:2.
[111] Jas. 3:17. Cf. No. 109, *The Trouble and Rest of Good Men*, II.3, where Wesley defines 'controversy' as 'the offspring of hell'. Cf. also, Nos. 138A and 138B, 'On Dissimulation'.
[112] Matt. 10:16.

With regard to you who are already engaged in this work, the first advice I would give you is calmly and deeply to consider the nature of your undertaking. Know what you are about; be throughly acquainted with what you have in hand. Consider the objections which are made to the whole of your undertaking. And 5 before you proceed, be satisfied that those objections have no real weight. Then may every man act as he is fully persuaded in his own mind.[113]

2. I advise you, secondly, be not in haste to increase your number. And in adding thereto regard not wealth, rank, or any 10 outward circumstance. Only regard the qualifications above described. Inquire diligently whether the person proposed be of an *unblameable carriage*, and whether he be a man of *faith, courage, patience, steadiness*, whether he be a *lover* of God and man. If so, he will add to your strength as well as number. If not, you will lose by 15 him more than you gain. For you will displease God. And be not afraid to purge out from among you any who do not answer the preceding character. By thus lessening your number you will increase your strength; you will be 'vessels meet for your master's use'.[114]   20

3. I would, thirdly, advise you narrowly to observe from what *motive* you at any time act or speak. Beware that your intention be not stained with any regard either to profit or praise. Whatever you do, 'do it to the Lord,'[115] as the servants of Christ.[116] Do not aim at pleasing yourself in any point, but pleasing him whose you 25 are, and whom you serve.[117] Let your eye be single[118] from first to last; eye God alone in every word and work.

4. I advise you, in the fourth place, see that you do everything in a right *temper*, with lowliness and meekness, with patience and gentleness, worthy the gospel of Christ. Take every step trusting 30 in God, and in the most tender, loving spirit you are able. Meantime *watch always* against all hurry and dissipation of spirit, and *pray always* with all earnestness and perseverance that your faith fail not. And let nothing interrupt that *spirit of sacrifice* which you make of all you have and are, of all you suffer and do, that it 35 may be an offering of a sweet smelling savour to God[119] through Jesus Christ.

[113] See Rom. 14:5.
[115] Cf. Col. 3:23.
[117] See Acts 27:23.
[119] See Eph. 5:2.

[114] Cf. 2 Tim. 2:21.
[116] Eph. 6:6.
[118] See Matt. 6:22.

5. As to the *manner* of acting and speaking, I advise you to do it with all innocence and simplicity, prudence, and seriousness. Add to these all possible calmness and mildness; nay, all the tenderness which the case will bear. You are not to behave as
5 butchers or hangmen, but as surgeons rather, who put the patient to no more pain than is necessary in order to the cure. For this purpose each of *you* likewise has need of 'a lady's hand with a lion's heart'.[120] So shall many even of them you are constrained to punish 'glorify God in the day of visitation'.[121]
10 6. I exhort all of you who fear God, as ever you hope to find mercy at his hands, as you dread being found (though you knew it not) 'even to fight against God',[122] do not on any account, reason, or pretence whatsoever, either directly or indirectly, oppose or hinder so merciful a design, and one so conducive to his glory.
15 But this is not all. If you are lovers of mankind, if you long to lessen the sins and miseries of your fellow-creatures, can you satisfy yourselves, can you be clear before God, by barely not opposing it? Are not *you* also bound by the most sacred ties, 'as you have opportunity to do good to all men'?[123] And is not here an
20 opportunity of doing good to many, even good of the highest kind? In the name of God, then, embrace the opportunity. Assist in doing this good, if no otherwise, yet by your earnest prayers for them who are immediately employed therein. Assist them, according to your ability, to defray the expense which necessarily
25 attends it, and which, without the assistance of charitable persons, would be a burden they could not bear. Assist them, if you can without inconvenience, by quarterly or yearly subscriptions. At least, assist them *now*: use the present hour, doing what God puts into your heart. Let it not be said that you saw your
30 brethren labouring for God and would not help them with one of your fingers.[124] In this way, however, 'come to the help of the Lord, to the help of the Lord against the mighty.'[125]

---

[120] Cf. *Oxford Dictionary of English Proverbs*, 'Surgeon', where the first citation is dated 1589, attributed to L. Wright, *Display of Dutie*, 37(a): 'In a good chirurgian a hawkes eye, a lyons heart, and a ladies hand.' See also Thomas Adams (*fl.* 1612–53; called by Robert Southey 'the prose Shakespeare of Puritan theologians'), *Sermons* (1861), I.43: 'We say of the chirurgian that he should have a lady's hand and a lion's heart; but the Christian soldier should have a lady's heart and a lion's hand.' Cf. also Wesley's letter to his brother Charles, dated twenty-five days earlier than this sermon, Jan. 5, 1763, where he also uses this proverb.
[121] 1 Pet. 2:12.   [122] Acts 5:39.   [123] Cf. Gal. 6:10.
[124] See Matt. 23:4.   [125] Cf. Judg. 5:23.

7. I have an higher demand upon you who love, as well as fear, God. He whom you fear, whom you love, has qualified *you* for promoting his work in a more excellent way.[126] Because you love God you love your brother also.[127] You love not only your friends, but your enemies;[128] not only the friends, but even the enemies of 5 God. You have 'put on, as the elect of God',[129] 'lowliness, gentleness, long-suffering'.[130] You have faith in God, and in Jesus Christ whom he hath sent[131]—faith which overcometh the world. And hereby you conquer both evil shame and that fear of man which 'bringeth a snare':[132] so that you can 'stand with boldness 10 before them that despise you and make no account of your labours'.[133] Qualified then as you are, and armed for the fight, will *you* be 'like the children of Ephraim, who being harnessed, and carrying bows, turned back in the day of battle'?[134] Will *you* leave a few of your brethren to stand alone against all the hosts of the 15 aliens? O say not, 'This is too heavy a cross: I have not strength or courage to bear it.' True; not of yourself. But you that believe 'can do all things through Christ strengthening'[135] you. 'If thou canst believe, all things are possible to him that believeth.'[136] No cross is too heavy for *him* to bear, knowing that they that 'suffer with him, 20 shall reign with him'.[137] Say not, 'Nay, but I cannot bear to be *singular.*'[138] Then you cannot enter into the kingdom of heaven. No one enters there but through the 'narrow way'.[139] And all that walk in this are singular. Say not, 'But I cannot endure the reproach, the odious name of an *informer.*' And did any man ever 25 save his soul that was not 'a by-word, and a proverb of reproach'?[140] Neither canst thou ever save thine, unless thou art willing that men should 'say all manner of evil of thee'.[141] Say not, 'But if I am active in this work I shall lose not only my reputation, but my friends, my customers, my business, my livelihood, so that 30 I shall be brought to poverty.' Thou shalt not; thou canst not; it is absolutely impossible unless God himself chooseth it. For 'his kingdom ruleth over all,'[142] and 'the very hairs of thy head are all

---

[126] Cf. No. 89 by this title.
[128] See Matt. 5:43-44.
[130] Cf. Eph. 4:2.
[132] Prov. 29:25.
[134] Ps. 78:10 (BCP).
[136] Mark 9:23.
[138] Cf. No. 31, 'Sermon on the Mount, XI', III.4 and n.
[139] Cf. Matt. 7:14.
[141] Cf. Matt. 5:11.

[127] See 1 John 4:21.
[129] Cf. Col. 3:12.
[131] See John 17:3.
[133] Cf. Wisd. 5:1.
[135] Phil. 4:13.
[137] Cf. 2 Tim. 2:12.

[140] Tobit 3:4.
[142] Ps. 103:19.

numbered.'[143] But if the wise, the gracious God choose it for thee,
wilt thou murmur or complain? Wilt thou not rather say, 'The cup
which my Father hath given me, shall I not drink it?'[144] If you
'suffer for Christ, happy are you; the spirit of glory and of Christ
5 shall rest upon you.'[145] Say not: 'I would suffer all things, but my
wife will not consent to it. And certainly a man ought to "leave
father and mother", and all, "and cleave to his wife".'[146] True,
all—but God; all—but Christ. But he ought not to leave *him* for
his wife. He is not to 'leave any duty undone'[147] for the dearest
10 relative. Our Lord himself hath said in this very sense, 'If any man
loveth father, or mother, or wife, or children, more than me, he is
not worthy of me!'[148] Say not: 'Well, I would forsake all for Christ.
But one duty must not hinder another. And this would frequently
hinder my attending public worship.' Sometimes it probably
15 would. 'Go', then, 'and learn what that meaneth, I will have mercy
and not sacrifice.'[149] And whatever is lost by showing this mercy,
God will repay sevenfold into thy bosom.[150] Say not: 'But I shall
hurt my own soul. I am a young man; and by taking up loose
women I should expose myself to temptation.' Yes, if you did this
20 in your own strength, or for your own pleasure. But that is not the
case. You trust in God: and you aim at pleasing him only. And if
he should call you even into the midst of a burning fiery furnace,[151]
'though thou walkest through the fire thou shalt not be burnt,
neither shall the flames kindle upon thee.'[152] 'True; if *he called me*
25 into the furnace. But I do not see that I am called to this.' Perhaps
thou art not willing to see it. However, if thou wast not called
before, I call thee *now*, in the name of Christ, 'Take up thy cross
and follow him.'[153] Reason no more with flesh and blood, but now
resolve to cast in thy lot with the most despised, the most
30 infamous of his followers, the filth and offscouring of the world.[154]
I call thee in particular who didst once strengthen their hands, but
since art drawn back. Take courage! Be strong! Fulfil their joy by
returning with heart and hand. Let it appear thou 'departedst for
a season, that they might receive thee again for ever'.[155] O be 'not

[143] Matt. 10:30.
[145] Cf. 1 Pet. 4:14.
[147] Cf. Matt. 23:23.
[149] Matt. 9:13.
[151] Dan. 3:6, 11, 15.
[153] Cf. Matt. 16:24, etc.
[154] See 1 Cor. 4:13.
[155] Cf. Philem. 15.

[144] John 18:11.
[146] Mark 10:7; cf. Gen. 2:24.
[148] Cf. Matt. 10:37.
[150] See Ps. 79:12.
[152] Cf. Isa. 43:2.

disobedient to the heavenly calling'![156] And as for all of you who know whereunto ye are called, count ye all things loss,[157] so ye may save one soul for which Christ died. And therein 'take no thought for the morrow',[158] but 'cast all your care on him that careth for you.'[159] 'Commit your souls', bodies, substance, all to him, 'as 5 unto a merciful and faithful Creator'.[160]

« « « « « « «

The original edition, as also that of 1778, appended:

The form of a Donation by Will.

Item. I, A. B., do hereby give and bequeath the sum of _____ unto the Treasurer for the time being of a voluntary society commonly called or known by 10 the name of 'The Society for Reformation of Manners' (which Society doth now usually meet in St. Martins le Grand, near Newgate Street, London) the same to be paid within _____ months after my decease, and to be applied to the uses and purposes of the said Society.

Subscriptions and donations are taken in by Messrs.   15
Williams and Bellamy, near the Mansion House, London.
Mr. Edward Webber, near the East India House.
Mr. William Park, in Holiwell Street, Strand.
Mr. Crook, Great Turn-Stile, Holbourn.
Mr. Osgood, in St. Martin's Court, near Leicester Fields.   20

« « « « « « «

Appendix to the *Works*, edition of 1771:

N.B. After this Society had subsisted several years, and done unspeakable good, it was wholly destroyed by a verdict given against it in the King's Bench, with three hundred pounds damages. I doubt a severe account remains for the witnesses, the jury, and all who were concerned in that dreadful affair.[161]   25

---

[156] Cf. Acts 26:19.
[157] See Phil. 3:8.
[158] Matt. 6:34.
[159] Cf. 1 Pet. 5:7.   [160] Cf. 1 Pet. 4:19.
[161] In JWJ, Feb. 2, 1766, Wesley wrote: 'I dined with W. Welsh, the father of the late Society for Reformation of Manners. But that excellent design is at a full stop. They have indeed convicted the wretch who by wilful perjury carried the cause against them in Westminster Hall; but they could never recover the expense of that suit. Lord, how long shall the ungodly triumph?'
A fresh beginning in the same cause, and under the same name, was made by William Wilberforce in 1787, and it flourished even more effectively than its predecessors, well into the latter half of the nineteenth century. See R. A. Soloway, *Prelates and People: Ecclesiastical Social Thought in England, 1783–1852* (Toronto, Univ. of Toronto Press, 1969), 354-56.

Betty Chider her Book

A

S E R M O N

On the DEATH of the

Rev. Mr GEORGE WHITEFIELD.

PREACHED

At the CHAPEL in *Tottenham-Court-Road,*

AND

At the TABERNACLE near *Moorfields,*

On SUNDAY, NOVEMBER 18, 1770.

By J O H N W E S L E Y, *M. A.*

Late FELLOW of *Lincoln-College, Oxon :* and
CHAPLAIN to the Right Honourable the Countefs
Dowager of *BUCHAN.*

2 SAM. XII. 23.

*Now he is dead, wherefore fhould I faft ? Can I bring him
back again ? I fhall go to him, but he fhall not return to me.*

L O N D O N:

Printed by J. and W. OLIVER, in *Bartholomew-Clofe.*
Sold by G. KEITH, in Gracechurch-fireet ; W. HARRIS, in St Paul's Church-
yard ; E. CABE, in Ave-Mary-Lane ; P. JONES, in Tottenham-Court-Road ;
M. ENGLEFIELD, in Weft-ftreet, Seven-Dials ; and at the Foundery.

M.DCC.LXX.

[Price SIXPENCE.]

Parson Greenwood 1771

ON THE DEATH OF GEORGE WHITEFIELD

AN INTRODUCTORY COMMENT

On its face, this is scarcely more than a heartfelt tribute from one great evangelist to another, a eulogy for a brother minister fallen before his time in a splendid career. Certainly, it was thus intended and thus may be read. But if one notices a certain formality in its tone or any lack of fervency, an understanding of its peculiar circumstances could be helpful. Actually, this sermon was the epilogue to a complex history of friendly rivalry and open conflict that would have been vivid in the memories of its first hearers and readers. This history has yet to be explored in sufficient depth, despite the massive but partisan biographical studies of Seymour, Countess of Huntingdon, *and Tyerman's twin 'Lives' of John Wesley (3 vols.) and George Whitefield (2 vols.). But it was a more decisive influence in the course of the Evangelical Revival than has been fully realized.*

Its occasion was not only solemn; it was downright awkward, and called for all the diplomacy and aplomb that Wesley could muster. Three months before (August 7-10, 1770), Wesley and his 'Conference' had issued a public warning to all Methodists who 'had leaned too much toward Calvinism'. This had given huge offence to Whitefield's closest friends and sponsors—the Countess of Huntingdon and her 'Connexion'. Even so, they had dutifully complied with Whitefield's expressed desire that Wesley be invited to preach his funeral sermon; and Wesley had accepted. Behind this lies a fascinating story, some parts of which bear directly upon an understanding of the sermon itself.

George Whitefield, close on his eighteenth birthday, had come up to Oxford in 1732 from his lowly origins in Gloucester to become a humble 'servitor' at Pembroke College, across St. Aldate's Street from lordly Christ Church. He soon heard about 'the Methodists' and admired them at a distance, but was not admitted to 'the Holy Club' until the winter of 1735. Thus, he was too young to be included in the Georgia expedition (and he was also not yet ordained). Instead, he spent a year of informal ministry in and around Gloucester and Bristol, experienced his 'new birth' long before the Wesleys, and was ordained deacon by Bishop Martin Benson in Gloucester Cathedral, June 20, 1736. Personally

*diffident and self-deprecating, he discovered an extraordinary talent for
dramatic preaching, and quickly became the most popular preacher in
England, with nine published sermons to his credit (one on 'New Birth',
another on 'The Almost Christian', and a third on 'Justification by
Faith'), all before his twenty-third birthday, and still only a deacon.
Moreover, he owed none of this success to the Wesleys, whom he had
quickly eclipsed in fame and notoriety.*

*Nevertheless, he was interested in their Georgia mission and at their
belated invitation decided to join them. The venture was, however,
delayed, for various reasons, until February 1738. Indeed, he was in
Deal harbour, ready to sail westward on February 7, his exuberantly
hopeful departure making a poignant contrast to the dispirited
homecoming of John Wesley. Wesley wrote Whitefield a hasty note,
advising him to abandon his mission and return to London; see
Tyerman, Life of Rev. George Whitefield (1876–77), I. 114-16.
Whitefield ignored this, of course, and thereafter was greatly vindicated
by his almost instant success in Georgia. The colonists responded eagerly
to his eloquence, and even William Stephens found his preaching
impressive:*

> May 21, 1738. Mr. Whitefield officiated this day at the church and made a sermon
> very engaging to the most thronged congregation I had ever seen there.
> May 28th. Mr. Whitefield manifests great ability in the ministry and his sermons
> today were very moving.
> July 2nd. Mr. Whitefield gains more and more on the affections of the people, by his
> labour and assiduity in the performance of divine offices [as a deacon!] to which an open
> and easy deportment without show of austerity or singularity of behaviour in
> conversation contribute not a little. . . . [Obviously, Stephens is here contrasting
> Whitefield with his predecessor.]

*By temperament, however, Whitefield was indisposed toward a settled
ministry, and was back in England before the year was out, preaching
and raising money for both his 'Charity Schools' and a projected
'Orphans' House' in Georgia. On January 14, 1739, he was ordained
priest in Christ Church Cathedral, Oxford, by Bishop Benson, who was
acting for Bishop Secker and also for Bishop Gibson of London, who had
agreed with the Georgia Trustees that Whitefield should return to
Savannah as rector. For this unusual ordination, Lady Huntingdon
and some of her noble friends (e.g., the Duchess of Marlborough) had
come as lay sponsors. Shortly thereafter, Whitefield began to preach in
the fields of Kingswood (February 17) and was promptly threatened
with excommunication by the Chancellor of the diocese (February 20).
Disregarding this, he went from success to success in his new irregular*

ministry—and even managed to involve a reluctant John Wesley in it.

Five months later, he was on his way back to America with a collection of £2,530 for his cherished Orphanage (on a five hundred acre tract of land donated by the Georgia Trustees). In the course of the next thirty years he raised more than £3,000 for this project. Moreover, he added five more evangelistic missions to America and, despite his untimely death at fifty-five, he had left a permanent mark on American Christianity as a part of the first 'Great Awakening'. It was a career more spectacular than Wesley's in almost all respects, save only that he left no organization to carry on his work and also that his message left a scant residue of original ideas. But, as a popular spokesman for the prevailing Puritan piety, he had no peer in his time.

In his doctrine, predestination was more presupposed than argued out, but he asserted it so vigorously that Wesley came to regard it not only as a denial of 'free-will' but as an encouragement to the relaxation of Christian discipline. This is what Stephens had noticed in Georgia—and had approved. Moreover, Whitefield's Journals, published in 1738–39, were candid beyond prudence and had made him an easy target for his critics. They pounced on his unguarded expressions of 'enthusiasms' (claims to 'direct inspiration') and on his equally unguarded invectives against the Establishment (cf. his comment that 'Archbishop Tillotson knew no more about true Christianity than Mahomet'). When 'Methodism' was attacked (as by Bishop Gibson), it was Whitefield who was more often in view than the brothers Wesley—somewhat to their exasperation.

Although his first protests against Whitefield's 'overemphasis' had been private, Wesley felt divinely led (in 1740) to preach and publish a harsh attack upon the doctrine and all its partisans, in a sermon called Free Grace (see No. 110). This caused an irreparable breach between what became 'two sorts of Methodists'. Wesley and Whitefield both sought reconciliation, short of compromise—and Whitefield never lost his personal admiration for Wesley and for his mission. But Seymour's insight on this point is shrewd: 'Mr. Wesley and Mr. Whitefield interchanged letters not very frequently, and they preached occasionally in each other's pulpits; but there was no cordial intercourse—no hearty cooperation. Such a wound as had been made in their friendship always leaves a scar. . . . Nevertheless, they did justice to each other's intentions and virtues . . .' (Seymour, Countess of Huntingdon, I.474).

Wesley reports two important approaches to reconciliation in 1766—in January (see JWJ for the 31st) and August (17 and 24), on

*the eve of Whitefield's departure for America, from which he never
returned. The latter is especially illuminating:*

> It was at the earnest request of the Countess of Huntingdon, whose heart God has
> turned again, that I came hither [to meet Whitefield in London]; and if no other good
> result from it but our firm union with Mr. Whitefield, it is abundant recompense for my
> labour. My brother and I conferred with him every day, and we resolved . . . by the grace
> of God, to go on hand in hand through honour and dishonour.

*They would not meet again on earth.
But tensions between Wesley and the Calvinists continued:*

> Many were not a little surprised in the evening [of Aug. 25] at seeing me in the
> Countess of Huntingdon's chapel. The congregation was not only large but serious, and I
> fully delivered my own soul. So I am in no concern whether I preach there again or no.

*He never did.
Whitefield's seventh mission to America ended in Newburyport,
Massachusetts, on September 30, 1770. His untimely death and the
extraordinary outpouring of grief and honour that followed are lovingly
recounted in John Gillies,* Memoirs of the Life of the Rev. G.
Whitefield, M. A., *in his collected edition of Whitefield's* Works
(1771–72), VII.269–346.

> The melancholy news of Mr. Whitefield's death reached London on Monday, Nov. 5,
> 1770, by the Boston Gazette and by three letters from different persons at Boston, to
> his friend Mr. Keen, who also by the same post received two of [Whitefield's] own
> handwriting, written in health (one seven and the other five days before his death). Mr.
> Keen had the melancholy event notified the same night at the Tabernacle [Moorfields]
> and the next night at Tottenham Court Chapel. His next step was to consider of the
> proper person to preach the funeral sermon; and recollecting he had often said to Mr.
> Whitefield, 'If you should die abroad, whom shall we get to preach your funeral sermon?
> Must it be your old friend, the Rev. Mr. John Wesley?' And having received constantly
> for answer, 'He is the man', Mr. Keen accordingly waited on the Rev. Mr. Wesley on the
> Saturday following [Nov. 10] and engaged him to preach it on the Lord's day, Nov. 18,
> which he did to a very large, crowded, and mournful auditory, many hundreds going
> away who could not possibly get in (p. 276).

Wesley's record of this is in the Journal *for November 10:*

> I returned to London and had the melancholy news of Mr. Whitefield's death
> confirmed by his executors, who desired me to preach his funeral sermon on Sunday the
> 18th. In order to write this, I retired to Lewisham on Monday, and on Sunday following
> went to the chapel in Tottenham Court Road. . . . It was an awful season. All were still
> as night; most appeared to be deeply affected; and an impression was made on many
> which one would hope will not speedily be effaced.
>   The time appointed for my beginning at the Tabernacle [in Upper Moorfields, three
> hundred yards from the Foundery] was half-hour after five, but it was quite filled at
> three, so I began at four. . . . Oh that all may hear the voice of him with whom are the

issues of life and death; and who so loudly, by this unexpected stroke, calls all his children to love one another. (See also Journal *entries for November 23.)*

The untypically fulsome title-page of this sermon suggests Wesley's sense that it was, in some sense or other, the official memorial. There were, however, dozens of others both in America and England by closer friends and colleagues than Wesley; see Gillies's Extracts from Some of the Funeral Sermons Preached on the Occasion of [Whitefield's] Death', Memoirs in Works, VII.292-346. What is obvious is that Wesley was 'thoroughly sensible how difficult it [was for him] to speak on so delicate a subject [under those circumstances]; what prudence is required . . . to say neither too little nor too much' (II.3). The bulk of the sermon is a summary of Whitefield's early career drawn chiefly from his Journals, to which are added excerpts from The Boston Gazette and The London Evening Post. The conclusion is a moving tribute to one whose talents for dramatic oratory were clearly greater than his own. The only inlet for controversy would come in Wesley's claim that the essence of Whitefield's gospel could be 'summed up in two words, "the new birth" and "justification by faith"'. His offer to edit and publish Whitefield's writings (see below, I.17) was quite sincere but quietly ignored. That assignment went to Dr. John Gillies.

One of Whitefield's most ardent admirers, William Romaine, had already been outraged by the anti-Calvinist 'Minute' and was further offended by what he regarded as Wesley's presumption. In the ensuing issue of The Gospel Magazine (January 1771) he attacked both the sermon and the preacher. His objection to the sermon was its text: 'How improper to apply the words of a mad prophet [Balaam] to so holy a man as Mr. Whitefield!' But his main complaint was Wesley's falsification, as he saw it, of Whitefield's essential teaching. 'On the contrary, the grand fundamental doctrines which [Whitefield] everywhere preached were the everlasting covenant between the Father and the Son and absolute predestination flowing therefrom.' Wesley's cool reply to this may be seen in his open letter to Lloyd's Evening Post, March 1, 1771.

This, and much more, lay behind what must have been, for Wesley, one of his most difficult 'occasions'. It was a labour of love, an exercise in honest candour, an unaccustomed venture in diplomacy. The sermon went through five editions in two years and was not thereafter reprinted in Wesley's lifetime; he omitted it from SOSO, I-VIII (1787–88). For this publishing history and a list of variant readings, see Appendix, Vol. 4; see also Bibliog, No. 324.

On the Death of George Whitefield

Numbers 23:10

*Let me die the death of the righteous, and let
my last end be like his!*

5   1. 'Let my last end be like his!' How many of you join in this
wish? Perhaps there are few of you who do not, even in this
numerous congregation. And Oh! that this wish may rest upon
your minds! That it may not die away till your souls also are
lodged 'where the wicked cease from troubling, and where the
10 weary are at rest'![1]
     2. An elaborate exposition of the text will not be expected
on this occasion. It would detain you too long from the
sadly-pleasing thought of your beloved brother, friend, and
pastor; yea, and father too; for how many are here whom he hath
15 'begotten in the Lord'![2] Will it not then be more suitable to your
inclinations, as well as to this solemnity, directly to speak of this
man of God whom you have so often heard speaking in this
place?—'the end of whose conversation' ye know, 'Jesus Christ,
the same yesterday, today, and for ever'.[3]
20   And may we not,
     First, observe a few particulars of his life and death;
     Secondly, take some view of his character; and,
     Thirdly, inquire how we may improve this awful providence,
his sudden removal from us.

25   I. 1. We may, in the first place, observe a few particulars of his
life and death. He was born at Gloucester in December 1714,[4]
and put to a grammar-school there when about twelve years old.[5]
When he was seventeen he began to be seriously religious, and
served God to the best of his knowledge. About eighteen he

---

[1] Cf. Job 3:17; the text and an echo of Wesley's early sermon, No. 109, *The Trouble and
Rest of Good Men.*
[2] Cf. 1 Cor. 4:15.   [3] Heb. 13:7-8.
[4] Dec. 16.   [5] St. Mary de Crypt.

removed to the university, and was admitted at Pembroke College in Oxford. And about a year after he became acquainted with the Methodists (so called), whom from that time he loved as his own soul.

2. By them he was convinced that we 'must be born again',[6] or outward religion will profit us nothing. He joined with them in fasting on Wednesdays and Fridays, in visiting the sick and the prisoners, and in gathering up the very fragments of time, that no moment might be lost; and he changed the course of his studies, reading chiefly such books as entered into the heart of religion, and led directly to an experimental knowledge of Jesus Christ and him crucified.[7]

3. He was soon tried as with fire. Not only his reputation was lost, and some of his dearest friends forsook him, but he was exercised with inward trials, and those of the severest kind. Many nights he lay sleepless upon his bed, many days prostrate on the ground. But after he had groaned several months under 'the spirit of bondage', God was pleased to remove the heavy load by giving him 'the spirit of adoption',[8] enabling him, through a living faith, to lay hold on 'the Son of his love'.[9]

4. However, it was thought needful for the recovery of his health, which was much impaired, that he should go into the country. He accordingly went to Gloucester, where God enabled him to awaken several young persons. These soon formed themselves into a little society, and were some of the first-fruits of his labour. Shortly after he began to read twice or thrice a week to some poor people in the town, and every day to read to and pray with the prisoners in the county gaol.

5. Being now about twenty-one years of age, he was solicited to enter into holy orders. Of this he was greatly afraid, being deeply sensible of his own insufficiency. But the bishop himself sending for him, and telling him, 'Though I had purposed to ordain none under three and twenty, yet I will ordain *you*.whenever you come;' and several other providential circumstances concurring, he submitted, and was ordained on Trinity Sunday, 1736.[10] The next Sunday he preached to a crowded auditory in the church wherein

---

[6] John 3:7.   [7] See 1 Cor. 2:2.
[8] Rom. 8:15.
[9] A paraphrase of ὁ υἱός μου ὁ ἀγαπητός (as in Matt. 3:17; 17:5; and 2 Pet. 1:17: 'my beloved son').
[10] June 20th.

he was baptized. The week following he returned to Oxford and took his bachelor's degree. And he was now fully employed; the care of the prisoners and the poor lying chiefly on him.

6. But it was not long before he was invited to London to serve
5 the cure of a friend going into the country.[11] He continued there two months, lodging in the Tower, reading prayers in the chapel twice a week, catechizing and preaching once, besides daily visiting the soldiers in the barracks and the infirmary. He also read prayers every evening at Wapping Chapel and preached at
10 Ludgate prison every Tuesday. While he was here letters came from his friends in Georgia which made him long to go and help them. But not seeing his call clear, at the appointed time he returned to his little charge at Oxford; where several youths met daily at his room to 'build up each other in their most holy faith'.[12]

15 7. But he was quickly called from hence again to supply the cure of Dummer in Hampshire.[13] Here he read prayers twice a day, early in the morning and in the evening after the people came from work. He also daily catechized the children, and visited from house to house. He now divided the day into three parts, allotting
20 eight hours for sleep and meals, eight for study and retirement, and eight for reading prayers, catechizing, and visiting the people. Is there a more excellent way for a servant of Christ and his church? If not, who will 'go and do likewise'?[14]

8. Yet his mind still ran on going abroad. And being now fully
25 convinced he was called of God thereto, he set all things in order, and in January 1737 went down to take leave of his friends in Gloucester. It was in this journey that God began to bless his ministry in an uncommon manner. Wherever he preached, amazing multitudes of hearers flocked together, in Gloucester, in
30 Stonehouse,[15] in Bath, in Bristol; so that the heat of the churches was scarce supportable. And the impressions made on the minds of many were no less extraordinary. After his return to London, while he was detained by General Oglethorpe[16] from week to

---

[11] Thomas Broughton (1712–77), curate of the Tower of London. He had been active in the Holy Club.

[12] Cf. Jude 20.

[13] As curate to Charles Kinchin (1711–42), another Oxford Methodist.

[14] Cf. Luke 10:37.

[15] Revd. Sampson Harris was the incumbent of St. Cyril's parish church in Stonehouse, Gloucestershire. Whitefield preached in his pulpit and then in the churchyard to overflowing crowds.

[16] A retrospective reference to James Edward Oglethorpe (1696–1785), one of the chief

week and from month to month, it pleased God to bless his word still more. And he was indefatigable in his labour: generally on Sunday he preached four times, to exceeding large auditories; besides reading prayers twice or thrice, and walking to and fro, often[17] ten or twelve miles.

9. On December 28 [1737] he left London. It was on the 29th that he first preached without notes. December 30 he went on board;[18] but it was above a month before they cleared the land. One happy effect of their very slow passage he mentions in April following: 'Blessed be God, we now live very comfortably in the great cabin. We talk of little else but God and Christ . [. . .] And scarce a word is heard among us when together but what has reference to our fall in the first, and our new birth in the Second Adam.'[19] It seems likewise to have been a peculiar providence that he should spend a little time at Gibraltar, where both citizens and soldiers, high and low, young and old, acknowledged the day of their visitation.

10. From Sunday, May 7, 1738, till the latter end of August following, he 'made full proof of his ministry'[20] in Georgia, particularly at Savannah. He read prayers and expounded twice a day, and visited the sick daily. On Sunday he expounded at five in the morning; at ten read prayers and preached, and at three in the afternoon; and at seven in the evening expounded the Church catechism. How much easier is it for our brethren in the ministry, either in England, Scotland, or Ireland, to find fault with such a labourer in our Lord's vineyard than to tread in his steps!

11. It was now that he observed the deplorable condition of many children here; and that God put into his heart the first thought of founding an orphan-house, for which he determined to raise contributions in England, if God should give him a safe return thither. In December following he did return to London, and on Sunday, January the 14th, 1739, he was ordained priest at Christ Church, Oxford. The next day he came to London again; and on Sunday 21st preached twice. But though the churches were large, and crowded exceedingly, yet many hundred stood in

---

promoters and defenders of the Georgia colony; Oglethorpe's promotion to brigadier-general did not come until 1743.

[17] 'Often' is inserted only in *Works*, 1771.

[18] The *Whitaker*, from Purfleet.

[19] Cf. *George Whitefield's Journals*, ed., Iain Murray (London, Banner of Truth Trust, 1960), p. 149.

[20] Cf. 2 Tim. 4:5.

the churchyard, and hundreds more returned home. This put him upon the first thought of preaching in the open air. But when he mentioned it to some of his friends, they judged it to be mere madness. So he did not carry it into execution till after he had left
5 London. It was on Wednesday, February 21, that finding all the church doors to be shut in Bristol (beside that no church was able to contain one half of the congregation) at three in the afternoon he went to Kingswood and preached abroad, to near two thousand people. On Friday he preached there to four or five
10 thousand; and on Sunday to (it was supposed) ten thousand. The number continually increased all the time he stayed at Bristol. And a flame of holy love was kindled, which will not easily be put out. The same was afterwards kindled in various parts of Wales, of Gloucestershire, and Worcestershire. Indeed wherever he
15 went God abundantly confirmed the word of his messenger.

12. On Sunday, April 29, he preached the first time in Moorfields, and on Kennington Common.[21] And the thousands of hearers were as quiet as they could have been in a church. Being again detained in England from month to month, he made
20 little excursions into several counties, and received the contributions of willing multitudes for an orphan-house in Georgia. The embargo which was now laid on the shipping[22] gave him leisure for more journeys through various parts of England, for which many will have reason to bless God to all eternity. At
25 length, on August 14, he embarked. But he did not land in Pennsylvania till October 30. Afterwards he went through Pennsylvania, the Jerseys, New York, Maryland, Virginia, North and South Carolina, preaching all along to immense congregations, with full as great effect as in England. On January 10, 1740,
30 he arrived at Savannah.

13. January 29 he added three desolate orphans to near twenty which he had in his house before. The next day he laid out the ground for the house, about ten miles from Savannah. February

---

[21] A then open tract of public ground on 'the Surrey side of the Thames' across from Pimlico and just beyond the celebrated Vauxhall 'pleasure gardens'. Cf. Earl of Egmont, *Diary of Viscount Percival, Afterwards First Earl of Egmont* (London, Historical Manuscripts Commission, 1920–23), III. 64, 67-69, for an eyewitness account of Whitefield's open air preaching on Woolwich Common (June 5, 1739) and on Charlton Green (June 8).

[22] Because of the tense situation in the West Indies, which led to open war (Oct. 19, 1739); it was 'the prelude to a struggle for dominion, lasting nearly a quarter of a century, between England and the Bourbon powers'; cf. Basil Williams, *The Whig Supremacy*, p. 203; see also, pp. 197-200, 220-21.

11 he took in four orphans more, and set out for Frederica[23] in order to fetch the orphans that were in the southern parts of the colony. In his return he fixed a school, both for children and grown persons, at Darien,[24] and took four orphans thence. March 25 he laid the first stone of the orphan-house, to which, with great 5 propriety, he gave the name of 'Bethesda'[25]—a work for which the children yet unborn shall praise the Lord. He had now about forty orphans, so that there were near an hundred mouths to be fed daily. But he was 'careful for nothing',[26] casting his care on him who 'feedeth the young ravens that call upon him'.[27]   10

14. In April he made another tour through Pennsylvania, the Jerseys, and New York. Incredible multitudes flocked to hear, among whom were abundance of Negroes. In all places the greater part of the hearers were affected to an amazing degree. Many were deeply convinced of their lost state; many truly 15 converted to God. In some places thousands cried out aloud; many as in the agonies of death; most were drowned in tears; some turned pale as death; others were wringing their hands; others lying on the ground; others sinking into the arms of their friends; almost all lifting up their eyes, and calling for mercy. 20

15. He returned to Savannah June 5. The next evening during the public service the whole congregation, young and old, were dissolved in tears. After service several of the parishioners, and all his family, particularly the little children, returned home crying along the street, and some could not help praying aloud. The 25 groans and cries of the children continued all night, and great part of the next day.

16. In August he set out again, and through various provinces came to Boston. While he was here and in the neighbouring places he was extremely weak in body. Yet the multitudes of 30 hearers were so great, and the effects wrought on them so astonishing, as the oldest men then alive in the town had never seen before. The same power attended his preaching at New York; particularly on Sunday, November 2, almost as soon as he began, crying, weeping, and wailing were to be heard on every 35

---

[23] On St. Simon's Island, where Charles Wesley had served briefly as minister. Cf. CWJ, Mar. 9–May 13, 1736.

[24] A settlement of Scottish Highlanders at the mouth of the Altamaha River, seventy-three miles southwest of Savannah. Cf. JWJ, Dec. 2, 1737.

[25] See John 5:2.   [26] Phil. 4:6.

[27] Ps. 147:9 (BCP).

side. Many sunk down to the ground, cut to the heart; and many were filled with divine consolation. Toward the close of his journey he made this reflection: 'It is the seventy-fifth day since I arrived at Rhode Island, exceeding weak in body. Yet God has
5 enabled me to preach an hundred and seventy-five times in public, beside exhorting frequently in private. Never did God vouchsafe me greater comforts. Never did I perform my journeys with less fatigue, or see such a continuance of the divine presence in the congregations to whom I preached.'[28] In December he
10 returned to Savannah, and in the March following arrived in England.

17. You may easily observe that the preceding account is chiefly extracted from his own *Journals*, which, for their artless and unaffected simplicity, may vie with any writings of the kind.
15 And how exact a specimen is this of his labours both in Europe and America for the honour of his beloved Master during the thirty years that followed! As well as of the uninterrupted shower of blessings wherewith God was pleased to succeed his labours! Is it not much to be lamented that anything should have prevented
20 his continuing this account till at least near the time when he was called by his Lord to enjoy the fruit of his labours? If he has left any papers of this kind, and his friends account me worthy of the honour, it would be my glory and joy to methodize, transcribe, and prepare them for the public view.
25 18. A particular account of the last scene of his life is thus given by a gentleman of Boston:

After being about a month with us in Boston and its vicinity, and preaching every day, he went to Old York,[29] preached on Thursday, September 27, there; proceeded to Portsmouth and preached there on Friday. On Saturday morning
30 he set out for Boston; but before he came to Newbury,[30] where he had engaged to preach the next morning, he was importuned to preach by the way. The house not being large enough to contain the people, he preached in an open field. But having been infirm for several weeks, this so exhausted his strength that when he came to Newbury he could not get out of the ferry-boat without the help of two
35 men. In the evening, however, he recovered his spirits and appeared with his usual cheerfulness. He went to his chamber at nine, his fixed time, which no company could divert him from; and slept better than he had done for some weeks before. He rose at four in the morning, September 30, and went into his closet; and his companion observed he was unusually long in private. He left his

---

[28] Cf. Whitefield, *Journals*, p. 499 (Dec. 1, 1740).
[29] Then in 'New Hampshire'; now York Village, Maine.
[30] Newburyport, Mass.

closet, returned to his companion, threw himself on the bed, and lay about ten minutes. Then he fell upon his knees, and prayed most fervently to God that if it was consistent with his will he might that day finish his Master's work. He then desired his man to call Mr. Parsons,[31] the clergyman at whose house he was; but in a minute, before Mr. Parsons could reach him, died without a sigh or groan. 5 On the news of his death, six gentlemen set out for Newbury in order to bring his remains hither, but he could not be moved, so that his precious ashes must remain at Newbury. Hundreds would have gone from this town to attend his funeral had they not expected he would have been interred here. . . . May this stroke be sanctified to the church of God in general, and to this province in 10 particular![32]

II. 1. We are, in the second place, to take some view of his character. A little sketch of this was soon after published in the *Boston Gazette,* an extract of which is subjoined:

Little can be said of him but what every friend to vital Christianity who has sat 15 under his ministry will attest. In his public labours he has for many years astonished the world with his eloquence and devotion. With what divine pathos did he persuade the impenitent sinner to embrace the practice of piety and virtue! Filled with the spirit of grace, he spoke from the heart, and with a fervency of zeal perhaps unequalled since the days of the apostles, adorned the 20 truths he delivered with the most graceful charms of rhetoric and oratory. From the pulpit he was unrivalled in the command of an ever-crowded auditory. Nor was he less agreeable and instructive in his private conversation: happy in a remarkable ease of address, willing to communicate, studious to edify. May the rising generation catch a spark of that flame which shone with such 25 distinguished lustre in the spirit and practice of this faithful servant of the most high God![33]

2. A more particular, and equally just character of him, has appeared in one of the English papers. It may not be disagreeable to you to add the substance of this likewise: 30

The character of this truly pious person must be deeply impressed on the heart of every friend to vital religion. In spite of a tender and delicate constitution he continued to the last day of his life preaching with a frequency and a fervour that seemed to exceed the natural strength of the most robust. Being called to the exercise of his function at an early age, when most young men are only 35 beginning to qualify themselves for it, he had not time to make a very considerable progress in the learned languages. But this defect was amply

---

[31] Jonathan Parsons (1705–76), minister of the Old South Church of Newburyport.

[32] Presumably from one of those 'three letters from different persons at Boston' which Robert Keen would have brought to Wesley, along with his copy of the *Boston Gazette*—see above, p. 328.

[33] Abridged from an editorial in *The Massachusetts Gazette, and Boston Post-Boy and The Advertiser,* No. 684 (Mon. Oct. 1, 1770), p. 3. The news itself had been reported in the same paper the day before.

supplied by a lively and fertile genius, by fervent zeal, and by a forcible and most persuasive delivery. And though in the pulpit he often found it needful by 'the terrors of the Lord to persuade men',[34] he had nothing gloomy in his nature, being singularly cheerful, as well as charitable and tender-hearted. He was as
5 ready to relieve the bodily as the spiritual necessities of those that applied to him. It ought also to be observed that he constantly enforced upon his audience every moral duty, particularly industry in their several callings, and obedience to their superiors. He endeavoured by the most extraordinary efforts of preaching in different places, and even in the open fields, to rouse the lower class of people
10 from the last degree of inattention and ignorance to a sense of religion. For this and his other labours the name of George Whitefield will long be remembered with esteem and veneration.[35]

3. That both these accounts are just and impartial will readily be allowed; that is, as far as they go. But they go little farther than
15 the *outside* of his character. They show you the *preacher*, but not the *man*, the *Christian*, the *saint* of God. May I be permitted to add a little on this head from a personal knowledge of near forty years? Indeed, I am thoroughly sensible how difficult it is to speak on so delicate a subject, what prudence is required to avoid both
20 extremes, to say neither too little nor too much. Nay, I know it is impossible to speak at all, to say either less or more, without incurring from some the former, from others the latter censure. Some will seriously think that too little is said, and others that it is too much. But without attending to this I will speak just what I
25 know, before him to whom we are all to give an account.

4. Mention has already been made of his unparalleled *zeal*, his indefatigable *activity*, his *tender-heartedness* to the afflicted, and *charitableness* toward the poor. But should we not likewise mention his deep *gratitude* to all whom God had used as
30 instruments of good to him? Of whom he did not cease to speak in the most respectful manner, even to his dying day? Should we not mention that he had a heart susceptible of the most generous and the most tender *friendship*? I have frequently thought that this, of all others, was the distinguishing part of his character. How few
35 have we known of so kind a temper, of such large and flowing affections! Was it not principally by this that the hearts of others were so strangely drawn and knit to him? Can anything but love

---

[34] Cf. 2 Cor. 5:11.
[35] An abridgement from *The London Evening Post* for Nov. 10, 1770 (No. 1607), p. 4. Sugden cites it as from *The London Chronicle* for Nov. 6, but that paper carried only an announcement of Whitefield's death without the eulogy quoted here. The *Post's* encomium was then reprinted in *The Scots Magazine* (Dec. 1770, XXXII. 574-75), as from a 'Lond[on] pap[er]'.

beget love? This shone in his very countenance, and continually breathed in all his words, whether in public or private. Was it not this, which, quick and penetrating as lightning, flew from heart to heart? Which gave that life to his sermons, his conversations, his letters? Ye are witnesses.   5

5. But away with the vile misconstruction of men of corrupt minds, who know of no love but what is 'earthly and sensual'.[36] Be it remembered at the same time that he was endued with the most nice and unblemished *modesty*. His office called him to converse very frequently and largely with women as well as men; and those 10 of every age and condition. But his whole behavior toward them was a practical comment on that advice of St. Paul to Timothy, 'Entreat the elder women as mothers, the younger as sisters, with all purity.'[37]

6. Meantime, how suitable to the friendliness of his spirit was 15 the *frankness* and *openness* of his conversation! Although it was as far removed from rudeness on the one hand as from guile and disguise on the other. Was not this frankness at once a fruit and a proof of his *courage* and *intrepidity*? Armed with these, he feared not the faces of men, but 'used great plainness of speech'[38] to 20 persons of every rank and condition, high and low, rich and poor; endeavouring only 'by manifestation of the truth' to 'commend himself to every man's conscience in the sight of God'.[39]

7. Neither was he afraid of labour or pain, any more than of 'what man could do unto him',[40] being equally   25

> *Patient* in bearing ill and doing well.[41]

And this appeared in the *steadiness* wherewith he pursued whatever he undertook for his Master's sake. Witness one instance for all, the orphan-house in Georgia, which he began and perfected in spite of all discouragements. Indeed, in whatever 30 concerned himself he was pliant and flexible. In this case he was 'easy to be entreated',[42] easy to be either convinced or persuaded. But he was immovable in the things of God, or wherever his

---

[36] Cf. Jas. 3:15.   [37] 1 Tim. 5:1-2.   [38] Cf. 2 Cor. 3:12.
[39] Cf. 2 Cor. 4:2.   [40] Cf. Heb. 13:6.
[41] Samuel Wesley, Jun., 'The Battle of the Sexes', st. xxxv, l. 8, in *Poems* (1736), p. 38; cf. John Wesley, *A Collection of Moral and Sacred Poems* (1744), III.33. See also, No. 83, 'On Patience', §7; his letters to Richard Morgan, Dec. 17, 1733, and Penelope Newman, Aug. 12, 1744. Cf. Wesley's obituary of Robert Swindells, *Minutes*, July 29, 1783.
[42] Jas. 3:17.

conscience was concerned. None could persuade, any more than affright him, to vary in the least point from that *integrity* which was inseparable from his whole character, and regulated all his words and actions. Herein he did

5   Stand as an iron pillar strong,
                 And steadfast as a wall of brass.[43]

8. If it be inquired what was the foundation of this integrity, or of his sincerity, courage, patience, and every other valuable and amiable quality, it is easy to give the answer. It was not the
10 excellence of his natural temper; not the strength of his understanding. It was not the force of education; no, nor the advice of his friends. It was no other than faith in a bleeding Lord: 'faith of the operation of God'.[44] It was 'a lively hope' of 'an inheritance incorruptible, undefiled, and that fadeth not away'.[45]
15 It was 'the love of God shed abroad in his heart by the Holy Ghost which was given unto him',[46] filling his soul with tender, disinterested love to every child of man. From this source arose that torrent of *eloquence* which frequently bore down all before it; from this that astonishing force of *persuasion*, which the most
20 hardened sinners could not resist. This it was which often made his 'head as waters' and his 'eyes a fountain of tears'.[47] This it was which enabled him to pour out his soul in *prayer* in a manner peculiar to himself, with such fullness and ease united together, with such strength and variety both of sentiment and expression.
25 9. I may close this head with observing what an honour it pleased God to put upon his faithful servant by allowing him to declare his everlasting gospel in so many various countries, to such numbers of people, and with so great an effect on so many of their precious souls! Have we read or heard of any person since
30 the apostles who testified the gospel of the grace of God through so widely extended a space, through so large a part of the habitable world? Have we read or heard of any person who called so many thousands, so many myriads of sinners to repentance? Above all, have we read or heard of any who has been a blessed
35 instrument in his hand of bringing so many sinners 'from

[43] John and Charles Wesley, *Hymns and Sacred Poems* (1739), p. 203 (*Poet. Wks.*, I.180). Cf. Wesley's letter to the Countess of Huntingdon, Sept. 16, 1773.
[44] Col. 2:12.   [45] Cf. 1 Pet. 1:3-4.
[46] Cf. Rom. 5:5.
[47] Cf. Jer. 9:1.

darkness to light, and from the power of Satan unto God'?[48] It is true, were we to talk thus to the gay world we should be judged to 'speak as barbarians'.[49] But *you* understand the language of the country to which you are going, and whither our dear friend is gone a little before us.   5

III. But how shall we improve this awful providence? This is the third thing which we have to consider. And the answer to this important question is easy (may God write it in all our hearts!): by keeping close to the *grand doctrines* which he delivered, and by drinking into his *spirit.*   10
1. And, first, let us keep close to the grand scriptural doctrines which he everywhere delivered. There are many doctrines of a less essential nature, with regard to which even the sincere children of God (such is the present weakness of human understanding!) are and have been divided for many ages. In 15 these we may think and let think;[50] we may 'agree to disagree'.[51] But meantime let us hold fast the essentials of 'the faith which was once delivered to the saints',[52] and which this champion of God so strongly insisted on at all times and in all places.
2. His fundamental point was: give God all the glory of 20 whatever is good in man. And in the business of salvation, set Christ as high and man as low as possible. With this point he and his friends at Oxford, the original Methodists[53] (so called), set out.

---

[48] Acts 26:18. On this same day (Nov. 18) Henry Venn was also preaching a similar sermon in the Countess of Huntingdon's Chapel in Bath (on the text, Isa. 8:18) and agreed with Wesley on this point especially: 'The greatness and intenseness of his labours . . . [and] their compass exceeds anything that others can pretend to' (see John Gillies, *Memoirs*, in Whitefield's *Works*, VII.332). Tyerman, *Whitefield*, II.619-28, lists seventeen memorial sermons preached and seven as published. At least six other published sermons are in MA. All of them stress the extraordinary impact of Whitefield's preaching. Augustus Toplady went so far as to declare Whitefield 'the Apostle of the English empire, . . . the prince of [all English] preachers' ('A Concise Character of the Late Rev. Mr. Whitefield', *Works* [1837], p. 494).

[49] Cf. 1 Cor. 14:11.

[50] Cf. No. 7, 'The Way to the Kingdom', I.6 and n.

[51] In his letter to his brother Charles, Aug. 19, 1785, Wesley wrote, 'We can (as Mr. Whitefield used to say) agree to disagree.' See also an earlier letter to Charles on Nov. 3, 1775. Cf. Ovid, *Metamorphoses*, i. 433: '*Discors concordia*' ('agreeing to differ'). St. Bernard of Clairvaux had already phrased the same notion in his letter to Cardinal Hugh of Ostia: 'It became a matter of discord. But why do I say discord? It was rather a matter of concord, for all the brethren were found to agree completely in disagreeing' (*Letters* [1953], p. 443).

[52] Jude 3.

[53] Wesley makes frequent autobiographical references to the Holy Club or 'the young gentlemen at Oxford'. Cf. Nos. 63, 'The General Spread of the Gospel', §13; 79, 'On

Their grand principle was: there is *no power* (by nature) and *no merit* in man. They insisted, all power to think, speak, or act right is in and from the Spirit of Christ; and all merit is (not in man, how high soever in grace, but merely) in the blood of Christ. So
5   he and they taught: there is no power in man, till it is given him from above, to do one good work, to speak one good word, or to form one good desire. For it is not enough to say all men are *sick of sin*. No, we are all '*dead* in trespasses and sins'.[54] It follows that all the children of men are 'by nature children of wrath'.[55] We are all
10   'guilty before God',[56] liable to death, temporal and eternal.
       3. And we are all helpless, both with regard to the power and to the guilt of sin. For, 'Who can bring a clean thing out of an unclean?'[57] None less than the Almighty. Who can raise those that are *dead*, spiritually dead in sin? None but he who raised us from
15   the dust of the earth. But on what consideration will he do this? 'Not for works of righteousness that we have done.'[58] 'The dead cannot praise thee, O Lord!'[59] Nor do anything for the sake of which they should be raised to life. Whatever therefore God does, he does it merely for the sake of his well-beloved Son: 'He was
20   wounded for our transgressions, he was bruised for our iniquities.'[60] 'He himself bore all our sins in his own body upon the tree.'[61] 'He was delivered for our offences, and rose again for our justification.'[62] Here then is the sole *meritorious cause* of every blessing we do or can enjoy; in particular of our pardon and
25   acceptance with God, of our full and free justification.[63] But by what means do we become interested in what Christ has done and suffered? 'Not by works, lest any man should boast;'[64] but by faith alone. 'We conclude', says the apostle, 'that a man is justified by faith, without the works of the law.'[65] And 'to as many as' thus
30   'receive him giveth he power to become the sons of God: even to those that believe in his name, who are born, not of the will of man, but of God.'[66]

Dissipation', §20; see also 89, 'The More Excellent Way', VI.4; 112, *On Laying the Foundation of the New Chapel*, I.2, II.15.

[54] Eph. 2:1.   [55] Eph. 2:3.   [56] Rom. 3:19.
[57] Job 14:4.   [58] Cf. Titus 3:5.   [59] Cf. Pss. 88:10; 115:17.
[60] Isa. 53:5.   [61] 1 Pet. 2:24.   [62] Cf. Rom. 4:25.
[63] But this conflict between 'meritorious' and 'formal' causes in justification was one of the controverted issues between Wesley and the Calvinists (including Whitefield). See Whitefield's Sermon XIV, 'The Lord Our Righteousness', in *Works*, V.216-34; and Sermon XV, *ibid.*, pp. 235-50; and cf. Wesley's No. 20, *The Lord our Righteousness*.
[64] Cf. Eph. 2:9.   [65] Cf. Rom. 3:28.
[66] Cf. John 1:12-13.

4. And 'except a man be thus born again he cannot see the kingdom of God.'[67] But all who are thus 'born of the Spirit'[68] have 'the kingdom of God within'[69] them. Christ sets up his kingdom in their hearts—'righteousness, peace, and joy in the Holy Ghost'.[70] That 'mind is in them which was in Christ Jesus',[71] enabling them 5 to 'walk as Christ also walked'.[72] His indwelling Spirit makes them both holy in heart and 'holy in all manner of conversation'.[73] But still, seeing all this is a free gift through the righteousness and blood of Christ, there is eternally the same reason to remember, 'he that glorieth, let him glory in the Lord.'[74] 10

5. You are not ignorant that these are the fundamental doctrines which he everywhere insisted on. And may they not be summed up, as it were, in two words—*the new birth*, and *justification by faith?* These let us insist upon with all boldness, at all times, and in all places; in public (those of us who are called 15 thereto) and, at all opportunities, in private. Keep close to these good, old, unfashionable doctrines, how many soever contradict and blaspheme. Go on, my brethren, 'in the name of the Lord, and in the power of his might';[75] with all care and diligence 'keep that safe which is committed to your trust;'[76] knowing that 'heaven 20 and earth shall pass away; but' this truth 'shall not pass away'.[77]

6. But will it be sufficient to keep close to his *doctrines*, how pure soever they are? Is there not a point of still greater importance than this, namely, to drink into his *spirit?* Herein to 'be a follower of' him, 'even as' he was 'of Christ'?[78] Without this the purity of 25 our doctrines would only increase our condemnation. This, therefore, is the principal thing, to copy after his spirit. And allowing that in some points we must be content to *admire* what we cannot *imitate;* yet in many others we may, through the same free grace, be partakers of the same blessing. Conscious then of your 30 own wants, and of his bounteous love who 'giveth liberally and upbraideth not',[79] cry to him that worketh all in all for a measure of the same precious faith; of the same zeal and activity, the same tender-heartedness, charitableness, bowels of mercies.[80] Wrestle

[67] Cf. John 3:3.
[69] Cf. Luke 17:21.
[71] Cf. Phil. 2:5.
[73] 1 Pet. 1:15.
[75] Cf. Eph. 6:10.
[77] Cf. Matt. 24:35, etc.
[79] Jas. 1:5.
[80] See Col. 3:12.

[68] Cf. John 3:5.
[70] Rom. 14:17.
[72] Cf. 1 John 2:6.
[74] 1 Cor. 1:31; 2 Cor. 10:17.
[76] Cf. 1 Tim. 6:20.
[78] Cf. 1 Cor. 11:1.

with God for some degree of the same grateful, friendly, affectionate temper; of the same openness, simplicity, and godly sincerity, 'love without dissimulation'.[81] Wrestle on, till the power from on high works in you the same steady courage and patience;
5 and above all, because it is the crown of all, the same invariable integrity.

7. Is there any other fruit of the grace of God with which he was eminently endowed, and the want of which among the children of God he frequently and passionately lamented? There is one, that
10 is, *catholic love:* that sincere and tender affection which is due to all those who, we have reason to believe, are children of God by faith; in other words, all those in every persuasion who 'fear God and work righteousness'.[82] He longed to see all who had 'tasted of the good word'[83] of a truly *catholic spirit*—a word little understood,
15 and still less experienced, by many who have it frequently in their mouth. Who is he that answers this character? Who is a man of a 'catholic spirit'?[84] One who loves as friends, as brethren in the Lord, as joint partakers of the present kingdom of heaven, and fellow-heirs of his eternal kingdom, all, of whatever opinion,
20 mode of worship, or congregation, who believe in the Lord Jesus; who love God and man; who, rejoicing to please and fearing to offend God, are careful to abstain from evil, and zealous of good works.[85] He is a man of a truly catholic spirit who bears all these continually upon his heart; who having an unspeak-
25 able tenderness for their persons, and an earnest desire of their welfare, does not cease to commend them to God in prayer, as well as to plead their cause before men; who speaks comfortably to them, and labours by all his words to strengthen their hands in God. He assists them to the uttermost of his power in all things,
30 spiritual and temporal. He is ready 'to spend and to be spent'[86] for them; yea, to 'lay down his life for his brethren'.[87]

8. How amiable a character is this! How desirable to every child of God! But why is it then so rarely found? How is it that there are so few instances of it? Indeed, supposing we have tasted of the
35 love of God, how can any of us rest till it is our own! Why, there is

---

[81] Rom. 12:9.
[82] See Ps. 15:2 (AV); Eccles. 12:13.
[83] Cf. Heb. 6:5.
[84] Cf. No. 39, 'Catholic Spirit'. Also Richard Baxter, *The True Catholick and Catholick Church Described.*
[85] Titus 2:14.   [86] 2 Cor. 12:15.   [87] Cf. John 15:13; 1 John 3:16.

a delicate device whereby Satan persuades thousands[88] that they may stop short of it, and yet be guiltless. It is well if many here present are not in this 'snare of the devil, taken captive at his will'.[89] 'O yes', says one, 'I have all this love for those I believe to be children of God. But I will never believe he is a child of God who belongs to that *vile congregation!* Can he, do you think, be a child of God who holds such *detestable opinions?* Or he that joins in such senseless and superstitious, if not idolatrous worship?' So we justify ourselves in one sin by adding a second to it! We excuse the want of love in ourselves by laying the blame on others. To colour our own devilish temper we pronounce our brethren children of the devil. O beware of this! And if you are already taken in the snare, escape out of it as soon as possible. Go and learn that truly catholic love which 'is not rash or hasty' in judging; that love which 'thinketh no evil', which 'believeth and hopeth all things';[90] which makes all the allowances for others that we desire others should make for us. Then we shall take knowledge of the grace of God which is in every man, whatever be his opinion or mode of worship. Then will all that fear God be near and dear unto us 'in the bowels of Jesus Christ'.[91]

9. Was not this the spirit of our dear friend? And why should it not be ours? O thou God of love, how long shall thy people be a by-word among the heathen?[92] How long shall they laugh us to scorn, and say, 'See how *these* Christians love one another!'[93] When wilt thou roll away our reproach?[94] 'Shall the sword devour for ever? How long will it be ere thou bid thy people return from following each other?' Now at least 'let all the people stand still, and pursue after' their brethren 'no more'![95] But whatever others do, let all of us, my brethren, hear the voice of him that 'being dead, yet speaketh'![96] Suppose ye hear him say: 'Now at least "be ye followers of me as I was of Christ!"'[97] Let brother "no more lift up sword" against brother, neither "know ye war any more"![98] Rather "put ye on, as the elect of God, bowels of mercies, humbleness of mind, brotherly kindness, gentleness, long-suffering, forbearing one another in love."[99] Let the time past

---

[88] Cf. No. 42, 'Satan's Devices'; cf. also Whitefield's Sermon XLVIII, 'Satan's Devices', in *Works*, VI. 241-56.
[89] 2 Tim. 2:26.   [90] Cf. 1 Cor. 13:4, 5, 7.
[91] Cf. Phil. 1:8.   [92] See Ps. 44:14 (AV).
[93] Tertullian, *Apology*, ch. 39, §7; see No. 22, 'Sermon on the Mount, II', III.18 and n.
[94] See Josh. 5:9.   [95] Cf. 2 Sam. 2:26, 28.   [96] Heb. 11:4.
[97] Cf. 1 Cor. 11:1.   [98] Cf. Isa. 2:4; Mic. 4:3.   [99] Cf. Col. 3:12-13.

suffice for strife, envy, contention, for "biting and devouring one another".[100] Blessed be God that ye have not long ago been "consumed one of another"![101] From henceforth hold ye "the unity of the Spirit in the bond of peace".'[102]

5   10. O God, with thee no word[103] is impossible: thou dost whatsoever pleaseth thee! O that thou wouldst cause the mantle of thy prophet, whom thou hast taken up, now to fall upon us that remain! 'Where is the Lord God of Elijah?'[104] 'Let' his 'spirit rest upon'[105] these thy servants! Show thou art the God that 'answerest
10   by fire'![106] Let the fire of thy love fall on every heart! And because we love thee, let us love one another with a 'love stronger than death'.[107] 'Take away from us all anger, and wrath, and bitterness; all clamour, and evil-speaking.'[108] Let thy Spirit so rest upon us that from this hour we may 'be kind to each other,
15   tender-hearted; forgiving one another, even as God for Christ's sake hath forgiven us'![109]

An H Y M N

I

Servant of God, well done!
20   Thy glorious warfare's past,
The battle's fought, the race is won,
And thou art crowned at last;
Of all thy heart's desire
Triumphantly possessed,
25   Lodged by the ministerial choir
In thy Redeemer's breast.

II

In condescending love
Thy ceaseless prayer He heard,
30   And bade thee suddenly remove
To thy complete reward:
Ready to bring the peace,
Thy beauteous feet were shod,
When mercy signed thy soul's release
35   And caught thee up to God.

---

[100] Cf. Gal. 5:15.
[101] *Ibid.*
[102] Eph. 4:3.
[103] All published edns. read 'word'; but is this a printer's misreading of 'work'?
[104] 2 Kgs. 2:14.   [105] 2 Kgs. 2:9, 15.
[106] Cf. 1 Kgs. 18:24.   [107] Cf. S. of S. 8:6.
[108] Cf. Eph. 4:31.   [109] Cf. Eph. 4:32.

III

With saints enthroned on high
Thou dost thy Lord proclaim,
And still *to God salvation* cry,
  Salvation to the Lamb!   5
O happy, happy soul!
In ecstasies of praise,
Long as eternal ages roll,
  Thou seest thy Saviour's face.

IV   10

Redeemed from earth and pain,
Ah! when shall we ascend,
And all in Jesus' presence reign
With our translated friend!
Come, Lord, and quickly come!   15
And when in thee complete,
Receive thy longing servants home,
  To triumph—at thy feet![110]

---

[110] By Charles Wesley (*Poet. Wks.*, VI. 316-17); this hymn, almost certainly included in the sermon as delivered, would have served as the rhetorical equivalent of an ascription.

SERMONS ON SEVERAL OCCASIONS
VOLUMES V–VIII

AN EDITORIAL COMMENT

We turn now to a much later collection of Wesley's sermons, that mirrors his mind and ministry in its last two decades. In the Works *of 1771–74, he had included fifty-three 'Sermons on Several Occasions' in the first four volumes (1771). In a prefatory note 'To the Reader' he had explained that in that edition (and one thinks especially of the sermons):*

There is scarce any subject of importance, either in practical or controversial divinity, which is not treated of, more or less, either professedly or occasionally. . . . So that in this edition, I present . . . my last and maturest thoughts, agreeable, I hope, to Scripture, reason, and Christian antiquity.[1]

This suggests an assumption on his part that in SOSO, *I–IV, he had rounded off his theological task, in so far as written sermons could have done that.*

Actually, of course, two more tumultuous and fruitful decades lay ahead for him; to his amazement, the Revival continued on from strength to strength. But this could only have the effect of raising old problems in new contexts. His health and vigour held up remarkably,[2] and so he went on, travelling, preaching, publishing—and arguing with the Calvinists. In the first decade (1771–81), he published eight 'new' sermons; but then in the second decade (1781–91) came an unexpected bumper crop of written sermons that exceeded the whole of SOSO, *I–IV, both in number and also in range of topics. It was as if he were building on the soteriological foundations securely laid so that, reacting to the mounting challenges from the Calvinists, he felt free to undertake a new sort of 'instruction in the faith' for second and third generation Methodists. It was a new kind of Christian paranesis for men and women who, though firmly grounded in their 'Christian assurance', were baffled by the new challenges to Christian belief and ethics thrown up by the drastic changes in the intellectual and cultural climate in Britain in the final quarter of the century.*

---

[1] §§2, 4.
[2] Cf. the birthday entries in JWJ, June 28, 1774 and 1788.

In response, and as a fresh new resource for the Methodists, Wesley had launched a serial publication, entitled The Arminian Magazine *(1778–). Its axial theme was defined by its sub-title:* Extracts and Original Treatises on Universal Redemption. *Its monthly instalments were collected into annual volumes, with a comprehensive table of 'Contents'. Its obvious design was to furnish extra help to the Methodists in their unending struggles 'with the patrons of* particular redemption'.[3] *It can rightly be seen as Wesley continuing his role as their theological tutor in yet another guise:*

Each number will therefore consist of four parts. First, a defence of that grand Christian doctrine, 'God willeth all men to be saved, and to come to the knowledge of the truth.' Secondly, an extract from the life of some holy man, whether Lutheran, Church of England man, Calvinist, or Arminian. Thirdly, accounts and letters containing the experience of pious persons, the greatest part of whom are still alive. And, fourthly, verses explaining or confirming the capital doctrines we have in view.[4]

To begin with, be it noted, there were to be no 'original sermons'. *Soon, however, he was persuaded to alter this format, and to add new sermons of his own. In this way he found a new 'pulpit' in the* Magazine. *His explanation of this development is given in the 'Preface' to Vol. IV (1781):*

Several of my friends have been frequently importuning me to write a few more sermons. I thought indeed I might now have been fairly excused, and have remitted that work to my younger brethren. But as they are not satisfied with this, I submit to their well-meant importunity, and design to write, with God's assistance, a few more plain, practical discourses on those which I judge to be the most necessary of the subjects I have not yet treated of. The former part of one of these is published this month; the latter will follow in February. And so, every two months, so long as God spares my life and health, I shall publish another.[5]

Thus it was that the Arminian Magazine *became a prod to the publication, in one decade, of more sermons than had thus far appeared in print in Wesley's whole career. Moreover, these new sermons are not old oral favourites reduced to writing; the correlation between the texts of the sermons written for the* Magazine *and those of his oral preaching is unaccountably low. The evangelical foundations of* SOSO, I–IV *are everywhere presupposed, and occasionally restated, but there is no announced 'programme' for their progression. The one common concern in them is Wesley's interest in dealing with specific issues as they had emerged in the later course of the Revival. Where earlier statements had*

---

[3] 'To the Reader', 1778, §4. [4] *Ibid.*, §7. [5] Pref. 1781, §6.

been misunderstood or un-understood, he took this new forum to redefine and to revise them in fresh terms. In every case, he is intent upon an updating of his message in the light of unfolding cultural changes in 'an age of transition'. This would seem to have been his warrant for the marked increase of various sorts of rhetorical ornamentations (quotations, allusions, illustrations, etc.).

Wesley's overloaded schedule and the lack of qualified assistants created special problems in the publishing operations of the Magazine: this helps to explain certain otherwise puzzling features here. First, and unavoidably, Wesley was writing in haste, against unaccustomed deadlines and, more often than not, without libraries to consult. Then, too, his advancing years were taking their inevitable toll.[6] Finally, Wesley's assistants were not always equal to their tasks. Thus, in 1789, he was compelled,

> however unwillingly, to drop Mr. [Thomas] O[livers], for only these two reasons: (1), the errata are unsufferable; I have borne them for these twelve years, but can bear it no longer; (2), several pieces are inserted without my knowledge, both in verse and prose.[7]

Further light on the situation comes from Olivers's successor, James Creighton (in a letter to his sister, August 22, 1789):

> . . . the chief difficulty [in my editorial tasks] is in the Magazine, a great part of which is made out from manuscripts badly written. They must be . . . reduced to grammar and sense. . . . Sometimes a whole page or leaf will be so blotted and interlined (as we must cross out some words and insert others) that the printer can hardly make it out. This is the case also with respect to these sermons of Mr. W[esley] written in his own hand [a hand so legible earlier on], which it is almost impossible for anyone now to make out. . . .

It may be doubted that Wesley had further plans for the republication of these Magazine sermons. After all, 'the first four volumes of sermons' (as they had been termed in the 'Model Deed' of 1763) remained in place as a doctrinal baseline. In 1787, however, his hand was forced by a move by others to publish an unauthorized collection of these later sermons. His response was a decision to do the job himself. The cover of the Magazine for January 1788 announces the publication of a new edition of SOSO, I–IV. This appeared with its original 'Preface' (1746) and in its original order of 1746–60. The notice added: 'There are also in the press, and will shortly be published in four volumes,

---

[6] See his belated admissions of this in JWJ, Jan. 1 and June 28, 1790.

[7] JWJ, Aug. 8, 1789. Actually Wesley was complaining in large measure about some of the 'fillers' used for otherwise empty spaces.

price 10s., all the sermons in the ten volumes of the Arminian Magazine'—*actually, as we have seen, in the* eight *volumes, IV–XI. This new quartet, numbered* SOSO, *V–VIII, have their own Preface, which affords a fresh revelation of Wesley's interests at this later stage. But it leaves some obvious questions unanswered. Why, for example, the reversion to the forty-four sermons of 1746–60, and therefore the discarding of all but one of the nine new sermons that had appeared in* SOSO, *I–IV in 1771? Only* The Lord Our Righteousness *was retained, inserted out of order in* SOSO, *V. 105–25. Again, why was the original design (twelve sermons per volume) enlarged to fourteen? And, even more crucially, why the particular ordering of this new collection? It is neither chronological, topical, nor in the original sequence in the* Magazine. *Wesley may have been, as he claimed, 'the properest person'* [8] *to supervise this new publication, but why, then, did he fail to follow through on his own announced principle of ordering—of 'placing those first which are intended to throw light on some important Christian doctrine, and afterwards those which more directly relate to some branch of Christian practice'?* [9] *One gets the impression of a good deal of improvisation, and this is confirmed by Wesley's letter from Chester to Peard Dickinson in London (April 15, 1788): 'Pray consult with T. Olivers where the additional sermons may be most properly inserted. I have another ready for the press and two more begun.' The last sermon for Vol. VIII was rushed to the printer in the barest nick of time.*

Of the fifty-six sermons in SOSO, *V–VIII, forty-three had already appeared in the* Magazine. *Six would appear in the concurrent volume (XI, 1788). Two more would appear in* SOSO, *VIII, before they did in the* Magazine *(XII, 1789). As we have seen, only one of the nine sermons from the 1760s survived in this new edition, although four of those that had been discarded had been published separately.*

SOSO, *V–VIII, are still 'plain truth for plain people': evangelical, strong on 'application'. Their 'Preface' stresses this even more emphatically than the 1746 'Preface' had done. There is, however, no mistaking the fact that Wesley's homiletical style and theological substance had acquired fresh nuances over the years. Thus, in V–VIII, the reader may expect more ornamentation, more speculative formulations, more show of learning, more of an emphasis upon a theology of culture. Salvation by faith alone is everywhere presupposed, but now the stress is upon its outworkings in the new circumstances of the*

---

[8] Pref. §2.   [9] *Ibid.,* §3.

Methodist people (social, economic, cultural). These new volumes are not a mere addendum to I–IV; they amount to a second major phase in Wesley's development as a 'folk theologian'.

They have, however, been sadly neglected by the generality of Wesley's interpreters. Joseph Benson, in the first posthumous edition of Wesley's collected Works *(in seventeen volumes, 1809–13) adopts a different rubric for the sermons.*[10] *In John Emory's 'first American edition' in seven volumes (1831), the first fifty-three sermons occupy Vol. I; the others are gathered into Vol. II. Thomas Jackson, in 1825, divided the sermons into five 'series'—the 'First' contains Sermons 1 through 53—and there is an obvious implication that the first series was by far the most important one.*[11] *This preoccupation had supported the tendency*[12] *to concentrate on* SOSO, *1-44 (or 1-53), at the expense of the much larger fraction of the sermon corpus.*

Such an imbalance needs redressing. Despite their uneven quality, these later sermons exhibit Wesley's ripened Christian wisdom in a quite remarkable fashion—its broadened scope, its ample theological perspective, its quickened sensitivities to Christian social imperatives. They are, therefore, a remarkable achievement by a phenomenally busy old man, still leading a still burgeoning Revival. They give us a sight of the continued stretching of his mind toward a fuller understanding of his faith. Thus, they enlarge our resources for understanding that faith and its lifelong passion for an integrated vision of the Christian order of salvation.

---

[10] E.g., Vol. VII, 'Thirty-seven Sermons on Various Subjects' (1811), and so on to Vol. XI, 'Sixteen Sermons and Tracts on Various Subjects' (1812).

[11] See Frank Baker, *Union Catalogue of the Publications of John and Charles Wesley*, No. 420 (pp. 190-97) for an exhibit of the overwhelming predominance of 'the standards' in subsequent edns. of Wesley's sermons; and see also E. H. Sugden's account of the elaborate *law suit* required by the British Conference to 'settle' their prolonged disputes as to the exact number implied by the phrase 'standard sermons' (*Wesley's Standard Sermons*, 1921, II.331-40).

[12] Even as in Schmidt, *op. cit.*

SERMONS

O N

Several Occasions.

By J. O H N W E S L E Y, M. A.
Fellow of *Lincoln-College*, OXFORD.

V O L. V.

L O N D O N:

Printed and fold at the NEW CHAPEL, *City-Road*, and at
the Rev. Mr. WESLEY's Preaching-Houfes
in Town and Country. 1788.

PREFACE

1. A gentleman in the west of England informed me a few days ago that a clergyman in his neighbourhood designed to print in two or three volumes the sermons which had been published in the ten volumes of the *Arminian Magazine*. I had been frequently 5 solicited to do this myself, and had as often answered, 'I leave this for my executors.' But if it must be done before I go hence, methinks I am the properest person to do it.

2. I intend therefore to set about it without delay. And if it pleases God to continue to me a little longer the use of my 10 understanding and memory, I know not that I can employ them better. And perhaps I may be better able than another to revise my own writings, in order either to retrench what is redundant, to supply what is wanting, or to make any farther alterations which shall appear needful. 15

3. To make these plain discourses more useful I purpose now to range them in proper order; placing those first which are intended to throw light on some important Christian doctrines, and afterwards those which more directly relate to some branch of Christian practice. And I shall endeavour to place them all in 20 such an order that one may illustrate and confirm the other.[1] There may be the greater need of this because they were occasionally written during a course of years, without any order or connection at all, just as this or the other subject either occurred to my own mind or was suggested to me at various times by one or 25 another friend.

4. To complete the number of twelve sermons in every volume I have added six sermons to those printed in the *Magazines*.[2] And I did this the rather because the subjects were important and cannot be too much insisted on. 30

5. Is there need to apologize to sensible persons for the plainness of my style?[3] A gentleman whom I much love and

---

[1] Cf. *Works* (1771), I. 'To the Reader', §2: 'I wanted to methodize these tracts, . . . placing those together which were on similar subjects, and in such order that one might illustrate another.'

[2] *On the Trinity* (1775; see No. 55); *On Predestination* (1776; see No. 58); *The Lord Our Righteousness* (1765; see No. 20); *The Important Question* (1775; see No. 84); *A Call to Backsliders* (1778; see No. 86); *The Reward of Righteousness* (1777; see No. 99).

[3] Cf. *Works* (1771), I. 'Preface'. But see also Vicesimus Knox, *Essays Moral and Literary*,

respect lately informed me, with much tenderness and courtesy, that 'men of candour made great allowance for the decay of my faculties, and did not expect me to write now, either with regard to sentiment or language, as I did thirty or forty years ago.' Perhaps
5 they are decayed, though I am not conscious of it. But is not this a fit occasion to explain myself concerning the style I use, from choice, not necessity? I *could* even now write as floridly and rhetorically as even the admired Dr. B[lair].[4] But I dare not; because I seek the honour that cometh of God only![5] What is the
10 praise of man to *me*, that have one foot in the grave, and am stepping into the land whence I shall not return?[6] Therefore I dare no more write in a 'fine style' than wear a fine coat. But were it otherwise, had I time to spare, I should still write just as I do. I should purposely decline what many admire, an highly
15 ornamented style. I cannot relish French oratory; I despise it from my heart.[7] Let those that please be in raptures at the pretty, elegant sentences of Massillon[8] or Bourdaloue.[9] But give me the

No. 15, p. 73. Toward the century's end, the vogue of the old 'plain style' had given place to things like Hervey's *Meditations*. Knox comments on 'the rhapsodic style which wearies by its constant efforts to elevate the mind to ecstasy. . . . Many modern sermons . . . aim at sublimity and highly figurative eloquence [but have, instead] become turgid and affected.'

[4] Dr. Hugh Blair (1718–1800), a famous Scottish orator for whom the first 'regius professorship of rhetoric and belles-lettres' at the University of Edinburgh was created in 1762. Samuel Johnson praised his eloquence; Leslie Stephen (*DNB*) speaks of 'his unimpassioned and rather affected style'. On another front, however (the controversy over the authorship of 'Ossian's' *Fingal*), Blair and Wesley had been allies in an unpopular cause—both espousing the claims of James Macpherson to the poem's 'antiquity'; cf. JWJ, July 17, 1767; May 15, 1784; and June 23, 1786.

[5] See John 5:44.

[6] See Job 10:21.

[7] It is not easy to explain Wesley's prejudice against French culture: 'French is the poorest, meanest language in Europe; it is no more comparable to the German or Spanish than a bagpipe is to an organ. . . . It is as impossible to write a fine poem in French as to make fine music upon a jew's harp' (JWJ, Oct. 11, 1756).

[8] Jean-Baptiste Massillon (1663–1742), celebrated preacher and reforming bishop of Clermont (1719–42). *The Catholic Encyclopedia* ranks him 'above Bossuet and Bourdaloue as a preacher' and speaks of his concern 'to speak to the heart in a language readily understood'. His *Works* (mostly sermons) were first published in 1745; there is no record that Wesley had actually read them. But Massillon's fame was immense, and this, apparently, was Wesley's point of reference.

[9] Louis Bourdaloue (1632–1704), the most famous court preacher in seventeenth-century France. Taine ranked him with Cicero, Livy, Bossuet, Burke, and Fox as an orator; Fénelon praised his lucid style and the clarity of the order in his sermons. There is no record of Wesley's having read him, either.

plain nervous style of Dr. South,[10] Dr. Bates,[11] or Mr. John Howe.[12] And for elegance, show me any French writer who exceeds Dean Young[13] or Mr. Seed.[14] Let who will admire the French frippery:[15] I am still for plain, sound English.

6. I think a preacher or a writer of sermons has lost his way 5
when he imitates any of the French orators, even the most famous of them—even Massillon or Bourdaloue. Only let his language be plain, proper, and clear, and it is enough. God himself has told us how to speak, both as to the matter and the manner: 'If any man speak' in the name of God 'let him speak as the oracles of God.'[16] 10
And if he would imitate any part of these above the rest, let it be the first Epistle of St. John. This is the style, the most excellent style, for every gospel preacher.[17] And let him aim at no more ornament than he finds in that sentence which is the sum of the whole gospel: 'We love him because he hath first loved us.'[18] 15

London, Jan. 1, 1788

[10] Robert South (1634–1716), the liveliest and most eloquent of the Caroline divines; cf. Irène Simon, *Three Restoration Divines*, I.228-74. He was a staunch Tory and ardent polemicist against the Puritans and Nonconformists. His style is 'nervous' in Johnson's sense of that term: 'well-strung, strong, vigorous'.

[11] William Bates (1625–99), famed as 'the silver-tongued preacher' of the Commonwealth, who continued as an influential leader among the Nonconformists. John Howe, in his sermon, 'On the Death of Dr. William Bates' (*Works*, VI. 301), speaks of his 'peculiar way of preaching and writing—especially his frequent most apt similitudes and allusions, . . . brisk and vivid fancy, regulated by judgment and sanctified by divine grace'.

[12] John Howe (1630–1705), one of Cromwell's favourite preachers and a leading spirit in the cause of 'comprehension' after the Restoration. Wesley gleaned some of his own 'catholic spirit' from Howe's active concern for Christian unity, as in *The Carnality of Religious Contention Among Christians* (1693). In Vol. XLVIII of the *Christian Lib.* (1755), he had extracted a 'Life' of Howe and also his *Living Temple* (1675), a Puritan essay on the theme of holy living.

[13] Edward Young (1643–1705), Dean of Salisbury, a plain style preacher, popular in his own age but already overshadowed in Wesley's time by the fame of his son (also Edward), 'the poet'. Wesley quotes from Dean Young's *Sermons on Several Occasions* in No. 144, 'The Love of God', III.4; his *exordium* and Young's are recognizably similar.

[14] Jeremiah Seed (1700–47), Fellow of Queen's College, Oxford, and rector of Knight's Enham, Hampshire, 1741-47. His works, in two volumes, were published posthumously in 1750. Johnson comments of him that 'he had a very fine style but was not very theological' (Boswell's *Life of Johnson*, pp. 913-14).

[15] The French preaching that Wesley affects to despise was chiefly aimed at courtly audiences in a culture in which style was highly prized. Laurence Sterne, who was no 'plain style preacher', had commented on 'the theatrical character' of French preaching in a letter to his wife from Paris, March 1762; cf. *Letters of Laurence Sterne*, ed. by L. P. Curtis (Oxford, Oxford Univ. Press, 1935), pp. 154-55.

[16] 1 Pet. 4:11.

[17] Cf. JWJ, Jan. 5, 1787: 'I do not admire [the] florid way of writing. Good sense does not need to be so studiously adorned. I love St. John's style as well as matter.'

[18] Cf. 1 John 4:19.

ON ETERNITY

AN INTRODUCTORY COMMENT

This is Wesley's deepest plunge into speculative theology up to this point in his career. It was not written until June 28, 1786; it had been printed in Vol. IX (1786) of the Magazine *(November and December) without a title, which seems to have been supplied (by Wesley?) when it appeared as the first sermon in* SOSO, *V (1788). There is no record of Wesley's ever having preached from Ps. 90:2 on any other occasion.*

On Eternity

Psalm 90:2

From everlasting to everlasting thou art God.

1. I would fain speak of that awful subject, eternity. But how
5 can we grasp it in our thought? It is so vast that the narrow mind of man is utterly unable to comprehend it. But does it not bear some affinity to another incomprehensible thing, immensity? May not space, though an unsubstantial thing, be compared with another unsubstantial thing, duration? But what is immensity? It is
10 boundless space. And what is eternity? It is boundless duration.

2. Eternity has generally been considered as divisible into two parts, which have been termed eternity *a parte ante*, and eternity *a parte post*[1]—that is, in plain English, that eternity which is past,

---

[1] The then familiar scholastic distinction (regarding 'boundless duration') between *aeternitas a parte ante* and *aeternitas a parte post*. Cf. the note (No. 25) in Cowley, *Pindarique Odes*, 'The Muse', on 'the two sorts of eternity: from the present backwards . . . and from the present forwards'. Wesley repeats this notion in §7, below. His two most important sources here are Locke, *Essay Concerning Human Understanding*, II. xvii. 10ff.; and Clarke,

and that eternity which is to come. And does there not seem to be an intimation of this distinction in the text? 'Thou art God from everlasting'—here is an expression of that eternity which is past; 'to everlasting'—here is an expression of that eternity which is to come. Perhaps indeed some may think it is not strictly proper to 5 say there is an eternity that is past. But the meaning is easily understood. We mean thereby duration which had no beginning; as by eternity to come we mean that duration which will have no end.

3. It is God alone who (to use the exalted language of 10 Scripture) 'inhabiteth eternity'[2] in both these senses. The great Creator alone (not any of his creatures) is 'from everlasting to everlasting': his[3] duration alone, as it had no beginning, so it cannot have any end. On this consideration it is that one speaks thus in addressing Immanuel, God with us,[4]   15

> Hail, God the Son, with glory crowned,
>   E'er time began to be;
> Throned with thy Sire through half the round
>   Of wide eternity![5]

Demonstration of the Being and Attributes of God, Propositions I-III. But see also Prior's *Solomon*, iii.613-18:

> Amid two seas on one small point of land,
> Wearied, uncertain, and amazed we stand;
> On either side our thoughts incessant turn,
> Forward we dread; and looking back we mourn;
> Losing the present in this dubious haste;
> And lost ourselves betwixt the future and the past.

And cf. Addison, *Evidences of the Christian Religion* (London, 'Cooke's edition', n.d.), p. 67: 'We consider eternity, or infinite duration, as a line that has neither a beginning nor end. . . . In our speculations of eternity we consider the time which is present to us as the middle, which divides the whole line into equal parts. For this reason, many witty authors compare the present time to an isthmus, or narrow neck of land, that rises in the midst of an ocean, immeasurably diffused on either side of it. . . . Philosophy (and indeed common sense) naturally throws eternity under two divisions: which we may call in English, that eternity which is past and that eternity which is to come. The learned terms of *aeternitas a parte ante* and *aeternitas a parte post* . . . can have no other ideas affixed to them. . . .'

[2] Isa. 57:15.

[3] *AM, SOSO*, 'it is', altered by Wesley in his MS annotations in *AM* to 'his'.

[4] Cf. Isa. 7:14; Matt. 1:23.

[5] Samuel Wesley, Jun., 'An Hymn to God the Son', *Poems* (1736), p. 3. Here Wesley follows his own version from his *Collection of Psalms and Hymns* (Charleston, 1737), pp. 12-13; in his *Collection of Moral and Sacred Poems* (1744), III.180-81, he restored his brother's orig. reading in st. 1, l. 3, 'through one half-round'.

And again,

> Hail, God the Son, with glory crowned,
> When time shall cease to be;
> Throned with the Father through the round
> Of whole eternity!⁶

5

4. 'E'er time began to be.'—But what is *time?* It is not easy to say, as frequently as we have had the word in our mouth. We know not what it properly is: we cannot well tell how to define it. But is it not in some sense a fragment of eternity, broken off at both ends?⁷ That portion of duration which commenced when the world began, which will continue as long as this world endures, and then expire for ever? That portion of it which is at present measured by the revolution of the sun and planets,⁸ lying (so to speak) between two eternities, that which is past, and that which is to come? But as soon as the heavens and the earth flee away from the face of him that sitteth on the great white throne,⁹ time will be no more, but sink for ever into the ocean of eternity.¹⁰

5. But by what means can a mortal man, the creature of a day,¹¹ form any idea of eternity? What can we find within the compass of nature to illustrate it by? With what comparison shall we compare it?¹² What is there that bears any resemblance to it? Does there not seem to be some sort of analogy between boundless duration and boundless space? The great Creator, the Infinite Spirit, inhabits both the one and the other. This is one of his peculiar prerogatives: 'Do not I fill heaven and earth? saith the Lord.'¹³ Yea, not only the utmost regions of creation, but all the expanse of boundless space! Meantime how many of the children of men may say,

---

⁶ *Ibid.*, p. 4, where the original and the anthologies of both 1737 and 1744 read, 'Hail, with essential glory crowned'.

⁷ Cf. Augustine, *Confessions*, XI. xiv-xxvi, XII. xxix. See also No. 58, *On Predestination*, §5.

⁸ I.e., sidereal time, time measured by reference to the motions of the stars. Cf. *OED* for this usage as early as 1681.

⁹ See Rev. 20:11.

¹⁰ Cf. Richard Blackmore, 'Essay on the Immortality of the Soul', in *Essays on Several Subjects* (London, 1716), p. 295: 'the boundless ocean of eternity'. See also Hervey, *Theron and Aspasio*, II.356: 'a fathomless abyss, a vast eternity'. Cf. also Nos. 21, 'Sermon on the Mount, I', II.6; and 33, 'Sermon on the Mount, XIII', III.7, where Wesley has already used this phrase.

¹¹ Pindar, *Pythian Odes*, viii. 95. Cf. Wesley's first Preface (1746), §5.

¹² Mark 4:30.   ¹³ Jer. 23:24.

Lo, on a narrow neck of land,
Midst two unbounded seas I stand,
Secure, insensible!
A point of time, a moment's space,
Removes me to that heavenly place, 5
Or shuts me up in hell![14]

6. But leaving one of these unbounded seas to the Father of eternity, to whom alone duration without beginning belongs, let us turn our thoughts on duration without end. This is not an incommunicable attribute of the great Creator; but he has been 10 graciously pleased to make innumerable multitudes of his creatures partakers of it. He has imparted this not only to angels, and archangels, and all the companies of heaven,[15] who are not intended to die, but to glorify him and live in his presence for ever, but also to the inhabitants of the earth who dwell in houses 15 of clay.[16] Their bodies indeed are 'crushed before the moth',[17] but their souls will never die. God made them, as an ancient writer speaks, to be 'pictures of his own eternity'.[18] Indeed all spirits, we have reason to believe, are clothed with immortality; having no inward principle of corruption, and being liable to no external 20 violence.

7. Perhaps we may go a step farther still. Is not matter itself, as well as spirit, in one sense eternal? Not indeed *a parte ante*, as some senseless philosophers, both ancient and modern, have dreamed. Not that anything had existed from eternity; seeing if so 25 it must be God. Yea, it must be the one God; for it is impossible

---

[14] Charles Wesley, 'An Hymn for Seriousness', ver. 2, *Hymns and Sacred Poems* (1749), I.34 (*Poet. Wks.*, IV.316). Orig., 'Twixt two unbounded seas' and 'A point of life'. Cf. Prior, *Solomon*, iii. 613-18; and Cowley, *Pindarique Odes*, 'Life and Fame', st. 1. See also William Reeves, *Fourteen Sermons . . .* , p. 327:

This *Jota* or *Tittle* of mortal life seems to rise up
Like a neck of land between two oceans.

Cf. also, George Lillo, *Arden of Feversham* (1739), Act III, sc. 3:

What shall we call this undetermined state,
This narrow isthmus 'twixt two boundless oceans,
That, whence we came, and that, to which we tend?

For a similar metaphor, cf. No. 146, 'The One Thing Needful', §3, where Wesley speaks of man 'placed on a narrow, weak, tottering bridge, whereof either end was swallowed up in eternity'.
[15] See BCP, Communion, Pref. to the Sanctus.
[16] Job 4:19. Cf. No. 28, 'Sermon on the Mount, VIII', §21 and n.
[17] *Ibid.*
[18] Cf. Wisd. 2:23. See No. 120, 'The Unity of the Divine Being', §8.

there should be two Gods, or two Eternals.[19] But although nothing beside the great God can have existed from everlasting, none else can be eternal, *a parte ante;* yet there is no absurdity in supposing that all creatures are eternal, *a parte post.*[20] All matter
5 indeed is continually changing, and that into ten thousand forms. But that it is changeable does in no wise imply that it is perishable. The substance may remain one and the same,[21] though under innumerable forms. It is very possible any portion of matter may be resolved into the atoms of which it was originally composed.
10 But what reason have we to believe that one of these atoms ever was or ever will be annihilated? It never can, unless by the uncontrollable power of its almighty Creator. And is it probable that ever he will exert this power in unmaking any of the things that he hath made? In this also God is 'not a son of man that he
15 should repent'.[22] Indeed every creature under heaven does and must continually change its form; which we can now easily account for, as it clearly appears from late discoveries that ethereal fire[23] enters into the composition of every part of the creation. Now this is essentially *edax rerum.*[24] It is the universal
20 menstruum,[25] the *discohere*[26] of all things under the sun. By the force of this even the strongest, the firmest bodies are dissolved. It appears from the experiment repeatedly made by the great Lord Bacon that even diamonds, by a high degree of heat, may be turned into dust.[27] And that in a still higher degree (strange as it
25 may seem) they will totally flame away. Yea, by this 'the heavens'

[19] Cf. Clarke, *Demonstration of the Being and Attributes of God*, Proposition VII; see also, Ralph Cudworth, *The True Intellectual System of the Universe* (1678), p. 119: '. . . all the ancient atheists . . . did at once deny both eternities to the world: past and future.'

[20] Cf. above, §2 and n. Both *AM* and *SOSO* read 'remain in one and the same', surely an uncorrected error.

[21] The notion of the conservation of matter had become a scientific commonplace by Wesley's time; cf. Cudworth, *op. cit.*, pp. 119-20. Wesley extended the principle to include organic life in his *Survey*, II.147. See also No. 15, *The Great Assize*, III.3 and n.

[22] Num. 23:19.

[23] Cf. No. 15, *The Great Assize*, III.4 and n.

[24] A switch from Ovid's *Metamorphoses*, xv. 234, where it is said that *time* is 'the devourer of all things'. Here 'ethereal fire' is identified as *edax rerum*.

[25] Johnson, *Dictionary*, defines 'menstruum' as a 'dissolvent', especially 'of metals'; in Wesley's *Dictionary* it is defined as 'any dissolving liquor'.

[26] I.e., 'disintegrating power'. Is this a typographical error for 'discoherence', or is it a neologism? Cf. *OED* for an adjectival use (from the Lat. verb *discohaere*) but none for the noun.

[27] See Bacon's analysis of 'Heat' under three 'Tables' (of 'Essence', 'Deviations', and 'Degrees') in *Works*, ed. by Spedding *et al.* (1869), I.354-84. But cf. Wesley's comment on *linum asbestum* in No. 73, 'Of Hell', II.6.

themselves 'will be dissolved; the elements shall melt with fervent heat.'[28] But they will be only dissolved, not destroyed: they will melt, but they will not perish. Though they lose their present form, yet not a particle of them will ever lose its existence; but every atom of them will remain under one form or other to all 5 eternity.

8. But still we would inquire, 'What is this eternity?' How shall we pour any light upon this abstruse subject? It cannot be the object of our understanding. And with what comparison shall we compare it?[29] How infinitely does it transcend all these! What are 10 any temporal things placed in comparison with those that are eternal? What is the duration of the long-lived oak, of the ancient castle, of Trajan's pillar,[30] of Pompey's amphitheatre;[31] what is the antiquity of the Tuscan urns,[32] though probably older than the foundation of Rome; yea, of the pyramids of Egypt,[33] suppose they 15 have remained upwards of three thousand years, when laid in the balance with eternity? It vanishes into nothing. Nay, what is the duration of 'the everlasting hills',[34] figuratively so called, which have remained ever since the general deluge, if not from the foundation of the world, in comparison of eternity? No more than 20 an insignificant cipher. Go farther yet. Consider the duration from the creation of the first-born sons of God, of Michael the archangel in particular, to the hour when he shall be commissioned to sound his trumpet, and to utter his mighty voice through the vault of heaven, 'Arise, ye dead, and come to the 25

[28] Cf. 2 Pet. 3:12.

[29] Mark 4:30.

[30] The votive column in the centre of the largest of the imperial fora in Rome, close by the present day Piazza Venezia; it still is very nearly intact. The column itself is ninety-seven feet high, dates from A.D. 113, and in a spiral frieze a yard wide and six hundred fifty feet long commemorates Trajan's conquest of Dacia.

[31] An imperial theatre dating from 52 B.C. The contour of its stage is traced now by the Via di Chiavari as it leads into the eighteenth-century Teatro Argentina. The Piazza de Teatro di Pompeo covers what was the seating space. Pompey's colossal statue is preserved in the Palazza Spada in the Campo di Fiori. ·

[32] I.e., Etruscan, the largest surviving collection of which is in the Villa Giulia in Rome; another is in the Etruscan Museum in Orvieto.

[33] Egypt was often included in 'the grand tour' by English travellers and scholars in the eighteenth century; there is a large literature on the then remaining monuments of ancient Egypt (espec. 'Grand Cairo', the Pyramids, and the Sphinx); cf., e.g., Richard Pococke, *A Description of the East and Some Other Countries* (1743), Vol. I; and Samuel Clarke, *A Mirrour or Looking-Glasse* (1654), pp. 608-11. See also, Charles Rollin, *Ancient History* (1738), I. 43-48. For other references to the pyramids, cf. Nos. 78, 'Spiritual Idolatry', I.7; 102, 'Of Former Times', §4. See also, *Survey*, I. 108, V. 142.

[34] Gen. 49:26.

judgment!' Is it not a moment, a point, a nothing in comparison of unfathomable eternity? Add to this a thousand, a million of years, add a million of million[35] of ages, before the mountains were brought forth, or the earth and the round world were
5 made[36]—what is all this in comparison of that eternity which is past? Is it not less, infinitely less, than a single drop of water to the whole ocean? Yea, immeasurably less than a day, an hour, a moment, to a million of ages. Go back a thousand millions still. Yet you are no nearer the beginning of eternity.
10 9. Are we able to form a more adequate conception of eternity to come? In order to this let us compare it with the several degrees of duration which we are acquainted with. An ephemeron fly lives six hours, from six in the evening to twelve.[37] This is a short life compared to that of a man, which continues threescore or
15 fourscore years. And this itself is short if it be compared to the nine hundred and sixty-nine years of Methuselah.[38] Yet what are these years, yea, all that have succeeded each other from the time that the heavens and the earth were erected, to the time when the heavens shall pass away, and the earth with the works of it shall be
20 burnt up, if we compare it to the length of that duration which never shall have an end!

10. In order to illustrate this a late author has repeated that striking thought of St. Cyprian. Suppose there were a ball of sand as large as the globe of earth; suppose a grain of this sand were to
25 be annihilated, reduced to nothing, in a thousand years; yet that whole space of duration wherein this ball would be annihilating, at the rate of one grain in a thousand years, would bear infinitely less proportion to eternity—duration without end—than a single grain of sand would bear to all that mass.[39]

---

[35] Orig., *AM*, 'add a million, a million of millions', altered in Wesley's MS annotations.
[36] See Ps. 90:2.
[37] This reference extends Chambers's *Cyclopaedia* estimate by an hour: '[The ephemeron fly] is born about six a clock in the evening and dies about eleven. . . . It never eats from the time of its change to death.' Cf. Oliver Goldsmith, *History of the Earth and Animated Nature* (1774), VII.361-62, and Eleazar Albin, *A Natural History of English Insects* (1724), p. 2. which cites William Derham's *Physico-Theology* (1716), Bk. VIII, for a discussion of the 'ichneumon fly-kind'. See also, Wesley's *Survey*, II.17.
[38] Cf. Gen. 5:27.
[39] This reference has not been located in the writings of St. Cyprian. The 'late author' here was almost certainly Addison, in *The Spectator*, No. 575 (Mon. Aug. 2, 1714), who cites as his source, not St. Cyprian, but 'one of the schoolmen'. Addison goes on: 'Supposing the whole body of the earth were a great ball or mass of the finest sand and that a single grain or particle of this sand should be annihilated every thousand years? Etc.' The same simile had been used earlier by John Flavell in *Navigation Spiritualized* (1682; see

11. To infix this important point the more deeply in your mind, consider another comparison. Suppose the ocean to be so enlarged as to include all the space between the earth and the starry heavens. Suppose a drop of this water to be annihilated once in a thousand years; yet that whole space of duration 5 wherein this ocean would be annihilating, at the rate of one drop in a thousand years, would be infinitely less in proportion to eternity than one drop of water to that whole ocean.

Look then at those immortal spirits, whether they are in this or the other world. When they shall have lived thousands of 10 thousands of years, yea, millions of millions of ages, their duration will be but just begun: they will be only upon the threshold of eternity.

12. But besides this division of eternity into that which is past and that which is to come, there is another division of eternity 15 which is of unspeakable importance. That which is to come, as it relates to immortal spirits, is either a happy or a miserable eternity.

13. See the spirits of the righteous that are already praising God in a happy eternity. We are ready to say, 'How short will it 20 appear to those who drink of the rivers of pleasure[40] at God's right hand!' We are ready to cry out,

> A day without night
> They dwell in his sight,
> And eternity seems as a day![41]   25

But this is only speaking after the manner of men. For the measures of long and short are only applicable to time, which admits of bounds, and not to unbounded duration. This rolls on (according to our low conceptions) with unutterable, inconceivable swiftness—if one would not rather say it does not roll or 30 move at all, but is one still, immovable ocean. For the inhabitants

Works, 1740, II.318), where the cited sources are 'both Gerhard and Drexelius', not Cyprian. Again, it appears in Thomas Boston, *Human Nature in Its Fourfold State* (1720; Edinburgh, 1812), State IV, Head, vi, p. 443, still with no attribution to Cyprian. More recently, as evidence of its belonging to a larger lore, one may find the simile in James Joyce, *A Portrait of the Artist as a Young Man* (London, J. Cape, 1956), pp. 131-32, with no attribution at all. Wesley would use it more than once again, as in Nos. 84, *The Important Question*, III.13; 103, 'What is Man? Ps. 8:3-4', II.3; and 118, 'On the Omnipresence of God', I.3.

[40] See Ps. 36:8 (AV).

[41] Charles Wesley, *Hymns and Sacred Poems* (1749), II. 314 (*Poet. Wks.*, V. 458). Orig., 'We feast in his sight.'

of heaven 'cease not day or night', but 'continually cry, Holy, holy, holy, is the Lord, the God, the Almighty; who was, and who is, and who is to come!'[42] And when millions of millions of ages are elapsed, their eternity is but just begun.

5   14. On the other hand, in what a condition are those immortal spirits who have made choice of a miserable eternity! I say, made choice; for it is impossible this should be the lot of any creature but by his own act and deed. The day is coming when every soul will be constrained to acknowledge in the sight of men and angels,

10   No dire decree of thine did seal,
                     Or fix the unalterable doom;
                     Confirm my unborn soul to hell,
                     Or damn me from my mother's womb.[43]

In what condition will such a spirit be after the sentence is
15 executed: 'Depart, ye cursed, into everlasting fire, prepared for the devil and his angels!'[44] Suppose him to be just now plunged into 'the lake of fire, burning with brimstone',[45] where 'they have no rest day or night,' but 'the smoke of their torment ascendeth up for ever and ever.'[46] For ever and ever! Why, if we were only to be
20 chained down one day, yea, one hour, in a lake of fire, how amazingly long would one day or one hour appear! I know not if it would not seem as a thousand years. But—astonishing thought—after thousands of thousands he has but just tasted of his bitter cup! After millions it will be no nearer the end than it
25 was the moment it began.

      15. What then is he—how foolish, how mad, in how unutterable a degree of distraction—who, seeming to have the understanding of a man, deliberately prefers temporal things to eternal? Who (allowing that absurd, impossible supposition that
30 wickedness is happiness—a supposition utterly contrary to all

---

[42] Cf. Rev. 4:8.

[43] John and Charles Wesley, *Hymns and Sacred Poems* (1740), p. 133 (*Poet Wks.*, III.33). Orig.:

> No dire decree obtained thy seal,
> Or fixed th' unalterable doom,
> Consigned my unborn soul to hell,
> Or damned me from my mother's womb.

See No. 84, *The Important Question*, III (proem) and n. Another hymn by this title appears at the end of No. 110, *Free Grace.*

[44] Matt. 25:41.   [45] Rev. 19:20.

[46] Rev. 14:11.

reason, as well as to matter of fact)[47] prefers the happiness of a year, say a thousand years, to the happiness of eternity; in comparison of which a thousand ages are infinitely less than a year, a day, a moment? Especially when we take this into the consideration (which indeed should never be forgotten), that the refusing of a happy eternity implies the choosing of a miserable eternity. For there is not, cannot be, any medium between everlasting joy and everlasting pain. It is a vain thought which some have entertained, that death will put an end to the soul as well as the body. It will put an end to neither the one nor the other; it will only alter the manner of their existence. But when the body 'returns to the dust as it was, the spirit will return to God that gave it'.[48] Therefore at the moment of death it must be unspeakably happy or unspeakably miserable. And that misery will never end.

> Never! Where sinks the soul at that dread sound?
> Into a gulf how dark, and how profound![49]

How often would he who had made the wretched choice wish for the death both of his soul and body! It is not impossible he might pray in some such manner as Dr. Young supposes—

> When I have writhed ten thousand years in fire,
> Ten thousand thousand, let me then expire![50]

16. Yet this unspeakable folly, this unutterable madness, of preferring present things to eternal is the disease of every man born into the world, while in his natural state.[51] For such is the constitution of our nature that as the eye sees only such a portion of space at once, so the mind sees only such a portion of time at once. And as all the space that lies beyond this is invisible to the eye, so all the time that lies beyond that compass is invisible to the mind. So that we do not perceive either the space or the time which is at a distance from us. The eye sees distinctly the space that is near it, with the objects which it contains. In like manner the mind sees distinctly those objects which are within such a

---

[47] Cf. No. 5, 'Justification by Faith', I.4 and n.   [48] Cf. Eccles. 12:7.

[49] Cf. Young, *The Last Day*, iii.156-57. See also, Wesley, *A Collection of Moral and Sacred Poems* (1744), II.89. Also No. 73, 'Of Hell', III.3, for another quotation of these lines.

[50] *Ibid.*, iii.206-7; orig., 'When I have raved . . . '. See also *A Collection of Moral and Sacred Poems* (1744), II.90.

[51] Cf. No. 9, 'The Spirit of Bondage and of Adoption', §5 and n.

distance of time. The eye does not see the beauties of China. They are at too great a distance. There is too great a space between us and them: therefore we are not affected by them. They are as nothing to us: it is just the same to us as if they had no 5 being. For the same reason the mind does not see either the beauties or the terrors of eternity. We are not at all affected by them, because they are so distant from us. On this account it is that they appear to us as nothing; just as if they had no existence. Meantime we are wholly taken up with things present, whether in 10 time or space; and things appear less and less as they are more and more distant from us, either in one respect or the other. And so it must be; such is the constitution of our nature, till nature is changed by almighty grace. But this is no manner of excuse for those who continue in their natural blindness to futurity; because 15 a remedy for it is provided, which is found by all that seek it. Yea, it is freely given to all that sincerely ask it.

17. This remedy is faith. I do not mean that which is the faith of a heathen, who believes that there is a God, and that he is a rewarder of them that diligently seek him;[52] but that which is 20 defined by the Apostle, an 'evidence' or conviction 'of things not seen';[53] a divine evidence and conviction of the invisible and the eternal world. This alone opens the eyes of the understanding[54] to see God and the things of God. This as it were takes away, or renders transparent, the impenetrable veil

25   Which hangs 'twixt mortal and immortal being.[55]

---

[52] Cf. Heb. 11:6. For 'the faith of a heathen', cf. No. 1, *Salvation by Faith*, I.2 and n.
[53] Heb. 11:1.
[54] Cf. Eph. 1:18; 1 Cor. 2:10-12.
[55] Another favourite quotation from a stage play; cf. John Hughes, *The Siege of Damascus* (first produced on the day of the author's death, Feb. 17, 1720), III.i. 205-11 [speaking of death]:

> What are thou, O thou great mysterious terror!
> The way to thee we know! diseases, famine.
> Sword, fire, and all thy ever-open gates,
> That day and night stand ready to receive us.
> But what's beyond them?—Who will draw that veil?
> Yet death's not there—No; 'tis a point of time,
> The verge 'twixt mortal and immortal being.

Note Hughes's use of 'verge' as a noun; Wesley changed the syntax to use 'hangs' as a verb. Wesley's version appears, in quotation marks, in No. 119, 'Walking by Sight and Walking by Faith', §6; and also in *Serious Thoughts on the Earthquake in Lisbon*. It also appears in No. 117, 'On the Discoveries of Faith', §8, without quotation marks.

When

> Faith lends its realizing light,
> The clouds disperse, the shadows fly;
> The invisible appears in sight,
> And God is seen by mortal eye.[56]   5

Accordingly a believer (in the scriptural sense) lives in eternity, and walks in eternity. His prospect is enlarged. His view is not any longer bounded by present things;[57] no, nor by an earthly hemisphere, though it were, as Milton speaks, 'tenfold the length of this terrene'.[58] Faith places the unseen, the eternal world, 10 continually before his face. Consequently he 'looks not at the things that are seen'—

> Wealth, honour, pleasure, or what else,
> This short-enduring world can give;[59]

these are not his aim, the object of his pursuit, his desire, or 15 happiness—'but at the things that are not seen'; at the favour, the image, and the glory of God; as well knowing that 'the things which are seen are temporal', a vapour, a shadow, a dream that vanishes away;[60] whereas 'the things that are not seen are eternal',[61] real, solid, unchangeable.   20

18. What then can be a fitter employment for a wise man than to meditate upon these things? Frequently to expand his thoughts 'beyond the bounds of this diurnal sphere',[62] and to expatiate above even the starry heavens, in the fields of eternity? What a means might it be to confirm his contempt of the poor, little 25 things of earth! When a man of huge possessions was boasting to

---

[56] Charles Wesley, 'The Life of Faith', ver. 6, in *Hymns and Sacred Poems* (1740), p. 7 (*Poet. Wks.*, I.210). See also No. 132, 'On Faith, Heb. 11:1', §18; and *Advice to the People called Methodists* (*Bibliog.* No. 108; Vol. 9 of this edn.).

[57] Cf. Addison, *Cato*, Act V, sc. 1; see also, No. 117, 'On the Discoveries of Faith', §8 and n.

[58] Milton, *Paradise Lost*, vi. 78. Cf. also Nos. 71, 'Of Good Angels', I.2; 115, 'Dives and Lazarus', I.6; and 132, 'On Faith, Heb. 11:1', §7.

[59] A translation from the French (of Antoinette Bourignon?) apparently provided the Wesleys by John Byrom; it appears in his *Miscellaneous Poems* (published posthumously in 1773), II. 211. The immediate source here would seem to be 'Renouncing All for Christ. From the French', ver. 7, in *Hymns and Sacred Poems* (1739), p. 124 (*Poet. Wks.*, I.111). Wesley used it again in No. 125, 'On a Single Eye', II.4; and in his letters to Ann Bolton, May 2, 1771; to Alexander Knox, Apr. 1, 1776; and to Mary Smith, Nov. 20, 1789.

[60] See Jas. 4:14.   [61] 2 Cor. 4:18.

[62] A paraphrase of Milton, *Paradise Lost*, vii. 21-22; see also No. 70, 'The Case of Reason Impartially Considered', II.4.

his friend of the largeness of his estate, Socrates desired him to bring a map of the earth, and to point out Attica therein. When this was done (although not very easily, as it was a small country) he next desired Alcibiades to point out his own estate therein.
5 When he could not do this, it was easy to observe how trifling the possessions were in which he had so prided himself in comparison of the whole earth![63] How applicable is this to the present case! Does anyone value himself on his earthly possessions? Alas, what is the whole globe of earth to the infinity
10 of space? A mere speck of creation.[64] And what is the life of man, yea, the duration of the earth itself, but a speck of time, if it be compared to the length of eternity? Think of this! Let it sink into your thought till you have some conception, however imperfect, of that

15
       boundless, fathomless abyss,
       Without a bottom or a shore.[65]

19. But if naked eternity, so to speak, be so vast, so astonishing an object as even to overwhelm your thought, how does it still enlarge the idea to behold it clothed with either happiness or
20 misery! Eternal bliss or pain! Everlasting happiness, or everlasting misery! One would think it would swallow up every other thought in every reasonable creature. Allow me only this: 'Thou art on the brink of either a happy or miserable eternity.'

[63] The point here (Socrates's deflation of Alcibiades's arrogance) is a theme of the pseudo-Platonic *Alcibiades I*, along with a reference to his 'huge possessions' (in §104) and a disparaging comparison between the vast landholdings of Persian royalty and Alcibiades's 'three hundred acre farm at Erchiae' (§123). But this is not the source of this anecdote of Wesley. Nor does it appear in Xenophon's *Memorabilia of Socrates*, nor Plutarch's 'Life of Alcibiades', nor even in John Gilbert Cooper, whose biography of Socrates (1739) was Wesley's source for his comment on Socrates's *daimon* (see No. 71, 'Of Good Angels', §2 and n.). One may guess that it belonged to a common stock of Socratic lore that Wesley shared. But whence?

[64] Cf. Young, *The Last Day*, ii. 221; and Wesley's *Collection of Moral and Sacred Poems* (1744), II. 80. See also Nos. 103, 'What is Man? Ps. 8:3-4', Proem; and 119, 'Walking by Sight and Walking by Faith', §4, where the phrase does appear as a quotation.

[65] This couplet, in its exact text here, has not been located. Its phrases, however, are familiar enough. E.g., Milton's 'The dark unbottomed infinite abyss' (*Paradise Lost*, ii. 405); Young's 'fathomless abyss' (*Night Thoughts*, I. 64-65); Watts's 'unfathomable sea/ Those deeps without a shore' in 'Death and Eternity' (*Works*, IV.343); and also his 'without a bottom or a shore' (*Works*, IV. 267). Other variations appear, as in Blackmore, *Essays on Several Subjects*,—a comparison between 'a little rill' and 'the boundless ocean of eternity'. Is this a composite quotation from memory? See No. 21, 'Sermon on the Mount, I', II.6.

Thy Creator bids thee now stretch out thy hand either to the one or the other—and one would imagine no rational creature could think on anything else. One would suppose that this single point would engross his whole attention. Certainly it ought so to do; certainly if these things are so there can be but one thing needful. 5 O let you and I at least, whatever others do, choose that better part which shall never be taken away from us![66]

20. Before I close this subject permit me to touch upon two remarkable passages in the Psalms (one in the eighth, the other in the one hundred and forty-fourth) which bear a near relation to it. 10 The former is: 'When I consider the heavens, the work of thy fingers, the moon and the stars which thou hast ordained; what is man that thou art mindful of him? Or the son of man that thou visitest him?'[67] Here man is considered as a cipher, a point, compared to immensity. The latter is: 'Lord, what is man, that 15 thou hast such respect unto him? [. . .] Man is like a thing of naught; his time passeth away like a shadow!'[68] In the new translation[69] the words are stronger still: 'What is man, that thou takest knowledge of him? Or the son of man, that thou makest account of him?' Here the Psalmist seems to consider the life of 20 man as a moment, a nothing, compared to eternity. Is not the purport of the former, 'How can he that filleth heaven and earth take knowledge of such an atom as man? How is it that he is not utterly lost in the immensity of God's works?' Is not the purport of the latter, 'How can he that inhabiteth eternity[70] stoop to regard 25 the creature of a day; one whose life passeth away like a shadow?' Is not this a thought which has struck many serious minds as well as it did David's, and created a kind of fear lest they should be forgotten before him who grasps all space and all eternity?[71] But does not this fear arise from a kind of supposition that God is such 30 an one as ourselves? If we consider boundless space or boundless duration, we shrink into nothing before it. But God is not a man. A day and [a] million of ages are the same with him. Therefore

---

[66] See Luke 10:42.
[67] Cf. Ps. 8:3-4.
[68] Ps. 144:3-4 (BCP).
[69] I.e., of 1611. Cf. also No. 103, 'What is Man? Ps. 8:3-4', II.4, where Wesley makes this point again. For other comments about the AV, cf. JWJ, Sept. 14, 1785, and Apr. 22, 1787; and No. 51, *The Good Steward*, II.8.
[70] Isa. 57:15.
[71] An echo here of that strange passage in the letter to Charles, June 27, 1766: 'Or if I have any fear, it is not of falling into hell but of falling into nothing.'

there is the same disproportion between him and any finite being as between him and the creature of a day. Therefore whenever that thought recurs, whenever you are tempted to fear lest you should be forgotten before the immense, the eternal God, remember that nothing is little or great, that no duration is long or short, before him. Remember that God *ita praesidet singulis sicut universis, et universis sicut singulis;* that he presides over every individual as over the universe; and the universe as over each individual.[72] So that you may boldly say—

> Father, how wide thy glories shine,
> Lord of the universe, and mine!
> Thy goodness watches o'er the whole,
> As all the world were but one soul:
> Yet counts my every sacred hair,
> As I remained thy single care![73]

Epworth, June 28, 1786

---

[72] Cf. Augustine, *Confessions*, III.xi; see No. 37, 'The Nature of Enthusiasm', n. 45.
[73] Charles Wesley, *Short Hymns on Select Passages of the Holy Scriptures* (1762), II.158, this one on Matt. 10:39 (*Poet. Wks.*, X.239). In l. 5 Charles borrowed his first line from Watts (see *Works*, IV.340, 353). In turn in l. 5 John has changed Charles's 'Yet *keeps* my every sacred hair'. John uses this stanza again in Nos. 67, 'On Divine Providence', §26; and 77, 'Spiritual Worship', I.8; and in *Some Observations on Liberty*, §57.

ON THE TRINITY

This sermon was written and published in Ireland in 1775 under the title, A Sermon on 1st John, v. 7, *and, despite its six further editions in Wesley's lifetime, it was not reprinted in the* Arminian Magazine. *(For details of its publishing history and variant readings, see Appendix, Vol. 4, and* Bibliog, No. 353.*) The text (1 John 5:7), and so also presumably the topic, must have been a favourite in Wesley's oral preaching, for its use is recorded twenty-three times. There are, however, very few references to the doctrine, as such, in Wesley's writings; this is his only extended comment on it. This suggests that for Wesley, as for pietists generally, abstruse doctrines are better believed devoutly than analysed rationally.*

Thus, the crucial point here is that the mystery of 'the Three-One God' is better left as mystery, to be pondered and adored. Speculations must not be overblown nor exalted to the rank of definitive statements. This, obviously, is a reaction to certain tendencies in Anglican rationalism (e.g., Richard Hooker, George Bull, Thomas Sherlock); it may have been a partial warrant for Wesley's mildly surprising judgment that 'one of the best tracts which that great man Dean [Jonathan] Swift ever wrote was his sermon upon the Trinity.' Swift had argued in that sermon for the reality of the Trinity and for implicit belief even as he insisted that its understanding lay beyond the range of reason. Some of Wesley's other references to Swift are less admiring (cf. JWJ, June 14, 1771; July 12, 1773; and especially October 27, 1775, five months after this sermon had been written).

Despite these disavowals of rationalism, however, it is plain enough that the substance *of Wesley's own trinitarian doctrine follows faithfully in the traditional Anglican line hewed out by Bishop John Pearson, of Chester, in* An Exposition of the Creed *(first edition, 1659; fifth edition [last in Pearson's lifetime], 1683; but see also the enlarged folio edition of 1732, which Wesley would have seen at Oxford). The admission of the problems about the textual evidence for 1 John 5:7 is interesting; so also is Wesley's appeal to J. A. Bengel's authority, rather than to such English critics as Matthew Poole, Matthew Henry, or Henry Hammond. Even more interesting, however, is the high incidence of 'learned allusions' in this particular sermon. Simplified as its argument may be, was it meant to be* ad populum? *But if not, why so blithe a disregard of the tradition?*

On the Trinity

Advertisement

Some days since I was desired to preach on this text. I did so yesterday morning. In the afternoon I was pressed to write down
5 and print my sermon; if possible before I left Cork. I have wrote it this morning: but I must beg the reader to make allowance for the disadvantages I am under, as I have not here any books to consult, nor indeed any time to consult them.

Cork, May 8, 1775

10 ## 1 John 5:7

There are three that bear record in heaven, the Father, the Word, and the Holy Ghost: and these three are one.

1. Whatsoever the generality of people may think, it is certain that opinion is not religion: no, not right opinion, assent to one or
15 to ten thousand truths. There is a wide difference between them: even right opinion is as distant from religion as the east is from the west. Persons may be quite right in their opinions, and yet have no religion at all. And on the other hand persons may be truly religious who hold many wrong opinions. Can anyone possibly
20 doubt of this while there are Romanists in the world? For who can deny, not only that many of them formerly have been truly

religious (as à Kempis,[1] Gregory Lopez,[2] and the Marquis de Renty[3]), but that many of them even at this day are real, inward Christians? And yet what an heap of erroneous opinions do they hold, delivered by tradition from their fathers! Nay, who can doubt of it while there are Calvinists in the world—asserters of 5

[1] One of the three principal influences mentioned by Wesley in his own spiritual autobiography (JWJ, May 24, 1738). He knew à Kempis (1380–1471) chiefly as the author of *De Imitatione Christi*, which in 1738 he said he had read 'in Dean Stanhope's translation' (see JWJ, *ibid.*). Born in Kempen, near Cologne, Thomas (Hemerken) lived most of his life in the Augustinian monastery of St. Agnes near Zwolle (Netherlands). He was a disciple of Groote and Ruysbroeck and became the most famous of the spokesmen for the '*Devotio Moderna*' (if, indeed, he *was* the author of the *Imitation*). Wesley translated and published the *Imitation* in 1735. (Moore writes that Wesley was 'dissatisfied with Stanhope's translation and determined to give a full view of the self-denying purity of his favourite guide'; cf. *Wesley*, II.401).

For some of Wesley's repeated references to à Kempis see Nos. 73, 'Of Hell', II.7; 79, 'On Dissipation', §17; 125, 'On a Single Eye', §1. Cf. also his letter to his mother, May 28, 1725; to Joseph Taylor, Sept. 24, 1782; and to James Macdonald, Oct. 23, 1790. He used Castellio's Ciceronian translation of it *(e Latino in Latinum)* as a Latin text for the students at Kingswood.

[2] An obscure Spanish mystic (1542–96), discovered by Wesley in Francisco Losa's *Holy Life of Gregory Lopez, A Spanish Hermite in the West Indies* (orig. in Spanish, 1618?; Eng. tr., 1675). This he abridged and published in the *Christian Lib.*, L. 337-406. Wesley must have been impressed by Lopez's 'conversion' in Toledo (age 20) and his resolution 'to quit both the court, his friends and native country'. Lopez arrived in 'New Spain' (Mexico) in 1562, and shortly found a hermitage in the wilderness of Amajac and lived in great austerity for seven years in *un alto puro y nudo di amore de Dios* ('in an exalted state of the pure, unadorned love of God'). Then came a period of itinerancy (Guasteca, Atrisco, Mexico City, etc.) but always in a severely ascetic lifestyle. His last seven years were spent in a little house near Santa Fé ('two leagues from the city' [Mexico City]) where he died. Before one of his infrequent communions, Losa records that Lopez 'fell on his knees before Fr. Vincent and, striking his breast, said, "Through the mercy of God, I do not remember to have offended him in anything. Give me, if you please, the most holy Sacraments." Fr. Vincent asked in amazement, "Is it possible a man should have attained so high a degree of virtue, as not to be conscious of [sin]?"'

It is easy to see how Lopez's example affected Wesley: (1) their mutual source in Scupoli's *Spiritual Combat;* (2) Lopez's voyage to Mexico had parallels to the Georgia mission; (3) 'holy living' as a lifelong quest; (4) stress on self-denial; (5) tranquillity of soul; (6) *contemptus mundi;* (7) identification with the poor; (8) Lopez's practice of 'primitive physick'; (9) 'perfection' as purity of intention *in this life;* (10) the equation of holiness and happiness.

Lopez's influence had already been acknowledged by Molinos and Madame Guyon. Cf. No. 114, *On the Death of John Fletcher*, III.12, as well as repeated references in JWJ and *Letters.*

[3] Gaston Jean Baptiste de Renty (1611–49), a highborn Frenchman turned ascetic, known to Wesley through the *Life* by Saint-Jure, (see No. 14, *The Repentance of Believers*, n. 70). A precocious youth, de Renty was 'converted' by a reading of à Kempis and resolved to become a Carthusian hermit. His parents dissuaded him from this, encouraging him to marry and enter a career of public service. In 1638, however, he abandoned his career to devote himself wholly to ascetic piety (e.g., wearing an iron girdle, etc.) and to charity. He also influenced Henry Buch (1590–1666) to found a religious congregation of *Les Frères*

absolute predestination? For who will dare to affirm that none of these are truly religious men? Not only many of them in the last century were burning and shining lights,[4] but many of them are now real Christians, loving God and all mankind. And yet what
5 are all the absurd opinions of all the Romanists in the world compared to that one, that the God of love, the wise, just, merciful Father of the spirits of all flesh, has from all eternity fixed an absolute, unchangeable, irresistible decree that part of mankind shall be saved, do what they will, and the rest damned, do what
10 they can![5]
2. Hence we cannot but infer that there are ten thousand mistakes which may consist with real religion; with regard to which every candid, considerate man will think and let think.[6] But there are some truths more important than others. It seems there
15 are some which are of deep importance. I do not term them *fundamental* truths, because that is an ambiguous word, and hence there have been so many warm disputes about the number of 'fundamentals'.[7] But surely there are some which it nearly concerns us to know, as having a close connection with vital
20 religion. And doubtless we may rank among these that contained in the words above cited: 'There are three that bear record in heaven, the Father, the Word, and the Holy Ghost: and these three are one.'
3. I do not mean that it is of importance to believe this or that
25 *explication* of these words. I know not that any well-judging man

---

Cordonniers, one of the models for Wesley's societies. Wesley's references to de Renty are numerous; cf. No. 14, *The Repentance of Believers*, I.15 and n.

[4] See John 5:35.

[5] A bitter echo of the Calvinist controversy and of Wesley's caricature of Augustus M. Toplady's *Doctrine of Absolute Predestination*, ch. 5, §9 (see *Bibliog*, No. 322): 'The sum of all is this: One in twenty (suppose) of mankind are *elected;* nineteen in twenty are *reprobated.* The *elect* shall be saved, do what they will. The *reprobate* shall be damned, do what they can. Reader, believe this, or be damned. Witness my hand, A*[ugustus]* T*[oplady].*'

[6] Cf. No. 7, 'The Way to the Kingdom', I.6 and n.

[7] An echo of another bitter controversy from the sixteenth and seventeenth centuries ('adiaphoristic'); cf. J. L. von Mosheim, *Institutiones Historiae Ecclesiasticae* (1726; Eng. tr. by J. Murdock, 1841), 'Century XVI', iii.2.28; see also Heppe, *Reformed Dogmatics*, p. 688. In England the Parliament of 1653 had drawn up a list of sixteen 'fundamental articles', which narrowly missed enactment as church law; cf. Daniel Neal, *History of the Puritans* (1754), II.143-44. In 1734 Daniel Waterland had also drawn up a list of seven 'fundamentals' which had not included a formal doctrine of the Trinity. Here, as elsewhere, Wesley is reacting against the tendencies of both orthodoxy and pietism (*viz.,* Lange, Spener, *et al.*); he is taking the narrowest possible view of the irreducible 'fundamentals' and a consciously tolerant view of a broad spectrum of theological opinions (i.e., *adiaphora*).

would attempt to explain them at all. One of the best tracts which that great man Dean Swift ever wrote was his sermon upon the Trinity.[8] Herein he shows that all who endeavoured to explain it at all have utterly lost their way; have above all other persons hurt the cause which they intended to promote, having only, as Job speaks, 'darkened counsel by words without knowledge'.[9] It was in an evil hour that these explainers began their fruitless work. I insist upon no explication at all; no, not even on the best I ever saw—I mean that which is given us in the creed commonly ascribed to Athanasius.[10] I am far from saying, he who does not assent to this 'shall without doubt perish everlastingly'. For the sake of that and another clause I for some time scrupled subscribing to that creed, till I considered, (1), that these sentences only relate to *wilful,* not involuntary unbelievers— to those who, having all the means of knowing the truth, nevertheless obstinately reject it; (2), that they relate only to the *substance* of the doctrine there delivered, not the philosophical *illustrations* of it.

4. I dare not insist upon anyone's using the word 'Trinity' or

---

[8] Jonathan Swift (1667–1745), Dean of St. Patrick's, Dublin, from 1713; his sermon 'On the Trinity' was first published in 1744, in *Three Sermons;* there is no record of when or where it was ever preached. The singling out of Swift's sermon for praise reflects Wesley's approval of Swift's contention that the doctrine of the Trinity is a 'mystery', so far above reason as precludes rational explication altogether. Here, they were both dissenting from men like Robert South ('The Doctrine of the Blessed Trinity Asserted', in *Sermons,* 1844, II.174-91) who, with many Anglicans, believed the doctrine could be shown as not contrary to reason. Cf. Joseph Trapp, 'On the Trinity' (London, 1730), where it was argued that the doctrine is demonstrably rational. See also Louis A. Landa, 'Swift, the Mysteries, and Deism', in *Studies in English* (Austin, Tex., Univ. of Texas Press, 1944), pp. 239-56; Landa's thesis is that Swift's 'antirationalism' with regard to the 'mystery' of the Trinity is aimed at the rationalism of the Deists.

[9] Cf. Job 38:2.

[10] Cf. BCP, Athanasian Creed, directing that it 'shall be said or sung at Morning Prayer instead of the Apostles' Creed on Christmas Day, the Epiphany', and eleven other festival days, including Trinity Sunday. Wesley was aware that Athanasian authorship of this Western creed had been abandoned by most scholars for more than a century (since G. J. Voss, 1642), and he must have known the conclusions of Daniel Waterland's *Critical History of the Athanasian Creed* (1723), where its date is placed in the decade A.D. 430-40 and its authorship attributed to St. Hilary of Arles; see the list of other possible authors in Philip Schaff, *The Creeds of Christendom* (New York, Harper and Harper, 1881–82), I, §10. The first certain witness to this creed is Caesarius of Arles (*c.* A.D. 542). What is noteworthy about Wesley's comments here is his qualified approval of this Creed's positive statement on the Trinity and his rejection of the 'damnatory clauses' with which it opens and closes. In 1755, he had declined to 'defend the *damnatory clauses* and the speaking of "this faith" (i.e., these opinions) as if it were the ground term of salvation'; see Frank Baker, *John Wesley and the Church of England,* pp. 18-19, 331. Cf. also Hooker, *Laws of Ecclesiastical Polity,* Bk. V, ch. 42.

'Person'. I use them myself without any scruple, because I know of none better. But if any man has any scruple concerning them, who shall constrain him to use them? I cannot; much less would I burn a man alive—and that with moist, green wood—for saying,
5 'Though I believe the Father is God, the Son is God, and the Holy Ghost is God, yet I scruple using the words "Trinity" and "Persons" because I do not find those terms in the Bible.' These are the words which merciful John Calvin cites as wrote by Servetus in a letter to himself.[11] I would insist only on the direct
10 words unexplained, just as they lie in the text: 'There are three that bear record in heaven, the Father, the Word, and the Holy Ghost: and these three are one.'

5. 'As they lie in the text'—but here arises a question. Is that text genuine? Was it originally written by the Apostle or inserted
15 in later ages? Many have doubted of this; and in particular that great light of the Christian church, lately removed to the church above, Bengelius—the most pious, the most judicious, and the most laborious, of all the modern commentators on the New Testament.[12] For some time he stood in doubt of its authenticity,

[11] A remote paraphrase, apparently based on *'Sententiae vel Propositionum Excerptae Ex Libris Michaelis Serveti'* in Calvin's *Defensio Orthodoxae Fidei de Sacra Trinitate* (1554); see *Calvini Opera*, VIII.501-8. These excerpts should be compared with Servetus's own words: 'The doctrine of the Trinity can be neither established by logic nor proved from Scripture. . . . The Scriptures and the Fathers teach one God the Father and Jesus Christ his Son; but scholastic philosophy has introduced terms which are not understood and do not accord with Scripture. Jesus taught that he himself was the Son of God. . . . But the doctrine of the Trinity incurs the ridicule of the Mohammedans [Servetus was a Spaniard] and the Jews. It arose out of Greek philosophy . . . , whereas the church should be founded on the belief that Jesus Christ is the Son of God' (*The Two Treatises of Servetus on the Trinity* [no date for the orig.; Eng. tr. by E. M. Wilbur, 1932], pp. 3-5). Wesley (JWJ, July 9, 1741) recounts his discovery of a history of the Calvin-Servetus affair in the Bodleian Library, and in *Some Remarks on a Defence of Aspasio Vindicated*, §6, cites 'Dr. Chandler, an eminent Presbyterian divine in London' as having given 'a circumstantial account of the whole affair' (Samuel Chandler, *The History of Persecution in Four Parts*, London, 1736, espec. pp. 315-25); in the same *Remarks*, §6, Wesley had already said very nearly what he repeats here.

Calvin has, of course, been condemned and defended for his part in Servetus's condemnation and death. In the 'Dedicatory Preface' to *The Eternal Predestination of God* (1552; Eng. tr. 1856), pp. 20-21, Calvin denies that he was responsible for Servetus's death and adds, in *The Secret Providence of God* (1558; Eng. tr. 1856), p. 346: 'That I myself earnestly entreated that Servetus might not be put to death, his judges themselves are witnesses.' See also *Actes du Procès de Michael Servète* (1553), in *Calvini Opera Omnia*, VIII.725-856. But see Sebastian Castellio in *Concerning Heretics*, ed. and tr. by R. H. Bainton (1935), pp. 265-87.

[12] John Albert Bengel (1687–1752), whose *Gnomon Novi Testamenti* (1742) was Wesley's principal source for his *Explanatory Notes Upon the New Testament* (1755). Bengel's comments on 1 John 5:7-9 run for sixteen pages in the *Gnomon* and conclude that

because it is wanting in many of the ancient copies. But his doubts were removed by three considerations: (1). That though it is wanting in many copies yet it is found in more, abundantly more, and those copies of the greatest authority. (2). That it is cited by a whole train of ancient writers from the time of St. John to that of 5 Constantine. This argument is conclusive; for they could not have cited it had it not then been in the sacred canon. (3). That we can easily account for its being after that time wanting in many copies when we remember that Constantine's successor[13] was a zealous Arian, who used every means to promote his bad cause, to 10 spread Arianism throughout the empire; in particular the erasing this text out of as many copies as fell into his hands. And he so far prevailed that the age in which he lived is commonly styled *seculum Arianum*, the Arian age; there being then only one eminent man who opposed him at the peril of his life. So that it 15 was a proverb, *Athanasius contra mundum*—'Athanasius against the world'.[14]

6. But it is objected: 'Whatever becomes of the text, we cannot believe what we cannot comprehend. When therefore you require us to believe mysteries, we pray you to have us excused.' 20

Here is a twofold mistake. (1). We do not require you to believe any mystery in this, whereas you suppose the contrary. But (2), you do already believe many things which you cannot comprehend.

7. To begin with the latter. You do already believe many things 25 which you cannot comprehend. For you believe there is a *sun* over your head. But whether he stands still in the midst of his system,

---

TR of 5:7 is required by the context rather than by the weight of MS evidence. Wesley's summary of Bengel's argument seems to have been based, not upon the *Gnomon*, but on a separate 'dissertation' in Bengel's *Apparatus Criticus* (1734). The words between 'bear record' (ver. 7) and 'the spirit' (ver. 8) are included in no modern critical edn.

[13] Constantius, who became sole ruler of the Empire in A.D. 353 and who died in A.D. 361; cf. the vivid and circumstantial account of this period in William Cave, *Ecclesiastici: Or, the History of the . . . Fathers of the Church* (1716), pp. 399-441 ('The Life of St. Athanasius').

[14] Dean Stanley, *Lectures on the History of the Eastern Church* (1884), pp. 224-29, quotes a long section from Hooker's *Law of Ecclesiastical Polity*, V. xlii.5, which concludes: 'So that this was the plain condition of those times: the whole world against Athanasius and Athanasius against it.' From which he then infers: 'It is probably from the Latin version of this celebrated passage that we derive the proverb, *Athanasius contra mundum*.' Cf. Wesley's letter to William Wilberforce (commending his heroic struggles against slavery), as well as Charles's letter to John, Jan. 2, 1738. Cf. also No. 88, 'On Dress', §23, where Wesley quotes from his brother Samuel's verse which makes this same point in different words.

or not only revolves on his own axis but 'rejoiceth as a giant to run his course',[15] you cannot comprehend either one or the other—*how* he moves, or *how* he rests. By what power, what natural, mechanical power, is he upheld in the fluid ether? You cannot deny the fact; yet you cannot account for it so as to satisfy a rational inquirer. You may indeed give us the hypotheses of Ptolemy, Tycho Brahe, Copernicus,[16] and twenty more. I have read them over and over. I am sick of them. I care not three straws for them all.

> Each new solution but once more affords
> New change of terms, and scaffolding of words:
> In other garb my question I receive,
> And take my doubt the very same I gave.[17]

Still I insist, the *fact* you believe, you cannot deny. But the *manner* you cannot comprehend.

8. You believe there is such a thing as *light*, whether flowing from the sun or any other luminous body. But you cannot

---

[15] Ps. 19:5(BCP).

[16] A shorthand reference to the knowledge explosion in the physical sciences in his own and preceding centuries and a reflection of his interest in the impact of the new science upon religion. The Ptolemaic (geocentric) model of astronomy had dominated medieval world views until the sixteenth century when they were challenged, less radically by the Danish astronomer Tycho Brahe (1546–1601) and much more radically by the heliocentrism of Nicolaus Copernicus (1473–1543). It is interesting that Wesley here ignores Brahe's more famous and influential assistant and successor, Johannes Kepler (1571–1630). What is important for him here is the development of the changing world views from the geocentrism of Ptolemy, the fixed earth theories of Brahe, to the radical heliocentrism of Copernicus. Wesley had also read (how carefully one can only guess) Sir Isaac Newton's *Opticks* (1704), and the *Principia Mathematica* (1687), along with Bernard Le Bovier de Fontenelle's *Conversations on the Plurality of Worlds* (1686). He was equally interested in the speculations of Thomas Burnet *(Sacred Theory of the Earth)* and John Keill's critique *(An Examination of Dr. Burnet's Theory,* 1698), as well as the controversies generated by William Whiston's *A New Theory of the Earth,* and John Woodward's *Natural History of the Earth* (1695). He was even drawn into the eccentric notions of John Hutchinson's *Moses's Principia* (1724), chiefly as a foil against what he regarded as the naturalistic tendencies of Newton and the Newtonians. His chief reliance, perhaps, was on John Rogers, *Dissertation on the Knowledge of the Antients in Astronomy* (1755). His gleanings from these various excursions into 'contemporary science' may be seen in Nos. 69, 'The Imperfection of Human Knowledge', I.5; 77, 'Spiritual Worship', I.6; 103, 'What is Man? Ps. 8:3-4', I.3-6, II.9-12; 132, 'On Faith, Heb. 11:1', §3; cf. also his letter 'To the Editor of *The London Magazine*', Jan. 1, 1765. His summary of 'modern astronomy' appears in the *Survey,* espec. III.279, 296, 328-40. His consistent point, in all these passages, is that science cannot penetrate the mysteries of faith and should not presume to try. Its positive function is to extend and verify our knowledge of creation as the exhibition of the Creator's providence, wisdom, and glory.

[17] Prior, *Solomon,* I. 477-80, beginning, 'Yet this solution . . .'. See also Wesley, *Moral and Sacred Poems* (1744), I.111.

comprehend either its nature or the manner wherein it flows. How does it move from Jupiter to the earth in eight minutes—two hundred thousand miles in a moment?[18] How do the rays of the candle brought into the room instantly disperse into every corner? Again: here are three candles, yet there is but one light. Explain 5 this, and I will explain the Three-One God.

9. You believe there is such a thing as *air*. It both covers you as a garment, and

Wide interfused
Embraces round this florid earth.[19]   10

But can you comprehend how? Can you give me a satisfactory account of its nature, or the cause of its properties? Think only of one, its elasticity. Can you account for this? It may be owing to electric fire[20] attached to each particle of it: it may not—and neither you nor I can tell. But if we will not breathe it till we can 15 comprehend it, our life is very near its period.

10. You believe there is such a thing as *earth*. Here, you fix your foot upon it. You are supported by it. But do you comprehend what it is that supports the earth? 'O, an elephant', says a Malabarian philosopher; 'and a bull supports him.'[21] But what 20 supports the bull? The Indian and the Briton are equally at a loss for an answer. We know it is God that 'spreadeth the north over the empty space, and hangeth the earth upon nothing'.[22] This is the fact. But how? Who can account for this? Perhaps angelic, but not human creatures.   25

I know what is plausibly said concerning the powers of

[18] Cf. Chambers's *Cyclopaedia*, on 'Jupiter', 'Planets', and 'Light'. Cf. also No. 69, 'The Imperfection of Human Knowledge', I.5 (where Wesley speaks of Rogers's efforts to discredit Newton) and n. Even so, Wesley maintains a sceptical attitude toward all these claims: 'With regard to [the planets'] distance from the earth, there is such an immense difference in the calculations of the astronomers . . . that it is wisest to confess our ignorance and to acknowledge we have nothing to rest on here but uncertain conjecture' (*Survey*, III.296). Thus Wesley stands closer to Rogers than he ever did to Newton.
[19] Milton, *Paradise Lost*, vii. 89-90. Cf. No. 89, 'The More Excellent Way', V.5.
[20] Cf. No. 15, *The Great Assize*, III.4 and n.
[21] Cf. Locke, *Essay Concerning Human Understanding*, II.xiii. 19, xxiii.2 (which discusses this Malabarian philosophy); cf. also Soame Jenyns, *A Free Inquiry into the Nature and Origin of Evil* (1757) for a later discussion of the 'fable'. Jeremy Taylor, *Works*, I. lix (intro.) makes mention of this 'sage system of Indian cosmogony'. See Wesley's 'Remarks on Mr. H.'s Account of the Gentoo Religion in Hindostan', first published in *Lloyd's Evening Post*, Nov. 30, 1774, and afterwards in *AM* (1785), VIII. 425-28, 474-76.
[22] Cf. Job 26:7.

projection and attraction.[23] But spin as fine as we can, matter of fact sweeps away our cobweb hypothesis. Connect the force[s] of projection and attraction how you can, they will never produce a circular motion. The moment the projected steel comes within
5 the attraction of the magnet, it does not form a curve, but drops down.

11. You believe you have a *soul*. 'Hold there', says the Doctor;[a] 'I believe no such thing. If you have an immaterial soul, so have the brutes too.' I will not quarrel with any that think they have;
10 nay, I wish he could prove it. And surely I would rather allow *them* souls than I would give up my own. In this I cordially concur in the sentiment of the honest heathen: *Si erro, libenter erro; et me redargui valde recusem*[24]—if I err, I err willingly; and I vehemently refuse to be convinced of it. And I trust most of those who do not
15 believe a Trinity are of the same mind. Permit me then to go on. You believe you have a soul connected with this house of clay.[25] But can you comprehend how? What are the ties that unite the heavenly flame with the earthly clod? You understand just nothing of the matter. So it is; but how none can tell.
20   12. You surely believe you have a *body* together with your soul, and that each is dependent on the other. Run only a thorn into your hand: immediately pain is felt in your soul. On the other side, is shame felt in your soul? Instantly a blush overspreads your cheek. Does the soul feel fear or violent anger? Presently the body

---

[a] Dr. Bl--ir, in his late tract [i.e., Patrick Blair, M.D., of Cork, *Thoughts on Nature and Religion* (1774); cf. pp. 61-63: '(since) all (animals) have a "mind" or faculty of thinking and judging . . . , they must have as equal a right to an immortal director as the human species.' Wesley and Blair, however, have little else in common in their assumptions and conclusions].

---

[23] Key terms in the wide-ranging debates about the 'new science', the theory of gravitation in particular. Cf. Chambers's *Cyclopaedia*, on 'Attraction' (running to eight quarto columns); see also 'Force', 'Projectile', 'Projection', and 'Gravitation'. The 'cobweb hypothesis' may refer here to the gossamer character of the various theories being spun out so profusely. One of them would have been the odd theory of biblical symbolism of John Hutchinson, who had found, in the *unpointed* text of the Hebrew Bible, clues to a complete cosmology based on the physical interaction of light, fire, and air (analogous to the Trinity). This was the project of *Moses's Principia* and his other prolific writings. Wesley appreciated Hutchinson as a counterweight to Newton, but the empirical turn of his mind quickly turned him away from Hutchinson's fanciful theorizings; cf. No. 77, 'Spiritual Worship', I.6 and n.
[24] A conflation of bits from two different passages in Cicero's *De Senectute (On Old Age)*, xxiii. 85 and xxiii. 83.
[25] See Job 4:19. Cf. No. 28, 'Sermon on the Mount, VIII', §21 and n.116.

trembles. There also are facts which you cannot deny; nor can you account for them.

13. I bring but one instance more. At the command of your soul your hand is lifted up. But who is able to account for this, for the connection between the act of the mind, and the outward actions? 5 Nay, who can account for 'muscular motion' at all, in any instance of it whatever? When one of the most ingenious physicians in England had finished his lecture upon that head he added: 'Now, gentlemen, I have told you all the discoveries of our enlightened age. And now, if you understand one jot of the matter, you 10 understand more than I do.'[26]

The short of the matter is this. Those who will not believe anything but what they can comprehend must not believe that there is a *sun* in the firmament, that there is *light* shining around them, that there is *air*, though it encompasses them on every side, 15 that there is any *earth*, though they stand upon it. They must not believe that they have a *soul*, no, nor that they have a *body*.

14. But, secondly, as strange as it may seem, in requiring you to believe, 'there are three that bear record in heaven, the Father, the Word, and the Holy Ghost; and these three are one,' you are 20 not required to believe any mystery. Nay, that great and good man, Dr. Peter Browne, sometime Bishop of Cork, has proved at large that the Bible does not require you to believe any mystery at all.[27] The Bible barely requires you to believe such *facts*, not the manner of them. Now the mystery does not lie in the *fact*, but 25 altogether in the *manner*.

For instance, 'God said, Let there be light; and there was light.'[28] I believe it: I believe the plain *fact;* there is no mystery at all

[26] A similar comment may be found in *Christ Crucified*, §II, the sermon preached by Wesley at Wakefield, Apr. 28, 1774 (see Appendix C, Vol. 1 of this edn.; also *Bibliog*, No. 624), attributed to a 'Dr. Hunter', which could have been either of the two brothers, William (1718–83) or John (1728–93). One may guess (on the basis of his reputation as a popular lecturer) that this anecdote came from William. The idea may be found, earlier, in James Keill (another Scottish physician), *Account of Animal Secretion: the Quantity of Blood in the Human Body and Muscular Motion* (1708), with its frequent disclaimers of definitive knowledge.

[27] Peter Browne (d. 1735), *The Procedure, Extent, and Limits of Human Understanding* (1728). Wesley read this in 1729 and drew up a précis of it for his further use. Cf. his letter to William Law, Jan. 6, 1756; his 'Remarks on Mr. Locke's Essay on Human Understanding', printed in the *AM* (1782–83), VI–VII; and his *Survey*, V.171-223. For Wesley, Browne's essay stood as the most effective rejoinder to Hume and to the faithless sort of scepticism that cuts even the nerve of rational analysis of religious mysteries.

[28] Gen. 1:3.

in this. The mystery lies in the *manner* of it. But of this I believe nothing at all; nor does God require it of me.

Again. 'The word was made flesh.'[29] I believe this fact also. There is no mystery in it; but as to the *manner, how* he was made flesh, wherein the mystery lies, I know nothing about it; I believe nothing about it. It is no more the object of my faith than it is of my understanding.

15. To apply this to the case before us. 'There are three that bear record in heaven . . . : and these three are one.' I believe this *fact* also (if I may use the expression)—that God is Three and One. But the *manner, how,* I do not comprehend; and I do not believe it. Now in this, in the *manner,* lies the mystery. And so it may; I have no concern with it. It is no object of my faith; I believe just so much as God has revealed and no more. But this, the *manner,* he has not revealed; therefore I believe nothing about it. But would it not be absurd in me to deny the fact because I do not understand the manner? That is, to reject *what God has revealed* because I do not comprehend *what he has not revealed?*

16. This is a point much to be observed. There are many things which 'eye hath not seen, nor ear heard, neither hath it entered into the heart of man to conceive'.[30] Part of these God hath 'revealed to us by his Spirit'[31]—*revealed,* that is, unveiled, uncovered. That part he requires us to believe. Part of them he has not revealed. That we need not, and indeed cannot, believe; it is far above, out of our sight.

Now where is the wisdom of rejecting what is revealed because we do not understand what is not revealed? Of denying the *fact* which God has unveiled because we cannot see the *manner,* which is veiled still?

17. Especially when we consider that what God has been pleased to reveal upon this head is far from being a point of indifference, is a truth of the last importance. It enters into the very heart of Christianity; it lies at the root of all vital religion.

Unless these three are one, how can 'all men honour the Son, even as they honour the Father'?[32] I know not what to do, says Socinus in a letter to his friend, with my untoward followers. They will not worship Jesus Christ. I tell them, it is written, 'Let

[29] John 1:14.
[30] Cf. 1 Cor. 2:9.
[31] 1 Cor. 2:10.
[32] John 5:23.

all the angels of God worship him.'[33] They answer, 'However that be, if he is not God we dare not worship him. "For it is written, Thou shalt worship the Lord thy God, and him only shalt thou serve." '[34]

But the thing which I here particularly mean is this: the knowledge of the Three-One God[35] is interwoven with all true Christian faith, with all vital religion.

I do not say that every real Christian can say with the Marquis de Renty, 'I bear about with me continually an experimental verity, and a plenitude of the presence of the ever blessed Trinity.'[36] I apprehend this is not the experience of *babes*, but rather *fathers in Christ*.[37]

But I know not how anyone can be a Christian believer till 'he hath' (as St. John speaks) 'the witness in himself';[38] till 'the Spirit of God witnesses with his spirit that he is a child of God'[39]–that is, in effect, till God the Holy Ghost witnesses that God the Father has accepted him through the merits of God the Son—and having this witness he honours the Son and the blessed Spirit 'even as he honours the Father'.[40]

18. Not that every Christian believer *adverts* to this; perhaps at first not one in twenty; but if you ask any of them a few questions you will easily find it is implied in what he believes.

---

[33] Heb. 1:6.
[34] Matt. 4:10. Cf. *Fausti Socini Senensis Opera Omnia* (Irenopoli, 1656), *'Epistolae ad amicos', Ad Matthaeum Radecium, Epistola III*, pp. 387-88. This would have been the Polish historian, Matthew Radecius.
[35] This phrase had been used by Samuel Wesley, Sen., in his *Life of Christ* (1697), ll. 778 (p. 53), VI. 62 (p. 185), IX. 833 (p. 318). It was repeated by Samuel Wesley, Jun., in his *Poems* (1736), p. 234. See also John Wesley's *Notes* on Luke 4:18.
[36] Cf. Saint-Jure, *Life*, p. 28. De Renty has 'ordinarily' for Wesley's 'constantly' and speaks of 'the most Holy Trinity'. Cf. Henri Bremond, *A Literary History of Religious Thought in France*, II. 431, where (in review of French mysticism, including de Renty) Bremond quotes Pére Poulain, from his *Les graces d'oraison* (5th edn.), p. 66: 'God no longer contents himself with helping us to think *of* him and putting us in mind of his Presence, but he imparts to us *an experimental intellectual knowledge of that Presence.*' Bremond adds: 'This indeed is the fundamental mystical phenomenon.' Cf. also No. 117, 'On the Discoveries of Faith', §17; and the ascriptions to Nos. 133, 'Death and Deliverance'; and 134, 'Seek First the Kingdom'; see also his letter to Hester Ann Roe, June 22, 1776; and the *Notes* on Matt. 3:17; 6:13; Luke 4:18.
[37] Cf. No. 13, *On Sin in Believers*, III.2 and n.
[38] 1 John 5:10.
[39] Cf. Rom. 8:16.
[40] Cf. John 5:23.

Therefore I do not see how it is possible for any to have vital religion who denies that these three are one. And all my hope for them is, not that they will be saved during their unbelief (unless on the footing of honest heathens, upon the plea of invincible ignorance),[41] but that God, before they go hence, will 'bring them to the knowledge of the truth'.[42]

[41] Cf. No. 39, 'Catholic Spirit', I.5 and n.
[42] Cf. 1 Tim. 2:4; 2 Tim. 3:7; Heb. 10:26.

GOD'S APPROBATION OF HIS WORKS

AN INTRODUCTORY COMMENT

This sermon was written expressly for the Arminian Magazine *and appeared in its issues for July and August 1782 (V.341-46, 397-403), as 'Sermon X. On Genesis i:31'. There is no record of Wesley's use of this text elsewhere (a rare instance of a text for a written sermon not already used in his oral preaching). It was then brought up to its present place in* SOSO, *V. 41-56, and given its new title.*

God's Approbation of His Works

Genesis 1:31

*And God saw everything that he had made;
and behold, it was very good.*

1. When God created the heavens and the earth and all that is 5 therein, at the conclusion of each day's work it is said, 'And God saw that it was good.' Whatever was created was good in its kind, suited to the end for which it was designed, adapted to promote the good of the whole and the glory of the great Creator. This sentence it pleased God to pass with regard to each particular 10 creature. But there is a remarkable variation of the expression with regard to all the parts of the universe taken in connexion with each other, and constituting one system: 'And God saw everything that he had made; and behold, it was very good!'

2. How small a part of this great work of God is man able to 15 understand! But it is our duty to contemplate what he has wrought, and to understand as much of it as we are able. For 'The merciful Lord', as the Psalmist observes, 'hath so done his marvellous works', of creation as well as of providence, 'that they

ought to be had in remembrance'[1] by all that fear him, which they cannot well be unless they are understood. Let us then by the assistance of that Spirit who giveth unto man understanding, endeavour to take a general survey of the works which God made
5 in this lower world as they were before they were disordered and depraved in consequence of the sin of man. We shall then easily see that as every creature was 'good' in its primeval state, so, when all were compacted in one general system, 'behold, they were very good.'[2] I do not remember to have seen any attempt of this kind,
10 unless in that truly excellent poem (termed by Mr. Hutchinson, 'that wicked farce'),[3] Milton's *Paradise Lost.*[4]

[I.]1. 'In the beginning God created the matter of the heavens and the earth.'[5] (So the words, as a great man observes,[6] may properly be translated.) He first created the four elements out of
15 which the whole universe was composed: earth, water, air, and fire, all mingled together in one common mass.[7] The grossest parts of this, the earth and water, were utterly without form till God infused a principle of motion, commanding the air to move 'upon the face of the waters'.[8] In the next place, 'The Lord God
20 said, Let there be light: and there was light.'[9] Here were the four constituent parts of the universe: the true, original, simple elements. They were all essentially distinct from each other, and yet so intimately mixed together in all compound bodies that we cannot find any, be it ever so minute, which does not contain them
25 all.

[1] Cf. Ps. 105:5.
[2] An echo of Wesley's earlier project, *A Survey of the Wisdom of God in Creation.*
[3] Hutchinson's actual words: 'that cursed farce of Milton, where he . . . makes the Devil his hero . . .'; cf. his *Works* (3rd edn., 1748–49), V.107; see also XII.xx-xxii.
[4] Cf. *Paradise Lost,* vii. 549-640. Wesley had already published *An Extract from Milton's Paradise Lost* in 1763 (322 pp.) with a commendation 'To the Reader': 'Of all the poems which have hitherto appeared in the world, in whatever age or nation, the preference has generally been given, by impartial judges, to Milton's *Paradise Lost.'* In the sermons Wesley quoted more than thirty-five different passages of *Paradise Lost,* many of them more than once. In an encomium on Matthew Prior, Wesley says he was equal to or superior to 'any English poet, except *Milton* . . .' (see *AM,* V.665).
[5] Cf. Gen. 1:1.
[6] In No. 57, 'On the Fall of Man', II.6, this 'great man' turns out to have been John Hutchinson. The idea of *creatio de nihilo* is, of course, patristic, as in Tertullian, *Against Hermogenes,* ii-xxxviii (espec. xviii); and in Augustine's *Confessions,* XI. vi-xxiii (espec. xx-xxii). Cf. No. 15, *The Great Assize,* III.3 and n.
[7] Cf. No. 57, 'On the Fall of Man', II.1.
[8] Gen. 1:2.
[9] Cf. Gen. 1:3.

2. 'And God saw that' every one of these 'was good',[10] was perfect in its kind. The *earth* was good: the whole surface of it was beautiful in a high degree. To make it more agreeable,

> He clothed
> The universal face with pleasant green.[11]   5

He adorned it with flowers of every hue, and with shrubs and trees of every kind. And every part was fertile as well as beautiful: it was nowhere deformed by rough or ragged rocks; it did not shock the view with horrid precipices, huge chasms, or dreary caverns, with deep, impassable morasses, or deserts of barren 10 sand. But we have not any authority to say, with some learned and ingenious authors, that there were no mountains on the original earth, no unevennesses on its surface.[12] It is not easy to reconcile this hypothesis with those words of Moses, 'The waters increased, . . . and all the high hills that were under the whole 15 heaven were covered. Fifteen cubits upward (above the highest) did the waters prevail; and the mountains were covered.'[a] We have no reason to believe that these mountains were produced by the deluge itself. Not the least intimation of this is given: therefore we cannot doubt but they existed before it. Indeed they 20 answered many excellent purposes, besides greatly increasing the beauty of the creation by a variety of prospects which had been totally lost had the earth been one extended plain. Yet we need not suppose their sides were abrupt, or difficult of ascent. It is highly probable that they rose and fell by almost insensible 25 degrees.

3. As to the internal parts of the earth, even to this day we have scarce any knowledge of them. Many have supposed the centre of the globe to be surrounded with an abyss of fire. Many others have imagined it to be encompassed with an abyss of water, which 30

---

[a] Gen. 7:[17,] 19-20.

[10] Gen. 1:10.
[11] Cf. Milton, *Paradise Lost*, vii.313, 315-16.
[12] The principal advocate of a world view such as this was Thomas Burnet, whom Wesley would have known as a former Master of the Charterhouse. His *Telluris Theoria Sacra* appeared in 1681, and an English revision, *Sacred Theory of the Earth* in 1684. Addison and Steele reviewed it enthusiastically; William Whiston countered with a different theory of a paradisiacal earth in his *A New Theory of the Earth*. The whole speculation was summarily dismissed by the scientists (e.g., John Keill and John Flamsteed, *et al.*) and remains as a sort of theological curio.

they supposed to be termed in Scripture 'the great deep',[b] all the
fountains of which were broken up in order to the general deluge.
But however this was, we are sure all things were disposed therein
with the most perfect order and harmony. Hence there were no
5 agitations within the bowels of the globe, no violent convulsions,
no concussions of the earth, no earthquakes, but all was unmoved
as the pillars of heaven. There were then no such things as
eruptions of fire: there were no volcanoes, burning mountains.
Neither Vesuvius, Etna, nor Hekla, if they had any being, then
10 poured out smoke and flame, but were covered with a verdant
mantle from the top to the bottom.[13]

4. The element of *water*, it is probable, was then mostly
confined within the great abyss. In the new earth (as we are
informed by the Apostle) 'there will be no more sea,'[c] none
15 covering as now the face of the earth, and rendering so large a part
of it uninhabitable by man. Hence it is probable there was no
external sea in the paradisiacal earth; none until the great deep
burst the barriers which were originally appointed for it. Indeed
there was not then that need of the ocean for navigation which
20 there is now. For either (as the poet supposes)

Omnis tulit omnia tellus—[14]

every country produced whatever was requisite either for the
necessity or comfort of its inhabitants; or man being then (as he
will be again at the resurrection) equal to angels, was able to
25 convey himself at his pleasure to any given distance. Over and
above that, those flaming messengers were always ready to
minister to the heirs of salvation. But whether there was sea or
not, there were rivers sufficient to water the earth and make it very
plenteous. These answered all the purposes of convenience and
30 pleasure, by

liquid lapse of murmuring stream.[15]

[b] Gen. 7:11.
[c] [Cf.] Rev. 21:1.

---

[13] Cf. No. 15, *The Great Assize*, III.4 and n.
[14] Cf. Virgil, *Eclogues*, iv. 39: 'each land shall bear all fruits.' See also, No. 64, 'The New Creation', §12.
[15] Cf. Milton, *Paradise Lost*, viii. 263; and see also Nos. 60, 'The General Deliverance', I.2; 64, 'The New Creation', §12; 78, 'Spiritual Idolatry', I.8; and a letter to Ann Granville, Aug. 14, 1731.

To which were added gentle, genial showers, with salutary mists and exhalations. But there were no putrid lakes, no turbid or stagnating waters; but only such as

> bore impressed
> Fair Nature's image on their placid breast.[16]   5

5. The element of *air* was then always serene, and always friendly to man. It contained no frightful meteor, no unwholesome vapours, no poisonous exhalations. There were no tempests, but only cool and gentle breezes,

> *genitabilis aura favoni,*[17]   10

fanning both man and beast, and wafting the fragrant odours on their silent wings.

6. The sun, the fountain of *fire*,

> of this great world both eye and soul,[18]

was situated at the most exact distance from the earth, so as to   15
yield a sufficient quantity of heat (neither too little nor too much) to every part of it. God had not yet

> bid his angels turn askance
> [. . .] this oblique globe.[19]

There was therefore then no country that groaned under   20

> The rage of Arctos, and eternal frost.[20]

There was no violent winter or sultry summer, no extreme either of heat or cold. No soil was burnt up by the solar heat, none uninhabitable through the want of it. Thus earth, water, air, and fire all conspired together to the welfare and pleasure of man.   25

7. To the same purpose served the grateful vicissitude of light and darkness, day and night. For as the human body, though not

---

[16] Cf. Thomas Parnell, 'The Hermit', ver. 2; see also *Moral and Sacred Poems* (1744), I.268.

[17] Cf. the whole of l.11 in Lucretius, *De Rerum Natura (On the Nature of Things)*, i.: 'and the breeze of the teeming southwind blows afresh.'

[18] Milton, *Paradise Lost*, v.171; see also, I.10, below.

[19] Cf. Milton, *Paradise Lost*, x.668-71; see also No. 64, 'The New Creation', §14.

[20] Cf. Prior, *Solomon*, I. 265; and *Moral and Sacred Poems* (1744), I. 106. Repeated in No. 64, 'The New Creation', §14; in a letter to Lawrence Coughlan, Aug. 27, 1768; and in JWJ of the same date.

liable to death or pain, yet needed continual sustenance by food, so although it was not liable to weariness, yet it needed continual reparation by sleep. By this the springs of the animal machine[21] were wound up from time to time, and kept always fit for the 5 pleasing labour for which man was designed by his Creator. Accordingly 'the evening and the morning were the first day'[22] before sin or pain was in the world. The first natural day had one part dark for a season of repose, one part light for a season of labour. And even in paradise Adam *slept*[d] before he sinned; sleep 10 therefore belonged to innocent human nature. Yet I do not apprehend it can be inferred from hence that there is either darkness or sleep in heaven.[23] Surely there is no darkness in that City of God. Is it not expressly said, 'There shall be no night there'? Indeed they have no light from the sun; but 'the Lord 15 giveth them light.'[e] So it is all day in heaven, as it is all night in hell. On earth we have a mixture of both. Day and night succeed each other till earth shall be turned to heaven. Neither can we at all credit the account given by the ancient poet concerning sleep in heaven, although he allows 'cloud-compelling Jove' to remain 20 awake while the inferior gods were sleeping.[24] 'Tis pity therefore that our great poet should copy so servilely after the old heathen as to tell us,

> Sleep had sealed
> All but the unsleeping eyes of God himself.[25]

25 Not so: they that are 'before the throne of God' serve 'him day and night' (speaking after the manner of men) 'in his temple.'[f] That is, without any interval. As wicked spirits are tormented day and night, without any intermission of their misery, so holy spirits enjoy God day and night, without any intermission of their 30 happiness.

---

[d] [Gen.] 2:21. [e] Rev. 22:5. [f] Rev. 7:15.

[21] Cf. No. 51, *The Good Steward*, I.4 and n. [22] Gen. 1:5*b*.
[23] Cf. No. 51, *The Good Steward*, II.10 and n.
[24] This translation of Homer's νεφεληγερέτα Ζεύς, as in the *Iliad*, i.511-12 and 517-18, or xiv. 312-13, 341-42 (more conventionally, 'cloud-gathering Zeus'), may be seen in Edmund Waller, 'Of the Danger of His Majesty . . . Escaped . . .', l.10, *Works* (1729), p. 2; and in Samuel Wesley, Jun., 'The Iliad in a Nutshell', in *Poems*, p. 345. See also Nicholas Rowe, *Lucan's Pharsalia*, V. 897; and Pope, *Iliad*, xiv. 388.
[25] Cf. Milton, *Paradise Lost*, v. 646-47; cf. also the *Iliad*, ii. 3-4, 5-8.

8. On the second day God encompassed the terraqueous globe[26] with that noble appendage the atmosphere, consisting chiefly of air, but replete with earthly particles of various kinds, and with huge volumes of water—sometimes invisible, sometimes visible—buoyed up with that ethereal fire,[27] a particle of 5 which cleaves to every particle of air. By this the water was divided into innumerable drops, which descending watered the earth and made it very plenteous, without incommoding any of its inhabitants. For there were then no impetuous currents of air, no tempestuous winds; no furious hail, no torrents of rain, no roll- 10 ing thunders or forky[28] lightnings. One perennial spring was perpetually smiling over the whole surface of the earth.

9. On the third day God commanded all kind of vegetables to spring out of the earth. It pleased him first to clothe

> The universal face with pleasant green.[29]   15

And then to add thereto innumerable herbs, intermixed with flowers of all hues. To these were added shrubs of every kind, together with tall and stately trees, whether for shade, for timber, or for fruit, in endless variety. Some of these were adapted to particular climates or particular exposures, while vegetables of 20 more general use (as wheat in particular) were not confined to one country, but would flourish almost in every climate. But among all these there were no weeds, no useless plants, none that encumbered the ground. Much less were there any poisonous ones, tending to hurt any one creature, but everything was 25 salutary in its kind, suitable to the gracious design of its great Creator.

10. The Lord now created 'the sun to rule the day, and the moon to govern the night'.[30] The sun was

> Of this great world both eye and soul.[31]   30

The eye, making all things visible, imparting light to every part of the system, and thereby rejoicing both earth and sky; and the soul, the principle of all life, whether to vegetables or animals. Some of

---

[26] Cf. I.10, below; and No. 15, *The Great Assize*, I.1 and n.
[27] Cf. *ibid.*, III.4 and n.
[28] *OED* traces this usage much further back (i.e., 1508) than 'forked' (1729).
[29] A repetition of I.2, above, omitted from the text of *SOSO*, V.
[30] Cf. Gen. 1:16; Ps. 136:8-9 (BCP).
[31] Milton. See above, I.6 and n.

the uses of the moon we are acquainted with: her causing the ebbing and flowing of the sea, and influencing in a greater or smaller degree all the fluids in the terraqueous globe.[32] And many other uses she may have, unknown to us, but known to the wise
5 Creator. But it is certain she had no hurtful, no unwholesome influence on any living creature.[33] 'He made the stars also:'[34] both those that move round the sun, whether of the primary or secondary order, or those that being at a far greater distance appear to us as fixed in the firmament of heaven. Whether *comets*[35]
10 are to be numbered among the stars, and whether they were parts of the original creation, is perhaps not so easy to determine, at least with certainty, as we have nothing but probable conjecture either concerning their nature or their use. We know not whether (as some ingenious men have imagined) they are ruined
15 worlds—worlds that have undergone a general conflagration—or whether (as others not improbably suppose) they are immense reservoirs of fluids, appointed to revolve at certain seasons, and to supply the still decreasing moisture of the earth. But certain we are that they did not either produce or portend any evil. They did
20 not (as many have fancied since)

> From their horrid hair
> Shake pestilence and war.[36]

11. The Lord God afterward peopled the earth with animals of every kind. He first commanded the waters to bring forth
25 abundantly: to bring forth creatures which, as they inhabited a grosser element, so they were in general of a more stupid nature, endowed with fewer senses and less understanding than other animals. The bivalved shell-fish in particular seem to have no sense but that of feeling, unless perhaps a low measure of taste, so

---

[32] Cf. I.8, above; and No. 15, *The Great Assize*, I.1 and n.
[33] Cf. Chambers's denial of the moon's causal influence on lunacy, in *Cyclopaedia*.
[34] Gen. 1:16.
[35] Chambers's *Cyclopaedia* has five columns for his entry on stars: 'The stars are distinguished, from the phenomena of their motion, etc., into "fixed" and "erratic" . . .' (i.e., planets and comets). His entry on comets runs to seven columns. Wesley was fascinated by astronomy, as most folk in the eighteenth century were (cf. No. 55, *On the Trinity*, §7 and n.). Cf. also his *Survey*, V.i.4, 'Comets and Fixed Stars' (III.272-73), and VI. i.3-5, 'Planets and Comets' (IV. 62-64). Cf. also Nos. 64, 'The New Creation', §8; 68, 'The Wisdom of God's Counsels', §3; 69, 'The Imperfection of Human Knowledge', I.5; 103, 'What is Man? Ps. 8:3-4', I. 4-5; 132, 'On Faith, Heb. 11:1', §3. See also No. 15, *The Great Assize*, III.4 and n.; and *Serious Thoughts on the Earthquake at Lisbon*.
[36] Cf. Milton, *Paradise Lost*, ii.710-11.

that they are but one degree above vegetables. And even the king
of the waters (a title which some give the whale because of his
enormous magnitude), though he has sight added to taste and
feeling, does not appear to have an understanding proportioned
to his bulk. Rather, he is inferior therein not only to most birds 5
and beasts but to the generality of even reptiles and insects.
However, none of these then attempted to devour or in any wise
hurt one another. All were peaceful and quiet, as were the watery
fields wherein they ranged at pleasure.

12. It seems the insect kinds were at least one degree above the 10
inhabitants of the waters. Almost all these too devour one another
and every other creature which they can conquer. Indeed, such is
the miserably disordered state of the world at present that
innumerable creatures can no otherwise preserve their own lives
than by destroying others.[37] But in the beginning it was not so. 15
The paradisiacal earth afforded a sufficiency of food for all its
inhabitants, so that none of them had any need of temptation to
prey upon the other. The spider was as harmless as the fly, and
did not then lie in wait for blood. The weakest of them crept
securely over the earth, or spread their gilded wings in the air, that 20
waved in the breeze and glittered in the sun without any to make
them afraid. Meantime the reptiles of every kind were equally
harmless, and more intelligent than they. Yea, one species of

---

[37] Cf. Nos. 60, 'The General Deliverance', II. 3; and 64, 'The New Creation', §17. This
notion of the predatory chain of the ladder of living things has a striking parallel in Bishop
Joseph Hall, *Soliloquies*, X, *Select Works*, III. 346: 'I cannot but observe, how universal it is,
in all kinds, for one creature to prey upon another: the greater fishes devour the less; the
birds of rapine feed upon the smaller fowls: the ravenous wild beasts sustain themselves
with the flesh of the weaker and tamer cattle: the dog pursues the hare; the cat, the mouse:
yea, the very mole, under the earth, hunts for the worm; and the spider, in our window, for
the fly. Whether it pleased God to ordain this antipathy in nature, or whether man's sin
brought this enmity upon the creature, I enquire not: this I am sure of, that both God hath
given unto man, the lord of this inferior world, leave and power, to prey upon all these his
fellow-creatures, and to make his use of them both for his necessity and lawful pleasure;
and that the God of this world is only he, that hath stirred up men to prey upon one
another: some, to eat their flesh, as the savage Indians; others, to destroy their lives,
estates, good names: this proceeds only from him that is a murderer from the beginning.
O my soul, do thou mourn in secret, to see the great enemy of mankind so woefully
prevalent, as to make the earth so bloody a shambles to the sons of men; and see Christians
so outrageously cruel to their own flesh. And O thou, that art the Lord of Hosts and the
God of Peace, restrain thou the violent fury of those, which are called by thy name; and
compose these unhappy quarrels, amongst them that should be brethren. Let me, if it may
stand with thy blessed will, once again see peace smile over the earth, before I come to see
thy face in glory.'

them 'was more subtle', or knowing, 'than any of the' brute creation 'which God had made'.[38]

13. But in general the *birds*, created to fly in the open firmament of heaven, appear to have been of an order far superior
5 to either insects or reptiles, although still considerably inferior to *beasts* (as we now restrain that word, to quadrupeds—four-footed animals—which two hundred years ago included every kind of living creatures).[39] Many species of these are not only endowed with a large measure of natural understanding, but are likewise
10 capable of much improvement by art, such as one would not readily conceive. But among all these there were no birds or beasts of prey, none that destroyed or molested another; but all the creatures breathed in their several kinds the benevolence of their great Creator.

15 14. Such was the state of the creation, according to the scanty ideas which we can now form concerning it, when its great Author, surveying the whole system at one view, pronounced it 'very good'! It was good in the highest degree whereof it was capable, and without any mixture of evil. Every part was exactly
20 suited to the others, and conducive to the good of the whole. There was 'a golden chain' (to use the expression of *Plato*) 'let down from the throne of God'[40]—an exactly connected series of

---

[38] Cf. Gen. 3:1.

[39] Cf. *OED*'s citation of Miles Coverdale's usage of 'beast' (1535): 'The Bey is but a small beast amonge the foules, yet is his fruit exceedinge swete.'

[40] The 'proof-text' here is Plato's *Thaeatetus*, 153C, where Plato cites Homer's *Iliad*, viii. 19, as a proof-text for the phrase, ἡ σειρὰ χρυσείη ('the golden chain'). The two texts are metaphors for Plato's pervasive and basic idea of 'the great chain of being' (i.e., the interconnectedness of all things in a single coherent whole). The classic survey of this idea is A. O. Lovejoy, *The Great Chain of Being: A Study of the History of an Idea* (Cambridge, Mass., Harvard Univ. Press, 1936). Long before Wesley's time, this monistic world view had become a philosophical commonplace celebrated by the Cambridge Platonists and by poets like Milton, Herbert, Pope, Thomson, *et al.* See, e.g., Herbert's *The Temple*, 'Providence', 133-36; or Pope, *Essay on Man*, i. 237-42:

> Vast chain of being! which from God began
> Natures ethereal, human, angel, man,
> Beast, bird, fish, insect, what no eye can see,
> No glass can reach; from Infinite to thee,
> From thee to nothing. . . .

See also James Thomson, *The Seasons*, 'Summer', ll. 333-36:

> Has any seen
> The mighty chain of being, lessening down
> From Infinite Perfection to the brink
> Of dreary nothing, desolate abyss!

beings, from the highest to the lowest: from dead earth, through fossils, vegetables, animals, to man, created in the image of God, and designed to know, to love, and enjoy his Creator to all eternity.

[II.]1. Here is a firm foundation laid on which we may stand 5 and answer all the cavils of minute philosophers;[41] all the objections which 'vain men who would be wise'[42] make to the goodness or wisdom of God in the creation. All these are grounded upon an entire mistake, namely, that the world is now in the same state it was at the beginning. And upon this 10 supposition they plausibly build abundance of objections. But all these objections fall to the ground when we observe this supposition cannot be admitted. The world at the beginning was in a totally different state from that wherein we find it now. Object therefore whatever you please to the present state either of the 15 animate or inanimate creation, whether in general or with regard to any particular instances, and the answer is ready: these are not now as they were in the beginning. Had you therefore heard that vain King of Castile crying out with exquisite self-sufficiency, 'If I had made the world I would have made it better than 20 God Almighty has made it,'[43] you might have replied: 'No: God Almighty—whether you know it or not—did not make it as it is

---

This idea is everywhere presupposed in Wesley, and yet without ever contradicting, in his mind, the premise of *creatio de nihilo*. Cf., e.g., Nos. 42, 'Satan's Devices', II.4; 60, 'The General Deliverance', III.6; 68, 'The Wisdom of God's Counsels', §2; 71, 'Of Good Angels' (*passim*, for the place of angels in the chain of being); 72, 'Of Evil Angels', §1. See also, Wesley's *Survey*, IV.57–333.

[41] See No. 15, *The Great Assize*, II.4 and n.

[42] Cf. Job 11:12.

[43] The 'vain king' was Alphonso X, '*El Sabio*' (1221–84), and his ironic aphorism survives in many different versions. Cf. Clarke, *A Mirrour or Looking-Glasse* (1654), p. 190, where Clarke cites Justus Lipsius, *De Cruce Libri Tres . . .* (1637). It surfaced as the motto for Dean Acheson's autobiography, *Present at the Creation* (New York, Norton, 1969): 'Had I been present at the creation I would have given some useful hints for the better ordering of the universe (Alphonso X, the Learned . . . King of Spain).' The original comment, however, seems not to have been aimed at the universe in general but more specifically at the complexities of the Ptolemaic astronomy. Cf. John Norris, 'Sermon Preached Before the University of Oxford, Mar. 29, 1685', p. 2, where mention is made of 'that arrogant and peevish mathematician who charged the grand architect with want of skill in the mechanism of the world' saying he could have done better. See also Pufendorf's *Introduction to the History of the Principal Kingdoms and States of Europe* (rev. edn., 1764), I.61, where it is also noted that 'Alphonso X, surnamed "The Wise," was universally esteemed for his learning and particularly for his skill in astronomy.' Cf. No. 90, 'An Israelite Indeed', II.10 and n.

now. He himself made it better, unspeakably better than it is at present. He made it without any blemish, yea, without any defect. He made no corruption, no destruction in the inanimate creation. He made not death in the animal creation, neither its harbingers, 5 sin and pain. If you will not believe his own account, believe your brother heathen. It was only

> Post ignem aetheria domo
> Subductum . . . ,

that is, in plain English, after man, in utter defiance of his Maker, 10 had eaten of the tree of knowledge, that

> macies et nova febrium
> Terris incubuit cohors—[44]

that a whole army of evils, totally new, totally unknown till then, broke in upon rebel man, and all other creatures, and overspread 15 the face of the earth.'

2. 'Nay' (says a bold man who has since personated a Christian, and so well that many think him one!):[g] 'God is not to blame for either the natural or moral evils that are in the world. For he made it as well as he could: seeing evil must exist, in the very nature of 20 things.' It must, in the *present* nature of things, supposing man to

---

[g] Mr. S_____J_____s. [I.e., Soame Jenyns (1704-87) in his *Free Inquiry into the Nature and Origin of Evil* (first published anonymously in 1757). Cf. p. 15: 'The true solution of this incomprehensible paradox must be this, that all evils owe their existence solely to the necessity of their own natures, by which I mean they could not possibly have been prevented without the loss of some Superior Good, or the permission of some greater evil than themselves; or that many (p. 16) evils will unavoidably insinuate themselves by the natural relations and circumstances of things into the most perfect system of created beings, even in opposition to the will of an almighty Creator . . . .' P. 17: 'All that infinite power and wisdom could do was to make choice of that method which was attended with the least and fewest (evils).' P. 108: 'If it be objected that this (general argument) makes God the author of sin, I answer, God is and must be the author of everything.' P. 109: 'If natural evil owes its existence to necessity, why not moral (evil as well)? If misery brings with it its utility, why not wickedness?' This was promptly denounced by Samuel Johnson (who readily recognized the author) in *The Literary Magazine*, 1757, and by others; cf. Richard Butterworth, 'Soame Jenyns', in WHS, XIII.3. See also, Nos. 57, 'On the Fall of Man', §1; 59, 'God's Love to Fallen Man', II.15; 62, 'The End of Christ's Coming', I.8. Cf. also Wesley's letter to his father, Dec. 19, 1729, where he refers to Humphrey Ditton (1675–1715), *Discourse on the Resurrection of Christ* (1714). And cf. Wesley's *Notes* on Matt. 13:28.]

---

[44] Cf. Horace, *Odes*, I. iii. 29-31: 'after fire was stolen from its home in heaven [by Prometheus], wasting disease and a new plague of fevers fell upon the earth.' See also No. 129, 'Heavenly Treasure in Earthen Vessels', II.1.

have rebelled against God. But evil did not exist at all in the original nature of things. It was no more the necessary result of matter than it was the necessary result of spirit. All things then, without exception, were very good. And how should they be otherwise? There was no defect at all in the power of God, any more than in his goodness or wisdom. His goodness inclined him to make all things good: and this was executed by his power and wisdom. Let every sensible infidel then be ashamed of making such miserable *excuses* for his Creator! He needs none of us to make *apologies*, either for him or for his creation! 'As for God, his way is perfect'[45]—and such originally were all his works. And such they will be again, when 'the Son of God' shall have 'destroyed all the works of the devil'.[46]

3. Upon this ground, then—that 'God made man upright', and every creature perfect in its kind, but that man 'found out to himself many inventions'[47] of happiness independent on God, and that by his apostasy from God he threw not only himself but likewise the whole creation, which was intimately connected with him, into disorder, misery, death—upon this ground, I say, we do not find it difficult to

Justify the ways of God with men.[48]

For although he left man in the hand of his own counsel, to choose good or evil, life or death; although he did not take away the liberty he had given him, but suffered him to choose death, in consequence of which the whole creation now groaneth together;[49] yet when we consider all the evils introduced into the creation may work together for our good—yea, may work out for us a far more exceeding and eternal weight of glory[50]—we may well praise God for permitting these temporary evils in order to our eternal good. Yea, we may well cry out: 'O the depth both of the wisdom and of the goodness of God![51] He hath done all things well.[52] Glory be unto God, and unto the Lamb for ever and ever!'[53]

---

[45] 2 Sam. 22:31.   [46] Cf. 1 John 3:8.   [47] Cf. Eccles. 7:29.
[48] Cf. Milton, *Paradise Lost*, i. 26. See No. 15, *The Great Assize*, II.10 and n.
[49] See Rom. 8:22.
[50] See 2 Cor. 4:17.
[51] Cf. Rom. 11:33.
[52] Mark 7:37.
[53] Rev. 5:13; for Wesley's usage of ascriptions as endings for his sermons, see No. 1, *Salvation by Faith*, III.9 and n.

ON THE FALL OF MAN

AN INTRODUCTORY COMMENT

This sermon is dated March 13, 1782, and was printed in the May and June issues of the Arminian Magazine *of that same year as 'Sermon IX. On Genesis iii. 19', but without any other title. It was then repositioned in* SOSO, V. *57-72, with its present title and a comment on sin as the basic cause of pain and evil, especially in view of the vision of a paradisiacal earth delineated in 'God's Approbation of His Works'. Wesley had preached from Gen. 3:19 four times before (twice in 1759, once in 1760, and once in 1761); he would return to it once more in 1789. This published sermon is a reprise of the main themes of Wesley's early manuscript sermon on Gen. 1:27 (see No. 141); thus, one may consider the consonance between his earliest reflections on the problems of creation and the Fall and his latest.*

On the Fall of Man

Genesis 3:19

Dust thou art, and unto dust thou shalt return.

1. Why is there *pain* in the world?[1] Seeing God is 'loving to
5 every man, and his mercy is over all his works'?[2] Because there is *sin:* had there been no sin there would have been no pain. But pain (supposing God to be just) is the necessary effect of sin. But why is there sin in the world? Because man was created in the image of God:[3] because he is not mere matter, a clod of earth, a
10 lump of clay, without sense or understanding, but a spirit like his Creator; a being endued not only with sense and understanding

[1] Cf. Jenyns, *Free Inquiry,* pp. 18, 53, 60, 62.
[2] Cf. Ps. 145:9 (BCP).   [3] See Gen. 1:27; 9:6.

but also with a will exerting itself in various affections. To crown all the rest, he was endued with liberty, a power of directing his own affections and actions, a capacity of determining himself, of choosing good or evil. Indeed had not man been endued with this, all the rest would have been of no use. Had he not been a free as 5 well as an intelligent being, his understanding would have been of no service. For he would have been as incapable of holiness, or any kind of virtue, as a tree or a block of marble. And having this power, a power of choosing good or evil, he chose the latter—he chose evil. Thus 'sin entered into the world,'[4] and pain of every 10 kind, preparatory to *death*.

2. This plain, simple account of the origin of evil, whether natural or moral, all the wisdom of man could not discover till it pleased God to reveal it to the world. Till then man was a mere enigma to himself, a riddle which none but God could solve.[5] And 15 in how full and satisfactory a manner has he solved it in this chapter! In such a manner as does not indeed serve to gratify vain curiosity, but as is abundantly sufficient to answer a nobler end, to

> Justify the ways of God with men.[6]

To this end I would, first, briefly consider the preceding part of 20 this chapter, and then, secondly, more particularly weigh the solemn words which have been already recited.

I.1. In the first place let us briefly consider the preceding part of this chapter. 'Now the serpent was more subtle' or knowing, 'than any beast of the field which the Lord had made'[a]—endued 25 with more understanding than any other animal in the brute creation. Indeed there is no improbability in the conjecture of an ingenious man,[b] that the serpent was then endued with that

---

[a] Ver. 1.
[b] The late Dr. Nicholas Robinson [1697?–1775, a Welsh physician with theological interests whose ingenious book, *The Christian Philosopher* (see its 2nd, enlarged edn., 1757), Wesley 'took some pains in correcting . . .' (JWJ, Feb. 10, 1757). Robinson's discussion of the serpent's speaking comes in *An Appendix to the First Book of the Christian Philosopher, Containing a Physico-Theological Discourse on the Nature, Attributes and Properties of the Serpent that Tempted Eve* . . . (1742), pp. 65-68: 'Now the serpent was more wise and prudent than all the animals of the earth which the Lord had made. . . . He was above

---

[4] Rom. 5:12.
[5] Cf. Nos. 128, 'The Deceitfulness of the Human Heart', II.8; 129, 'Heavenly Treasure in Earthen Vessels', §1; 140, 'The Promise of Understanding', I.2.
[6] Cf. Milton, *Paradise Lost*, i.26. See No. 15, *The Great Assize*, II.10 and n.

reason which is now the property of man. And this accounts for the circumstance which on any other supposition would be utterly unintelligible. How comes Eve not to be surprised, yea, startled and affrighted, at hearing the serpent *speak* and *reason?* Unless
5 she knew that reason, and speech in consequence of it, were the original properties of the serpent? Hence without showing any surprise she immediately enters into conversation with him. 'And he said unto the woman, Yea, hath God said, Ye shall not eat of every tree of the garden?' See how he who was a liar from the
10 beginning mixes truth and falsehood together! Perhaps on purpose, that she might be the more inclined to speak, in order to clear God of the unjust charge. Accordingly 'the woman said unto the serpent, We may eat of the fruit of the trees of the garden: but of the tree which is in the midst of the garden God hath said, Ye
15 shall not eat of it; neither shall ye touch it, lest ye die.'ᶜ Thus far she appears to have been clear of blame. But how long did she continue so? 'And the serpent said unto the woman, Surely ye shall not die. For God doth know, in the day ye eat thereof your eyes shall be opened, and ye shall be as gods, knowing good and
20 evil.'ᵈ Here sin began, namely, unbelief. 'The woman was deceived,'⁷ says the Apostle. She believed a lie: she gave more credit to the word of the devil than to the word of God. And

man himself. . . . And if he spoke to Eve, in consequence of that superiority, then it follows that she had no reason to be surprised at the speech of the serpent; since language was natural to the state and condition of that species of animals. From whence I deduce the following proposition: Proposition I: That the serpent who spoke to Eve was of a species of creatures superior to every class of brutes that was in nature; and very nearly approaching if not entirely coming up to the privileges that the individuals of the human nature obtain in this imperfect state of things, save that he was endued with innocence (which we lost upon the Fall) and also clear of guilt and crime. . . . Speech was a faculty inherent in the serpent, by the rights of his creation. . . . Had the faculty of speech been a new thing, then the surprise must have terrified Eve. . . .'

[The same idea, however, had received a rather different interpretation in Joseph Mede, *Works* (1677); cf. his Discourse XL, p. 223: 'I think none so unreasonable as to believe it was the "unreasonable and brute serpent"; . . . for whence should he learn or how should he understand God's commandment to our first parents? And how is it possible a serpent should speak? . . . If we say she (Eve) thought the tempter to be "the brute serpent", how will this stand with the perfection of man's knowledge in his integrity to think a serpent could speak like a reasonable creature, who would not judge her a silly woman now that should think so. And yet, the wisest of us all is far short of Eve in regard of her knowledge then.' Cf. below, No. 62, 'The End of Christ's Coming', I.9].

ᶜ Ver. 2[-3].
ᵈ Ver. 4-5.

⁷ Cf. 1 Tim. 2:14.

unbelief brought forth actual sin. 'When the woman saw that the tree was good for food, and pleasant to the eyes, and to be desired to make one wise, she took of the fruit and did eat,'[8] and so completed her sin. But 'the man', as the Apostle observes, 'was not deceived.'[9] How then came he to join in the transgression? 'She gave unto her husband, and he did eat.'[10] He sinned with his eyes open. He rebelled against his Creator, as is highly probable,

> Not by stronger reason moved,
> But fondly overcome with female charms.[11]

And if this was the case there is no absurdity in the assertion of a great man that 'Adam sinned in his heart before he sinned outwardly, before he ate of the forbidden fruit;'[12] namely by inward idolatry, by loving the creature more than the Creator.

2. Immediately pain followed sin. When he lost his innocence he lost his happiness. He painfully feared that God in the love of whom his supreme happiness before consisted. 'He said, I heard thy voice in the garden; and I was afraid.'[e] He fled from him who was till then his desire, and glory, and joy. He 'hid himself from the presence of the Lord God, among the trees of the garden'![13] Hid himself! What, from the all-seeing eye? The eye which with one glance pervades heaven and earth! See how his understanding likewise was impaired! What amazing folly was this! Such as one would imagine very few even of his posterity could have fallen into. So dreadfully was his 'foolish heart darkened'[14] by sin, and guilt, and sorrow, and fear! His innocence was lost; and at the same time his happiness and his wisdom! Here is the clear, intelligible answer to that question, how came evil into the world?

3. One cannot but observe throughout this whole narration the inexpressible tenderness and lenity of the almighty Creator from

[e] Ver. 10.

---

[8] Gen. 3:6.   [9] Cf. 1 Tim. 2:14.   [10] Gen. 3:6.
[11] Cf. Milton, *Paradise Lost*, ix. 998-99:

> Against his better knowledge, not deceived,
> But fondly overcome with female charm.

[12] The source of this idea (although not the actual quotation given here) is Augustinian. Cf. *Enchiridion*, ch. xiii, 'Baptism and Original Sin'; see also, *ibid.*, ch. xvii, 'On Forgiveness of Sins', *passim;* and cf. N. P. Williams, *The Ideas of the Fall and Original Sin* (London, New York, Longmans, Green, and Co., Ltd., 1927), pp. 362-66.
[13] Cf. Gen. 3:8.   [14] Rom. 1:21.

whom they had revolted, the sovereign against whom they had
rebelled. 'And the Lord God called unto Adam, and said unto
him, Where art thou?'¹⁵ Thus graciously calling him to return who
would otherwise have eternally fled from God. 'And he said, I
5 heard thy voice in the garden, and I was afraid, because I was
naked.'¹⁶ Still here is no acknowledgement of his fault, no
humiliation for it. But with what astonishing tenderness does
God lead him to make that acknowledgement! 'And he said, Who
told thee that thou wast naked?' How camest thou to make this
10 discovery? 'Hast thou eaten of the tree whereof I commanded
thee that thou shouldst not eat? And the man said' (still
unhumbled, yea, indirectly throwing the blame upon God
himself), 'The woman whom thou gavest to be with me, she gave
me of the tree, and I did eat. And the Lord God', still
15 endeavouring to bring them to repentance, 'said unto the woman,
What is this that thou hast done? And the woman said', nakedly
declaring the thing as it was, 'The serpent beguiled me, and I did
eat.ᶠ And the Lord God said unto the serpent', to testify his utter
abhorrence of sin by a lasting monument of his displeasure in
20 punishing the creature that had been barely the instrument of it,
'Thou art cursed above all cattle, and above every beast of the
field. . . . And I will put enmity between thee and the woman,
and between thy seed and her seed: it shall bruise thy head, and
thou shalt bruise his heel.'¹⁷ Thus in the midst of judgment hath
25 God remembered mercy,¹⁸ from the beginning of the world!
Connecting the grand promise of salvation with the very sentence
of condemnation.

　　4. 'Unto the woman he said, I will greatly multiply thy sorrow
and' (or *in*) 'thy conception; in sorrow', or pain, 'thou shalt bring
30 forth children;' yea, above any other creature under heaven:
which original curse we see is entailed on her latest posterity.
'And thy desire shall be to thy husband, and he shall rule over
thee.'¹⁹ It seems the latter part of this sentence is explanatory of
the former. Was there till now any other inferiority of the woman
35 to the man than that which we may conceive in one angel to
another? 'And unto Adam he said, Because thou hast hearkened

ᶠ Ver. [11-] 13.

---

¹⁵ Gen. 3:9.　　　　　　　¹⁶ Ver. 10.　　　　　　　¹⁷ Ver. 14-15.
¹⁸ See Hab. 3:2.　　　　　　　　　　　　　　　　　¹⁹ Gen. 3:16.

unto the voice of thy wife, and hast eaten of the tree of which I commanded thee saying, Thou shalt not eat of it; cursed is the ground for thy sake.'[20] 'Thorns and thistles shall it bring forth unto thee'—useless, yea, and hurtful productions: whereas nothing calculated to hurt or to give pain had at first any place in the creation. 'And thou shalt eat the herb of the field'—coarse and vile compared to the delicious fruits of paradise. 'In the sweat of thy face shalt thou eat bread, till thou return unto the ground; for out of it wast thou taken. For dust thou art, and unto dust thou shalt return.'[21]

II.1. Let us now, in the second place, weigh these solemn words in a more particular manner. 'Dust thou art.' But how fearfully and wonderfully wrought into innumerable fibres, nerves, membranes, muscles, arteries, veins, vessels of various kinds! And how amazingly is this dust connected with *water*, with enclosed, circulating fluids, diversified a thousand ways by a thousand tubes and strainers! Yea, and how wonderfully is air impacted into every part, solid or fluid, of the animal machine![22] *Air*, not elastic, which would tear the machine in pieces, but as fixed as water under the pole! But all this would not avail were not ethereal *fire* intimately mixed both with this earth, air, and water.[23] And all these elements are mingled together in the most exact proportion; so that while the body is in health no one of them predominates in the least degree over the others.

2. Such was man, with regard to his corporeal part, as he came out of the hands of his Maker. But since he sinned he is not only dust but mortal, corruptible dust. And by sad experience we find that this 'corruptible body presses down the soul'.[24] It very frequently hinders the soul in its operations, and at best serves it very imperfectly. Yet the soul cannot dispense with its service, imperfect as it is. For an embodied spirit cannot form one thought but by the mediation of its bodily organs. For thinking is not (as many suppose) the act of a pure spirit, but the act of a spirit

---

[20] Gen. 3:17.

[21] Gen. 3:18-19.

[22] Cf. No. 51, *The Good Steward*, I.4 and n. For 'body-soul dualism', cf. No. 41, *Wandering Thoughts*, III.5 and n.

[23] Cf. No. 15, *The Great Assize*, III.4 and n. Cf. also No. 56, 'God's Approbation of His Works' I.1, where Wesley also speaks of the four primal elements.

[24] Cf. Wisd. 9:15. Cf. below, II.5 and, above, No. 41, *Wandering Thoughts*, II.3 and n.

connected with a body, and playing upon a set of material keys.[25] It cannot possibly therefore make any better music than the nature and state of its instruments allow it. Hence every disorder of the body, especially of the parts more immediately subservient to
5 thinking, lays an almost insuperable bar in the way of its thinking justly. Hence the maxim received in all ages, *Humanum est errare et nescire.*[26] Not ignorance alone (that belongs more or less to every *creature* in heaven and earth; seeing none is omniscient, none knoweth all things, save the *Creator*), but error is entailed on every
10 child of man. Mistake as well as ignorance is, in our present state, inseparable from humanity. Every child of man is in a thousand mistakes, and is liable to fresh mistakes every moment. And a mistake in judgment may occasion a mistake in practice, yea, naturally leads thereto. I mistake, and possibly cannot avoid
15 mistaking, the character of this or that man. I suppose him to be what he is not; to be better or worse than he really is. Upon this wrong supposition I behave wrong[27] to him, that is, more or less affectionately than he deserves. And by the mistake which is occasioned by the defect of my bodily organs I am naturally led so
20 to do. Such is the present condition of human nature, of a mind dependent on a mortal body. Such is the state entailed on all human spirits while connected with flesh and blood!

3. 'And unto dust thou shalt return.' How admirably well has the wise Creator secured the execution of this sentence on all the
25 offspring of Adam! It is true he was pleased to make one exception from this general rule, in a very early age of the world, in favour of an eminently righteous man. So we read: after Enoch had 'walked with God three hundred, sixty and five years, he was not: for God took him'.[g] He exempted him from the sentence
30 passed upon all flesh, and took him alive into heaven. Many ages after he was pleased to make a second exception, ordering the prophet Elijah to be taken up into heaven in a chariot of fire—very probably by a convoy of angels assuming that appearance.[28] And it is not unlikely that he saw good to make a

---

[g] Gen. 5:23-24.

[25] The repetition of a passage from Wesley's letter to Mrs. Bennis, Oct. 28, 1771. See also, No. 51, *The Good Steward*, II.10 and n.
[26] See No. 39, 'Catholic Spirit', I.4 and n.
[27] Used adverbially, although 'wrongly' also had long been in common use.
[28] See 2 Kgs. 2:11.

third exception in the person of the beloved disciple. There is transmitted to us a particular account of the apostle John's old age. But we have not any account of his death, and not the least intimation concerning it. Hence we may reasonably suppose that he did not die, but that after he had finished his course, and 5 'walked with God' for about a hundred years, 'the Lord took him,' as he did Enoch—not in so open and conspicuous a manner as he did the prophet Elijah.[29]

4. But setting these two or three instances[30] aside, who has been able in the course of near six thousand years to evade the 10 execution of this sentence passed on Adam and all his posterity? Be men ever so great masters of the art of healing, can they prevent or heal the gradual decays of nature? Can all their boasted skill heal old age, or hinder dust from returning to dust? Nay, who among the greatest masters of medicine has been able to add a 15 century to his own years? Yea, or to protract his own life any considerable space beyond the common period? The days of man for above three thousand years, from the time of Moses at least, have been fixed by a middling computation at threescore years and ten. How few are there that attain to fourscore years! Perhaps 20 hardly one in five hundred. So little does the art of man avail against the appointment of God!

5. God has indeed provided for the execution of his own decree in the very principles of our nature. It is well known, the human body when it comes into the world consists of innumerable 25 membranes, exquisitely thin, that are filled with circulating fluids, to which the solid parts bear a very small proportion. Into the tubes composed of these membranes nourishment must be continually infused; otherwise life cannot continue, but will come to an end almost as soon as it is begun. And suppose this 30 nourishment to be liquid, which as it flows through those fine canals continually enlarges them in all their dimensions, yet it

---

[29] All the standard references (Polycarp, Irenaeus, Jerome, and even the best MSS of the apocryphal *Acts of John*) speak of John's death in natural terms. A couple of inferior Greek MSS of the *Acts*, however, have 'appendices' which describe St. John's 'removal' much as Wesley does here. See 'The Acts of John', §115, *The Apocryphal New Testament*, tr. by M. R. James (Oxford, Clarendon Press, 1953), p. 270. Cf. Nos. 68, 'The Wisdom of God's Counsels', §8; and 104, 'On Attending the Church Service', §1.

[30] *AM*, 'these rare instances', altered in 1788 to what appears to have been an only partially successful attempt at a revision, reproduced by the compositor as 'these rare or three instances'. Wesley's personal copy, however, (in MA), sets the matter straight by substituting 'two' for 'rare'.

contains innumerable solid particles, which continually adhere to
the inner surface of the vessels through which they flow; so that in
the same proportion as any vessel is enlarged it is stiffened also.
Thus the body grows firmer as it grows larger, from infancy to
5 manhood. In twenty, five and twenty, or thirty years, it attains its
full measure of firmness. Every part of the body is then stiffened
to its full degree: as much earth adhering to all the vessels as gives
the solidity they severally need to the nerves, arteries, veins,
muscles, in order to exercise their functions in the most perfect
10 manner. For twenty, or it may be thirty years following, although
more and more particles of earth continually adhere to the inner
surface of every vessel in the body, yet the stiffness caused
thereby is hardly observable, and occasions little inconvenience.
But after sixty years (more or less, according to the natural
15 constitution, and a thousand accidental circumstances) the
change is easily perceived, even at the surface of the body.
Wrinkles show the proportion of the fluids to be lessened, as does
also the[31] dryness of the skin, through a diminution of the blood
and juices which before moistened and kept it smooth and soft.
20 The extremities of the body grow cold, not only as they are remote
from the centre of motion, but as the finer vessels[32] are filled up,
and can no longer admit the circulating fluid. As age increases
fewer and fewer of the vessels are pervious, and capable of
transmitting the vital stream; except the larger ones, most of
25 which are lodged within the trunk of the body. In extreme old age
the arteries themselves—the grand instruments of circulation—
by the continual apposition of earth, become hard and as it were
bony, till having lost the power of contracting themselves they can
no longer propel the blood, even through the largest channels, in
30 consequence of which death naturally ensues. Thus are the seeds
of death sown in our very nature. Thus from the very hour when
we first appear on the stage of life we are travelling toward death:
we are preparing, whether we will or no, to return to the dust from
whence we came![33]

---

[31] Wesley's MS annotations and errata add 'the' to the orig. text of *AM*.

[32] Orig., *AM*, 'but as more remote, the inner vessels'. The *AM* errata and Wesley's
annotations in his personal copy delete 'more remote' and alter to 'the finer vessels'. In
turn this is altered in *SOSO* to 'the smaller vessels'.

[33] This account of aging, and especially of the process of arterial hardening, is a
repetition of Wesley's much earlier account of the fatal effects of eating the forbidden fruit
in Eden (a vivid description of atherosclerosis!); see No. 141, 'The Image of God', on
Gen. 1:27. See also, above, II.1; and No. 51, *The Good Steward*, I.4 and n. Cf. also

6. Let us now take a short review of the whole, as it is delivered with inimitable simplicity, what an unprejudiced person might even from hence infer to be the word of God. In that period of duration which he saw to be most proper (of which he alone could be the judge whose eye views the whole possibility of things from 5 everlasting to everlasting) the Almighty, rising in the greatness of his strength, went forth to create the universe. 'In the beginning he created', made out of nothing, 'the matter of the heavens and the earth.'[34] (So Mr. Hutchinson[35] observes the original words properly signify.) Then 'the spirit or breath from the Lord', that is 10 the air, 'moved upon the face of the waters.'[36] Here were earth, water, air, three of the elements or component parts of the lower world. 'And God said, Let there be light: and there was light.'[37] By his omnific word light, that is, fire, the fourth element, sprang into being. Out of these, variously modified and proportioned to each 15 other, he composed the whole universe. 'The earth brought forth grass, and herb yielding seed, and the tree yielding fruit after its kind:'[38] and then the various tribes of animals to inhabit the waters, the air, and the earth. But the very heathen could observe,

> *Sanctius his animal mentisque; capacius altae*   20
> *Deerat adhuc!*[39]

There was still wanting a creature of a higher rank, capable of wisdom and holiness. *Natus homo est.*[40] 'So God created man in his own image: in the image of God created he him!'[41] Mark the emphatical repetition! God did not make him mere matter, a 25 piece of senseless, unintelligent clay, but a spirit like himself (although clothed with a material vehicle). As such he was endued with understanding, with a will, including various affections, and with liberty, a power of using them in a right or wrong manner, of choosing good or evil. Otherwise neither his understanding nor 30

Chambers's *Cyclopaedia*, on 'Blood', 'Circulation', etc. Wesley knew of Dr. Andrew Wilson's work on the circulation of the blood, *Medical Researches* (1777), as well as that of William Harvey, *Exercitatio anatomica de motu cordis et sanguinis in animalibus* (Frankfurt, 1628), which he noted in the intro. to his *Survey;* cf. No. 116, 'What is Man? Ps. 8:4', §4.
[34] Cf. Gen. 1:1.
[35] See No. 56, 'God's Approbation of His Works', I.1 and n.
[36] Cf. Gen. 1:2.   [37] Gen. 1:3.   [38] Cf. Gen. 1:12.
[39] Cf. Ovid, *Metamorphoses*, i. 76-77: 'A holier animal was wanting still/With mind of wider grasp.'
[40] *Ibid.*, i. 78; 'Man was born.'
[41] Gen. 1:27. Cf. No. 1, *Salvation by Faith*, §1 and n.

his will would have been to any purpose; for he must have been as incapable of virtue or holiness as the stock of a tree. Adam, in whom all mankind were then contained, freely preferred evil to good. He chose to do his own will rather than the will of his
5 Creator. He 'was not deceived',[42] but knowingly and deliberately rebelled against his Father and his King. In that moment he lost the moral image of God, and, in part, the natural. He commenced unholy, foolish, and unhappy. And 'in Adam all died.'[43] He entitled all his posterity to error, guilt, sorrow, fear; pain,
10 diseases, and death.

7. How exactly does matter of fact, do all things round us, even the face of the whole world, agree with this account? Open your eyes! Look round you! See darkness that may be felt; see ignorance and error; see vice in ten thousand forms; see
15 consciousness of guilt, fear, sorrow, shame, remorse, care, covering the face of the earth! See misery, the daughter of sin. See on every side sickness and pain, inhabitants of every nation under heaven, driving on the poor, helpless sons of men, in every age, to the gates of death! So they have done wellnigh from the
20 beginning of the world. So they will do till the consummation of all things.

8. But can the Creator despise the work of his own hands? Surely that is impossible! Hath he not then, seeing he alone is able, provided a remedy for all these evils? Yea, verily he hath!
25 And a sufficient remedy, every way adequate to the disease. He hath fulfilled his word: he hath given 'the seed of the woman to bruise the serpent's head'.[44] 'God so loved the world that he gave his only-begotten Son, that whosoever believeth in him might not perish, but have everlasting life.'[45] Here is a remedy provided for
30 all our guilt: he 'bore all our sins in his body on the tree'.[46] And 'if any man have sinned, we have an advocate with the Father, Jesus Christ the righteous.'[47] And here is a remedy for all our disease, all the corruption of our nature. For 'God hath also', through the intercession of his Son, 'given us his Holy Spirit',[48] to 'renew'
35 us both 'in knowledge',[49] in his natural image, 'opening the eyes of our understanding, and enlightening'[50] us with all such knowledge as is requisite to our pleasing God; and also in his

---

[42] 1 Tim. 2:14. [43] Cf. 1 Cor. 15:22. [44] Cf. Gen. 3:15.
[45] Cf. John 3:16. [46] Cf. 1 Pet. 2:24.
[47] Cf. 1 John 2:1. [48] Cf. 1 Thess. 4:8.
[49] Cf. Col. 3:10. [50] Cf. Luke 24:45; Eph. 1:18.

moral image, namely, 'righteousness and true holiness'.[51] And supposing this is done, we know that 'all things will work together for our good.'[52] We know by happy experience that all natural evils change their nature and turn to good; that sorrow, sickness, pain, will all prove medicines to heal our spiritual sickness. They will all be 'to our profit'; will all tend to our unspeakable advantage, making us more largely 'partakers of his holiness'[53] while we remain on earth, adding so many stars to that crown[54] which is reserved in heaven for us.

9. Behold then both the justice and mercy of God! His justice in punishing sin, the sin of him in whose loins we were then all contained, on Adam and all his whole posterity! And his mercy, in providing an universal remedy for an universal evil! In appointing the Second Adam to die for all who had died in the first: that 'as in Adam all died, so in Christ all might be made alive;'[55] that 'as by one man's offence judgment came upon all men to condemnation, so by the righteousness of one' the free gift 'might come upon all, unto justification of life'.[56] 'Justification of life', as being connected with the new birth, the beginning of spiritual life,[57] which leads us through the life of holiness to life eternal, to glory.

10. And it should be particularly observed that 'where sin abounded, grace does much more abound.'[58] For 'not as the condemnation' so 'is the free gift;'[59] but we may gain infinitely more than we have lost. We may now attain both higher degrees of holiness and higher degrees of glory than it would have been possible for us to attain if Adam had not sinned. For if Adam had not sinned, the Son of God had not died.[60] Consequently that amazing instance of the love of God to man had never existed which has in all ages excited the highest joy, and love, and gratitude from his children. We might have loved God the

---

[51] Eph. 4:24.   [52] Cf. Rom. 8:28.

[53] Cf. Heb. 12:10.

[54] This metaphor of 'stars' added to our heavenly 'crown' was a favourite of Wesley; cf. Nos. 59, 'God's Love to Fallen Man', II.11; 89, 'The More Excellent Way', §8; and 144, 'The Love of God', II.10. Cf. also Samuel Wesley, Sen., *Life of Christ* (1697), V. 278 (p. 152): 'Stript from my robes of light and starry crowns'. See also the 1780 *Collection* (Vol. 7 of this edn.) 487:23, 'And each a starry crown receive'; and 496:30, 'Till all receive the starry crown'.

[55] Cf. 1 Cor. 15:22.   [56] Cf. Rom. 5:18.

[57] Cf. No. 14, *The Repentance of Believers*, III.2 and n.

[58] Cf. Rom. 5:20.   [59] Cf. Rom. 5:15, 18.

[60] An echo of Wesley's long-time commitment to the *felix culpa* tradition. Cf. No. 59, 'God's Love to Fallen Man', I.1 and n.

Creator, God the Preserver, God the Governor. But there would have been no place for love to God the Redeemer: this could have had no being. The highest glory and joy of saints on earth and saints in heaven, Christ crucified, had been wanting. We could not then have praised him that, 'thinking it no robbery to be equal with God, yet emptied himself, took upon him the form of a servant, and was obedient to death, even the death of the cross'![61] This is now the noblest theme of all the children of God on earth; yea, we need not scruple to affirm, even of angels, and archangels, and all the company of heaven:[62]

> Hallelujah they cry
> To the King of the sky,
> To the great, everlasting I Am;
> To the Lamb that was slain,
> And liveth again,
> Hallelujah to God and the Lamb.[63]

Bristol, March 13, 1782[64]

---

[61] Cf. Phil. 2:6-8 (*Notes*).
[62] BCP, Communion, Sanctus.
[63] Charles Wesley, *Hymns and Sacred Poems* (1749), II.314 (*Poet. Wks.*, V.458).
[64] Place and date as in *AM* only.

ON PREDESTINATION

AN INTRODUCTORY COMMENT

Wesley's aversion to the range of various Calvinist explications of predestination (and there were many of them) ran back to childhood and had been reinforced by his mother's reflections on the problem. In his early Oxford days mother and son had shared their misgivings, and Susanna had summarized her conclusions with admirable clarity:

The doctrine of predestination, as maintained by the rigid Calvinists, is very shocking, and ought utterly to be abhorred; because it directly charges the most h[igh] God with being the author of sin. And I think you reason very well and justly against it. For 'tis certainly inconsistent with the justice and goodness of God to lay any man under either a physical or moral necessity of committing sin, and then to punish him for doing it. 'Far be this from thee, O Lord. . . . Shall not the Judge of all the earth do right?' [Cf. Gen. 18:25]

I do firmly believe that God from eternity hath elected some to everlasting life. But then I humbly conceive that this election is founded on his foreknowledge, according to that in the 8th of Romans: [. . .] 'Whom in his eternal prescience God saw would make a right use of their powers, and accept of offered mercy, . . . he did predestinate, adopt for his children, his peculiar treasure. And that they might be conformed to the image of his Son, he called them to himself, by his external Word, the preaching of the gospel, and internally by his Holy Spirit. Which call they obeying, by faith and repentance, he justifies them, absolves them from the guilt of all their sins, and acknowledges them as just persons, through the merits and mediation of Jesus Christ. And having thus justified, he receives them to glory—to heaven.

This is the sum of what I believe concerning predestination, which I think is agreeable to the analogy of faith, since it never derogates from God's free grace, nor impairs the liberty of man. Nor can it with more reason be supposed that the prescience of God is the cause that so many finally perish, than that our knowing the sun will rise tomorrow is the cause of its rise.[1]

The reader may judge how far John Wesley had moved from the essence of this opinion in this sermon here, half a century later.

Even so, through his career, his polemic against predestination was less of a preoccupation than has been supposed, although he could always depend upon an outcry from the Calvinists whenever he broached the issue (as with his sermon, Free Grace *[1739], and with his treatise,* Predestination Calmly Considered *[1755]). But he was able*

---

[1] Susanna Wesley to John, Aug. 18, 1725 (25:179-80 in this edn.)

sincerely to deny to John Newton (May 14, 1765) that he had been opposing predestination with more 'frequency and vehemence' than other opinions with which he disagreed. 'Taking one year with another for twenty years past, I have not preached eight sermons a year [out of 800] upon the subject.' And the record would seem to bear him out, since for the crucial texts of Rom. 8:29, 30; and 9:15, 18, 21, there are surprisingly few entries in the records of his oral preaching. For Rom. 8:29, 30, we have only two (one in 1741 and the other in 1773). He reports having preached on Rom. 9:18 only once (May 31, 1741) but never on Rom. 9:15 or 21. In 1741 (March 17) he had 'preached a sermon . . . directly on predestination' from Gen. 18:25. There is only one reference specifically for 1 Pet. 1:2 (December 25, 1757), though there are six recorded texts which include this verse (one each in 1740, 1757, 1759, 1761, and two in 1784).

After the fresh outbreak of hostilities between the Calvinists and the Wesleyans in 1770, Wesley still held his peace as far as we can tell from the record. In the early summer of 1773, however, he was in Ireland, where he seems to have preached, and then written out, a sermon 'On Romans 8:29, 30', dating it 'Armagh, June 5, 1773'. Later, in 1782, he recalls:

Several years ago I delivered the following discourse at Londonderry, in Ireland. It was printed at the request of several of the clergy. As it is little known in England, I believe the inserting it here will be acceptable to many serious persons.[2]

If there was a first printing in Ireland (as there may have been), no copy of it is extant. Our 'first edition' is dated three years later, and in London; its publishing history and variant readings are set out in Appendix Vol. 4. See also Bibliog, *No. 362. When in 1788 it was included, unnumbered, in* SOSO, *V, it was given its present title and placed here in this order.*

Given the turmoils of the controversy, it should be noted how much more irenic the tone of Wesley's statements here are compared with most of his others. This, then, is a conscious exercise in 'catholic spirit', and important against the grim background of the controversy as it was remembered by its partisans. Actually, the centerpiece of this sermon is a summary of Wesley's understanding of the ordo salutis *as a whole, with a sort of predestinarian doctrine of his own based on divine prescience and human free will. It re-presents his mother's teaching from long ago,*

---

[2] *AM* (1782), V.505.

together with echoes from his extended comment in the Notes *on 1 Pet. 1:2, which would be worth comparing with this 'Discourse'.*

On Predestination

Romans 8:29-30

Whom he did foreknow, he did predestinate to be conformed to the image of his Son: . . . whom he did predestinate, them he also called; whom he called, them he also justified; and whom he justified, them he also 5 *glorified.*

1. 'Our beloved brother Paul', says St. Peter, 'according to the wisdom given to him, hath written unto you; as also in all his epistles, speaking in them of these things; in which are some things hard to be understood, which they that are unlearned and 10 unstable wrest, as they do also the other scriptures, to their own destruction.'[a]

2. It is not improbable that among those things spoken by St. Paul which are 'hard to be understood', the Apostle Peter might place what he speaks on this subject in the eighth and ninth 15 chapters of his Epistle to the Romans. And it is certain, not only 'the unlearned', but many of the most learned men in the world, and not 'the unstable' only, but many who seemed to be well established in the truths of the gospel, have for several centuries 'wrested' these passages 'to their own destruction'. 20

3. 'Hard to be understood' we may well allow them to be, when we consider how men of the strongest understanding, improved by all the advantages of education, have continually differed in judgment concerning them. And this very consideration, that there is so wide a difference upon the head between men of the 25 greatest learning, sense, and piety, one might imagine would make all who now speak upon the subject exceedingly wary and self-diffident. But I know not how it is that just the reverse is observed in every part of the Christian world. No writers upon earth appear more positive than those who write on this difficult 30 subject. Nay, the same men who writing on any other subject are

[a] 2 Pet. 3:15-16.

remarkably modest and humble, on this alone lay aside all self-distrust,

And speak *ex cathedra* infallible.[1]

This is peculiarly observable of almost all those who assert the
5   absolute decrees.[2] But surely it is possible to avoid this: whatever
we propose may be proposed with modesty, and with deference to
those wise and good men who are of a contrary opinion. And the
rather because so much has been said already on every part of the
question, so many volumes have been written, that it is scarce
10 possible to say anything which has not been said before. All I
would offer at present, not to the lovers of contention, but to men
of piety and candour, are a few short hints which perhaps may cast
some light on the text above recited.

4. The more frequently and carefully I have considered it, the
15 more I have been inclined to think that the Apostle is not here (as
many have supposed) describing a chain of causes and effects
(this does not seem to have entered into his heart) but simply
showing *the method in which God works—the order* in which the
several branches of salvation constantly follow each other. And
20 this, I apprehend, will be clear to any serious and impartial
inquirer surveying the work of God either forward or
backward—either from the beginning to the end, or from the end
to the beginning.[3]

5. And first, let us look forward on the whole work of God in
25 the salvation of man, considering it from the beginning, the first

---

[1] This sounds like a line of verse, from a source so far untraced. Among several other allusions by Wesley to a supposedly infallible utterance, as from the papal throne, cf. 'pronounce *ex cathedra*' (letter to *Monthly Review*, Oct. 5, 1756), and 'speak as it were *ex cathedra*, with an air of infallibility' *(A Letter to a Gentleman at Bristol*, Jan. 6, 1758, ¶7).

[2] Cf. Chambers's *Cyclopaedia*, on 'Predestination'. See also, *Early Nonconformity, 1566–1800: A Catalogue of Books in Dr. Williams' Library, London*, Subject Catalogue, 'Calvinism', 'Predestination', 'England, Church of—Doctrines', for a conspectus of the literature of this tormented question. But, more specifically, see Augustus M. Toplady, *The Doctrine of the Church of England* (1771), *Historic Proof of the Doctrinal Calvinism of the Church of England* (1774), 2 vols., and Toplady's direct personal attack upon Wesley in *An Old Fox Tarr'd and Feathered* (2nd edn., corrected, 1775). On the other side, Wesley would also have known of Samuel Harsnet's swingeing denunciation of predestination as a 'monstrous doctrine' in his sermon at St. Paul's Cross in 1584, as reported by Jeremy Collier, *Ecclesiastical History*, II.646; Harsnet ended up as Archbishop of York.

[3] An echo of Wesley's special interest in the *ordo salutis* and his citation of Jonathan Edwards's emphasis upon the Scripture as 'the *history* of salvation'; see No. 67, 'On Divine Providence', §4 and n. See also the opening arguments in Wesley's *Predestination Calmly Considered*, §§1-4; and his *Thoughts upon God's Sovereignty*.

point, till it terminates in glory. The first point is the foreknowledge of God. God *foreknew* those in every nation who would believe, from the beginning of the world to the consummation of all things. But in order to throw light upon this dark question it should be well observed that when we speak of 5 God's *foreknowledge* we do not speak according to the nature of things, but after the manner of men.[4] For if we speak properly there is no such thing as either *foreknowledge* or *after-knowledge* in God. All time, or rather all eternity (for time is only that small fragment of eternity which is allotted to the children of men)[5] 10 being present to him at once, he does not know one thing before another, or one thing after another, but sees all things in one point of view, from everlasting to everlasting.[6] As all time, with everything that exists therein, is present with him at once, so he sees at once whatever was, is, or will be to the end of time. But 15 observe: we must not think they *are* because he *knows* them. No; he knows them because they are. Just as I (if one may be allowed to compare the things of men with the deep things of God) now know the sun shines. Yet the sun does not shine because I know it: but I know it because he shines. My knowledge *supposes*[7] the sun 20 to shine, but does not in any wise *cause* it. In like manner God knows that man sins; for he knows all things. Yet we do not sin because he knows it: but he knows it because we sin. And his knowledge *supposes* our sin, but does not in any wise *cause* it. In a word, God looking on all ages from the creation to the 25 consummation as a moment, and seeing at once whatever is in the hearts of all the children of men, knows everyone that does or does not believe in every age or nation. Yet what he knows, whether faith or unbelief, is in no wise caused by his knowledge. Men are as *free* in believing, or not believing, as if he did not know 30 it at all.

6. Indeed if man were not free he could not be accountable either for his thoughts, words, or actions. If he were not free, he would not be capable either of reward or punishment. He would be incapable either of virtue or vice, of being either morally good 35 or bad. If he had no more freedom than the sun, the moon, or

---

[4] Rom. 6:19; 1 Cor. 15:32; Gal. 3:15.
[5] See No. 54, 'On Eternity', §4 and n.
[6] Ps. 90:2; 103:17; 106:48 (AV).
[7] I.e., to regard as a matter of fact; cf. *OED* for this as a familiar eighteenth-century usage.

the stars, he would be no more accountable than they. On supposition that he had no more freedom than they, the stones of the earth would be as capable of reward and as liable to punishment as man—one would be as accountable as the other.
5 Yea, and it would be as absurd to ascribe either virtue or vice to him as to ascribe it to the stock of a tree.

7. But to proceed. 'Whom he did foreknow, them he did predestinate to be conformed to the image of his Son.' This is the second step (to speak after the manner of men: for in fact there is
10 nothing *before* or *after* in God). In other words, God decrees from everlasting to everlasting that all who believe in the Son of his love shall be conformed to his image, shall be saved from all inward and outward sin[8] into all inward and outward holiness. Accordingly it is a plain, undeniable fact: all who truly believe in
15 the name of the Son of God[9] do now 'receive the end of their faith, the salvation of their souls';[10] and this in virtue of the unchangeable, irreversible, irresistible decree of God: 'He that believeth shall be saved; he that believeth not shall be damned.'[11]

8. 'Whom he did predestinate, them he also called.' This is the
20 third step (still remembering that we speak after the manner of men). To express it a little more largely: according to his fixed decree that believers shall be saved, those whom he foreknows as such he calls both outwardly and inwardly; outwardly by the word of his grace, and inwardly by his Spirit.[12] This inward application
25 of his word to the heart seems to be what some term 'effectual calling'. And it implies the calling them children of God; the 'accepting' them 'in the Beloved';[13] the justifying them 'freely by his grace, through the redemption that is in Jesus Christ'.[14]

9. 'Whom he called, those he justified.' This is the fourth step.
30 It is generally allowed that the word 'justified' here is taken in a peculiar sense, that it means, he made them just or righteous. He executed his decree, 'conforming them to the image of his Son', or (as we usually speak) 'sanctified them'.

10. It remains, 'whom he justified, those he glorified.' This is
35 the last step. Having made them 'meet to be partakers of the inheritance of the saints in light',[15] he gives them 'the kingdom which was prepared for them before the world began'.[16] This is

---

[8] See No. 13, *On Sin in Believers*, intro., III.1-9, and n.
[9] See 1 John 5:13.   [10] Cf. 1 Pet. 1:9.   [11] Cf. Mark 16:16.
[12] Cf. Acts 14:3; 20:32; Rom. 1:7; 1 Cor. 1:2.   [13] Cf. Eph. 1:6.
[14] Rom. 3:24.   [15] Col. 1:12.   [16] Cf. Matt. 25:34.

the order wherein, 'according to the counsel of his will'[17]—the
plan he has laid down from eternity—he saves those whom he
foreknew, the true believers in every place and generation.

11. The same great work of salvation by faith, according to the
foreknowledge and decree of God, may appear in a still clearer
light if we view it backward, from the end to the beginning.
Suppose then you stood with the 'great multitude which no man
can number, out of every nation, and tongue, and kindred, and
people', who 'give praise unto him that sitteth upon the throne
and unto the Lamb for ever and ever';[18] you would not find one
among them all that were entered into glory who was not a witness
of that great truth, 'Without holiness no man shall see the
Lord'[19]—not one of all that innumerable company who was not
sanctified before he was *glorified*. By holiness he was prepared for
glory,[20] according to the invariable will of the Lord, that the crown
purchased by the blood of his Son should be given to none but
those who are renewed by his Spirit. He is become 'the author of
eternal salvation' only 'to them that obey him';[21] that obey him
inwardly and outwardly; that are holy in heart, and holy in all
manner of conversation.[22]

12. And could you take a view of all those upon earth who are
now *sanctified*, you would find, not one of these had been
sanctified till after he was *called*. He was first called, not only with
an outward call by the Word and the messengers of God, but
likewise with an inward call by his Spirit applying his Word,
enabling him to believe in the only-begotten Son of God,[23] and
bearing testimony with his spirit that he was a child of God.[24] And
it was by this very means they were all sanctified. It was by a sense
of the love of God shed abroad in his heart[25] that every one of
them was enabled to love God. Loving God, he loved his
neighbour as himself, and had power to walk in all his
commandments blameless.[26] This is a rule which admits of no
exception. God *calls* a sinner his own, that is, justifies him, before
he sanctifies. And by this very thing, the consciousness of his

[17] Cf. Eph. 1:11.   [18] Cf. Rev. 7:9-10.
[19] Cf. Heb. 12:14.
[20] Cf. *Notes* on Rom. 9:23.
[21] Cf. Heb. 5:9.
[22] 1 Pet. 1:15.
[23] See John 3:18.
[24] See Rom. 8:16. Cf. No. 5, 'Justification by Faith', IV.2 and n.
[25] See Rom. 5:5.   [26] See Luke 1:6.

favour,[27] he works in him that grateful, filial affection from which spring every good temper, and word, and work.

13. And who are they that are thus *called* of God but those whom he had before 'predestinated', or decreed to 'conform to 5 the image of his Son'? This decree (still speaking after the manner of men) precedes every man's calling. Every believer was predestinated before he was called. For God calls none but 'according to the counsel of his will', according to this πρόθεσις, or plan of acting,[28] which he had laid down before the foundation 10 of the world.[29]

14. Once more: as all that are called were predestinated, so all whom God has predestinated he *foreknew*. He knew, he saw them as believers, and as such predestinated them to salvation, according to his eternal decree, 'He that believeth shall be 15 saved.'[30] Thus we see the whole process of the work of God from the end to the beginning. Who are glorified? None but those who were first sanctified. Who are sanctified? None but those who were first justified. Who are justified? None but those who were first predestinated. Who are predestinated? None but those 20 whom God foreknew as believers. Thus the purpose and work of God stand unshaken as the pillars of heaven: 'He that believeth shall be saved: he that believeth not shall be damned.'[31] And thus God is clear from the blood of all men; since whoever perishes, perishes by his own act and deed. 'They will not come unto me,'[32] 25 says the Saviour of men; and 'there is no salvation in any other.'[33] They *will not believe;* and there is no other way either to present or eternal salvation. Therefore their blood is upon their own head;[34] and God is still 'justified in his saying'[35] that he 'willeth all men to be saved, and to come to the knowledge of his truth'.[36]

30   15. The sum of all is this: the almighty all-wise God sees and knows from everlasting to everlasting all that is, that was, and that is to come, through one eternal now. With him nothing is either past or future, but all things equally present. He has, therefore, if we speak according to the truth of things, no 35 foreknowledge, no after-knowledge. This would be ill consistent

---

[27] See No. 3, '*Awake, Thou That Sleepest*', III.8 and n.
[28] See Rom. 8:28; Eph. 1:11; 2 Tim. 1:9.
[29] John 17:24; Eph. 1:4; 1 Pet. 1:20.
[31] *Ibid.*
[33] Cf. Acts 4:12.
[35] Cf. Rom. 3:4.
[30] Mark 16:16.
[32] Cf. John 5:40; 6:44.
[34] See 2 Sam. 1:16.
[36] Cf. 1 Tim. 2:4.

with the Apostle's words, 'With him is no variableness or shadow of turning;'[37] or with the account he gives of himself by the prophet, 'I the Lord change not.'[38] Yet when he speaks to us, knowing whereof we are made, knowing the scantiness of our understanding, he lets himself down to our capacity and speaks of 5 himself after the manner of men. Thus in condescension to our weakness he speaks of his own 'purpose', 'counsel', 'plan', 'foreknowledge'. Not that God has any need of 'counsel', of 'purpose', or of 'planning' his work beforehand. Far be it from us to impute these to the Most High, to measure him by ourselves: It 10 is merely in compassion to us that he speaks thus of himself as 'foreknowing' the things in heaven or earth, and as 'predestinating' or 'foreordaining' them. But can we possibly imagine that these expressions are to be taken literally? To one who was so gross in his conceptions might he not say, 'Thinkest thou I am 15 such an one as thyself?' Not so. 'As the heavens are higher than the earth, so are my ways higher than thy ways.'[39] I know, decree, work, in such a manner as it is not possible for thee to conceive. But to give thee some faint, glimmering knowledge of my ways I use the language of men, and suit myself to thy apprehensions, in 20 this thy infant state of existence.

16. What is it then that we learn from this whole account? It is this and no more: (1), God knows all believers; (2), wills that they should be saved from sin; (3), to that end justifies them; (4), sanctifies; and (5), takes them to glory. 25

O that men would praise the Lord for this his goodness![40] And that they would be content with this plain account of it, and not endeavour to wade into those mysteries which are too deep for men to fathom!

Armagh 30
June 5, 1773

---

[37] Cf. Jas. 1:17.
[38] Mal. 3:6.
[39] Isa. 55:9.
[40] See Ps. 107:8.

GOD'S LOVE TO FALLEN MAN

AN INTRODUCTORY COMMENT

This sermon was written in Birmingham and first appeared in the Arminian Magazine, *V. 453-59, 509-15, for September and October 1782, numbered 'XI'. Its theme, though not its text, is a constant in Wesley's soteriology (see below, I.1 and n.): that without creating man to sin, God's omnipotent grace has wrought an even more wonderful glory for creation than if man had continued in his original innocence and obedience ('if Adam had not fallen, Christ had not died'). As an obvious source, he had already extracted a sizeable fraction of Samuel Hoard's* God's Love to Mankind *(1633) and printed it in five instalments in the first year of the* Magazine *(1778, Vol. I). There is, however, only one reference to his oral preaching from 'Romans 5:14, etc.' (January 23, 1741), with no certain indication of his topic.*

In its first form the sermon had no title. In SOSO, *V. 85, Wesley had entitled it 'God's Love to Fallen Man:' A Sermon on Romans v. 15. It was twice reprinted in separate pamphlets in 1791; for further details and also variant readings see Appendix, Vol. 4; and* Bibliog, *No. 375.ii. That its message lay close to Wesley's heart is confirmed by Elizabeth Ritchie's memoir of his last days (Curnock, VIII. 139): 'The next pleasing, awful scene was the great exertion he made in order to make Mr. Broadbent understand that he fervently desired a sermon he had written on the Love of God should be scattered abroad and given away to everybody.' We also have James Rogers's note to this: 'He said, "Where is my sermon on The Love of God? Take it and spread it abroad; give it to everyone."' Ten thousand were printed and given away.*

God's Love to Fallen Man

Romans 5:15

Not as the transgression, so is the free gift.[1]

1. How exceeding common, and how bitter, is the outcry against our first parent for the mischief which he not only brought upon himself, but entailed upon his latest posterity! It was by his wilful rebellion against God that 'sin entered into the world'.[2] 'By one man's disobedience', as the Apostle observes, 'the many', οἱ πολλοί, as many as were then in the loins of their forefather, 'were made', or constituted, 'sinners:'[3] not only deprived of the favour of God, but also of his image; of all virtue, righteousness, and true holiness; and sunk partly into the image of the devil, in pride, malice, and all other diabolical tempers; partly into the image of the brute, being fallen under the dominion of brutal passions and grovelling appetites. Hence also death entered into the world, with all his forerunners and attendants, pain, sickness, and a whole train of uneasy as well as unholy passions and tempers.

2. 'For all this we may thank Adam,' has echoed down from generation to generation. The selfsame charge has been repeated in every age, and in every nation where the oracles of God are known, in which alone this grand and important event has been discovered to the children of men. Has not *your* heart, and probably your lips too, joined in the general charge? How few are there of those who believe the scriptural relation of the fall of man that have not entertained the same thought concerning our first parent! Severely condemning him that through wilful disobedience to the sole command of his Creator

Brought death into the world, and all our woe.[4]

---

[1] 'Transgression' is Wesley's own translation here of παράπτωμα. Wycliffe had translated it 'gilte', Tyndale and Cranmer as 'synne', Geneva, Rheims, and AV as 'offence'. Even Wesley, in his *Notes*, had followed the AV. But notice that modern lexicographers (see Arndt and Gingrich, Schmoller) tend to favour 'transgression', as do some modern translations (e.g., Conybeare, Montgomery). NEB translates it 'wrongdoing'.

[2] Rom. 5:12.   [3] Rom. 5:19.   [4] Milton, *Paradise Lost*, i.3.

3. Nay, it were well if the charge rested here: but it is certain it does not. It cannot be denied that it frequently glances from Adam to his Creator. Have not thousands, even of those that are called Christians, taken the liberty to call his mercy, if not his
5 justice also, into question on this very account? Some indeed have done this a little more modestly, in an oblique and indirect manner. But others have thrown aside the mask and asked, 'Did not God foresee that Adam would abuse his liberty? And did he not know the baneful consequences which this must naturally
10 have on all his posterity? And why then did he permit that disobedience? Was it not easy for the Almighty to have prevented it?' He certainly did foresee the whole. This cannot be denied. For 'known unto God are all his works from the beginning of the world.'⁵ (Rather, from all eternity, as the words ἀπ᾽ αἰῶνος
15 properly signify.) And it was undoubtedly in his power to prevent it: for he hath all power both in heaven and earth. But it was known to him at the same time that it was best, upon the whole, not to prevent it. He knew that 'not as the transgression, so the free gift'; that the evil resulting from the former was not as the
20 good resulting from the latter, not worthy to be compared with it. He saw that to permit the fall of the first man was far best for mankind in general; that abundantly more good than evil would accrue to the posterity of Adam by his fall; that if 'sin abounded' thereby over all the earth, yet 'grace would much more abound';⁶
25 yea, and that to every individual of the human race, unless it was his own choice.

4. It is exceeding strange that hardly anything has been written, or at least published, on this subject; nay, that it has been so little weighed or understood by the generality of Christians; especially
30 considering that it is not a matter of mere curiosity, but a truth of the deepest importance; it being impossible on any other principle

> To assert a gracious providence,
> And justify the ways of God with men;⁷

35 and considering withal how plain this important truth is to all sensible and candid inquirers. May the Lover of men open the

---

⁵ Acts 15:18. ⁶ Cf. Rom. 5:20.
⁷ Cf. Milton, *Paradise Lost*, i.25-26. See No. 56, 'God's Approbation of His Works', II.3 and n.

eyes of our understanding to perceive clearly that by the fall of
Adam mankind in general have gained a capacity,
    First, of being more holy and happy on earth; and
    Secondly, of being more happy in heaven, than otherwise they
could have been.[8]   5

[I.] 1. And, first, mankind in general have gained by the fall of
Adam a capacity of attaining more holiness and happiness on
earth than it would have been possible for them to attain if Adam
had not fallen. For if Adam had not fallen Christ had not died.[9]
Nothing can be more clear than this; nothing more undeniable.   10
The more thoroughly we consider the point, the more deeply
shall we be convinced of it. Unless all the partakers of human
nature had received that deadly wound in Adam it would not have
been needful for the Son of God to take our nature upon him. Do
you not see that this was the very ground of his coming into the 15
world? 'By one man sin entered into the world, and death by sin.
And thus death passed upon all', through him 'in whom all men
sinned.'[a] Was it not to remedy this very thing that 'the Word was
made flesh'?[10] That 'as in Adam all died, so in Christ all might be
made alive'?[11] Unless then *many* had been made sinners by the   20

[a] Rom. 5:12.

---

[8] Wesley's own conclusion to the controversy which, despite his typical complaint
against the literature on the subject, had actually been the issue in a long and earnest
debate, running back into patristic theology.

[9] This tradition *(O felix culpa!)* was familiar to Augustine; it was a favourite theme of
Rupert of Deutz and Hugh of St. Victor; Wesley was summing up and simplifying a
complex controversy. See the excellent synopsis in B. F. Westcott, *The Epistles of John,
International Critical Commentary* (1909), *addendum*, 'The Gospel of Creation', pp.
286-328. John Donne in a sermon preached at Whitehall, Apr. 19, 1618, on 1 Tim. 1:15,
had laid out the options between the Incarnation as a natural outworking of creation
(which would have happened even if the first Adam had not sinned) and the view that
Christ came because of man's sin and fallen state. Donne had come down on the same side
that Wesley would later take. Cf. Donne's *Sermons*, ed. by George R. Potter and Evelyn M.
Simpson (Berkeley and Los Angeles, Univ. of California Press, 1962), I. 303-6. See also
Milton, *Paradise Lost*, xii.469-72:

> O Goodness infinite, Goodness immense!
> That all this good of evil shall produce,
> And evil turn to good; more wonderful
> Than that which by creation first brought forth.

For Wesley's other comments on this theme, cf. Nos. 57, 'On the Fall of Man', II.10; and
64, 'The New Creation', §16.

[10] John 1:14.

[11] Cf. 1 Cor. 15:22.

disobedience of one, by the obedience of one many would not
have been 'made righteous'.[b] So there would have been no room
for that amazing display of the Son of God's love to mankind.
There would have been no occasion for his 'being obedient unto
5 death, even the death of the cross'.[12] It could not then have been
said, to the astonishment of all the hosts of heaven, 'God so loved
the world,' yea, the ungodly world which had no thought or desire
of returning to him, 'that he gave his Son' out of his bosom, his
only-begotten Son, 'to the end that whosoever believeth on him
10 should not perish, but have everlasting life.'[13] Neither could we
then have said, 'God was in Christ reconciling the world unto
himself;'[14] or that he 'made him to be sin' (that is, a sin-offering)
'for us who knew no sin, that we might be made the righteousness
of God through him'.[15] There would have been no such occasion
15 for such 'an advocate with the Father' as 'Jesus Christ the
righteous';[16] neither for his appearing 'at the right hand of God to
make intercession for us'.[17]

2. What is the necessary consequence of this? It is this—there
could then have been no such thing as faith in God, 'thus loving
20 the world', giving his only Son for us men and for our salvation.
There could have been no such thing as faith in the Son of God,
'as loving us and giving himself for us'.[18] There could have been
no faith in the Spirit of God, as renewing the image of God in our
hearts,[19] as raising us from the death of sin unto the life of
25 righteousness.[20] Indeed the whole privilege of justification by
faith could have had no existence; there could have been no
redemption in the blood of Christ;[21] neither could Christ have
been 'made of God unto us either wisdom, righteousness,
sanctification, or redemption'.[22]

30 3. And the same grand blank which was in our faith must
likewise have been in our love. We might have loved the Author of
our being, the Father of angels and men, as our Creator and
Preserver; we might have said, 'O Lord, our Governor, how

---

[b] Ver. 18[-19].

[12] Cf. Phil. 2:8.   [13] Cf. John 3:16.
[14] 2 Cor. 5:19.   [15] Cf. 2 Cor. 5:21.
[16] 1 John 2:1.   [17] Cf. Rom. 8:34.
[18] Cf. Gal. 2:20.   [19] See Col. 3:10.
[20] See Rom. 6:4.   [21] See Eph. 1:7; Col. 1:14.
[22] 1 Cor. 1:30.

excellent is thy name in all the earth.'[23] But we could not have loved him under the nearest and dearest relation, as 'delivering up his Son for us all'.[24] We might have loved the Son of God as being 'the brightness of his Father's glory, the express image of his person'[25] (although this ground seems to belong rather to the inhabitants of heaven than of earth). But we could not have loved him as 'bearing our sins in his own body on the tree',[26] and 'by that one oblation of himself once offered making a full oblation, sacrifice, and satisfaction for the sins of the whole world'.[27] We could not have been 'made conformable to his death', nor have 'known the power of his resurrection'.[28] We could not have loved the Holy Ghost as revealing to us the Father and the Son, as opening the eyes of our understanding,[29] bringing us out of darkness into his marvellous light,[30] renewing the image of God in our soul,[31] and sealing us unto the day of redemption.[32] So that in truth what is now 'in the sight of God, even the Father', not of fallible men, 'pure religion and undefiled',[33] would then have had no being; inasmuch as it wholly depends on those grand principles 'By grace ye are saved through faith;'[34] and 'Jesus Christ is of God made unto us wisdom and righteousness, and sanctification and redemption.'[35]

4. We see then what unspeakable advantage we derive from the fall of our first parent, with regard to faith—faith both in God the Father, who spared not his own Son,[36] his only Son, but 'wounded him for our transgressions, and bruised him for our iniquities';[37] and in God the Son, who poured out his soul for us transgressors, and washed us in his own blood.[38] We see what advantage we derive therefrom with regard to the love of God, both of God the Father and God the Son. The chief ground of this love, as long as we remain in the body, is plainly declared by the Apostle: 'We love him, because he first loved us.'[39] But the greatest instance of his love had never been given if Adam had not fallen.

[23] Cf. Ps. 8:1, 9. Note the conflation here of words from the BCP Psalter and from the AV: e.g., 'earth' for 'world'.

[24] Cf. Rom. 8:32.   [25] Cf. Heb. 1:3.
[26] Cf. 1 Pet. 2:24.   [27] Cf. BCP, Communion, Consecration.
[28] Cf. Phil. 3:10.   [29] See Luke 24:45; Eph. 1:18.
[30] 1 Pet. 2:9.   [31] See Col. 3:10.
[32] See Eph. 4:30.   [33] Cf. Jas. 1:27.
[34] Eph. 2:8.   [35] Cf. 1 Cor. 1:30.
[36] Rom. 8:32.   [37] Cf. Isa. 53:5.
[38] See Rev. 1:5.   [39] 1 John 4:19.

5. And as our faith both in God the Father and the Son receives an unspeakable increase, if not its very being, from this grand event, as does also our love both of the Father and the Son; so does the love of our neighbour also, our benevolence to all
5 mankind, which cannot but increase in the same proportion with our faith and love of God. For who does not apprehend the force of that inference drawn by the loving Apostle, 'Beloved, if God so loved us, we ought also to love one another.'[40] 'If God *so* loved us'—observe, the stress of the argument lies on this very point—
10 'so loved us' as to deliver up his only Son to die a cursed death for our salvation! 'Beloved, what manner of love is this', wherewith God hath loved us! So as to give his *only Son!* In glory equal with the Father; in majesty coeternal! What manner of love is this wherewith the only-begotten Son of God hath loved us! So as to
15 'empty himself', as far as possible, of his eternal Godhead! As to divest himself of that glory which he had with the Father before the world began! As to 'take upon him the form of a servant, being found in fashion as a man'! And then to humble himself still farther, 'being obedient unto death, yea, the death of the cross'![41]
20 If God *so* loved us, how ought we to love one another! But this motive to brotherly love had been totally wanting if Adam had not fallen. Consequently we could not then have loved one another in so high a degree as we may now. Nor could there have been that height and depth in the command of our blessed Lord, 'As I have
25 loved you, so love one another.'[42]

6. Such gainers may we be by Adam's fall with regard both to the love of God and of our neighbour. But there is another grand point which, though little adverted to, deserves our deepest consideration. By that one act of our first parent not only 'sin
30 entered into the world',[43] but pain also, and was alike entailed on his whole posterity. And herein appeared not only the justice but the unspeakable goodness of God! For how much good does he continually bring out of this evil! How much holiness and happiness out of pain!

35 7. How innumerable are the benefits which God conveys to the children of men through the channel of sufferings! So that it might well be said, 'What are termed afflictions in the language of

---

[40] 1 John 4:11.
[41] Cf. Phil. 2:7-8. A conflation of the AV and Wesley's translation in his *Notes*.
[42] Cf. John 13:34; 15:12.
[43] Rom. 5:12.

men are in the language of God styled blessings.' Indeed had
there been no suffering in the world a considerable part of
religion, yea, and in some respects the most excellent part, could
have had no place therein; since the very existence of it depends
on our suffering; so that had there been no pain it could have had 5
no being. Upon this foundation, even our suffering, it is evident
all our passive graces[44] are built—yea, the noblest of all Christian
graces, love 'enduring all things'.[45] Here is the ground for
resignation to God, enabling us to say from the heart, in every
trying hour, 'It is the Lord: let him do what seemeth him good.'[46] 10
'Shall we receive good at the hand of the Lord, and shall we not
receive evil?'[47] And what a glorious spectacle is this! Did it not
constrain even a heathen to cry out, *Ecce spectaculum Deo dignum!:*
'See a sight worthy of God—a good man struggling with adversity
and superior to it.'[48] Here is the ground for confidence in God, 15
both with regard to what we feel, and with regard to what we
should fear, were it not that our soul is calmly stayed on him.
What room could there be for trust in God if there was no such
thing as pain or danger? Who might not say then, 'The cup which
my Father hath given me, shall I not drink it?'[49] It is by sufferings 20
that our faith is tried, and therefore made more acceptable to
God. It is in the day of trouble that we have occasion to say,
'Though he slay me, yet will I trust in him.'[50] And this is
well-pleasing to God, that we should own him in the face of
danger, in defiance of sorrow, sickness, pain, or death. 25

8. Again: had there been neither natural nor moral evil in the
world, what must have become of patience, meekness,
gentleness, long-suffering? It is manifest they could have had no
being, seeing all these have evil for their object. If therefore evil

---

[44] A technical phrase to match the phrase, 'passive virtues', in II.11, below. Cf. St.
Thomas, *Summa Theologia*, IIa-IIae, *Qq.* 136-40. For other comments on the virtue of
suffering, cf. No. 83, 'On Patience', §3 and n.

[45] Cf. 1 Cor. 13:7.   [46] 1 Sam. 3:18.

[47] Cf. Job 2:10.

[48] Cf. Seneca, *Moral Essays: 'De Providentia'* ('On Providence'), where Seneca is moved
to 'wonder if God who most dearly loves the good . . . allots to them a fortune that forces
them into a struggle' (ii.7). His comment, cited by Wesley, is in ii.9: *'Ecce spectaculum
dignum ad quod respiciat intentus operi suo deus, ecce par deo dignum, vir si et provocabit.* Behold
a spectacle worthy of God in contemplating his works; behold a contest worthy of God: a
brave man ranged against ill-fortune; and all the more if he is also the challenger.' Cf. also
Martial, *Epigrams*, I. civ. 11; *'quis spectacula non putet deorum'.* And see No. 149, 'On Love',
III.8.

[49] John 18:11.   [50] Job 13:15.

had never entered into the world, neither could these have had any place in it. For who could have 'returned good for evil' had there been no evil-doer in the universe? How had it been possible on that supposition to 'overcome evil with good'?[51] Will you say,
5   'But all these graces might have been divinely infused into the hearts of men.' Undoubtedly they might: but if they had, there would have been no use or exercise for them. Whereas in the present state of things we can never long want occasion to exercise them. And the more they are exercised, the more all our
10 graces are strengthened and increased. And in the same proportion as our resignation, our confidence in God, our patience and fortitude, our meekness, gentleness, and long-suffering, together with our faith and love of God and man increase, must our happiness increase, even in the present world.
15 9. Yet again: as God's permission of Adam's fall gave all his posterity a thousand opportunities of *suffering*, and thereby of exercising all those passive graces which increase both their holiness and happiness; so it gives them opportunities of *doing good* in numberless instances, of exercising themselves in various
20 good works which otherwise could have had no being. And what exertions of benevolence, of compassion, of godlike mercy, had then been totally prevented! Who could then have said to the Lover of men,

       Thy mind throughout my life be shown,
25   While listening to the wretch's cry,
       The widow's or the orphan's groan,
         On mercy's wings I swiftly fly,
       The poor and needy to relieve;
         Myself, my all, for them to give?[52]

30 It is the just observation of a benevolent man,

       All worldly joys go less,
     Than that one joy of doing kindnesses.[53]

Surely 'in keeping' this commandment, if no other, 'there is great

---

[51] Rom. 12:21.
[52] Cf. Charles Wesley, *Scripture Hymns* (1762), II.380 *(Poet. Wks.,* XIII.167), on Jas. 1:27, beginning 'Father, on me the grace bestow,' st. 2. A more exact quotation of this stanza appears in No. 99, *The Reward of Righteousness,* III.2.
[53] George Herbert. Cf. *The Temple,* 'The Church Porch', st. 55, ll.5-6: 'All worldly joys go lesse/To the one joy of doing kindnesses.' See also, No. 84, *The Important Question,* III.5.

reward'.[54] 'As we have time, let us do good unto all men;'[55] good of
every kind, and in every degree. Accordingly the more good we do
(other circumstances being equal) the happier we shall be. The
more we deal our bread to the hungry, and cover the naked with
garments, the more we relieve the stranger, and visit them that are 5
sick or in prison;[56] the more kind offices we do to those that groan
under the various evils of human life; the more comfort we
receive even in the present world; the greater recompense we
have in our own bosom.

10. To sum up what has been said under his head. As the more 10
holy we are upon earth the more happy we must be (seeing there
is an inseparable connection between holiness and happiness); as
the more good we do to others the more of present reward
redounds into our own bosom; even as our sufferings for God
lead us to 'rejoice' in him 'with joy unspeakable and full of glory'.[57] 15
Therefore the fall of Adam, first, by giving us an opportunity of
being far more holy; secondly, by giving us the occasions of doing
innumerable good works which otherwise could not have been
done; and thirdly, by putting it into our power to suffer for God,
whereby 'the spirit of glory and of God rests upon us;'[58] may be 20
of such advantage to the children of men, even in the present life,
as they will not thoroughly comprehend till they attain life
everlasting.

[II.] 11. It is then we shall be enabled fully to comprehend, not
only the advantages which accrue at the present time to the sons 25
of men by the fall of their first parent, but the infinitely greater
advantages which they may reap from it in eternity. In order to
form some conception of this we may remember the observation
of the Apostle: 'As one star differeth from another star in glory, so
also is the resurrection of the dead.'[59] The most glorious stars will 30
undoubtedly be those who are the most holy; who bear most of
that image of God wherein they were created. The next in glory
to these will be those who have been most abundant in good
works; and next to them those that have suffered most according
to the will of God. But what advantages in every one of these re- 35
spects will the children of God receive in heaven by God's per-

---

[54] Cf. Ps. 19:11.   [55] Cf. Gal. 6:10.
[56] See Matt. 25:35-36.   [57] 1 Pet. 1:8.
[58] Cf. 1 Pet. 4:14.
[59] Cf. 1 Cor. 15:41-42.

mitting the introduction of pain upon earth, in consequence of
sin! By occasion of this they attained many holy tempers which
otherwise could have had no being: resignation to God, confidence in him in times of trouble and danger, patience,
5 meekness, gentleness, long-suffering, and the whole train of
passive virtues.[60] And on account of this superior holiness they
will then enjoy superior happiness. Again: everyone will then
'receive his own reward according to his own labour'.[61] Every
individual will be 'rewarded according to his works'.[62] But the fall
10 gave rise to innumerable good works which could otherwise never
have existed, such as ministering to the necessities of saints, yea,
relieving the distressed in every kind. And hereby innumerable
stars will be added to their eternal crown.[63] Yet again. There will
be an abundant reward in heaven for *suffering* as well as for *doing*
15 the will of God: 'These light afflictions, which are but for a
moment, work out for us a far more exceeding and eternal weight
of glory.'[64] Therefore that event which occasioned the entrance of
suffering into the world has thereby occasioned to all the children
of God an increase of glory to all eternity. For although the suf-
20 ferings themselves will be at an end; although

> The pain of life shall then be o'er,
> The anguish and distracting care;
> There sighing grief shall weep no more;
> And sin shall never enter there;[65]

25 yet the joys occasioned thereby shall never end, but flow at God's
right hand for evermore.

12. There is one advantage more that we reap from Adam's fall
which is not unworthy our attention. Unless in Adam all had
died,[66] being in the loins of their first parent, every descendant of
30 Adam, every child of man, must have personally answered for
himself to God. It seems to be a necessary consequence of this
that if he had once fallen, once violated any command of God,

---

[60] See above, I.7.
[61] 1 Cor. 3:8.
[62] Cf. Matt. 16:27.
[63] Cf. No. 57, 'On the Fall of Man', II.8 and n.
[64] Cf. 2 Cor. 4:17.
[65] Charles Wesley, *Hymns and Sacred Poems* (1749), I.21, published earlier in John and
Charles Wesley, *Hymns and Sacred Poems* (1739), p. 223. In both the first line reads, 'The
pain of life shall there be o'er.'
[66] 1 Cor. 15:22.

there would have been no possibility of his rising again; there was no help, but he must have perished without remedy. For that covenant knew not to show mercy: the word was, 'The soul that sinneth, it shall die.'[67] Now who would not rather be on the footing he is now? Under a covenant of mercy? Who would wish 5 to hazard a whole eternity upon one stake? Is it not infinitely more desirable to be in a state wherein, though encompassed with infirmities, yet we do not run such a desperate risk, but if we fall we may rise again? Wherein we may say,

> My trespass is grown up to heaven! 10
> But far above the skies,
> In Christ abundantly forgiven,
> I see thy mercies rise![68]

13. In Christ! Let me entreat every serious person once more to fix his attention here. All that has been said, all that can be said 15 on these subjects, centres in this point. The fall of Adam produced the death of Christ! Hear, O heavens, and give ear, O earth![69] Yea,

> Let earth and heaven agree,
> Angels and men be joined, 20
> To celebrate with me
> The Saviour of mankind;
> T' adore the all-atoning Lamb,
> And bless the sound of Jesu's name![70]

If God had prevented the fall of man, 'the Word' had never been 25 'made flesh'; nor had we ever 'seen his glory, the glory as of the only-begotten of the Father'.[71] Those mysteries never had been displayed 'which the very angels desire to look into'.[72] Methinks this consideration swallows up all the rest, and should never be out of our thoughts. Unless 'by one man judgment had come 30 upon all men to condemnation'[73] neither angels nor men could ever have known 'the unsearchable riches of Christ'.[74]

---

[67] Ezek. 18:4, 20.
[68] Charles Wesley, *Hymns and Sacred Poems* (1749), I.164 (*Poet. Wks.*, IV.446).
[69] Isa. 1:2.
[70] Charles Wesley, *Hymns on God's Everlasting Love* (1741), p. 31 (*Poet. Wks.*, III.71). The poem had been reprinted in *AM* (1778), I.191-92, with the title, 'The Universal Love of Christ'.
[71] Cf. John 1:14.
[72] Cf. 1 Pet. 1:12.
[73] Cf. Rom. 5:17, 18.
[74] Eph. 3:8.

14. See then, upon the whole, how little reason we have to repine at the fall of our first parent, since herefrom we may derive such unspeakable advantages both in time and eternity. See how small pretence there is for questioning the mercy of God in
5 permitting that event to take place! Since therein mercy, by infinite degrees, rejoices over judgment! Where then is the man that presumes to blame God for not preventing Adam's sin? Should we not rather bless him from the ground of the heart for therein laying the grand scheme of man's redemption, and
10 making way for that glorious manifestation of his wisdom, holiness, justice, and mercy? If indeed God had decreed before the foundation of the world[75] that millions of men should dwell in everlasting burnings[76] because Adam sinned hundreds or thousands of years before they had a being, I know not who could
15 thank him for this, unless the devil and his angels;[77] seeing on this supposition all those millions of unhappy spirits would be plunged into hell by Adam's sin, without any possible advantage from it. But, blessed be God, this is not the case. Such a decree never existed. On the contrary, every one born of a woman may be
20 an unspeakable gainer thereby; and none ever was or can be a loser but by his own choice.

15. We see here a full answer to that plausible account 'of the origin of evil' published to the world some years since, and supposed to be unanswerable—'that it necessarily resulted from
25 the nature of matter, which God was not able to alter'.[78] It is very kind in this sweet-tongued orator to make an excuse for God! But there is really no occasion for it: God hath answered for himself. He made man in his own image, a spirit endued with understanding and liberty. Man abusing that liberty produced
30 evil, brought sin and pain into the world. This God permitted in order to a fuller manifestation of his wisdom, justice, and mercy, by bestowing on all who would receive it an infinitely greater happiness than they could possibly have attained if Adam had not fallen.

35 16. 'O the depth of the riches both of the wisdom and knowledge of God!'[79] Although a thousand particulars of 'his

---

[75] John 17:24; Eph. 1:4; 1 Pet. 1:20.
[76] See Isa. 33:14.   [77] Matt. 25:41.
[78] Cf. Jenyns, *Free Inquiry*. Cf. above, No. 56, 'God's Approbation of His Works', II.2 and n.
[79] Rom. 11:33.

judgments, and of his ways, are unsearchable' to us, and 'past' our 'finding out',[80] yet may we discern the general scheme running through time into eternity. 'According to the counsel of his own will',[81] the plan he had laid before the foundation of the world, he created the parent of all mankind in his own image. And he 5 permitted 'all men' to be 'made sinners by the disobedience of' this *one* man, that 'by the obedience of one' all who receive 'the free gift'[82] may be infinitely holier and happier to all eternity!

Birmingham, July 9, 1782[83]

---

[80] *Ibid.*
[81] Cf. Eph. 1:11.
[82] Rom. 5:15, 16.
[83] This place and date as in *AM*.

THE GENERAL DELIVERANCE

AN INTRODUCTORY COMMENT

This sermon first appeared in the Arminian Magazine *in 1782, V. 8-14, 61-69 (January and February), under the title 'Free Thoughts on the Brute Creation'. The title had been borrowed from an essay by John Hildrop, D. D. (1680?–1756), theologian and satirist, published in 1742. Hildrop's essay ('In Two Letters to a Lady') had been a rejoinder to a* jeu d'esprit *by a French Jesuit, G. H. Bougeant,* Amusement Philosophique sur le Langage des Bêtes, *1739 (Eng. tr. also in 1739). Wesley thought well enough of Hildrop's essay to abridge and publish it with its original title in the* Arminian Magazine *for 1783, in twelve instalments.[1] Thus, when he prepared to reprint his own sermon for the 1788 collection, he had to give it a new title, and chose 'The General Deliverance'.*

Bougeant's Aristotelian presupposition as to the immutability of animal species had prompted Hildrop to apply the Platonic 'chain of being' to the theory that the human fall set off the degradation of 'the brute creation' in tragic sequence. Wesley, sharing Hildrop's cosmology, differs from him in three respects: (1) whereas for Hildrop the 'chain of being' idea implies a continuum, *Wesley interprets it as a series in which* man *is the crucial link of 'conveyance' or 'communication' between the Creator and his 'brute creation'; (2) man has a 'capacity for God', a gift not bestowed on creatures below him in the chain; (3) in the 'general deliverance' God may well enhance the status and glory of all creatures above their originals. This, obviously, expands Wesley's point that 'God's Love to Fallen Man' is such that, in his sovereign grace, God will turn even the Fall into the final advantage not only of 'fallen man' but of the entire creation as well. This essay may thus be correlated with the cognate eschatological notions of Nos. 15, The Great Assize; and 59, 'God's Love to Fallen Man'.*

Wesley mentions having preached from Rom. 8:19-22 five times (1747, 1748, 1750, 1754, 1755), which is not to say that all of those sermons had the same topic as this one. It is, however, a reasonable guess that his basic vision of a cosmic redemption had come to him as part of his heritage from Christian Platonism.

[1] VI. 33-36, 90-92, 141-44, 202-4, 259-61, 315-17, 370-72, 424-27, 487-89, 538-40, 596-98, 654-57.

The General Deliverance

Romans 8:19-22

The earnest expectation of the creature waiteth for the manifestation of the sons of God.

For the creature was made subject to vanity, not willingly, but by 5
reason of him that subjected it.

Yet in hope that the creature itself also shall be delivered from the bondage of corruption, into the glorious liberty of the sons of God.

For we know that the whole creation groaneth, and travaileth in pain together until now.[1]   10

1. Nothing is more sure than that, as 'the Lord is loving to every man', so 'his mercy is over all his works'[2]—all that have sense, all that are capable of pleasure or pain, of happiness or misery. In consequence of this 'he openeth his hand and filleth all things living with plenteousness:'[3] 'he prepareth food for cattle,' as well 15 as 'herbs for the children of men.'[4] He provideth for the fowls of the air, 'feeding the young ravens when they cry unto him'.[5] 'He sendeth the springs into the rivers that run among the hills,' to give drink to every beast of the field, and that even 'the wild asses may quench their thirst.'[6] And suitably to this he directs us to be 20 tender of even the[7] meaner creatures, to show mercy to these also. 'Thou shalt not muzzle the ox that treadeth out the corn'[8]—a custom which is observed in the eastern countries even to this day. And this is by no means contradicted by St. Paul's question, 'Doth God take care for oxen?'[9] Without doubt he does. We 25 cannot deny it without flatly contradicting his word. The plain meaning of the Apostle is—Is this all that is implied in the text? Hath it not a farther meaning? Does it not teach us we are to feed the bodies of those whom we desire to feed our souls? Meantime it is certain God 'giveth grass for the cattle', as well as 'herbs for 30 the use of men'.[10]

---

[1] Cf. AV, and Wesley's translation in his *Notes*.   [2] Ps. 145:9 (BCP).
[3] Cf. Ps. 145:16 (BCP).   [4] Cf. Pss. 104:14; 147:8-9 (BCP).
[5] Cf. Ps. 147:9 (BCP).   [6] Cf. Ps. 104:10-11 (BCP).
[7] Orig., *AM* and *SOSO*, 'even', to which Wesley added 'the' in his MS annotations of *SOSO*.
[8] Cf. Deut. 25:4.   [9] 1 Cor. 9:9.   [10] Cf. Ps. 147:8-9 (BCP).

2. But how are these Scriptures reconcilable to the present
state of things? How are they consistent with what we daily see
round about us in every part of the creation? If the Creator and
Father of every living thing is rich in mercy towards all; if he does
5 not overlook or despise any of the works of his own hands;[11] if he
wills even the meanest of them to be happy according to their
degree—how comes it to pass that such a complication of evils
oppresses, yea, overwhelms them? How is it that misery of all
kinds overspreads the face of the earth? This is a question which
10 has puzzled the wisest philosophers in all ages. And it cannot be
answered without having recourse to the oracles of God. But
taking these for our guide we may inquire,
  I. What was the original state of the brute creation?[12]
  II. In what state is it at present? And
15 III. In what state will it be at the manifestation of the children
  of God?

I.1. We may inquire, in the first place, What was the original
state of the brute creation? And may not we learn this even from
the place which was assigned them, namely, the garden of God?
20 All the beasts of the field, and all the fowls of the air, were with
Adam in paradise. And there is no question but their state was
suited to their place: it was paradisiacal, perfectly happy.[13]
Undoubtedly it bore a near resemblance to the state of man
himself. By taking therefore a short view of the one we may
25 conceive the other. Now 'man was made in the image of God.'[14]
But 'God is a spirit.'[15] So therefore was man. Only that spirit,
being designed to dwell on earth, was lodged in an earthly
tabernacle.[16] As such he had an innate principle of *self-motion*.
And so, it seems, has every spirit in the universe; this being the
30 proper distinguishing difference between spirit and matter,
which is totally, essentially passive and inactive, as appears from a

---

[11] See Job 10:3.

[12] Cf. *OED* for eighteenth-century (and prior) usages of this phrase.

[13] This passage (I.1-4) is an earlier statement of the same thesis (with some of the same
text) that would then be expanded a year later into 'God's Approbation of His Works',
passim (see No. 56). In *AM*, 'The General Deliverance' had preceded 'God's
Approbation'; here Wesley has reversed and repeated himself. For other references to the
idea of 'adamic perfection', see also No. 5, 'Justification by Faith', I.4 and n.

[14] Cf. Gen. 1:27; 9:6. Cf. below, III.11, 12; and cf. also, No. 1, *Salvation by Faith*, §1
and n.

[15] John 4:24.

[16] See 2 Cor. 5:1; and cf. No. 28, 'Sermon on the Mount, VIII', §21 and n.

thousand experiments.[17] He was, after the likeness of his Creator, endued with *understanding*, a capacity of apprehending whatever objects were brought before it, and of judging concerning them. He was endued with a *will*, exerting itself in various affections and passions; and, lastly, with *liberty*, or freedom of choice, without 5 which all the rest would have been in vain, and he would have been no more capable of serving his Creator than a piece of earth or marble. He would have been as incapable of vice or virtue as any part of the inanimate creation. In these, in the power of self-motion, understanding, will, and liberty, the natural image of 10 God consisted.

2. How far his power of self-motion then extended it is impossible for us to determine. It is probable that he had a far higher degree both of swiftness and strength than any of his posterity ever had, and much less any of the lower creatures. It is 15 certain he had such strength of understanding as no man ever since had. His understanding was perfect in its kind; capable of apprehending all things clearly, and judging concerning them according to truth, without any mixture of error. His will had no wrong bias of any sort, but all his passions and affections were 20 regular, being steadily and uniformly guided by the dictates of his unerring understanding; embracing nothing but good, and every good in proportion to its degree of intrinsic goodness. His liberty likewise was wholly guided by his understanding: he chose or refused according to its direction. Above all (which was his 25 highest excellence, far more valuable than all the rest put together) he was a creature capable of God,[18] capable of knowing, loving, and obeying his Creator. And in fact he did know God, did unfeignedly love and uniformly obey him. This was the supreme perfection of man, as it is of all intelligent beings—the continually 30 seeing and loving and obeying the Father of the spirits of all flesh.[19] From this right state, and right use of all his faculties, his happiness naturally flowed. In this the essence of his happiness consisted; but it was increased by all the things that were round about him. He saw with unspeakable pleasure the order, the 35 beauty, the harmony of all the creatures: of all animated, all inanimate nature—the serenity of the skies, the sun walking in

---

[17] Cf. No. 15, *The Great Assize*, III.3 and n.
[18] See below, III.11; also No. 1, *Salvation by Faith*, §1 and n.
[19] See Num. 16:22; 27:16.

brightness,[20] the sweetly variegated clothing of the earth; the trees, the fruits, the flowers,

And liquid lapse of murmuring streams.[21]

Nor was this pleasure interrupted by evil of any kind. It had no
5 alloy of sorrow or pain, whether of body or mind. For while he was innocent he was impassive, incapable of suffering. Nothing could stain his purity of joy. And to crown all, he was immortal.

3. To this creature, endued with all these excellent faculties, thus qualified for his high charge, God said, 'Have thou
10 dominion over the fish of the sea, and over the fowl of the air, and over every living thing that moveth upon the earth.'[a] And so the Psalmist: 'Thou madest him to have dominion over the works of thy hands; thou hast put all things under his feet: all sheep and oxen, yea, and the beasts of the field; the fowl of the air, and the
15 fish of the sea, and whatsoever passeth through the paths of the seas!'[b] So that man was God's vicegerent upon earth, the prince and governor of this lower world; and all the blessings of God flowed through him to the inferior creatures. Man was the channel of conveyance between his Creator and the whole brute
20 creation.

4. But what blessings were those that were then conveyed through man to the lower creatures? What was the original state of the brute creatures when they were first created? This deserves a more attentive consideration than has been usually given it. It
25 is certain these, as well as man, had an innate principle of *self-motion;* and that at least in as high a degree as they enjoy it at this day. Again: they were endued with a degree of *understanding* not less than that they are possessed of now. They had also a *will*, including various passions, which likewise they still enjoy. And
30 they had *liberty*,[22] a power of choice, a degree of which is still

---

[a] Gen. 1:28.   [b] Ps. 8:6-8 (AV).

---

[20] See Job 31:26.

[21] Milton, *Paradise Lost*, viii. 263. See No. 56, 'God's Approbation of His Works', I.4 and n.

[22] An echo of a longstanding controversy over the distinctions between *arbitrium* ('will' or 'judgment') and *voluntas* ('liberty' or 'choice') and their implications for the vexed question of grace and free will. Wesley's views in this matter had been influenced directly by Locke, *Essay Concerning Human Understanding*, Bk. II, chs. 5, 10, 11, and 21, but they rest back further on Erasmus, *Diatribe de Libero Arbitrio* (1524); cf. his *Opera Omnia* (1706), IX. 1220-24, 1245-48. See Nos. 9, 'The Spirit of Bondage and of Adoption', I.3;

found in every living creature. Nor can we doubt but their understanding too was in the beginning perfect in its kind. Their passions and affections were regular, and their choice always guided by their understanding.

5. What then makes the barrier between men and brutes? The line which they cannot pass? It was not reason. Set aside that ambiguous term: exchange it for the plain word, understanding, and who can deny that brutes have this? We may as well deny that they have sight or hearing. But it is this: man is capable of God;[23] the inferior creatures are not.[24] We have no ground to believe that they are in any degree capable of knowing, loving, or obeying God. This is the specific difference between man and brute—the great gulf which they cannot pass over. And as a loving obedience to God was the perfection of men, so a loving obedience to man was the perfection of brutes. And as long as they continued in this they were happy after their kind; happy in the right state and the right use of their respective faculties. Yea, and so long they had some shadowy resemblance of even *moral goodness*. For they had gratitude to man for benefits received, and a reverence for him. They had likewise a kind of benevolence to each other, unmixed with any contrary temper. How *beautiful* many of them were we may conjecture from that which still remains; and that not only in the noblest creatures, but in those of the lowest order. And they were all surrounded not only with plenteous food, but with everything that could give them pleasure; pleasure unmixed with pain; for pain was not yet—it had not entered into paradise. And they too were immortal. For 'God made not death: neither hath he pleasure in the death of any living.'[25]

6. How true then is that word, 'God saw everything that he had made: and behold it was very good.'[26] But how far is this from

14, *The Repentance of Believers*, I.4; 43, *The Scripture Way of Salvation*, I.2; 62, 'The End of Christ's Coming', I.4-5; 63, 'The General Spread of the Gospel', §9; 67, 'On Divine Providence', §15; 71, 'Of Good Angels', I.1; 95, 'On the Education of Children', §§15-16; 116, 'What is Man? Ps. 8:4', §11; 118, 'On the Omnipresence of God', II.1; 135, 'On Guardian Angels', §1; 140, 'The Promise of Understanding', II.1.

[23] Note the reiteration here of the same key phrase (an echo of the Lutheran *capax infiniti?*) from I.2, above. See also an even bolder use of it in III.6, below.

[24] This thesis, together with the cognate notion of 'man as the channel of conveyance (or communication) between his Creator and the whole brute creation' (above, I.3; below, II.1), differentiates Wesley's interpretation of the 'chain of being' idea from Hildrop's. Cf. No. 1, *Salvation by Faith*, §1 and n.

[25] Cf. Wisd. 1:13. See No. 64, 'The New Creation', §17; also Ezek. 18:32, 23; 33:11.

[26] Gen. 1:31.

being the case now!²⁷ In what a condition is the whole lower world! To say nothing of inanimate nature, wherein all the elements seem to be out of course, and by turns to fight against man. Since man rebelled against his Maker, in what a state is all 5 animated nature! Well might the Apostle say of this, 'The whole creation groaneth together, and travaileth together in pain until now.'²⁸ This directly refers to the brute creation. In what state this is at present we are now to consider.

II.1. As all the blessings of God in paradise flowed through 10 man to the inferior creatures; as man was the great channel of communication between the Creator and the whole brute creation; so when man made himself incapable of transmitting those blessings, that communication was necessarily cut off. The intercourse between God and the inferior creatures being 15 stopped, those blessings could no longer flow in upon them. And then it was that 'the creature', every creature, 'was subject to vanity',²⁹ to sorrow, to pain of every kind, to all manner of evils. 'Not' indeed 'willingly'; not by its own choice, not by any act or deed of its own; 'but by reason of him that subjected it';³⁰ by the 20 wise permission of God, determining to draw eternal good out of this temporary evil.

2. But in what respects was 'the creature', every creature, then 'made subject to vanity'? What did the meaner creatures suffer when man rebelled against God? It is probable they sustained 25 much loss even in the lower faculties, their vigour, strength, and swiftness. But undoubtedly they suffered far more in their understanding, more than we can easily conceive. Perhaps insects and worms had then as much understanding as the most intelligent brutes have now; whereas millions of creatures have at 30 present little more understanding than the earth on which they crawl or the rock to which they adhere. They suffered still more in their will, in their passions, which were then variously distorted, and frequently set in flat opposition to the little understanding that was left them. Their liberty likewise was greatly impaired, 35 yea, in many cases totally destroyed. They are still utterly

---

²⁷ Orig., 'the case', altered in the *AM* errata and Wesley's annotated copy to 'the case now'. *SOSO* alters orig. to 'the present case'.
²⁸ Cf. Rom. 8:22.
²⁹ Cf. Rom. 8:20.
³⁰ *Ibid.*

enslaved to irrational appetites which have the full dominion over them. The very foundations of their nature are out of course, are turned upside down. As man is deprived of *his* perfection, his loving obedience to God, so brutes are deprived of *their* perfection, their loving obedience to man. The far greater part of 5 them flee from him, studiously avoid his hated presence. The most of the rest set him at open defiance, yea, destroy him if it be in their power. A few only, those we commonly term domestic animals, retain more or less of their original disposition, and (through the mercy of God) love him still and pay obedience to 10 him.

3. Setting these few aside, how little shadow of good, of gratitude, of benevolence, of any right temper is now to be found in any part of the brute creation! On the contrary, what savage fierceness, what unrelenting cruelty, are invariably observed in 15 thousands of creatures, yea, are[31] inseparable from their natures! Is it only the lion, the tiger, the wolf, among the inhabitants of the forest and plains; the shark and a few more voracious monsters among the inhabitants of the waters; or the eagle among birds; that tears the flesh, sucks the blood, and crushes the bones of 20 their helpless fellow-creatures? Nay, the harmless fly, the laborious ant, the painted butterfly, are treated in the same merciless manner even by the innocent songsters of the grove![32] The innumerable tribes of poor insects are continually devoured by them. And whereas there is but a small number, comparatively, 25 of beasts of prey on the earth, it is quite otherwise in the liquid element: there are but few inhabitants of the waters, whether of the sea or of the rivers, which do not devour whatsoever they can master. Yea, they exceed herein all the beasts of the forest, and all the birds of prey. For none of these have been ever observed to 30 prey upon their own species,

> *Saevis inter se convenit ursis*[33]—
> Even savage bears will not each other tear.

But the water savages swallow up all, even of their own kind, that are smaller and weaker than themselves. Yea, such at present 35

---

[31] Orig., *AM* and *SOSO*, 'is', altered in Wesley's printed errata and MS annotations in *AM* to 'are'.
[32] A paraphrase of James Thomson, *The Castle of Indolence* (1748), I, st. 10: 'The swarming songsters of the careless grove'.
[33] Juvenal, *Satires*, xv.164.

is the miserable constitution of the world, to such 'vanity' is it now 'subjected',[34] that an immense majority of creatures, perhaps a million to one, can no otherwise preserve their own lives than by destroying their fellow-creatures.[35]

5   4. And is not the very form, the outward appearance of many of the creatures, as horrid as their dispositions? Where is the beauty which was stamped upon them when they came first out of the hands of their Creator? There is not the least trace of it left: so far from it that they are shocking to behold! Nay, they are not only
10 terrible and grisly to look upon, but deformed, and that to a high degree. Yet their features, ugly as they are at best, are frequently made more deformed than usual when they are distorted by pain, which they cannot avoid any more than the wretched sons of men. Pain of various kinds, weakness, sickness, diseases innumerable,
15 come upon them, perhaps from within, perhaps from one another, perhaps from the inclemency of seasons, from fire, hail, snow, or storm, or from a thousand causes which they cannot foresee or prevent.

5. Thus 'as by one man sin entered into the world, and death by
20 sin; even so death passed upon all men.'[36] And not on man only, but on those creatures also that 'did not sin after the similitude of Adam's transgression'.[37] And not death alone came upon them, but all of its train of preparatory evils: pain, and ten thousand sufferings. Nor these only, but likewise all those irregular
25 passions, all those unlovely tempers (which in men are sins, and even in the brutes are sources of misery) 'passed upon all' the inhabitants of the earth, and remain in all, except the children of God.

6. During this season of 'vanity', not only the feebler creatures
30 are continually destroyed by the stronger; not only the strong are frequently destroyed by those that are of equal strength; but both the one and the other are exposed to the violence and cruelty of him that is now their common enemy—man. And if his swiftness or strength is not equal to theirs, yet his art more than supplies

---

[34] Cf. Rom. 8:20.
[35] Cf. No. 56, 'God's Approbation of His Works', I.12 and n.
[36] Cf. Rom. 5:12.
[37] Cf. Rom. 5:14; note that the identification of 'those creatures' here had been variously interpreted—by Poole, *Annotations*, as infants (who could not have sinned as Adam did), and by Henry, *Exposition*, as the fallen angels (who also sinned in a different way).

that defect. By this he eludes all their force, how great so ever it be; by this he defeats all their swiftness, and notwithstanding their various shifts and contrivances, discovers all their retreats. He pursues them over the widest plains, and through the thickest forests. He overtakes them in the fields of air, he finds them out in 5 the depths of the sea. Nor are the mild and friendly creatures who still own his sway, and are duteous to his commands, secured thereby from more than brutal violence, from outrage and abuse of various kinds. Is the generous horse, that serves his master's necessity or pleasure with unwearied diligence, is the faithful dog, 10 that waits the motion of his hand or his eye, exempt from this? What returns for their long and faithful service do many of these poor creatures find? And what a dreadful difference is there between what they suffer from their fellow brutes and what they suffer from the tyrant, man! The lion, the tiger, or the shark, give 15 them pain from mere necessity, in order to prolong their own life; and put them out of their pain at once. But the human shark, without any such necessity, torments them of his free choice; and perhaps continues their lingering pain till after months or years death signs their release. 20

III.1. But will *the creature*, will even the brute creation, always remain in this deplorable condition? God forbid that we should affirm this; yea, or even entertain such a thought! While 'the whole creation groaneth together' (whether men attend or not) their groans are not dispersed in idle air, but enter into the ears of 25 him that made them. While his creatures 'travail together in pain', he knoweth all their pain, and is bringing them nearer and nearer to the birth which shall be accomplished in its season. He seeth 'the earnest expectation' wherewith the whole animated creation 'waiteth for' that final 'manifestation of the sons of God': in which 30 'they themselves also shall be delivered' (not by annihilation: annihilation is not deliverance) 'from the' present 'bondage of corruption, into' a measure of 'the glorious liberty of the children of God.'

2. Nothing can be more express. Away with vulgar prejudices, 35 and let the plain word of God take place. They 'shall be delivered from the bondage of corruption into glorious liberty'; even a measure, according as they are capable, of 'the liberty of the children of God'.

A general view of this is given us in the twenty-first chapter of 40

the Revelation. When he that 'sitteth on the great white throne'[38] hath pronounced, 'Behold I make all things new;'[39] when the word is fulfilled, 'The tabernacle of God is with men, [. . .] and they shall be his people, and God himself shall be with them and
5 be their God;'[40] then the following blessing shall take place (not only on the children of men—there is no such restriction in the text—but) on every creature according to its capacity: 'God shall wipe away all tears from their eyes. And there shall be no more death, neither sorrow nor crying. Neither shall there be any more
10 pain: for the former things are passed away.'[41]

3. To descend to a few particulars. The whole brute creation will then undoubtedly be restored, not only to the vigour, strength, and swiftness which they had at their creation, but to a far higher degree of each than they ever enjoyed. They will be
15 restored, not only to that measure of understanding which they had in paradise, but to a degree of it as much higher than that as the understanding of an elephant is beyond that of a worm. And whatever affections they had in the garden of God will be restored with vast increase, being exalted and refined in a manner which
20 we ourselves are not now able to comprehend. The liberty they then had will be completely restored, and they will be free in all their motions. They will be delivered from all irregular appetites, from all unruly passions, from every disposition that is either evil in itself or has any tendency to evil. No rage will be found in any
25 creature, no fierceness, no cruelty or thirst for blood. So far from it that 'the wolf shall dwell with the lamb, the leopard shall lie down with the kid, the calf and the young lion together; and a little child shall lead them. The cow and the bear shall feed together, and the lion shall eat straw like the ox. [. . .] They shall not hurt or
30 destroy in all my holy mountain.'[c]

4. Thus in that day all the 'vanity' to which they are now helplessly 'subject' will be abolished; they will suffer no more either from within or without; the days of their groaning are ended. At the same time there can be no reasonable doubt but all
35 the horridness of their appearance, and all the deformity of their aspect, will vanish away, and be exchanged for their primeval

[c] Isa. 11:6, 7, 9.

---

[38] Cf. Rev. 20:11.   [39] Rev. 21:5.
[40] Cf. Rev. 21:3.   [41] Rev. 21:4.

beauty. And with their beauty their happiness will return; to which there can then be no obstruction. As there will be nothing within, so there will be nothing without, to give them any uneasiness—no heat or cold, no storm or tempest, but one perennial spring. In the new earth, as well as in the new heavens, 5 there will be nothing to give pain, but everything that the wisdom and goodness of God can create to give happiness. As a recompense for what they once suffered while under 'the bondage of corruption', when God has 'renewed the face of the earth',[42] and their corruptible body has put on incorruption,[43] they 10 shall enjoy happiness suited to their state, without alloy, without interruption, and without end.

5. But though I doubt not that the Father of all has a tender regard for even his lowest creatures, and that in consequence of this he will make them large amends for all they suffer while 15 under their present bondage, yet I dare not affirm that he has an *equal regard* for them and for the children of men. I do not believe that

> He sees *with equal eyes*, as Lord of all,
> A hero perish or a sparrow fall![44]   20

By no means. This is exceeding pretty; but it is absolutely false. For though

> Mercy, with truth and endless grace,
> O'er all his works doth reign,
> Yet chiefly he delights to bless   25
> His favourite creature, man.[45]

God regards his meanest creatures much; but he regards man much more. He does not *equally regard* a hero and a sparrow, the best of men, and the lowest of brutes. 'How *much more* does your heavenly Father care for you'![46] says he who is 'in the bosom of the 30 Father'.[47] Those who thus strain the point are clearly confuted by his question, 'Are not ye *much better* than they?'[48] Let it suffice that

---

[42] Ps. 104:30.   [43] See 1 Cor. 15:53, 54.

[44] Cf. Pope, *Essay on Man*, i.87-88:

> Who sees with equal eye, as God of all,
> A hero perish or a sparrow fall.

Wesley has added his own italics; see No. 67, 'On Divine Providence', §19 (the same couplet without italics). See also Wesley, *A Collection of Moral and Sacred Poems* (1744), I. 305.

[45] Cf. Charles Wesley, 'Of God', in *Hymns for Children* (1763), p. 4 (*Poet Wks.*, VI. 372).

[46] Cf. Matt. 7:11.   [47] John 1:18.   [48] Cf. Matt. 6:26.

God regards everything that he hath made in its own order, and in proportion to that measure of his own image which he has stamped upon it.

6. May I be permitted to mention here a conjecture concerning
5 the brute creation? What if it should then please the all-wise, the all-gracious Creator, to raise them higher in the scale of beings?[49] What if it should please him, when he makes us 'equal to angels',[50] to make them what we are now? Creatures capable of God? Capable of knowing, and loving, and enjoying the Author of their
10 being? If it should be so, ought our eye to be evil because he is good?[51] However this be, he will certainly do what will be most for his own glory.

7. If it be objected to all this (as very probably it will): 'But of what use will those creatures be in that future state?' I answer this
15 by another question—'What use are they of now?' If there be (as has commonly been supposed) eight thousand species of insects, who is able to inform us of what use seven thousand of them are? If there are four thousand species of fishes, who can tell us of what use are more than three thousand of them? If there are six
20 hundred sorts of birds, who can tell of what use five hundred of those species are? If there be four hundred sorts of beasts, to what use do three hundred of them serve? Consider this; consider how little we know of even the present designs of God;[52] and then you will not wonder that we know still less of what he designs to do in
25 the new heavens and the new earth.[53]

8. 'But what end does it answer to dwell upon this subject which we so imperfectly understand?' To consider so much as we do understand, so much as God has been pleased to reveal to us, may answer that excellent end—to illustrate that mercy of God
30 which is 'over all his works'.[54] And it may exceedingly confirm our belief that much more he is 'loving to every man'.[55] For how well

---

[49] See No. 56, 'God's Approbation of His Works', I.14 and n.

[50] Luke 20:36.

[51] See Matt. 20:15; note the rejection here of the anthropocentric notion of creation that blinds us to the interesting possibility that God can still make of 'the brute creation' whatever may please his 'all-wise, all-gracious' providence, quite beyond the present range of human imagination.

[52] Cf. Wesley's *Survey*, I. 191 ff., II. 56 ff.; and Goldsmith's *History of the Earth*. Here, as everywhere, Wesley presupposes that scientific knowledge is merely instrumental to faith and its acknowledgement of God's omniscient wisdom. Cf. No. 69, 'The Imperfection of Human Knowledge', I.12.

[53] See 2 Pet. 3:13; Rev. 21:1.

[54] Ps. 145:9 (BCP).   [55] *Ibid.*

may we urge our Lord's word, 'Are not ye much better than they?'[56] If then the Lord takes such care of the fowls of the air and of the beasts of the field, shall he not much more take care of *you*, creatures of a nobler order? If 'the Lord will save' (as the inspired writer affirms) 'both man and beast' in their several degrees, surely 'the children of men may put their trust under the shadow of his wings'![57]

9. May it not answer another end, namely, furnish us with a full answer to a plausible objection against the justice of God in suffering numberless creatures that never had sinned to be so severely punished? They could not sin, for they were not moral agents. Yet how severely do they suffer! Yea, many of them, beasts of burden in particular, almost the whole time of their abode on earth. So that they can have no retribution here below. But the objection vanishes away if we consider that something better remains after death for these poor creatures also! That these likewise shall one day be delivered from this bondage of corruption, and shall then receive an ample amends for all their present sufferings.

10. One more excellent end may undoubtedly be answered by the preceding considerations. They may encourage us to imitate him whose mercy is over all his works. They may soften our hearts towards the meaner creatures, knowing that the Lord careth for them. It may enlarge our hearts towards those poor creatures to reflect that, as vile as they appear in our eyes, not one of them is forgotten in the sight of our Father which is in heaven. Through all the vanity to which they are now subjected, let us look to what God hath prepared for them. Yea, let us habituate ourselves to look forward, beyond this present scene of bondage, to the happy time when they will be delivered therefrom into the liberty of the children of God.

11. From what has been said I cannot but draw one inference, which no man of reason can deny. If it is this which distinguishes men from beasts, that they are creatures capable of God,[58] capable of knowing, and loving, and enjoying him; then whoever is 'without God in the world'[59]—whoever does not know, or love, or enjoy God, and is not careful about the matter—does in effect

[56] Matt. 6:26.
[57] Cf. Ps. 36:7 (BCP).
[58] Cf. above, I.1-2 and n.; see also III.6.
[59] Eph. 2:12.

disclaim the nature of man, and degrade himself into a beast. Let such vouchsafe a little attention to those remarkable words of Solomon: 'I said in my heart concerning the estate of the sons of men, . . . they might see that they themselves are beasts.'ᵈ *These*
5 sons of men are undoubtedly beasts—and that by their own act and deed. For they deliberately and wilfully disclaim the sole characteristic of human nature. It is true they may have a share of reason—they have speech and they walk erect. But they have not the mark, the only mark, which totally separates man from the
10 brute creation. 'That which befalleth beasts, the same thing befalleth them.'⁶⁰ They are equally without God in the world, 'so that a man' of this kind 'hath no pre-eminence above a beast.'⁶¹

12. So much more let all those who are of a nobler turn of mind assert the distinguishing dignity of their nature! Let all who are of
15 a more generous spirit know and maintain their rank in the scale of beings. Rest not till you enjoy the privilege of humanity—the knowledge and love of God. Lift up your heads, ye creatures capable of God. Lift up your hearts to the Source of your being!

Know God, and teach your souls to know
20 The joys that from religion flow.⁶²

Give your hearts to him who, together with ten thousand blessings, has 'given you his Son, his only Son'!⁶³ Let your continual 'fellowship be with the Father, and with his Son, Jesus Christ'!⁶⁴ Let God be in all your thoughts, and ye will be men
25 indeed. Let him be your God and your all! The desire of your eyes, the joy of your heart, and your portion for ever!

November 30, 1781⁶⁵

ᵈ Eccles. 3:18.

---

⁶⁰ Cf. Eccles. 3:19.
⁶¹ *Ibid.*
⁶² Cf. Thomas Parnell, 'A Hymn to Contentment', ll. 45-46:

Know God—and bring thy heart to know
The joys which from religion flow.

See also Wesley, *A Collection of Moral and Sacred Poems* (1744), I. 266; and cf. 'A Thought Upon Marriage', §7, in *AM* (1785), V.535 (Vol. 14 of this edn.).
⁶³ Cf. John 3:16.
⁶⁴ Cf. 1 John 1:3.
⁶⁵ This note was added in *AM* only. Cf. JWJ on Wesley's visit to Shoreham and the Revd. Vincent Perronet on this day.

THE MYSTERY OF INIQUITY

AN INTRODUCTORY COMMENT

Wesley had a dramatic 'theology of history'. Its plot revolved around the grim discrepancies that stretch out between the perfections of the original creation and of its eventual restoration—between what history should (and could) have been and what had, in fact, transpired. Within this perspective, he could see the whole of history as a tragic drama of fallings away and partial restorations from each of which, in its turn, there then followed yet another falling away. And yet such is the power of sovereign grace that God's design is never nullified by any of these outworkings of 'the mystery of iniquity'. Consequently, both the Christian's hopes for the human future and the imperatives to holy living are bolstered by the assurance that God's designs will yet be realized. This sermon is a comment on some of the dramatic moments in the dismal story, climaxed by a ringing cry of hope.

Wesley's first recorded use of 2 Thess. 2:7 is in 1756 (September 19); he returned to it twice in 1782 (December 20, 22) and twice more in 1783 (March 7, 10). This suggests a closer correlation than usual between his oral preaching and a written sermon, for this one first appeared (without a title and numbered XV) in the Arminian Magazine *for May and June 1783 (VI. 229-37, 285-94). In 1788 it was placed in a different order in* SOSO, *V. 147-70, and given the title it has carried since. It was not published separately, but Wesley records yet another oral sermon on the text in 1790 (July 15).*

The Mystery of Iniquity

2 Thessalonians 2:7

The mystery of iniquity doth already work.

1. Without inquiring how far these words refer to any particular
5 event in the Christian church, I would at present take occasion
from them to consider that important question—in what manner
'the mystery of iniquity' hath 'wrought' among us till it hath
wellnigh covered the whole earth.

2. It is certain that God 'made man upright',[1] perfectly holy and
10 perfectly happy.[2] But by rebelling against God he destroyed
himself, lost the favour and the image of God, and entailed sin,
with its attendant pain, on himself and all his posterity. Yet his
merciful Creator did not leave him in this helpless, hopeless state.
He immediately appointed his Son, his well-beloved Son, 'who is
15 the brightness of his glory, the express image of his person',[3] to be
the Saviour of men, 'the propitiation for the sins of the whole
world';[4] the great Physician, who by his almighty Spirit should
heal the sickness of their souls, and restore them not only to the
favour but to 'the image of God wherein they were created'.[5]
20 3. This great 'mystery of godliness'[6] began to work from the
very time of the original promise. Accordingly the Lamb, being
(in the purpose of God) 'slain from the beginning of the world',[7]
from the same period his sanctifying Spirit began to renew the
souls of men. We have an undeniable instance of this in Abel, who
25 'obtained a testimony' from God 'that he was righteous'.[a] And
from that very time all that were partakers of the same faith were
partakers of the same salvation; were not only reinstated in the
favour, but likewise restored to the image of God.

4. But how exceeding small was the number of these, even from

---

[a] Heb. 11:6[cf. 5 and 4].

---

[1] Eccles. 7:29.
[2] Another typical conjunction of holiness and happiness; see No. 5, 'Justification by Faith', I.4 and n.
[3] Cf. Heb. 1:3.　　　　[4] 1 John 2:2.　　　　[5] Cf. Col. 3:10.
[6] 1 Tim. 3:16.　　　　　　　　　　　　　　　　　[7] Cf. Rev. 13:8.

the earliest ages! No sooner did 'the sons of men multiply upon the face of the earth' than 'God', looking down from heaven, 'saw that the wickedness of man was great upon earth;' so great 'that every imagination of the thoughts of his heart was evil, only evil', and that 'continually'.[b] And so it remained without any intermission till God executed that terrible sentence, 'I will destroy man, whom I have created, from the face of the earth.'[c]

5. 'Only Noah found grace in the eyes of the Lord,' being 'a just man and perfect in his generations.'[8] Him therefore, with his wife, his sons, and their wives, God preserved from the general destruction. And one might have imagined that this small remnant would likewise have been 'perfect in their generations'. But how far was this from being the case! Presently after this signal deliverance we find one of them, Ham, involved in sin, and under his father's curse. And how did the mystery of iniquity afterwards work, not only in the posterity of Ham, but in the posterity of Japhet; yea, and of Shem—Abraham and his family only excepted!

6. Yea, how did it work even in the posterity of Abraham, in God's chosen people! Were not these also, down to Moses, to David, to Malachi, to Herod the Great, 'a faithless and stubborn generation'?[9] 'A sinful nation, a people laden with iniquity', continually 'forsaking the Lord, and provoking the Holy One of Israel'?[10] And yet we have no reason to believe that these were worse than the nations that surrounded them, who were universally swallowed up in all manner of wickedness, as well as in damnable idolatries, not having the God of heaven 'in all their thoughts',[11] but working all uncleanness with greediness.[12]

7. In the fullness of time, when iniquity of every kind, when ungodliness and unrighteousness had spread over all nations, and covered the earth as a flood; it pleased God to lift up a standard against it, by 'bringing his first-begotten into the world'.[13] Now, then, one would expect the mystery of godliness would totally prevail over the mystery of iniquity—the Son of God would be 'a light to lighten the Gentiles', as well as 'salvation to his people Israel'.[14] All Israel, one would think, yea, and all the earth, will

[b] Gen. 6:1-5.   [c] Ver. 7.

---

[8] Gen. 6:8-9.   [9] Ps. 78:9 (BCP).   [10] Cf. Isa. 1:4.
[11] Cf. Ps. 10:4.   [12] See Eph. 4:19.
[13] Cf. Heb. 1:6.   [14] Luke 2:32; cf. Jer. 3:23.

soon be filled with the glory of the Lord.[15] Nay; the mystery of
iniquity prevailed still, wellnigh over the face of the earth. How
exceeding small was the number of those whose souls were
healed by the Son of God himself! 'When Peter stood up in the
5 midst of them, the number of names was about a hundred and
twenty.'[d] And even these were but imperfectly healed; the chief of
them being a little before so weak in faith that though they did
not, like Peter, forswear their Master, yet 'they all forsook him
and fled.'[16] A plain proof that the sanctifying 'Spirit was not' then
10 'given', because 'Jesus was not glorified.'[17]

8. It was then, when he had 'ascended up on high, and led
captivity captive',[18] that 'the promise of the Father' was fulfilled,
'which they had heard from him'.[19] It was then he began to work
like himself, showing that 'all power was given to him in heaven
15 and earth.'[20] 'When the day of Pentecost was fully come, suddenly
there came a sound from heaven, as of a rushing mighty wind, and
there appeared tongues as of fire, and they were all filled with
the Holy Ghost.'[e] In consequence of this three thousand souls
received 'medicine to heal their sickness',[21] were restored to the
20 favour and the image of God, under one sermon of St. Peter's.[f]
'And the Lord added to them daily' (not 'such as should be
saved'—a manifest perversion of the text—but) 'such as were
saved.'[22] The expression is peculiar; and so indeed is the position
of the words, which run thus, 'And the Lord added those that
25 were saved daily to the church.' First, *they were saved* from the
guilt and power of sin; then *they were added* to the assembly of the
faithful.

9. In order clearly to see how they were already saved we need
only observe the short account of them which is recorded in the
30 latter part of the second and in the fourth chapter. 'They

---

[d] Acts 1:15.
[e] Chap. 2:1-4.
[f] [Cf.] Chap. 2, ver. 41.

---

[15] See Num. 14:21.　　　　　　　　　　　　　[16] Mark 14:50.
[17] Cf. John 7:39.　　　　　　　　　　　　　　[18] Cf. Eph. 4:8.
[19] Cf. Acts 1:4.　　　　　　　　　　　　　　　[20] Cf. Matt. 28:18.
[21] Ps. 147:3 (BCP).
[22] Cf. Acts 2:47 in the AV and in Wesley's *Notes;* this is Wesley's correction of the AV's
translation of σωζομένους (AV: 'such as should be saved'). Even so, Greek participles
usually imply a *process;* thus, most modern translations (e.g., NEB) have it, 'such as were
being saved'.

continued steadfastly in the apostles' doctrine, and in the fellowship, and in the breaking of bread, and in the prayers:'[23] that is, they were daily taught by the apostles, and had all things common, and received the Lord's Supper, and attended all the public service.[g] 'And all that believed were together, and had all things common; and sold their possessions, and parted them to all men, as every man had need.'[h] And again: 'The multitude of them that believed', now greatly increased, 'were of one heart and of one soul. Neither said any of them that ought of the things which he possessed was his own, but they had all things common.'[i] And yet again: 'Great grace was upon them all; neither was there any among them that lacked. For as many as were possessors of lands or houses sold them, and brought the price of the things that were sold, and laid them at the apostles' feet. And distribution was made unto every man according as he had need.'[j]

10. But here a question will naturally occur. How came they to act thus, to have all things in common, seeing we do not read of any positive command to do this? I answer, there needed no outward command: the command was written on their hearts. It naturally and necessarily resulted from the degree of love which they enjoyed. Observe! 'They were of one heart and of one soul: and not so much as one' (so the words run) 'said' (they could not, while their hearts so overflowed with love) 'that any of the things which he possessed was his own.' And wheresoever the same cause shall prevail the same effect will naturally follow.

11. Here was the dawn of the proper gospel day. Here was a proper Christian church. It was now 'the Sun of righteousness rose' upon the earth, 'with healing in his wings.'[24] He did now 'save his people from their sins':[25] he 'healed' all 'their sickness'.[26] He not only taught that religion which is the true 'healing of the soul',[27] but effectually planted it in the earth; filling the souls of all that believed in him with *righteousness*, gratitude to God, and goodwill to man, attended with a *peace* that surpassed all understanding, and with *joy* unspeakable and full of glory.[28]

[g] Chap. 2.   [h] Chap. 2:41, 44-45.
[i] Chap. 4:31-32[4:32].   [j] Ver. 34-35[ver. 33-35].

---

[23] Cf. Acts 2:42.
[24] Cf. Mal. 4:2.   [25] Matt. 1:21.
[26] Matt. 9:35.   [27] Cf. Ps. 41:4.
[28] 1 Pet. 1:8.

12. But how soon did 'the mystery of iniquity' work again and obscure the glorious prospect! It began to work (not openly indeed, but covertly) in two of the Christians, Ananias and Sapphira. 'They sold their possession' like the rest, and probably
5 for the same motive. But afterwards, giving place to the devil, and reasoning with flesh and blood, they 'kept back part of the price'.[29] See the first Christians that 'made shipwreck of faith and a good conscience'![30] The first that 'drew back to perdition', instead of continuing to 'believe to the' final 'salvation'[31] of the soul. Mark
10 the first plague which infected the Christian church! Namely, the love of money! And will it not be the grand plague in all generations, whenever God shall revive the same work? O ye believers in Christ, take warning! Whether you are yet but 'little children', or 'young men' that 'are strong'[32] in the faith. See the
15 snare! *Your* snare in particular![33] That which you will be peculiarly exposed to after you have escaped from gross pollutions. 'Love not the world, neither the things of the world. If any man love the world', whatever he was in times past, 'the love of the Father is not' now 'in him.'[34]

20   13. However, this plague was stayed in the first Christian church by instantly cutting off the infected persons. And by that signal judgment of God on the first offenders, 'great fear came upon all',[k] so that for the present at least no one dared to follow their example. Meantime *believers*, men full of faith and love, who
25 rejoiced to have all things in common, 'were the more added to the Lord, multitudes both of men and women'.[l]

   14. If we inquire in what manner the mystery of iniquity, the energy of Satan, began to work again in the Christian church, we shall find it wrought in quite a different way, putting on quite
30 another shape. Partiality crept in among the Christian believers. Those by whom the distribution to everyone was made had respect of persons, largely supplying those of their own nation, while the other 'widows' who were not Hebrews 'were neglected in the daily administration'.[m] Distribution was not made to them
35 according as everyone had need. Here was a manifest breach of

---

[k] Acts 5:11.   [l] Ver. 14.   [m] Chap. 6:1.

---

[29] Acts 5:1-2.   [30] Cf. 1 Tim. 1:19.   [31] Cf. Heb. 10:39.   [32] 1 John 2:12-14.
[33] Another echo of Wesley's mounting frustration with his own Methodists in their new-found affluence. Cf. intro. to No. 50, 'The Use of Money'.
[34] 1 John 2:15.

brotherly love in the Hebrews, a sin both against justice and mercy; seeing the Grecians, as well as the Hebrews, had 'sold all that they had, and laid the price at the apostles' feet'.[35] See the second plague that broke in upon the Christian church—partiality: respect of persons, too much regard for those of our own side, and too little for others, though equally worthy.

15. The infection did not stop here, but one evil produced many more. From partiality in the Hebrews 'there arose in the Grecians a murmuring against them;'[36] not only discontent and resentful thoughts, but words suitable thereto; unkind expressions, hard speeches, evil-speaking, and backbiting naturally followed. And by the 'root of bitterness' thus 'springing up', undoubtedly 'many were defiled'.[37] The apostles indeed soon found out a means of removing the occasion of this murmuring; yet so much of the evil root remained that God saw it needful to use a severer remedy. He let loose the world upon them all, if haply by their sufferings, by the spoiling of their goods, by pain, imprisonment, and death itself, he might at once punish and amend them. And persecution, God's last remedy for a backsliding people, had the happy effect for which he intended it. Both the partiality of the Hebrews ceased, and the murmuring of the Grecians. And 'then had the churches rest, and were edified,' built up in the love of God and one another. 'And walking in the fear of the Lord, and in the comforts of the Holy Ghost, were multiplied.'[n]

16. It seems to have been some time after this that the mystery of iniquity began to work in the form of *zeal*.[38] Great troubles arose by means of some who zealously contended for circumcision and the rest of the ceremonial law, till the apostles and elders put an end to the spreading evil by that final determination: 'It seemed good unto the Holy Ghost, and to us, to lay on you no greater burden than these necessary things, that ye abstain from meats offered to idols, and from blood, and from things strangled, and from fornication.'[o] Yet was not this evil so

---

[n] Acts 9:31.   [o] Chap. 15:28-29.

---

[35] Cf. Acts 4:37.   [36] Cf. Acts 6:1.   [37] Heb. 12:15.
[38] Cf. the comment on misguided zeal, in the rather different context, in Wesley's sermon 'On Zeal', §1, written earlier (1781) but placed in a different order in *SOSO*, VII (see No. 92); note Wesley's suggestions as to how even zeal may be corrupted in 'the mystery of iniquity'.

thoroughly suppressed but that it frequently broke out again, as we learn from various parts of St. Paul's epistles, particularly that to the Galatians.

17. Nearly allied to this was another grievous evil which at the
5 same time sprang up in the church: want of mutual forbearance, and of consequence anger, strife, contention, variance. One very remarkable instance of this we find in this very chapter. When 'Paul said to Barnabas, Let us visit the brethren where we have preached the word, Barnabas determined to take with him
10 John,'[39] because he was 'his sister's son'.[40] 'But Paul thought it not good to take him who had deserted them before.'[41] And he had certainly reason on his side. But Barnabas resolved to have his own way. Καὶ ἐγένετο παροξυσμός, 'And there was a fit of anger.'[42] It does not say on St. Paul's side. Barnabas only[43] had
15 passion, to supply the want of reason. Accordingly he departed from the work, and went home, while St. Paul 'went' forward 'through Syria and Cilicia, confirming the churches'.[p]

18. The very first society of Christians at Rome were not altogether free from this evil leaven. There were 'divisions and
20 offences'[q] among them also, although in general they seem to have 'walked in love'.[44] But how early did the mystery of iniquity work, and how powerfully, in the church at Corinth! Not only 'schisms'[45] and 'heresies',[46] animosities, fierce and bitter contentions were among them, but open, actual sins; yea, 'such
25 fornication as was not named among the heathens'.[r] Nay, there was need to remind them that 'neither adulterers, nor thieves, nor drunkards' could 'enter into the kingdom of heaven'.[s] And in all

---

p Ver. 41.
q [Rom.] 16:17.
r 1 Cor. 5:1[; cf. Wesley's tr. in his *Notes*].
s Chap. 6:9-10.

---

[39] Acts 15:36-37. [40] Cf. Col. 4:10.
[41] Cf. Acts 15:38.
[42] Cf. Acts 15:39, where the text reads ἐγένετο δὲ παροξυσμός. Another instance of Wesley's insistence that Barnabas alone was caught up in this 'fit of anger'; cf. No. 22, 'Sermon on the Mount, II', III.10 and n.
[43] The *AM* text does not have this 'only', which may have been a printer's error. It appears in 1788 and obviously fills out the sense. In the MS errata to that vol. Wesley did not challenge it.
[44] Eph. 5:2.
[45] 1 Cor. 12:25.
[46] 1 Cor. 11:19.

St. Paul's epistles we meet with abundant proof that tares grew up with the wheat in all the churches, and that the mystery of iniquity did everywhere in a thousand forms counterwork the mystery of godliness.

19. When St. James wrote his Epistle, directed more immediately 'to the twelve tribes scattered abroad',[47] to the converted Jews, the tares sown among his wheat had produced a plentiful harvest. That grand pest of Christianity, a faith without works,[48] was spread far and wide, filling the church with a wisdom from beneath which was 'earthly, sensual, devilish';[49] and which gave rise not only to rash judging and evil-speaking but to 'envy, strife, confusion, and every evil work'.[50] Indeed whoever peruses the fourth and fifth chapters of this Epistle with serious attention will be inclined to believe that even in this early period the tares had nigh choked the wheat, and that among most of those to whom St. James wrote no more than the form of godliness, if so much, was left.

20. St. Peter wrote about the same time to 'the strangers', the Christians 'scattered abroad through' all those spacious provinces of 'Pontus, Galatia, Cappadocia, Asia (Minor) and Bithynia'.[51] These probably were some of the most eminent Christians that were then in the world. Yet how exceeding far were even these from being 'without spots and blemishes'![52] And what grievous tares were here also growing up with the wheat! Some of them were 'bringing in damnable heresies, even denying the Lord that bought them'.[t] And 'many followed their pernicious ways,' of whom the Apostle gives that terrible character, they 'walk after the flesh, in the lust of uncleanness, [. . .] like brute beasts, made to be taken and destroyed. [. . .] Spots they are, and blemishes, while they feast with you' (in the 'feasts of charity'[53] then celebrated throughout the whole church); 'having eyes full of adultery, and that cannot cease from sin. [. . .] These are wells without water, clouds that are carried with a tempest, for whom the mist of darkness is reserved for ever.'[54] And yet these very men

[t] 2 Pet. 2:1, etc.

---

[47] Jas. 1:1.
[48] Jas. 2:26; cf. No. 35, 'The Law Established through Faith, I', §4 and n.; see also intro. to Nos. 33–35.
[49] Jas. 3:15.   [50] Cf. Jas. 3:16.   [51] Cf. 1 Pet. 1:1.
[52] Cf. 1 Pet. 1:19.   [53] Jude 12.   [54] 2 Pet. 2:14, 17.

were called Christians, and were even then in the bosom of the church! Nor does the Apostle mention them as infesting any one particular church only, but as a general plague, which even then was dispersed far and wide among all the Christians to whom he
5 wrote.

21. Such is the authentic account of the mystery of iniquity, working even in the apostolic churches! An account given, not by the Jews or heathens, but by the apostles themselves. To this we may add the account which is given by the Head and Founder of
10 the church—him 'who holds the stars in his right hand',[55] who is 'the faithful and true witness'.[56] We may easily infer what was the state of the church in general from the state of the seven churches in Asia. One of these, indeed, the Church of Philadelphia, had 'kept his word, and had not denied his name'.[u] The Church of
15 Smyrna was likewise in a flourishing state. But all the rest were corrupted more or less; insomuch that several of them were not a jot better than the present race of Christians; and our Lord then threatened, what he has long since performed, to 'remove the candlestick'[57] from them.
20 22. Such was the real state of the Christian church, even during the first century, while not only St. John, but most of the apostles, were present with and presided over it. But what a mystery is this! That the all-wise, the all-gracious, the Almighty should suffer it so to be! Not in one only, but as far as we can learn
25 in every Christian society, those of Smyrna and Philadelphia excepted. And how came these to be excepted? Why were these less corrupted (to go no farther) than the other churches of Asia? It seems, because they were less wealthy. The Christians in Philadelphia were not literally 'increased in goods',[58] like those in
30 Ephesus or Laodicea; and if the Christians at Smyrna had acquired more wealth, it was swept away by persecution. So that these, having less of this world's goods, retained more of the simplicity and purity of the gospel.

23. But how contrary is this scriptural account of the ancient
35 Christians to the ordinary apprehensions of men! We have been apt to imagine that the primitive church was all excellence and

[u] Rev. 3:8.

---

[55] Cf. Rev. 2:1.
[57] Cf. Rev. 2:5.

[56] Rev. 3:14.
[58] Cf. Rev. 3:17.

perfection! Answerable to that strong description which St. Peter cites from Moses: 'Ye are a chosen generation, a royal priesthood, a holy nation, a peculiar people.'[59] And such, without all doubt, the first Christian church which commenced at the day of Pentecost was. But how soon did the fine gold become dim![60] How soon was the wine mixed with water![61] How little time elapsed before the god of this world[62] so far regained his empire that Christians in general were scarce distinguishable from heathens, save by their opinions and modes of worship!

24. And if the state of the church in the very first century was so bad, we cannot suppose it was any better in the second. Undoubtedly it grew worse and worse. Tertullian,[63] one of the most eminent Christians of that age, has given us an account of it in various parts of his writings, whence we learn that real, internal religion was hardly found; nay, that not only the *tempers* of the Christians were exactly the same with those of their heathen neighbours (pride, passion, love of the world reigning alike in both), but their lives and manners also. The bearing a faithful testimony against the general corruption of Christians seems to have raised the outcry against Montanus;[64] and against Tertullian himself, when he was convinced that the testimony of Montanus was true. As to the heresies fathered upon Montanus, it is not easy to find what they were. I believe his grand heresy was the maintaining that 'without' inward and outward 'holiness no man shall see the Lord.'[65]

25. Cyprian, Bishop of Carthage,[66] in every respect an unexceptionable witness, who flourished about the middle of the

---

[59] 1 Pet. 2:9; cf. Exod. 19:6.   [60] Lam. 4:1.
[61] Isa. 1:22.   [62] 2 Cor. 4:4.
[63] (*c.* 160–*c.* 220); a gifted pioneer in Latin Christianity, famous both for his apologetic writings (e.g., *Apology* [*c.* 198]) and polemics (e.g., *Against Marcion* [207 *et seq.*]). Wesley knew, of course, that Tertullian had become a Montanist and a fierce critic of the spiritual apathy and moral laxity of the generality of nominal Christians in his day, labelling them 'psychics' (which would come close to Wesley's 'almost Christians'). Cf. his essays *On Modesty, On Fasting,* and *Against Praxeas,* espec. §1; see also Ernest Evans, *Tertullian's Treatise Against Praxeas* (1948), pp. 81, 187.

[64] Wesley had read John Lacy's critical account of Montanus in his *General Delusions of Christians . . .* (1713); see pp. 242ff. But see also a sympathetic appraisal of Montanism in Gottfried Arnold's *Unparteyische Kirchen–und ketzer–historie . . .* (1668), Pt. 1, Bk. II, ch. 4. See No. 68, 'The Wisdom of God's Counsels', §9; and also No. 15, *The Great Assize,* II.2 and n.

[65] Cf. Heb. 12:14; the parallels here between Montanus and Wesley are obvious enough and also certainly self-conscious.

[66] The chief problems of St. Cyprian's letters centre around the terms on which 'lapsed Christians' may be received back into communion with the Catholic church, on the unity

third century, has left us abundance of letters in which he gives a large and particular account of the state of religion in this time. In reading this, one would be apt to imagine he was reading an account of the present century; so totally void of true religion 5 were the generality both of the laity and clergy;[67] so immersed in ambition, envy, covetousness, luxury, and all other vices, that the Christians of Africa were then exactly the same as the Christians of England are now.

26. It is true that during this whole period, during the first three 10 centuries, there were intermixed longer or shorter seasons wherein true Christianity revived. In those seasons the justice and mercy of God let loose the heathens upon the Christians. Many of these were then called to resist unto blood. And the blood of the martyrs was the seed of the church.[68] The apostolical spirit 15 returned; and many 'counted not their lives dear unto themselves, so they might finish their course with joy'.[69] Many others were reduced to happy poverty; and being stripped of what they had loved too well, they 'remembered from whence they were fallen, and repented, and did their first works'.[70]

20   27. Persecution never did, never could give any lasting wound to genuine Christianity. But the greatest it ever received, the grand blow which was struck at the very root of that humble, gentle, patient love, which is the fulfilling of the Christian law, the

of the church and her episcopacy, the baptism of infants, etc. Wesley has exaggerated Cyprian's passing criticisms of 'the *generality* of both the laity and the clergy' and has misinterpreted Cyprian's *defence* of the Christians against the charge by a Roman official (Demetrianus, pro-consul of Africa) that the Christians are to blame for all the woes of 'the declining world' (cf. Treatise V, *An Address to Demetrianus* [*ANF*, V. 457-65]). Cyprian agrees that the world is declining and that human affairs are desperate ('the world has now grown old'). But he denies that the Christians are the *cause* of the decline, and suggests that the Romans have hastened the end by their unjust persecution of the Christians among whom (§20) 'there flourishes the strength of hope and the firmness of faith' (cf. the triumphant peroration in §25). For other references to St. Cyprian, cf. Nos. 102, 'Of Former Times', §17; 104, 'On Attending the Church Service', §14; and see also 54, 'On Eternity', §10 and n.

[67] For other references to the church as a 'mixed society', cf. No. 104, 'On Attending the Church Service', §13 and n.

[68] An aphorism so familiar that Wesley omits quotation marks; cf. John Favour's *Antiquity Triumphing Over Novelty* (1619), p. 469; or Samuel Purchas, *Pilgrimes* (1625); and Thomas Fuller's *Church History*. It is a paraphrase from Tertullian's *Apologeticus*, L. 13: '*Plures efficimur, quotiens metimur a vobis; semen est sanguis christianorum*' ('We increase, even while we are being mown down by you [pagans]; the blood of the Christians is seed'). See No. 23, 'Sermon on the Mount, III', III.5 and n.

[69] Cf. Acts 20:24.

[70] Cf. Rev. 2:5.

whole essence of true religion, was struck in the fourth century by Constantine the Great, when he called himself a Christian, and poured in a flood of riches, honours, and power upon the Christians, more especially upon the clergy.[71] Then was fulfilled in the Christian church what Sallust says of the people of Rome: *Sublata imperii aemula, non sensim sed praecipiti cursu, a virtutibus descitum, ad vitia transcursum.*[72] Just so, when the fear of persecution was removed, and wealth and honour attended the Christian profession, the Christians did not gradually sink, but rushed headlong into all manner of vices. Then the mystery of iniquity was no more hid, but stalked abroad in the face of the sun. Then, not the golden, but the iron age of the church commenced: then one might truly say,

---

[71] Wesley's negative view of the Constantinian 'fall of the church' grew emphatic over the years; cf., e.g., Nos. 64, 'The New Creation', §4; 66, 'The Signs of the Times', II.7; 89, 'The More Excellent Way', §2; 97, 'On Obedience to Pastors', I.3; 102, 'Of Former Times', §§15, 16; 104, 'On Attending the Church Service', §14; 112, *On Laying the Foundation of the New Chapel*, II.6; 121, 'Prophets and Priests', §8. Cf. also, *A Farther Appeal*, Pt. III, I.7 (11:276 in this edn.), and 'Thoughts Upon a Late Phenomenon' (*AM*, 1789, XII. 46-49). But see No. 68, 'The Wisdom of God's Counsels', §8, where Wesley speaks of the 'fall of the church' coming (long before Constantine) when the love of money caused the first breach in the 'community of goods'.

This was in sharp contrast to Thomas Newton's triumphalist view in his *Dissertations on the Prophecies, which have remarkably been fulfilled, and at this time are fulfilling the world* (2nd edn., London, 1760), III. 69-74. Newton, at this time Bishop of Bristol, had made the point that Constantine's reign fulfilled the Apocalypse prophecy of 'the sixth seal, or period'—of 'a great earthquake or rather a great concussion (σεισμος μεγας) . . . And where was ever a greater concussion or removal than when Christianity was advanced to the throne of paganism and idolatry gave place to true religion? . . . [This was] one of the greatest and most memorable revolutions which ever was in the world . . . .' Later (pp. 210-14), Newton portrays the struggle between Christianity and paganism as the earthly counterpart of 'the war in heaven between the angels of darkness and the angels of light'; (p. 212), 'Constantine himself and the Christians of his time describe his conquests under the same image; as if they had understood that this prophecy had received its accomplishment in him.'

William Weston had also seen the hand of providence in the Constantinian liberation; cf. his *Dissertation on Some of the Most Remarkable Wonders of Antiquity* (Cambridge, 1748). Cf. also Joseph Milner, *The History of the Church of Christ from the Days of the Apostles to 1753*, espec. II.38-41. Cf. also Laurence Echard, *A General Ecclesiastical History*, (5th edn., 1719), Bk. III, v-vi.467-72; William Cave, *Ecclesiastici*, pp. 267-78; and Mosheim, *Institutiones Historiae Ecclesiasticae*, I. i. 10.

[72] A lapse of memory here; this is not Sallust but a garbled version, to the same point, of Velleius Paterculus, *History of Rome*, '*Liber Posterior*', II. i. 2-5: '*Quippe remoto Carthaginis metu sublataque imperii aemula non gradu, sed praecipiti cursu a virtute descitum, ad vitia transcursum*' ('When Rome was freed of the fear of Carthage and her rival for empire was out of her way, the path of [civic] virtue was abandoned for that of corruption, not gradually but in headlong haste').

Protinus irrupit venae peioris in aevum
Omne nefas; fugere pudor, verumque fidesque;
In quorum subiere locum fraudesque, dolusque,
Insidiaeque, et vis, et amor sceleratus habendi.[73]

5 At once in that unhappy age broke in
All wickedness and every deadly sin:
Truth, modesty, and love fled far away,
And force, and thirst of gold claimed universal sway.

28. And this is the event which most Christian expositors
10 mention with such triumph! Yea, which some of them suppose to
be typified in the Revelation by the 'New Jerusalem coming down
from heaven'![74] Rather say it was the coming of Satan and all his
legions from the bottomless pit: seeing from that very time he
hath set up his throne over the face of the whole earth, and
15 reigned over the Christian as well as the pagan world with hardly
any control. Historians indeed tell us very gravely of nations in
every century who were by such and such (*saints*, without doubt!)[75]
converted to Christianity. But still these converts practised all
kinds of abominations, exactly as they did before; no way differing
20 either in their tempers or in their lives from the nations that were
still called heathens. Such has been the deplorable state of the
Christian church from the time of Constantine till the
Reformation. A Christian nation, a Christian city (according to
the scriptural model) was nowhere to be seen; but every city and
25 country, a few individuals excepted, was plunged in all manner of
wickedness.

29. Has the case been altered since the Reformation? Does the
mystery of iniquity no longer work in the church? No. The
Reformation itself has not extended to above one-third even of
30 the western church. So that two-thirds of this remain as they
were;[76] so do the eastern, southern, and northern churches. They

[73] A more nearly accurate quotation of Ovid, *Metamorphoses*, i. 128-31 (except for
'*fugere*', which should read '*fugitque*', and '*dolusque*', a printer's error for '*dolique*'). The
verse translation may be Wesley's own; it is not in the standard translations of his time by
Arthur Golding (1565–67) and Dryden (Garth's edn., 1717). Cf. the slightly different
version of these lines in No. 128, 'The Deceitfulness of the Human Heart', §1, and yet
another verse translation—again, probably, by Wesley.

[74] Rev. 21:2; cf. Thomas Newton, *op. cit.*, p. 212. See also No. 102, 'Of Former Times',
§15.

[75] An echo of Juan de Valdes's ironic phrase about 'the saints of the world'; see No. 4,
Scriptural Christianity, II.5 and n.

[76] Cf. No. 63, 'The General Spread of the Gospel', §7, where Wesley again makes the
same point, and §16 for his reference to Luther's saying that revivals last no longer than

are as full of heathenish, or worse than heathenish, abominations as ever they were before. And what is the condition of the reformed churches? It is certain that they were reformed in their opinions as well as their modes of worship. But is not this all? Were either their tempers or lives reformed? Not at all. Indeed 5 many of the reformers themselves complained that the Reformation was not carried far enough. But what did they mean? Why, that they did not sufficiently reform the *rites* and *ceremonies* of the church.[77] Ye fools and blind![78] To fix your whole attention on the circumstantials of religion! Your complaint ought to have 10 been, the essentials of religion were not carried far enough. You ought vehemently to have insisted on an entire change of men's *tempers* and *lives;* on their showing they had 'the mind that was in Christ',[79] by 'walking as he also walked'.[80] Without this how exquisitely trifling was the reformation of opinions and rites and 15 ceremonies! Now let anyone survey the state of Christianity in the reformed parts of Switzerland; in Germany or France; in Sweden, Denmark, Holland; in Great Britain and Ireland. How little are any of these reformed Christians better than heathen nations! Have they more (I will not say communion with God, 20 although there is no Christianity without it) but have they more justice, mercy, or truth, than the inhabitants of China or Indostan?[81] O no! We must acknowledge with sorrow and shame that we are far beneath them!

> That we, who by thy name are named, 25
> The heathens unbaptized out-sin![82]

30. Is not this the 'falling away' or 'apostasy' from God foretold

one generation. For population statistics, cf. No. 15, *The Great Assize*, II.4 and n. on Edward Brerewood.

[77] A comment on the surface issues, at least, of the Puritan controversy (i.e., over vestments, the Prayer Book, and prelacy).
[78] Matt. 23:17, 19.
[79] Cf. Phil. 2:5.
[80] Cf. 1 John 2:6.
[81] I.e., Hindustan or India. Addison also used the term 'Indostan' as Wesley does here; cf. R. W. Harris, *Reason and Nature in Eighteenth Century Thought* (London, Blandford Press, 1968), p. 107. See also No. 69, 'The Imperfection of Human Knowledge', II.4.
[82] Cf. John and Charles Wesley, *Hymns on the Lord's Supper* (1745), p. 128:

> And those who by thy Name are named,
> The sinners unbaptized out-sin.

by St. Paul in his Second Epistle to the Thessalonians?[v] Indeed I would not dare to say with George Fox[83] that this apostasy was universal; that there never were any real Christians in the world from the days of the apostles till his time. But we may boldly say
5 that wherever Christianity has spread, the apostasy has spread also. Insomuch that although there are now, and always have been, individuals who were real Christians, yet the whole world never did, nor can at this day, show a Christian country or city.

31. I would now refer it to every man of reflection who believes
10 the Scriptures to be of God whether this general apostasy does not imply the necessity of a general reformation? Without allowing this, how can we possibly justify either the wisdom or goodness of God? According to Scripture the Christian religion was designed 'for the healing of the nations';[84] for the saving from
15 sin, by means of the Second Adam, all that were *constituted sinners* by the first. But it does not answer this end: it never did, unless for a short time at Jerusalem. What can we say but that if it *has not* yet, it surely *will* answer it. The time is coming when not only 'all Israel shall be saved,'[85] but 'the fullness of the Gentiles will come
20 in.'[86] The time cometh when 'violence shall no more be heard in the earth, wasting or destruction within our borders;' but every city shall 'call her walls salvation, and her gates praise'; when the people, saith the Lord, 'shall be all righteous; they shall inherit the land for ever, the branch of my planting, the work of my
25 hands, that I may be glorified.'[w]

32. From the preceding considerations we may learn the full answer to one of the grand objections of infidels against Christianity, namely, *the lives of Christians.* Of Christians, do you say? I doubt whether you ever knew a *Christian* in your life. When

---

[v] Chap. 2, ver. 3. [See also No. 1, *Salvation by Faith*, II.4 and n.]
[w] Isa. 60:18, 21.

---

[83] Founder of the Society of Friends, 1624–91, whose career, doctrines, and *Journal* suggest more than a few striking comparisons with Wesley's. The citation here of Fox's assertion of a 'universal apostasy' appears to have been Wesley's *inference* from passages in the *Journal* (1832 edn.), p. 116—in 1652: (1) 'I shewed also the state of apostasy since the apostles' days;' (2) pp. 599-600 (1686): 'the long night of apostasy'; (3) pp. 364-65 (1633): '. . . to shew that now the everlasting gospel was preached over the head of the whore, beast, false prophets, and anti-christs which had arose since the apostles' days . . . '. See also some of Fox's broadsheets; e.g., 'For Your Whoredoms in the City of London is the Hand of the Lord Stretched Forth Against Thee' (1660?). For another reference to Fox, cf. No. 68, 'The Wisdom of God's Counsels', §9 and n.
[84] Rev. 22:2.   [85] Rom. 11:26.   [86] Rom. 11:25.

Tomo Chachi,[87] the Indian chief, keenly replied to those who spoke to him of being a Christian: 'Why, these are Christians at Savannah! These[88] are Christians at Frederica!'—the proper answer was, 'No, they are not; they are no more Christians than you and Sinauky.' 'But are not those Christians in Canterbury, in London, in Westminster?' No, no more than they are angels. None are Christians but they that have the mind which was in Christ, and walk as he walked. 'Why, if these only are Christians', said an eminent wit, 'I never saw a Christian yet.'[89] I believe it: you never did. And perhaps you never will. For you will never find them in the grand or the gay world. The few Christians that are upon the earth are only to be found where *you* never look for them. Never therefore urge this objection more: never object to Christianity the lives or tempers of heathens. Though they are *called* Christians, the name does not imply the thing: they are as far from this as hell from heaven.

33. We may learn from hence, secondly, the extent of the fall, the astonishing spread of original corruption. What! among so many thousands, so many millions, is there none righteous, no not one?[90] Not by nature. But including the grace of God I will not say with the heathen poet,

> *Rari quippe boni: numera, vix sunt totidem quot*
> *Thebarum portae vel divitis ostia Nili.*[91]

As if he had allowed too much in supposing there were a hundred good men in the Roman Empire he comes to himself, and affirms there are hardly seven. Nay, surely there were seven thousand! There were so many long ago in one small nation where Elijah supposed there were none at all. But, allowing a few exceptions, we are authorized to say, 'The whole world lieth in wickedness;'[92] yea, 'in the wicked one' (as the words properly signify). 'Yes, the whole heathen world.' Yea, and the Christian, too (so called); for where is the difference, save in a few externals? See with your own

---

[87] Cf. JWJ, Feb. 13, 1736, and the diary for Easter 1736; June 29, 1736; and Apr. 11, 1737.

[88] *AM* orig., here and in the preceding sentence, 'there', altered by Wesley to 'these' in his errata and MS annotations.

[89] π; Cf. No. 63, 'The General Spread of the Gospel', §22.

[90] See Rom. 3:10.

[91] Juvenal, *Satires*, xiii. 26-27: 'Good men are rare; scarcely more in number than the gates of Thebes or the mouths of the enriching Nile' (i.e., seven).

[92] 1 John 5:19 (cf. *Notes*).

eyes. Look into that large country, Indostan.[93] There are Christians and heathens too. Which have more justice, mercy, and truth? The Christians or the heathens? Which are most corrupt, infernal, devilish in their tempers and practice? The 5 English or the Indians? Which have desolated whole countries, and clogged the rivers with dead bodies?

> O sacred name of Christian! how profaned![94]

O earth, earth, earth![95] How dost thou groan under the villainies of thy *Christian* inhabitants!

10   34. From many of the preceding circumstances we may learn, thirdly, what is the genuine tendency of riches: what a baleful influence they have had in all ages upon pure and undefiled religion. Not that money is an evil of itself: it is applicable to good as well as bad purposes. But nevertheless it is an undoubted truth
15 that 'the love of money is the root of all evil;'[96] and also that the possession of riches naturally breeds the love of them. Accordingly it is an old remark,

> *Crescit amor nummi, quantum ipsa pecunia crescit:*[97]

'As money increases, so does the love of it'—and always will, 20 without a miracle of grace. Although therefore other causes may concur, yet this has been in all ages the principal cause of the decay of true religion in every Christian community. As long as the Christians in any place were poor they were devoted to God. While they had little of the world they did not love the world; but 25 the more they had of it the more they loved it. This constrained the Lover of their souls at various times to unchain their persecutors, who by reducing them to their former poverty reduced them to their former purity. But still remember: riches have in all ages been the bane of genuine Christianity.

30   35. We may learn hence, fourthly, how great watchfulness they need who desire to be real Christians, considering what a state the world is in! May not each of them well say,

---

[93] Cf. §29 above, and n.
[94] Cf. Milton, *Paradise Lost*, iv. 951, 'O sacred name of faithfulness profaned!'
[95] Jer. 22:29.
[96] 1 Tim. 6:10.
[97] Juvenal, *Satires*, xiv.139: 'the love of money grows in proportion as wealth accumulates.' This same line is repeated in No. 131, 'The Danger of Increasing Riches', II.14, with still another translation by Wesley.

> Into a world of ruffians sent,
> I walk on hostile ground:
> Wild, human bears on slaughter bent,
> And ravening wolves surround.[98]

They are the most dangerous because they commonly appear in 5
sheep's clothing.[99] Even those who do not pretend to religion yet
make fair professions of goodwill, of readiness to serve us, and
perhaps of truth and honesty. But beware of taking their word.
Trust not any man until he fears God. It is a great truth,

> He that fears no God, can love no friend![100]   10

Therefore stand upon your guard against everyone that is not
earnestly seeking to save his soul. We have need to keep both our
heart and mouth 'as with a bridle, while the ungodly are in our
sight'.[101] Their conversation, their spirit, is infectious, and steals 15
upon us unawares, we know not how. 'Happy is the man that
feareth always'[102] in this sense also, lest he should partake of other
men's sins! 'O keep thyself pure!'[103] 'Watch and pray, that thou
enter not into temptation!'[104]

36. We may learn from hence, lastly, what thankfulness 20
becomes those who have escaped the corruption that is in the
world, whom God hath chosen out of the world to be holy and
unblameable. 'Who is it that maketh thee to differ? And what hast
thou which thou hast not received?'[105] 'Is it not God' alone 'who
worketh in thee both to will and to do for his good pleasure?'[106] 25
'And let those give thanks whom the Lord hath redeemed and
delivered from the hand of the enemy.'[107] Let us praise him that
he hath given us to see the deplorable state of all that are round
about us; to see the wickedness which overflows the earth, and yet
not be borne away by the torrent! We see the general, the almost 30

---

[98] Charles Wesley, *Hymns and Sacred Poems* (1749), II. 126 (*Poet. Wks.*, V. 268). The orig. text reads, 'Wild human beasts'; the present reading is John's 'improvement', as printed in *AM*. See also No. 69, 'The Imperfection of Human Knowledge', II.4, where Wesley has linked 'ruffians', 'wolves', and 'bears'.

[99] Matt. 7:15.

[100] Torquato Tasso, *Godfrey of Bulloigne; or the Recoverie of Jerusalem* (tr. by Edward Fairfax, 1600), Bk. IV, st. 65, l. 5: 'He knows, who fears no God, he loves no friend.' Cf. also Wesley's letter to Miss March, June 17, 1774.

[101] Cf. Ps. 39:2 (BCP).   [102] Prov. 28:14.
[103] Cf. 1 Tim. 5:22.   [104] Cf. Matt. 26:41.
[105] 1 Cor. 4:7 (*Notes*).   [106] Cf. Phil. 2:13.
[107] Cf. Ps. 107:2 (BCP).

universal contagion; and yet it cannot approach to hurt us! Thanks be unto him 'who hath delivered us from so great a death', and 'doth' *still* 'deliver'![108] And have we not farther ground for thankfulness, yea, and strong consolation, in the blessed hope 5 which God hath given us that the time is at hand when righteousness shall be as universal as unrighteousness is now? Allowing that 'the whole creation now groaneth together'[109] under the sin of man, our comfort is, it will not always groan: God will arise and maintain his own cause. And the whole creation shall 10 then be delivered both from moral and natural corruption. Sin, and its consequence, pain, shall be no more; holiness and happiness will cover the earth. Then shall all the ends of the world see the salvation of our God.[110] And the whole race of mankind shall know and love and serve God, and reign with him 15 for ever and ever!

---

[108] Cf. 2 Cor. 1:10.
[109] Cf. Rom. 8:22.
[110] See Ps. 98:3.

THE END OF CHRIST'S COMING

AN INTRODUCTORY COMMENT

This is yet another explanatory comment on 'the problem of evil' and on 'Christ's coming' as its saving remedy. It was finished on January 20, 1781, and published in the July and August issues of the Arminian Magazine *of that same year (IV. 360-66, 408-14), numbered IV, without a title. It was then placed ninth in Vol. V of* SOSO *(1788). Judging from the record of use of 1 John 3:8 in Wesley's oral preaching, it was a staple theme; twenty-seven instances are reported, spread rather evenly over the years from 1742 to 1789 (six in 1758). This confirms the impression of Wesley's serious preoccupation, both early and late, with the problem of evil, and especially* moral *evil.*

The End Of Christ's Coming

1 John 3:8

For this purpose was the Son of God manifested, that he might destroy the works of the devil.

1. Many eminent writers, heathen as well as Christian, both in 5 earlier and later ages, have employed their utmost labour and art in painting the beauty of virtue. And the same pains they have taken to describe, in the liveliest colours, the deformity of vice; both of vice in general, and of those particular vices which were most prevalent in their respective ages and countries. With equal 10 care they have placed in a strong light the happiness that attends virtue and the misery which usually accompanies vice, and always follows it. And it may be acknowledged that treatises of this kind are not wholly without their use. Probably hereby some on the one hand have been stirred up to desire and follow after virtue, and 15 some on the other hand checked in their career of vice; perhaps

reclaimed from it, at least for a season. But the change effected in men by these means is seldom either deep or universal. Much less is it durable: in a little space it vanishes away as the morning cloud.[1] Such motives[2] are far too feeble to overcome the
5 numberless temptations that surround us. All that can be said of the beauty and advantage of virtue and the deformity and ill effects of vice cannot resist, and much less overcome and heal, one irregular appetite or passion.

> All these fences, and their whole array,
10 > One cunning bosom-sin sweeps quite away.[3]

2. There is therefore an absolute necessity, if ever we would conquer vice, or steadily persevere in the practice of virtue, to have arms of a better kind than these; otherwise we may *see* what is right, but we cannot attain it. Many of the men of reflection
15 among the very heathens were deeply sensible of this. The language of their heart was that of Medea:

> *Video meliora proboque,*
> *Deteriora sequor.*[4]

How exactly agreeing with the words of the Apostle (personating
20 a man convinced of sin, but not yet conquering it): 'The good that I would I do not; but the evil I would not, that I do.'[5] The impotence of the human mind even the Roman philosopher could discover: 'There is in every man', says he, 'this weakness (he might have said, this sore disease) *gloriae sitis*—a thirst for glory.
25 Nature points out the disease; but nature shows us no remedy.'[6]

---

[1] See Job 7:9; Hos. 6:4.
[2] Orig., *AM* and *SOSO*, 'motions', corrected in Wesley's annotated copies of both.
[3] Cf. Herbert, 'Sinne', in *Poetical Works* (London, James Nisbet and Co., 1857), p. 53. It is included in Wesley's *Select Parts of Mr. Herbert's Sacred Poems* (1773), p. 12. Such phrases as 'bosom sin', 'darling sin', etc., were old-time clichés; see above, No. 48, 'Self-denial', II.2 and n.
[4] Cf. Medea's pathetic complaint in Ovid's *Metamorphoses*, vii. 20-21: 'Ah, if I could, I should be more myself. But some strange power holds me down against my will. Desire persuades me one way, reason another. *I see the better and approve it, but I follow the worse.*' This apothegm (reminiscent of Rom. 7:18-23, as Wesley notes) is a commonplace in seventeenth- and eighteenth-century theologians (William Pemble, Robert Fell, John Norris, Henry More, William Beveridge, Robert Sanderson, Robert South, and William Jones). Wesley had earlier used this in *Thoughts Upon Necessity*, IV.3.
[5] Cf. Rom. 7:19.
[6] π; Wesley speaks often of the desire or 'thirst for glory'; see Nos. 14, *The Repentance of Believers*, I.7 and n.; and 84, *The Important Question*, I.4, where he quotes from Virgil's *Aeneid*, vi.823: '*laudumque immensa cupido*' ('the immense thirst of praise').

3. Nor is it strange that though they sought for a remedy, yet they found none. For they sought it where it never was and never will be found, namely, in themselves—in reason, in philosophy. Broken reeds! Bubbles! Smoke! They did not seek it in God, in whom alone it is possible to find it. In God! No; they totally 5 disclaim this, and that in the strongest terms. For although Cicero, one of their oracles, once stumbled upon that strange truth, *Nemo unquam vir magnus sine afflatu divino fuit*[7] ('there never was any great man who was not divinely inspired'), yet in the very same tract he contradicts himself, and totally overthrows his 10 own assertion by asking, *Quis pro virtute aut sapientia gratias dedit Deis unquam?*[8]—whoever returned thanks to God for his virtue or wisdom? The Roman poet is (if possible) more express still; who, after mentioning several outward blessings, honestly adds:

> *Haec satis est orare Jovem, quae donat et aufert:*   15
> *Det vitam, det opes: aequum, mi animum ipse parabo.*[9]
> We ask of God, what he can give or take—
> Life, wealth: but virtuous I myself will make.

4. The best of them either sought virtue partly from God and[10] partly from themselves; or sought it from those gods who were 20 indeed but devils, and so not likely to make their votaries better than themselves. So dim was the light of the wisest of men till 'life and immortality were brought to light by the gospel;'[11] till 'the Son of God was manifested, to destroy the works of the devil.'[12]

But what are 'the works of the devil' here mentioned? How was 25 'the Son of God manifested' to destroy them? And how, in what manner, and by what steps, does he actually destroy them? These three very important points we may consider in their order.

I.[1.] And, first, what these works of the devil are we learn from the words preceding and following the text: 'We know that he was 30

---

[7] Cf. Cicero, *De Natura Deorum* (*On the Nature of the Gods*), ii. 66: '*Nemo igitur vir magnus sine aliquo afflatu divino unquam fuit.*'

[8] Cf. *ibid.*, iii.36, where Cicero's point is that human virtue (by contrast with good fortune) is *humanly* achieved. Wesley had earlier used quotations, to the same effect, in *The Doctrine of Original Sin*, Pt. I, I.12.

[9] Cf. Horace, *Epistles*, I.xviii. 111-12; the orig. has *ponit* in place of Wesley's *donat*. The translation is also probably Wesley's. See also *The Doctrine of Original Sin*, I.12.

[10] Orig., *AM* and *SOSO*, 'or', corrected in Wesley's annotated copy of *SOSO*.

[11] Cf. 2 Tim. 1:10.

[12] Cf. 1 John 3:8.

manifested to take away our sins.'ᵃ 'Whosoever abideth in him, sinneth not: whosoever sinneth, seeth him not, neither knoweth him.'ᵇ 'He that committeth sin is of the devil; for the devil sinneth from the beginning. For this purpose was the Son of God
5 manifested, that he might destroy the works of the devil.'ᶜ 'Whosoever is born of God doth not commit sin.'ᵈ From the whole of this it appears that 'the works of the devil' here spoken of are sin and the fruits of sin.

2. But since the wisdom of God has now dissipated the clouds
10 which so long covered the earth, and put an end to the childish conjectures of men concerning these things, it may be of use to take a more distinct view of these 'works of the devil', so far as the oracles of God instruct us. It is true, the design of the Holy Spirit was to assist our faith, not gratify our curiosity. And therefore the
15 account he has given in the first chapters of Genesis is exceeding short. Nevertheless, it is so clear that we may learn therefrom whatsoever it concerns us to know.

3. To take the matter from the beginning: 'The Lord God' (literally 'Jehovah, the Gods'; that is, One and Three) 'created
20 man in his own image'¹³—in his own *natural* image (as to his better part) that is, a spirit, as God is a spirit: endued with *understanding*, which, if not the essence, seems to be the most essential property of a spirit. And probably the human spirit, like the angelical, then discerned truth by intuition.¹⁴ Hence he
25 named every creature as soon as he saw it according to its inmost nature.¹⁵ Yet his knowledge was limited, as he was a creature; ignorance therefore was inseparable from him. But error was not: it does not appear that he was mistaken in anything. But he was capable of mistaking, of being deceived, although not necessitat-
30 ed to it.

4. He was endued also with a *will*, with various affections (which are only the will exerting itself various ways) that he might love, desire, and delight in that which is good; otherwise his understanding had been to no purpose. He was likewise endued

---

ᵃ [1 John 3:8] Ver. 5.   ᵇ Ver. 6.
ᶜ Ver. 8.   ᵈ Ver. 9.

---

¹³ Cf. Gen. 1:27; cf. also No. 141, 'The Image of God', on this text.
¹⁴ Cf. below, III.1; and No. 10, 'The Witness of the Spirit, I', I.12 and n.
¹⁵ Cf. No. 141, 'The Image of God', II.2, as well as Wesley's extract from John Hildrop, 'Free Thoughts on the Brute Creation', in *AM* (1783), VI.35.

with *liberty*,[16] a power of choosing what was good, and refusing what was not so. Without this both the will and the understanding would have been utterly useless. Indeed without liberty man had been so far from being a *free agent* that he could have been no *agent* at all. For every *unfree being* is purely passive, not active in any 5 degree. Have you a sword in your hand? Does a man stronger than you seize your hand, and force you to wound a third person? In this you are no agent, any more than the sword: the hand is as passive as the steel. So in every possible case. He that is not free is not an *agent*, but a *patient*.[17]   10

5. It seems therefore that every spirit in the universe, as such, is endued with *understanding*, and in consequence with a will and with a measure of *liberty*; and that these three are inseparably united in every intelligent nature. And observe: 'liberty necessitated', or overruled, is really no liberty at all. It is a 15 contradiction in terms. It is the same as 'unfree freedom', that is, downright nonsense.

6. It may be farther observed (and it is an important observation) that where there is no liberty there can be no moral good or evil, no virtue or vice. The fire warms us, yet it is not 20 capable of virtue; it burns us, yet this is no vice. There is no virtue but where an intelligent being knows, loves, and chooses what is good; nor is there any vice but where such a being knows, loves, and chooses what is evil.

7. And God created man, not only in his *natural*, but likewise in 25 his own *moral* image.[18] He created him not only in *knowledge*, but also in righteousness and true holiness.[19] As his understanding was without blemish, perfect in its kind, so were all his affections. They were all set right, and duly exercised on their proper objects. And as a free agent he steadily chose whatever was good, 30 according to the direction of his understanding. In so doing he was unspeakably happy, dwelling in God and God in him, having an uninterrupted fellowship with the Father and the Son through

---

[16] Cf. No. 60, 'The General Deliverance', I.4 and n.

[17] I.e., one who is *acted upon*. Cf. Addison, *Spectator*, No. 486 (Sept. 17, 1712), and his allusion to bachelors versus married men: 'Let them not pretend to be free . . . and laugh at us poor married patients.' See also *OED*. The same usage occurs in No. 82, 'On Temptation', I.11.

[18] Cf. No. 1, *Salvation by Faith*, §1 and n.

[19] Eph. 4:24.

the eternal Spirit; and the continual testimony of his conscience that all his ways were good and acceptable to God.[20]

8. Yet his liberty (as was observed before) necessarily included a power of choosing or refusing either good or evil. Indeed it has been doubted whether man could then choose evil, knowing it to be such. But it cannot be doubted he might mistake evil for good. He was not infallible; therefore not impeccable. And this unravels the whole difficulty of the grand question, *unde malum?*[21] 'How came evil into the world?' It came from 'Lucifer, son of the morning':[22] it was 'the work of the devil'. 'For the devil', saith the Apostle, 'sinneth from the beginning;'[23] that is, was the first sinner in the universe; the author of sin; the first being who by the abuse of his liberty introduced evil into the creation.

> He, of the first,
> If not the first archangel,[24]

was self-tempted to think too highly of himself. He freely yielded to the temptation, and gave way first to pride,[25] then to self-will. He said, 'I will sit upon the sides of the north; I will be like the Most High.'[26] He did not fall alone, but soon drew after him a third part of the stars of heaven; in consequence of which they lost their glory and happiness, and were driven from their former habitation.

9. 'Having great wrath',[27] and perhaps envy at the happiness of the creatures whom God had newly created, it is not strange that he should desire and endeavour to deprive them of it. In order to this he concealed himself in the serpent, who was 'the most subtle',[28] or intelligent, of all the brute creatures, and on that

---

[20] Cf. No. 5, 'Justification by Faith', I.4 and n.; see also No. 56, 'God's Approbation of His Works'.

[21] Cf. A. G. Sertillanges, *Le problème du mal*, Vol. I, *L'histoire* (Paris, Aubier, 1948); and R. A. Tsanoff, *The Nature of Evil* (New York, Macmillan, 1931), chs. I-II. A perennial, tormented question for thoughtful people in every age; see Linwood Urban and Douglas N. Walton, eds., *The Power of God: Readings on Omnipotence and Evil* (Oxford, Oxford Univ. Press, 1978). In Wesley's case, it ran back to Hesiod's *Theogony* and to Plato (e.g., *Politicus*, *Theaetetus*, *Timaeus);* he would have also known of Marcion's central question *(Unde malum et quare?)* and his answer ('two gods, one good, the other evil') from Tertullian's *Against Marcion*, I.2. But see also his comments on Jenyns, *et al.*, in No. 56, 'God's Approbation of His Works', II.2 and n.

[22] Isa. 14:12.   [23] 1 John 3:8.

[24] Milton, *Paradise Lost*, v. 659-60. See also No. 128, 'The Deceitfulness of the Human Heart', I.1.

[25] Cf. III.2, below; and No. 14, *The Repentance of Believers*, I.3 and n.

[26] Cf. Isa. 14:13-14.   [27] Rev. 12:12.   [28] Cf. Gen. 3:1.

account the least liable to raise suspicion. Indeed some have (not improbably) supposed that the serpent was then endued with reason and speech.[29] Had not Eve known he was so, would she have admitted any parley with him? Would she not have been frighted rather than 'deceived', as the Apostle observes she was?[30] To deceive her Satan mingled truth with falsehood: 'Hath God said, ye may not eat of every tree of the garden?'[31] And soon after persuaded her to disbelieve God, to suppose his threatening should not be fulfilled. She then lay open to the whole temptation: to 'the desire of the flesh', for the tree was 'good for food'; to 'the desire of the eyes', for it was 'pleasant to the eyes'; and to 'the pride of life', for it was 'to be desired to make one wise',[32] and consequently honoured. So unbelief begot pride. She thought herself wiser than God, capable of finding a better way to happiness than God had taught her. It begot self-will: she was determined to do her own will, not the will of him that made her. It begot foolish desires, and completed all by outward sin: 'she took of the fruit and did eat.'[33]

10. She then 'gave to her husband, and he did eat'.[34] And 'in that day' yea, that moment, he 'died'.[35] The life of God was extinguished in his soul. The glory departed from him. He lost the whole moral image of God, righteousness and true holiness.[36] He was unholy; he was unhappy; he was full of sin, full of guilt and tormenting fears. Being broke off from God, and looking upon him as an angry judge, 'he was afraid.'[37] But how was his understanding darkened, to think he could 'hide himself from the presence of the Lord among the trees of the garden'![38] Thus was his soul utterly dead to God! And in that day his body likewise began to die; became obnoxious[39] to weakness, sickness, pain—all preparatory to the death of the body, which naturally led to eternal death.

II. Such are 'the works of the devil', sin and its fruits, considered in their order and connection. We are in the second place to consider how 'the Son of God was manifested' in order to 'destroy' them.

---

[29] Cf. No. 57, 'On the Fall of Man', I.1 and n.   [30] See 1 Tim. 2:14.
[31] Gen. 3:1.   [32] Gen. 3:6; 1 John 2:16 (*Notes*).
[33] Cf. Gen. 3:6.   [34] *Ibid.*   [35] Cf. Gen. 2:17.
[36] Eph. 4:24.   [37] Cf. Gen. 3:10.   [38] Cf. Gen. 3:8.
[39] I.e., 'susceptible to'; see No. 7, 'The Way to the Kingdom', II.4 and n.

1. He was manifested as the only-begotten Son of God,[40] in glory equal with the Father, to the inhabitants of heaven, before and at the foundation of the world.[41] These 'morning-stars sang together', all these 'sons of God shouted for joy',[42] when they
5 heard him pronounce, 'Let there be light; and there was light;'[43] when he 'spread the north over the empty space',[44] and 'stretched out the heavens like a curtain'.[45] Indeed it was the universal belief of the ancient church that God the Father none hath seen, nor can see; that from all eternity he hath dwelt in light un-
10 approachable; and it is only in and by the Son of his love that he hath at any time revealed himself to his creatures.

2. How the Son of God was manifested to our first parents in paradise it is not easy to determine. It is generally, and not improbably, supposed that he appeared to them in the form of a
15 man, and conversed with them face to face. Not that I can at all believe the ingenious dream of Dr. Watts[46] concerning 'the glorious humanity of Christ', which he supposes to have existed before the world began, and to have been endued with I know not what astonishing powers. Nay, I look upon this to be an exceeding
20 dangerous, yea, mischievous hypothesis, as it quite excludes the force of very many Scriptures which have been hitherto thought to prove the Godhead of the Son. And I am afraid it was the grand means of turning that great man aside from the faith once delivered to the saints;[47] that is, if he was turned aside, if that
25 beautiful soliloquy be genuine which is printed among his posthumous works, wherein he so earnestly beseeches the Son of God not to be displeased 'because he cannot believe him to be coequal and coeternal with the Father'.[48]

---

[40] John 3:18.   [41] See Eph. 1:4; 1 Pet. 1:20.   [42] Job 38:7.
[43] Gen. 1:3.   [44] Cf. Job 26:7.   [45] Cf. Ps. 104:2; Isa. 40:22.
[46] Isaac Watts (1674–1748), one of Nonconformity's most eminent preachers and their greatest poet and hymnist; cf. Horton Davies, *Worship and Theology in England*, Vol. III. For his notion of Christ's 'glorious humanity', cf. Watts's *Useful and Important Questions, Q.*VI (*Works*, VI. 706), and *The Glory of Christ as God-Man Displayed (idem)*, Discourse II, 'An Enquiry into the extensive powers of the human nature of Christ . . .', pp. 772-79. Watts's doctrine of Christ's *pre-existent* humanity is developed in Discourse III (pp. 802-43) 'by tracing out the early existence of [Christ's] human nature as the first-born of God . . . before the formation of the world'. Wesley had warned against this doctrine in a letter to his brother (June 8, 1780) and would repeat the same warning in a letter to Joseph Benson (Sept. 17, 1788). Cf. the survey of the discussion of pre-existence in I. A. Dorner, *History . . . of the Doctrine of the Person of Christ* (1870), II.ii.329-33.
[47] Jude 3.
[48] Cf. Watts's brief pamphlet, *A Solemn Address to the Great and Ever Blessed God*, first published in 1745; then suppressed, but republished in *The Posthumous Works* (1779), Vol.

3. May we not reasonably believe it was by similar appearances that he was manifested in succeeding ages to Enoch, while he 'walked with God';[49] to Noah, before and after the deluge; to Abraham, Isaac, and Jacob on various occasions; and, to mention no more, to Moses. This seems to be the natural meaning of the 5 word: 'My servant Moses is faithful in all my house. With him will I speak mouth to mouth, even apparently, and not in dark speeches; and the similitude of Jehovah shall he behold'[50] —namely, the Son of God.

4. But all these were only types of his grand manifestation. It 10 was in the fullness of time[51] (in just the middle age of the world, as a great man largely proves)[52] that God 'brought his first-begotten into the world, made of a woman',[53] by the power of the Highest overshadowing her.[54] He was afterwards manifested to the shepherds; to devout Simeon; to Anna, the prophetess; and to 'all 15 that waited for redemption in Jerusalem'.[55]

5. When he was of due age for executing his priestly office he was manifested to Israel, 'preaching the gospel of the kingdom of God in every town and in every city'.[56] And for a time he was glorified by all, who acknowledged that he 'spake as never man 20 spake';[57] that he 'spake as one having authority',[58] with all the wisdom of God, and the power of God. He was manifested by numberless 'signs and wonders, and mighty works which he did';[59] as well as by his whole life, being the only one born of a woman 'who knew no sin';[60] who from his birth to his death 'did 25 all things well',[61] doing continually 'not his own will, but the will of him that sent him'.[62]

II. H. L. Burnett (in *DNB*, 'I. Watts') speaks of this as 'a very pathetic piece'. On the strength of it Nathaniel Lardner had laid claim to Watts as 'a Unitarian'; see Thomas Belsham, *Memoirs of Theophilus Lindsey* . . . (1812), 161-64. But Thomas Milner, in his *Life of Watts* (1834), p. 35, stoutly denied this. Dorner, *op. cit.*, III, Appendix, 404-5, dismisses the pamphlet as an unrepresentative product of Watts's dotage.

[49] Gen. 5:22, 24.
[50] Cf. Num. 12:7-8.
[51] Gal. 4:4.
[52] Cf. Jonathan Edwards, *A History of the Work of Redemption* (1774), pp. 207 ff.
[53] Cf. Heb. 1:6.   [54] See Luke 1:35.
[55] Cf. Luke 2:38 (*Notes*).   [56] Cf. Matt. 4:23; 9:35.
[57] Cf. John 7:46.
[58] Cf. Matt. 7:29.
[59] Cf. 2 Cor. 12:12.
[60] 2 Cor. 5:21.
[61] Cf. Mark 7:37.
[62] Cf. John 6:38.

6. After all, 'Behold the Lamb of God, taking away the sin of the world!'[63] This was a more glorious manifestation of himself than any he had made before. How wonderfully was he manifested to angels and men when he 'was wounded for *our*
5 transgressions',[64] when he 'bore all our sins in his own body on the tree';[65] when, having by that one oblation of himself once offered, made a full, perfect, and sufficient sacrifice, oblation, and satisfaction for the sins of the whole world,[66] he cried out, 'It is finished; and bowed his head, and gave up the ghost.'[67] We need
10 but just mention those farther manifestations—his resurrection from the dead, his ascension into heaven, into the glory which he had before the world began;[68] and his pouring out the Holy Ghost on the day of Pentecost; both of which are beautifully described in those well-known words of the Psalmist: 'He hath ascended up
15 on high; he hath led captivity captive; he hath received gifts for men; yea, even for his enemies, that the Lord God might dwell among, or in them.'[69]

7. 'That the Lord God might dwell in them.' This refers to a yet farther manifestation of the Son of God, even his inward
20 manifestation of himself. When he spoke of this to his apostles, but a little before his death, one of them immediately asked, 'Lord, how is it that thou wilt manifest thyself to us, and not unto the world?'[70] By enabling us to believe in his name. For he is then inwardly manifested to us when we are enabled to say with con-
25 fidence, 'My Lord, and my God!'[71] Then each of us can boldly say, 'The life which I now live, I live by faith in the Son of God, who loved *me* and gave himself for *me*.'[72] And it is by thus manifesting himself in our hearts that he effectually 'destroys the works of the devil'.

30 III.1. How he does this, in what manner, and by what steps he does actually destroy them, we are now to consider. And, first, as Satan began his work in Eve by tainting her with unbelief, so the

---

[63] Cf. John 1:29.
[64] Isa. 53:5.
[65] Cf. 1 Pet. 2:24.
[66] Cf. BCP, Communion, Consecration.
[67] John 19:30.
[68] See John 17:5.
[69] Cf. Ps. 68:18 (BCP).
[70] Cf. John 14:22.
[71] John 20:28.   [72] Cf. Gal. 2:20.

Son of God begins his work in man by enabling us to believe in him. He both opens and enlightens the eyes of our understanding. Out of darkness he commands light to shine, and takes away the veil which the god of this world had spread over our hearts. And we then see, not by a chain of *reasoning*, but by a kind of intuition,[73] by a direct view, that 'God was in Christ, reconciling the world to himself, not imputing to them their former trespasses,'[74] not imputing them to *me*. In that day 'we know that we are of God,'[75] children of God by faith, 'having redemption through the blood' of Christ, 'even the forgiveness of sins'.[76] 'Being justified by faith, we have peace with God, through our Lord Jesus Christ:'[77] that peace which enables us in every state therewith to be content;[78] which delivers us from all perplexing doubts, from all tormenting fears, and in particular from that 'fear of death whereby we were all our lifetime subject to bondage'.[79]

2. At the same time the Son of God strikes at the root of that grand work of the devil, pride;[80] causing the sinner to humble himself before the Lord, to abhor himself as it were in dust and ashes.[81] He strikes at the root of self-will, enabling the humbled sinner to say in all things, 'Not as I will, but as thou wilt.'[82] He destroys the love of the world, delivering them that believe in him from 'every foolish and hurtful desire';[83] from 'the desire of the flesh, the desire of the eyes, and the pride of life'.[84] He saves them from seeking or expecting to find happiness in any creature. As Satan turned the heart of man from the Creator to the creature; so the Son of God turns his heart back again from the creature to the Creator.[85] Thus it is, by manifesting himself, he destroys the works of the devil, restoring the guilty outcast from God to his favour, to pardon and peace; the sinner in whom dwelleth no good thing,[86] to love and holiness; the burdened, miserable sinner, to joy unspeakable,[87] to real, substantial happiness.

---

[73] Cf. above, I.3; also No. 10, 'The Witness of the Spirit, I', I.12 and n.
[74] 2 Cor. 5:19 (*Notes*). [75] 1 John 5:19.
[76] Cf. Col. 1:14. [77] Rom. 5:1.
[78] See Phil. 4:11. [79] Cf. Heb. 2:15.
[80] Cf. I.8 above; and No. 14, *The Repentance of Believers*, I.3 and n.
[81] See Job 42:6.
[82] Matt. 26:39.
[83] Cf. 1 Tim. 6:9.
[84] Cf. 1 John 2:16 (*Notes*).
[85] An echo of St. Irenaeus's doctrine of recapitulation; cf. *Against Heresies*, III.18 (1-7), 21(10); V.21-23.
[86] Rom. 7:18. [87] 1 Pet. 1:8.

3. But it may be observed that the Son of God does not destroy
the whole work of the devil in man, as long as he remains in this
life. He does not yet destroy bodily weakness, sickness, pain, and
a thousand infirmities incident to flesh and blood.[88] He does not
5 destroy all that weakness of understanding which is the natural
consequence of the soul's dwelling in a corruptible body; so that
still

Humanum est errare et nescire:[89]

both ignorance and error belong to humanity. He entrusts us with
10 only an exceeding small share of knowledge in our present state,
lest our knowledge should interfere with our humility, and we
should again affect to be as gods. It is to remove from us all
temptation to pride, and all thought of independency (which is
the very thing that men in general so earnestly covet, under the
15 name of 'liberty') that he leaves us encompassed with all these
infirmities—particularly weakness of understanding—till the
sentence takes place, 'Dust thou art, and unto dust thou shalt
return!'[90]

4. Then error, pain, and all bodily infirmities cease: all these
20 are destroyed by death. And death itself, 'the last enemy'[91] of man,
shall be destroyed at the resurrection. The moment that we hear
the voice of the archangel and the trump of God, 'then shall be
fulfilled the saying that is written, Death is swallowed up in
victory. This corruptible body shall put on incorruption; this
25 mortal body shall put on immortality;'[92] and the Son of God,
manifested in the clouds of heaven, shall destroy this last work of
the devil.

5. Here then we see in the clearest, strongest light, what is real
religion: a restoration of man, by him that bruises the serpent's
30 head, to all that the old serpent deprived him of; a restoration not
only to the favour, but likewise to the image of God; implying not
barely deliverance from sin but the being filled with the fullness of
God.[93] It is plain, if we attend to the preceding considerations,

---

[88] See No. 39, 'Catholic Spirit', I.4 and n.
[89] Cf. No. 13, *On Sin in Believers*, intro., III.1-9, and n.
[90] Cf. Gen. 3:19.
[91] 1 Cor. 15:26.
[92] 1 Cor. 15:54.
[93] Eph. 3:19.

that nothing short of this is Christian religion. Everything else, whether negative or external, is utterly wide of the mark. But what a paradox is this! How little is it understood in the Christian world! Yea, or this enlightened age,[94] wherein it is taken for granted, the world is wiser than ever it was from the beginning of 5 the world. Among all our discoveries, who has discovered this? How few either among the learned or unlearned? And yet, if we believe the Bible, who can deny it? Who can doubt of it? It runs through the Bible from the beginning to the end, in one connected chain. And the agreement of every part of it with every 10 other is properly the *analogy* of *faith*.[95] Beware of taking anything else, or anything less than this for religion. Not anything else: do not imagine an *outward form*, a round of duties, both in public and private, is religion. Do not suppose that honesty, justice, and whatever is called 'morality' (though excellent in its place) is 15 religion. And least of all dream that orthodoxy, right opinion[96] (vulgarly called 'faith'), is religion. Of all religious dreams this is the vainest, which takes hay and stubble for gold tried in the fire!

6. O do not take anything less than this for the religion of Jesus Christ! Do not take part of it for the whole. What God hath joined 20 together, put not asunder.[97] Take no less for his religion than the 'faith that worketh by love'[98] all inward and outward holiness. Be not content with any religion which does not imply the destruction of all the works of the devil, that is, of all sin. We know weakness of understanding, and a thousand infirmities, will 25 remain while this corruptible body remains. But sin need not remain: this is that work of the devil, eminently so called, which the Son of God was manifested to destroy in this present life. He is able, he is willing, to destroy it now in all that believe in him. Only be not straitened in your own bowels![99] Do not distrust his 30

---

[94] Cf. Immanuel Kant, *What is Enlightenment?*: 'If we are asked, "Do we now live in *an enlightened age?*", the answer is "No", but we do live in *an age of enlightenment.*' (In L. W. Beck, ed., *Critique of Practical Reason and Other Writings in Moral Philosophy* [Chicago, Univ. of Chicago Press, 1949], pp. 286-92.) See also Peter Gay, *The Enlightenment.*

[95] Cf. Wesley's definition of this in his *Notes* on Rom. 12:6: 'according to the general tenor of [Scripture]'. He goes on to explain that 'the analogy of faith' comprehends 'that grand scheme of doctrine which is delivered therein, touching original sin, justification by faith, and present inward salvation'. The whole note is worth analysis and comparison with No. 5, 'Justification by Faith', §2 and n.

[96] Cf. No. 7, 'The Way to the Kingdom,' I.6 and n.

[97] See Matt. 19:6.

[98] Cf. Gal. 5:6. See also No. 2, *The Almost Christian*, II.6 and n.

[99] 2 Cor. 6:12.

power or his love! Put his promise to the proof! He hath spoken: and is he not ready likewise to perform? Only 'come boldly to the throne of grace,'[100] trusting in his mere mercy: and you shall find, 'He saveth to the uttermost all those that come to God through
5 him!'[101]

Jan. 20, 1781[102]

---

[100] Heb. 4:16.
[101] Cf. Heb. 7:25.
[102] This date is omitted from the text in *SOSO*, V (1788).

THE GENERAL SPREAD OF THE GOSPEL

AN INTRODUCTORY COMMENT

This sermon is a study in shadow and light. Wesley's survey of the 'condition of the world at present' yields a dismal picture. It is, of course, drawn from seventeenth- and eighteenth-century sources and reflects their general estimates of non-European lands and peoples. But Wesley's hopes for the universal redemption of even such a world remain as high as ever, and he takes the Methodist Revival both as a sign of hope and a model of God's final design for 'the general spread of the Gospel'. He had preached from Isa. 11:9 seven times before (from 1747 to 1755); this sermon was written in Dublin in April 1783, and then promptly printed in the Arminian Magazine *for July and August of that year (numbered XVI), without a title and with the text given mistakenly as 'Isaiah ix. 11'. Its present title appears in the reprint in* SOSO, *V.189-207. These were its only two editions in Wesley's lifetime.*

The General Spread of the Gospel

Isaiah 11:9

*The earth shall be full of the knowledge of the Lord,
as the waters cover the sea.*

1. In what a condition is the world at present! How does 5
darkness, intellectual darkness, ignorance, with vice and misery
attendant upon it, cover the face of the earth! From the accurate
inquiry made with indefatigable pains by our ingenious
countryman, Mr. Brerewood[1] (who travelled himself over a great
part of the known world in order to form the more exact 10
judgment), supposing the world to be divided into thirty parts,

---

[1] Brerewood, *Enquiries touching the Diversities of Languages and Religions Through the Chief Parts of the Earth;* see No. 15, *The Great Assize,* II.4 and n.

nineteen of them are professed heathens, altogether as ignorant of Christ as if he had never come into the world. Six of the remaining parts are professed Mahometans: so that only five in thirty are so much as nominally Christians!

5   2. And let it be remembered that since this computation was made many new nations have been discovered—numberless islands, particularly in the South Seas, large and well inhabited. But by whom? By heathens of the basest sort, many of them inferior to the beasts of the field. Whether they eat men or no
10 (which indeed I cannot find any sufficient ground to believe) they certainly kill all that fall into their hands. They are therefore more savage than lions, who kill no more creatures than are necessary to satisfy their present hunger. See the real dignity of human nature!² Here it appears in its genuine purity; not polluted either
15 by those 'general corrupters, kings',³ or by the least tincture of religion! What will Abbé Raynal⁴ (that determined enemy to monarchy and revelation) say to this?

3. A little, and but a little, above the heathens in religion are the Mahometans. But how far and wide has this miserable delusion
20 spread over the face of the earth! Insomuch that the Mahometans are considerably more in number (as six to five) than Christians. And by all the accounts which have any pretence to authenticity these are also in general as utter strangers to all true religion as their four-footed brethren. As void of mercy as lions and tigers, as
25 much given up to brutal lusts as bulls or goats; so that they are in truth a disgrace to human nature, and a plague to all that are under their iron yoke.

4. It is true, a celebrated writer (Lady Mary Wortley M[ontagu]),⁵ gives a very different character of them. With the

---

² The deists generally insisted on the inborn dignity of human nature; see James Burgh, *The Dignity of Human Nature* (1745), in particular. Wesley vigorously rejected this view, espec. in his *Doctrine of Original Sin.* In 1762, he reprinted Pt. I of this as a separate pamphlet, and gave it Burgh's title as a touch of sarcasm; see also No. 128, 'The Deceitfulness of the Human Heart', §2.

³ A sentiment widely shared by the French *lumières* and anti-monarchists; cf. Diderot's 'kings' and 'tyranny' in the *Encyclopédie* ('*roi*' in Vol. XIV; '*tyrannie*' in Vol. XVI). See also Abbé G. T. F. Raynal's anti-monarchist sentiments in his *Histoire philosophique et politique des éstablissements et du commerce des Européens dan les deux Indies* (1770); Eng. tr. by J. Justamond (1776); cf. Vol. IV, V.397-445, 'On Government'.

⁴ Orig., 'Resnal'.

⁵ 1689–1762. She spent some eighteen months in Turkey (1717–18) with her husband, who was England's ambassador to the Turkish Porte. She travelled extensively and recounts her enthusiasm for the Turkish people and Turkish culture in her *Letters*, published posthumously in 1763.

finest flow of words, in the most elegant language, she labours to wash the Ethiop white. She represents them as many degrees above the Christians, as some of the most amiable people in the world, as possessed of all the social virtues, as some of the most accomplished of men. But I can in no wise receive her report: I 5 cannot rely upon her authority. I believe those round about her had just as much religion as their admirer had when she was admitted into the interior parts of the Grand Signior's seraglio.[6] Notwithstanding therefore all that such a witness does or can say in their favour, I believe the Turks in general are little, if at all, 10 better than the generality of the heathens.

5. And little, if at all, better than the Turks are the Christians in the Turkish dominions, even the best of them, those that live in the Morea,[7] or are scattered up and down in Asia. The more numerous bodies of Georgian, Circassian, Mingrelian[8] Chris- 15 tians, are a proverb of reproach to the Turks themselves; not only for their deplorable ignorance, but for their total, stupid, barbarous irreligion.

6. From the most authentic accounts we can obtain of the southern Christians, those in Abyssinia, and of the northern 20 churches, under the jurisdiction of the Patriarch of Moscow, we have reason to fear they are much in the same condition, both with regard to knowledge and religion, as those in Turkey. Or if those in Abyssinia[9] are more civilized and have a larger share of knowledge, yet they do not appear to have any more religion than 25 either the Mahometans or pagans.

7. The western churches seem to have the pre-eminence over all these in many respects. They have abundantly more knowledge; they have more scriptural and more rational modes of worship. Yet two-thirds of them are still involved in the 30 corruptions of the Church of Rome;[10] and most of these are entirely unacquainted with either the theory or practice of religion. And as to those who are called Protestants or Reformed,

---

[6] This is described in detail in Letter 39 (Mar. 10, 1718).

[7] I.e., the Peloponnesus. Morea ('mulberry-leaf') was the old designation for the peninsula south of the isthmus of Corinth.

[8] These were regions within 'Transcaucasia' on the eastern extremity of the Black Sea; they passed from Turkish to Russian possession in 1804. In Wesley's time the majority of the inhabitants were Greek Orthodox; see No. 122, 'Causes of the Inefficacy of Christianity', §4.

[9] I.e., Ethiopia, where the state religion was 'Coptic' (i.e., Monophysite).

[10] Cf. No. 61, 'The Mystery of Iniquity', §29 and n.

what acquaintance with it have they? Put Papists and Protestants, French and English together, the bulk of one and of the other nation; and what manner of Christians are they? Are they 'holy, as he that hath called them is holy'?[11] Are they filled with
5 'righteousness, and peace, and joy in the Holy Ghost'?[12] Is there 'that mind in them which was also in Christ Jesus'?[13] And do they 'walk as Christ also walked'?[14] Nay, they are as far from it as hell is from heaven.

8. Such is the present state of mankind in all parts of the world!
10 But how astonishing is this, if there is a God in heaven![15] And if his eyes are over all the earth! Can he despise the work of his own hand?[16] Surely this is one of the greatest mysteries under heaven! How is it possible to reconcile this with either the wisdom or goodness of God? And what can give ease to a thoughtful mind
15 under so melancholy a prospect? What but the consideration that things will not always be so; that another scene will soon be opened. God will be jealous of his honour: he will arise and maintain his own cause.[17] He will judge the prince of this world, and spoil him of his usurped dominion. He will 'give' his Son 'the
20 heathen for his inheritance, and the uttermost parts of the earth for his possession'.[18] 'The earth shall be filled with knowledge of the Lord, as the waters cover the sea.'[19] The loving knowledge of God, producing uniform, uninterrupted holiness and happiness, shall cover the earth, shall fill every soul of man.
25 9. 'Impossible!' will some men say. 'Yea, the greatest of all impossibilities! That we should see a Christian world! Yea, a Christian nation, or city! "How can these things be?"'[20] On one supposition, indeed, not only all impossibility but all difficulty vanishes away. Only suppose the Almighty to act *irresistibly*, and
30 the thing is done; yea, with just the same ease as when 'God said, Let there be light; and there was light.'[21] But then man would be man no longer; his inmost nature would be changed.[22] He would no longer be a moral agent, any more than the sun or the wind, as

[11] Cf. 1 Pet. 1:15.
[13] Cf. Phil. 2:5.
[15] See Dan. 2:28.
[17] See Ps. 74:23 (BCP).
[18] Cf. Ps. 2:8.
[19] Hab. 2:14.
[20] John 3:9.
[21] Gen. 1:3.
[22] Cf. No. 60, 'The General Deliverance', I.4 and n.

[12] Rom. 14:17.
[14] Cf. 1 John 2:6.
[16] See Job 10:3.

he would no longer be endued with liberty, a power of choosing or self-determination. Consequently he would no longer be capable of virtue or vice, of reward or punishment.

10. But setting aside this clumsy way of cutting the knot which we are not able to untie, how can all men be made holy and 5 happy[23] while they continue men? While they still enjoy both the understanding, the affections, and the liberty which are essential to a moral agent? There seems to be a plain, simple way of removing this difficulty without entangling ourselves in any subtle, metaphysical disquisitions. As God is one, so the work of 10 God is uniform in all ages. May we not then conceive how he *will* work on the souls of men in times to come by considering how he *does* work *now?* And how he *has* wrought in times past?

11. Take one instance of this, and such an instance as you cannot easily be deceived in. You know how God wrought in *your* 15 *own* soul when he first enabled you to say, 'The life I now live, I live by faith in the Son of God, who loved me, and gave himself for me.'[24] He did not take away your understanding, but enlightened and strengthened it. He did not destroy any of your affections; rather they were more vigorous than before. Least of all did he 20 take away your liberty, your power of choosing good or evil; he did not *force* you; but being *assisted* by his grace you, like Mary, *chose* the better part.[25] Just so has he *assisted* five in one house to make that happy *choice,* fifty or five hundred in one city, and many thousands in a nation, without depriving any of them of that 25 liberty which is essential to a moral agent.[26]

12. Not that I deny that there are exempt cases wherein

The o'erwhelming power of saving grace[27]

does, for a time, work as irresistibly as lightning falling from heaven.[28] But I speak of God's general manner of working, of 30

[23] Cf. No. 5, 'Justification by Faith', I.4 and n.
[24] Gal. 2:20.	[25] Luke 10:42.
[26] This, of course, is the work of prevenient grace, not unaided human initiative. Cf. No. 43, *The Scripture Way of Salvation,* I.2 and n.; see also, No. 85, 'On Working Out Our Own Salvation', I.2-3, II.1, III.3-4.
[27] Charles Wesley, 'The Invitation', st. 10, in *Hymns on the Great Festivals* (1746), p. 46; reprinted in *Hymns and Sacred Poems* (1749), I. 260 (*Poet. Wks.,* V. 64); and as No. 9 in the *Collection,* Vol. 7 of this edn. This was one of Wesley's favourite expressions during his later years; cf. JWJ, June 20, 1769; Apr. 6, 1785; July 8, 1786; June 7, 1788; and June 21, 1789. Cf. also his letter to Mary Cooke, Oct. 30, 1785.
[28] See Luke 10:18.

which I have known innumerable instances; perhaps more within fifty years last past than anyone in England or in Europe. And with regard even to these exempt cases: although God does work irresistibly *for the time*, yet I do not believe there is any human soul
5 in which God works irresistibly *at all times*.[29] Nay, I am fully persuaded there is not. I am persuaded there are no men living that have not many times 'resisted the Holy Ghost',[30] and 'made void the counsel of God against themselves'.[31] Yea, I am persuaded every child of God has at some time 'life and death set
10 before him',[32] eternal life and eternal death, and has in himself the casting voice. So true is that well-known saying of St. Austin (one of the noblest he ever uttered), *Qui fecit nos sine nobis, non salvabit nos sine nobis*—he that made us *without ourselves* will not save us *without ourselves*.[33] Now in the same manner as God *has* converted
15 so many to himself without destroying their liberty, he *can* undoubtedly convert whole nations, or the whole world. And it is as easy to him to convert a world as one individual soul.

13. Let us observe what God has done already.

Between fifty and sixty years ago God raised up a few young
20 men in the University of Oxford, to testify those grand truths which were then little attended to:[34]

That without holiness no man shall see the Lord;[35]

That this holiness is the work of God, who worketh in us both to will and to do;[36]

25 That he doth it of his own good pleasure, merely for the merits of Christ;

---

[29] Cf. *Predestination Calmly Considered*, §§1-4. Note the echoes here of the crucial distinction, emphasized by the Second Council of Orange (529; cf. Seeberg, *Doctrines*, I. 379-82) between the irresistibility of the sovereign grace of the Father and the resistibility of the prevenient grace of the Holy Spirit. This is a linch-pin in Wesley's doctrine of grace; see below, No. 68, 'The Wisdom of God's Counsels', §4.

[30] Cf. Acts 7:51.

[31] Luke 7:30 *(Notes)*.

[32] Cf. Deut. 30:19.

[33] Cf. Augustine, Sermon 169, on Phil. 3:3-16, xi (13): '*Qui ergo fecit te sine te, non te justificat sine te*' (Migne, *PL*, XXXVIII.923). Cf. Wesley, No. 85, 'On Working Out Our Own Salvation', II. 7. See also Peter Heylyn, *Historia Quinquarticularis*, Pt. II, ch. i, §10, 509; and Richard Baxter, *Aphorisms*, Prop. XII, p. 13, which Wesley abridged in 1745.

[34] A retrospective summary of the essence of Wesley's early 'gospel'; note his inclusion of *sola fide* and the evangelical emphasis on justification as antecedent to sanctification. It is, however, doubtful that Wesley had come to this view of the *ordo salutis* before 1738. This does, however, contradict Wesley's claim that he had not even heard of the *sola fide* before his contact with the Moravians (cf. his letters to William Law, May 14 and May 20, 1738). Cf. also No. 53, *On the Death of George Whitefield*, III.2 and n.

[35] See Heb. 12:14.   [36] See Phil. 2:13.

That this holiness is the mind that was in Christ,[37] enabling us to walk as Christ also walked;[38]

That no man can be thus sanctified till he is justified; and

That we are justified by faith alone. These great truths they declared on all occasions in private and in public; having no 5 design but to promote the glory of God, and no desire but to save souls from death.

14. From Oxford, where it first appeared,[39] the little leaven spread wider and wider. More and more saw the truth as it is in Jesus, and received it in the love thereof. More and more 'found 10 redemption through the blood of Jesus, even the forgiveness of sins'.[40] They were born again of his Spirit, and filled with righteousness, and peace, and joy in the Holy Ghost.[41] It afterwards spread to every part of the land, and a little one became a thousand.[42] It then spread into north Britain[43] and Ireland, 15 and, a few years after, into New York, Pennsylvania, and many other provinces in America, even as high as Newfoundland and Nova Scotia. So that although at first this 'grain of mustard seed' was 'the least of all the seeds', yet in a few years it grew into a 'large tree, and put forth great branches'.[44]   20

15. Generally when these truths—justification by faith in particular—were declared in any large town, after a few days or weeks there came suddenly on the great congregation, not in a corner (at London, Bristol, Newcastle upon Tyne in particular) a violent and impetuous power, which   25

> Like mighty wind or torrent fierce,
> Did then opposers all o'errun.[45]

And this frequently continued, with shorter or longer intervals, for several weeks or months. But it gradually subsided, and then

---

[37] See Phil. 2:5.   [38] See 1 John 2:6.

[39] Note this reinvention of the history of the Revival. However, see Sermons 1-4 and their dissociation of the Holy Club from the general religious life of the university. Wesley's old age has mellowed these memories.

[40] Cf. Col. 1:14.   [41] Rom. 14:17.   [42] See Isa. 60:22.

[43] A reference both to the northern half of England and also to Scotland (a usage developed after the coronation of James VI of Scotland as James I of England [1604]). John Wilkes's newspaper, *The North Briton*, was published in Berwick-upon-Tweed, Northumberland.

[44] Cf. Matt. 13:31-32.

[45] Cf. Henry More, 'An Hymn Upon the Descent of the Holy Ghost at the Day of Pentecost', st. 12, in *Theological Works* (London, 1708), p. 826:

> Like mighty wind and torrent fierce,
> Let it withstanders all o'errun.

the work of God was carried on by gentle degrees; while that Spirit, in watering the seed that had been sown, in confirming and strengthening them that had believed,

> deigned his influence to infuse,
> 5   Secret, refreshing as the silent dews.[46]

And this difference in his usual manner of working was observable not only in Great Britain and Ireland, but in every part of America, from south to north, wherever the word of God came with power.

10   16. Is it not then highly probable that God will carry on his work in the same manner as he has begun? That he *will* carry it on I cannot doubt; however Luther may affirm that a revival of religion never lasts above a generation, that is, thirty years[47] (whereas the present revival has already continued above fifty);[48]
15 or however prophets of evil may say, 'All will be at an end when

It was altered by John Wesley and published in *Hymns and Sacred Poems* (1739), p. 187 (*Poet. Wks.*, I. 167):

> Like mighty wind, or torrent fierce
> Let it opposers all o'er-run.

Cf. also, JWJ, July 11, 1779.

[46] Cf. Mark Le Pla, *The Song of the Three Children Paraphrased*, st. 16, last 2 lines:

> Bless God, who deigns his influence to infuse,
> Secret, refreshing, as the silent dews.

Cf. Wesley, *A Collection of Moral and Sacred Poems* (1744), II. 116. See also, JWJ, Mar. 3, 1740.

[47] 'So it is the case that in no one spot in the world hath the Gospel stayed clean and pure beyond one man's memory. . . . [After a generation] there followed at once thereon a pack of rabble spirits and false teachers.' Cf. Luther, *Fastenpostillen*, 1525 (Weimar Edn., 17/2: 179, ll. 28-29; see also, Karl Barth, *Church Dogmatics*, I/1: 53). For other references to this effect, cf. Nos. 94, 'On Family Religion', §3; and 122, 'Causes of the Inefficacy of Christianity', §17. See also Wesley's letter to Elizabeth Ritchie, Feb. 12, 1779; and his 'Thoughts Upon a Late Phenomenon', §4, in *AM* (1789), XII.47.

Jonathan Edwards, in his *Faithful Narrative* (1736), refers to the revival of religion in Saxony which began by the labours of the famous Professor Francke and had then been carried on for more than thirty years. For Wesley's extract from Edwards's *Narrative* see *Bibliog*, No. 85.

It is interesting that Horace Walpole would presently make the same prediction about the Methodists; see his letter to Mary Berry, June 23, 1791: 'The patriarchess of the Methodists, Lady Huntingdon, is dead. Now that she and Whitefield and Wesley are gone, the sect will probably decline: a second crop of apostles seldom acquire the influence of the founders.' See also *The Gospel Magazine* (1774), p. 350: 'An attentive observer of men and things will notice that almost every revival of true religion has subsided soon after the death of its original promoters.'

[48] I.e., prior to 1739. For other examples where Wesley dates the Revival from 1729 and the Holy Club, cf. Nos. 94, 'On Family Religion', §3; and 107, 'On God's Vineyard', proem, I.1. See also his letter to William Black, Nov. 26, 1786.

the first instruments are removed.' There will then very probably be a great shaking;[49] but I cannot induce myself to think that God has wrought so glorious a work to let it sink and die away in a few years. No; I trust this is only the beginning of a far greater work—the dawn of 'the latter day glory'.[50]

17. And is it not probable, I say, that he will carry it on in the same manner as he has begun? At the first breaking out of his work in this or that place there may be a shower, a torrent of grace; and so at some other particular seasons which 'the Father has reserved in his own power'.[51] But in general it seems the kingdom of God will not 'come with observation',[52] but will silently increase wherever it is set up, and spread from heart to heart, from house to house, from town to town, from one kingdom to another. May it not thus spread, first through the remaining provinces, then through the isles of North America?[53] And at the same time from England to Holland, where there is already a blessed work in Utrecht, Harlem, and many other cities? Probably it will spread from these to the Protestants in France, to those in Germany, and those in Switzerland. Then to Sweden, Denmark, Russia, and all the other Protestant nations in Europe.

18. May we not suppose that the same leaven of pure and undefiled religion, of experimental knowledge and love of God, of inward and outward holiness, will afterwards spread to the Roman Catholics, in Great Britain, Ireland, Holland; in Germany, France, Switzerland; and in all other countries where Romanists and Protestants live intermixed and familiarly converse with each other? Will it not then be easy for the wisdom of God to make a way for religion, in the life and power thereof, into those countries that are merely[54] popish, as Italy, Spain, Portugal? And may it not be gradually diffused from thence to all that name the name of Christ in the various provinces of Turkey, in Abyssinia, yea, and in the remotest parts, not only of Europe, but of Asia, Africa, and America?

19. And in every nation under heaven we may reasonably believe God will observe the same order which he hath done from

---

[49] Ezek. 38:19.
[50] Cf. Job 19:25.
[51] Cf. Acts 1:7.
[52] Cf. Luke 17:20.
[53] Is this an indirect reference to Thomas Coke's plans for a missionary venture to North America, especially to the West Indies? Cf. John Vickers, *Thomas Coke* (New York, Abingdon, 1969), chs. 9-10.
[54] I.e., exclusively; cf. Johnson's *Dictionary*.

the beginning of Christianity. 'They shall all know *me*,' saith the
Lord, not from the greatest to the least (this is that wisdom of the
world which is foolishness with God) but 'from the least to the
greatest,'[55] that the praise may not be of men, but of God.[56] Before
5 the end even the rich shall enter into the kingdom of God.
Together with them will enter in the great, the noble, the
honourable; yea, the rulers, the princes, the kings of the earth.
Last of all the wise and learned, the men of genius, the
philosophers, will be convinced that they are fools; will 'be
10 converted and become as little children, and enter into the
kingdom of God'.[57]

20. Then shall be fully accomplished to 'the house of Israel',[58]
the spiritual Israel, of whatever people or nation, that gracious
promise: 'I will put my laws in their mind, and write them in their
15 hearts; and I will be to them a God, and they shall be to me a
people. And they shall not teach every man his neighbour, and
every man his brother, saying, Know the Lord; for they shall all
know me, from the least to the greatest. For I will be merciful to
their unrighteousness, and their sins and their iniquities will I
20 remember no more.'[59] Then shall 'the times of' universal
'refreshment come from the presence of the Lord'.[60] The grand
Pentecost shall 'fully come', and 'devout men in every nation
under heaven', however distant in place from each other, shall 'all
be filled with the Holy Ghost'.[61] And they will 'continue steadfast
25 in the apostles' doctrine and in the fellowship, and in the breaking
of bread, and in prayers'.[62] They will 'eat their meat', and do all
that they have to do, 'with gladness and singleness of heart'.[63]
'Great grace' will be 'upon them all'; and they will be all 'of one
heart and of one soul'.[64] The natural, necessary consequence of
30 this will be the same as it was in the beginning of the Christian
church. 'None of them will say that ought of the things which he
possesses is his own, but they will have all things common.
Neither will there be any among them that want; for as many as
are possessed of lands or houses will sell them, and distribution
35 will be made to every man, according as he has need.'[65] All their
desires, meantime, and passions, and tempers will be cast in one

---

[55] Heb. 8:11.   [56] See Rom. 2:29.   [57] Cf. Matt. 18:3.
[58] Heb. 8:10.   [59] Heb. 8:10-12.
[60] Cf. Acts 3:19.   [61] Cf. Acts 2:1, 4, 5.
[62] Cf. Acts 2:42.   [63] Acts 2:46.
[64] Acts 4:32-33.   [65] Cf. Acts 4:32, 34-35.

mould, while all are doing the will of God on earth as it is done in heaven.[66] All their 'conversation will be seasoned with salt',[67] and will 'minister grace to the hearers';[68] seeing it will not be so much they that speak 'as the Spirit of their Father that speaketh in them'.[69] And there will be no 'root of bitterness springing up', 5 either to 'defile' or trouble them.[70] There will be no Ananias or Sapphira, to bring back the cursed love of money[71] among them. There will be no partiality; no 'widows neglected in the daily ministration'.[72] Consequently there will be no temptation to any murmuring thought or unkind word of one against another, while 10

> They all are of one heart and soul,
> And only love informs the whole.[73]

21. The grand stumbling-block being thus happily removed out of the way, namely, the lives of the Christians, the Mahometans will look upon them with other eyes, and begin to 15 give attention to their words. And as their words will be clothed with divine energy, attended with the demonstration of the Spirit and of power, those of them that fear God will soon take knowledge of the Spirit whereby the Christians speak. They will 'receive with meekness the engrafted word',[74] and will bring forth 20 fruit with patience.[75] From them the leaven will soon spread to those who till then had no fear of God before their eyes.[76] Observing 'the Christian dogs', as they used to term them, to have changed their nature, to be sober, temperate, just, benevolent— and that in spite of all provocations to the contrary—from 25 admiring their lives they will surely be led to consider and embrace their doctrine. And then the Saviour of sinners will say: 'The hour is come. I will glorify my Father. I will seek and save

---

[66] See Matt. 6:10.   [67] Cf. Col. 4:6.   [68] Eph. 4:29.
[69] Cf. Matt. 10:20.   [70] See Heb. 12:15.
[71] Cf. intro. to No. 50, 'The Use of Money'.
[72] Acts 6:1.
[73] Cf. Charles Wesley, 'Primitive Christianity', *Hymns and Sacred Poems* (1749), II. 333 (*Poet. Wks.*, V. 480):

> They all were of one heart and soul,
> And only love inspired the whole.

This poem was first published as an appendix to the 2nd edn. of *An Earnest Appeal*, 1743 (11: 90-101 in this edn.); cf. also Nos. 68, 'The Wisdom of God's Counsels', §7; and 109, *The Trouble and Rest of Good Men*, II.3; where Wesley uses the same thought though not in verse. In No. 4, *Scriptural Christianity*, IV.2, Wesley uses part of the first line.
[74] Jas. 1:21.   [75] Luke 8:15.   [76] Rom. 3:18.

the sheep that were wandering on the dark mountains. Now will I avenge myself of my enemy, and pluck the prey out of the lion's teeth. I will resume my own for ages lost: I will claim the purchase of my blood.' So he will go forth in the greatness of his strength,[77]
5 and all his enemies shall flee before him. All the prophets of lies shall vanish away, and all the nations that had followed them shall acknowledge the great Prophet of the Lord, 'mighty in word and deed';[78] and 'shall honour the Son, even as they honour the Father'.[79]

10 22. And then the grand stumbling-block being removed from the heathen nations also, the same spirit will be poured out upon them, even those that remain in the uttermost parts of the sea.[80] The poor American savage will no more ask, 'What, are the Christians better than us?'[81] when they
15 see their steady practice of universal temperance, and of justice, mercy, and truth. The Malabarian heathen will have no more room to say: 'Christian man take my wife; Christian man much drunk; Christian man kill man! *Devil-Christian!* Me no Christian.'[82] Rather, seeing how far the Christians exceed their
20 own countrymen in whatsoever things are lovely and of good report,[83] they will adopt a very different language, and say, '*Angel-Christian!*' The holy lives of the Christians will be an argument they will not know how to resist; seeing the Christians steadily and uniformly practise what is agreeable to the law
25 written in their own hearts,[84] their prejudices will quickly die away, and they will gladly receive 'the truth as it is in Jesus'.[85]

23. We may reasonably believe that the heathen nations which are mingled with the Christians, and those that bordering upon

---

[77] Isa. 63:1.
[78] Cf. Luke 24:19.
[79] Cf. John 5:23.
[80] Ps. 139:9 (AV).
[81] Cf. No. 61, 'The Mystery of Iniquity', §32.
[82] For the Malabarians Wesley was dependent on a book which greatly influenced his mother, by Bartholomew Ziegenbalg, *The Propagation of the Gospel in the East; being an Account of the Success of two Danish Missionaries, lately sent to the East Indies for the Conversion of the Heathens in Malabar* (tr. by A. W. Boehme, edn. of 1718): 'One of [their] most obstinate prejudices is the abominable, wicked life of the Christians here' (p. 57); the spread of the Gospel is greatly hampered 'by the scandalous life of our Christians' (p. 51). For the actual quotation, however, Wesley's memory was surely filling out what he had reported in a similar context about his experiences in Georgia and South Carolina: '[Immoral "Christians"] cause the very savages in the Indian woods to cry out, "Christian much drunk, Christian beat men, Christian tell lies, devil Christian. Me no Christian." ' (*A Farther Appeal*, Pt. I, VII. 4 (11:189 in this edn.); cf. Frank Baker, *From Wesley to Asbury*, Durham, N.C., Duke Univ. Press, 1976, pp. 8-9).
[83] See Phil. 4:8.
[84] See Rom. 2:15.
[85] Cf. Eph. 4:21.

Christian nations have constant and familiar intercourse with them, will be some of the first who learn to worship God in spirit and in truth;[86] those, for instance, that live on the continent of America, or in the islands that have received colonies from Europe. Such are likewise all those inhabitants of the East Indies 5 that adjoin to any of the Christian settlements. To these may be added numerous tribes of Tartars, the heathen parts of the Russias, and the inhabitants of Norway, Finland, and Lapland. Probably these will be followed by those more distant nations with whom the Christians trade; to whom they will impart what is of 10 infinitely more value than earthly pearls, or gold and silver. The God of love will then prepare his messengers and make a way into the polar regions, into the deepest recesses of America, and into the interior parts of Africa; yea, into the heart of China and Japan, with the countries adjoining to them. And 'their sound' will then 15 'go forth into all lands, and their voice to the ends of the earth'.[87]

24. But one considerable difficulty still remains. There are very many heathen nations in the world that have no intercourse either by trade or any other means with Christians of any kind. Such are the inhabitants of the numerous islands in the South Sea, and 20 probably in all large branches of the ocean. Now what shall be done for these poor outcasts of men? 'How shall they believe', saith the Apostle, 'in him of whom they have not heard? And how shall they hear without a preacher?' You may add, 'And how shall they preach, unless they be sent?'[88] Yea, but is not God able to 25 send them? Cannot he raise them up, as it were, out of the stones?[89] And can he ever want means of sending them? No: were there no other means, he 'can take them by his Spirit' (as he did Ezekiel),[a] or by 'his angel', as he did Philip,[b] and set them down wheresoever it pleaseth him. Yea, he can find out a thousand 30 ways, to foolish man unknown. And he surely will: for heaven and earth may pass away; but his word shall not pass away.[90] He will 'give his Son the uttermost part of the earth for his possession'.[91]

25. 'And so all Israel' too 'shall be saved.' For 'blindness has happened to Israel' (as the great Apostle observes) 'till the 35

[a] Ezek. 11:24.
[b] Acts 8[:26].

---

[86] See John 4:23, 24.
[88] Rom. 10:14-15.
[90] See Matt. 24:35, etc.

[87] Cf. Rom. 10:18.
[89] See Matt. 3:9.
[91] Cf. Ps. 2:8.

fullness of the Gentiles be come in.' Then 'the Deliverer that cometh out of Zion shall turn away iniquity from Jacob. [. . .] God hath' now 'concluded them all in unbelief, that he may have mercy upon all.'ᶜ Yea, and he will so have mercy upon all Israel as
5 to give them all temporal with all spiritual blessings. For this is the promise: 'For the Lord thy God will gather thee from all nations, whither the Lord thy God hath scattered thee. [. . .] And the Lord thy God will bring thee into the land which thy fathers possessed, and thou shalt possess it. And the Lord thy God will
10 circumcise thy heart, and the heart of thy seed, to love the Lord thy God with all thy heart, and with all thy soul.'ᵈ Again: 'I will gather them out of all countries whither I have driven them; and I will bring them again to this place, and I will cause them to dwell safely. [. . .] And I will give them one heart, and one way, that they
15 may fear me forever. I will put my fear into their hearts, that they shall not depart from me. And I will plant them in this land assuredly, with all my heart, and with all my soul.'ᵉ

Yet again: 'I will take you from among the heathen, and gather you out of all countries, and will bring you into your own land.
20 Then will I sprinkle clean water upon you, and ye shall be clean; from all your filthiness and from all your idols will I cleanse you. [. . .] And ye shall dwell in the land that I gave to your fathers; and ye shall be my people, and I will be your God.'ᶠ

26. At that time will be accomplished all those glorious
25 promises made to the Christian church, which will not then be confined to this or that nation, but will include all the inhabitants of the earth. 'They shall not hurt nor destroy in all my holy mountain.'ᵍ 'Violence shall no more be heard in thy land, wasting nor destruction within thy borders; but thou shalt call thy walls,
30 Salvation, and thy gates, Praise.'⁹² Thou shalt be encompassed on every side with salvation, and all that go through thy gates shall praise God. 'The sun shall be no more thy light by day; neither for brightness shall the moon give light unto thee; but the Lord shall be unto thee an everlasting light, and thy God thy glory.'⁹³ The
35 light of the sun and moon shall be swallowed up in the light of his countenance shining upon thee. 'Thy people also shall be all⁹⁴

ᶜ Rom. 11:25-26, 32.   ᵈ Deut. 30:3, 5-6.   ᵉ Jer. 32:37, 39-41.
ᶠ Ezek. 36:24-25, 28.   ᵍ Isa. 11:9.

---

⁹² Isa. 60:18.   ⁹³ Isa. 60:19.
⁹⁴ Only in Wesley's own errata to *Sermons*, V, p. 206, in MA, is 'all' added.

righteous, [. . .] the work of my hands, that I may be glorified.'[95] 'As the earth bringeth forth her bud, and the garden causeth the things that are sown in it to spring forth; so the Lord God will cause righteousness and praise to spring forth before all the nations.'[h]   5

27. This I apprehend to be the answer, yea, the only full and satisfactory answer that can be given, to the objection against the wisdom and goodness of God, taken from the present state of the world. It will not always be thus: these things are only permitted for a season by the great Governor of the world, that he may draw   10 immense, eternal good out of this temporary evil. This is the very key which the Apostle himself gives us in the words above recited, 'God hath concluded them all under sin, that he might have mercy upon all!'[96] In view of this glorious event how well may we cry out, 'O the depth of the riches both of the wisdom and   15 knowledge of God!' Although for a season 'his judgments were unsearchable, and his ways past finding out.'[i] It is enough we are assured of this one point, that all these transient evils will issue well, will have a happy conclusion, and that 'Mercy first and last will reign.'[97] All unprejudiced persons may see with their eyes that   20 he is already renewing the face of the earth.[98] And we have strong reason to hope that the work he hath begun he will carry on unto the day of his Lord Jesus;[99] that he will never intermit this blessed work of his Spirit until he has fulfilled all his promises; until he hath put a period to sin and misery, and infirmity, and death; and   25 re-established universal holiness and happiness, and caused all the inhabitants of the earth to sing together, 'Hallelujah! The Lord God omnipotent reigneth!'[100] 'Blessing, and glory, and wisdom, and honour, and power, and might be unto our God for ever and ever!'[j]   30

Dublin, April 22, 1783[101]

---

[h] Isa. 61:11.   [i] Rom. 11:33.
[j] Rev. 7:12. [Note the ascription; cf. No. 1, *Salvation by Faith*, III.9 and n.]

---

[95] Isa. 60:21.   [96] Cf. Rom. 11:32. See §25 above.
[97] Cf. Milton, *Paradise Lost*, iii. 132-34:

> In mercy and justice both,
> Through heaven and earth, so shall my glory excel;
> But mercy, first and last, shall brightest shine.

[98] See Ps. 104:30.   [99] 1 Cor. 5:5; 2 Cor. 1:14.   [100] Cf. Rev. 19:6.
[101] This note omitted from the 2nd edn.

THE NEW CREATION

AN INTRODUCTORY COMMENT

The aged Wesley returned again and again to his vision of cosmic redemption: the restoration of all creation, including the entire human family, as the final, full benefit of God's unbounded love. This sermon was written in 1785 for inclusion in the November and December issues of the Arminian Magazine *for that year (Vol. VIII), numbered XXX, without a title and no further indication of place or date. The only prior reference to a sermon on Rev. 21:5 comes just two years earlier (January 1, 1783); the only other recorded instance comes five years later (August 4, 1790). This present sermon was placed in* SOSO *(V.209-22), with its present title and in the series of essays in Wesleyan eschatology that had begun with 'God's Love to Fallen Man'. It is remarkable for its unusual level of speculation (more than Wesley was wont to allow himself) and for its numerous allusions to the speculations of others, including an almost casual passing reference to a then quite lively controversy about 'the plurality of [inhabited] worlds'. Wesley's endorsement of the then novel idea of progress reflects his unfaltering optimism, in his case an optimism of grace rather than of nature.*

The New Creation

Revelation 21:5

Behold, I make all things new.

1. What a strange scene is here opened to our view! How
5 remote from all our natural apprehensions! Not a glimpse of what is here revealed was ever seen in the heathen world.[1] Not only the modern, barbarous, uncivilized heathens have not the least

---

[1] Wesley would, as a matter of course, have known the myth of Er which stands as the apocalyptic climax of Plato's *Republic*; why would he have regarded this as radically noncomparable with the biblical apocalypse?

conception of it; but it was equally unknown to the refined, polished heathens of ancient Greece and Rome. And it is almost as little thought of or understood by the generality of Christians: I mean, not barely those that are nominally such, that have the form of godliness without the power;[2] but even those that in a measure 5 fear God and study to work righteousness.

2. It must be allowed that after all the researches we can make, still our knowledge of the great truth which is delivered to us in these words is exceedingly short and imperfect. As this is a point of mere[3] revelation, beyond the reach of all our natural faculties, 10 we cannot penetrate far into it, nor form any adequate conception of it. But it may be an encouragement to those who have in any degree tasted of the powers of the world to come[4] to go as far as we can go, interpreting Scripture by Scripture, according to the analogy of faith.[5] 15

3. The Apostle, caught up in the visions of God, tells us in the first verse of the chapter, 'I saw a new heaven and a new earth;'[6] and adds, 'He that sat upon the throne said (I believe the only words which he is said to utter throughout the whole book), Behold, I make all things new.'[a] 20

4. Very many commentators entertain a strange opinion that this relates only to the present state of things, and gravely tell us that the words are to be referred to the flourishing state of the church, which commenced after the heathen persecutions. Nay, some of them have discovered that all which the Apostle speaks 25 concerning the 'new heaven and the new earth' was fulfilled when Constantine the Great poured in riches and honours upon the Christians.[7] What a miserable way is this of making void the whole counsel of God[8] with regard to all that grand chain of events, in reference to his church, yea, and to all mankind, from the time 30 that John was in Patmos unto the end of the world! Nay, the line of this prophecy reaches farther still. It does not end with the

---

[a] [Rev. 21,] ver. 5.

---

[2] See 2 Tim. 3:5.
[3] Cf. Johnson's definition of 'mere' as 'this only; such and nothing else'.
[4] See Heb. 6:5.
[5] Cf. No. 5, 'Justification by Faith', §2 and n.; but see also No. 62, 'The End of Christ's Coming', III.5 and n.
[6] Rev. 21:1.
[7] Cf. No. 61, 'The Mystery of Iniquity', §27 and n.
[8] See Luke 7:30.

present world, but shows us the things that will come to pass when this world is no more.

5. Thus saith the Creator and Governor of the universe, 'Behold, I make all things new:' all which are included in that expression of the Apostle, 'a new heaven and a new earth'. 'A new heaven': the original word in Genesis (chapter one) is in the plural number. And indeed this is the constant language of Scripture—not *heaven*, but *heavens*. Accordingly the ancient Jewish writers are accustomed to reckon three heavens. In conformity to which the apostle Paul speaks of his being 'caught up into the third heaven'.[9] It is this, the third heaven, which is usually supposed to be the more immediate residence of God—so far as any residence can be ascribed to his omnipresent Spirit, who pervades and fills the whole universe. It is here (if we speak after the manner of men) that the Lord sitteth upon his throne, surrounded by angels and archangels, and by all his flaming ministers.

6. We cannot think that this heaven will undergo any change, any more than its great inhabitant. Surely this palace of the Most High was the same from eternity, and will be world without end.[10] Only the inferior heavens are liable to change; the highest of which we usually call the starry heaven.[11] This, St. Peter informs us, is 'reserved unto fire, against the day of judgment and destruction of ungodly men'.[12] In that day, 'being on fire', it shall first shrivel as a parchment scroll; then it shall 'be dissolved', and 'shall pass away with a great noise';[13] lastly it shall 'flee from the face of him that sitteth on the throne',[14] 'and there shall be found no place for it.'[15]

7. At the same time 'the stars shall fall from heaven,'[16] the secret chain being broken which had retained them in their several orbits from the foundation of the world. In the meanwhile the lower or sublunary 'heaven',[17] with 'the elements' (or

---

[9] Cf. 2 Cor. 12:2.   [10] Eph. 3:21.

[11] Orig., 'heavens'; Wesley deletes the 's' in his annotated copy.

[12] Cf. Wesley's *Notes* on 2 Pet. 3:7, where he prefers the reading, 'destruction', in the Geneva Bible rather than the AV reading, 'perdition'.

[13] Cf. 2 Pet. 3:10-12; and note Wesley's paraphrase and conflation of the text.

[14] Cf. Rev. 6:16.   [15] Cf. Rev. 20:11.   [16] Matt. 24:29.

[17] I.e., this earth and its 'heaven' (atmosphere) as in Aristotelian and Ptolemaic astronomy; for this whole passage, cf. John Ray's third discourse in *Three Physico-Theological Discourses . . . III. The Dissolution of the World* (4th edn. by William Derham, 1732).

principles that compose it), 'shall melt with fervent heat,' while 'the earth with the works that are therein shall be burnt up.'[18] This is the introduction to a far nobler state of things, such as it has not yet entered into the heart of men to conceive—the universal restoration which is to succeed the universal destruction. For 'we 5 look for', says the Apostle, 'new heavens and a new earth, wherein dwelleth righteousness.'[b]

8. One considerable difference there will undoubtedly be in the starry heaven when it is created anew; there will be no blazing stars, no comets there.[19] Whether those horrid, eccentric orbs are 10 half-formed planets, in a chaotic state (I speak on the supposition of a plurality of worlds)[20] or such as have undergone their general conflagration, they will certainly have no place in the new heaven, where all will be exact order and harmony. There may be many other differences between the heaven that now is and that which 15 will be after the renovation. But they are above our apprehension: we must leave eternity to explain them.

9. We may more easily conceive the changes which will be wrought in the lower heaven, in the region of the air. It will be no more torn by hurricanes, or agitated by furious storms or 20 destructive tempests. Pernicious or terrifying meteors will have no more place therein. We shall have no more occasion to say,

> There like a trumpet, loud and strong,
> Thy thunder shakes our coast;
> While the red lightnings wave along, 25
> The banners of thy host![21]

[b] 2 Pet. 3:7, etc. [i.e., 7, 13].

---

[18] Cf. 2 Pet. 3:10.

[19] Cf. No. 56, 'God's Approbation of His Works', I.10 and n.

[20] Speculation as to the plurality of habitable worlds has a long history. Cicero, *De Natura Deorum (On the Nature of the Gods)*, I. x .25, quotes Anaximenes as having held 'that there are [inhabited] worlds, countless in number'; cf. *ibid.* I. xxxix. 98. See also Henry More, *Democritus Platonissans; Or An Essay Upon the Infinity of Worlds Out of Platonic Principles* (Cambridge, 1647); and Christian Huygens, *The Celestial Worlds Discovered, Or Conjectures on the Planetary Worlds* (1722), p. 18. Wesley's interest in this is reflected in his quotation from Louis Dutens, *Inquiry into the Origin of the Discoveries Attributed to the Moderns* (1769), about 'the notion of the plurality of worlds' lately popularized 'thanks to the elegant work of Mr. de Fontenelle'; see Wesley's *Survey*, V. 114. This was Bernard Le Bovier de Fontenelle, whose *Conversations On the Plurality of Worlds* had become a conversation piece in eighteenth-century England. It had had four separate English translations (the first by the English novelist, Mrs. Aphra Behn) from 1688 to 1760. It is not known which of these Wesley had read.

[21] Watts, 'A Song to Creating Wisdom', Pt. II, st. vii, in *Horae Lyricae* (1705). Twelve stanzas of this appear in Wesley's *A Collection of Psalms and Hymns* (1738); it reappears

No; all will be then light, fair, serene—a lively picture of the eternal day.

10. All the elements (taking that word in the common sense for the principles of which all natural beings are compounded)[22] will be new indeed; entirely changed as to their qualities, although not as to their nature. *Fire* is at present the general destroyer of all things under the sun; dissolving all things that come within the sphere of its action, and reducing them to their primitive atoms. But no sooner will it have performed its last great office of destroying the heavens and the earth (whether you mean thereby one system only, or the whole fabric of the universe—the difference between one and millions of worlds being nothing before the great Creator); when, I say, it has done this, the destruction wrought by fire will come to a perpetual end. It will destroy no more; it will consume no more; it will forget its power to burn, which it possesses only during the present state of things, and be as harmless in the new heavens and earth as it is now in the bodies of men and other animals, and the substance of trees and flowers; in all which (as late experiments show) large quantities of ethereal fire[23] are lodged—if it be not rather an essential component part of every material being under the sun. But it will probably retain its vivifying power, though divested of its power to destroy.

11. It has been already observed that the calm, placid *air* will be no more disturbed by storms and tempests. There will be no more meteors with their horrid glare, affrighting the poor children of men. May we not add (though at first it may sound like a paradox) that there will be no more rain. It is observable that there was none in paradise; a circumstance which Moses particularly mentions: 'The Lord God had not caused it to rain upon the earth. But there went up a mist from the earth,' which then covered up the abyss of waters, 'and watered the whole face of the ground'[c] with moisture sufficient for all the purposes of vegetation. We have all reason to believe that the case will be the same when paradise is restored. Consequently there will be no

---

[c] Gen. 2:5-6.

---

in *A Collection of Hymns for the Use of the People Called Methodists* (1780), No. 217 (Vol. 7 of this edn.).

[22] *Viz.*, earth, air, fire, and water.
[23] See No. 15, *The Great Assize*, III.3 and n.

more clouds or fogs; but one bright, refulgent day. Much less will there be any poisonous damps or pestilential blasts. There will be no sirocco in Italy; no parching or suffocating winds in Arabia; no keen north-east winds in our own country,

> Shattering the graceful locks of yon fair trees;[24]   5

but only pleasing, healthful breezes,

> Fanning the earth with odoriferous wings.[25]

12. But what change will the element of *water* undergo when all things are made new? It will be in every part of the world clear and limpid, pure from all unpleasing or unhealthful mixtures; rising 10 here and there in crystal fountains to refresh and adorn the earth 'with liquid lapse of murmuring stream'.[26] For undoubtedly, as there were in paradise, there will be various rivers gently gliding along, for the use and pleasure of both man and beast. But the inspired writer has expressly declared, 'there will be no more 15 sea.'[d] We have reason to believe that at the beginning of the world, when God said, 'Let the waters under the heaven be gathered together unto one place, and let the dry land appear,'[e] the dry land spread over the face of the water, and covered it on every side. And so it seems to have done till, in order to the general deluge 20 which he had determined to bring upon the earth at once, 'the windows of heaven were opened, and the fountains of the great deep broken up.'[27] But the sea will then retire within its primitive bounds, and appear on the surface of the earth no more. Neither indeed will there be any more need of the sea. For either as the 25 ancient poet supposes,

[d] Rev. 21:1.
[e] Gen. 1:9.

---

[24] Cf. Milton, *Paradise Lost*, x.1065-67:

> . . . while the winds
> Blow, moist and keen, shattering the graceful locks
> Of these fair spreading trees; . . .

[25] Cf. *ibid.*, iv.156-58:

> Now gentle gales,
> Fanning their odoriferous wings, dispense
> Native perfumes . . .

[26] *Ibid.*, viii. 263. See No. 56, 'God's Approbation of His Works', I.4 and n.
[27] Cf. Gen. 7:11.

Omnis feret omnia tellus[28]—

every part of the earth will naturally produce whatever its
inhabitants want—or all mankind will procure what the whole
earth affords by a much easier and readier conveyance. For all the
inhabitants of the earth, our Lord informs us, will then be
5 ἰσάγγελοι,[29] 'equal to angels'; on a level with them in swiftness as
well as strength; so that they can quick as thought transport
themselves or whatever they want from one side of the globe to
the other.

13. But it seems a greater change will be wrought in the *earth*
10 than even in the air and water. Not that I can believe that
wonderful discovery of Jacob Behmen,[30] which many so eagerly
contend for, that the earth itself with all its furniture and
inhabitants will then be transparent as glass.[31] There does not
seem to be the least foundation for this, either in Scripture or
15 reason. Surely not in Scripture: I know not one text in the Old
or[32] New Testament which affirms any such thing. Certainly it
cannot be inferred from that text in the Revelation, chapter the
fourth, verse the sixth: 'And before the throne there was a sea of
glass, like unto crystal.' And yet, if I mistake not, this is the chief,
20 if not the only Scripture which has been urged in favour of this
opinion! Neither can I conceive that it has any foundation in
reason. It has indeed been warmly alleged that all things would be
far more beautiful if they were quite transparent. But I cannot
apprehend this; yea, I apprehend quite the contrary. Suppose
25 every part of a human body were made transparent as crystal,
would it appear more beautiful than it does now? Nay, rather it
would shock us above measure. The surface of the body, and in
particular 'the human face divine',[33] is undoubtedly one of the
most beautiful objects that can be found under heaven. But could
30 you look through the rosy cheek, the smooth, fair forehead, or the
rising bosom, and distinctly see all that lies within, you would turn
away from it with loathing and horror.

---

[28] Virgil, *Eclogues*, iv. 39; see No. 56, 'God's Approbation of His Works', I.4 and n.
[29] Luke 20:36.
[30] An English spelling of Jakob Boehme (1575–1624), the famous German theosophist, widely influential in England, espec. in the later works of William Law. Cf. No. 15, *The Great Assize*, III.3. and n.
[31] *Ibid.*
[32] *AM* orig., 'and', altered in Wesley's errata and MS annotations.
[33] Milton, *Paradise Lost*, iii. 44.

14. Let us next take a view of those changes which we may reasonably suppose will then take place in the *earth*. It will no more be bound up with intense cold, nor parched up with extreme heat; but will have such a temperature as will be most conducive to its fruitfulness. If in order to punish its inhabitants God did 5 of old

> Bid his angels turn askance
> This oblique globe,[34]

thereby occasioning violent cold on one part, and violent heat on the other; he will undoubtedly then order them to restore it to its 10 original position; so that there will be a final end, on the one hand of the burning heat which makes some parts of it scarce habitable; and on the other of

> The rage of Arctos, and eternal frost.[35]

15. And it will then contain no jarring or destructive principles 15 within its own bosom. It will no more have any of those violent convulsions in its own bowels. It will no more be shaken or torn asunder by the impetuous force of *earthquakes;* and will therefore need neither Vesuvius nor Etna, nor any *burning mountains*[36] to prevent them. There will be no more horrid rocks or frightful 20 precipices; no wild deserts or barren sands; no impassable morasses or unfaithful[37] bogs to swallow up the unwary traveller. There will doubtless be inequalities on the surface of the earth, which are not blemishes, but beauties. For[38] though I will not affirm that 25

> earth hath this variety from heaven
> Of pleasure situate in hill and dale;[39]

---

[34] Cf. Milton, *Paradise Lost*, x. 668-71; cf. No. 56, 'God's Approbation of His Works', I.6 and n.

[35] Prior, *Solomon*, i. 265; cf. No. 56, 'God's Approbation of His Works', I.6 and n.

[36] Cf. Thomas Burnet, *Sacred Theory of the Earth*, II. 55 (a favourite of Wesley; cf. JWJ, Jan. 17, 1770), where among the features of the primal catastrophe are 'burning mountains or volcanoes of the earth'. See Wesley's echo of this in No. 15, *The Great Assize*, III.4 and n.

[37] Orig., *AM* and *SOSO*, 'unfruitful', altered by Wesley in *AM* errata and his MS annotations to 'unfaithful'.

[38] Orig., *AM* and *SOSO*, 'And', but altered by Wesley in *AM* errata and MS annotations to 'For'.

[39] Milton, *Paradise Lost*, vi. 640-41. See No. 124, 'Human Life a Dream', §7.

yet I cannot think gently rising hills will be any defect, but an ornament of the new-made earth. And doubtless we shall then likewise have occasion to say:

> Lo there his wondrous skill arrays
> The fields in cheerful green!
> A thousand herbs his hand displays,
> A thousand flowers between![40]

16. And what will the general produce of the earth be? Not thorns, briars, or thistles. Not any useless or fetid weed; not any poisonous, hurtful, or unpleasant plant; but every one that can be conducive in any wise either to our use or pleasure. How far beyond all that the most lively imagination is now able to conceive! We shall no more regret the loss of the terrestrial paradise, or sigh at that well-devised description of our great poet;

> Then shall this mount
> Of paradise by might of waves be moved
> Out of his place, pushed by the horned flood,
> With all its verdure spoiled, and trees adrift,
> Down the great river to the opening gulf,
> And there take root, an island salt and bare![41]

For all the earth shall then be a more beautiful paradise than Adam ever saw.[42]

17. Such will be the state of the new earth with regard to the meaner, the inanimate parts of it. But great as this change will be, it is little, it is nothing, in comparison of that which will then take place throughout all animated nature. In the living part of the creation were seen the most deplorable effects of Adam's apostasy. The whole animated creation, whatever has life, from leviathan to the smallest mite, was thereby 'made subject' to such 'vanity'[43] as the inanimate creatures could not be. They were

---

[40] Cf. Watts, above, §9. Watts's own text reads:

> How did his wondrous skill array
> Your fields in charming green;
> A thousand herbs his art display,
> A thousand flowers between!

[41] Milton, *Paradise Lost,* xi.829-34.
[42] Cf. No. 59, 'God's Love to Fallen Man', I.1 and n.
[43] Rom. 8:20.

subject to that fell[44] monster, death, the conqueror of all that breathe. They were made subject to its forerunner, pain, in its ten thousand forms; although 'God made not death, neither hath he pleasure in the death of any living.'[45] How many millions of creatures in the sea, in the air, and on every part of the earth, can 5 now no otherwise preserve their own lives than by taking away the lives of others; by tearing in pieces and devouring their poor, innocent, unresisting fellow-creatures! Miserable lot of such innumerable multitudes, who, insignificant as they seem, are the offspring of one common Father, the creatures of the same God 10 of love! It is probable not only two-thirds of the animal creation, but ninety-nine parts out of a hundred, are under a necessity of destroying others in order to preserve their own life![46] But it shall not always be so. He that sitteth upon the throne[47] will soon change the face of all things, and give a demonstrative proof to all 15 his[48] creatures that 'his mercy is over all his works.'[49] The horrid state of things which at present obtains will soon be at an end. On the new earth no creature will kill or hurt or give pain to any other. The scorpion will have no poisonous sting, the adder no venomous teeth. The lion will have no claws to tear the lamb; no 20 teeth to grind his flesh and bones. Nay, no creature, no beast, bird, or fish, will have any inclination to hurt any other. For cruelty will be far away, and savageness and fierceness be forgotten. So that violence shall be heard no more, neither wasting or destruction seen on the face of the earth. 'The wolf 25 shall dwell with the lamb' (the words may be literally as well as figuratively understood) 'and the leopard shall lie down with the kid.'[50] 'They shall not hurt or destroy,'[51] from the rising up of the sun to the going down of the same.

18. But the most glorious of all will be the change which then 30

[44] Johnson, *Dictionary*, defines 'fell' as 'cruel, barbarous, inhuman, savage, ravenous'. It occurs frequently in the literature of the time, referring to 'war' (as in Nicholas Rowe, *Tamerlane*, Act I, sc. 1; see No. 128, 'The Deceitfulness of the Human Heart', II.4), 'anger' and 'destruction' (cf. Beaumont and Fletcher, *Bonduca*, Act III, sc. 5), 'revenge' (Beattie, *The Minstrel*, II. xlvi. 6), and even to 'love' (as in Spenser, *Faerie Queene*, Bk. II, Canto IV. xxxv. 3).
[45] Cf. Wisd. 1:13. See also No. 60, 'The General Deliverance', I.5 and n.
[46] Cf. No. 56, 'God's Approbation of His Works', I.12 and n.
[47] See Rev. 5:13; 6:16; 7:15.
[48] Wesley adds 'his' only in the MS annotations to *SOSO*.
[49] Ps. 145:9 (BCP).
[50] Isa. 11:6.
[51] Cf. Isa. 11:9.

will take place on the poor, sinful, miserable children of men. These had fallen in many respects, as from a greater height, so into a lower depth than any other part of the creation. But they shall 'hear a great voice out of heaven, saying, Behold, the
5 tabernacle of God is with men, and he will dwell with them, and they shall be his people, and God himself shall be their God.' Hence will arise an unmixed state of holiness and happiness far superior to that which Adam enjoyed in paradise.[52] In how beautiful and affecting a manner is this described by the Apostle!
10 'God shall wipe away all tears from their eyes; and there shall be no more death, neither sorrow nor crying, neither shall there be any more pain: for the former things are done away.'[f] As there will be no more death, and no more pain or sickness preparatory thereto; as there will be no more grieving for or parting with
15 friends; so there will be no more sorrow or crying. Nay, but there will be a greater deliverance than all this; for there will be no more sin. And to crown all, there will be a deep, an intimate, an uninterrupted union with God; a constant communion with the Father and his Son Jesus Christ, through the Spirit; a continual
20 enjoyment of the Three-One God,[53] and of all the creatures in him![54]

---

[f] Rev. 21:3-4.

---

[52] Cf. No. 5, 'Justification by Faith', I.4 and n.
[53] Cf. No. 55, *On the Trinity*, §17 and n.
[54] For other summaries of Wesley's eschatology, cf. No. 15, *The Great Assize*, intro., II.4, and n.

THE DUTY OF REPROVING OUR NEIGHBOUR

AN INTRODUCTORY COMMENT

In this sermon we have an abrupt change of theme and climate. It was written in July 1787, but not published in the Arminian Magazine *until the beginning of the following year (Vol. XI, January and February 1788) as number XLIII, and without a title. It was then promptly reprinted with its present title in* SOSO *(V. 223-36). Note that it is the fifteenth sermon in a volume already advertised as planned for fourteen. This rather sudden shift in plans might account for the fact that it is not a logical sequel to 'The New Creation'. It was not published again in Wesley's lifetime.*

Its theme is reminiscent of an older Puritan concern that in view of their rejection of traditional forms of confession, and also in light of their discovery that self-examination is not enough for life together in Christian fellowship. Christians should therefore serve as 'consciences' to each other. Wesley had before him the example of Richard Baxter, The Saints' Everlasting Rest *(1649/50), and even more specifically the sermon of John Kitchin on 'How Must We Reprove That We May Not Partake of Other Men's Sinnes', which his grandfather, Samuel Annesley, had included in* The Morning-Exercise at Cripplegate *(1661); cf. Robert C. Monk,* John Wesley: His Puritan Heritage, *pp. 233-36. The only two recorded instances of Wesley's use of Lev. 19:17 in his oral preaching occur in 1784 and 1787.*

The Duty of Reproving our Neighbour

Leviticus 19:17

Thou shalt not hate thy brother in thy heart: thou shalt in any wise rebuke thy neighbour, and not suffer sin upon him.

A great part of the book of Exodus, and almost the whole of the 5 book of Leviticus, relate to the ritual or ceremonial law of Moses, which was peculiarly given to the children of Israel; but was such 'a yoke', says the apostle Peter, 'as neither our fathers nor we were able to bear'.[1] We are therefore delivered from it: and this is one branch of 'the liberty wherewith Christ hath made us free'.[2] Yet it is easy to observe that many excellent moral precepts are 5 interspersed among these ceremonial laws. Several of them we find in this very chapter. Such as, 'Thou shalt not gather every grape of thy vineyard; thou shalt leave them for the poor and stranger. I am the Lord your God.'[a] 'Ye shall not steal, neither deal falsely,'[3] 'neither lie one to another.'[b] 'Thou shalt not 10 defraud thy neighbour, neither rob him: the wages of him that is hired shall not abide with thee till the morning.'[c] 'Thou shalt not curse the deaf, nor put a stumbling-block before the blind, but shalt fear thy God: I am the Lord.'[d] As if he had said, I am he whose eyes are over all the earth, and whose ears are open to their 15 cry. 'Ye shall do no unrighteousness in judgment; thou shalt not respect the person of the poor,' which compassionate men may be tempted to do, 'nor honour the person of the mighty', to which there are a thousand temptations.[e] 'Thou shalt not go up and down as a talebearer among thy people'[f]—although this is a sin 20 which human laws have never yet been able to prevent. Then follows, 'Thou shalt not hate thy brother in thy heart: thou shalt in any wise rebuke thy neighbour, and not suffer sin upon him.'

In order to understand this important direction aright, and to apply it profitably to our own souls, let us consider, 25 First, what it is that we are to rebuke or reprove. What is the thing that is here enjoined? Secondly, who are they whom we are commanded to reprove? And, thirdly, how are we to reprove them?

I.1. Let us consider, first, What is the duty that is here 30 enjoined? What is it we are to rebuke or reprove? And what is it 'to reprove'? What is it to reprove? To tell anyone of his faults, as clearly appears from the following words, 'Thou shalt not suffer sin upon him.' Sin is therefore the thing we are called to reprove, or rather him that commits sin. We are to do all that in us lies to 35 convince him of his fault, and lead him into the right way.

---

[a] [Lev. 19,] ver. 10. [b] Ver. 11. [c] Ver. 13.
[d] Ver. 14. [e] Ver. 15. [f] Ver. 16.

---

[1] Cf. Acts 15:10. [2] Gal. 5:1.
[3] This phrase from Leviticus was present in *AM*, but omitted from *SOSO*.

2. Love indeed requires us to warn him, not only of sin (although of this chiefly), but likewise of any error which if it were persisted in would naturally lead to sin. If we do not hate him in our heart, if we love our neighbour as ourselves, this will be our constant endeavour—to warn him of every evil way and of every 5 mistake which tends to evil.

3. But if we desire not to lose our labour,[4] we should rarely reprove anyone for anything that is of a disputable nature, that will bear much to be said on both sides. A thing may possibly appear evil to me; therefore I scruple the doing of it. And if I were 10 to do it while that scruple remains I should be a sinner before God. But another is not to be judged by my conscience;[5] to his own master he standeth or falleth.[6] Therefore I would not reprove him but for what is clearly and undeniably evil. Such, for instance, is profane cursing and swearing, which even those who practise it 15 most will not often venture to defend, if one mildly expostulates with them. Such is drunkenness, which even a habitual drunkard will condemn when he is sober. And such, in the account of the generality of people, is the profaning of the Lord's day. And if any which are guilty of these sins for a while attempt to defend them, 20 very few will persist to do it if you look them steadily in the face, and appeal to their own conscience in the sight of God.

II.1. Let us, in the second place, consider, Who are those that we are called to reprove? It is the more needful to consider this because it is affirmed by many serious persons that there are some 25 sinners whom the Scripture itself forbids us to reprove. This sense has been put on that solemn caution of our Lord in his Sermon on the Mount: 'Cast not your pearls before swine, lest they trample them under foot, and turn again and rend you.'[7] But

---

[4] See below, III.3. Cf. the anecdote in Boswell's *Life of Johnson* (in 1772), 'On School Chastisement', recalled from Locke's *Treatise on Education* (1693), about the mother who corrected her daughter for an eighth time because, said she, 'I would have lost my labour if I had stopped at the seventh.' A similar story is told of Samuel and Susanna Wesley and their eldest son. Samuel had asked his wife why she was repeating a lesson 'to that dull child for the twentieth time'; Susanna's reply: 'Because the nineteenth would not have been enough.' See George J. Stevenson, *Memorials of the Wesley Family* (London, 1876), p. 169; and Eliza Clarke, *Susanna Wesley* (1886), p. 28. The same theme reappears in Nos. 91, 'On Charity', III.8; 93, 'On Redeeming the Time', III.3; 95, 'On the Education of Children', §15; and 96, 'On Obedience to Parents', II.1. Cf. also Wesley's letter to Philothea Briggs, Oct. 16, 1771.

[5] See 1 Cor. 10:29.   [6] Rom. 14:4.

[7] Cf. Matt. 7:6; see also the *Notes* on this verse.

the plain meaning of these words is, Do not offer the pearls, the sublime doctrines or mysteries of the gospel, to those whom you know to be brutish men, immersed in sins, and having no fear of God before their eyes.[8] This would expose those precious jewels
5 to contempt, and yourselves to injurious treatment. But even those whom we know to be, in our Lord's sense, dogs and swine, if we saw them do or heard them speak what they themselves know to be evil, we ought in any wise to reprove them; else we 'hate our brother in our heart'.

10 2. The persons intended by 'our neighbour' are every child of man,[9] everyone that breathes the vital air, all that have souls to be saved. And if we refrain from performing this office of love to any because they are sinners above other men, they may persist in their iniquity, but their blood will God require at our hands.[10]

15 3. How striking is Mr. Baxter's reflection on this head, in his *Saints' Everlasting Rest:* 'Suppose thou wert to meet one in the lower world to whom thou hadst denied this office of love when ye were both together under the sun; what answer couldst thou make to his upbraiding? At such a time and place, while we were
20 under the sun, God delivered me into thy hands. I then did not know the way of salvation, but was seeking death in the error of my life.[11] And therein thou sufferedst me to remain, without once endeavouring to awake me out of sleep! Hadst thou imparted to me thy knowledge, and warned me to flee from the wrath to
25 come,[12] neither I nor thou need ever have come into this place of torment.'[13]

4. Everyone therefore that has a soul to be saved is entitled to this good office from thee. Yet this does not imply that it is to be done in the same degree to everyone. It cannot be denied that

8 Rom. 3:18.
9 Cf. No. 7, 'The Way to the Kingdom', I.8 and n.
10 See 2 Sam. 4:11; Ezek. 3:18, 20; 33:6, 8.
11 Cf. Wisd. 1:12; and No. 6, 'The Righteousness of Faith', §2 and n.
12 Matt. 3:7.
13 Cf. Baxter, *The Saints' Everlasting Rest*, Pt. III, §7 in *Works*, III. 226: 'Consider, what a thing it will be to look upon your poor friends eternally in those flames, and to think that your neglect was a great cause of it! And that there was a time when you might have done much to prevent it! If you should there perish with them, it would be no small aggravation of your torment; if you be in heaven, it would sure be a sad thought, were it possible that any sorrow could dwell there, to hear a multitude of poor souls there to cry out for ever, Oh! if you would but have told me plainly of my sin and danger, and dealt roundly with me, and set it home, I might have escaped all this torment, and been now in rest. Oh! what a sad voice will this be!'

there are some to whom it is particularly due. Such, in the first place, are our parents, if we have any that stand in need of it; unless we should place our consorts and our children on an equal footing with them. Next to these we may rank our brothers and sisters, and afterwards our relations, as they are allied to us in a 5 nearer or more distant manner, either by blood or by marriage. Immediately after these are our servants, whether bound to us for a term of years or any shorter term. Lastly, such in their several degrees are our countrymen, our fellow-citizens, and the members of the same society, whether civil or religious. The 10 latter have a particular claim to our service; seeing these societies are formed with that very design, to watch over each other for this very end, that we may not suffer sin upon our brother.[14] If we neglect to reprove any of these when a fair opportunity offers we are undoubtedly to be ranked among those that 'hate their 15 brother in their heart'. And how severe is the sentence of the Apostle against those who fall under this condemnation! 'He that hateth his brother', though it does not break out into words or actions, 'is a murderer. And ye know', continues the Apostle, 'that no murderer hath eternal life abiding in him.'[15] He hath not that 20 seed planted in his soul which groweth up unto everlasting life. In other words, he is in such a state that if he dies therein he cannot see life. It plainly follows that to neglect this is no small thing, but eminently endangers our final salvation.

III. We have seen what is meant by reproving our brother, and 25 who those are that we should reprove. But the principal thing remains to be considered. How, in what manner, are we to reprove them?

1. It must be allowed that there is a considerable difficulty in performing this in a right manner. Although at the same time it is 30 far less difficult to some than it is to others. Some there are who are particularly qualified for it, whether by nature, or practice, or grace. They are not encumbered either with evil shame or that sore burden, the fear of man.[16] They are both ready to undertake this labour of love, and skilful in performing it. To these therefore 35

---

[14] An echo of the *General Rules*, §5: '. . . doing good . . . by instructing, reproving, or exhorting . . .'.

[15] Cf. 1 John 3:15.

[16] An echo of Francke's *Nicodemus: Or A Treatise Against the Fear of Man* (1706); cf. No. 14, *The Repentance of Believers*, I.7 and n.

it is little or no cross; nay, they have a kind of relish for it, and a satisfaction therein over and above that which arises from a consciousness of having done their duty. But be it a cross to us, greater or less, we know that hereunto we are called.[17] And be the difficulty ever so great to us, we know in whom we have trusted; and that he will surely fulfil his word, 'As thy day, so shall thy strength be.'[18]

2. In what manner then shall we reprove our brother, in order that our reproof may be most effectual? Let us first of all take care that whatever we do may be done in the spirit of *love;*[19] in the spirit of tender goodwill to our neighbour, as for one who is the son of our common Father, and one for whom Christ died, that he might be a partaker of salvation. Then, by the grace of God, love will beget love. The affection of the speaker will spread to the heart of the hearer; and you will find in due time that your labour hath not been in vain in the Lord.[20]

3. Meantime the greatest care must be taken that you speak in the spirit of *humility.* Beware that you do not think of yourself more highly than you ought to think.[21] If you think too highly of yourself, you can scarce avoid despising your brother. And if you show, or even feel, the least contempt of those whom you reprove, it will blast your whole work and occasion you to lose all your labour.[22] In order to prevent the very appearance of pride it will be often needful to be explicit on the head—to disclaim all preferring yourself before him; and at the very time you reprove that which is evil, to own and bless God for that which is good in him.

4. Great care must be taken, in the third place, to speak in the spirit of *meekness,*[23] as well as *lowliness.* The Apostle assures us that 'the wrath of men worketh not the righteousness of God.'[24] Anger, though it be adorned with the name of zeal, begets anger; not love or holiness. We should therefore avoid with all possible care the very appearance of it. Let there be no trace of it either in the eyes, the gesture, or the tone of voice; but let all of these concur in manifesting a loving, humble, and dispassionate spirit.

---

[17] See 1 Pet. 2:21.　　　　　　　　　　　　　　　　　[18] Cf. Deut. 33:25.
[19] Cf. No. 17, 'The Circumcision of the Heart,' I.2 and n.
[20] See 1 Cor. 15:58.
[21] Rom. 12:3. See also, No. 21, 'Sermon on the Mount, I,' I.7 and n.
[22] Cf. above, I.3 and n.
[23] Cf. No. 22, 'Sermon on the Mount, II', I.4 and n.
[24] Cf. Jas. 1:20.

5. But all this time see that you do not trust in yourself. Put no confidence in your own wisdom, or address, or abilities of any kind. For the success of all you speak or do, trust not in yourself, but in the great Author of every good and perfect gift.[25] Therefore while you are speaking continually lift up your heart to him that 5 worketh all in all.[26] And whatsoever is spoken in the spirit of *prayer* will not fall to the ground.

6. So much for the *spirit* wherewith you should speak when you reprove your neighbour. I now proceed to the outward *manner*. It has been frequently found that the prefacing a reproof with a 10 frank profession of goodwill has caused what was spoken to sink deep into the heart. This will generally have a far better effect than that grand fashionable engine, flattery,[27] by means of which the men of the world have often done surprising things. But the very same things, yea, far greater, have much oftener been 15 effected by a plain and artless declaration of disinterested love. When you feel God has kindled this flame in your heart, hide it not; give it full vent. It will pierce like lightning. The stout, the hard-hearted, will melt before you, and know that God is with you of a truth.[28] 20

7. Although it is certain that the main point in reproving is to do it with a right spirit, yet it must also be allowed there are several little circumstances with regard to the outward manner which are by no means without their use, and therefore are not to be despised. One of these is—whenever you reprove, do it with great 25 *seriousness;* so that as you really are in earnest you may likewise appear so to be. A ludicrous[29] reproof makes little impression, and is soon forgot. Besides, that many times is taken ill, as if you ridiculed the person you reprove. And indeed those who are not accustomed to make jests do not take it well to be jested upon. 30 One means of giving a serious air to what you speak is, as often as may be, to use the very words of Scripture. Frequently we find the word of God, even in a private conversation, has a peculiar energy; and the sinner, when he expects it least, feels it 'sharper than a two-edged sword'.[30] 35

8. Yet there are some exceptions to this general rule of

---

[25] Jas. 1:17. [26] 1 Cor. 12:6.
[27] Cf. No. 14, *The Repentance of Believers*, I.7 and n. for Wesley's comments on the 'praise of men'.
[28] See 1 Cor. 14:25.
[29] I.e., 'jesting' or 'sportive'; cf. Johnson, *Dictionary*. [30] Cf. Heb. 4:12.

reproving seriously. There are some exempt cases, wherein, as a good judge of human nature observes,

Ridiculum acri fortius[31]—

a little well-placed raillery will pierce deeper than solid argument.
5 But this has place chiefly when we have to do with those who are strangers to religion. And when we condescend to give a ludicrous reproof to a person of this character it seems we are authorized so to do by that advice of Solomon, 'Answer a fool according to his folly, lest he be wise in his own eyes.'[32]
10   9. The manner of the reproof may in other respects too be varied according to the occasion. Sometimes you may find it proper to use many words to express your sense at large. At other times you may judge it more expedient to use few words; perhaps a single sentence. And at others it may be advisable to use no
15 words at all, but a gesture, a sigh, or a look. Particularly when the person you would reprove is greatly your superior. And frequently this silent kind of reproof will be attended by the power of God, and consequently have a far better effect than a long and laboured discourse.
20   10. Once more. Remember the remark of Solomon, 'A word spoken *in season,* how good is it!'[33] It is true, if you are providentially called to reprove anyone whom you are not likely to see any more, you are to snatch the present opportunity, and to speak 'in season' or 'out of season'.[34] But with them whom you
25 have frequent opportunities of seeing you may wait for a fair occasion. Here the advice of the poet has place. You may speak

Si validus, si laetus erit, si denique poscet[35]—

when he is in a good humour, or when he asks it you. Here you may catch the

30   *mollia tempora fandi*[36]—

---

[31] Cf. Horace, *Satires*, I.x.14-15: '*Ridiculum acri/Fortius et melius magnas plerumque secat res.*' Compare this approving reference to Horace with Wesley's more typical disapproval, as in No. 2, *The Almost Christian*, I.9 and n.

[32] Cf. Prov. 26:5.   [33] Prov. 15:23.   [34] 2 Tim. 4:2.

[35] Horace, *Epistles*, I. xiii. 3: '*if* he's well, *if* he's in good spirits, *if*—in fine—he asks for them' (Loeb, 194: 334-35). Addison quotes this in *The Spectator*, No. 553, Dec. 4, 1712.

[36] Cf. Virgil, *Aeneid*, iv. 293-94, '*mollissima fandi / tempora*', 'the happiest season for speech' (Loeb, 1:414-15). See also Wesley's letter to George Whitefield and his friends at Oxford, Sept. 10, 1736, and his *Journal* for the same date.

the time when his mind is in a soft, mild frame. And then God will both teach you how to speak, and give a blessing to what is spoken.

11. But here let me guard you against one mistake. It passes for an indisputable maxim, 'Never attempt to reprove a man when he is intoxicated with drink.'[37] Reproof, it is said, is then thrown 5 away, and can have no good effect. I dare not say so. I have seen not a few clear instances of the contrary. Take one. Many years ago, passing by a man in Moorfields, who was so drunk he could hardly stand, I put a paper into his hand. He looked at it and said, '*A Word—A Word to a Drunkard*[38]—that is me—Sir, Sir! I am 10 wrong.—I know I am wrong—Pray let me talk a little with you.' He held me by the hand a full half-hour. And I believe he got drunk no more.

12. I beseech you, brethren, by the mercies of God,[39] do not despise poor drunkards. Have compassion on them. Be instant 15 with them in season and out of season![40] Let not shame or fear of men prevent your pulling these brands out of the burning;[41] many of them are[42] self-condemned:

> Nor do they not discern the evil plight
> That they are in.[43]   20

But they despair; they have no hope of escaping out of it. And they sink into it still deeper, because none else has any hope for them! 'Sinners of every other sort', said a venerable old clergyman, 'have I frequently known converted to God. But an habitual drunkard I have never known converted.' But I have known five 25 hundred, perhaps five thousand. Ho! Art thou one, who readest these words? Then hear thou the words of the Lord! I have a message from God unto thee,[44] O sinner! Thus saith the Lord, Cast not away thy hope.[45] I have not forgotten thee. He that tells

---

[37] E.g., Pliny the Elder, *Natural History*, XXIII. i. 23, '*In proverbium cessit, sapientiam vino obumbrari*', 'It has passed into a proverb that wisdom is clouded by wine;' cf. 'When the wine is in, the wit is out,' 'Wine counsels seldom prosper,' and other apothegms in the same vein.

[38] Cf. Wesley's little tract under this title; see *Bibliog*, No. 111; Vol. 14 of this edn.
[39] See Rom. 12:1.   [40] See 2 Tim. 4:2.
[41] See Zech. 3:2. Cf. No. 4, *Scriptural Christianity*, II.2 and n.
[42] Orig., *AM* and *SOSO*, 'not', altered in Wesley's MS annotations to each work.
[43] Cf. Milton, *Paradise Lost*, i. 335-36:
> Nor did they not perceive the evil plight
> In which they were.

[44] Judg. 3:20.   [45] See Heb. 10:35.

thee, 'There is no help,' is a liar from the beginning.[46] Look up!
Behold the Lamb of God who taketh away the sin of the world![47]
This day is salvation come to thy soul.[48] Only see that thou despise
not him that speaketh! Just now he saith unto thee: 'Son, be of
5 good cheer! Thy sins are forgiven thee!'[49]

13. Lastly, you that are diligent in this labour of love, see that
you be not discouraged, although after you have used your best
endeavours you should see no present fruit. You 'have need of
patience', and then, 'after ye have done the will of God'[50] herein,
10 the harvest will come. Never be 'weary of well-doing; in due time
ye shall reap, if ye faint not.'[51] Copy after Abraham, who 'against
hope, still believed in hope'.[52] 'Cast thy bread upon the waters,
and after many days thou shalt find it again.'[53]

14. I have now only a few words to add, unto you, my brethren,
15 who are vulgarly called 'Methodists'. I never heard or read of any
considerable revival of religion which was not attended with a
spirit of reproving. I believe it cannot be otherwise; for what is
faith unless it worketh by love?[54] Thus it was in every part of
England when the present revival of religion began about fifty
20 years ago: all the subjects of that revival—all the Methodists, so
called, in every place—were reprovers of outward sin.[55] And
indeed so are all that 'being justified by faith, have peace with
God through Jesus Christ'.[56] Such they are at first; and if they use
that precious gift it will never be taken away. Come, brethren! In
25 the name of God, let us begin again! Rich or poor, let us all arise
as one man! And in any wise let every man 'rebuke his neighbour,
and not suffer sin upon him'! Then shall all Great Britain and
Ireland know that we do not go 'a warfare at our own cost'.[57] Yea,
'God shall bless us, and all the ends of the world shall fear him.'[58]

30 Manchester, July 28, 1787

[46] See John 8:44.
[47] John 1:29.
[48] See Luke 19:9.
[49] Cf. Matt. 9:2.
[50] Heb. 10:36.
[51] Cf. Gal. 6:9.
[52] Rom. 4:18.
[53] Eccles. 11:1.
[54] See Gal. 5:6; cf. No. 2, *The Almost Christian*, II.6 and n.
[55] See No. 13, *On Sin in Believers*, intro., III.1-9, and n.
[56] Cf. Rom. 5:1.
[57] Cf. 1 Cor. 9:7.
[58] Ps. 67:7 (BCP).

THE SIGNS OF THE TIMES

AN INTRODUCTORY COMMENT

Since childhood Wesley had understood himself as having a providential vocation, and by the 1780s he was convinced that the Methodist Revival, with its parallels in Britain and America, was one of the landmark events in the whole of church history. He was, therefore, baffled (and offended?) by the steadfast indifference to it on the part of the leaders of the Church of England. The Revival had survived its days of violent persecution by local mobs and magistrates, but the day of recognition of its import for spiritual renewal in England and the world had not yet come—and might never. It was in something of this mood of complaint in the late summer of 1787, at St. Helier, Isle of Jersey, that he 'finished [this present] sermon on Discerning the Signs of the Times' *(cf. JWJ, August 25, 1787). It is one of the rare examples of the cult-hero taking himself seriously as such, with an elaborate parallelism between the blindness of the* Pharisees *and* Sadducees *to 'the signs of their times' and equivalent myopias in his own day. It is clear, however, that the main point to the sermon is its concluding appeal to the Methodists that they not fail in their discernment of the signs of their times, but respond appropriately.*

This was, apparently, the only time he ever preached from this particular text (Matt. 16:3); the sermon was published in the Arminian Magazine *the following year in the March and April issues without title (Vol. XI. 115-20, 172-78), and then immediately, with its present title, as the concluding item in* SOSO, *V. 237-52, the sixteenth in a work advertised for fourteen parts). Like 'The Duty of Reproving our Neighbour', it seems to have been placed here to fill out a volume rather than as a link in Wesley's programme as advertised in the preface to* SOSO, *V-VIII.*[1]

---

[1] See above, pp. 455-57.

The Signs of the Times

Matthew 16:3

Ye can discern the face of the sky; but can ye not discern the signs of the times?

5   1. The entire passage runs thus: 'The Pharisees also, with the Sadducees, came, and tempting, desired him that he would show them a sign from heaven. He answered and said, When it is evening, ye say, It will be fair weather, for the sky is red; and in the morning, It will be foul weather today, for the sky is red and 10 lowering. O ye hypocrites, ye can discern the face of the sky; but can ye not discern the signs of the times?'

  2. 'The Pharisees also, with the Sadducees, came.' In general these were quite opposite to each other; but it is no uncommon thing for the children of the world to lay aside their opposition to each other (at least for a season) and cordially to unite in opposing 15 the children of God. 'And tempting', that is, making a trial whether he was indeed sent of God, 'desired him that he would show them a sign from heaven', which they believed no false prophet was able to do. It is not improbable they imagined this 20 would convince them that he was really sent from God. 'He answered and said unto them, When it is evening, ye say, It will be fair weather, for the sky is red; and in the morning, It will be foul weather today, for the sky is red and lowering.' Probably there were more certain signs of fair and foul weather in their climate 25 than there are in ours. 'O ye hypocrites', making profession of love while you have enmity in your hearts; 'ye can discern the face of the sky,' and judge thereby what the weather will be; 'but can ye not discern the signs of the times,' when God brings his first-begotten Son into the world?

30   3. Let us more particularly inquire, first, What were 'the times' whereof our Lord speaks? And what were 'the signs' whereby those times were to be distinguished from all others? We may then inquire, secondly, what are 'the times' which we have reason to believe are *now* at hand? And how is it that all who are called 35 Christians do not discern 'the signs of these times'?

522

I.1. Let us in the first place inquire, What times were those concerning which our Lord is here speaking? It is easy to answer: the times of the Messiah, the times ordained before the foundation of the world wherein it pleased God to give his only-begotten Son[1] to take our nature upon him, to be 'found in fashion as a man', to live a life of sorrow and pain, and at length to be 'obedient unto death, even the death of the cross';[2] to the end 'that whosoever believeth on him should not perish, but have everlasting life'.[3] This was the important time, the signs whereof the Pharisees and Sadducees could not discern. Clear as they were in themselves, yet so thick a veil was upon the heart of these men that they did not discern the tokens of his coming, though foretold so long before.

2. But what were those signs of the coming of that Just One[4] which had been so long and so clearly foretold? And whereby they might easily have discerned those times, had not the veil been on their heart? They are many in number; but it may suffice to mention a few of them. One of the first is that pointed out in the solemn words spoken by Jacob a little before his death: 'The sceptre shall not depart from Judah, nor a lawgiver from between his feet, until Shiloh come.'[a] All, both ancient and modern Jews, agree that by 'Shiloh' we are to understand the Messiah;[5] who was therefore to come, according to the prophecy, 'before the sceptre', that is, the sovereignty, 'departed from Judah'. But it did without controversy depart from Judah at this very time; an infallible sign that at this very time 'Shiloh', that is the Messiah, 'came'.

3. A second eminent sign of those times, the times of the coming of the Messiah, is given us in the third chapter of the prophecy of Malachi: 'Behold, I send my messenger, and he shall prepare my way before me; and the Lord whom ye seek shall suddenly come to his temple.'[b] How manifestly was this fulfilled, first, by the coming of John the Baptist; and then by our blessed Lord himself, 'coming suddenly to his temple'! And what sign

---

[a] Gen. 49:10. [b] Ver. 1.

[1] See John 3:16. [2] Cf. Phil. 2:8.
[3] Cf. John 3:16. [4] See Acts 7:52.
[5] The Hebrew text here is notoriously obscure. Modern commentators tend to reject the translation, 'Shiloh', whether as a place or Messianic metaphor; cf. E. A. Speiser, *Genesis*, The Anchor Bible (1964). But Wesley is right about the traditions of rabbinical

could be clearer to those that impartially considered the words of the prophet Isaiah: 'The voice of one crying in the wilderness, Prepare ye the way of the Lord, make his paths straight!'[c]

4. But yet clearer signs than these (if any could be clearer) were
5 the mighty works that he wrought. Accordingly he himself declares, 'The works which I do, they testify of me.'[6] And to these he explicitly appeals in his answer to the question of John the Baptist (not proposed, as some have strangely imagined, from any doubt which he had himself; but from a desire of confirming his
10 disciples who might possibly waver when their master was taken from their head): 'Art thou he that should come,' the Messiah? 'Or look we for another?'[7] No bare verbal answer could have been so convincing as what they saw with their own eyes. Jesus therefore referred them to this testimony: 'He answered and said
15 unto them, Go and show John the things which ye hear and see: the blind receive their sight, and the lame walk; the lepers are cleansed, and the deaf hear; the dead are raised up, and the poor have the gospel preached unto them.'[d]

5. But how then came it to pass that those who were so
20 sharp-sighted in other things, who could 'discern the face of the sky', were not able to discern those signs which indicated the coming of the Messiah? They could not discern them, not for want of evidence—this was full and clear—but for want of integrity in themselves; because they were a 'wicked and
25 adulterous generation';[8] because the perverseness of their hearts spread a cloud over their understanding. Therefore although the Sun of righteousness[9] shone bright, yet they were insensible of it.

[c] Chap. 40, ver. 3.   [d] Matt. 11:4-5.

interpretation up to his day; cf. Menahem M. Kasher, *Encyclopedia of Biblical Interpretation*, Vol. VI: *Genesis* (New York, American Encyclopedia Society, 1965), p. 169, §§75-77: '. . . until Shiloh—i.e., the royal Messiah—comes . . .'. See also Abraham Ben-Isaiah and Benjamin Sharfman, *The Pentateuch and Rashi's Commentary* (Brooklyn, S. S. and R. Publishing Company, 1949–50), I. 489: 'I.e., Messiah, the King, for the Kingdom is his, and thus does Onkelos render it.' Abraham Cohen confirms this in his *Soncino Chumash . . . An Exposition Based on the Classical Jewish Commentaries* (London, Soncino Press, 1956). John Skinner, in his *Genesis* (1910) in the *International Critical Commentary*, had realized this: 'the Messianic acceptation of this passage prevailed in Jewish circles from the earliest times.'

[6] Cf. John 5:36 *(Notes)*.
[7] Luke 7:19, 20; cf. Henry, *Exposition*, for a comment on the basis for John's implied doubts here.
[8] Matt. 16:4.   [9] Mal. 4:2.

They were not willing to be convinced; therefore they remained in ignorance. The light was sufficient; but they shut their eyes that they might not see it. So that they were without excuse, till vengeance came upon them to the uttermost.[10]

II.1. We are in the second place to consider, What are 'the times' which we have reason to believe are *now* at hand? And how is it that all who are called Christians do not discern 'the signs of these times'?

'The times' which we have reason to believe are at hand (if they are not already begun) are what many pious men have termed the time of 'the latter-day glory';[11] meaning the time wherein God would gloriously display his power and love in the fulfilment of his gracious promise that 'the knowledge of the Lord shall cover the earth, as the waters cover the sea.'[12]

2. 'But are there in England, or in any part of the world, any *signs* of such a time approaching?' It is not many years since that a person of considerable learning, as well as eminence in the Church (then Bishop of London), in his pastoral letter made this observation: 'I cannot imagine what persons mean by talking of "a great work of God" at this time. I do not see any work of God now, more than has been at any other time.'[13] I believe it. I believe

---

[10] See 1 Thess. 2:16.   [11] Cf. Jer. 49:39; Hag. 2:9.   [12] Cf. Isa. 11:9; Hab. 2:14.

[13] A blurred memory of Bishop Edmund Gibson's general disapproval of the early Methodists; cf. CWJ, Oct. 21, 1738 (the date is in error; the meeting between John and Charles and the bishop took place on Friday, Oct. 20), and John's diary for Oct. 20—he does not mention the event in his *Journal*. Cf. also CWJ, Feb. 21, 1739; see also John's diary, Saturday, Mar. 24, 1739, and his reply to the bishop's 'Charge to the Clergy', June 11, 1747, in which the bishop had attacked Wesley, the Moravians, and Whitefield; Gibson's *Pastoral Letter to the People of His Diocese . . . by way of Caution against Lukewarmness on the one Hand and Enthusiasm on the other* (1739, 55pp.), and three other of Gibson's 'pastoral letters'. Wesley's alleged quotation does not appear, verbatim, in any of them. Yet is a clear *inference* from Gibson's letters that he did not regard the Methodist Revival as an especially 'great work of God', and rejected their claims (Whitefield's in particular) to 'a special and immediate mission from God', etc. (cf. pp. 27–41). It was this inference that Wesley felt free to place here in quotation marks.

Another of Gibson's pamphlets that comes nearer to Wesley's mark appeared in 1744, *Observations Upon the Conduct and Behaviour of a Certain Sect Usually Distinguished by the Name of Methodists* (folio and quarto), Pt. III, *Q.* 3, 1, 'Imagination of some great work of which God makes them the instruments'; pp. 22–23: 'Whether . . . their astonishment that God should make such "poor mean" creatures as they are his instruments in an extraordinary work which he is bringing about upon the earth is not a means to keep up an opinion in their hearers that *all* they do and say is directed and dictated immediately by God . . .'. For Wesley's reply, see his *Farther Appeal*, Pt. I, III.2-9 (11:119-30 in this edn.). See also No. 112, *On Laying the Foundation of the New Chapel*, §2. For other references to Bishop Gibson, cf. II.10, below; and No. 68, 'The Wisdom of God's Counsels', §21.

that great man did not see any extraordinary work of God. Neither he nor the generality of Christians, so called, saw any signs of the glorious day that is approaching. But how is this to be accounted for? How is it that those who can now 'discern the face
5 of the sky', who are not only great philosophers, but great divines, as eminent as ever the Sadducees, yea, or the Pharisees, were, do not discern the signs of those glorious times, which if not begun, are nigh, even at the door?

3. We allow indeed that in every age of the Church, 'the
10 kingdom of God came not with observation;'[14] not with splendour and pomp, or with any of those outward circumstances which usually attend the kingdoms of this world. We allow this 'kingdom of God is within us';[15] and that consequently when it begins either in an individual or in a nation it 'is like a grain of mustard seed',
15 which at first 'is the least of all seeds'; but nevertheless gradually increases till 'it becomes a great tree.'[16] Or, to use the other comparison of our Lord, it is like a little 'leaven, which a woman took and hid in three measures of meal, till the whole was leavened'.[17]

20 4. But may it not be asked, Are there now any signs that the day of God's power is approaching? I appeal to every candid, unprejudiced person, whether we may not at this day discern all those signs (understanding the words in a spiritual sense) to which our Lord referred to John's disciples. 'The blind receive
25 their sight.'[18] Those who were blind from their birth, unable to see their own deplorable state, and much more to see God and the remedy he has prepared for them in the Son of his love, now see themselves, yea, and 'the light of the glory of God in the face of Jesus Christ'.[19] 'The eyes' of their 'understanding' being now
30 'opened',[20] they see all things clearly. 'The deaf hear.'[21] Those that were before utterly deaf to all the outward and inward calls of God now hear, not only his providential calls, but also the whispers of his grace. 'The lame walk.'[22] Those who never before arose from the earth, or moved one step toward heaven, are now
35 walking in all the ways of God; yea, running the race that is set before them.[23] 'The lepers are cleansed.'[24] The deadly leprosy of

---

[14] Cf. Luke 17:20.   [15] Cf. Luke 17:21.
[16] Matt. 13:31-32.   [17] Cf. Matt. 13:33.
[18] Matt. 11:5.   [19] 2 Cor. 4:6.
[20] Cf. Luke 24:45; Eph. 1:18.   [21] Matt. 11:5.
[22] *Ibid.*   [23] See Heb. 12:1.   [24] Matt. 11:5.

sin, which they brought with them into the world, and which no art of man could ever cure, is now clean departed from them. And surely never in any age or nation since the apostles have those words been so eminently fulfilled, 'The poor have the gospel preached unto them,'[25] as it is at this day. At this day the gospel 5 leaven—faith working by love,[26] inward and outward holiness, or (to use the terms of St. Paul) 'righteousness, and peace, and joy in the Holy Ghost'[27]—hath so spread in various parts of Europe, particularly in England, Scotland, Ireland, in the islands,[28] in the north and south, from Georgia to New England and Newfound- 10 land, that sinners have been truly converted to God, throughly changed both in heart and in life; not by tens, or by hundreds only, but by thousands, yea, by myriads![29] The fact cannot be denied: we can point out the persons, with their names and places of abode. And yet the wise men of the world, the men of 15 eminence, the men of learning and renown, 'cannot imagine what we mean by talking of any extraordinary work of God'! They cannot discern the signs of *these times!* They can see no sign at all of God's arising to maintain his own cause and set up his kingdom over the earth! 20

5. But how may this be accounted for? How is it that they cannot discern the signs of these times? We may account for their want of discernment on the same principle we accounted for that of the Pharisees and Sadducees; namely, that they likewise were what those were, an 'adulterous and sinful generation'.[30] If their 25 eye was single, their whole body would be full of light.[31] But suppose their eye be evil, their whole body must be full of darkness.[32] Every evil temper darkens the soul; every evil passion clouds the understanding. How then can we expect that those should be able to discern the signs of the times who are full of all 30 disorderly passions, and slaves to every evil temper? But this is

---

[25] *Ibid.*   [26] See Gal. 5:6.   [27] Rom. 14:17.

[28] An interesting ambiguity here. This sermon was written on the Isle of Jersey, and Wesley may have had in mind the Channel Islands, the Isle of Wight, the Isle of Man, etc., since the revival had spread to all of them in the period, 1753–83. But the reference to America also suggests the American West Indies, where Nathaniel Gilbert had pioneered in 1760 and where Thomas Coke had carried the work forward in 1786.

[29] In Wesley's personal copy of *AM*, this phrase, 'yea, by myriads', has been crossed out—another instance, one supposes, of Wesley's instinct for compression.

[30] Mark 8:38.

[31] See Matt. 6:22. Cf. No. 31, 'Sermon on the Mount, XI', III.4 and n.

[32] See Matt. 6:23. Cf. No. 125, 'On a Single Eye', on this text.

really the case. They are full of pride; they think of themselves far more highly than they ought to think.[33] They are vain; they 'seek honour one of another, and not the honour that cometh of God only'.[34] They cherish hatred and malice in their hearts: they give
5 place to anger, to envy, to revenge. They return evil for evil, and railing for railing.[35] Instead of overcoming evil with good,[36] they make no scruple of demanding an eye for an eye, and a tooth for a tooth.[37] They 'savour not the things that are of God, but the things that are of men'.[38] They set their affections, not on things above,
10 but on things that are of the earth.[39] They 'love the creature more than the Creator':[40] they are 'lovers of pleasure more than lovers of God'.[41] How then should they discern the signs of the times? The god of this world whom they serve has blinded their hearts,[42] and covered their minds with a veil of thick darkness. Alas! What
15 have these 'souls of flesh and blood' (as one speaks)[43] to do with God or the things of God?

6. St. John assigns this very reason for the Jews not understanding the things of God, namely, that in consequence of their preceding sins and wilful[44] rejecting the light, God had now
20 delivered them up to Satan, who had blinded them past recovery. Over and over, when they might have seen they would not; they shut their eyes against the light. And now they cannot see, God having given them up to an undiscerning mind; therefore they do not believe because of the reason given in that saying of Isaiah,[45]
25 'He hath blinded their eyes, and hardened their hearts; that they should not see with their eyes, nor understand with their hearts, and be converted, and I should heal them.'[46] The plain meaning

---

[33] See Rom. 12:3.
[34] Cf. John 5:44.
[35] See 1 Pet. 3:9.
[36] See Rom. 12:21.
[37] Matt. 5:38.
[38] Cf. Mark 8:33.
[39] See Col. 3:2.
[40] Cf. Rom. 1:25.
[41] 2 Tim. 3:4.
[42] See 2 Cor. 4:4.

[43] This may be a garbled echo from Law's *Spirit of Prayer* (*Works*, VII. 76); cf. Wesley's long 'open letter' to Law, Jan. 6, 1756: 'That angels have bodies you affirm elsewhere. But are you sure they have flesh and blood? Are not angels spirits? And surely a spirit hath not flesh and blood.' Cf. No. 124, 'Human Life a Dream', §7, where Wesley speaks of 'eyes of flesh and blood' and where the term, 'eyes', connotes the immaterial self.

[44] Actually an adverbial usage, as in Shakespeare's *Winter's Tale*, I. ii. 255: 'If ever I were wilful negligent'.

[45] In both published texts this passage reads: 'therefore they do not believe because that Isaiah said (that is, because of the reason given in that saying of Isaiah)'. This is obviously awkward; one may suppose that the proofreader failed to realize that the parenthesis was actually an emendation and not an addition.

[46] John 12:40, alluding to Isa. 6:10.

is, not that God did this by his own immediate power—it would be flat blasphemy to say that God in this sense hardens any man—but his Spirit strives with them no longer, and then Satan hardens them effectually.

7. And as it was with them in ancient times, so it is with the present generation. Thousands of those who bear the name of Christ are now given up to an undiscerning mind. The god of this world hath so blinded their eyes that the light cannot shine upon them,[47] so that they can no more discern the signs of the times than the Pharisees and Sadducees could of old. A wonderful instance of this spiritual blindness, this total inability to discern the signs of the times mentioned in Scripture, is given us in the very celebrated work of a late eminent writer, who supposes 'the new Jerusalem came down from heaven'[48] when Constantine the Great called himself a Christian.[49] I say, 'called himself a Christian'; for I dare not affirm that *he was one*, any more than Peter the Great.[50] I cannot but believe he would have come nearer the mark if he had said, that was the time when a huge cloud of infernal brimstone and smoke came up from the bottomless pit.[51] For surely there never was a time wherein Satan gained so fatal an advantage over the church of Christ as when such a flood of riches, and honour, and power broke in upon it, particularly on the clergy.[52]

8. By the same rule, what signs would this writer have expected of the approaching conversion of the heathens? He would doubtless have expected a hero, like Charles of Sweden,[53] or

---

[47] See 2 Cor. 4:4.

[48] Cf. Rev. 21:2, 10.

[49] Bishop Thomas Newton. See No. 61, 'The Mystery of Iniquity', §27 and n.

[50] In JWJ, Jan. 30, 1756, Wesley had voiced his doubt that Peter the Great was a Christian: 'Undoubtedly, he was a soldier, a general, and a statesman scarce inferior to any. But why was he called a Christian? What has Christianity to do either with deep dissimulation or savage cruelty?' The probable source of Wesley's main knowledge of Peter the Great was Alexander Gordon's two-volume *History of Peter the Great* (1755), together with John Banks's *History of the Life and Reign of. . . Peter the Great* (1740), both of which Wesley had read. Peter had been a favourite subject for English biographers in the eighteenth century. Daniel Defoe in 1723 and John Mottley in 1739 had also published histories of his life.

[51] See Rev. 9:11; 20:1. Cf. also No. 32, 'Sermon on the Mount, XII', I.7 and n.

[52] For other references to the church as a 'mixed society', see No. 104, 'On Attending the Church Service', §13 and n.

[53] Charles XII (1682–1718), one of Sweden's great warrior heroes, whose untimely death at Frederickshall is cited by way of illustration in No. 124, 'Human Life a Dream', §9.

Frederick of Prussia,[54] to carry fire, and sword, and Christianity through whole nations at once. And it cannot be denied that since the time of Constantine many nations have been converted in this way. But could it be said concerning such conversions as these,

5 'The kingdom of heaven cometh not with observation'?[55] Surely everyone must observe a warrior rushing through the land at the head of fifty or sixty thousand men! But is this the way of spreading Christianity which the author of it, the Prince of Peace,[56] has chosen? Nay, it is not in this manner that a grain of

10 mustard seed grows up into a great tree.[57] It is not thus that 'a little leaven leavens the whole lump.'[58] Rather, it spreads by degrees farther and farther, till the whole is leavened. We may form a judgment of what will be hereafter by what we have seen already. And this is the way wherein true Christian religion, the faith that

15 worketh by love,[59] has been spreading, particularly through Great Britain and its dependencies, for half a century.

9. In the same manner it continues to spread at the present time also, as may easily appear to all those whose eyes are not blinded. All those that experience in their own hearts the power of God

20 unto salvation[60] will readily perceive how the same religion which they enjoy is still spreading from heart to heart. They take knowledge of the same grace of God, strongly and sweetly[61] working on every side; and rejoice to find another and another sinner, first inquiring, 'What must I do to be saved?'[62] and then

25 testifying, 'My soul doth magnify the Lord, and my spirit doth rejoice in God my Saviour.'[63] Upon a fair and candid inquiry they find more and more, not only of those who had some form of religion, but of those who had no form at all, who were profligate, abandoned sinners, now entirely changed, truly fearing God and

30 working righteousness.[64] They observe more and more, even of

---

[54] Frederick II ('the Great') of Prussia (1712–86), whose 'infernal subtlety' (despite his genius) had lately been commented on by Wesley in JWJ, Aug. 26, 1784; see also Dec. 10, 1787, and May 7, 1789.

[55] Luke 17:20.

[56] Isa. 9:6.

[57] See Matt. 13:31-32.

[58] Cf. 1 Cor. 5:6; Gal. 5:9; also Matt. 13:33.

[59] See Gal. 5:6. Cf. No. 2, *The Almost Christian*, II.6 and n.

[60] Rom. 1:16.

[61] Cf. No. 15, *The Great Assize*, II.10 and n.

[62] Acts 16:30.

[63] Cf. Luke 1:46-47.

[64] See Acts 10:35.

these poor outcasts of men, who are inwardly and outwardly changed, loving God and their neighbour; living in the uniform practice of justice, mercy, and truth; as they have time, doing good to all men;[65] easy and happy in their lives, and triumphant in their death.   5

10. What excuse then have any that believe the Scriptures to be the Word of God for not discerning the signs of these times, as preparatory to the general call of the heathens? What could God have done which he hath not done[66] to convince you that the day is coming, that the time is at hand, when he will fulfil his glorious 10 promises; when he will arise to maintain his own cause, and to set up his kingdom over all the earth? What, indeed, unless he had *forced* you to believe? And this he could not do without destroying the nature which he had given you. For he made you free agents; having an inward power of self-determination, which is essential 15 to your nature. And he deals with you as free agents from first to last. As such, you may shut or open your eyes as you please. You have sufficient light shining all around you; yet you need not see it unless you will. But be assured God is not well-pleased with your shutting your eyes and then saying, 'I cannot see.' I counsel you to 20 bestow an impartial examination upon the whole affair. After a candid inquiry into matter of fact, consider deeply, 'What hath God wrought?'[67] 'Who hath seen such a thing? Who hath heard such a thing? Hath not a nation', as it were, been 'born in a day?'[68] How swift, as well as how deep, and how extensive a work has 25 been wrought in the present age! And certainly, 'not by might, neither by power, but by the Spirit of the Lord'.[69] For how utterly inadequate were the means! How insufficient were the instruments to work any such effect! At least those of which it has pleased God to make use of in the British dominions and in 30 America. By how unlikely instruments has God been pleased to work from the beginning! 'A few, young, raw heads!' said the Bishop of London, 'What can they pretend to do?'[70] They

---

[65] See Gal. 6:10. Notice, however, that Wesley has softened the Pauline 'as we have therefore *opportunity*' to 'as they have time'—a considerable difference.

[66] See Isa. 5:4; see also No. 107, 'On God's Vineyard', on this text.

[67] Num. 23:23, the text of Wesley's sermon (No. 112) on laying the foundation stone for the New Chapel, City Road, London, Apr. 21, 1777.

[68] Cf. Isa. 66:8.   [69] Cf. Zech. 4:6.

[70] Another blurred memory. What Gibson had asked in his *Observations* (see above, II.2) is as follows: 'Whether it does not savour of self-sufficiency and presumption, when a few young heads, without any colour of a divine commission, set up their own schemes as the

pretended to be *that* in the hand of God that a pen is in the hand of a man. They pretended (and do so at this day) to do the work whereunto they are sent; to do just what the Lord pleases. And if it be his pleasure to throw down the walls of Jericho, the
5 strongholds of Satan, not by the engines of war[71] but by the blasts of rams' horns,[72] who shall say unto him, 'What dost thou?'[73]

11. Meantime, 'Blessed are your eyes, for they see. [. . .] Many prophets and righteous men have desired to see the things you see, and have not seen them, and to hear the things that you hear,
10 and have not heard them.'[74] You see and acknowledge the day of your visitation—such a visitation as neither you nor your fathers had known. You may well say, 'This is the day which the Lord hath made; we will rejoice and be glad therein.'[75] You see the dawn of that glorious day whereof all the prophets have spoken.
15 And how shall you most effectually improve this day of your visitation?

12. The first point is—see that you yourselves receive not the blessing of God in vain. Begin at the root, if you have not already. Now repent and believe the gospel.[76] If you have believed, 'Look
20 to yourselves, that ye lose not what you have wrought, but that ye receive a full reward!'[77] 'Stir up the gift of God that is in you!'[78] 'Walk in the light, as he is in the light.'[79] And while you 'hold fast'[80] 'that which you have attained',[81] 'go on unto perfection.'[82] Yea, and when you are 'made perfect in love',[83] still, 'forgetting the

great standard of Christianity. And, how it can be reconciled to Christian humility, prudence, or charity, to indulge their own notions to such a degree as to perplex, unhinge, terrify, and distract the minds of multitudes of people, who have lived from their infancy under a gospel ministry, and in the regular exercise of a gospel worship; and all this, by persuading them that they have never yet heard the true Gospel, nor been instructed in the true way of salvation before; and that they neither are, nor can be true Christians, but by adhering to *their* doctrines and discipline, and embracing Christianity upon *their* schemes: All the while, for the sake of those schemes and in pursuance of them, violating the wholesome rules, which the powers spiritual and temporal have wisely and piously established, for the preservation of peace and order in the church.' Cf. No. 68, 'The Wisdom of God's Counsels', §21, where Wesley quotes Gibson more accurately. See Wesley's other account of the revival in A *Short History of the People Called Methodists*, §54, where he speaks of 'a handful of raw young men'. The added term 'raw' may have lodged in Wesley's memory from Robert South's contemptuous reference to the Commonwealth preachers as 'raw, unlearned, ill-bred persons'; cf. South, *Sermons* (1844), I.111.

[71] Ezek. 26:9.   [72] See Josh. 6:5.   [73] Cf. John 6:30.
[74] Cf. Matt. 13:16-17.   [75] Cf. Ps. 118:24.
[76] Mark 1:15.   [77] Cf. 2 John 8.
[78] Cf. 2 Tim. 1:6.   [79] 1 John 1:7.
[80] Heb. 3:6, etc.   [81] Cf. Phil. 3:12, 16; 1 Tim. 4:6.
[82] Heb. 6:1.   [83] 1 John 4:18.

things that are behind, press on to the mark for the prize of the high calling of God in Christ Jesus.'[84]

13. It behoves you in the next place to help your neighbours. 'Let your light so shine before men that they may see your good works, and glorify your Father which is in heaven.'[85] As you have time, do good unto all men, but especially unto them that are of the household of faith.[86] Proclaim the glad tidings of salvation ready to be revealed, not only to those of your own household, not only to your relations, friends, and acquaintance, but to all whom God providentially delivers into your hands. 'Ye', who already know in whom you have believed,[87] 'are the salt of the earth.'[88] Labour to season, with the knowledge and love of God, all that you have any intercourse with. 'Ye are a city set upon a hill;' ye 'cannot', ye ought not to 'be hid'.[89] 'Ye are the light of the world.' 'Men do not light a candle and put it under a bushel;' how much less the all-wise God. No, let it 'shine to all that are in the house',[90] all that are witnesses of your life and conversation. Above all, continue instant in prayer,[91] both for yourselves, for all the church of God, and for all the children of men, that they may remember themselves and be turned unto our God. That they likewise may enjoy the gospel blessing on earth, and the glory of God in heaven.

St. Helier, Isle of Jersey, Aug. 27, 1787[92]

---

[84] Cf. Phil. 3:13-14.
[85] Matt. 5:16.
[86] See Gal. 6:10; and n. 65, above.
[87] See 2 Tim. 1:12.
[88] Matt. 5:13.
[89] Cf. Matt. 5:14.
[90] Cf. Matt. 5:14-15.
[91] See Rom. 12:12.
[92] The place and date appear only in *AM* (1788), XI.178, with the spelling, 'St. Helliers'.

ON DIVINE PROVIDENCE

AN INTRODUCTORY COMMENT

Wesley placed this sermon as the first item in SOSO, *VI; it sums up his views on one of his favourite themes. From 1744 through 1785 he had used this present text (Luke 12:7) no fewer than forty-five times. Finally, in March 1786, he set down his thoughts in sermon form, as if in order to supply needed material for the* Arminian Magazine. *In any case, the sermon was published straightway (March and April) in Vol. IX.125-32, 185-93. Its only other publication in Wesley's lifetime was in* SOSO, *VI.3-27.*

Wesley had read David Hume's 'insolent book on miracles' (cf. JWJ, March 5, 1769; cf. also No. 10, 'Of Miracles', in Philosophical Essays Concerning Human Understanding, *1748) and was sufficiently incensed by its stringent denials of the* miracula *in general that, later, he would denounce Hume as 'the most insolent despiser of truth and virtue that ever appeared in the world' (JWJ, May 5, 1772). But, as this sermon will show (together with its notes on Wesley's sources), the force of Hume's destructive analysis, powerful as it was in later generations, never really registered on Wesley's mind. His arguments here, and the theological substance of the sermon, are in direct line with the classical Anglican statements of the doctrine of providence (e.g., Hooker, Pearson, Ussher). Special notice, however, might well be paid to John Wilkins,* Discourse Concerning the Beauty of Providence *(sixth edition 1680); there are resemblances between Wilkins and Wesley that are too obvious to be explained merely by reference to their shared tradition.*

On Divine Providence

Luke 12:7

Even the very hairs of your head are all numbered.

1. The doctrine of divine providence has been received[1] by wise men in all ages. It was believed by many of the eminent heathens, not only philosophers, but orators and poets. Innumerable are the testimonies concerning it which are scattered up and down in their writings; agreeable to that well-known saying in Cicero, *deorum moderamine cuncta geri*,[2] that all things, all events in the[3] world, are under the management of God. We might bring a cloud of witnesses to confirm this, were any so hardy as to deny it.

2. The same truth is acknowledged at this day in most parts of the world; yea, even in those nations which are so barbarous as not to know the use of letters. So when Paustoobee, an Indian chief of the Chickasaw nation in North America, was asked, 'Why do you think the Beloved Ones (so they term God) take care of *you?*' he answered without any hesitation, 'I was in the battle with the French, and the bullet went on this side, and the bullet went on that side; and this man died, and that man died; but I am alive still: and by this I know that the Beloved Ones take care of me.'[4]

3. But although the ancient as well as modern heathens had some conception of a divine providence, yet the conceptions which most of them entertained concerning it were dark, confused, and imperfect; yea, the accounts which the most enlightened among them gave were usually contradictory to each

---

[1] Orig., *AM* and *SOSO*, 'renewed', but altered by Wesley's MS annotations in *AM*.

[2] Cf. *De Natura Deorum (On the Nature of the Gods)*, II. xxx. 75; see also Apuleius, *De Mundo*, 30. See No. 69, 'The Imperfection of Human Knowledge', II.2. Wesley's quotation is not really close to Cicero's own text; had he picked it up as an aphorism of the schools? He repeats another version of it in *An Estimate of the Manners of the Present Times*, §13, and translates it 'the providence of God directs all things' (cf. *Bibliog*, No. 426; Vol. 15 of this edn.).

[3] Orig., *AM* and *SOSO*, 'this', altered by Wesley's MS annotations in *AM*.

[4] This interview with Paustoobee by the Wesleys and the Moravians is reported in *Gent's Mag.*, May 1737; and also in *JWJ*, July 20, 1736 (with the usual discrepancies in details). Both accounts associate 'Beloved Ones' with 'four beloved things above: the clouds, the sun, the clear sky, and He that lives in the clear sky'.

other. Add to this that they were by no means assured of the truth
of those very accounts. They hardly dared to affirm anything, but
spoke with the utmost caution and diffidence. Insomuch that
what Cicero himself, the author of that noble declaration,
5 ventures to affirm in cool blood at the end of his long dispute
upon the subject, amounts to no more than this lame and
impotent conclusion, *Mihi verisimilior videbatur Cottae oratio*—
'what Cotta said (the person that argued in the defence of the
being and providence of God) *seemed* to me *more probable* than
10 what his opponent had advanced to the contrary.'[5]

4. And it is no wonder. For only God himself can give a clear,
consistent, perfect account (that is, as perfect as our weak
understanding can receive in this our infant state of existence; or
at least, as is consistent with the designs of his government) of his
15 manner of governing the world. And this he hath done in his
written Word: all the oracles of God,[6] all the Scriptures both of
the Old Testament and the New describe so many scenes of
divine providence. It is the beautiful remark of a fine writer:
'Those who object to the Old Testament, in particular, that it is
20 not a connected history of nations, but only a congeries of broken
unconnected events, do not observe the nature and design of
these writings. They do not see that Scripture is *the history of
God.*'[7] Those who bear this upon their minds will easily perceive
that the inspired writers never lose sight of it, but preserve one
25 unbroken, connected chain, from the beginning to the end. All
over that wonderful book, as 'life and immortality' (immortal life)
is gradually 'brought to light',[8] so is 'Immanuel, God with us',[9]
and his kingdom ruling over all.

5. In the verses preceding the text our Lord has been arming
30 his disciples against the fear of man. 'Be not afraid (says he, verse

[5] Cf. Cicero, *De Natura Deorum (Of the Nature of the Gods)*, III. xl. 95: '*Haec cum essent dicta, ita discessimus ut Velleio Cottae disputatio verior, mihi Balbi ad veritatis similitudinem videretur esse propensior*' ('Here the conversation ended, and we parted, Velleius thinking Cotta's discourse to be the truer, while I felt that that of Balbus approximated more nearly to a semblance of the truth').

[6] Cf. No. 5, 'Justification by Faith', §2 and n.

[7] This idea, though not the phrase itself, informs the whole of Jonathan Edwards, *A History of the Work of Redemption;* cf. espec. X.v.436-38. The idea was one of the premises of the 'federal theology' of Johann Cocceius that had influenced both Edwards and Wesley; cf. his *Summa doctrinae de Foedere et Testamento Dei* (1648). See also No. 58, *On Predestination*, §4.

[8] Cf. 2 Tim. 1:10.

[9] Matt. 1:23; note Wesley's use of Isaiah's spelling of Immanuel rather than Matthew's.

4) of them that can kill the body, and after [that] have no more that they can do.' He guards them against this fear, first, by reminding them of what was infinitely more terrible than anything which man could inflict: 'fear him who after he hath killed hath power to cast into hell.'[10] He guards them farther against it by the 5 consideration of an overruling providence. 'Are not five sparrows sold for two farthings? And not one of them is forgotten before God.'[11] Or, as the words are repeated by St. Matthew with a very inconsiderable variation, 'Not one of them shall fall to the ground without your Father. But even the very hairs of your head are all 10 numbered.'[a]

6. We must indeed observe that this strong expression, though repeated by both the Evangelists, need not imply (though if anyone thinks it does he may think so very innocently) that God does literally number all the hairs that are on the heads of all his 15 creatures. But it is a proverbial expression, implying that nothing is so small or insignificant in the sight of men as not to be an object of the care and providence of God, before whom nothing is small that concerns the happiness of any of his creatures.

7. There is scarce any doctrine in the whole compass of 20 revelation which is of deeper importance than this. And at the same time there is scarce any that is so little regarded, and perhaps so little understood. Let us endeavour, then, with the assistance of God, to examine it to the bottom, to see upon what foundation it stands, and what it properly implies. 25

8. The eternal, almighty, all-wise, all-gracious God, is the Creator of heaven and earth. He called out of nothing by his all-powerful word the whole universe, all that is.[12] 'Thus the heavens and the earth were created, and all the hosts of them.'[13] And after he had set all things else in array, the plants after their 30 kinds, fish and fowl, beasts and reptiles, after their kinds, 'he created man after his own image.'[14] And the Lord saw that every

---

[a] Matt. 10:29, 30.

---

[10] Luke 12:5.
[11] Luke 12:6.
[12] For a very earnest argument in favour of the doctrine of the *creatio de nihilo*, cf. Arthur Collier, *Clavis Universalis: Or a New Inquiry After Truth. Being a Demonstration of the Non-Existence, or Impossibility of an External World* (1713); Collier was a disciple of Berkeley and a source for Wesley. See No. 15, *The Great Assize*, III.3 and n.
[13] Cf. Gen. 2:1.
[14] Cf. Gen. 1:27.

distinct part of the universe was good. But when he saw everything he had made, all in connection with each other, 'behold it was very good.'[15]

9. And as this all-wise, all-gracious Being created all things, so
5 he sustains all things. He is the preserver as well as the creator of everything that exists. 'He upholdeth all things by the word of his power,'[16] that is, by his powerful word. Now it must be that he knows everything he has made, and everything he preserves from moment to moment. Otherwise he could not preserve it: he could
10 not continue to it the being which he has given it. And it is nothing strange that he who is omnipresent, who 'filleth heaven and earth',[17] who is in every place, should see what is in every place, where he is intimately present. If the eye of man discerns things at a small distance, the eye of an eagle what is at a greater, the eye of
15 an angel what is at a thousand times greater distance (perhaps taking in the surface of the earth at one view) how shall not the eye of God see everything through the whole extent of creation? Especially considering that nothing is distant from him, in whom we all 'live and move and have our being'.[18]
20 10. It is true our narrow understandings but imperfectly comprehend this. But whether we comprehend it or no, we are certain that so it is. As certain as it is that he created all things, and that he still sustains all that he has created, so certain it is that he is present at all times, in all places; that he is above, beneath; that he
25 'besets us behind and before', and as it were 'lays his hand upon us'. We allow, 'such knowledge is too high and wonderful for us; we cannot attain unto it.'[19] The manner of his presence no man can explain, nor probably any angel in heaven. Perhaps what the ancient philosopher speaks of the soul in regard to its residence in
30 the body, that it is *tota in toto, et tota in qualibet parte,*[20] might in some sense be spoken of the omnipresent Spirit in regard to the universe—that he is not only 'all in the whole, but all in every

---

[15] Gen. 1:31.   [16] Cf. Heb. 1:3.
[17] Cf. Jer. 23:24. See No. 118, 'On the Omnipresence of God'.
[18] Acts 17:28.
[19] Cf. Ps. 139:5-6 (AV).
[20] A Latin translation of Plotinus, *Enneads*, IV. ii.1. Cf. Stephen MacKenna's Eng. tr. (Boston, Mass., Charles T. Branford Company, 1916), II. 4: '[The soul] does not consist of separate sections; its divisibility lies in its presence at every point in the recipient, but it is indivisible as dwelling *entire in the total and entire in every part*' (italics added). See also Nos. 69, 'The Imperfection of Human Knowledge', I.13; and 116, 'What is Man? Ps. 8:4', §6.

part'. Be this as it may, it cannot be doubted but he sees every atom of his creation, and that a thousand times more clearly than we see the things that are close to us: even of these we see only the surface, while he sees the inmost essence of everything.

11. The omnipresent God sees and knows all the properties of all the beings that he hath made. He knows all the connections, dependencies, and relations, and all the ways wherein one of them can affect another. In particular he sees[21] all the inanimate parts of the creation, whether in heaven above or in the earth beneath. He knows how the stars, comets, or planets above influence the inhabitants of the earth beneath; what influence the lower heavens, with their magazines of fire, hail, snow, and vapours, winds and storms, have on our planet. And what effects may be produced in the bowels of the earth by fire, air, or water; what exhalations may be raised therefrom, and what changes wrought thereby; what effects every mineral or vegetable may have upon the children of men: all these lie naked and open to the eye of the Creator and Preserver of the universe.

12. He knows all the animals in this lower world, whether beasts, birds, fishes, reptiles, or insects. He knows all the qualities and powers he hath given them, from the highest to the lowest. He knows every good angel and every evil angel in every part of his dominions; and looks from heaven upon the children of men over the whole face of the earth.

He knows all the hearts of the sons of men, and understands all their thoughts. He sees what any angel, any devil, any man, either thinks, or speaks, or does; yea, and all they feel. He sees all their sufferings, with every circumstance of them.

13. And is the Creator and Preserver of the world unconcerned for what he sees therein? Does he look upon these things either with a malignant or heedless eye? Is he an Epicurean god? Does he sit at ease in the heaven, without regarding the poor inhabitants of earth? It cannot be. He hath made us, not we ourselves;[22] and he cannot despise the work of his own hands.[23] We are his children. And can a mother forget the children of her womb? Yea, she may forget; yet will not God forget us.[24] On the contrary, he hath expressly declared that as his 'eyes are over all

---

[21] *AM* and *SOSO,* 'saw', altered only in Wesley's MS annotations to *AM.*
[22] See Ps. 100:3 (AV).
[23] See Job 10:3.
[24] See Isa. 49:15.

the earth';[25] so he 'is loving to every man, and his mercy is over all his works'.[26] Consequently he is concerned every moment for what befalls every creature upon earth; and more especially for everything that befalls any of the children of men. It is hard
5 indeed to comprehend this; nay, it is hard to believe it, considering the complicated wickedness and the complicated misery which we see on every side. But believe it we must unless we will make God a liar, although it is sure no man can comprehend it. It behoves us then to humble ourselves before
10 God, and to acknowledge our ignorance. Indeed how can we expect that a man should be able to comprehend the ways of God? Can a worm comprehend a worm? How much less can it be supposed that a man can comprehend God!

For how can finite measure Infinite?[27]

15   14. He is infinite in wisdom as well as in power; and all his wisdom is continually employed in managing all the affairs of his creation for the good of all his creatures. For his wisdom and goodness go hand in hand; they are inseparably united, and continually act in concert with almighty power for the real good of
20 all his creatures. His power, being equal to his wisdom and goodness, continually co-operates with them. And to him all things are possible. He doth whatsoever pleaseth him, in heaven and earth, and in the sea and all deep places. And we cannot doubt of his exerting all his power, as in sustaining, so in
25 governing all that he has made.
     15. Only he that can do all things else cannot deny himself; he cannot counteract himself, or oppose his own work. Were it not for this he would destroy all sin, with its attendant pain, in a moment. He would abolish wickedness out of his whole creation,
30 and suffer no trace of it to remain. But in so doing he would counteract himself, he would altogether overturn his own work, and undo all that he has been doing since he created man upon the earth. For he created man in his own image:[28] a spirit, like himself; a spirit endued with understanding, with will, or

---

[25] Cf. Pss. 34:15; 83:18 (BCP).   [26] Ps. 145:9 (BCP).
     [27] Nathaniel Lee and John Dryden, *Oedipus, A Tragedy*, III. i. 240: 'But how can Finite measure Infinite?' See also, Dryden, 'The Hind and the Panther' i.105: 'But how can finite grasp Infinity?' See also Nos. 142, 'The Wisdom of Winning Souls', I; and 103, 'What is Man? Ps. 8:3-4', I.6.
     [28] Gen. 1:27.

affections, and liberty—without which neither his understanding nor his affections could have been of any use, neither would he have been capable either of vice or virtue. He could not be a moral agent, any more than a tree or a stone. If therefore God were thus to exert his power there would certainly be no more vice; but it is 5 equally certain, neither could there be any virtue in the world. Were human liberty taken away men would be as incapable of virtue as stones.[29] Therefore (with reverence be it spoken) the Almighty himself cannot do this thing. He cannot thus contradict himself, or undo what he has done. He cannot destroy out of the 10 soul of man that image of himself wherein he made him. And without doing this he cannot abolish sin and pain out of the world. But were it to be done it would imply no wisdom at all, but barely a stroke of omnipotence. Whereas all the manifold wisdom of God (as well as all his power and goodness) is displayed in 15 governing man as man; not as a stock or a stone, but as an intelligent and free spirit, capable of choosing either good or evil. Herein appears the depth of the wisdom of God in his adorable providence! In governing men so as not to destroy either their understanding, will, or liberty! He commands all things both in 20 heaven and earth to assist man in attaining the end of his being, in working out his own salvation—so far as it can be done without compulsion, without overruling his liberty. An attentive inquirer may easily discern, the whole frame of divine providence is so constituted as to afford man every possible help, in order to his 25 doing good and eschewing evil, which can be done without turning man into a machine; without making him incapable of virtue or vice, reward or punishment.

16. Meantime it has been remarked by a pious writer[30] that there is (as he expresses it) a threefold circle of divine providence 30

---

[29] One of Wesley's unvarying theses; cf. No. 60, 'The General Deliverance', I.4 and n.

[30] Cf. Thomas Crane, *Isagoge ad Dei Providentiam, Or a Prospect of Divine Providence* (1672), Observation XXIV. i. 271-72: '(1) There is the outermost circle of common or general providence: here all men . . . may be placed (Matt. 5:45; Acts 14:17); (2) There is an intermediate circle of special or limited providence, which respects members in common of the visible Church. Unto the Jews were committed the oracles of God (Rom. 3:2); they are called the children of the kingdom, inasmuch as God honoured them with his worship and ordinances (Matt. 8:12); (3) There is the inmost circle of peculiar and singular providence. In this circle are the elect of God, and called of him in Christ Jesus. The former [is] of larger circumference that this latter (Matt. 22:14). . . . Quarrel not with God because all are not within the inmost circle of providence. . . .'

Wesley extracted this for the *Christian Lib.* XXXVIII.184-86 (Observation XIII). The idea is repeated in No. 77, 'Spiritual Worship', I. 9. But see also Stephen Charnock, *Works*

over and above that which presides over the whole universe. We do not now speak of that overruling hand which governs the inanimate creation; which sustains the sun, moon, and stars in their stations, and guides their motions; we do not refer to his care
5 of the animal creation, every part of which we know is under his government who 'giveth food unto the cattle, and feedeth the young ravens that call upon him'[31]—but we here speak of that superintending providence which regards the children of men. Each of these is easily distinguished from the others by those who
10 accurately observe the ways of God. The outermost circle includes the whole race of mankind, all the descendants of Adam, all the human creatures that are dispersed over the face of the earth. This comprises not only the Christian world, those that name the name of Christ,[32] but the Mahometans also, who
15 considerably outnumber even the nominal Christians; yea, and the heathens likewise, who very far outnumber the Mahometans and Christians put together. 'Is he the God of the Jews', says the Apostle, 'and not of the Gentiles also?'[33] And so we may say, Is he the God of the Christians, and not of the Mahometans and
20 heathens also? Yea, doubtless of the Mahometans and heathens also. His love is not confined: 'The Lord is loving unto every man, and his mercy is over all his works.'[34] He careth for the very outcasts of men: it may truly be said,

> Free as the air thy bounty streams
25 > O'er all thy works: thy mercies' beams
> Diffusive as thy sun's arise.[35]

17. Yet it may be admitted that he takes more immediate care of those that are comprised in the second, the smaller circle, which

(1684), I. 696, where God's dominion is spoken of as 'threefold': (1) over all creatures; (2) over the church as in the Covenant of Grace; (3) over the blessed and, negatively, the damned.

[31] Cf. Ps. 147:9 (BCP).
[32] See 2 Tim. 2:19. Wesley is relying on the demography of Edward Brerewood; see No. 63, 'The General Spread of the Gospel', §1 and n.
[33] Cf. Rom. 3:29.
[34] Ps. 145:9 (BCP).
[35] John and Charles Wesley, *Hymns and Sacred Poems* (1739), p. 160, a translation (almost certainly by John Wesley) from the German of J. A. Scheffler:

> Yet free as air thy bounty streams
> On all thy works; thy mercy's beams,
> Diffusive as thy sun's, arise.

(Cf. *Poet. Wks.*, I.142.)

includes all that are called Christians, all that profess to believe in Christ. We may reasonably think that these in some degree honour him, at least more than the heathens do. God does likewise in some measure honour them, and has a nearer concern for them. By many instances it appears that the prince of this 5 world has not so full power over these as over the heathens. The God whom they even profess to serve does in some measure maintain his own cause. So that the spirits of darkness do not reign so uncontrolled over them as they do over the heathen world. 10

18. Within the third, the innermost circle, are contained only the real Christians, those that worship God, not in form only, but in spirit and in truth.[36] Herein are comprised all that love God, or at least truly fear God and work righteousness,[37] all in whom is the mind which was in Christ,[38] and who walk as Christ also walked.[39] 15 The words of our Lord above recited peculiarly refer to these. It is to these in particular that he says, 'Even the very hairs of your head are all numbered.' He sees their souls and their bodies: he takes particular notice of all their tempers, desires, and thoughts, all their words and actions. He marks all their sufferings, inward 20 and outward, and the source whence they arise; so that we may well say,

> Thou know'st the pains thy servants feel,
> Thou hear'st thy children's cry;
> And their best wishes to fulfil, 25
> Thy grace is ever nigh.[40]

Nothing relative to these is too great, nothing too little, for his attention. He has his eye continually, as upon every individual person that is a member of this his family, so upon every circumstance that relates either to their souls or bodies, either to 30 their inward or outward state, wherein either their present or eternal happiness is in any degree concerned.

19. But what say the wise men of the world to this? They answer with all readiness, 'Who doubts of this? We are not

[36] John 4:23-24.
[37] See Acts 10:35.
[38] See Phil. 2:5.
[39] See 1 John 2:6.
[40] Cf. Watts, *The Psalms of David*, Ps. 145:14, 17, etc., Pt. 3, st. 4. See also *A Collection of Psalms and Hymns* (London, 1741) p. 88.

atheists. We all acknowledge a providence. That is, a general providence, for indeed the particular providence of which some talk, we know not what to make of.[41] Surely the little affairs of men are far beneath the regard of the great Creator and Governor of
5 the universe! Accordingly,

> He sees with equal eyes, as Lord of all,
> A hero perish, or a sparrow fall.'[42]

Does he indeed? I cannot think it; because (whatever that fine poet did, or his patron, whom he so deeply despised and yet
10 grossly flattered)[43] I believe the Bible; wherein the Creator and Governor of the world himself tells me quite the contrary. That he has a tender regard for the brute creatures I know: he does in a measure 'take care for oxen';[44] 'he provideth food for the cattle,'[45] as well as 'herbs for the use of men'.[46] 'The lions roaring after
15 their prey do seek their meat from God.'[47] 'He openeth his hand and filleth all things living with plenteousness.'[48]

> The various troops of sea and land
> In sense of common want agree:
> All wait on thy dispensing hand,
20 > And have their daily alms from thee.
> They gather what thy stores disperse,
> Without their trouble to provide,
> Thou op'st thy hand: the universe,
> The craving world is all supplied.[49]

25 Our heavenly Father 'feedeth the fowls of the air'.[50] But mark! 'Are not ye much better than they? Shall he not then much more feed you,'[51] who are pre-eminent by so much odds?[52] He does not

---

[41] *AM*, orig., 'of it', altered in Wesley's MS annotation.

[42] Pope, *Essay on Man*, i. 87-88. See No. 60, 'The General Deliverance', III.5 and n.

[43] Most probably Addison, whose favour greatly aided Pope's early rise to fame. In turn, Pope's praise of Addison's *Cato* was enthusiastic (at first); their friendship later foundered; cf. Leslie Stephen's account of this in *DNB*.

[44] 1 Cor. 9:9.   [45] Cf. Ps. 147:9 (BCP).   [46] Cf. Ps. 147:8 (BCP).
[47] Ps. 104:21 (BCP).   [48] Cf. Ps. 145:16 (BCP).

[49] Wesley implies in §20 that this is by 'the same elegant poet' as the quotation there, namely Pope. This is not the case; the source remains unidentified.

[50] Cf. Matt. 6:26.   [51] Matt. 6:26, 30.

[52] Orig., *AM* (1786), IX.188, 'who are pre-eminently so much odds'; the text here is Wesley's alteration in his own annotated copy, found also in *Sermons* (1788). Neither is altogether clear. It is possible that Wesley's MS may have read, 'who are pre-eminently so much [at] odds'—i.e., who are so very different? This would conform to a familiar current usage of 'at odds'; cf. *OED*.

in that sense look upon *you* and *them* 'with equal eyes', set you on a level with *them*. Least of all does he set you on a level with brutes in respect of life and death. 'Right precious in the sight of the Lord is the death of his saints.'[53] Do you really think the death of a sparrow is equally precious in his sight? He tells us, indeed, that 'not a sparrow falleth on the ground without your Father.'[54] But he asks at the same time, 'Are ye not of more value than many sparrows?'[55]

20. But in support of a general in contradistinction[56] to a particular providence the same elegant poet lays it down as an unquestionable maxim,

> the Universal Cause
> Acts not by partial, but by general laws—[57]

plainly meaning that he never deviates from those general laws in favour of any particular person. This is a common supposition, but which is altogether inconsistent with the whole tenor of Scripture. For if God never deviates from these general laws then there never was a miracle in the world, seeing every miracle is a deviation from the general laws of nature. Did the Almighty confine himself to these general laws when he divided the Red Sea?[58] When he commanded the waters to stand on a heap,[59] and make a way for his redeemed to pass over? Did he act by general laws when he caused the sun to stand still for the space of a whole day?[60] No, nor in any of the miracles which are recorded either in the Old or New Testament.

21. But it is on supposition that the Governor of the world never deviates from those general laws that Mr. Pope adds those beautiful lines in full triumph, as having now clearly gained the point:

---

[53] Ps. 116:13 (BCP); and Ps. 116:15 (AV); a conflation.
[54] Cf. Matt. 10:29.
[55] Cf. Matt. 10:31.
[56] Orig., *AM* and *SOSO*, 'contradiction', altered in Wesley's MS annotations to *AM*.
[57] Pope, *Essay on Man*, iv. 35-36. Cf. Wesley, *A Collection of Moral and Sacred Poems* (1744), I.336, where he adds a footnote to the couplet: 'God governs by *general*, not *particular*, laws; intends happiness to be *equal*, and to be so it must be *social*, since all particular happiness depends on general.' Cf. also below, §29.
[58] Cf. Exod. 14:21.
[59] See Ps. 78:14 (BCP).
[60] Cf. Josh. 10:12-13.

> Shall burning Etna, if a sage requires,
> Forget to thunder and recall her fires?
> On air or sea new motions be impressed,
> O blameless Bethel! to relieve thy breast?
> 5 When the loose mountain trembles from on high,
> Shall gravitation cease, if you go by?
> Or some old temple, nodding to its fall,
> For Chartres' head reserve the hanging wall?[61]

We answer: if it please God to continue the life of any of his
10 servants he will suspend that or any other law of nature. The
stone shall not fall, the fire shall not burn, the floods shall not
flow. Or he will give his angels charge, and in their hands shall
they bear him up,[62] through and above all dangers.

22. Admitting then that in the common course of nature God
15 does act by general laws, he has never precluded himself from
making exceptions to them whensoever he pleases; either by
suspending that law in favour of those that love him, or by
employing his mighty angels: by either of which means he can
deliver out of all danger them that trust in him.

20 'What! You expect miracles, then!' Certainly I do, if I believe
the Bible. For the Bible teaches me that God hears and answers
prayer. But every answer to prayer is properly a miracle. For if
natural causes take their course, if things go on in their natural
way, it is no answer at all. Gravitation therefore shall cease, that is,
25 cease to operate, whenever the Author of it pleases. Cannot the
men of the world understand these things? That is no wonder: it
was observed long ago, 'An unwise man doth not consider this,
and a fool doth not understand it.'[63]

23. But I have not done with this same *general providence* yet. By
30 the grace of God I will sift it to the bottom. And I hope to show it is
such stark, staring nonsense as every man of sense ought to be
utterly ashamed of.

You say, 'You allow a *general* providence, but deny a *particular*
one.'[64] And what is a general (of whatever kind it be) that includes

---

[61] Pope, *Essay on Man*, iv.123-30. Cf. Wesley's extract in his *Collection of Moral and Sacred Poems* (1744), I.338, from which this particular passage is omitted.

[62] See Ps. 91:11-12; Matt. 4:6; Luke 4:10-11.   [63] Ps. 92:6 (BCP).

[64] Cf. No. 37, 'The Nature of Enthusiasm', §28, where Wesley also discusses 'general' and 'particular' providence; and No. 23, 'Sermon on the Mount, III', III.5 (for a summary of Wesley's doctrine of special providence); see also No. 41, *Wandering Thoughts*, III.1; *An Estimate of the Manners of the Present Times*, §13. Cf. Thomas Crane, *op. cit.*, in §16 above, as well as Bishop John Wilkins's Sermon on Eccles. 3:11, *Discourse Concerning the Beauty of Providence.*

no particulars? Is not every general necessarily made up of its several particulars? Can you instance in any general that is not? Tell me any genus, if you can, that contains no species. What is it that constitutes a genus but so many species added together?[65] What, I pray, is a 'whole that contains no parts'? Mere nonsense 5 and contradiction! Every whole must in the nature of things be made up of its several parts; insomuch that if there be no parts there can be no whole.

24. As this is a point of the utmost importance we may consider it a little farther. What do you mean by a general providence 10 contradistinguished from a particular? Do you mean a providence which superintends only the larger parts of the universe? Suppose the sun, moon, and stars. Does it not regard the earth too? You allow it does. But does it not likewise regard the inhabitants of it? Else what doth the earth, an inanimate lump of matter, signify? Is 15 not one spirit, one heir of immortality, of more value than all the earth? Yea, though you add to it[66] the sun, moon, and stars? Nay, and the whole inanimate creation? Might we not say, 'These shall perish, but this remaineth; these all shall wax old as doth a garment;' but this (it may be said in a lower sense even of the 20 creature) 'is the same, and his years shall not fail'.[67]

25. Or do you mean when you assert a general providence distinct from a particular one that God regards only some parts of the world, and does not regard others? What parts of it does he regard? Those without, or those within, the solar system? Or does 25 he regard some parts of the earth and not others? Which parts? Only those within the temperate zones? What parts then are under the care of his providence? Where will you lay the line? Do you exclude from it those that live in the torrid zone? Or those that dwell within the Arctic Circles? Nay, rather say, 'The Lord is 30 loving to every man,' and his care is 'over all his works'.[68]

26. Do you mean (for we would fain find out your meaning, if you have any meaning at all) that the providence of God does indeed extend to all parts of the earth with regard to great and singular events, such as the rise and fall of empires; but that the 35

---

[65] Cf. the definitions of 'genus' and 'species' in Wesley's *Compendium of Logic* (1750), ch. 1, sect. v. (*Bibliog*, No. 186; Vol. 15 of this edn.).

[66] *AM*, orig., 'you add these to', and his MS annotation 'you add to these', finally altered in *SOSO*.

[67] Cf. Heb. 1:11-12, quoting Ps. 102:26-27.

[68] Cf. Ps. 145:9 (BCP).

little concerns of this or that man are beneath the notice of the Almighty? Then you do not consider that 'great' and 'little' are merely relative terms, which have place only with respect to men? With regard to the Most High, man and all the concerns of men
5 are nothing, less than nothing before him. And nothing is 'small' in his sight that in any degree affects[69] the welfare of any that fear God and work righteousness.[70] What becomes then of your general providence, exclusive of a particular? Let it be for ever rejected by all rational men as absurd, self-contradictory
10 nonsense. We may then sum up the whole scriptural doctrine of providence in that fine saying of St. Austin, *Ita praesides singulis sicut universis, et universis sicut singulis!* [71]

> Father, how wide thy glories shine!
> Lord of the universe—and mine.
15 > Thy goodness watches o'er the whole,
> As all the world were but one soul;
> Yet keeps my every sacred hair,
> As I remained thy single care.[72]

27. We may learn from this short view of the providence of
20 God, first, to put our whole trust in him who hath never failed them that seek him. Our blessed Lord himself makes this very use of the great truth now before us. 'Fear not, therefore'[73]—if you truly fear God you need fear none beside. He will be a strong tower to all that trust in him, from the face of your enemies. What
25 is there either in heaven or in earth that can harm you while you are under the care of the Creator and Governor of heaven and earth? Let all earth and all hell combine against you—yea, the whole animate and inanimate creation—they cannot harm while God is on your side; his favourable kindness covers you 'as a
30 shield'![74]

28. Nearly allied to this confidence in God is the thankfulness we owe for his kind protection. Let those give thanks whom the Lord thus delivers from the hand of all their enemies. What an

---

[69] Orig., *AM*, 'And nothing is "small" in his sight, not in any degree affects', to which in his MS annotations he added 'which' before 'affects'. The orig. text was altered in *SOSO*, however, by changing 'not' to 'that'—probably a closer approximation to the misread orig. MS.
[70] See Acts 10:35.
[71] Cf. Augustine, *Confessions*, III. xi; see No. 37, 'The Nature of Enthusiasm', n. 45.
[72] Charles Wesley, *Scripture Hymns* (1762), II.158; see No. 54, 'On Eternity', §20 and n.
[73] Luke 12:7.
[74] Ps. 5:12 (AV); 5:13 (BCP).

unspeakable blessing it is to be the peculiar care of him that has all power in heaven and earth! How can we sufficiently praise him while we are under his wings, and 'his faithfulness and truth are our shield and buckler'![75]

29. But meantime we should take the utmost care to walk 5 humbly and closely with our God.[76] Walk humbly: for if you in any wise rob God of his honour, if you ascribe anything to yourself, the things which should have been for your wealth will prove to you 'an occasion of falling'.[77] And walk closely! See that you have 'a conscience void of offence toward God and toward man'.[78] It is 10 so long as you do this that you are the peculiar care of your Father which is in heaven. But let not the consciousness of his caring for you make you careless, indolent, or slothful: on the contrary, while you are penetrated with that deep truth, 'the help that is done upon earth, he doth it himself,'[79] be as earnest and diligent in 15 the use of all the means as if you were your own protector.

Lastly, in what a melancholy condition are those who do not believe there is any providence; or, which comes to exactly the same point, not a particular one! Whatever station they are in, as long as they are in the world they are exposed to numberless 20 dangers which no human wisdom can foresee, and no human power can resist. And there is no help! If they trust in men they find them 'deceitful upon the weights'.[80] In many cases they cannot help; in others they will not. But were they ever so willing, they will die: therefore vain is the help of man. And God is far 25 above, out of their sight: they expect no help from him. These modern (as well as the ancient) Epicureans have learnt that

the Universal Cause
Acts not by partial, but by general laws.[81]

He only takes care of the great globe itself, not of its puny 30 inhabitants. He heeds not how those

vagrant emmets crawl
At random on the air-suspended ball.[82]

[75] Cf. Ps. 91:4 (BCP).   [76] See Mic. 6:8.
[77] Ps. 69:23 (BCP).   [78] Acts 24:26.
[79] Ps. 74:13 (BCP). Cf. No. 71, 'Of Good Angels', II.9.
[80] Ps. 62:9 (BCP).
[81] Pope, *Essay on Man*, iv. 35-36; cf. §20, above.
[82] 'Emmets'—i.e., ants; see Young, *The Last Day*, ii. 219-20. This had been included in Wesley, *A Collection of Moral and Sacred Poems* (1744), II.80.

How uncomfortable is the situation of that man who has no farther hope than this! But on the other hand, how unspeakably 'happy' is the man 'that hath the Lord for his help, and whose hope is in the Lord his God'![83] Who can say, 'I have set the Lord 5 always before me: because he is on my right hand I shall not be moved.'[84] Therefore, 'though I walk through the valley of the shadow of death, I will fear no evil; for thou art with me; thy rod and thy staff, they comfort me.'[85]

Bristol, March 3, 1786[86]

---

[83] Cf. Ps. 146:5 (AV).
[84] Cf. Ps. 16:8 (AV).
[85] Ps. 23:4 (AV).
[86] Omitted from *SOSO*, VI.

THE WISDOM OF GOD'S COUNSELS

AN INTRODUCTORY COMMENT

The Journal *for April 1784 recounts Wesley's journeyings from London to Scotland by way of Chester, Liverpool, Manchester, Stockport, Carlisle. He was in Edinburgh on the 25th. The report also manages to reflect Wesley's mixed feelings about the uneven progress of the Revival, his alarm over various signs of weakened discipline within the Methodist ranks; cf. JWJ, April 5: 'We are labouring to secure the [Methodist] preaching-houses to the next generation! In the name of God, let us, if possible, secure the present generation from drawing back to perdition' (one of his favourite clichés in such warnings). There is no record in the* Journal *or the diary of his writing a sermon during this period but, according to his entry in the* Arminian Magazine *for August 1784 (VII.410), he finished one on Rom. 9:33 in Glasgow on April 28. It was a text from which he had not preached before, as far as our records go.*

As already in 'The Mystery of Iniquity' (see No. 61), he is here concerned with the vagaries of revivals as instruments of God's providence; this may account for this sermon's place in Wesley's revised order of SOSO, *VI—after 'On Divine Providence'. There is an asymmetry in its rhetorical form; its proem (§§1-7) takes a very broad view of God's wisdom at work in creation and history. Thereafter, the sermon descends quickly into a series of comments on the uneven course of church history in general, 'the deceitfulness of riches' (especially in the case of the Methodists), and the waning of their religious zeal. It was first published without a title in the* Arminian Magazine *for July and August (VII.346-52, 402-10); its present title was added in the collection of 1788 (VI.29-52). It was not published again in Wesley's lifetime, although he does mention preaching from Rom. 9:33 again on January 11, 1789.*

The Wisdom of God's Counsels

Romans 11:33

O the depth of the riches both of the wisdom and knowledge of God.

5   1. Some apprehend the 'wisdom' and the 'knowledge' of God to mean one and the same thing. Others believe that the wisdom of God more directly refers to his appointing the ends of all things, and his knowledge to the means which he hath prepared and made conducive to those ends. The former seems to be the
10 most natural explication; as the wisdom of God in its most extensive meaning must include the one as well as the other, the means as well as the ends.

  2. Now the wisdom, as well as the power of God, is abundantly manifested in his creation, in the formation and arrangement of
15 all his works, in heaven above and in the earth beneath; and in adapting them all to the several ends for which they were designed; insomuch that each of them apart from the rest is good, but all together are *very good;*[1] all conspiring together in one connected system,[2] to the glory of God in the happiness of his
20 intelligent creatures.

  3. As this wisdom appears even to short-sighted men (and much more to spirits of a higher order) in the creation and disposition of the whole universe, and every part of it, so it equally appears in their preservation, in his 'upholding all things by the
25 word of his power'.[3] And it no less eminently appears in the permanent government of all that he has created. How admirably does his wisdom direct the motions of the heavenly bodies! Of all the stars in the firmament, whether those that are *fixed* or those that *wander,* though never out of their several orbits![4] Of the sun
30 in the midst of heaven! Of those amazing bodies, the comets, that shoot in every direction through the immeasurable fields of ether! How does he superintend all the parts of this lower world, this

[1] Gen. 1:31.
[2] Cf. No. 56, 'God's Approbation of His Works', I.14 and n.
[3] Heb. 1:3.
[4] Cf. No. 56, 'God's Approbation of His Works', I.10 and n.

'speck of creation',[5] the earth! So that all things are still as they were at the beginning, 'beautiful in their seasons';[6] and summer and winter, seed-time and harvest, regularly follow each other. Yea, all things serve their Creator: 'fire and hail, snow and vapour, wind and storm, are fulfilling his word.'[7] So that we may 5 well say, 'O Lord, our Governor, how excellent is thy name in all the earth!'[8]

4. Equally conspicuous is the wisdom of God in the government of nations, of states and kingdoms; yea, rather more conspicuous—if infinite can be allowed to admit of any degrees. 10 For the whole inanimate creation, being totally passive and inert,[9] can make no opposition to his will. Therefore in the natural world all things roll on in an even, uninterrupted course. But it is far otherwise in the moral world. Here evil men and evil spirits continually oppose the divine will, and create numberless ir- 15 regularities. Here therefore is full scope for the exercise of all the riches both of the wisdom and knowledge of God, in counteracting all the wickedness and folly of men, and all the subtlety of Satan, to carry on his own glorious design, the salvation of lost mankind. Indeed were he to do this by an absolute 20 decree, and by his own irresistible power, it would imply no wisdom at all. But his wisdom is shown by saving man in such a manner as not to destroy his nature, not to take away the liberty which he has given him.[10]

5. But the riches both of the wisdom and the knowledge of 25 God[11] are most eminently displayed in his church; in planting it like a grain of mustard seed, the least of all seeds;[12] in preserving and continually increasing it till it grew into a great tree, notwithstanding the uninterrupted opposition of all the powers of darkness. This the Apostle justly terms 'the manifold wisdom'— 30 πολυποίκιλος σοφία—'of God'.[13] It is an uncommonly expressive word, intimating that this wisdom in the manner of its operation is diversified a thousand ways, and exerts itself with infinite varieties. These things the highest 'angels desire to look

---

[5] Young, *The Last Day*, ii.221.
[6] Cf. Eccles. 3:11.
[7] Cf. Ps. 148:8 (BCP).
[8] Cf. Ps. 8:1, 9 (BCP).
[9] Cf. No. 15, *The Great Assize*, III.3 and n.
[10] See above, No. 63, 'The General Spread of the Gospel', §12 and n.
[11] See Rom. 11:33.
[12] See Matt. 13:31-32.   [13] Eph. 3:10. Cf. below, §24.

into',[14] but can never fully comprehend. It seems to be with regard to these chiefly that the Apostle utters that strong exclamation, 'How unsearchable are his judgments!'[15] His counsels, designs, impossible to be fathomed! 'And his ways' of accomplishing them
5 'past finding out'[16]—impossible to be traced! According to the Psalmist, 'His paths are in the deep waters, and his footsteps are not known.'[17]

6. But a little of this he has been pleased to reveal unto us. And by keeping close to what he has revealed, meantime comparing
10 the word and the work of God together, we may understand a part of his ways. We may in some measure trace this manifold wisdom from the beginning of the world: from Adam to Noah, from Noah to Moses, and from Moses to Christ. But I would now consider it (after just touching on the history of the church in past ages) only
15 with regard to what he has wrought in the present age, during the last half century; yea, and in this little corner of the world, the British islands only.[18]

7. In the fullness of time, just when it seemed best to his infinite wisdom, God brought his first-begotten into the world. He then
20 laid the foundation of his church, though it hardly appeared till the day of Pentecost. And it was then a glorious church; all the members thereof being 'filled with the Holy Ghost',[19] 'being of one heart and of one mind',[20] 'and continuing steadfastly in the apostles' doctrine, and in fellowship, in the breaking of bread,
25 and in the prayers'.[21] 'In fellowship', that is, having 'all things in common', no man counting 'anything he had his own'.[22]

> Meek, simple followers of the Lamb,
> They lived, and thought, and spake the same;
> They all were of one heart and soul,
30 > And only love inspired the whole.[23]

---

[14] 1 Pet. 1:12.
[15] Rom. 11:33.
[16] *Ibid.*
[17] Cf. Ps. 77:19.
[18] Note how this swift passage from a universal perspective to a quite personal focus is paralleled in No. 107, 'On God's Vineyard', proem; and No. 63, 'The General Spread of the Gospel'.
[19] Acts 2:4, etc.
[20] Cf. Acts 4:32.
[21] Cf. Acts 2:42.　　　　　　　　　　　　　[22] Cf. Acts 2:44; 4:32.
[23] Charles Wesley, 'Primitive Christianity', *Hymns and Sacred Poems* (1749), II.333 *(Poet. Wks.,* V. 480); John has conflated the opening couplet of st. 2 and the closing couplet of st. 6. See No. 63, 'The General Spread of the Gospel', §20 and n.

8. But their happy state did not continue long. See Ananias and Sapphira,[24] through the love of money ('the root of all evil'[25]) making the first breach in the community of goods. See the partiality, the unjust respect of persons on the one side, the resentment and murmuring on the other, even while the apostles 5 themselves presided over the church at Jerusalem! See the grievous spots and wrinkles that were found in every part of the church, recorded not only in the Acts but in the Epistles of St. Paul, James, Peter, and John. A still fuller account we have in the Revelation: and according to this, in what a condition was the 10 Christian church even in the first century, even before St. John was removed from the earth;[26] if we may judge (as undoubtedly we may) of the state of the church in general from the state of those particular churches (all but that of Smyrna)[27] to which our Lord directed his epistles! And from this time, for fourteen hundred 15 years, it was corrupted more and more, as all history shows, till scarce any either of the power or form of religion was left.

9. Nevertheless it is certain that the gates of hell did never totally prevail against it.[28] God always reserved a seed for himself, a few that worshipped him in spirit and in truth.[29] I have often 20 doubted whether these were not the very persons whom the rich and honourable Christians, who will always have number as well as power on their side, did not stigmatize from time to time with the title of 'heretics'. Perhaps it was chiefly by this artifice of the devil and his children, that the good which was in them being evil 25 spoken of,[30] they were prevented from being so extensively used as otherwise they might have been. Nay, I have doubted whether that arch-heretic, Montanus,[31] was not one of the holiest men in the second century. Yea, I would not affirm that the arch-heretic

---

[24] Acts 5:1-11.
[25] Cf. 1 Tim. 6:10. See intro., No 50, 'The Use of Money'. Note espec. that here Wesley is saying that the first fall of the church came *before* Constantine, but see No. 61, 'The Mystery of Iniquity', §27 and n., for Wesley's more typical view that 'the fall' came with Constantine.
[26] Cf. No. 57, 'On the Fall of Man', II.3 and n.
[27] Jackson's 3rd edn., possibly based on Wesley's annotated Vol. VI of *SOSO*, since lost, which has 'those of Smyrna and Philadelphia'.
[28] Cf. Matt. 16:18.   [29] Cf. John 4:24.   [30] See Rom. 14:16.
[31] Traditionalist though he was, Wesley was also critical of traditional condemnations of those he recognized as kindred spirits in one degree or another. Montanus was a Phrygian charismatic of the second century who had professed to be called, under the direct guidance of the Holy Spirit, to restore the church to its primitive spirituality—thus, the prototype of many later enthusiasts. Cf. No. 61, 'The Mystery of Iniquity', §24 and n.

of the fifth century[32] (as plentifully as he has been bespattered for many ages) was not one of the holiest men of that age, not excepting St. Augustine himself—a wonderful saint! as full of pride, passion, bitterness, censoriousness, and as foul-mouthed
5 to all that contradicted him as George Fox himself.[33] I verily believe the real heresy of Pelagius was neither more nor less than this, the holding that Christians may by the grace of God (not without it; that I take to be a mere slander) 'go on to perfection';[34] or, in other words, 'fulfil the law of Christ'.[35]
10 'But St. Augustine says'—When St. Augustine's passions were heated his word is not worth a rush. And here is the secret. St. Augustine was angry at Pelagius. Hence he slandered and abused him (as his manner was) without either fear or shame. And St. Augustine was then in the Christian world what Aristotle was
15 afterwards. There needed no other proof of any assertion than *ipse dixit*—'St. Augustine said it.'
    10. But to return. When iniquity had overspread the church as a flood, the Spirit of the Lord lifted up a standard against it. He raised up a poor monk, without wealth, without power, and at that
20 time without friends, to declare war, as it were, against all the world; against the Bishop of Rome and all his adherents. But this little stone, being chosen of God, soon grew into a great mountain; and increased more and more till it had covered a considerable part of Europe. Yet even before Luther was called
25 home the love of many was waxed cold.[36] Many that had once run well turned back from the holy commandment delivered to them; yea, the greater part of those that once experienced the power of faith made shipwreck of faith and a good conscience.[37] The observing this was supposed to be the occasion of that illness (a

---

[32] I.e., Pelagius (*c.* 355–420), a fellow Briton who may or may not have been a 'Pelagian' in the sense in which he was so fiercely condemned by Augustine, Pope Zosimus, *et al.;* cf. Evans, *Pelagius.* Wesley's plaudits here overlook the crucial distinction that, for Pelagius, prevenience is not emphasized, whereas for Wesley the Spirit's initiative is the dynamic essence of all grace. Cf. his letter to John Fletcher, Aug. 18, 1775, as well as an earlier letter to Alexander Coates, July 7, 1761.

[33] Cf. Fox's broadsheet of 1660(?), *For Your Whoredoms in the City of London is the Hand of the Lord Stretched Forth Against Thee . . . :* 'Whores and Whoremongers, . . . you stink before the Lord . . . the noisome smell of your flesh stinks . . .'. See also, Fox's *The Great Mystery of the Great Whore Unfolded and Antichrist's Kingdom Revealed Unto Destruction* (1659). Cf. No. 48, 'Self-denial', I.1. For another reference to Fox, cf. No. 61, 'The Mystery of Iniquity', §30.

[34] Heb. 6:1.   [35] Gal. 6:2.
[36] See Matt. 24:12.   [37] 1 Tim. 1:19.

fit of the stone) whereof Luther died; after uttering these melancholy words: 'I have spent my strength for nought. Those who are called by my name are, it is true, reformed in opinions and modes of worship; but in their hearts and lives, in their tempers and practice, they are not a jot better than the Papists.'[38] 5

11. About the same time it pleased God to visit Great Britain. A few in the reign of King Henry VIII, and many more in the three following reigns, were real witnesses of true scriptural Christianity. The number of these exceedingly increased in the beginning of the following century. And in the year 1627 there 10 was a wonderful pouring out of the Spirit in several parts of England, as well as in Scotland and the north of Ireland.[39] But from the time that riches and honour poured in upon them that feared and loved God, their hearts began to be estranged from him, and to cleave to the present world; no sooner was 15 persecution ceased, and the poor, despised, persecuted Christians invested with power, and placed in ease and affluence, but a change of circumstances brought a change of spirit. Riches and honour soon produced their usual effects. Having the world, they quickly loved the world. They no longer breathed after heaven, 20 but became more and more attached to the things of earth; so that in a few years one who knew and loved them well, and was an unexceptionable judge of men and manners, Dr. Owen,[40] deeply lamented over them, as having lost all the life and power of religion, and being become just of the same spirit with those 25 whom they despised as the mire in the streets.

[38] Luther suffered from 'the stone' (i.e., renal calculus); cf. *Table Talk*, Nos. 3522, 3733, 5047, etc., but he died of a heart attack, as Samuel Clarke had already reported in his *Marrow of Ecclesiastical Historie* (1650), p. 93. Cf. J. G. Walch, *Dr. Martin Luthers Sämtliche Schriften* (1740), XXI.277 ff.; and E. G. Schwiebert, *Luther and His Times* (St. Louis, Concordia Publishing House, 1950), pp. 747-50. Wesley had found the story of Luther's dying lament in J. D. Herrnschmid, *Life of Martin Luther* (1742), X.10, extracts of which had been published in *AM* (1778, see espec. I.272). For Herrnschmid's quotation (uncited), see *An Earnest Exhortation* . . . (1522) [Weimar edn., 8:685]; this had no relation to Luther's dying words. See also No. 102, 'Of Former Times', §14; and for Wesley's other references to Luther, see No. 14, *The Repentance of Believers*, I.9 and n.

[39] Cf. Gillies, *Historical Collections*. It is interesting that this outpouring is not mentioned in the standard church historical surveys (e.g., Mosheim, Gee and Hardy, Williston Walker, etc.). But it must have been what Wesley regarded as the flowering of the Puritan movement and the forerunner of the charismatic renewals later seen amongst the Quakers and other 'spirituals'.

[40] Cf. *The Works of John Owen* (1842), VI, 'Of Temptation', p. 112: 'We [Puritans] have by Providence shifted places with the men of the world, we have by sin shifted spirits with them also . . . we are cast into the mould of them that went before us . . .'.

12. What little religion was left in the land received another deadly wound at the Restoration, by one of the worst princes that ever sat on the English throne,[41] and by the most abandoned court in Europe. And infidelity now broke in amain, and overspread the
5 land as a flood. Of course all kind of immorality came with it, and increased to the end of the century. Some feeble attempts were made to stem the torrent during the reign of Queen Anne.[42] But it still increased till about the year 1725,[43] when Mr. Law published his *Practical Treatise on Christian Perfection;* and not long after his
10 *Serious Call to a Devout and Holy Life.*[44] Here the seed was sown which soon grew up, and spread to Oxford, London, Bristol, Leeds, York, and within a few years to the greatest part of England, Scotland, Ireland.[45]

13. But what means did the wisdom of God make use of in
15 effecting this great work? He thrust out such labourers into his harvest as the wisdom of man would never have thought on. He chose the weak things to confound the strong, and the foolish things to confound the wise.[46] He chose a few young, poor, ignorant men, without experience, learning, or art; but simple of

---

[41] I.e., Charles II (1660–85). Gilbert Burnet, *History of His Own Times* (1724), I.611, says, 'And finding it not easy to reward [his friends] as they deserved, he forgot them all *alike.* . . . This was an equal return. . . . He never troubled his thoughts with the sense of any of the services that had been done him.' Richard Steele, writing in *The Spectator,* No. 462 (1712), has a kinder assessment: 'He pursued pleasure more than ambition, but was a good king, loved by his subjects.' Cf. Sir George Clark, *The Later Stuarts, 1660–1714,* Vol. 10, in *Oxford History of England* (1955), especially the French Ambassador, Pomponne's, comment on 'this perpetually agitated state of England', p. 109. See also No. 79, 'On Dissipation', §1.

[42] Such as her fund for the poorer clergy ('Queen Anne's Bounty', 1704, *et seq.*) and her attempts to counter the Whig and Latitudinarian monopolies in the episcopacy.

[43] Cf. Wesley's references to 1725 as the year of his first conversion, as in his recollection in *A Plain Account of Christian Perfection* (1766): 'In the year 1725 [in reading 'several parts of' Jeremy Taylor's *Holy Living* and *Holy Dying*] . . . I was exceedingly affected—that part in particular which relates to purity of intention. Instantly I resolved to dedicate *all my life* to God, *all* my thoughts, and words, and actions: being throughly convinced, there was no medium; but that *every part* of my life (not *some* only) must either be a sacrifice to God or to myself, that is, in effect, to the devil.'

[44] The 1st edn. of *Christian Perfection* bears the date 1726; *Serious Call* is dated 1729. See Wesley's remembrance of his experience of these in JWJ, May 24, 1738, §5: 'The light flowed in so mightily upon my soul that everything appeared in a new view. . . . I was persuaded that I should be accepted of him and that I was even then [1729?] in a state of salvation.'

[45] Cf. Gillies, *Historical Collections,* and Joseph Milner, *History of the Church of Christ.* . . . Cf. also John Walsh, 'Methodism at the End of the Eighteenth Century', in *A History of the Methodist Church in Great Britain,* I.275-315.

[46] See 1 Cor. 1:17.

heart, devoted to God, full of faith and zeal, seeking no honour, no profit, no pleasure, no ease, but merely to save souls; fearing neither want, pain, persecution; nor whatever man could do unto them; yea, not counting their lives dear unto themselves, so they might finish their course with joy.[47] Of the same spirit were the people whom God by their word called out of darkness into his marvellous light,[48] many of whom soon agreed to join together in order to strengthen each others' hands in God. These also were simple of heart, devoted to God, zealous of good works;[49] desiring neither honour, nor riches, nor pleasure, nor ease, nor anything under the sun but to attain the whole image of God, and to dwell with him in glory.

14. But as these young preachers grew in years they did not all grow in grace. Several of them indeed increased in other knowledge; but not proportionably in the knowledge of God. They grew less simple, less alive to God, and less devoted to him. They were less zealous for God, and consequently less active, less diligent in his service. Some of them began to desire the praise of men and not the praise of God only;[50] some to be weary of a wandering life, and so [to] seek ease and quietness. Some began again to fear the faces of men; to be ashamed of their calling; to be unwilling to deny themselves, to take up their cross daily and 'endure hardship as good soldiers of Jesus Christ'.[51] Wherever these preachers laboured there was not much fruit of their labours. Their word was not as formerly clothed with power: it carried with it no demonstration of the Spirit.[52] The same faintness of spirit was in their private conversation. They were no longer 'instant in season, out of season',[53] 'warning every man and exhorting every man',[54] 'if by any means they might save some'.[55]

15. And as some preachers 'declined from their first love',[56] so did many of the people. They were likewise assaulted on every side, encompassed with manifold temptations. And while many of them triumphed over all, and were 'more than conquerors

---

[47] See Acts 20:24. Cf. No. 66, 'The Signs of the Times', II.10 and n.
[48] 1 Pet. 2:9.
[49] Titus 2:14.
[50] See John 12:43.
[51] Cf. 2 Tim. 2:3.
[52] See 1 Cor. 2:4.
[53] 2 Tim. 4:2.
[54] Cf. Col. 1:28.
[55] Cf. 1 Cor. 9:22.
[56] Cf. Rev. 2:4.

through him that loved them',[57] others gave place to the world, the flesh, or the devil, and so 'entered into temptation';[58] some of them 'made shipwreck of their faith'[59] at once; some by slow, insensible degrees. Not a few, being in want of the necessaries of
5 life, were overwhelmed with the cares of the world. Many relapsed into the desires of other things, which choked the good seed, 'and it became unfruitful'.[60]

16. But of all temptations none so struck at the whole work of God as 'the deceitfulness of riches'[61]—a thousand melancholy
10 proofs of which I have seen within these last fifty years. Deceitful are they indeed! For who will believe they do him the least harm? And yet I have not known threescore rich persons, perhaps not half the number, during threescore years, who, as far as I can judge, were not less holy than they would have been had they been
15 poor. By *riches* I mean, not thousands of pounds; but any more than will procure the conveniences of life.[62] Thus I account him a rich man who has food and raiment for himself and family without running into debt, and something over. And how few are there in these circumstances who are not hurt, if not destroyed there-
20 by? Yet who takes warning? Who seriously regards that awful declaration of the Apostle, even 'they that desire to be rich fall into temptation and a snare, and into divers foolish and hurtful desires, which drown men in destruction and perdition.'[63] How many sad instances have we seen of this in London, in Bristol,
25 in Newcastle, in all the large trading towns throughout the kingdoms where God has lately caused his power to be known! See how many of those who were once simple of heart, desiring nothing but God, are now gratifying 'the desire of the flesh',[64] studying to please their senses, particularly their taste—endeav-
30 ouring to enlarge the pleasures of tasting[65] as far as possible. Are not *you* of that number? Indeed you are no drunkard, and no

---

[57] Cf. Rom. 8:37.
[58] Cf. Mark 14:38.
[59] 1 Tim. 1:19.
[60] Cf. Mark 4:19.   [61] Matt. 13:22; Mark 4:19.
[62] An increasingly insistent theme of Wesley's last two decades; for this consistent definition of riches, see No. 30, 'Sermon on the Mount, X', §26 and n. Cf. also intro. to No. 50, 'The Use of Money'.
[63] Cf. 1 Tim. 6:9.
[64] Gal. 5:16; 1 John 2:16. Cf. No. 7, 'The Way to the Kingdom', II.2 and n.
[65] Law, *Christian Perfection* (*Works*, III. 38); cf. No. 50, 'The Use of Money', II.2 and n.

glutton. But do you not indulge yourself in a kind of regular sensuality? Are not eating and drinking the greatest pleasures of your life, the most considerable part of your happiness? If so I fear St. Paul would have given you a place among those 'whose god is their belly'![66] How many of them are now again indulging 'the desire of the eye'?[67] Using every means which is in their power to enlarge the pleasures of the imagination?[68] If not in grandeur, which as yet is out of their way, yet in new or beautiful things? Are not you seeking happiness in pretty or elegant apparel, or furniture? Or in new clothes, or books, or in pictures, or gardens? 'Why, what harm is there in these things!' There is this harm, that they gratify 'the desire of the eye', and thereby strengthen and increase it; making you more and more dead to God, and more alive to the world. How many are indulging 'the pride of life'?[69] Seeking the honour that cometh of men? Or 'laying up treasures on earth'?[70] They *gain all they can*, honestly and conscientiously. They *save all they can*, by cutting off all needless expense, by adding frugality to diligence. And so far all is right. This is the duty of everyone that fears God. But they do not *give all they can;* without which they must needs grow more and more earthly-minded.[71] Their affections will cleave to the dust[72] more and more, and they will have less and less communion with God. Is not this *your* case? Do not *you* seek the praise of men more than the praise of God?[73] Do not *you* lay up, or at least desire and endeavour to 'lay up, treasures on earth'? Are you not then (deal faithfully with your own soul!) more and more alive to the world? And consequently more and more dead to God? It cannot be otherwise. That *must* follow unless you give all you can, as well as gain and save all you can. There is no other way under heaven to prevent your money from sinking you lower than the grave; for 'if any man love the world, the love of the Father is not in him.'[74] And if it *was* in him in ever so high a degree, yet if he slides into the love of the world, by the same degrees that this enters in, the love of God will go out of the heart.

---

[66] Phil. 3:19.   [67] 1 John 2:16; cf. n. 64 above.

[68] Cf. Addison, who wrote at least nine essays for *The Spectator* on 'The Pleasures of the Imagination'; cf. No. 44, *Original Sin*, II.10 and n.

[69] 1 John 2:16.

[70] Cf. Matt. 6:19, 20. Cf. intro. to No. 28, 'Sermon on the Mount, VIII'.

[71] A reprise of Wesley's three 'rules' for ;the use of money'; see No. 50, 'The Use of Money', I.1 and n.

[72] See Ps. 119:25.   [73] John 12:43.   [74] 1 John 2:15.

17. And perhaps there is something more than all this contained in those words, 'Love not the world, neither the things of the world.'[75] Here we are expressly warned against 'loving the world' as well as against loving 'the things of the world'. 'The world' is the men that know not God, that neither love nor fear him. To love these with a love of delight or complacence, to set our affections upon them, is here absolutely forbidden; and by parity of reason to converse or have intercourse with them farther than necessary business requires. Friendship or intimacy with them St. James does not scruple to term adultery. 'Ye adulterers and adulteresses, know ye not that the friendship of the world is enmity with God? Whosoever therefore will be a friend of the world is an enemy of God.'[76] Do not endeavour to shuffle away, or evade the meaning of these strong words. They plainly require us to stand aloof from them, to have no needless commerce with unholy men. Otherwise we shall surely slide into conformity to the world, to their maxims, spirit, and customs. For not only their words, harmless as they seem, do eat as doth a canker, but their very breath is infectious; their spirit imperceptibly influences our spirit. It steals 'like water into our bowels, and like oil into our bones'.[77]

18. But all rich men are under a continual temptation to acquaintance and conversation with worldly men. They are likewise under a continual temptation to pride, to think more highly of themselves than they ought to think.[78] They are strongly tempted to revenge when they are ever so little affronted. And having the means in their own hands, how few are there that resist the temptation! They are continually tempted to sloth, indolence, love of ease, softness, delicacy; to hatred of self-denial and taking up the cross, even that of *fasting* and *rising early*, without which it is impossible to grow in grace. If *you* are increased in goods, do not you know that these things are so? Do you contract no intimacy with worldly men? Do not you converse with them more than duty requires? Are you in no danger of pride? Of thinking your-self better than your poor, dirty neighbours? Do you never resent, yea, and revenge an affront? Do you never render evil for evil?[79]

---

[75] *Ibid.*
[76] Cf. Jas. 4:4.
[77] Cf. Ps. 109:18 (AV); cf. ver. 17 (BCP).
[78] See Rom. 12:3.
[79] 1 Thess. 5:15.

Do not you give way to indolence or love of ease? Do you deny
yourself, and take up your cross daily?[80] Do you constantly rise as
early as you did once? Why not? Is not your soul as precious now
as it was then? How often do you fast? Is not this a duty to *you* as
much as to a day labourer? But if you are wanting in this, or any   5
other respect, who will tell you of it? Who dares tell you the plain
truth but those who neither hope nor fear anything from you? And
if any venture to deal plainly with you, how hard is it for you to
bear it! Are not you far less reprovable, far less advisable, than
when you were poor? It is well if you can bear reproof even from   10
me. And in a few days you will see me no more.

Once more therefore I say, having gained and saved all you
can, give all you can; else your money will eat your flesh as fire,
and will sink you to the nethermost hell!

O beware of 'laying up treasures upon earth'! Is it not   15
treasuring up wrath against the day of wrath?

Lord! I have warned them; but if they will not be warned, what
can I do more? I can only 'give them up unto their own heart's
lusts, and let them follow their own imaginations'![81]

19. By not taking this warning it is certain many of the   20
Methodists are already fallen. Many are falling at this very time.
And there is great reason to apprehend that many more will fall,
most of whom will rise no more!

But what method may it be hoped the all-wise God will take
to repair the decay of his work? If he does not remove the   25
candlestick[82] from this people and raise up another people who
will be more faithful to his grace, it is probable he will proceed in
the same manner as he has done in time past. And this has
hitherto been his method. When any of the old preachers 'left
their first love',[83] lost their simplicity and zeal, and departed from   30
the work, he raised up young men, who *are* what they *were*, and
sent them into the harvest in their place. The same he has done
when he was pleased to remove any of his faithful labourers
into Abraham's bosom. So when Henry Millard,[84] Edward

---

[80] See Matt. 16:24, etc.
[81] Cf. Ps. 81:13 (BCP); note this rare instance of the directly personal appeal of
Wesley's oral preaching carried over into his written style.
[82] See Rev. 2:5.   [83] Cf. Rev. 2:4.
[84] A young preacher who had been in the thick of the Cornish anti-Methodist
persecutions in 1744; in 1745 he was named as one of the 'Assistants' or supervising
preachers, but died from smallpox not long afterwards (JWJ, Sept. 16, 1744; *AM* [1778],
I.230-31; MS Minutes, 1745).

Dunstone,[85] John Manners,[86] Thomas Walsh,[87] or any others, rested from their labours, he raised up other young men from time to time, willing and able to perform the same service. It is highly probable he will take the very same method for the time to 5 come. The place of those preachers who either die in the Lord, or lose the spiritual life which God had given them, he will supply by others that are alive to God, and desire only to spend and be spent for him.[88]

20. Hear ye this, all ye preachers who have not the same life, 10 the same communion with God, the same zeal for his cause, the same burning love to souls, that you had once! 'Take heed unto yourselves, that ye lose not the things ye have wrought, but that ye receive a full reward.'[89] Beware lest God swear in his wrath that ye shall bear his standard no more! Lest he be provoked to take the 15 word of his grace[90] utterly out of your mouth! Be assured the Lord hath no need of *you: his* work doth not depend upon *your* help. As he is able 'out of the stones to raise up children to Abraham',[91] so he is able out of the same to raise up preachers after his own heart! O make haste! 'Remember from whence you are fallen; 20 and repent and do the first works!'[92]

21. Would it not provoke the Lord of the harvest to lay you altogether aside if you *despised* the labourers he had raised up, merely because of their *youth?* This was commonly done to us when *we* were first sent out between forty and fifty years ago. Old, 25 wise men asked, 'What will these *young* heads do?' So the then

---

[85] Edward Dunstone (or Dunstan) died Jan. 6, 1748/9, and Charles Wesley read an edifying account of his death to the London societies. In a letter to his betrothed that month he speaks of Dunstone as 'the extraordinary youth you heard of' (Charles Wesley, MS letter to Sally Gwynne [Jan. 23, 1749], MA).

[86] John Manners (1731–63), converted 1755, served as an itinerant preacher both in Ireland and the north of England; he died in York (Charles Atmore, *The Methodist Memorial; being an Impartial Sketch of the Lives and Characters of the Preachers* [Bristol, Edwards, 1801], pp. 247-50; Thomas Jackson, *Lives of Early Methodist Preachers,* II.112, IV.24, 26, 76; C. H. Crookshank, *History of Methodism in Ireland,* I.152; MS *Minutes,* 1758).

[87] Thomas Walsh (*c.* 1730–59), a converted Irish Roman Catholic who became a saintly preacher and a fine Hebrew scholar. In a letter to Dean William Digby, written in the early 1780's, Wesley would say of him that he was 'the best Hebraean I ever knew'. Wesley wrote a foreword for James Morgan's biography of Walsh, 1762, and included an abridgement of it in his own *Works* (1772), XI. 129-36, XII. 3-26 (see *Bibliog,* No. 252).

[88] See 2 Cor. 12:15.

[89] Cf. 2 John 8.

[90] Acts 14:3; 20:32.

[91] Cf. Matt. 3:9.

[92] Cf. Rev. 2:5.

Bishop of London in particular.[93] But shall we adopt their language? God forbid! Shall we teach him whom he shall send? Whom he shall employ in his own work? Are we then the men, and shall 'wisdom die with us'?[94] Does the work of God hang upon us? O humble yourselves before God, lest he pluck you away and 5 there be none to deliver![95]

22. Let us next consider, What method has the wisdom of God taken for these five and forty years, when thousands of the people that once ran well, one after another 'drew back to perdition'?[96] Why, as fast as any of the poor were overwhelmed with world- 10 ly care, so that the seed they had received became unfruitful; and as fast as any of the rich gave way to the love of the world, to foolish and hurtful desires,[97] or to any other of those innumerable temptations which are inseparable from riches, God has constantly from time to time raised up men endued with the spirit 15 which they had lost. Yea, and generally this change has been made with considerable advantage. For the last were not only (for the most part) more numerous than the first, but more watchful, profiting by their example; more spiritual, more heavenly-minded; more zealous, more alive to God, and more dead to all things 20 here below.[98]

23. And, blessed be God, we see he is now doing the same thing in various parts of the kingdom. In the room of those that have fallen from their steadfastness, or are falling at this day, he is continually raising up out of the stones other children to 25 Abraham. This he does at one or another place according to his own will; pouring out his quickening Spirit on this or another people just as it pleaseth him. He is raising up those of every age and degree—young men and maidens, old men and children[99]— to be 'a chosen generation, a royal priesthood, a holy nation, a 30 peculiar people, to show forth his praise who has called them out of darkness into his marvellous light'.[100] And we have no reason to doubt but he will continue so to do till the great promise is fulfilled, till 'the earth is filled with the knowledge of the glory of the Lord, as the waters cover the sea';[101] 'till all Israel is saved, and 35 the fullness of the Gentiles is come in'.[102]

---

[93] Edmund Gibson, *Observations* . . . ; see No. 66, 'The Signs of the Times', II.10 and n.

[94] Cf. Job 12:2.   [95] See Ps. 50:22 (BCP).   [96] Cf. Heb. 10:39.
[97] 1 Tim. 6:9.   [98] See Rom. 6:11.   [99] See Ps. 148:12.
[100] Cf. 1 Pet. 2:9.   [101] Cf. Isa. 11:9; Hab. 2:14.   [102] Cf. Rom. 11:26, 25.

24. But have all those that have sunk under manifold temptations[103] so fallen that they can rise no more? 'Hath the Lord
cast them all off for ever, and will he be no more entreated? Is
his promise come utterly to an end for evermore?'[104] God forbid
5 that we should affirm this! Surely he is able to heal all their
backslidings;[105] for with God no word is impossible. And is he
not willing, too? He is 'God, and not man';[106] 'therefore his
compassions fail not.'[107] Let no backslider despair: 'return unto
the Lord, and he will have mercy upon you; unto our God, and
10 he will abundantly pardon.'[108]

Meantime, thus saith the Lord to you that now supply their
place, 'Be not high-minded, but fear!' If the 'Lord spared not' thy
elder brethren, 'take heed lest he spare not thee!'[109] *Fear*, though
not with a servile, tormenting fear, lest thou fall by any of the same
15 temptations, by either the cares of the world, the deceitfulness of
riches, or the desire of other things.[110] Tempted you will be in ten
thousand different ways, perhaps as long as you remain in the
body; but as long as you continue to watch and pray, you will not
'enter into temptations'.[111] His grace has been hitherto sufficient
20 for you,[112] and so it will be unto the end.

25. You see here, brethren, a short and general sketch of the
manner wherein God works upon earth in repairing his work[113] of
grace wherever it is decayed through the subtlety of Satan, and
the unfaithfulness of men, giving way to the fraud and malice of
25 the devil. Thus he is now carrying on his own work, and thus he
will do to the end of time. And how wonderfully plain and simple
is his way of working, in the spiritual as well as the natural world!
That is, his general plan of working, of repairing whatsoever is
decayed. But as to innumerable particulars we must still cry out,
30 'O the depth! How unfathomable are his counsels! And his paths
past tracing out!'[114]

Glasgow, April 28, 1784[115]

---

[103] See 1 Pet. 1:6; and No. 47, 'Heaviness through Manifold Temptations'; on this text.
[104] Cf. Ps. 77:7-8 (AV and BCP conflated).
[105] See Jer. 3:22.   [106] Hos. 11:9.
[107] Cf. Lam. 3:22.   [108] Cf. Isa. 55:7.
[109] Cf. Rom. 11:20-21.   [110] See Mark 4:19.
[111] Cf. Mark 14:38.   [112] See 2 Cor. 12:9.
[113] Orig., *AM* and *SOSO*, 'this work', corrected by Wesley in his errata and MS
annotations in *AM*.
[114] Cf. Rom. 11:33.
[115] Place and date of writing are omitted from the collected *Sermons*.

THE IMPERFECTION OF HUMAN KNOWLEDGE

THE CASE OF REASON IMPARTIALLY CONSIDERED

AN INTRODUCTORY COMMENT

These next two sermons were paired in this order in SOSO, *VI (1788), even though they had been written earlier and in reverse sequence. 'The Case of Reason . . . ' dates from July 6, 1781, and from Langham Row in Lincolnshire (cf. the* Journal *entry for that day for Wesley's critical remarks on the then famous historian, William Robertson). He then had the sermon published as No. VI in the* Arminian Magazine *for November and December of that year (IV. 574-80, 630-36) without a title. Wesley had preached from its text, 1 Cor. 14:20, only twice before (January 8, 1753, and March 20, 1772). 'Imperfection . . . ' had been written in early March 1784 in Bristol and then promptly printed in the* Arminian Magazine *as No. XXI in June and July (VII. 233-41, 290-98), also without a title and with an error in citation of the text ('. . . we know in part' is cited as 1 Cor. 13:10 instead of 13:9, and this error is faithfully repeated twice by Paramore in* SOSO, *VI. 53-54). That this was a problem still much on Wesley's mind is suggested by the fact that he had preached on 1 Cor. 13:9 four times in 1783.*

Wesley brought both sermons together in SOSO, *VI, and quite logically, since both are comments on the actual limitations of 'human understanding' and on the practical implications for Christian living of an intellectual modesty deeply grounded in a religious understanding of transcendence. Wesley had grown up in the fading days of an Anglican rationalism (Ray, Butler, Clarke, Paley) which took for granted that a sincere 'faith seeking understanding' would surely be richly rewarded, since faith and reason are finally consonant. And, as we have seen, he was himself a rationalist of sorts. But as deism and 'the Enlightenment' had progressed and, even more particularly, as a certain confidence in human rationality had filtered down to ordinary folk, Wesley recognized a growing threat both to Christian faith and to any proper sense of Christian reverence and awe.*

*These two sermons are therefore intended as antidotes and alter-
natives to what Wesley regarded as a* false *rationalism. Even so, and
not accidentally, Wesley also reflects here his undiminished interest
in a valid 'theology of culture.' It is worth noting and comparing the
higher than average number of his passing allusions here to 'contemporary' science, philosophy, and literature. If this is 'plain truth
for plain people', the Methodists were no longer as 'plain' as they had
been in their earlier, humbler beginnings.*

SERMON 69

The Imperfection of Human Knowledge

1 Corinthians 13:9[1]

We know in part.

1. The desire of knowledge is an universal principle in man,
5 fixed in his inmost nature.[2] It is not variable, but constant in every
rational creature, unless while it is suspended by some stronger
desire. And it is insatiable: 'the eye is not satisfied with seeing, nor
the ear with hearing;'[3] neither the mind by any degree of
knowledge which can be conveyed into it. And it is planted in
10 every human soul for excellent purposes. It is intended to hinder
our taking up our rest in anything here below; to raise our
thoughts to higher and higher objects, more and more worthy of
our consideration, till we ascend to the source of all knowledge
and all excellence, the all-wise and all-gracious Creator.
15 2. But although our desire of knowledge has no bounds, yet our
knowledge itself has. It is indeed confined within very narrow
bounds, abundantly narrower than common people imagine or

---

[1] All edns. up to and including that of Joseph Benson (1809–13) read 1 Cor. 13:10
here—an unnoticed succession of the same error. The misreading was first corrected by
Thomas Jackson in 1825.
[2] Cf. Aristotle, *Metaphysics*, I. i [980]: 'All men, by nature, desire to know.' But see also
à Kempis's qualification (to which Wesley subscribed) in *Imitation*, I.ii.1: 'All men
naturally desire to know, but what availeth knowledge without the fear of God?' Cf. No.
140, 'The Promise of Understanding', proem, §2.
[3] Eccles. 1:8.

men of learning are willing to acknowledge—a strong intimation (since the great Creator doth nothing in vain) that there will be some future state of being wherein that now insatiable desire will be satisfied, and there will be no longer so immense a distance between the appetite and the object of it.   5

3. The present knowledge of man is exactly adapted to his present wants. It is sufficient to warn us of, and preserve us from, most of the evils to which we are now exposed, and to procure us whatever is necessary for us in this our infant state of existence. We know enough of the nature and sensible qualities of the things 10 that are round about us, so far as they are subservient to the health and strength of our bodies. We know how to procure and prepare our food; we know what raiment is fit to cover us; we know how to build our houses, and to furnish them with all necessaries and conveniences. We know just as much as is conducive to our living 15 comfortably in this world. But of innumerable things above, below, and round about us, we know little more than that they exist. And in this our deep ignorance is seen the goodness as well as the wisdom of God, in cutting short his knowledge on every side on purpose to 'hide pride from man.'[4]   20

4. Therefore it is that by the very constitution of their nature the wisest of men 'know' but 'in part'. And how amazingly small a part do they know either of the Creator or of his works! This is a very needful, but a very unpleasing theme; for 'vain man would be wise.'[5] Let us reflect upon it for a while. And may the God of 25 wisdom and love open our eyes to discern our own ignorance!

I.1. To begin with the great Creator himself. How astonishingly little do we know of God! How small a part of his nature do we know! Of his essential attributes! What conception can we form of his omnipresence? Who is able to comprehend how God 30 is in this and every place? How he fills the immensity of space? If philosophers, by denying the existence of a vacuum,[6] only meant that there is no place empty of God, that every point of infinite space is full of God, certainly no man could call it in question. But still, the fact being admitted, what is omnipresence or ubiquity? 35

---

[4] Job 33:17; cf. No. 45, 'The New Birth', I.4 and n.
[5] Job 11:12.
[6] I.e., the Cartesians; cf. articles on 'Vacuum' in Chambers's *Cyclopaedia;* together they run past four folio columns, suggesting how general and exigent the arguments about space and matter were in the eighteenth century.

Man is no more able to comprehend this than to grasp the universe.

2.[7] The omnipresence or immensity of God Sir Isaac Newton endeavours to illustrate by a strong expression, by terming infinite
5 space 'the sensorium of the Deity'.[8] And the very heathens did not scruple to say, 'All things are full of God'[9]—just equivalent with his own declaration, 'Do not I fill heaven and earth, saith the Lord?'[10] How beautifully does the Psalmist illustrate this! 'Whither shall I flee from thy presence? If I go up into heaven,
10 thou art there: if I go down to hell, thou art there also. If I take the wings of the morning, and remain in the uttermost parts of the sea: even there thy hand shall find me, and thy right hand shall hold me.'[11] But in the meantime, what conception can we form either of his eternity or immensity? Such knowledge is
15 too wonderful for us: we cannot attain unto it.[12]

3. A second essential attribute of God is eternity. He existed before all time. Perhaps we might more properly say, he *does exist* from everlasting to everlasting. But what is eternity? A celebrated author says that the divine eternity is, *Vitae interminabilis tota simul*
20 *et perfecta possessio*—'the at once entire and perfect possession of never-ending life'.[13] But how much wiser are we for this definition? We know just as much of it as we did before. 'The at once entire and perfect possession'! Who can conceive what this means?

25   4. If indeed God had stamped (as some have maintained) an

---

[7] The order here of §§2, 3 is that of the text of *Sermons* (1788), a reversal of the order in *AM*.

[8] Cf. H. G. Alexander, ed., *The Leibniz-Clarke Correspondence, With Extracts from Newton's* Principia *and* Opticks (Manchester, Univ. of Manchester, 1970), pp. 12-13 (§3), 16-17 (§3), 28-29 (§§10-12), 40-41 (§24). An even more likely direct source of this phrase and its attribution, for Wesley, is Addison, *The Spectator*, No. 565 (July 9, 1714): 'The noblest and most exalted way of considering this infinite space is that of Sir Isaac Newton, who calls it the "Sensorium" of the Godhead.' There is a rather different reference in Luis Vaz de Camoens, *The Lusiad* (tr. by W. J. Mickle in 1776), Bk.X, pp. 537-38 (see Mickle's n.): '[Infinite space was] called by the old philosophers and school divines, "The Sensorium of the Deity".' The common source of the idea, of course, is Plato's notion of a 'Receptacle' (τὸ ὑποχείμενον), as in the *Timaeus*, 51*A*, 57*C*, etc. See also No. 10, 'The Witness of the Spirit, I', I.12 and n.

[9] Attributed to Thales by Aristotle and Cicero; see No. 23, 'Sermon on the Mount, III', I.6 and n.

[10] Jer. 23:24.

[11] Cf. Ps. 139:7-10 (AV and BCP conflated).

[12] See Ps. 139:6.

[13] Cf. Boethius, *The Consolation of Philosophy*, V.6 (10): '*Aeternitas igitur est interminabilis vitae tota simul et perfecta possessio.*'

idea of himself on every human soul, we must certainly have understood something of these, as well as his other attributes; for we cannot suppose he would have impressed upon us either a false or imperfect idea of himself.[14] But the truth is, no man ever did, or does now find any such idea stamped upon his soul. The little which we do know of God (except what we receive by the inspiration of the Holy One) we do not gather from an inward impression, but gradually acquire from without. 'The invisible things of God', if they are known at all, 'are known from the things that are made;'[15] not from what God hath written in our hearts, but from what he hath written in all his works.

5. Hence then, from his works, particularly his works of creation, we are to learn the knowledge of God.[16] But it is not easy to conceive how little we know even of these. To begin with those that are at a distance. Who knows how far the universe extends? What are the limits of it?[17] The morning stars can tell, who sang together when the lines of it were stretched out,[18] when God said, 'This be thy just circumference, O world!'[19] But all beyond the fixed stars is utterly hid from the children of men. And what do we know of the *fixed stars?*[20] Who telleth the *number* of them? Even of that small portion of them that by their mingled light form what we call *the Milky Way?* And who knows the *use* of them? Are they so many suns that illuminate their respective planets? Or do they only minister to this (as Mr. Hutchinson[21] supposes) and contribute in some unknown way to the perpetual circulation of

[14] Christian Platonists in general had maintained this notion of innate ideas of God, and Wesley follows them since 'our knowledge of God and the things of God' are not 'empirical' but rather intuitive. Cf. Richard Bentley's Boyle Lecture, No. 4 (1692): 'The commonly received notion of an innate idea of God, imprinted upon every soul. . . .' See also Nos. 95, 'On the Education of Children,' §5; 96, 'On Obedience to Parents', §1; 117, 'On the Discoveries of Faith', §1; and 'Remarks Upon Mr. Locke's *Essay on Human Understanding*' (*AM*, 1783–84, Vols. VI-VII).

[15] Cf. Rom. 1:20.

[16] The central theme of Wesley's *Survey;* see espec. his closing summary, 1st edn. (1763), II.244-56; 3rd edn. (1777), V.235-55.

[17] For Wesley's interest in astronomy, cf. No. 55, *On the Trinity,* §7 and n.

[18] Cf. Job 38:5-7.

[19] Milton, *Paradise Lost,* vii. 231; repeated in Nos. 103, 'What is Man? Ps. 8:3-4', I.5; and 132, 'On Faith, Heb. 11:1', §7.

[20] Cf. No. 56, 'God's Approbation of His Works', I.10 and n.

[21] Cf. John Hutchinson, *Works,* II ('D'): '. . . the light is pressed *out* by the influx of spirit and spirit is pressed *in* by the influx of light; and so the whole matter of the heavens is perpetually changing conditions and circulating. . . .' See Wesley's account of 'The Hutchinsonian System' in his *Survey,* 1st edn. (1763), II.136-39; 3rd edn. (1777), III. 276-80. Cf. also No. 57, 'On the Fall of Man', II.6 and n.

light and spirit? Who knows what *comets* are? Are they planets not fully formed? Or planets destroyed by a conflagration? Or are they bodies of a wholly different nature, of which we can form no idea? Who can tell what is the *sun?* Its use we know; but who knows of
5 what *substance* it is composed? Nay, we are not yet able to determine whether it be fluid or solid! Who knows what is the precise *distance* of the sun from the earth? Many astronomers are persuaded it is a hundred millions of miles; others that it is only eighty-six millions, though generally accounted ninety. But
10 equally great men say it is no more than fifty; some of them that it is but twelve. Last comes Dr. Rogers, and *demonstrates* that it is just two millions, nine hundred thousand miles![22] So little do we know even of this glorious luminary, the eye and soul of the lower world! And just as much of the planets that surround him; yea, of
15 our own planet, the *moon.* Some indeed have discovered

Rivers and mountains on her spotty globe;[23]

yea, have marked out all her seas and continents! But after all we know just nothing of the matter. We have nothing but mere uncertain conjecture concerning the nearest of all the heavenly
20 bodies.

6. But let us come to the things that are still nearer home, and inquire what knowledge we have of them. How much do we know of that wonderful body, *light?* How is it communicated to us? Does it flow in a continued stream from the sun? Or does the sun
25 impel the particles next his orb, and so on and on, to the extremity of his system? Again, does light gravitate, or not? Does it attract or repel other bodies? Is it subject to the *general* laws which obtain in

[22] John Rogers, M.D., *Dissertation on the Knowledge of the Antients in Astronomy;* cf. JWJ, May 12, 1757: 'I finished Dr. Rogers' essay on the learning of the ancients. I think he has clearly proved that they had microscopes and telescopes, and knew all that is valuable in modern astronomy.' Wesley's doubts about the latter were reinforced by the gross variations in their calculations. E.g., for the distance between sun and earth, their estimates range from Rogers's 2,910,164 miles to Copernicus' 4,302,625, to Kepler's 12,907,876, to De la Hire's 136,923,591; see Rogers, p. 75. But see also A. Wolf, *A History of Science, Technology, and Philosophy in the 18th Century* (New York, Harper Torchbooks, 1961), pp. 144, 175-76. It is now known that the earth's distance from the sun is not constant, due to the changes in the earth's orbit, but that the mean (with less than 2 percent variation) is about 93,000,000 miles (or a parallax of 8.79″). Unsurprisingly, Newton's calculation (86,051,398) came closest to this. There is an interesting comment on the role of astronomy in England in Williams, *The Whig Supremacy*, pp. 354-56. In any case, one may hope that Dr. Rogers was a better physician than astronomer.

[23] Cf. Milton, *Paradise Lost,* i. 291; in No. 103, 'What is Man? Ps. 8:3-4', II.10, Wesley repeats the phrase without quotation marks. Cf. also JWJ, Sept. 20, 1759.

all other matter? Or is it a body *sui generis*, altogether different from all other matter? Is it the same with the *electric fluid* or not? Who can explain the phenomenon of electricity? Who knows why some bodies *conduct* the electric fluid and others arrest its course? Why is the phial capable of being charged to such a point and no 5 farther?[24] A thousand more questions might be asked on this head, which no man living can answer.

7. But surely we understand the *air* we breathe, and which encompasses us on every side. By that admirable property of elasticity it is the general spring of nature. But is elasticity 10 essential to air, and inseparable from it? Nay, it has been lately proved by numberless experiments that air may be fixed, that is, divested of its elasticity, and *generated*, or restored to it again. Therefore it is no otherwise elastic than as it is connected with electric fire![25] And is not this electric or ethereal fire the only true, 15 essential elastic in nature? Who knows by what power dew, rain, and other vapours rise and fall in the air? Can we account for the phenomenon of them upon the common principles? Or must we own with a late ingenious author that those principles are utterly insufficient, and that they cannot be rationally accounted for but 20 upon the principle of electricity?[26]

8. Let us now descend to the *earth* which we tread upon, and which God has peculiarly given to the children of men. Do the children of men understand this? Suppose the terraqueous globe to be seven or eight thousand miles in diameter,[27] how much of 25 this do we know? Perhaps a mile or two of its surface: so far the art of man has penetrated. But who can inform us what lies beneath this? Beneath the region of stones, metals, minerals, and other fossils? This is only a thin crust which bears an exceeding small

[24] The phenomenon of the Leyden jar; cf. *Survey*, 3rd edn. (1777), III.218-25.
[25] See No. 15, *The Great Assize*, III.3 and n.
[26] Probably Benjamin Franklin, whose *Experiments and Observations on Electricity* (1751) Wesley had read, Feb. 17, 1753. Fascinated with this newly discovered mystery, Wesley also read Hoadly and Wilson, *Observations on a Series of Electrical Experiments* (1756); William Watson, *Observations Upon the Effects of Electricity* (1763); Richard Lovett, *Philosophical Essays* (1766); John Freke, *An Essay to Shew the Cause of Electricity* (2nd edn., 1746), *et al.* (see the Preface to Wesley's *Desideratum; or Electricity Made Plain and Useful* [1760]), all of whom had tended to regard electrical phenomena in cosmic terms. Cf. Wesley's *Survey* (1777), III.215-47, espec. p. 242: 'Electricity will probably soon be considered as the great vivifying principle of nature by which she carries on most of her operations. It is a fifth element distinct from and of a superior nature to the other four.' See also No. 15, *The Great Assize*, III.4 and n.
[27] Another measurement about which the geographers of Wesley's time still differed; cf. William Pemble, *A Brief Introduction to Geography* (1675), p. 9: 'The thickness of half the

proportion to the whole. Who can acquaint us with the inner parts of the globe? Whereof do these consist? Is there a central fire, a grand reservoir which not only supplies the burning mountains,[28] but also ministers (though we know not how) to the ripening
5 of gems and metals; yea, and perhaps to the production of vegetables, and the well-being of animals too? Or is the great deep still contained in the bowels of the earth, a central abyss of waters? Who hath seen? Who can tell? Who can give any solid satisfaction to a rational inquirer?
10   9. How much of the very *surface* of the globe is still utterly unknown to us! How very little do we know of the polar regions, either north or south, either in Europe, or Asia! How little of those vast countries, the inland parts either of Africa or America! Much less do we know what is contained in the broad sea, the
15 great abyss which covers so large a part of the globe. Most of its chambers are inaccessible to man, so that we cannot tell how they are furnished. How little do we know of those things on the dry land which fall directly under our notice! Consider even the most simple metals or stones: how imperfectly are we acquainted with
20 their nature and properties! Who knows what it is that distinguishes metals from all other fossils? It is answered, 'Why, they are heavier.' Very true, but what is the cause of their being heavier? What is the specific difference between metals and stones? Or between one metal and another? Between gold and
25 silver? Between tin and lead? It is all mystery to the sons of men!
     10. Proceed we to the *vegetable* kingdom. Who can demonstrate that the sap in any vegetable performs a regular circulation through its vessels or that it does not? Who can point out the specific difference between one kind of plant and another? Or the
30 peculiar internal conformation and disposition of their component parts? Yea, what man living thoroughly understands the nature and properties of any one plant under heaven?
     11. With regard to *animals*. Are *microscopic animals*[29] (so called)

earth [i.e., the radius] is about 4,000 miles;' George Cheyne, *Philosophical Principles of Religion* (4th edn., 1734), I. 71-72: 'The earth's middle diameter is 7,846 miles, each of which contain 5,000 feet . . .;' and Thomas Salmon, *A New Geographical and Historical Grammar* (6th edn., 1758), p. 17: 'the circumference of the earth is 24,840 English miles' and 'the diameter almost a third, or 7,900 miles'. Current measurements push Wesley's upper limit: i.e., 7,917.4 miles (12,742 km.).
     [28] Cf. above, No. 15, *The Great Assize*, III.4 and n.
     [29] Cf. the section on 'microscopic animalculae' in Wesley's *Survey* (4th edn., 1784), II. 70-71: 'As to some of the animalculae observed by Leewenhoeck [1632–1723], he

real animals or no? If they are, are they not essentially different from all other animals in the universe, as not requiring any food, nor generating or being generated? Are they no animals at all, but merely inanimate particles of matter in a state of fermentation? How totally ignorant are the most sagacious of men touching the 5 whole affair of *generation!* Even the generation of men. 'In the book' of the Creator indeed 'were all our members written, which day by day were fashioned, when as yet there were none of them.'[30] But by what rule were they fashioned? In what manner? By what means was the first motion communicated to the *punctum* 10 *saliens?*[31] When and how was the immortal spirit superadded to the senseless clay? 'Tis mystery all. And we can only say, 'I am fearfully and wonderfully made.'[32]

12. With regard to *insects,* many are the discoveries which have been lately made.[33] But how little is all that is discovered yet in 15 comparison of what is undiscovered! How many millions of them, by their extreme minuteness, totally escape all our inquiries! And indeed the minute parts of the largest animals elude our utmost diligence. Have we a more complete knowledge of *fishes* than we have of insects? A great part, if not the greatest part of the 20 inhabitants of the waters, are totally concealed from us. It is probable the species of sea animals are full as numerous as the land animals. But how few of them are known to us! And it is very little we know of those few. With *birds* we are a little better acquainted; and indeed it is but little. For of very many we know 25 hardly anything more than their outward shape. We know a few of

computed that three or four hundred of them placed close together in a line would equal the diameter of a grain of sand. . . . But [Nicolaas] Hartsoeker [*Meditationes in Oeconomiam Generationis Animalium* (1715)] carries the matter still farther [and asks] according to our present system of generation . . . how minute the animalculae produced now may have been at the beginning.' See also Chambers's *Cyclopaedia,* 'Animalcule'.
    [30] Cf. Ps. 139:15-16.
    [31] 'Salient point'; cf. *Survey,* V. 248 (Appendix), where the same rhetorical question had been asked. Cf. also Aristotle, *Historia Animalium,* VI. iii.: τοῦτο δὲ τὸ σημεῖον πηδᾷ καὶ κινεῖται. The Latin phrase had come to be a technical term for that 'point' in an egg or embryo where vital motion begins (spontaneously, as most naturalists agreed). Cf. Edward Phillips, *The New World of English Words* (ed. J. Kersey, 1706). But see also Ray, *The Wisdom of God Manifested in the Works of Creation,* p. 59; Arthur Collier, *Clavis Universalis,* p. 148; and Sir Richard Blackmore, 'Creation, A Philosophical Poem' (1712), p. 359.
    [32] Ps. 139:14.
    [33] All the seventeenth- and eighteenth-century naturalists had sections on 'Insects'. Cf. Ray, *op. cit.,* pp. 6-7; Derham, *Physico-Theology;* Goldsmith, *History of the Earth . . . ;* and Wesley's *Survey* (4th edn., 1784), II. 56-135. Cf. also No. 60, 'The General Deliverance', III.7.

the obvious properties of others, chiefly those that frequent our houses. But we have not a thorough, adequate knowledge even of them. How little do we know of *beasts!* We do not know whence the different tempers and qualities arise, not only in different
5 species of them, but in individuals of the same species: yea, and frequently in those who spring from the same parents, the same both male and female animal. Are they mere machines? Then they are incapable either of pleasure or pain. Nay, they can have no senses: they neither see nor hear; they neither taste nor smell.
10 Much less can they know or remember, or move any otherwise than they are impelled from without. But all this (as daily experiments show) is quite contrary to matter of fact.

13. Well, but if we know nothing else, do not we know ourselves? Our bodies and our souls? What is our *soul?* It is a
15 spirit, we know. But what is a spirit? Here we are at a full stop. And where is the soul lodged? In the pineal gland?[34] In the whole brain? In the heart? In the blood? In any single part of the body? Or (if anyone can understand those terms) 'all in all, and all in every part'?[35] How is the soul *united* to the body? A spirit to a clod?
20 What is the secret, imperceptible chain that couples them together? Can the wisest of men give a satisfactory answer to any of these plain questions?

And as to our *body* itself, how little do we know![36] During a night's sleep a healthy man perspires one part in four less when he
25 sweats than when he does not.[37] Who can account for this? What

---

[34] Cf. Descartes's discovery that the point of jointure of body and soul is 'a certain very small gland . . . situated in the middle of its substance [the brain] and which is so suspended above the duct whereby the animal spirits in its anterior cavities have communication with those in the posterior that the slightest movements which take place in it alter very greatly the course of these spirits; and reciprocally so that the smallest changes which occur in the course of these spirits may do much to change the movements of this gland' *(Passions of the Soul,* I. 30-31). This idea had become familiar in England; cf. Addison's essay in *The Spectator,* No. 275 (Jan. 15, 1712): 'The pineal gland, which many of our modern philosophers suppose to be the seat of the soul'. Cf. also No. 116, 'What is Man? Ps. 8:4', §6; Wesley's *Survey* (4th edn., 1784), I.52; 'Remarks on the Limits of Human Knowledge', *Survey,* V. 252; and 'A Thought on Necessity' *(AM,* 1780, III. 487).
[35] Cf. No. 67, 'On Divine Providence', §10 and n. Cf. also Thomas Hobbes, *Human Nature* (1684), XI.72: 'It is a plain contradiction in natural discourse to say of the soul of man that it is *tota in toto et tota in qualibet parte corporis.*'
[36] For the body as a machine, cf. No. 51, *The Good Steward,* I.4 and n.
[37] A distinction between 'insensible perspiration' (exhalation) and sweat ('sensible perspiration'). Wesley had borrowed it from Joseph Rogers, M.D., *An Essay on Epidemic Disease* (Dublin, 1734), 'Appendix'. He uses it in the *Survey* (4th edn., 1784), I.47: 'An ingenious physician, Dr. Rogers, has found by numerous experiments that a person perspires abundantly less when he sweats than when he does not: that one who perspires

is *flesh?* That of the muscles in particular? Are the fibres that compose it of a determinate size? So that they can be divided only so far? Or are they resolvable *in infinitum?*[38] How does a muscle *act?* By being inflated, and consequently shortened? But what is it inflated with? If with blood, how and whence comes that blood? 5 And whither does it go the moment the muscle is relaxed? Are the *nerves* pervious or solid? How do they act? By vibration, or transmission of the animal spirits?[39] Who knows what the animal spirits are? Are they electric fire? What is *sleep?* Wherein does it consist? What is *dreaming?*[40] How can we know dreams from 10 waking thoughts? I doubt no man knows. O how little do we know even concerning ourselves! What then can we expect to know concerning the whole creation of God?

II.1. But are we not better acquainted with his *works of providence* than with his works of creation? It is one of the first 15 principles of religion that his kingdom ruleth over all; so that we may say with confidence, 'O Lord our Governor, how excellent is thy name over all the earth!'[41] It is a childish conceit to suppose chance governs the world, or has any part in the government of it;[42] no, not even in those things that to a vulgar eye appear to be 20

twenty-four ounces in seven hours of sleep, if he sweats does not perspire above six. . . . Whence he infers that it is not the same matter which is evacuated by insensible perspiration and by sweat. . . . What a field does this open!'

[38] An allowable alternative to *ad infinitum;* cf. *A Farther Appeal,* Pt. II, II.5 (11:219 in this edn.); and Wesley's letter to Samuel Furly, May 21, 1762.

[39] For some of Wesley's other discussions of animal spirits, cf. No. 80, 'On Friendship with the World', §17; his 'Thoughts on Nervous Disorders' (*AM*, 1786, IX.52-54, 94-97); his letter 'To an old Friend', Nov. 27, 1750. For other references, cf. Dr. Edward Young (father of the poet), Sermon V, 'The Heavenly Pattern', which Wesley extracted for the *Christian Lib.*, XLVI. 91-113 (see espec. p. 98); Bishop Berkeley discussed the matter in an essay for *The Guardian,* No. 35 (Apr. 21, 1713), as did Addison in *The Spectator,* No. 128 (July 27,1711). Locke, in his *Essay Concerning Human Understanding,* I.118, 121, 139, 143, spoke of them. So did Samuel Annesley in his sermon on 'Universal Conscientiousness', in *The Morning-Exercise at Cripplegate* (1661), p. 7. Cf. also, 'Essay on Learning', in *The Young Students Library* (1692), p. iii. Johnson, *Dictionary,* cites Bacon's *Natural History* as an illustration of 'spirit' (No. 17).

[40] For 'sleep', cf. No 93, 'On Redeeming the Time', *passim;* for 'dreams' and 'dreaming', cf. No. 124, 'Human Life a Dream', §4 and n.

[41] Cf. Ps. 8:1, 9 (BCP).

[42] A counter-thesis to Wesley's emphatic faith in providence and moral agency; cf. Cicero, *De Natura Deorum (On the Nature of the Gods),* II. xxxvii. 93: 'The world's order cannot be the result of some fortuitous concourse of atoms;' and Richard Lucas, *Enquiry After Happiness,* I. 101: ' 'Tis beneath the dignity of a soul . . . to hug chance and wind and waves the arbitrary disposers of his happiness. . . . Oh, how I hug the memory of those honest heathens who in a ragged gown and homely cottage bade defiance to fortune.' This notion is repeated endlessly by Wesley; cf., e.g., Nos. 71, 'Of Good Angels', II.3; 95, 'On

perfectly casual. 'The lot is cast into the lap; but the disposal
thereof is from the Lord.'[43] Our blessed Master himself has put
this matter beyond all possible doubt. 'Not a sparrow', saith he,
'falleth to the ground without the will of your Father which is in
5 heaven.'[44] Yea (to express the thing more strongly still) 'Even the
very hairs of your head are all numbered.'[45]

2. But although we are well apprised of this general truth, that
all things are governed by the providence of God (the very
language of the heathen orator, *deorum moderamine cuncta geri*),[46]
10 yet how amazingly little do we know of the particulars contained
under this general! How little do we understand of his providential dealings, either with regard to nations, or families, or
individuals! There are heights and depths in all these which our
understanding can in no wise fathom. We can comprehend but a
15 small part of his ways now; the rest we shall know hereafter.

3. Even with regard to entire nations, how little do we
comprehend of God's providential dealings with them! What
innumerable nations in the eastern world once flourished, to the
terror of all around them, and are now swept away from the face
20 of the earth; and their memorial is perished with them![47] Nor has
the case been otherwise in the west. In Europe also we read of
many large and powerful kingdoms of which the names only are
left: the people are vanished away, and are as though they had
never been. But why it has pleased the almighty Governor of the
25 world to sweep them with the besom of destruction[48] we cannot
tell; those who succeeded them being many times little better
than themselves.

4. But it is not only with regard to ancient nations that the
providential dispensations of God are utterly incomprehensible
30 to us: the same difficulties occur now. We cannot account for his
present dealings with the inhabitants of the earth. We know, the

the Education of Children', §14; his *Notes* on Luke 10:31 and Acts 17:18. See JWJ, July
6, 1781, where Wesley says, 'So far as fortune or chance governs the world, God has no
place in it.' Also his letter to Hester Ann Roe, Feb. 11, 1779: 'Chance has no share in the
government of the world.' Cf. also, *An Estimate of Manners of the Present Times*, §14.

[43] Cf. Prov. 16:33. [44] Cf. Matt. 10:29.

[45] Luke 12:7.

[46] Cicero, *De Natura Deorum* ('On the Nature of the Gods'), II. xxx. 75; cf. No. 67, 'On
Divine Providence', §1 and n.

[47] Ps. 9:6.

[48] Cf. Isa. 14:23; a 'besom' was, originally, a bundle of twigs and rods used for
punishment, then for sweeping (hence, 'broom'); fig., a weapon to sweep away something
undesirable.

Lord is loving unto every man, and that his mercy is over all his works.[49] But we know not how to reconcile this with the present dispensations of his providence. At this day is not almost every part of the earth full of darkness and cruel habitations? In what a condition, in particular, is the large and populous empire of Indostan?[50] How many hundred thousands of the poor, quiet people have been destroyed, and their carcases left as the dung of the earth! In what a condition (though they have no English ruffians there) are the numberless islands in the Pacific Ocean? How little is their state above that of wolves and bears! And who careth either for their souls or their bodies? But does not the Father of men care for them? O mystery of providence!

5. And who cares for thousands, myriads, if not millions of the wretched Africans? Are not whole droves of these poor sheep (human if not rational beings!) continually driven to market, and sold like cattle into the vilest bondage, without any hope of deliverance but by death?[51] Who cares for those outcasts of men, the well-known Hottentots? It is true, a late writer has taken much pains to represent them as a respectable people.[52] But from what motive it is not easy to say; since he himself allows (a specimen of

---

[49] Ps. 145:9 (BCP).

[50] I.e., Hindustan, or India. Besides the general reports, Wesley was much impressed by William Bolt's melancholy *Considerations on the Affairs of India* (1772–75); cf. JWJ, Feb. 23, 1776. Home criticism of British rule in India had begun to mount, with the seven-year-long impeachment of Warren Hastings already foreshadowed. Cf. No. 61, 'The Mystery of Iniquity', §33. Notice also how, in §35, 'ruffians', 'wolves', and 'bears' are linked in Charles's hymn (where he uses 'beasts'); see below, John's revision in this same paragraph.

[51] A detestation of slavery was part of Wesley's lifelong concern for the oppressed. Cf., e.g., his comment on 1 Tim. 1:10 in *Notes*, denouncing 'traders in Negroes, procurers of servants for America'. He borrowed heavily from Anthony Benezet's *Historical Account of Guinea* (1771). They both agreed that 'slavery under the pagan Romans and infidel Turks was more tolerable than in the Christian exploitation of African slaves for the Spanish and English colonies' (Benezet, VI. 63-71); see also, Wesley's extract of Benezet in *Thoughts Upon Slavery*, 1774 (*Bibliog*, No. 350; Vol. 15 of the edn.). In *A Seasonable Address to the Inhabitants of Great Britain* (*Bibliog*, No. 359; Vol. 15 of this edn.), he argues that 'one principal sin of our nation is the blood we have shed in Asia, Africa, and America. . . . The African [slave] trade is iniquitous from first to last. It is the price of blood! It is a trade of blood, and has stained our land with blood!'
Cf. also JWJ, Apr. 14, 1777, and Mar. 1788; and his letters to Samuel Hoare, Aug. 18, 1787; Granville Sharp, Oct. 11, 1787; Henry Moore, Mar. 14, 1790; and William Wilberforce, Feb. 24, 1791.

[52] 'Hottentots' was the generic label for natives of southern Africa. Much had been written about them by the frequent travellers who stopped over at the Cape of Good Hope. 'The late writer' cited here was Peter Kolben, in *The Present State of the Cape of Good Hope* (1731); cf. IV. 36. But even Kolben's evaluation of them is ambivalent; see, e.g., pp. 47, 56, 330-31. Cf. Wesley's No. 28, 'Sermon on the Mount, VIII', §9 and n.

their elegance of manners) that the raw guts of sheep and other cattle are not only some of their choicest food but also the ornaments of their arms and legs; and (a specimen of their religion) that the son is not counted a man till he has beat his
5 mother almost to death. And when his father grows old he fastens him in a little hut and leaves him there to starve![53] O Father of mercies! Are these the works of thy own hands? The purchase of thy Son's blood?

6. How little better is either the civil or religious state of the
10 poor American Indians![54] That is, the miserable remains of them; for in some provinces not one of them is left to breathe. In Hispaniola,[55] when the Christians came thither first, there were three millions of inhabitants. Scarce twelve thousand of them now survive. And in what condition are these? Or the other
15 Indians who are still scattered up and down in the vast continent of South or North America? Religion they have none; no public worship of any kind. God is not in all their thoughts. And most of them have no civil government at all—no laws, no magistrates— but every man does what is right in his own eyes; therefore they
20 are decreasing daily. And very probably in a century or two there will not be one of them left.

7. However, the inhabitants of Europe are not in so deplorable a condition. They are in a state of civilization. They have useful laws and are governed by magistrates. They have religion. They
25 are Christians. I am afraid, whether they are called Christians or not, many of them have not much religion. What say you to thousands of Laplanders,[56] of Finlanders? Samoyeds,[57] and Greenlanders? Indeed of all who live in high northern latitudes? Are they as civilized as sheep or oxen? To compare them with

---

[53] Cf. Kolben, *ibid.*, pp. 331-32. In Bond's edn. of *The Spectator*, III. 461, n. 1, there is a reference to John Maxwell's comment in his 'Account of the Cape of Good Hope' (*Philos. Trans.* No. 310, 1707), that the Hottentots have 'no notion of God'. They are also discussed in William Dampier's *Voyages* (1703), and by various writers in the *Collection of Voyages* (1704) or A. and J. Churchill. Cf. also, Adam Smith, *Wealth of Nations*, I.2. (intro.). See also No. 105, 'On Conscience', I.4; and the *Doctrine of Original Sin*, I. ii. 2 (Vol. 12 of this edn.).

[54] Cf. No. 38. 'A Caution against Bigotry', I.9 and n.

[55] The second largest island in the Caribbean (after Cuba) named Española by Columbus; it is now divided between the Dominican Republic and Haiti.

[56] Cf. No. 38, 'A Caution against Bigotry', I.4 and n.

[57] Wesley's spelling: 'Samoeids'—i.e., the Finno-Asian neighbours of the Laplanders and Finns in the Archangel district (Nenets) of what is now the extreme northwest corner of the USSR.

horses or any of our domestic animals would be doing them too much honour. Add to these myriads of human savages that are freezing among the snows of Siberia; and as many, if not more, who are wandering up and down in the deserts of Tartary. Add thousands upon thousands of Poles and Muscovites, and of 5 Christians, so called, from Turkey in Europe. And did 'God so love' these that 'he gave his Son, his only begotten Son, to the end they might not perish but have everlasting life'?[58] Then why are they thus? O wonder above all wonders!

8. Is there not something equally mysterious in the divine 10 dispensation with regard to Christianity itself? Who can explain why Christianity is not spread as far as sin? Why is not the medicine sent to every place where the disease is found? But alas! it is not; 'the sound of it is' not now 'gone forth into all lands'![59] The poison is diffused over the whole globe; the antidote is not 15 known in a sixth part of it.[60] Nay, and how is it that the wisdom and goodness of God suffer the antidote itself to be so grievously adulterated, not only in Roman Catholic countries, but almost in every part of the Christian world? So adulterated by mixing it frequently with useless, frequently with poisonous ingredients, 20 that it retains none, or at least a very small part of its original virtue. Yea, it is so thoroughly adulterated by many of those very persons whom he has sent to administer it that it adds tenfold malignity to the disease which it was designed to cure! In consequence of this there is little more mercy or truth to be found 25 among Christians than among pagans. Nay, it has been affirmed, and I am afraid truly, that many called Christians are far worse than the heathens that surround them: more profligate, more abandoned to all manner of wickedness, neither fearing God, nor regarding man![61] O who can comprehend this! Doth not he who 30 is higher than the highest regard it?

9. Equally incomprehensible to us are many of the divine dispensations with regard to particular families. We cannot at all comprehend why he raises some to wealth, honour, and power; and why in the meantime he depresses others with poverty and 35

---

[58] Cf. John 3:16.   [59] Cf. Ps. 19:4 (BCP).

[60] Another echo of Brerewood; see No. 15, *The Great Assize*, II.4 and n. In any of his value judgments, the Wesley whose conscious evangel was 'Universal Redemption' (as on the masthead of his *Magazine*) also makes an unselfconscious correlation between British Christianity at its best and Christianity as such.

[61] See Luke 18:4.

various afflictions. Some wonderfully prosper in all they take in hand, and the world pours in upon them; while others with all their labour and toil can scarce procure daily bread. And perhaps prosperity and applause continue with the former to their death; 5 while the latter drink the cup of adversity to their life's end—although no reason appears to us either for the prosperity of the one or the adversity of the other.

10. As little can we account for the divine dispensations with regard to *individuals*. We know not why the lot of this man is cast 10 in Europe, the lot of that man in the wilds of America; why one is born of rich or noble, the other of poor parents; why the father and mother of one are strong and healthy, those of another weak and diseased; in consequence of which he drags a miserable being all the days of his life, exposed to want, and pain, and a 15 thousand temptations from which he finds no way to escape. How many are from their very infancy hedged in with such relations that they seem to have no chance (as some speak), no possibility of being useful to themselves or others? Why are they, antecedent to their own choice, entangled in such connections? Why are hurtful 20 people so cast in their way that they know not how to escape them? And why are useful persons hid out of their sight, or snatched away from them at their utmost need? O God, how unsearchable are thy judgments or counsels! Too deep to be fathomed by our reason: 'and thy ways' of executing those counsels 'not to be 25 traced'⁶² by our wisdom!

III.1. Are we able to search out his works of *grace* any more than his works of providence? Nothing is more sure than that 'without holiness no man shall see the Lord.'⁶³ Why is it then that so vast a majority of mankind are, so far as we can judge, cut off from all 30 means, all possibility of holiness, even from their mother's womb? For instance: what possibility is there that a Hottentot, a New Zealander, or an inhabitant of Nova Zembla,⁶⁴ if he lives and dies there, should ever know what holiness means? Or consequently ever attain it? Yea, but one may say: 'He sinned 35 before he was born, in a *pre-existent state*. Therefore he was placed

---

⁶² Cf. Rom. 11:33.
⁶³ Cf. Heb. 12:14.
⁶⁴ 'New Land'. Two bleak islands in the Barents Sea off the northern coast of Siberia; now spelt Novaya Zemlya. Cf. Addison, *The Free-Holder*, No. 5 (Jan. 6, 1716), where he compares the inhabitants of Nova Zembla and the Hottentots of the Cape of Good Hope.

here in so unfavourable a situation. And it is mere mercy that he should have a second trial.' I answer: supposing such a pre-existent state, this which you call a second trial is really no trial at all. As soon as he is born into the world he is absolutely in the power of his savage parents and relations, who from the first 5 dawn of reason train him up in the same ignorance, atheism, and barbarity with themselves. He has no chance, so to speak; he has no possibility of any better education. What trial has he then? From the time he comes into the world till he goes out of it again he seems to be under a dire necessity of living in all ungodliness 10 and unrighteousness. But how is this? How can this be the case with so many millions of the souls that God has made? Art thou not the God 'of all the ends of the earth, and of them that remain in the broad sea'?[65]

2. I desire it may be observed that if this be improved into an 15 objection against revelation it is an objection that lies full as much against natural as revealed religion.[66] If it were conclusive it would not drive us into deism but into flat atheism.[67] It would conclude not only against the Christian revelation but against the being of a God. And yet I see not how we can avoid the force of it but by 20 resolving all into the unsearchable wisdom of God, together with a deep conviction of our ignorance and inability to fathom his counsels.

3. Even among us who are favoured far above these—to whom are entrusted the oracles of God,[68] whose word is a lantern to 25 our feet, and a light in all our paths[69]—there are still many circumstances in his dispensations which are above our comprehension. We know not why he suffered us so long to go on in our own ways before we were convinced of sin. Or why he made use of this or the other instrument, and in this or the other 30 manner. And a thousand circumstances attended the process of our conviction which we do not comprehend. We know not why he suffered us to stay so long before he revealed his Son in our

[65] Ps. 65:5 (BCP).

[66] For Wesley's comments on 'natural religion', see No. 1, *Salvation by Faith*, I.1 and n. But notice the resemblance between this turn of Wesley's argument and the central thesis of Joseph Butler's *Analogy of Religion, Natural and Revealed* (1736); thus far had it become standard and thus far Wesley shared this aspect of Anglican rationalism; see Irène Simon, *Three Restoration Divines*, I.i.75-148.

[67] Cf. No. 23, 'Sermon on the Mount, III', I.11 and n.

[68] Cf. No. 5, 'Justification by Faith', §2 and n.

[69] See Ps. 119:105 (BCP).

hearts; or why this change from darkness to light was accompanied with such and such particular circumstances.

4. It is doubtless the peculiar prerogative of God to reserve the 'times and seasons in his own power'.[70] And we cannot give any
5 reason why of two persons equally athirst for salvation one is presently taken into the favour of God and the other left to mourn for months or years. One, as soon as he calls upon God, is answered, and filled with peace and joy in believing. Another seeks after him—and it seems with the same degree of sincerity
10 and earnestness—and yet cannot find him, or any consciousness of his favour, for weeks, or months, or years. We know well this cannot possibly be owing to any absolute decree, consigning one before he was born to everlasting glory, and the other to everlasting fire. But we do not know what is the reason for it: it is
15 enough that God knoweth.

5. There is likewise great variety in the manner and time of God's bestowing his *sanctifying grace*,[71] whereby he enables his children to give him their whole heart, which we can in no wise account for. We know not why he bestows this on some even be-
20 fore they ask for it (some unquestionable instances of which we have seen); on some after they have sought it but a few days; and yet permits other believers to wait for it perhaps twenty, thirty, or forty years; nay, and others till a few hours or even minutes before their spirits return to him. For the various circumstances also
25 which attend the fulfilling of that great promise, 'I will circumcise thy heart, to love the Lord thy God with all thy heart and with all thy soul,'[72] God undoubtedly has reasons; but those reasons are generally hid from the children of men. Once more: some of those who are enabled to love God with all their heart and with all
30 their soul, retain the same blessing without any interruption till they are carried to Abraham's bosom. Others do not retain it, although they are not conscious of having grieved the Holy Spirit of God.[73] This also we do not understand: we do not herein 'know the mind of the Spirit'.[74]

35   IV.[1.] Several valuable lessons we may learn from a deep consciousness of this our own ignorance. First, we may learn

---

[70] Cf. Acts 1:7.
[71] Note the definition here, and cf. No. 19, 'The Great Privilege of those that are Born of God', §2 and n.
[72] Cf. Deut. 30:6.   [73] Cf. Eph. 4:30.   [74] Cf. Rom. 8:27.

hence a lesson of humility: not to think of ourselves, particularly with regard to our understanding, 'more highly than we ought to think'; but 'to think soberly',[75] being thoroughly convinced that we are not sufficient of ourselves to think one good thought; that we should be liable to stumble at every step, to err every moment 5 of our lives, were it not that we have 'an anointing from the Holy One' which 'abideth with us'[76]—were it not that he who knoweth what is in man helpeth our infirmities; that 'there is a spirit in man which giveth wisdom,' and the inspiration of the Holy One which giveth understanding.[77]   10

[2.] From hence we may learn, secondly, a lesson of faith, of confidence in God. A full conviction of our own ignorance may teach us a full trust in his wisdom. It may teach us (what is not always so easy as one would conceive it to be) to trust the invisible God farther than we can see him! It may assist us in learning that 15 difficult lesson, 'to cast down' our own 'imaginations' (or reasonings rather, as the word properly signifies), to 'cast down every high thing that exalteth itself against the knowledge of God, and bring into captivity every thought to the obedience of Christ.'[78] There are at present two grand obstructions to our 20 forming a right judgment of the dealings of God with respect to men. The one is, there are innumerable *facts* relating to every man which we do not and cannot know. They are at present hid from us, and covered from our search by impenetrable darkness. The other is, we cannot see the *thoughts* of men, even when we know 25 their actions. Still we know not their *intentions;* and without this we can but ill judge of their outward actions. Conscious of this, 'judge nothing before the time' concerning his providential dispensations; till he shall bring to light the 'hidden things of darkness', and manifest 'the thoughts and intent of the heart.'[79] 30

[3.] From a consciousness of our ignorance we may learn, thirdly, a lesson of resignation.[80] We may be instructed to say at all times and in all instances, 'Father, not as I will; but as thou wilt.'[81] This was the last lesson which our blessed Lord (as man) learnt

---

[75] Cf. Rom. 12:3.
[76] Cf. 1 John 2:20, 27.
[77] See Job 32:8.
[78] Cf. 2 Cor. 10:5.
[79] Cf. 1 Cor. 4:5.
[80] Cf. No. 22, 'Sermon on the Mount, II', I.4 and n.
[81] Matt. 26:39.

while he was upon earth. He could go no higher than, 'Not as I will, but as thou wilt,' till he bowed his head and gave up the ghost.[82] Let us also herein be made conformable to his death, that we may know the full 'power of his resurrection'.[83]

5 Bristol, March 5, 1784[84]

---

[82] John 19:30.
[83] Phil. 3:10.
[84] Place and date as given in *AM*.

The Case of Reason Impartially Considered

1 Corinthians 14:20

Brethren, be not children in understanding: in wickedness be ye children; but in understanding be ye men.[1]

1. It is the true remark of an eminent man, who had made many 5 observations on human nature, 'If reason be against a man, a man will always be against reason.'[2] This has been confirmed by the experience of all ages. Very many have been the instances of it in the Christian as well as the heathen world; yea, and that in the earliest times. Even then there were not wanting well-meaning 10 men who, not having much reason themselves, imagined that reason was of no use in religion; yea, rather, that it was a hindrance to it. And there has not been wanting a succession of men who have believed and asserted the same thing. But never was there a greater number of these in the Christian church, at 15 least in Britain, than at this day.

2. Among them that despise and vilify reason you may always expect to find those enthusiasts who suppose the dreams of their own imagination to be revelations from God. We cannot expect that men of this turn will pay much regard to reason. Having an 20 infallible guide, they are very little moved by the reasonings of fallible men. In the foremost of these we commonly find the whole herd of antinomians; all that, however they may differ in other respects, agree in 'making void the law through faith'.[3] If you oppose reason to these, when they are asserting propositions 25 ever so full of absurdity and blasphemy, they will probably think it

---

[1] This translation of κακία as 'wickedness' seems peculiar to Wesley; cf. his *Notes* for still further revisions of the AV. Wycliffe, Tyndale, Cranmer, Geneva, Rheims, and AV all render it as 'malice' or 'maliciousness'.

[2] Thomas Hobbes; cf. *The Last Sayings, or Dying Legacy of Mr. Thomas Hobbes of Malmesbury, Who Departed This Life on Thursday, December 4, 1679.* Printed for the Author's Executors (1680), p.39: 'In matters of right or interest, where reason is against a man, a man will be against reason.' See also Jonathan Swift, *A Letter to a Young Clergyman*, §3. See also, below, II.4.

[3] Cf. Rom. 3:31.

a sufficient answer to say, 'Oh, this is your reason!' Or, your carnal reason. So that all arguments are lost upon them: they regard them no more than stubble or rotten wood.

3. How natural is it for those who observe this extreme to run
5 into the contrary! While they are strongly impressed with the absurdity of undervaluing reason, how apt are they to overvalue it! So much easier it is to run from east to west than to stop at the middle point! Accordingly we are surrounded with those— we find them on every side—who lay it down as an undoubted
10 principle that reason is the highest gift of God. They paint it in the fairest colours: they extol it to the skies. They are fond of expatiating in its praise: they make it little less than divine. They are wont to describe it as very near, if not quite infallible. They look upon it as the all-sufficient director of all the children of
15 men, able by its native light to guide them into all truth, and lead them into all virtue.[4]

4. They that are prejudiced against the Christian revelation, who do not receive the Scriptures as the oracles of God, almost universally run into this extreme. I have scarce known any ex-
20 ception: so do all, by whatever name they are called, who deny the Godhead of Christ. (Indeed some of these say, they do not deny his Godhead, but only his supreme Godhead. Nay, this is the same thing; for in denying him to be the supreme God they deny him to be any God at all—unless they will assert that there
25 are two gods, a great one and little one!) All these are vehement applauders of reason as the great unerring guide. To these overvaluers of reason we may generally add men of eminently strong understanding; who, because they do know more than most other men, suppose they can know all things. But we may
30 likewise add many who are in the other extreme, men of eminently weak understanding; men in whom pride (a very common case) supplies the void of sense; who do not suspect themselves to be blind, because they were always so.[5]

5. Is there then no medium between these extremes,[6]
35 undervaluing and overvaluing reason? Certainly there is. But who

---

[4] Cf. Irène Simon, *Three Restoration Divines*, I. ii, espec. the references to Lord Falkland of Great Tew, Chillingworth, Stillingfleet, *et al.* But see also Joseph Butler, *Analogy of Religion, passim.*

[5] The prime example here would be, of course, David Hume; cf. also Nos. 120, 'The Unity of the Divine Being', §§19, 20; 128, 'The Deceitfulness of the Human Heart', §3, II.7; and 'Remarks on Count de Buffon's Natural History' (*AM*, 1782, V.546-48).

[6] Cf. No. 27, 'Sermon on the Mount, VII', §4 and n.

is there to point it out? To mark down the middle way? That great master of reason, Mr. Locke, has done something of the kind, something applicable to it, in one chapter of his *Essay concerning Human Understanding*.[7] But it is only remotely applicable to this: he does not come home to the point. The good and great Dr. 5 Watts has wrote admirably well both concerning reason and faith.[8] But neither does anything he has written point out the medium between valuing it too little and too much.

6. I would gladly endeavour in some degree to supply this grand defect: to point out, first, to undervaluers of it, what reason can 10 do; and then to the overvaluers of it, what reason cannot do.

But before either the one or the other can be done it is absolutely necessary to define the term, to fix the precise meaning of the word in question. Unless this is done men may dispute to the end of the world without coming to any good conclusion. This 15 is one great cause of the numberless altercations which have been on the subject. Very few of the disputants thought of this—of defining the word they were disputing about.[9] The natural consequence was, they were just as far from an agreement at the end as at the beginning. 20

I. 1. First, then, *reason* is sometimes taken for *argument*. So. 'Give me a *reason* for your assertion.' So in Isaiah, 'Bring forth your strong reasons;'[10] that is, your strong *arguments*. We use the word in nearly the same sense when we say, 'He has good *reasons* for what he does.' It seems here to mean: he has sufficient *motives*, 25 such as ought to influence a wise man. But how is the word to be understood in the celebrated question concerning 'the reasons of

---

[7] Wesley had read Locke's *Essay* (1690) in Oxford in 1725, and he had published a digest of it, with critical comments, in *AM* (1782–84), V–VII. Locke's empiricism was never more than partially satisfying to Wesley, as in the sections 'Of Reason' (IV. xvii) and 'Of Faith and Reason and Their Distinct Provinces' (IV. xviii). See also *The Reasonableness of Christianity* (1695), which still fell short of Wesley's concern for intuition in matters of 'our knowledge of God and of the things of God.'

[8] Wesley had read Watts, *The Strength and Weakness of Human Reason*, in the year of its publication (1731), and in 1734 he records having read the better known *Logic, or, the Right Use of Reason in the Enquiry After Truth* (1725). Watts had died (1748) before Wesley got round to *The Improvement of the Mind* (1741). It would take a sharp-eyed critic to detect as much of a difference between Watts and Wesley as Wesley here implies, save for the latter's greater stress on faith as noetic.

[9] But see Locke's 'Epistle to the Reader' in his *Essay*, and his comments in I. i. 7–8; see also his 'Second Letter to the Bishop of Worcester', in *Works* (London, 1823, Scientia Verlag Aalen, 1963), I. 7ff.

[10] Isa. 41:21.

things'?[11] Particularly when it is asked, *An rationes rerum sint aeternae?*[12]—whether the reasons of things are eternal. Do not the 'reasons of things' here mean the *relations* of things to each other? But what are the *eternal relations* of *temporal* things? Of things
5 which did not exist till yesterday? Could the relations of these things exist before the things themselves had any existence? Is not then the talking of such relations a flat contradiction? Yea, as palpable a one as can be put into words.

2. In another acceptation of the word, reason is much the same
10 with *understanding.* It means a faculty of the human soul; that faculty which exerts itself in three ways: by simple apprehension, by judgment, and by discourse. *Simple apprehension* is barely conceiving a thing in the mind, the first and most simple act of understanding. *Judgment* is the determining that the things before
15 conceived either agree with or differ from each other. *Discourse* (strictly speaking) is the motion of progress of the mind from one judgment to another. The faculty of the soul which includes these three operations I here mean by the term *reason.*

3. Taking the word in this sense, let us now impartially
20 consider, first, what it is that reason can do. And who can deny that it can do much, very much, in the affairs of common life? To begin at the lowest point, it can direct servants how to perform the various works wherein they are employed; to discharge their duty either in the meanest offices or in any of a higher nature. It can
25 direct the husbandman at what time and in what manner to cultivate his ground: to plough, to sow, to reap, to bring in his corn, to breed and manage his cattle, and to act with prudence and propriety in every part of his employment. It can direct artificers how to prepare the various sorts of apparel, and the
30 thousand necessaries and conveniences of life, not only for themselves and their households, but for their neighbours, whether nigh or afar off. It can direct those of higher abilities to plan and execute works of a more elegant kind. It can direct the

---

[11] Cf. Eccles. 7:25.

[12] A perennial question in Western philosophical theology. Cf. Augustine, *De diversis quaestionibus* LXXXIII (*q.* LXVI, *'De ideis'*), in Migne, *PL*, XL.29-31, where he speaks of *rationes aeternae* as subsisting in God. On the medieval influence of this text (and its thesis), see Martin Grabmann, *'Des H. Augustinus Quaestio "de ideis"* . . . *in ihrer inhaltlichen Bedeutung und mittelalterlichen Weiterwirkung'*, in *Mittelalterliches Geistesleben* (München, Max Huber Verlag, 1936), II. 25-34. Thomas treats the question in his *Super Sent.* I. 36; in *Summa Contra Gentiles*, I. 54; *Summa Theologica*, I, *Qg.* 55, 56, 93; in *De Veritate, Q.* 3; and in *Quodlibeta*, IV, *Q.* 1. Cf. *An Earnest Appeal*, §§28-32 (11:55-56 in this edn.).

painter, the statuary, the musician, to excel in the stations wherein providence has placed them. It can direct the mariner to steer his course over the bosom of the great deep. It enables those who study the laws of their country to defend the property or life of their fellow-subjects; and those who study the art of healing to 5 cure most of the maladies to which we are exposed in our present state.[13]

4. To ascend higher still, it is certain reason can assist us in going through the whole circle of arts and sciences: of grammar, rhetoric, logic, natural and moral philosophy, mathematics, al- 10 gebra, metaphysics. It can teach whatever the skill or industry of man has invented for some thousand years. It is absolutely necessary for the due discharge of the most important offices, such as are those of magistrates, whether of an inferior or superior rank; and those of subordinate or supreme governors, 15 whether of states, provinces, or kingdoms.

5. All this few men in their senses will deny. No thinking man can doubt but reason is of considerable service in all things relating to the present world. But suppose we speak of higher things, the things of another world. What can reason do here? Is it 20 a help or a hindrance of religion? It may do much in the affairs of men. But what can it do in the things of God?

6. This is a point that deserves to be deeply considered. If you ask, What can reason do in religion? I answer, It can do exceeding much, both with regard to the foundation of it, and the 25 superstructure.

The foundation of true religion stands upon the oracles of God.[14] It is built upon the prophets and apostles, Jesus Christ

---

[13] An echo of a familiar Puritan theme already reiterated, e.g., in the anonymous pamphlet of 1687, entitled, *An Occasional Discourse Concerning God's Fore-Knowledge and Man's Free-Agency: Being an Attempt to reconcile their seeming Opposition and to assert the Truth of both from the Holy Scriptures:* '. . . we see plainly that, by the good providence and disposal of Almighty God, men have power to do many things, as namely, to cultivate the earth, to build houses, to provide against hunger and cold, to educate their children, to exercise [their] several arts and trades, for the benefit of human life, and to manage all these according to certain rules, methods, and observations, arising partly from experience, and partly from men's consulting one another. In short, I conceive that God, having indued man with an understanding to judge, and a will to choose, and continually supplying him with power to act according to his nature, he doth not ordinarily overpower or impel his faculties, but leaves them to the free use and exercise thereof in things within his proper sphere. And this [power to judge and to choose] is what I mean by free will. Now, I address to my [second] province, which is to assert this, together with God's foreknowledge of future events from Scriptures' (pp. 25-26).

[14] Cf. No. 5, 'Justification by Faith', §2 and n.

himself being the chief corner-stone.[15] Now of what excellent use is reason if we would either understand ourselves, or explain to others, those living oracles! And how is it possible without it to understand the essential truths contained therein? A beautiful
5 summary of which we have in that which is called the Apostles' Creed. Is it not reason (assisted by the Holy Ghost) which enables us to understand what the Holy Scriptures declare concerning the being and attributes of God? Concerning his eternity and immensity, his power, wisdom, and holiness? It is by reason that
10 God enables us in some measure to comprehend his method of dealing with the children of men; the nature of his various dispensations, of the Old and New Covenant, of the law and the gospel. It is by this we understand (his Spirit opening and enlightening the eyes of our understanding)[16] what that re-
15 pentance is, not to be repented of;[17] what is that faith whereby we are saved; what is the nature and the condition of justification; what are the immediate and what the subsequent fruits of it. By reason we learn what is that new birth, without which we cannot enter into the kingdom of heaven, and what that holiness is,
20 without which no man shall see the Lord.[18] By the due use of reason we come to know what are the tempers implied in inward holiness, and what it is to be outwardly holy, holy in all manner of conversation[19]—in other words, what is the mind that was in Christ,[20] and what it is to walk as Christ walked.[21]
25   7. Many particular cases will occur, with respect to several of the foregoing articles, in which we shall have occasion for all our understanding if we would keep a conscience void of offence.[22] Many cases of conscience are not to be solved without the utmost exercise of our reason. The same is requisite in order to
30 understand and to discharge our ordinary relative duties; the duties of parents and children, of husband and wives, and (to name no more) of masters and servants. In all these respects, and in all the duties of common life, God has given us our reason for a guide. And it is only by acting up to the dictates of it, by using all
35 the understanding which God hath given us, that we can have a conscience void of offence towards God and towards man.[23]

---

[15] See Eph. 2:20.   [16] See Eph. 1:18.
[17] See 2 Cor. 7:10.   [18] See Heb. 12:14.
[19] 1 Pet. 1:15.   [20] See Phil. 2:5.
[21] See 1 John 2:6.   [22] Acts 24:16.
[23] *Ibid.*

8. Here then there is a large field indeed wherein reason may expatiate and exercise all its powers. And if reason can do all this, both in civil and religious things, what is it that it cannot do? We have hitherto endeavoured to lay aside all prejudice, and to weigh the matter calmly and impartially. The same course let us take still: let us now coolly consider, without prepossession on any side, what it is, according to the best light we have, that reason cannot do.

II. 1. And, first, reason cannot produce faith. Although it is always consistent with reason, yet reason cannot produce faith in the scriptural sense of the word. Faith, according to Scripture, is 'an evidence or conviction of things not seen'.[24] It is a divine evidence, bringing a full conviction of an invisible, eternal world.[25] It is true there was a kind of shadowy persuasion of this, even among the wiser heathens (probably from tradition, or from some gleams of light reflected from the Israelites). Hence many hundred years before our Lord was born, the Greek poet uttered that great truth,

> Millions of spiritual creatures walk the earth
> Unseen, whether we wake, or if we sleep.[26]

But this was little more than faint conjecture. It was far from a firm conviction; which reason in its highest state of improvement could never produce in any child of man.

2. Many years ago I found the truth of this by sad experience. After carefully heaping up the strongest arguments which I could find either in ancient or modern authors for the very being of a God and (which is nearly connected with it) the existence of an

---

[24] Cf. Heb. 11:1.

[25] Cf. No. 3, *'Awake, Thou That Sleepest'*, I.11 and n.

[26] The couplet is misremembered from Milton, *Paradise Lost*, iv. 677-78 (where 678 reads, 'Unseen, both when we wake and when we sleep'). The Greek poet is Hesiod, who in *Works and Days*, ll. 252-55, speaks of Zeus as having 'thrice ten thousand spirits [who] keep watch on the judgments and deeds of wrong, as they roam, clothed in mist, all over the earth'. Cf. also Plato, *Symposium*, 202, D12 (203, A6): 'through the demons there is intercourse between men and gods whether in the waking state or during sleep.' Also, Juvenal speaks of spirits of another realm, and Wesley quotes this in No. 73, 'Of Hell', §3 and n.

Wesley repeats the Miltonic version (citing Hesiod) in Nos. 71, 'Of Good Angels', §3; 117, 'On the Discoveries of Faith', §6; 119, 'Walking by Sight and Walking by Faith', §5 (where, incidentally, Wesley quotes I.678 correctly). Cf. also *An Earnest Appeal*, §10 (11:48 in this edn.).

invisible world, I have wandered up and down, musing with myself: What if all these things which I see around me, this earth and heaven, this universal frame,[27] has existed from eternity?[28] What if that melancholy supposition of the old poet be the real
5 case.

Οἴη περ φύλλων γενεή, τοίη δὲ καὶ ἀνδρῶν.[29]

What if the generation of men be exactly parallel with the generation of leaves? If the earth drops its successive inhabitants just as the tree drops its leaves? What if that saying of a great man
10 be really true,

Post mortem nihil est ipsaque mors nihil?[30]
Death is nothing and nothing is after death?

How am I sure that this is not the case? That I have not followed cunningly devised fables? And I have pursued the thought till
15 there was no spirit in me, and I was ready to choose strangling rather than life.[31]

3. But in a point of so unspeakable importance do not depend on the word of another; but retire for a while from the busy world,

---

[27] See Dryden, 'A Song for St. Cecilia's Day, 1687', ll.1-2:

> From Harmony, from heav'nly Harmony
> This universal Frame began.

[28] Cf. No. 15, *The Great Assize*, III.3 and n.

[29] Cf. Homer, *Iliad*, vi. 146. But see also the continuing lines (147-49): 'Even as are the generations of leaves, such are those also of men. As for the leaves, the wind scattereth some upon the earth, but the forest, as it burgeons, putteth forth others when the spring is come; even so of men one generation springeth up and another passeth away.' See Ecclus. 14:17-18.

> All flesh grows old, like a garment;
> The age-old law is: All must die.
> As with the leaves that grow on a vigorous tree:
> One falls off and another sprouts—
> So with the generations of flesh and blood:
> One dies and another is born.

The metaphor is repeated in JWJ, July 10, 1779: 'Taking a solitary walk in the churchyard, I felt the truth of "One generation goeth, and another cometh." See how the earth drops its inhabitants as the tree drops its leaves!' Cf. also, *ibid.*, Oct. 13, 1786; and No. 29, 'Sermon on the Mount, IX', §28.

[30] Cf. Seneca, *Troades*, II. ii. 397; more exactly: 'There is nothing after death, and even death itself is nothing.' This passage had been repeated by John Hawkins in a sermon in a London church that Welsey knew well (St. James, Clerkenwell), *The Certainty and Evidence of a Future State, being the Substance of Two Sermons Preached in the Parish Church of St. James, Clerkenwell, Sunday, August 29, 1725*, p. 7.

[31] See Job 7:15.

and make the experiment yourself. Try whether *your* reason will give you a clear, satisfactory evidence of the invisible world. After the prejudices of education are laid aside, produce your strong reasons for the existence of this. Set them all in array; silence all objections, and put all your doubts to flight. Alas, you cannot, 5 with all your understanding. You may perhaps repress them for a season. But how quickly will they rally again, and attack you with redoubled violence! And what can poor reason do for your deliverance? The more vehemently you struggle, the more deeply you are entangled in the toils. And you find no way to escape. 10

4. How was the case with that great admirer of reason, the author of the maxim above cited? I mean the famous Mr. Hobbes. None will deny that he had a strong understanding. But did it produce in him a full and satisfactory conviction of an invisible world? Did it open the eyes of his understanding to see 15

Beyond the bounds of this diurnal sphere?[32]

Oh no! Far from it! His dying words ought never to be forgotten. 'Where are you going, sir?' said one of his friends. He answered, 'I am taking a leap in the dark,' and died.[33] Just such an evidence of the invisible world can bare reason give to the wisest of men! 20

5. Secondly, reason alone cannot produce hope in any child of man; I mean scriptural hope, whereby we 'rejoice in hope of the glory of God';[34] that hope which St. Paul in one place terms, 'tasting of the powers of the world to come';[35] in another, the 'sitting in heavenly places with Christ Jesus'.[36] That which 25 enables us to say, 'Blessed be the God and Father of our Lord Jesus Christ, who hath begotten us again unto a lively hope, . . . to an inheritance incorruptible, and undefiled, and that fadeth not away, which is reserved in heaven for us.'[37] This hope can only spring from Christian faith: therefore where there 30 is not faith, there is not hope. Consequently reason, being unable to produce faith, must be equally unable to produce hope. Experience confirms this likewise. How often have I laboured,

---

[32] Milton, *Paradise Lost*, vi. 212; see No. 54, 'On Eternity', §18 and n.
[33] A legend that had already appeared in Samuel Wesley, Jun., *Poems*, p. 84, and earlier in a 'broadside' sheet dated 1680, entitled *The Last Saying, or Dying Legacy of Mr. Thomas Hobbes* (see also above, §1); and see John Watkins, *Characteristic Anecdotes* (1808), *loc. cit.*
[34] Rom. 5:2.   [35] Cf. Heb. 6:5.
[36] Cf. Eph. 2:6.
[37] Cf. 1 Pet. 1:3-4.

and that with my might, to beget this hope in myself? But it was lost labour. I could no more acquire this hope of heaven than I could touch heaven with my hand. And whoever of you makes the same attempt will find it attended with the same success. I do not
5 deny that a self-deceiving enthusiast may work in himself a kind of hope. He may work himself up into a lively imagination, into a sort of pleasing dream. He may 'compass himself about', as the prophet speaks, 'with sparks of his own kindling'. But this cannot be of long continuance; in a little while the bubble will surely
10 break. And what will follow? 'This shall ye have at my right hand,' said the Lord, 'ye shall lie down in sorrow.'[38]

6. If reason could have produced a hope full of immortality in any child of man, it might have produced it in that great man whom Justin Martyr scruples not to call, 'a Christian before
15 Christ'.[39] For who that was not favoured with the written Word of God ever excelled, yea, or equalled Socrates? In what other heathen can we find so strong an understanding, joined with so consummate virtue?[40] But had he really this hope? Let him answer for himself. What is the conclusion of that noble apology which he
20 made before his unrighteous judges? 'And now, O judges, ye are going hence to live; and I am going hence to die. Which of these is best the gods know; but I suppose no man does.'[41] No man knows! How far is this from the language of the little Benjamite?[42] 'I desire to depart and to be with Christ; for it is far better.'[43] And
25 how many thousands are there at this day, even in our own nation, young men and maidens, old men and children, who are able to witness the same good confession!

---

[38] Cf. Isa. 50:11.

[39] Cf. *The Second Apology*, ch. 10; and see also Robert Barclay, *Apology* (1736), Prop. V-VI, 'The Universal and Saving Light', where a similar allusion is made to Socrates. For other references in the sermons to Socrates, cf. Nos. 54, 'On Eternity', §18; 71, 'Of Good Angels', §2; and 119, 'Walking by Sight and Walking by Faith', §10.

[40] This allusion to Socrates's 'consummate virtue' calls to mind Wesley's sarcastic reference to Dr. John Taylor's applying the same to Jesus, as in Nos. 105, 'On Conscience', I.10; and 123, 'On Knowing Christ after the Flesh', §4.

[41] Cf. Plato, *Apology*, 42: 'I go to die and you to live; but which of us goes to the better lot is known only to God.' Note that Wesley has magnified the distance between Socrates and Christianity by rendering Plato's singular τῷ θεῷ as 'the gods'. See No. 119, 'Walking by Sight and Walking by Faith', §10.

[42] St. Paul, whose pride of tribal membership is reflected in Phil. 3:5 and Rom. 11:1. In his *Notes* also (Acts 19:21), Wesley uses the phrase, 'the little Benjamite' to apply to St. Paul. But he himself was 'little', and he had been brought up with the tradition (now proved incorrect) that his own middle name was Benjamin.

[43] Cf. Phil. 1:23.

7. But who is able to do this by the force of his reason, be it ever so highly improved? One of the most sensible and most amiable heathens that have lived since our Lord died, even though he governed the greatest empire in the world, was the Emperor Adrian.[44] It is his well-known saying, 'A prince ought to resemble 5 the sun: he ought to shine on every part of his dominion, and to diffuse his salutary rays in every place where he comes.'[45] And his life was a comment upon his word: wherever he went he was executing justice and showing mercy. Was not he then, at the close of a long life, full of immortal hope? We are able to answer 10 this from unquestionable authority, from his own dying words. How inimitably pathetic!

> *Adriani morientis ad animam suam*
> *(Dying Adrian to his soul):*
>
> *Animula, vagula, blandula,*   15
> *Hospes, comesque corporis,*
> *Quae nunc abibis in loca,*
> *Pallidula, rigida, nudula,*
> *Nec, ut soles, dabis jocos!*[46]

Which the English reader may see translated into our own 20 language with all the spirit of the original:

> Poor, little, pretty, fluttering thing,
>   Must we no longer live together.
> And dost thou prune thy trembling wing,
>   To take thy flight thou know'st not whither?   25
>
> Thy pleasing vein, thy humorous folly,
>   Lies all neglected, all forgot!
> And pensive, wav'ring, melancholy,
>   Thou hop'st, and fear'st, thou know'st not what.[47]

---

[44] I.e., Publius Aelius Hadrianus, Emperor A.D. 117–38, in succession to Trajan.

[45] Cf. Laurence Echard, *Ecclesiastical History*, III. i. 304: 'Staying at Rome a short time, he [the Emperor Hadrian] took a resolution to visit the whole empire in person, and see if all things were well regulated and established; and taking with him a splendid retinue and a considerable force, he first entered Gaul, where he made a lustration of the inhabitants, viewed the cities and forts, giving marks of his favour, as in all other places of the empire. In his travels he usually said that an emperor ought to imitate the sun, who carried his light through all the regions of the earth; and he generally travelled on foot always with head bare, making no difference between the frozen Alps and the scorching sands of Egypt.'

[46] Cf. *Minor Latin Poets*, Loeb, 284, p. 444. Wesley's text here is verbatim.

[47] Cf. Prior, '*Adriani morientis ad animam suam*' (cf. Aelius Spartianus, *De Vita Hadriani*, §xxv); here, Wesley's memory is less accurate. He had already published Pope's experiments with this passage in *A Collection of Moral and Religious Poems* (1744), II. 184-85; see also Pope, *Works* (1964), VI.91-94. The passage is repeated with further

8. Thirdly, reason, however cultivated and improved, cannot produce the love of God; which is plain from hence: it cannot produce either faith or hope, from which alone this love can flow. It is then only when we 'behold' by faith 'what manner of love the
5   Father hath bestowed upon us',[48] in giving his only Son that we might not perish but have everlasting life,[49] that 'the love of God is shed abroad in our heart, by the Holy Ghost which is given unto us.'[50] It is only then, when we 'rejoice in hope of the glory of God',[51] that 'we love him because he first loved us.'[52] But what can
10 cold reason do in this matter? It may present us with fair ideas: it can draw a fine picture of love; but this is only a painted fire![53] And farther than this reason cannot go. I made the trial for many years. I collected the finest hymns, prayers, and meditations which I could find in any language; and I said, sung, or read them over
15 and over with all possible seriousness and attention; but still I was like the bones in Ezekiel's vision: 'The skin covered them above; but there was no breath in them.'[54]

9. And as reason cannot produce the love of God, so neither can it produce the love of our neighbour, a calm, generous,
20 disinterested benevolence to every child of man. This earnest, steady goodwill to our fellow-creatures never flowed from any fountain but gratitude to our Creator. And if this be (as a very ingenious man supposes)[55] the very essence of virtue, it follows that virtue can have no being unless it spring from the love of
25 God. Therefore as reason cannot produce this love, so neither can it produce virtue.

10. And as it cannot give either faith, hope, love, or virtue, so it cannot give happiness, since separate from these there can be no happiness for any intelligent creature. It is true, those who are
30 void of all virtue may have pleasures such as they are; but happiness they have not, cannot have. No:

---

alterations in No. 119, 'Walking by Sight and Walking by Faith', §10; cf. Also *A Farther Appeal*, Pt. II. III.19 (11:267 in this edn.).
[48] 1 John 3:1.
[49] John 3:16.
[50] Rom. 5:5.
[51] Rom. 5:2.
[52] 1 John 4:19.
[53] Cf. *OED* for an instance of this metaphor in Middle English as early as 1300.
[54] Ezek. 37:8.
[55] Probably Francis Hutcheson, professor of philosophy at Glasgow, whose stress on disinterested benevolence, transcending religious or utilitarian motives, struck Wesley as both wrong and dangerous. Cf. No. 12, 'The Witness of Our Own Spirit', §5 and n.

Their joy is all sadness,
Their mirth is all vain:
Their laughter is madness:
Their pleasure is pain![56]

Pleasures? Shadows! Dreams! Fleeting as the wind; unsubstan- 5
tial as the rainbow! As unsatisfying to the poor, gasping soul,

As the gay colours of an eastern cloud.[57]

None of these will stand the test of reflection: if thought comes,
the bubble breaks.

Suffer me now to add a few, plain words; first to you who 10
undervalue reason. Never more declaim in that wild, loose,
ranting manner against this precious gift of God. Acknowledge
'the candle of the Lord',[58] which he hath fixed in our souls for
excellent purposes. You see how many admirable ends it answers,
were it only in the things of this life; of what unspeakable use is 15
even a moderate share of reason in all our worldly employments,
from the lowest and meanest offices of life, through all the
intermediate branches of business, till we ascend to those that are
of the highest importance and the greatest difficulty. When
therefore you despise or depreciate reason you must not imagine 20
you are doing God service; least of all are you promoting the
cause of God when you are endeavouring to exclude reason out of
religion. Unless you wilfully shut your eyes, you cannot but see of
what service it is both in laying the foundation of true religion,
under the guidance of the Spirit of God, and in raising the whole 25
superstructure. You see it directs us in every point both of faith
and practice: it guides us with regard to every branch both of
inward and outward holiness. Do we not glory in this, that the
whole of our religion is a 'reasonable service'.[59] Yea, and that
every part of it, when it is duly performed, is the highest exercise 30
of our understanding.

Permit me to add a few words to you likewise who overvalue

[56] Charles Wesley, *Hymns for Those That Seek Redemption* (1747), p. 32 (*Poet. Wks.*, IV. 241).
[57] See James Thomson, *The Seasons*, 'Spring', I. 203: 'Meantime refracted from yon eastern cloud'.
[58] Prov. 20:27. A slogan of the Cambridge Platonists; cf. Benjamin Whichcote, *Moral and Religious Aphorisms* (1753), No. 916; and Nathaniel Culverwell, *Discourse on the Light of Nature* (1661; 2nd edn., 1669), I.1.
[59] Rom. 12:1.

reason. Why should you run from one extreme into the other? Is not the middle way best?[60] Let reason do all that reason can: employ it as far as it will go. But at the same time acknowledge it is utterly incapable of giving either faith, or hope, or love; 5 and consequently of producing either real virtue or substantial happiness. Expect these from a higher source, even from the Father of the spirits of all flesh.[61] Seek and receive them not as your own acquisition, but as the gift of God. Lift up your hearts to him who giveth to all men liberally, and upbraideth not.[62] He 10 alone can give that faith which is the evidence and 'conviction of things not seen'.[63] He alone can 'beget you unto a lively hope'[64] of an inheritance eternal in the heavens.[65] And he alone can 'shed abroad his love in your heart by the Holy Ghost given unto you'.[66] Ask, therefore, and it shall be given you;[67] cry unto him, and you 15 shall not cry in vain. How can you doubt! 'If ye, being evil, know how to give good gifts unto your children, how much more shall your Father who is in heaven give the Holy Ghost unto them that ask him!'[68] So shall you be living witnesses that wisdom, holiness, and happiness are one,[69] are inseparably united; and are indeed 20 the beginning of that 'eternal life which God hath given us in his Son'.[70]

Langham Row, July 6, 1781[71]

---

[60] Cf. No. 27, 'Sermon on the Mount, VII', §4 and n.
[61] See Num. 16:22; 27:16.
[62] Jas. 1:5.
[63] Cf. Heb. 11:1.
[64] Cf. 1 Pet. 1:3.
[65] 2 Cor. 5:1.
[66] Cf. Rom. 5:5.
[67] See Matt. 7:7.
[68] Cf. Luke 11:13.
[69] Cf. No. 5, 'Justification by Faith', I.4 and n.
[70] Cf. 1 John 5:11.
[71] Place and date as in *AM*.

APPENDIX A

The Sermons as Ordered in this Edition

(Included is the location of the text as it is to be found in Jackson's edition of Wesley's *Works* (1829-31), Vols. V-VII, which has been popularly reproduced during this generation from the 1872 edition.)

[This edition, Vol. 1]

Sermons on Several Occasions (1771), I-IV

Jackson
(1872)

Preface (1746)..V. 1-6

1. Salvation by Faith..V. 7-16
   Eph. 2:8
2. The Almost Christian..V. 17-25
   Acts 26:28
3. 'Awake, Thou That Sleepest'..V. 25-36
   Eph. 5:14
4. Scriptural Christianity...V. 37-52
   Acts 4:31
5. Justification by Faith..V. 53-64
   Rom. 4:5
6. The Righteousness of Faith..V. 65-76
   Rom. 10:5-8
7. The Way to the Kingdom...V. 76-86
   Mark 1:15
8. The First-fruits of the Spirit...V. 87-97
   Rom. 8:1
9. The Spirit of Bondage and of Adoption.....................................V. 98-111
   Rom. 8:15
10. The Witness of the Spirit, Discourse I....................................V. 111-23
    Rom. 8:16
11. The Witness of the Spirit, Discourse II...................................V. 123-34
    Rom. 8:16
12. The Witness of Our Own Spirit..V. 134-44
    2 Cor. 1:12
13. On Sin in Believers..V. 144-56
    2 Cor. 5:17
14. The Repentance of Believers..V. 156-70
    Mark 1:15

Sermons on Several Occasions (1788), V-VIII

*Sermons not by John Wesley, but included
in Jackson's edition (see Appendices B and C, Vol. 4)*

Appendix A
(Wesley's text: editions, transmission, presentation, and variant readings)

Appendix B
(Sermons ascribed to Wesley on inconclusive grounds)

Appendix C
(Manuscript sermons abridged from other authors)

Appendix D
(Samples of Wesley's sermon registers)

Bibliography

Indexes

APPENDIX B

The Sermons
in Chronological Sequence

APPENDIX C

The Sermons
in Alphabetical Order

(N.B. Where a title is italicized, the sermon was published as a separate item before being issued in a collection. Some of the titles thus italicized here, however, abridge the titles under which Wesley originally published them; others (Nos. 3, 55, 58, 99, 109, 111) are quite different. For detailed descriptions of all Wesley's contemporary editions of each sermon see the Bibliography in this edition, here noted as 'B.50', etc. Titles supplied by the editor, whether to sermons separately published or to those first appearing in collected editions, or from manuscript sources, are given in this listing only within parentheses. These parentheses, however, are dropped from other listings, as from running titles and footnotes. Frequently the titles come from a lengthy tradition, which is noted, along with all the original titles used, in the introductory comment to the appropriate sermon. In alphabetizing the words 'a', 'an', 'of', 'on', 'the' are ignored. F.B.)

The Distribution of the Sermons in this Edition

Vol. 1, Nos. 1–33
Vol. 2, Nos. 34–76
Vol. 3, Nos. 77–114
Vol. 4, Nos. 115–51